This SO-BJF-970

THE VIRTUES AND STATES OF LIFE

THE THEOLOGY LIBRARY

The translation of the entire library
is under the direction of the Rev.
Louis J. Putz, C.S.C., University
of Notre Dame

THE VIRTUES
AND STATES
OF LIFE

08693

By a group of theologians
under the editorship of
A. M. Henry, O.P.

Translated by Robert J. Olsen and Genevieve T. Lennon
under the direction of Louis J. Putz, C.S.C.

Fides Publishers Association

Chicago, Illinois

Library of Congress Catalog Number: 54-10891

NIHIL OBSTAT:
Albert L. Schlitzer, C.S.C., S.T.D.
University of Notre Dame

IMPRIMATUR:
✠ Leo A. Pursley, D.D., Bishop of
Fort Wayne, Indiana

NIHIL OBSTAT:
Parisiis, die 19a *dec.* 1952
Th. Camelot, O.P.
Stud. reg. in Fac. "Le Saulchoir"
J. Tonneau, O.P.
Mag. in S. Theol.

IMPRIMI POTEST:
Parisiis, die 19a *dec.* 1952
A.-M. Avril, O.P.
Prior prov.

IMPRIMATUR:
Parisiis, die 19a *dec.* 1952
M. Potevin
Vic. gen.

Published originally by Les Editions du Cerf, 29,
Boulevard Latour-Maubourg, Paris 7, France

© COPYRIGHT: Fides Publishers Association
Chicago, Illinois, 1957

Manufactured by American Book–Stratford Press, Inc., New York
55

Faithfully Dedicated

to

Our Lady Immaculate

PLAN OF THE THEOLOGY LIBRARY

VOLUME FOUR

The Virtues and States of Life

CONTENTS

INTRODUCTION

Up to this point we have studied moral matters in a comprehensive way in their general principles: voluntary acts and passions, virtues and vices, law and grace (Vol. III). But general considerations would not be very useful if we went no further in our study. The moralist is definitively interested in the concrete action and the particular situation. We have now arrived at the study of this "particular" in human activity.

There are two ways of studying the particular in morality: on the one hand, we can consider each of the moral principles one after the other: a particular virtue, a particular vice, a particular law; on the other hand, we may consider the particular situations of men which would now be called "existential": the situations of the subordinate person and his superior, of the bishop and the Religious, of the active and the contemplative, of the man or woman who is trained in prayer and the person who has great social responsibilities, etc. The first consideration applies to all situations, the second must take into account all the virtues operative in every situation. These two considerations will be covered under two headings, "Virtues" and "States of Life."

However, a remark is necessary on the subject of the first. If we wanted to study each virtue, and then every vice, and then every precept, one after the other, we would often have to repeat ourselves. The sixth commandment of the Decalogue, for example, "Thou shalt not commit adultery," requires that we mention adultery. But adultery is also a sin and the sin cannot be known properly unless we refer to the virtue to which it is opposed. There is therefore a means of simplifying the matter of our study which is to range everything under the consideration of the virtues. From virtue we shall proceed each time to the gift of the Holy Spirit which may correspond to it, and to the vice which is opposed to it, to the precept concerning it, and if necessary to the passion which it may affect and the special grace that it requires.

All moral matters thus being reduced to the study of virtue, there are still two ways to simplify it.

First of all, we must note, in fact, that the virtues, like the vices, are distinguished according to their object and not according to certain accidental differences, as for example when a sin is a sin of thought, of word, of deed, or yet a sin of weakness, ignorance or malice. The same sin, against temperance for example, may possess one or another of these qualifications without being changed in itself. Therefore, we shall not take account of these differences in general. We shall study the virtues according to their matter or their object.

In the second place, we must note that all the virtues, classified according to their object, can be reduced, for the convenience of study, to seven in number: the three theological virtues and the four cardinal virtues. "Cardinal" comes from a Latin word meaning hinge; the cardinal virtues are the *axes* around which may be referred, more or less closely, the consideration of all the virtues, whether moral or intellectual. Among the latter we may consequently note that prudence is classified among the cardinal virtues, and that understanding, knowledge and wisdom may be studied in connection with the corresponding gifts of the Holy Spirit. With regard to art, we know that it does not directly pertain to morality.

This study of the "particular" by the consideration of the virtues alone permits morality to be authentically human and moral. Modern treatises on morality often begin with the principle of obligation which is a social concept and is infra-moral. Our theology, let us repeat once again, begins with the idea of the good which alone is capable of setting us in motion interiorly. The total good for man, a spiritual creature, is happiness, and it is happiness which governs all the dynamism of the virtues.

Chapter I

FAITH

by A. Liégé, O.P.

I. FAITH AS CONVERSION AND JUSTIFICATION

1. Conversion
2. The faith of Abraham and our faith
3. The faith as personal commitment
4. Man's decision and the grace of God
5. Faith and hope
6. Faith that justifies
7. Faith and baptism

II. THE ANTECEDENTS OF FAITH

1. The affirmations of the magisterium
2. The signs in revelation
3. The miracle: a divine deed and symbol
4. Man in the presence of the miraculous
5. Must we believe in miracles?
6. Physical miracle and moral miracle
7. Discernment of signs and grace
8. From the sign to the act of faith
9. Antecedents of faith and conditions of faith
10. Theology of faith and psychology of conversion
11. Concluding remarks

III. THE FAITH OF CONTEMPLATION

1. From the faith of conversion to the virtue of faith
   (a) Promises and grace
   (b) Faith, hope, charity
   (c) Intellectual faith
2. The world of faith
   (a) Jesus Christ, the fulness of the Word of God
   (b) The stages of catechesis
   (c) The rule of faith

1

Chapter I

FAITH

I. Faith as Conversion and Justification

1. CONVERSION

What happens when a man becomes a believer? In a very general way it may be said that he once thought of his life as a task to complete, and believed that success depended upon himself alone. The present world was the scene of his endeavor. He had to cope with many problems which he tried to solve within the limits of the world as he knew it, deciding that a man should perhaps be satisfied with every ordinary achievement. And then one day everything was changed in the life of this man. God had intervened, and had said to him, "Your whole life is at stake, together with everything you call your life: your joy and sorrow, your loves and your relations with other men, your work and your accomplishments, your body as well as your soul, your death and all the tragedies that lead up to it. But I am the Living God and the Friend of Man, and I will give you a life that will take up and infinitely surpass your laborious existence, a life transcending death and all the limitations of your carnal condition. I will be your Master, and your whole destiny will be in My hands. You will become My obedient and faithful collaborator in the fulfillment of your destiny." And the man said, "Yes!"—not through weakness or fear—but only because God's strength and life were so much greater than his own.

2. THE FAITH OF ABRAHAM AND OUR FAITH

Ever since Abraham's day, and for as long as there are men who are faithful to God, the adventure of faith begins with God's promise and gift of life to every man who makes the right about-face of conversion. In order that God may have first place, the whole course of his life is changed.

Abraham . . . is the father of us all; as it is written, "I have appointed thee the father of many nations." He is our father in the sight of God, whom

3

he believed, who gives life to the dead and calls things that are not as though they were. Abraham hoping against hope believed, so that he became the father of many nations, according to what was said, "So shall thy offspring be." And without weakening in faith, he considered his own deadened body (for he was almost a hundred years old) and the deadened womb of Sara; and yet in view of the promise of God, he did not waver through unbelief but was strengthened in faith, giving glory to God, being fully aware that whatever God has promised he is able also to perform. Therefore it was credited to him as justice. Now not for his sake only was it written that "It was credited to him," but for the sake of us also, to whom it will be credited if we believe in him who raised Jesus our Lord from the dead, who was delivered up for our sins, and rose again for our justification (Rom. 4:16-26).

Abraham in surrendering his life to God completely abandoned himself to Him, being certain that divine generosity would match his sacrifice in spite of immediate appearances. Since the word of Almighty God had promised it, it mattered little that Abraham knew nothing of the fulness of life contained in this promise. He took God's word seriously and staked his whole destiny upon this promise. He had faith in God, and so likewise did all our spiritual ancestors, the great believers of the Old Covenant, whom the Epistle to the Hebrews acclaimed in chapter eleven, before turning our eyes to "the author and finisher of faith, Jesus." Their faith was spelled out in their very words, for the Hebrew root "haman" (translated "pisteuein" by the Septuagint) in referring to the act of the believer, evokes very precisely the attitude of the child who lets himself be carried in his mother's arms. In the Hebrew language, to believe (causative mode: heemin) always means: to make someone else carry one's burden, that is to say, to put one's trust in another person, or to entrust oneself to some stable person. Now who can this stable one be? Who is completely self-sustaining, if not the One whom the Bible calls the Rock? Surrendering his whole being to God, the believer sharing in the stability of God Himself becomes stable and secure. "If you will not believe, you shall not continue" (Is. 7:9). Let us remember that *Amen,* an adverb that grew out of the same root, is the cry of faith: It is certain! It is firm and true!

Abraham still did not know how truly the God to whom he had devoted himself was the faithful and living God. But after the resurrection of Jesus Christ, we know how His promise of eternal life has been wonderfully fulfilled among men. Since then, the faith rests upon the coming of Jesus Christ, for the power of God shown forth in Jesus Christ has become a promise for every man coming into this world. "How shall they believe," asks St. Paul, "unless the gospel be preached to them?" However, to preach the gospel is to proclaim that God has summoned all men to accept His plan of salvation, manifested in the teaching, the life, death and resurrection of Jesus Christ. This is to proclaim a joyful message which decides everyone's destiny. One must take sides, either acknowledging that Jesus Christ comes from God, and therefore that His coming gives a divine meaning to human history, or else refuse to recognize its transcendent significance. But how could God have shown men more clearly His plan of love and life? At the beginning of His ministry Jesus declared, "The time is fulfilled, and the kingdom of God is at hand. Repent and believe in the gospel" (Mk. 1:15). In this respect it would be quite impossible to indicate more plainly the realism and the coherence with which St. Paul centers missionary preaching and conversion in the Risen Christ. "And if Christ has not risen, vain then is our preaching, vain too is your faith" (I Cor. 15:14). "The word is near thee, in thy mouth and in thy heart (that is, the word of faith, which we preach). For if thou confess with thy mouth that Jesus is the Lord, and believe in thy heart that God has raised him from the dead, thou shalt be saved. For with the heart a man believes unto justice, and with the mouth profession of faith is made unto salvation" (Rom. 10:8-11). At the central point of all history, the life-giving spirit of God was gloriously manifested in Jesus Christ. This manifestation becomes the promise of eternal life for every man who becomes one with Christ by uniting himself with Christ, Power of God, and by seeking that glory which comes from God alone. This is the echo of Our Lord's own words, "I am the resurrection and the life; he who believes in me, even if he die, shall live; and whoever lives and believes in me, shall never die" (Jn. 11:25-26). Abraham is our father in the faith, for he was the "type" of our belief in the death and resurrection of Christ.

3. THE FAITH AS PERSONAL COMMITMENT

We have spoken of risk in regard to the faith of conversion. Is risk the right word? Certainly not if it were the equivalent of wager, or if it raised any doubts concerning the faithfulness of God. However, we may say that the life of faith is a risk insofar as the believer puts his entire trust in a promise of life that depends upon God alone. Man in renouncing his self-sufficiency and in acknowledging the inconsistency of stressing his own capacity for immediate life, makes everything depend upon the gratuitous omnipotence of God. This is a decision which breaks with the selfish hoarding up of life and with the sufficiency of man, and for carnal man this uprooting seems like a risk indeed. "For he who would save his life will lose it: but he who loses his life for my sake will save it" (Lk. 9:24). It is clear that the faith involves the whole man and, particularly, his freedom. It is with the heart that man believes—in the biblical meaning of "heart" which designates the center of personality, that place in man from which comes forth everything that we mean when we speak of responsibility or commitment or destiny. We need only read again the parable of the Sower in Luke 8:5-16: "But that upon good ground, these are they who, with a right and good heart, having heard the word, hold it fast, and bear fruit in patience."

4. MAN'S DECISION AND THE GRACE OF GOD

Man is free to commit himself to God and to Christ, and his whole destiny hinges upon this. However, freedom alone is not sufficient to account for this conversion that makes God the real axis of an existence that was formerly centered entirely in itself. Freedom expresses itself in the response to the divine call (cf. Rom. 1:5-6). The call to faith is first, and expresses itself by the external word of Christ's Gospel. But God's Word is not only a message. It carries with it a power of conviction and of fecundity which acts upon the heart at the same time that the senses receive the message. Christ makes Himself known by this interior witness of which St. John spoke, without in any way violating the freedom of man. Consequently, the man who refuses the divine call does so freely, and whoever receives it gladly is able to make this acceptance by grace. St. Paul wrote to the Thessalonians, "God has chosen you as firstfruits unto salvation through the sanctification of the Spirit and belief of the truth. For this purpose he also called you by our gospel to gain the glory of our Lord Jesus Christ" (II Thess. 2:13-14). And the Church firmly contended against the semi-Pelagians that the act of conversion was primarily the work of the Holy Spirit in man. In the decrees of the second council of Orange, in 529, (canons 5 and 7, in *Denz.* 178 and 180) we read:

Let him be considered as contradicting the apostolic teaching, who denies that the first act of faith, and the loving gift of self that accompanies it, whereby we believe in Him Who justifies the ungodly in order to bring about the new birth of holy baptism, as well as the subsequent life of faith,[1] are all in us by grace, that is to say, by the inspiration of the Holy Spirit who rectifies our will and leads it from unbelief to faith, and from unrighteousness to godliness, as though attributing these things on the contrary to our own nature instead. If anyone persists in affirming that it is possible, by our natural powers alone, to reflect rightly upon any of the blessings that pertain to eternal life, or to make the choice of these blessings by our own decision, or claim that one can receive salvation, in this instance the preaching of the gospel, without the illumination and inspiration of the Holy Spirit whose anointing gives us the ability to receive and believe the truth, such a person is the victim of the heretical spirit, for he does not understand the Word of God recorded in the Gospel, "For without me you can do nothing" (Jn. 15:5), nor the affirmation of the Apostle, "Not that we are sufficient of ourselves to think anything, as from ourselves, but our sufficiency is from God" (II Cor. 3:5).

5. FAITH AND HOPE

Someone will surely ask how the faith of conversion may be distinguished from hope. This question is of greater importance when the believer's new life has larger dimension, but at this early stage of first response to the divine call, it is by complete self-giving, involving the whole person with all his faculties simultaneously, that the believer's act is expressed. This is the acknowledgement of Christ and of His function, and absolute confidence in the salvation that comes from Him, together with the love that responds to the divine love that He manifests, for all of this is contained in the single act. "Through him you are believers in God who raised him up from the dead and gave him glory, so that your faith and hope might be in God" (I Pet. 1:21). For this reason, admitting the truth of God's Word cannot be separated from the discovery of the holy Person of Christ and receiving the promise of eternal life. Man submits and obeys with his whole being.

6. FAITH THAT JUSTIFIES

We have devoted much time to the consideration of the act of faith as conversion because, as the Council of Trent expressed it, this act is "the foundation and root of all justification" (fundamentum et radix omnis justificationis)—omnis indicating that it does not pertain exclusively to the first moment of justification. The act of

[1] This phrase, because it has not been situated in its historical context, has given rise to contrary and tenaciously held interpretations among the theologians. We refer ourselves to the study made by J. Chénée: *Que signifiaient Initium fidei et* Affectus credulitatis *pour les semipélagiens?* in R. S. R., 1948, pp. 566-588.

conversion whereby man gives himself to God in Christ, coincides with the act of grace by which God begins to actualize the promise in the believer. God makes him righteous, and this implies purification and a whole new life, a state of friendship with God, and the enduring gift of the Holy Spirit. According to the Apostle, "Having been justified therefore by faith, let us have peace with God through our Lord Jesus Christ, through whom we also have access by faith unto that grace in which we stand, and exult in the hope of the glory of the sons of God" (Rom. 5:1-2). By the same power that filled the life of Jesus with the Spirit of God, and resurrected Him, the believing man participates in the mystery of Christ, interiorly sharing the risen life of the Lord. Faith has introduced him into a new existence and a new world.

7. FAITH AND BAPTISM

What does baptism add to faith if the believer is justified by faith. It completes and expands the work of justification. Baptism and faith are two aspects of a unique incorporation into Christ, intimately bound together. The act of conversion finds expression in the baptismal confession of faith, and justification is accomplished by the baptismal rite that makes the believer a member of the Church. If the first step in the act of faith is personal decision (although the Church has already participated through her external witness) it is baptism that gives a communal dimension to faith, and the faith thereafter is lived within the unity of God's people. St. Paul strongly emphasizes the complementary nature of faith and baptism. "For you are all the children of God through faith in Christ Jesus. For all you who have been baptized into Christ, have put on Christ" (Gal. 3:26-27; cf. Eph. 1:13-14; Col. 2:12). From this is derived the traditional name of baptism: the sacrament of faith.

We have been considering the case of baptized adults following their conversion. But what shall we say about children baptized before conversion? The bond between faith and baptism remains firm, on the one hand because the baptism of the child supposes a community of converts by whose mediation an organic link is established between baptism and the faith of the Church. On the other hand, thanks to the Christian community, the child will have to ratify his baptism by an act of conversion quite as personal as that of the adult.

II. The Antecedents of Faith

Faith is an absolute beginning in a man's life because it depends far more upon the action of God than upon the action of man. However, there must be the will to believe. Some men welcome the Word of God and others do not. In this section we will consider how a man prepares himself for conversion.

Two sets of factors obviously lead man toward conversion. There are the subjective factors that work upon his moral being and eventually bring about the break with the past in response to the call of God. And there are the objective factors by which we are able to verify the truly divine origin of the coming of God's Word. In actual experience we can see the influence of these two series of factors whenever a man begins to move in the direction of faith. It is at this point that all the problems of Catholic apologetics arise.

1. THE AFFIRMATIONS OF THE MAGISTERIUM

God's Word and His Grace are transcendent realities, but they are received deep within man's heart. That is why the faith requires roots and human guarantees. God calls us to receive His Word, but He has left us the means whereby we may objectively verify the claim that He has spoken to all men through Jesus Christ. The position of the Church with regard to all the various fideist theories is summed up in these terms, reaffirmed by the Vatican Council:

> Nevertheless (it had just been stated that the faith is supernatural reality), in order that our faith might be in conformity with reason's desire, God united the interior aids of the Holy Spirit with the external proofs of revelation. Among these proofs, first of all, were the miracles and prophecies that were a wonderful manifestation of the omnipotence and infinite wisdom of God, and these constitute the certain signs of divine revelation especially adapted to the understanding of all men (Session 3, chap. 3, *De Fide; in Denz.* 1790).

Here the Church takes a purely objective point of view, without requiring that all personal faith should be based upon these reasonable guarantees, or specifying the noetic conditions that lead to certitude with regard to revelation. When it becomes necessary to assure a man's progress toward belief, a canon of the same Session affirms that we should not disregard these rational guarantees in order to exalt subjective experience and feeling as the only valid criteria of certitude (canon 3; in *Denz.* 1813).

The Church does not want to sacrifice the mysticism of the faith to its humanism, nor should this be done inversely, for the manifestation of the living God took place in history and under a social form. The substance of the faith is finally a direct dialogue between the believer and God, but not without reference to the historical coming of revelation. How can we attribute a transcendent meaning to the coming of Jesus Christ if we are not previously sure of the historic reality of His coming? But this verified historic reality does not constitute the object or the essential motive of our act of faith. It is only the condition of belief. On this point the Vatican Council declares:

Let him be anathema who maintains that the assent to Christian faith is necessarily produced by the arguments of human reason (*Ibid.,* canon 5; in *Denz.* 1814).

2. THE SIGNS IN REVELATION

"Many other signs also Jesus worked in the sight of his disciples which are not written in this book. But these are written that you may believe that Jesus is the Christ, the Son of God, and that believing you may have life in his name" (Jn. 20:30-31). St. John ends his Gospel with these words, and it is this Gospel which effectively shows us that Jesus always accompanied His preaching with signs, and that conversions took place because of these signs (cf. Jn. 10:37-38; Acts 2:22). Even in the Old Testament we see that God always used signs together with His Word to lead men to faith. It has ever been so in the long missionary life of the Church. The external witness of the prophetic Word and the interior witness of the Holy Spirit have always been concurrent with the external witness of the signs (cf. Heb. 2:4; I Thess. 1:5).

What is a sign, and why is there a connection between the sign and the Word of God? A sign is a concrete reality, a gesture or an event, based upon sensory experience but charged with deeper meaning. There is an empirical consistency, but beyond this, and closely identified with it, there is a second point of intelligibility which refers the witness to another reality of the spiritual order, or at least to something that is invisible at the time. These facts are full of meaning for the person who can penetrate them profoundly. The understanding of signs and symbols is the very basis of all human communication, and of all relations between men. It is essential to the philosophy of language. When the invisible and transcendent God addresses His message to men of this world, it is not surprising, therefore, that He uses signs and symbols adapted to their understanding. It is the purpose of divine symbols to show that it is really God Who is speaking (cf. Jn. 3:2) and consequently, those who understand the symbols are both able and required to receive the Word which they accompany, for they are symbols of transcendence and signs of credibility.

3. THE MIRACLE: A DIVINE DEED AND SYMBOL

The deeper meaning of the sign is closely linked to its empirical reality. A fact or event of unusual nature which contrasts with ordinary experience must correspond with the religious meaning of the sign. This should be an event of divine origin which can serve as a symbol of the divine presence for the sake of the Word. Obviously a miracle is the sign, *par excellence,* of revelation. The miracle's religious meaning must never be separated from the reality of the extraordinary or preternatural event. Every miracle is a sign, although every sign or symbol is not objectively a miracle, for God does not act capriciously in the physical world by confounding the immanent laws which are His secondary causes. Such action on the part of God always pre-supposes an intention which transcends the physical world and pertains directly to the moral universe. It is not by accident that the divine event witnesses in favor of the Word, and even if we try to verify the transcendent event, we cannot separate the miracle from the sign. A definition of miracles that is truly theological must always begin with the religious sign. Let us consider a possible definition: For the witness who is able to understand its meaning, a miracle is a divine sign or symbol that visibly accompanies the coming of the Word in history, and the miracle's unusual and inexplicable nature in the entire network of natural causes humanly accredits the divine purpose which is manifested in relation to the Word.

4. MAN IN THE PRESENCE OF THE MIRACULOUS

The Vatican Council condemns anyone who would make the following claim: "It is impossible ever to have any certain knowledge of miracles or to prove properly the divine origin of Christ's religion with their help" (*ibid.,* canon 4, *Denz.* 1813). This condemnation presupposes that it is possible to recognize a miracle, even without Christian faith, but it does not deny that God's help can assist the human mind in this recognition. But help of this kind is not yet the interior revelation that takes place during the act of conversion. A further question still remains. Apart from the believer, who will recognize the miracle? The scientist? The metaphysician? Or someone else who may have noetic competence?

In the presence of a miraculous occurrence, the pure scientist would be wrong to make a flat denial, but we should not ask anything more of him than a suspension of judgment. He is obliged to be a determinist by method, and therefore we should not expect any positive conclusion from him, especially with reference to a unique event that will not occur again. Is there any evidence that anything ever transcends the order of natural causation? This question cannot be answered in *a priori* terms, and there is no scientist who can claim to have established the total enumeration of all natural possibilities. Consequently, when a miracle is attributed to "unknown causes" there is nothing irreverent in this remark of the scientist, for it is wholly consistent with his technical competence.

The philosopher is not restricted to the methodological determinism of the scientist, but with regard to the verified data of science we can hardly expect anything more from him than a highly probable judgment in favor of a causality which he would define as natural in the widest meaning of the term. This would include the possible activity of superhuman beings. It would be necessary to have a complete enumeration of all universal causalities in order to affirm that any particular occurrence transcends the whole order of creation. Consequently, there is always a margin of uncertainty, and even when the occurrence is spontaneously attributed to a divine origin and there is hardly any room for argument, the pure metaphysician will tend to take refuge within the minimal limits of the general explanation which admits that God is truly free and omnipotent, but does not see why His wisdom would require Him to act in a miraculous way without purpose.

It is therefore within the perspective of a definite perception of God's purpose in history that the miracle will be recognized with certainty. When all critical verification has been undertaken by others—and this is absolutely required—it is within the competence of the *religious man* to proceed from the ambiguous conclusion of the philosopher to the affirmation of the divinity of the miraculous event. Consequently, there is no absolute certainty that the event is divine until its religious meaning is recognized by those who are capable of that perception. It is therefore in the concordance of the event and of the sign that the miracle is concretely recognized as a sign and also as a transcendent event. This explains the attitude of the implacable adversaries of Jesus who, not wanting to acknowledge His miracles as signs (which would have condemned their unbelief), attributed them to a preternatural power (Mk. 3:22) or took refuge in agnosticism (Jn. 9:29). In the presence of delusive appearances or of prodigies and marvelous happenings, it is only the moral context and the meaningful relationship with the economy of salvation that will enable us to discern the truly divine causality of any event that is authentically miraculous. Christian authors of the first centuries, who witnessed the occurrence of many prodigious events, always insist on this.

We must not suppose that a miracle is a purely subjective reality, for when we attribute a determining value to the religious purpose, we are not dispensed from seeking the greatest possible assurances regarding the event itself. However, if the religious meaning alone makes for absolute certainty, thereby surpassing the rather considerable limitations of unoriented critical inquiry, it does not create this attitude of certainty, but rather assumes and confirms it in synthesis. This brings us to the problem of the specificity of religious knowledge, which does not attain to real objectivity except through the mediation of the perceiving subject.

5. MUST WE BELIEVE IN MIRACLES?

This question, commonly asked, is certainly equivocal in view of the affirmation of the Vatican Council previously cited. However, although belief and Christian faith would be synonymous in this instance, the question clearly indicates how spontaneously the concrete affirmation of a miracle is attributed to a religious faculty. We are now studying the miracle as antecedent to conversion, but at this point we find ourselves confronting the antecedents of the miracle, and these are the antecedents that immediately precede the faith of conversion.

To believe in miracles, is it sufficient for us to have certain antecedents of a purely rational kind; for example, a firm conviction regarding the existence of a Supreme Being and belief in the immortality of the human soul? It is easy to see that these logical antecedents are not sufficient, and the history of philosophical thought gives us considerable information regarding the spiritualistic rationalism, closed to all revelation, which these purely rational convictions produce. We have considered the normal attitude of the philosopher in the presence of a miracle, and we know that his rational affirmations do not indicate any acknowledgement of the religious sign in a positive way. Referring to the use of purely rational arguments in the effort to convert other men, Newman writes, "I say plainly that I do not care to overcome their reason without touching their hearts. I wish to deal, not with controversialists, but with inquirers" (*Grammar of Assent*, London, 1947, pp. 323-324). In the same essay, Newman continues, "And how, after all, is a man better for Christianity, who has never felt the need of it or the desire? . . . Men are too well inclined to sit at home, instead of stirring themselves to inquire whether a revelation has been given; they expect its evidences to come to them without their trouble; they act, not as suppliants, but as judges."

As a matter of fact, the religious sign is intended for the whole man, just as faith in Christ will eventually involve his whole being. The antecedents will necessarily derive from the order of human behavior. This certainly implies objective affirmations, for how could any man believe in miracles if he denies the existence and omnipotence of God? But these objective affirmations will be included in the existential affirmation of the whole person in opening the whole of life to the intervention of God without requiring that they be transposed to the level of reflexive consciousness. It is in the heart of the religious man that the Word of God will bring forth belief. Before this occurs, however, there must be an awareness of the transcendent and immanent God Whose voice he is preparing to hear.

The religious man is one whose actions show that his life is built around the central purpose of moral aspiration. This inspires him to make a positive submission to everything sacred, and is the preface to a dialogue in which the Other would have the initiative. This "sacred" and this "Other" designate no other being than the God of the metaphysician, but it is very important for man to acknowledge Him as the transcendent subject with whom he is in necessary personal relationship. He is the being whom man may address in the second person rather than a being of whom one would speak in the third person. It is the task of a philosophy of religion to establish with dialectical rigour, by an analysis of the primitive adhesion of the will, how the profound purposiveness of the moral conscience is of a religious nature. But every man is bound to experience the difficulty of being faithful to the transcendent demands of his conscience; there is no need to do any philosophizing about this, because it is man's conscience that orients him toward his true destiny and makes him aware of his insufficiency in the effort to reach his final end.

It is by a deepening of his moral life that man prepares himself for the hypothesis of God's personal intervention in human destiny for the sake of salvation, and that he becomes disposed to recognize the signs of the desired coming of God. Self-examination and a break with the past, personalizing freedom and a troubled conscience, and the affirmation of the sacred along with the discontinuity of existence, all take place, together. It is within these simultaneous occurrences of behavior that the entreating call to man's transcendent destiny is secretly instilled. But it sometimes happens that the unusual character of the sign will abruptly arouse a moral dynamism, together with a gravity of the heart and anxious expectation, not previously experienced, in the sudden collapse of an unenlightened moral life. The passing of a saint often brings about a moral disturbance of this kind.

6. PHYSICAL MIRACLE AND MORAL MIRACLE

When men speak of a miracle, they usually mean a miracle of the physical order; we have been spontaneously using the term in this sense. However, we should not limit the manifestation of divine signs to the physical world or to the psychical world either. The *moral miracle* is of capital importance as an antecedent of faith. What is the divine activity implied in the moral miracle? Here we will observe the preternatural occurrence that manifests an astonishing variation from the norm of ordinary human behavior expressed in a kind of moral transcendence that surpasses the whole moral person in duration and is finally summed up in self-surrender. This can only be explained as something dependent upon divine energy.

It is easy to admit the superiority of the moral miracle as a religious sign, in spite of its apparent vagueness at the level of scientific criticism. (1) Each of us can be a witness and judge of this kind of miracle because of our own moral experience. It takes place over a period of time and not all in a moment. Technical competence is not necessary in order to discern it; a moral consciousness is sufficient for this purpose. However, a moral miracle inevitably

brings us face to face with another question in regard to our concern for personalization. (2) The moral miracle is immediately and
intrinsically related to the Word of God, and constitutes its visible
fecundity. God promises the Kingdom and sanctity, and the sign
shows by visible effects that the divine power is already fulfilling the
promise. The sign is homogeneous with what is signified. The living
God directs the sign to the religious man and penetrates to the very
heart of his liberty and destiny by the conjunction of the Word and
the sign. Consequently, the numerous signs of credibility which lead
men to conversion generally begin with the holiness of a Christian
or of a Christian community, which is best shown forth in true charity, inspired by the extraordinary moral character of Jesus which the
Gospels present for our imitation. Our Lord said, "By this will all
men know that you are my disciples, if you have love for one another" (Jn. 13:35; cf. 17:21). Wherever evangelization and a collective acceptance of the Christian faith occur, the ecclesiastical
community constitutes a public and unequivocal sign of the divine
origin of the Word to which it bears witness. It was the Vatican
Council that saw in the miracle of the Church a recapitulated and
perpetual sign of revelation (*Ibid.,* chap. 3; *Denz.* 1794). From her
present faith the Church draws the message of salvation, and from
this same faith the signs emanate which necessarily accompany its
preaching.

7. DISCERNMENT OF SIGNS AND GRACE

We have considered the dispositions that make a man religious
and that are necessary for the recognition of divine signs. But are
these dispositions the result of purely natural behavior or do they
proceed primarily from the personal action of the God of the Word
preparing a man for the faith? The Church, specifying the affirmations of Holy Scripture on the gratuity of faith, teaches us that the
grace of God is primary in the call and preparation that precede
belief, in cooperation with man's freedom (Council of Trent, Session VI, canon 3; *Denz.* 813). It has already been noted that the
subjective antecedents of faith are the same as those that pertain to
recognition of the sign. Doubtless the philosopher will be tempted
to see in this attitude of the religious man nothing more than the
practical consequence of ethical reflection whereby, because of his
spiritual nature, the man places his ultimate destiny in a hereafter
created wholly out of his own ideas—a supernatural world in the

broad and negative meaning of the term. But the theologian will reply that this conclusion, to be effectively realized, requires that the candidate for faith have the secret help of the Holy Spirit that he may be made righteous in preparation for the salvation that will be received when he has faith in the Gospel. All this takes place in such a way that the religious attitude is really the result of all the moral dynamism of the man in search of his true destiny, but already inspired by the unperceived presence of God. The refusal of this grace of call to the faith will bring about the refusal of the signs and eventually the rejection of the faith itself. In this respect, we see in the Gospels, those men who did not have a pure heart or who were not men of good will. These were the evil men who were scandalized by the miracles of Our Lord as they were also offended by His parables (cf. Mt. 13:13; Lk. 16:27-31; Jn. 5:44; 8:43-47; 12:37). The sign is the test of our subjective dispositions, and it is the sign that obliges a man to show what spirit is in him.

8. FROM THE SIGN TO THE ACT OF FAITH

"Miracles enable us to judge of doctrine, and doctrine enables us to judge of miracles" said Pascal (*Br.,* frag. 803). We have effectively seen how the well-disposed witness of a miracle proceeded by immediate inference from the miracle to its meaning because of a positive but hypothetical attitude in favor of the Gospel. This inference, however rapidly made, also includes an analyzable proof since the sign includes the preternatural occurrence. Furthermore, in certain cases, the sign may contain a proof that is objectively weak, but even if the recognition of the divine origin of the Word is therefore summary, it is never doubtful for the subject who is disposed to belief. All believers have their reasons for believing, founded upon signs, but not all of them can give reasons for their belief in a satisfactory way. A particular event wherein the most summarily critical analysis finds no evidence of a miracle will constitute a personal sign for the witness whose moral dynamism tends entirely toward conversion; in this sign the witness will clearly recognize the call of God. This should not be a cause for scandal, for the sign that is objectively weak is nevertheless sufficient for the subject to establish his own certainty of credibility which ultimately faith will consolidate. It is not the materiality of the sign that matters most in regard to the individual's approach to belief. As Pascal says further, "Our religion is wise and foolish. Wise, because it is the most learned, and the most founded on miracles, prophecies, etc. Foolish because it is not all this which makes us belong to it. This makes us indeed condemn those who do not belong to it; but it does not cause belief in those who do belong to it" (Frag. 587).

What has just been said concerning the acquired certainty that follows the sign and which has for its object the historical fact of the coming of God in Jesus Christ and in the Church, does not mean that this certainty of credibility must constitute a marked and distinct stage in the psychological process. The effective recognition of the sign supposes that one already accepts what is signified with all one's desire; and the desire is transformed at once into real adhesion as the waters of a river lose themselves in an estuary. As soon as the sign has appeared, the individual finds himself seized by the revealed mystery to which he is converted interiorly by the Holy Spirit. This is the *moment of Christian faith,* a real beginning, for he was exterior to the mystery only a moment before, although tending toward belief and ready to welcome its coming. The action of God and man's active response have been so mingled since the call to faith, and more especially since hearing the Word accompanied by the sign, that one would be tempted, in reading St. John's Gospel, or in considering various conversion experiences, to judge everything at the phenomenal level and attribute the causality of faith to the sign. But the psychological quasi-coincidence of the recognition of the sign and the act of faith which often occurs should not prevent our recognition of the interior revelation of the Spirit as the principal cause of the grace of faith in Christ. We must be careful to distinguish the motives for believing which are the signs recognized as such, and the intrinsic motive of the act of faith which gives it a divine quality following the action of divine causality that produces it.

9. ANTECEDENTS OF FAITH AND CONDITIONS OF FAITH

Is every man capable of the deepening of personal life in which we found the remote subjective antecedent of faith? It is obvious that many social, economic, and cultural conditionings either favor or hinder that deepening process. It seems that numerous men of good will do not arrive at Christian faith because of certain inhuman conditions of life; this is particularly true on a vaster scale than ever before in our time of technical evolution. A double task therefore becomes necessary together with evangelization. We must create a climate of human truth in which men become attentive to everything sacred in their existence. In this respect, we must work for the amelioration of the material conditions of life. This double task of pre-evangelization pertains especially to the laity. We must be careful, however, not to place the antecedents and the conditions of faith on the same level. It sometimes happens that men find their way to belief in spite of very unfavorable living conditions. Inversely, the mere transformation of these living conditions will never suffice to open a man's heart to the advent of God. Riches of all kinds can become idols which separate a man more radically from the faith than the worst conditions of distress.

After what we have said regarding subjective antecedents necessary for the concrete recognition of signs, one cannot identify, purely and simply, the climate of human truth which we have just considered, with any institutional action of Christianity, nor with a cartel of Christian morality. To make the human milieu morally healthy does not imply the imposition of a code of obligations which cannot be justified apart from the faith, but rather requires the genesis of a moral aspiration which is conducive to high moral standards, even though they are far below the moral ideals of a Christian man. On the other hand, this moral aspiration cannot be separated from the initial practice of an authentic fraternal love which is creative of true human communities in which God will be able to reveal Himself because love has preceded Him there. "But he who does the truth comes to the light" (Jn. 3:21).

10. THEOLOGY OF FAITH AND PSYCHOLOGY OF CONVERSION

In speaking of conversion, it is particularly the act of conversion to Jesus Christ which held our interest. And however much that act emerges in the personal duration of a man with reference to perceptible mediations of Transcendence, we have been led to speak of the antecedents of this act. Yet our view-point has been theological. A psychologist or a phenomenologist of religion would designate by conversion only those things which pertain to subjective antecedents in regard to natural religion. The fact that we have integrated in the theological analysis certain psychological elements common to the two sciences calls forth the following remarks:

(a) The pole of theological analysis being the specifically Christian act, we have concentrated our attention upon an ultimate stage in which the dispositions of religious consciousness and the Word and sign meet together. Certain conversions have this rapid climax, but in other cases a long ripening process is necessary for the combined Word and sign and the religious acceptance to meet in full clarity. Some accounts of conversion really cover a whole lifetime.

(b) In the analysis of the consciousness of the "religious man" we limited ourselves to a clarification. A psychological classification would give consideration to the multiplicity of specific types. There are temperaments that are more or less religious. For some people the expression of religious consciousness will appear as a call to a transcendence of light; for others, preferably as a desire for purification and adoration. It would certainly be wrong to see oppositions where there are only various complementary expressions.

(c) In considering first of all the affirmation of the Sacred in the extension of the world of Values, we have neglected the numerous ambiguous fixations of the sacred, whether conscious or unconscious, which menace with impurity the religious consciousness and implicitly the Christian consciousness. The criticism of the sacred on the cosmological, sociological and psychological planes is most often beneficial because of the equivocal problems that are solved and the evaluation effected regarding the categorical irreducibility of the religious sentiment defined in relation to everything that is authentically sacred.

(d) The signs which, in specific instances, humanly motivate Christian conversions, are obviously very diverse, from the most traditional to the most unusual. In the course of the preceding pages we have spoken *about* the sign that produces the certainty of credibility. But having done this, we have still left a great deal unsaid. It often happens in the concrete genesis of faith that the decisive sign is presented as the interior synthesis of a number of significant elements. While no particular element is essential, and each could be criticized on the basis of complementary facts, the meaningful totality possesses a persuasive power which qualitatively outweighs the sum-total of the elements. Therefore, in the moral miracle of which the Church is an example, the convergence of probable signs finally produces certain conviction thanks to the presence of subjective antecedents. This fact has often been noted.

"Finally," says Paul Claudel, "the Catholic religion must be proved by a catholic demonstration, that is to say, a total demonstration, and by this very totality itself. It is true because it is catholic, i.e., complete, and because it is the key to everything and the crowning of everything. It is not triumphant unless it is forever setting up its indivisible whole in opposition to every partial criticism" (Positions et propositions, II, p. 73).

11. CONCLUDING REMARKS

In all of this section we have placed ourselves in the perspective of the adult who is approaching the faith. Perhaps we have been asking ourselves, "What about the person who was baptized in infancy?" The answer is simple. In the preceding section we noted that such a person must experience a real conversion in order to ratify the sacrament of faith. He must now also ground his faith in his moral and historical existence. The only difference from the unbaptized consists in the conditions of this grounding which will be effected in the interior of a world of grace. This does not destroy the human effort, but greatly simplifies the procedure.

III. The Faith of Contemplation

1. FROM THE FAITH OF CONVERSION TO THE VIRTUE OF FAITH

"O Lord, illumine Thy people, and inflame their hearts with the splendor of Thy grace, that they may always acknowledge their Savior (faith of conversion), and worship Him in Truth (faith of contemplation)." (From the *Roman Missal,* Post-communion for the Vigil of the Epiphany.)

(a) *Promises and Grace*

St. Paul tells us that Abraham is the father of believers. This means that he is the father of all who have been converted. But the faith, which is the gift, in the Holy Spirit, of the final Covenant, goes beyond the stage of conversion. The Christian finds his justification in the resurrection of Jesus Christ (Rom. 4:25) and consequently he enters immediately into the mystery of Christ. In the act of conversion this mystery was still external to him, but now it is partly realized within himself, for Christ now lives in him by faith (Eph. 3:16-17), and the Spirit is given to him interiorly (Eph. 1:13; Gal. 3:14); thus he is enabled to enter into the immediate but partial possession of the heritage anciently promised and marvellously realized in Jesus Christ, the Amen of God.

Before conversion, and in the very act of conversion, except in the case of a baptized person, the Holy Spirit acted only in a transitory way in man. But now He is given to man, and because of this presence the believer will possess (in a stable manner), a power that assimilates him to Our Lord. This does not mean that the believer possesses the Spirit in a proprietary way, but rather that God is faithful to His Covenant. Scripture calls this gift and presence the Faith, and it is still the heart, as the conscious center of the whole person and the source of the act of conversion, which is now made an integral part of Christ Himself. In our modern theological vocabulary we speak quite spontaneously of grace (sanctifying or habitual) to describe this implanting of divine reality in the believer's heart. We speak of faith as the first of the powers, or theological virtues, in which this new existence finds active expression. But the language of Scripture has the advantage of preserving the larger meaning of *faith* with the connotation of totality which was apparent to us when we considered the origins of faith.

(b) *Faith, Hope, Charity*

In conversion the believer was united to the Word of God by his whole being. All of his faculties cooperated with the power of the Holy Spirit to lead him to acceptance of the Gospel. Will the same thing occur in this further stage of belief? The answer seems very simple to anyone who has learned his catechism and has become familiar with the satisfying tripartite division of the fundamental virtues of Christian activity. Everyone knows that this division often recurs in the writings of St. Paul. However, careful attention compels us to declare that the Apostle doesn't always say exactly what theological tradition attributes to him. When charity is mentioned along with faith, it is usually love for the brethren that is meant. This is the power of loving the brethren by imitation of Christ, a power that is supremely the work of faith which is also love of God. Hope designates the tension of faith impatient to see the whole Body of Christ sharing in the reign of the Risen Lord when His last manifestation takes place. This is a faith which hopes for what it does not yet possess, but which finds its final fulfillment, here and now, in the daily practice of the Christian love of the brethren. Apparently this is the Paulinian idea, concordant with the thought of St. John (I Jn. 2:9-12; 4:7-14). St. Paul uses the word love very rarely to designate our relationship with God (Rom. 8:28; I Cor. 2:9; 16:22; Eph. 6:24), whereas he uses it constantly to designate the attitude of God toward ourselves. The faith of the Christian responds to this love of God, *a faith acting through brotherly love*. The numerous texts in the Epistles that mention charity together with faith and hope are clear in this respect. For example, we may consider Col. 1:3-5: "We give thanks to the God and Father of our Lord Jesus Christ, praying always for you, for we have heard of your faith in Christ Jesus and of the love that you bear towards all the saints because of the hope that is laid up for you in heaven." [2]

It is "faith" that hopes, and it is "faith" that practices fraternal charity. This way of seeing the intimate relationship of the three theological virtues once again emphasizes how greatly faith unites the whole man to God, and why it could only have a personal Reality for its object. We communicate only with persons, and the faith is man's total communion with Christ. Fraternal love is intimately related to faith only because it is intrinsically theological and Christian, like faith itself. It is through ourselves and our brethren that Christ loves. And we also see that hope comes forth from this same faith-love of Christ. If we desire and wait for the reign of Christ, it should be evident that we have given our hearts entirely to this hope, and that we have gone far beyond the self-centered stage of individual salvation.

(c) *Intellectual Faith*

In reflecting upon Christian faith, and with the connections so marked and constantly maintained, we can now legitimately isolate the faith as intellectual consciousness and intelligible communion from within the "faith" as a whole. This provides a double grasp of reciprocal implications which are, nonetheless, formally distinguishable. Theological analysis has not failed in this respect, and the Church has encouraged it, for in this the Church has found the means of safeguarding more surely the objective determinants of Christian assent, and the Church holds to this above everything else. In her estimate there is nothing that escapes from illusion, especially nothing that passes for Christian, unless it be in accord with doctrinal affirmation. Even in his day St. John could write, "If that abides in you which you have heard from the beginning, you also will abide in the Son and the Father" (I Jn. 2:24). It was with this same concern that the Vatican Council formulated the well-known definition of faith in these terms: "A supernatural virtue whereby

---

[2] Cf. Rom. 5:1-2; I Cor. 13:2,13; II Cor. 8:7; Gal. 5:5-6; Eph. 1:15; 6:23; I Thess. 3:6; II Thess. 1:3; I Tim. 1:13; II Tim. 1:13; Titus 1:1-2; 2:2.

we believe, with the help of God's grace and by His inspiration, that whatever God has revealed is true, not because of any intrinsic truth grasped by the light of natural reason, but rather because of the authority of the revealing God Who can neither deceive nor be deceived" (*Ibid.*, chap. 3; *Denz.* 1789). Therefore, it is in this sense that we will refer to faith hereafter. We must never forget, however, that this lasting perfection of faith is impossible except upon the basis of a continuing conversion. Intellectual faith becomes abstract, and then runs the risk of becoming a purely formal "orthodoxy," if the actuality of conversion ceases.

2. THE WORLD OF FAITH

When we refer to the world of faith we shall include everything that pertains to the object of the faith. Scholastics would call this the material object. It has a content, presented under certain forms and formulas (which creates a problem of presentation). All of this must be studied.

(a) *Jesus Christ, the Fulness of the Word of God*

The faith of conversion implies an aspect of intellectual assent which the faith of contemplation only serves to develop, whereas the religious and vital context of the first assent remains the same as the knowledge of ulterior faith. This does not mean that there are two kinds of faith, but only two stages of the same faith. The object of the faith of conversion was Jesus Christ embracing the life of all men in His sacrifice. This object of faith was first received in a complete affirmation which did not require further development. However, the progress of subjective faith gradually interiorizes the implications. One cannot go beyond the mystery of Christ, and the believer of many years can say with the catechumen, summing up his entire faith, "I believe in Jesus Christ." The mystery of Jesus Christ constitutes, in fact, the fulness of the Word of God in three ways: (1) In Christ's Resurrection the whole divine intent of glorious vitality for all men, foretold by the prophets, was realized; no action of God in human history could be more decisive. (2) In the realization of the mystery of Christ, the living God has let us have a glimpse, in the greatest possible measure, of what we can now receive from the heart of Divinity. (3) The mystery of the personal Christ is continued in the mystery of the mystical Christ and constitutes the present work of salvation.

However, there are some who will say that the mystery of the Holy Trinity is perhaps more central in revelation than the mystery of Christ. In God Himself this is certainly true, but not in the revelation that tells of His mercy toward us. It is through Christ and in Christ that we are led to the threshold of the Trinitarian mystery by the successive manifestation of the divine Persons in the work of salvation. In eternity, perhaps, a Trinitarian synthesis of the glorious Universe will be allowed us, but in this present time our synthesis of faith can only be Christocentric. The writings of the New Testament and the very life of the Church are the certain guarantors of this truth against the various constructions and verbal affirmations of idealism.

It is therefore in Jesus Christ that the whole world of faith is recapitulated. To affirm any aspect of the faith will always be an affirmation of Jesus Christ. The mysteries of our faith are not successive affirmations which are added to one another like the links of a chain. They are more like the flowering of a blossom beginning with the seed, or like the display of coloring that follows the decomposition of light. There is essentially only one mystery, an organic mystery which gathers together the whole Word of God in the unity of living logic, profoundly perceived by the believer. Not all aspects of the world of faith have the same importance; it is only with reference to the central mystery of Jesus Christ that their hierarchy can be established.

In Jesus Christ the whole of history enters into the mystery as a component part in the world of faith. The believer sees and judges everything and all events, whether personal or social, from the viewpoint of the mystery of Christ. Nothing is really profane any longer, for everything is intended for the glorious recapitulation in Jesus Christ (Eph. 1:9-13; Col. 1:20). Even as a man might see the same landscape successively under cloudy skies and then in full sunshine, so likewise the new believer sees the same world and the same human history. For in Jesus we see the inseparable association of God and of human life, but we do not see God "in Himself."

(b) *The Stages of Catechesis*

Our comments concerning the organic unity of the Christian mystery points to an important consequence regarding its transmission. The Church of the first centuries, in her evangelizing activity, seems to have clearly distinguished the first preaching about Jesus Christ, the *kerygma,* from the later religious instruction—called catechetics in the strict meaning of the term—which presented the doctrinal and moral conclusions derived from the first preaching. The recent convert may be unaware of certain important points of the Church's faith for a while, although he really proclaims his belief in all of them when he makes his submission to Christ. This should not be considered as doctrinal minimizing. St. Paul himself did not act otherwise when, in first proclaiming the Good News of the Gospel, his primary purpose was to form communities of converts, delaying until later the detailed instructions which we find set forth in the great Epistles that are a model for us. One also finds in the Epistle to the Hebrews the distinction between elementary teaching about Christ and a more complete instruction (Heb. 6:1-2). Similarly, the historian Eusebius tells us about evangelization during the course of the first centuries. Regarding the evangelists, he writes, "They emulated one another in preaching and transmitting the Book of the divine teachings of the Gospel to all those who had not yet heard anything of the word of the faith. They were content to lay the foundations of faith among foreign peoples, and then they appointed pastors in whose care they left all whom they had just brought to belief" (*Ecclesiastical History,* 3, 37).

With regard to the Church's prophetic mission, it is the function of the priesthood to transmit religious instruction to converts, while the laity fulfill their proper function in the *kerygma,* although not exclusively. The history of evangelization during the first centuries shows the place they held in this respect.

(c) *The Rule of Faith*

When we insist upon the unity of the object of faith in Jesus Christ, it is not meant that the Catholic *Credo* should be minimized in any way. From the very beginning the Church has had the conviction that one of her first tasks was to maintain the objective integrity of the doctrine contained in the Word of God. It is the work of the Holy Spirit to assure the inward and personal character of the believer's faith, but the Church must be the guardian and teacher of that faith with the greatest possible precision. St. Paul's warning is clear on this point: "But even if we or an angel from heaven should preach a gospel to you other than that which we have preached to you, let him be anathema"! (Gal. 1:8) And this intransigeance echoes the teaching which the Apocalypse attributes to Jesus: "I testify to everyone who hears the words of the prophecy of this book. If anyone shall add to them, God will add unto him the plagues that are written in this book. And if anyone shall take away from the words of the book of this prophecy, God will take away his portion from the tree of life, and from the holy city, and from the things that are written in this book." [3]

The Church's concern for orthodox belief is not therefore of recent date. Her prophetic function is not limited to this concern, but the authenticity of its exercise is certainly dependent upon it. The Church was inspired to formulate her faith in dogmas and symbols for the communal expression of what she believes, and to allow each believer to compare the interior affirmation of his belief with the orthodox expression. The necessities of the liturgy, public confessions of faith in the times of persecution, and polemical writings were originally dogmatic and symbolical formulae whose primitive elements are found in the New Testament (cf. Mat. 28:19; I Cor. 8:8; Eph. 4:4-6; I Tim. 2:5; etc.).

In Volume I of this work (chap. 1) the difficult problems of the Church's mediation of the Word of God were set forth. We must now remember that the Church is only the custodian of the revealed Word—mistress of its formulation, but wholly subject to its content. The Vatican Council declares, "The doctrine of faith revealed by God is committed to the Spouse of Christ as a divine deposit to be faithfully kept and infallibly promulgated. Therefore, the meaning of the sacred dogmas which must always be preserved is that which our holy mother Church has declared once and for always . . ." (*Ibid.,* chap. IV; *Denz.* 1800). The believer must be able to combine the living and personal unity of the unique affirmation of the Christian mystery with the multiplicity of dogmatic proclamations which the Magisterium of the Church has had to make in affirming the faith in its fulness. However, the formal definitions do not limit the act of faith which embraces the whole of reality in Jesus Christ. It is to be feared that the undeniable pedagogical advantage of symbolical or catechetical expositions of the faith is sometimes off-set by the loss of a living and personal unity of the object of faith. This could be remedied, at least in part, if we were careful to mention God or Christ as the active subject in every analytical proposition of doctrine. For instance, the Apostles' Creed

[3] Apoc. 22:18-20; cf. Col. 2:6-7; I Tim. 6:3-6; 20; II Tim. 1:12-14; 2:14-20; 4:1-6; Jude 3.

declares the *actions* of God for the salvation of the world, rather than concepts which make these actions objective. It was Jesus Christ Who was made man, and not the Incarnation.

The Christian faith is therefore an affirmation of reality. It demands an affirmative and negative response of the human mind. This affirmation is a supernatural act. It is nevertheless true that the act embraces the structures of objective affirmation which the human intellect has made. A theory of knowledge which denied the possibility of realistic affirmation of objects distinct from the knowing mind, like the theories proposed by philosophies of idealist identity or the various subjectivist systems, however mystical they may be, would be radically opposed to the orthodox faith. And that is why the Church has often been involved in philosophical controversy. She must claim an objective power and a background of eternity at the level of human affirmation. This condition is implicit in the maintenance in human consciousness of the eternal import of God's Word. For those men whose intellectual reflections are exacting, it is essential to think well in order to believe well.[4]

3. THE KNOWLEDGE OF FAITH

How does the world of faith become the object of intelligible communion in the believer's mind? For the intelligence to know anything, it is necessary to make reality alive within one's self by the assimilation of its content of being. This is the source of certitude. We shall now try to understand how this knowing activity is verified at the level of faith.

(a) *The Theological Virtue of Faith*

It is very important to understand what is meant by a theological virtue. For it is nothing less than the active power given to the believer that enables him to live in communion with the living God and to base all his activity in God. By revelation God was manifested outwardly to the world while using human mediations of the Word. But that is only one aspect of God's act of love for us, which constitutes revelation. What would it matter to man that God had given Himself if man could not recognize Him or enter into communion with Him? However, it is only God Who can open man's heart interiorly so that man may know Him. It is in the same act

---

[4] Cf. the Encyclical *Pascendi* of Pius X, in Denz. 2071-2081, and *Humani Generis* of Pius XII, of August 21, 1950.

of benevolent communication that God repeats externally the Word of Salvation deposited in the historical mediations, and also predisposes man to accept it inwardly (I Thess. 2:13). St. Matthew calls this *revelation* (Mt. 11:25; 16:17), and St. John, in his Gospel, refers to the *drawing-power of the Father* (Jn. 6:44-46, 65) and in his first Epistle he mentions the *witness* of God (5:10). St. Paul tells of the *illumination of the heart* (II Cor. 4:6; Eph. 1:17-18). In God revelation is a personal act, a manifestation of light and love. The interior power which lifts the believer to divine communion also affects the whole personality, and therefore it may be said that there is only one theological activity. For however much we have legitimately distinguished the aspect of knowledge in faith, we must attribute to God the source and energy of the act of faith in so far as He is the Revealer of Truth. Theologians call this the primal Truth, the source of all supernatural intelligibility. But here again we must be careful to recognize that which unites the theological virtues as well as the things that distinguish them.

To believe because God has revealed it will be adherence to the world of faith because God now endows us with the principle of grace whereby we can enter into intelligible contact with this divine world. This is the efficient first cause and the formal cause of the act of faith. Because of this principle, which is the light of faith, the intelligence of the believer finds itself in a certain continuity with the very activity of the divine Intelligence. It is not the empirical manifestation of the fact of revelation, nor the signs which have verified it, which motivate the act of faith in an immediate way. It is rather the eternal and contemporary act that is the cause of the historical manifestation itself, the living and blessed God in the very act of communication with men. Attributing this virtue of illumination particularly to the Holy Spirit, St. Paul writes, "And no one can say 'Jesus is Lord' except in the Holy Spirit" (I Cor. 12:3; cf. I Cor. 2:5; Eph. 2:8). It is consequently unnecessary to demonstrate that faith is a supernatural activity, for it is supernatural in its very principle. It is with the vision that God has given that the believer receives everything that God manifests to him. The believer is in the light (cf. Jn. 12:36; II Cor. 4:6; Eph. 5:8; Thess. 5:4-5).

(b) *The Faith, Knowledge of Assent*

The believer, in the light of God, adheres to the world of faith. But what does this mean? Adherence implies more than assent. It is not merely an external agreement with regard to affirmations about God, but a judgment of truth brought forth from within, concerning the mystery in all its aspects, that accompanies the conviction that this is reality, continuous with the witness of God.

This assent which the light of faith produces in the believer becomes the adherence of the whole person, avid to enter more completely into the mystery to which the believer was converted. For it is always conversion which is the basis of the knowledge of faith, a conversion which has become more profound and has passed from an avid love of Christ to a love that is more disinterested. Conversion makes this adherence more penetrating and enjoyable even if the mystery remains quite incomprehensible. Once more we find that fulness of communion in which the intellectual elements of faith are inserted.

The assent of faith comprises a large number of intelligible representations, but these representations, which have a human meaning when referred to experience, are assumed in the act of faith whenever we make an affirmation of truth of which God is always the subject. This is why there is no empirical evidence for our belief. The affirmations of the believer concerning the Mystery of Christ transcend human mediations and acquire their reality and their savor of truth in God Himself, quite beyond all experience of the senses. If we possessed a full understanding of the world of faith, we would be seeing God as He is in Himself. But the believer has for his portion only a mysterious affinity of his judgment with the affirmation of the Word of God, together with the consciousness of the inadequacy of any recourse to rational experience. "Now faith is the substance of things to be hoped for, the evidence of things that are not seen" (Heb. 11:1).

Adherence of this kind obviously produces certitude. This is immediately apparent to anyone who understands that God Himself is the immanent assurance rather than the proof of credibility assumed by the act of faith. It is because of God that faith is certain, in spite of the lack of evidence. This is a certainty that does not always allow for psychological consciousness or the appeasement which follows upon evidence, but rather presents its claims to the consideration of believers. At this point we should remember with Newman that "ten thousand difficulties do not make a doubt" and the greatest saints have experienced, at certain moments, the psychological disappearance of their certainty without in any way relaxing their steadfast adherence to the Faith. For example, St. Therese of the Child Jesus could say, "Jesus allowed my soul to be filled with the deepest darkness, and the very thought of heaven which had been so sweet ever since my earliest childhood, became for me a subject of struggle and torment. I wish that I could express what I feel, but it's quite impossible! One must have traveled through this dark tunnel to understand its obscurity. . . . However, I don't want to write more about it. I should be afraid of blaspheming. I am even afraid that I have said too much about it now. But may God forgive me! He knows very well that I force myself to perform the good works of faith, even when I do not possess the enjoyment of belief. I have pronounced more acts of faith in the course of the past year than during all my life" (Histoire d'une âme, 1946, pp. 136-138).

(c) *The Faith, Interior Knowledge*

This dark stage of belief does not describe the habitual state of communion with God which is the consequence of the light of faith. On the basis of an adherence penetrating deep into the world of faith in which he becomes wholly absorbed, the believer is called to a certain interior experience of the spiritual world which is the fruit of the presence of the Spirit of Christ: "And as for you, let the anointing which you have received from him, dwell in you, and you have no need that anyone teach you. But as his anointing teaches you concerning all things, and is true and is no lie, even as he has taught you, abide in him" (I Jn. 2:26-28). Here again there is a re-inforcement of the reciprocal causality of affective communion and intelligible communion which we previously considered under the form of conversion-adherence. Just as one advances in the knowledge of a person by a close relationship with the other's center of personality through love, similarly with regard to the Christian mystery it is through adherence to God and to Christ in the practice of a Christian life, and especially fraternal charity, that we are able to progress in our knowledge of God.

In reading the apostolic writings one should be careful not to identify with intellectual consciousness all of the texts that pertain to knowledge. In line with the Old Testament tradition, when knowing God meant belonging to His chosen people, doing His Will, confessing His presence and the power of His works, it was only the converted man—the man who lived in Christ—who could know God. To know truth has the same meaning. This does not exclude an affirmation of intelligible communion in favor of the faith of conversion. But the emphasis is not placed there. The assent of faith originally had the connotation of knowledge in a more exact sense than we use the term today. The knowledge of assent and interior knowledge are closely bound together, for the latter is really a perfection of the former, being more like the knowledge of philosophical language. This perfection in the order of knowledge is deeply rooted in conversion and in the Christian life. Preference is still made to the knowledge of Old Testament usage rather than that of philosophical intellectualism.

In a partial way the fatih is already a definitive perfection of the believer in so far as it accomplishes his salvation and unites him interiorly to God. This is an anticipation of the glory to come. On the other hand, faith is an imperfection because it requires that we make our journey far from Our Lord. For however deeply the believer may be able to penetrate the world of faith, there can be no escape from the essential darkness that prevents the vision of God, and there must always be a dependence upon the witness of the Word. "We see now through a mirror in an obscure manner," says St. Paul, "but then face to face. Now I know in part, but then I shall know even as I have been known" (I Cor. 13:12). And again, "for we walk by faith and not by sight" (II Cor. 5:7; cf. Rom. 8:24-25; 11:33-36).

Somewhere between pure assent and clear vision lies the believer's area of knowledge. Let us lay hold upon the luminous rays of that knowing faith.

1. Apart from contemplation of the world of faith, beginning with the vision of God Himself, the believer can nevertheless acquire a satisfying understanding of the whole plan of salvation in Jesus Christ. For everyone who enters into this world of faith there is a revelation that is marvellously coherent in which all human reality acquires a desired meaning. And in the center is the Person of Christ as the sustaining power of the universe and the revelation of infinite love. Is not this what St. Paul desired for the Ephesians when he wrote, ". . . and to have Christ dwelling through faith in your hearts: so that, being rooted and grounded in love, you may be able to comprehend with all the saints what is the breadth and length and height and depth, and to know Christ's love which surpasses knowledge, in order that you may be filled unto all the fulness of God" (Eph. 3:17-20; cf. Eph. 1:17-20; Col. 2:2).

2. In the time of the Old Covenant God made Himself known through His external acts of power, and in the same way He now reveals Himself through the inward working of His power of holiness in Jesus Christ. The Christian experiences the power of Christ's resurrection upon himself. He is conscious of the mysterious energy that enables him to love in a superhuman way; he perceives a presence of love in his life and in the life of the Church. How can anyone fail to identify the gifts of Christ with Christ Himself, in a vital relationship, or fail to anticipate an eventual immediate contact with Him? We do this in the same way as a man who traces his personal acts back to his soul as the source of all his activity. "So that I may know him," writes St. Paul to the Philippians, referring to Christ, "and the power of his resurrection and the fellowship of his sufferings: become like to him in death, in the hope that somehow I may attain to the resurrection from the dead" (Phil. 3:10; cf. I Jn. 4:7-9; 5:19-20). The fervent believer knows the realism that gradually impregnates his assent to the *Credo* when he has related it to Christian experience in the Holy Spirit. The prophecy of Jeremias is then fulfilled: "And they shall teach no more every man his neighbor, and every man his brother, saying: Know the Lord: for all shall know me from the least of them even to the greatest" (Jer. 31:31-34).

3. There is a final aspect of knowledge derived from faith that we must now consider. This is the power of contemplating one's own life from within the mystery of Christ, and of judging consequently what is according to God's Will. This is a kind of power of spontaneous discernment that enables us to know what is really Christian and what is not. Paul desired this power also for the Christians of his day. "This is why we too have been praying for you . . . asking that you may be filled with the knowledge of his will, in all spiritual wisdom and understanding. May you walk worthily of God and please him in all things" (Col. 1:9-10).

If the Christian is normally called to such a deepening of his faith, we can better understand that all his anterior motives for believing are resolved in his experience as a believer, and this now becomes a personal sign for him. This does not mean that he has denied or renounced his earlier motives, but that he discovers they are no longer adequate because they are too external. Is not the vital and intellectual harmony resulting from the faith an irrefutable proof for a man that he has not put his belief in a myth? The proof of all truth is that it gives life.

4. THE AGES OF FAITH (Faith of the Child, the Adolescent and the Adult)

In the preceding pages we have been considering faith in its mature stage. But the faith is a living reality which develops along with the personality. It is not in vain that God has given man thirty years for the full development of self and the fixing of his choices. Christ Himself wanted to experience all the ages of man. It is only in maturity that faith takes on all its dimensions. This does not mean that the faith of a child or an adolescent is untrue, but only that such faith is in the growing stage and is therefore still incomplete. The use of psychological principles to characterize in a general way the various ages of faith can be a very interesting study.

(a) *The Faith of the Child*

The child is naturally religious by temperament; faith is easy for him. This aptitude is due to two factors in his psychological make-up. He seeks protection and yet lives dependently. He has a sense of the invisible and the symbolical. These two traits certainly bring him into relationship with the sacred. But however authentic the child's abandonment to God may be, it is almost too simple to be solid. His faith will have to mature. And this will be achieved as he passes from an ambiguous religious sentiment to an acceptance of the Word of God in Jesus Christ, as he becomes capable of distinguishing more clearly the mystery from the myth.

(b) *The Faith of the Adolescent*

A breaking with the world of childhood and the affirmation of personal autonomy, exuberant human vitality, introspective attention, and the beginnings of rationalism, are the psychological factors underlying the faith of the adolescent. It is easy to see how they contrast with the faith of a child. This is the source of the crisis which generally marks the passage from one age to another, especially from the religious point of view.

The crisis surrounding the ties of human dependence (family, teachers, church) and of the forms of authority (an obligatory religion) makes possible a new bond with Christ freely chosen in the degree that this bond can be made to seem personal.

The adolescent's eagerness for life is not necessarily pagan. It is concurrent with a call to the infinite. This will induce the adolescent to submit himself to Christ if he has discovered that the faith leads him into the world of vitality and eternal youth of the Risen One. "It is to the glory of God that men should have life."

Introspective fixation can lead to egoism, but it also constitutes a possible factor of personalizing and interiorizing the faith. Growing rationalism in regard to the mystery will be easily overcome if we present the mystery as a personal reality and the faith as a meeting of persons rather than an acceptance of enigmas.

We must also keep in mind that moral difficulties and the accompanying sense of guilt will open the adolescent to the hope of an inward liberation which the faith brings him, but we must not exploit such difficulties morbidly.

Consequently a new synthesis of faith is built upon the critical consideration of the faith of childhood. It is not definitive, however, and we can plainly see how such faith must yet mature. There will have to be the passage from acceptance of God under the sign of the humanist affirmation of self to a more self-giving submission, and the passage from the joy of believing and the emotional sentiment of belief to the unromantic decision to unite one's whole life to Christ, to integrate human sacrifice and failure with eternal life. There must also be a discovery of the social dimensions of the faith, with the understanding that these are not contrary to the personal dimensions. But the most essential thing is an affirmation of the purpose of personal conversion to Christ.

(c) *The Adult's Faith*

The reality and harshness of life discovered in maturity delivers the severest blow against the optimistic and humanistic faith of the young man. But through this crisis the maturing factors mentioned in the preceding section will be fully operative. A certain number of purifications will enable the adult to go beyond the enthusiasms of sentiment, intelligence and action which were bound up with adolescent faith. A synthesis of adult faith can be summed up in three major points:

1. This new synthesis has now integrated human reality. The mature man knows that he must abandon his youth and give serious thought to the fact of death. He experiences tragedy at the very heart of his existence. He has become aware of sin, and he has become capable of accepting himself for what he is. All of this leads

to a more complete dependence of his entire destiny in his relationship with Christ in the act of Faith.

2. Faith is no longer preoccupied with the need to protect itself. It is now a sure faith, fearing nothing that is true or real in human values, because it is never a mere evasion or weakness. A great peace accompanies this kind of faith.

3. The adult believer lives by the faith, whereas the adolescent merely possessed the faith. The adult's whole life is essentially related to the mystery of Christ in a lucidity that is more and more continuous, going far beyond human references and the security of good works. Jesus Christ becomes wholly transcendent while interiorizing His presence at the same time. The words of St. Paul to the Philippians illustrate this deepening of faith: "But the things that were gain to me, these, for the sake of Christ, I have counted loss. Nay more, I count everything loss because of the excelling knowledge of Jesus Christ, my Lord. For his sake I have suffered the loss of all things, and I count them as dung that I may gain Christ and be found in him, not having a justice of my own, which is from the Law, but that which is from faith in Christ, the justice from God based upon faith" (Phil. 3:7-10).

(d) *Maturity of Faith*

Hereafter the adult must live maturely in the faith. He must "with a right and good heart, having heard the word, hold it fast, and bear fruit in patience" (Luke 8:15). The faith is more and more impregnated with hope and becomes fidelity. One enters wholly into the Beatitudes promulgated by Our Lord. The apostolic action deepens; it becomes more radiant although less dynamic.

(e) *Crises of Faith*

We have used the word crisis on several occasions. But we need not be afraid of this term. There are mortal crises and there are crises of growth. The critical passage from one age of belief to another will be mortal if the system of religious instruction has been an attempt to construct fallaciously upon ambiguous elements of childish or adolescent faith, without demonstrating the ulterior synthesis and supposing consequently that all risk has been avoided. All human growth has the element of risk. But these risks must be integrated in a positive manner. The faith is no exception to this rule. It may even happen that it becomes a duty to provoke the breaks that determine crises, if only to hasten the passage to mature belief. Too many adults still live very poorly upon adolescent faith, or even childish faith. On the other hand it sometimes happens that the action of God Himself burns all the bridges behind us. St. Therese of Lisieux is a wonderful example. Her experience of faith prematurely unfolded a human experience which ordinarily precedes.

IV. Varieties of Unbelief

This last section will be devoted to the study of attitudes contrary to the Faith. One can be opposed to the Christian faith by refusal to embrace it—this is called incredulity—or by defection, which is apostasy and heresy. Finally, there is the opposition of inconsistency, which is formalism in belief.

1. INCREDULITY, UNBELIEF AND INFIDELITY

Incredulity, unbelief and infidelity are three words which express a very similar reality. Incredulity is an emphatic refusal to believe in Christ. Infidelity and unbelief simply mean that one does not believe, either because of a refusal or because of involuntariness. Unbelief, however, is more Godless than infidelity, for this latter term includes the religious pagan.

(a) *Rejection of the Faith*

The whole Gospel of St. John is built around the drama that contrasts light and darkness, faith and unbelief. This drama, in which man's destiny is at stake, continues to be played around the Word that manifests the Lord just as it was formerly played around His historical person, and in this drama certain men refuse to believe the Gospel for reasons that are diametrically opposed to the motives that lead others to the light. These are intellectual motives primarily, but their only value is derived from insufficient or evil moral dispositions. It is with the heart that one believes, and with the heart one may refuse to believe. The refuge of the unbeliever in agnosticism, scepticism, or dilettantism is rarely a simple attitude, and may even be provisionally among some men a real illness of the mind inherited from some school of thought. "And if our gospel also is veiled," writes St. Paul to the Corinthians, "it is veiled only to those who are perishing. In their case, the god of this world has blinded their unbelieving minds, that they should not see the light of the gospel of the glory of Christ, who is the image of God" (II Cor. 4:3-4).

It is with respect to the person of Jesus Christ that incredulity is concretely affirmed. This supposes that His claims have been authentically proclaimed and that signs have accompanied the proclaiming. But this does not happen as often as we might expect. The refusal will be a simultaneous rejection of the external teaching and indocility toward the interior grace that would lead to belief after help had been given to recognize the signs. The permanent causes of incredulity are pride and the avid desire for unrestricted liberty, together with the darkness that is the consequence of sensual living or false living.

It is impossible to exaggerate the seriousness of the sin of unbelief. In the Book of Acts, which records the first Christian preaching, a tragic background envelops the preaching of the Good News, for the judgment of God is operative and the salvation of all who hear the preaching is at stake if they do not open their hearts. When Jesus sent His apostles on their first preaching mission, He said, "he who does not believe shall be condemned" (Mark 16:16, cf. Mt. 10:14-15; Lk. 10:10-12; Jn. 15:22-26; Apoc. 21:8). St. John tells us the reason for this gravity: "He who believes in the Son of God has the testimony of God in himself. *He who does not believe the Son, makes him a liar*" (I Jn. 5:10). And just as we cannot believe in Christ except through the Holy Spirit (I Cor. 12:3), it is also true that the man who refuses to believe in Christ is sinning against the Holy Spirit. For this reason incredulity is commonly identified with blasphemy against the Holy Spirit, and this is the unforgiveable sin.

(b) *Incredulity and Indifference*

Incredulity is so serious that the Church is obliged to denounce it and to protect individuals from it. She must also prevent the propagation of those social trends which are favorable to it. A certain intolerance in principle is commonly bound up with belief. Indifference and dogmatic liberalism would never be acceptable to a believer. But how can this intransigeance be reconciled with respect for the unbeliever? We must also consider the problem of reconciling the rights of truth with free access to the faith. The attitude of the fanatic and the totalitarian is quite as contrary to the reign of true Christian faith as liberalism itself.

In her opposition to the factors of incredulity the Church has certainly expressed her unchanging position in ways that are both practical and variable. The use of external means of constraint which she formerly encouraged in one particular context of Christian history seemed to her more and more inadmissible and finally inefficacious. Furthermore, since the Middle Ages there has developed a sense of respect for conscience, even for the erring conscience, together with a concern for the subjective elements of the affirmation of truth. The Church has accepted this development, but this must not be confused with liberalism. There are certain distinctions to be kept in mind, however, because the protection of the erring man who rejects the faith is not to be extended to the errors themselves. According to the code of canon law (canon 1351), no one can be compelled to profess the Catholic faith. It is true, nevertheless, that Christians and the Church have the obligation to witness prophetically in the midst of a pagan world, especially when there is militant and persecuting incredulity (cf. I Peter, 2:11-13). The affirmation of a living faith and a vigorous evangelization—unlike proselytism based upon human power—constitute the best combative armament against the rejection of God. The various defenses and institutional protections are only secondary.

(c) *Credulity*

When we denounce rejection of the Faith, we must likewise repudiate credulity, an attitude that is almost equally serious. As a kind of revenge against rationalism, credulity has increased considerably in modern times, just as it developed in the period of decadence of Greek civilization. Refusing to serve the only true God, many people seek the formulae of salvation from the pseudo-prophets and pseudo-revelations that require no conversion. The credulity of the masses seems to be unlimited. It responds to the religious yearnings of the human heart in an illusory manner and disintegrates personalities at the very point where the Word of God would ensure their fulfillment in the truth. This is nothing more than a parody of Christian faith and a degradation of the religious spirit which is the basis of man's essential greatness. The Apostle denounced this evil prophetically; writing to Timothy he said, "For there will come a time when they will not endure the sound doctrine; but having itching ears, will heap up to themselves teachers according to their own lusts, and they will turn away their hearing from the truth and turn aside rather to fables" (II Tim. 4:3-5). Peter contrasts real faith with that kind of credulity in his second Epistle: "For we were not following fictitious tales when we made known to you the power and coming of our Lord Jesus

Christ, but we had been eyewitnesses of his grandeur" (II Pet. 1:16; cf. I Jn. 4:1; I Cor. 12:2-3; I Thess. 5:19-21).

(d) *Faith Without Evangelization*

"For whoever calls upon the name of the Lord shall be saved," writes St. Paul to the Romans. "How then are they to call upon him in whom they have not believed? But how are they to believe him whom they have not heard? And how are they to hear, if no one preaches?" (Rom. 10:12-15). We have already mentioned the unbelievers who have heard the Word and rejected it. But what can be said about the involuntary infidels whom the Gospel has never reached? We know that it is not necessary to suppose that only a desert island, untouched by any kind of preaching, could be in such a condition. The historical character of Word-bearing mediations and of signs is not limited exclusively in a spatial manner, but also by sociological and psychological structures. Every day we meet men of good will who have never had occasion to reject the Gospel for the simple reason that they have never heard it.

The text of St. Paul, quoted above, like all revelation closely unites faith and salvation (cf. Mk. 16:16; Jn. 3:5; Heb. 11:6). The Church has simply continued this necessary identification. "Because it is impossible," declares the Vatican Council, "to please God without the faith (Heb. 11:6) and to be received into the society of its children; justification is not possible for anyone without the faith, and nobody will obtain eternal life if he does not persevere unto the end (Mat. 10:22). In order that we may satisfy the duty of embracing the true faith and persevere therein with steadfastness, God instituted the Church by His only Son and provided visible signs surrounding this institution in such a way that this same Church might be recognized by all men as the guardian and dispenser of the revealed Word" (chap. 3; *Denz.* 1793). However, it may seem that we are arguing in circles, for we are now particularly concerned about those men who have never had any contact with the Church's mediation.

Elsewhere revelation teaches us that all men are called to salvation in Jesus Christ. Let us hear St. Paul again: "God our Savior . . . wishes all men to be saved and to come to the knowledge of the truth" (I Tim. 2:3-4). And in the same Epistle he also writes, "we hope in the living God, who is the savior of all men, especially of believers" (*ibid.*, 4:10). His message to the Romans is similar:

Tribulation and anguish shall be visited upon the soul of every man who works evil; of Jew first and then of Greek. But glory and honor and peace shall be awarded to everyone who does good, to Jew first and then to Greek. Because with God there is no respect of persons. For whoever have sinned without the Law, will perish without the Law; and whoever have sinned under the Law, will be judged by the Law. For it is not they who hear the Law that are just in the sight of God; but it is they who follow the Law that will be justified. When the Gentiles who have no law do by nature what the Law prescribes, these having no law are a law unto themselves. They show the work of the Law written in their hearts. Their conscience bears witness to them, even when conflicting thoughts accuse or defend them. This will take place on the day when, according to my gospel, God will judge the hidden secrets of men through Jesus Christ (Rom. 2:9-17).

In this passage St. Paul makes no mention of the faith, and we must find some way to reconcile these affirmations with his previous insistence upon the mediation of faith as necessary to salvation. This question would present a great difficulty to anyone who failed to conceive of faith in Christ except in terms of an explicit dogmatic confession. After what was said about the faith of conversion, and remembering St. Paul's comments, as these pertain to the faith of Abraham and our own, it seems normal to see in obedience to the witness of moral conscience a real beginning of faith and the first stage of conversion whereby the unevangelized person touches the mystery of salvation in Jesus Christ. When St. Thomas Aquinas affirms that the immanent dialectic of the first act of real moral freedom 'points to a commitment so profound in regard to a man's egoism or his conversion to the Other that he finds himself either condemned or justified in the sight of God (I^a II^{ae}, q. 89, a. 6), he is simply expressing the same thought as the Apostle.

This faith, implicitly Christian, coincides with the state of mind of the religious man, open to the Word and the signs. A man discovers the seriousness of every human act, although this discovery may require many years to become precise. He learns that these acts pertain to values that are beyond the moral phenomenon. There follows an attitude of truthfulness in life and obedience to moral aspiration. In the human behavior of such a man there is something consistent, unifying and real for the moral world. But this something does not equal the purposiveness of the voluntary movement in itself. The absolute Value now appears as an empirical inference, immanent in the other values, and these are immanent in the moral phenomena, as though underlying them, and certifying them in a transcendent manner. This is so true that it is in reference to this moral absolute that every man, perhaps unconsciously, is called to plan his existence willingly and gladly in accord with an obedience to the attraction of the transcendent factor that accounts for all his moral élan. In this way of life the man no longer does only what is pleasing to himself; he is no longer concentrating upon himself. He experiences fidelity and infidelity. Ordinarily it will be in his relations with other men that the essential part of that fidelity will be concretely demonstrated (cf. Mat. 13).

If a human life is to be lived in this way consistently, in spite of occasional slips and failures, there must be conversion to the truth and attentiveness to the interior voice of conscience, and for this the influence of grace is necessary. Revelation is an external gift of the Word and an interior grace of conversion to the Word. Even those who have not heard the Word must nevertheless take their stand with regard to the interior gift of God. They must accept or refuse. And when there is consent there is a beginning of true communion with the unseen but present God. It is not absolutely necessary that the God Whom we have chosen to obey should be clearly identified or named. It may sometimes happen that a man who is the victim of prejudice will reject the name of God, but a man reveals his true self in his activity more than in declaration. Objectively, therefore, it is in relation to the Church's faith in Jesus Christ that this moral faith acquires saving value. We may continue to speak of natural religion, but we must remember that grace is already the artisan that makes a man profoundly faithful to himself. We may go on speaking of unbelievers, but we know that already this expression has begun to be contradicted by an act of faith of some kind or other.

At this point we face the question of faith in the non-Christian religions, and this is a complex question, for while it is true that a truly pure spiritual attitude may be developed in a pagan cult, in other cases it will be a matter of credulity and magic. In the vocabulary of Bergson this would be called open religion or closed religion. Modern research in religious ethnology tends to emphasize the presence of a primitive attitude of religious consciousness with respect to a unique principle of holiness. This is apparent even when the forms of this consciousness are very impure, and is observable in almost all positive religions. It is certain that truly religious men of these different religions, especially the mystics, have verified this conclusion by the distinctions they make between human deformations and authentic affirmations of religious consciousness. Providentially the non-Christian religions

seem to be religions of transition which facilitate the spiritual decision that leads to salvation when there has been no evangelization.

In the chapter that pertains to the Church we shall consider the
real status of these secret believers.

2. APOSTASY AND HERESY

(a) *Apostasy*

Apostasy is essentially a complete "deconversion." The apostate is
a renegade. Primarily it means a denial of the affirmations of the
faith. But it is evident, if we consider what the faith really is, that
intellectual denial rarely occurs without an accompanying moral
denial also. Christian tradition is very severe toward apostasy. "For
if after escaping the defilements of the world through the knowledge
of our Lord and Savior Jesus Christ, they are again entangled therein
and overcome, their latter state has become worse for them than the
former. For it were better for them not to have known the way of
justice, than having known it, to turn back from the holy commandment delivered to them" (II Pet. 2:20-21). And St. Paul tells us:
"if we endure, we shall also reign with him; if we disown him, he
also will disown us" (II Tim. 2:12). The Vatican Council echoes
the apostolic teaching in these terms:

> They who have held fast to Catholic truth by the heavenly gift of faith,
> and those who, influenced by human opinions, follow a false religion, are far
> from finding themselves on equal footing. Those, in fact, who have received
> the faith under the Magisterium of the Church, can never have a just cause
> for modifying it or for questioning it again.

> If anyone says that the faithful and those who have not yet received the
> only true faith are in the same situation, so that Catholics have a just cause
> to question the faith they have received under the Magisterium of the Church,
> withholding their full assent until they have completed a scientific demonstra-
> tion of the credibility and truthfulness of their faith, let him be anathema
> (chap. 3 and canon 6; *Denz.* 1794, 1815).

In this text the Council points out how greatly the grace of faith
interiorly connaturalizes the believer with the mystery, and to what
extent, exteriorly, the motives for belief are serious. This is so true
that, in principle, the man who has the faith could hardly turn away
from it with good cause. The Catholic Faith, for the believer, is not
a probability which one may discuss on the same level as other human
certitudes. This reveals the serious guilt of most apostates, but it does

not exclude the exceptional possibility of an apostasy in good faith for intellectual reasons or because of weaknesses of character.

Our consideration of the conciliar affirmation raises the question of *those who have been brought to the only true faith under the Magisterium of the Church.* It is evident that quite a number of baptized people do not receive sufficient religious instruction or participate explicitly enough in the Church's life to fulfill these special conditions. Shall we brand as apostates all baptized persons who profess unbelief or positive indifference, even claiming that they have never had any real faith at all? From a canonical point of view the Church will consider them as apostates, but she does not pronounce upon the guilt of an act in which social responsibility and personal responsibility are intermingled.

(b) *Heresy*

The heretic exercises a choice in the complex object of Christian assent. He claims to commit himself to Christ and to believe in His Word, but at the same time he rejects certain affirmations of that Word, or at least he rejects the way in which the charismatic Magisterium of the Church presents them. It is easy to see the nature of the sin of heresy. If the faith is essentially a union with the Spirit of God Who reveals Himself, the man who exercises private judgment in matters of faith constitutes himself a judge of the truth of salvation on an equal level with the Holy Spirit. If his rejection of any particular point of faith is formal, this is sufficient to taint his entire faith at its very source of light. O man, who are you to judge the secrets that God delivers to thee?

This fundamental gravity of heresy is paralleled by a separation from the community of the faithful, for it is through the faith primarily that the Church is one, and it is to safeguard that precious unity of faith that Our Lord first founded the Church. We have already said that the doctrinal intransigeance of the Catholic Church is based upon this fact. The Vatican Council affirmed this very forcefully:

The Church which has received, together with the apostolic charge of teaching, the mandate to conserve the deposit of faith, is acting by divine right when she proscribes false doctrines that usurp the name of knowledge (I Tim. 6:20). That is why it is forbidden to all faithful Christians to hold or defend as legitimate conclusions of science the opinions that reveal themselves as contrary to the doctrine of the faith, especially if they have been condemned by the Church.

If anyone says that human disciplines may be pursued with such liberty that their assertions, even contrary to revealed doctrine, may be held as true, and that the Church may not contradict them, let him be anathema (chap. 4 and canon 2; *Denz.* 1798 and 1817).

Faith is one, but heresy is multiple. One heresy is of the rationalist type. Another is mystical. Some reject a fundamental dogma, and others are opposed to a secondary element of the *Credo*. But in these variations it is the mixture of human pattern and the divine pattern of faith that is especially characteristic. "Anyone," says St. John, "who advances and does not abide in the doctrine of Christ, has not God" (II Jn. 9).

(c) *The Heretic and Heresy*

Heresy of the kind that we have been considering implies a rejection of certain elements of the faith and an act of emphatic obstinacy. It is quite a different matter when a poorly informed believer commits some error in matters of faith. And it is still another thing in the case of the multitude of dissident Christians who, unlike the heretics who engendered them, have never made an act of positive heresy. They have inherited only a part of the dogmatic tradition and are not generally in a position to verify the origins of their profession of faith. The Catholic Church cannot side with them, however. She is obliged to fight against heresy without judging the interior dispositions of those who are heretics only de facto, and these are the same distinctions to be made in practice as the distinctions of tolerance previously mentioned.

Without accepting any opposition in the dogmatic tradition between fundamental dogmas and secondary dogmas—which would be called facultative—we know that our understanding of the unity of the Christian mystery now permits us to see how heretics can be in communion with the Catholic faith, although it is obvious that this presupposes good faith. We pointed out that the mystery of Christ is an organic reality, originally affirmed in its entirety and then fully developed progressively. The external unity of the mystery that is professed is combined with the interior unity of the supernatural faculty of assent. And in the case of separated Christians, although heretics, we know that they keep the dual unity of the light of grace and implicit affirmation. If their hearts are right with God, their profession of everything that is implicitly essential in the Christian mystery comprises all that God has revealed to His Church in Jesus Christ, regardless of their irregular negations. However, this is an abnormal kind of faith which Catholic witness and the inquiry and study of the dissidents must try to terminate.

3. FORMALISM IN BELIEVING

During all of our study, faith has been shown as something bound up with the total behavior of the believer. Its connection with fraternal charity, itself a résumé of the whole of Christian practice (Rom. 13:9-10) constitutes a necessary condition of its fulness, for it is "faith which works through charity" (Gal. 5:6) and "He who is just lives by faith" (Rom. 1:17). The experience of believers confirms that the coherence of Christian conduct conditions the life of faith and its progress. Every sin is finally a sin against the faith, whether by inattention or lack of momentary lucidity, or by making exceptions to the rule. There is no greater illusion than when we claim to be intensifying our faith, or simply to be conserving it, while failing to be obedient to the faith in practice. Little by little such faith becomes abstract; the world of faith will seem unreal and its light will disappear. This is an infirmity in regard to belief.

We may wonder what may be the real faith of a believer whose only cares are earthly and who lives habitually in a selfish way, while always maintaining his adherence to orthodoxy. In the tradition of that living faith which, for them, was purely and simply the Christian faith, the apostolic authors would lead us to assume that there really is no longer anything there which resembles true faith.

> What will it profit, my brethren, if a man says he has faith, but does not have works? Can the faith save him? And if a brother or a sister be naked and in want of daily food, and one of you say to them, "Go in peace, be warmed and filled," yet you do not give them what is necessary for the body, what does it profit? So faith too, unless it has works, is dead in itself. But someone will say, "Thou hast faith, and I have works." Show me thy faith without works, and I from my works will show thee my faith (James 2:14-19).

When we think about all this, we must nevertheless admit that all is not lost. There has been no actual apostasy. The worldly person has not necessarily rejected the Word of God. He may even remain convinced that it is true and feel certain that those who believe in it with fervor are entirely right. But for himself, it is the *World* that matters, and nothing remains of the faith except the affirmation of orthodox truth. This is an affirmation without communion, and is coldly objective. Theologians wonder if this intellectual residue could still be called faith in any sense of the term, and what might be its exact nature. But we shall not tarry over this monstrous kind of Christian belief. Let us only remember the firm position of the Church which tells us that however abnormal this kind of faith may be, it still constitutes a gift of God and He, at least, remains faithful so long as man does not deny Him completely.

The faith in itself, and by its very nature, is a gift of God, even when it does not work through charity (Gal. 5:6). And the act of faith whereby man consents and cooperates with grace, which however he could resist, renders to God Himself a free obedience, and this is a work which pertains to salvation (Vatican Council, session 3, chap. 3; Denz. 1791 and 1814; cf. Council of Trent, session 6, chap. 6; Denz. 797).

Such a "faith" subsists only in the precariousness of a motive of fear or habit, and suffers from an internal contradiction which, unless there is a deep concern and desire for re-conversion, makes it tend toward extinction, a consummated apostasy, in a gradual way, without sudden breach, in the slow darkening of man's heart.

CONCLUSION

The faith must live. It must be deepened. And this deepening will be effected by three related means. The first is prayer which, with faith, constitutes a vital circle. By prayer faith becomes penetrating. It unifies itself and acquires a really fervent foundation. The second is the study of the Word of God in Scripture and in the life of the Church. Faith must be clarified, and more especially if we possess an extensive secular culture. The third, more or less necessary according to certain believers and various periods, is the reinforcement by study and by experience, of the human motives that accompany assent. This is a work of integration which will profit greatly from the work of prayer and study. All of this will help to deepen the intensity of the believer's commitment.

"Because all that is born of God overcomes the world; and this is the victory that overcomes the world, our faith" (I Jn. 5:4).

REFLECTIONS AND PERSPECTIVES

Our reflections will first be directed to the ensemble of theological virtues, and will then center upon faith in particular.

The Theological Virtues. Two points. It is important to remember, as pointed out in the course of this chapter, that the words Faith, Hope and Charity do not always have the technical sense in the New

Testament which they have acquired at least since the Middle Ages in Latin theology. Most of the time, in the writings of St. Paul and St. John, as in the synoptic gospels also, faith signifies adhesion of the whole of man's being to *God the Savior*. In this respect, exceptions are rare and they are disputed among exegetes. Faith then includes what we call charity toward God. It seems that the New Testament faith is incompatible with the notion of "dead faith" mentioned by theologians. Hope signifies the confident expectation of faith in a total salvation to be manifested by the *Return of Christ* and the *Resurrection of the Body*. Charity has the meaning of communion with our neighbor in Christ. The New Testament trilogy of faith, hope and charity coresponds to the trilogy of the "objects" which are God the Savior, the Return of Christ and our Neighbor.

It is obvious that the ideas expressed by these three words are accepted entirely and without any ambiguity in the thought of the Church. But the language of the Church (in the Councils as well as in Theology) uses the three words somewhat differently. In our adherence to God, faith is instead a virtue of the intelligence. It is divine light and knowledge. Hope and charity are virtues of the Will, for hope is the expectation of divine blessings and a confidence in the merciful power of God; nor can we ever become too dependent upon this power. Charity is the love of God for His own sake, and consequently the love of our neighbor also. If these three meanings enable the mind to see things in a new dimension and give us a better understanding of the profound implanting in the soul of what the New Testament calls faith, hope and charity, they should not make us forget that they are nevertheless the result of reflection and therefore, even in the New Testament, they are a theological elaboration.

The second point underlines the friendly and even sponsal character within us which corresponds to the theological virtues. If, in fact, grace gives to every spiritual creature the character of a spouse of Christ, the theological virtues simply correspond to the exercise of that grace, for this is the divine life which we have received, a life we share with Christ. And while religion has a servile aspect (in the etymological meaning of the term which has no pejorative connotation), faith, hope and charity have an aspect that is friendly, sponsal and filial. These are the virtues of the friend, the spouse, and the son.

The theological virtues, however, do not suppress the virtue of religion. Nor does the creature's sponsal character abolish his debt of service when God has united Himself to man by the gift of grace.

For however united interiorly to God we may be, we must always render to Him the service of our deeds, our words, our possessions, and all that we are in ourselves. The more we are united to God, the more greatly this debt of service and reverence is felt within us, and the more urgently it presents itself to us. No matter how vital our faith may be, it will inspire deeds and words that are equally derived from the virtue of prudence and the virtue of religion. Fervent faith will make this even more certain. For faith normally tends to express itself in prayer and "religious" demeanor. On the other hand, in the measure that the soul, in love with God through the activity of the theological virtues, spends itself in exercises of religion (prayers, acts, offerings and adorations, etc.), faith, hope and charity find in these religious exercises a renewal of fervor and life. There is the interaction of the acts of the friend (acts of the theological virtues) upon the acts of the servant (religious acts), and the interaction of the acts of the servant upon those of the friend. Obviously, however, the acts of the friend are, absolutely speaking, primary in relation to those of the servant.

Faith in Particular. A sound theology of faith must keep itself at all times from two temptations, or from two excesses, which are also two errors.

There is the temptation of *disinterestedness*, presenting the faith as a pure obedience. God speaks and I obey as a believer, or I believe because I obey. My mind is convinced because of the divine witness. It submits itself. It is true, of course, that faith may be considered under a certain aspect as obedience. St. Paul speaks of "the obedience of faith" (Rom. 1:5), and St. Luke refers to priests who "obey the faith" (Acts, 6:7); that is to say, they submit unreservedly to the full content of the faith. But faith means more than obedience. The mind cannot obey purely and simply by becoming disinterested in the content of the faith, because the faith is also a life for the intelligence. It is a light which opens the mind and enables it to reach out beyond natural knowledge, fulfilling it and giving it an increase of life and of the substance of the happiness it hopes for.

The other temptation is found in the idea of *immanence*. (These terms are only approximate, of course.) This is the exact opposite of transcendence. Instead of presenting the faith as a pure obedience, in an absolute heterogeneity between the message of faith and the believer, it is presented as the fulfillment of the believer, in a homogeneous continuity between the hunger of the mind and the revealed truth. Faith is here defined as a kind of natural intuition of the soul which turns toward God itself, or as the affective knowledge of the soul that is approaching God. There is a certain amount of truth in this position, for the Truth to which the believer adheres is not just any kind of truth. It pertains definitely to the mind, and it is this Truth alone which can bring fulfillment and obtain that happiness for which the mind of man was created. The mind cannot therefore be indifferent to such truth, nor can it accept without desire, as might happen in the acceptance of other knowledge, for this Truth is the mind's greatest treasure, indeed it is everything. But this position is also false, for we know that the Word of God not only satisfies our desire for knowledge, but far exceeds this desire. The Word of God is transcendent. There is a breach of continuity between our understanding and that which God has revealed to us. There may be continuity in the Thought of God Who is the unique author of our natural being and of our being as sons of God, and a continuity with regard to our natural intelligence and the light of faith which He communicates to us in His grace. There may also be continuity for the theologian who tries to see all things in the Thought of God, and considers the fulfillment of the believer's intelligence as the final purpose of the act of faith. But the faith comes from above; it is transcendent. It is false to consider it as the mature fruition of the mind in its natural quest for God. For faith is not naturally continuous with desire.

A sound theology will extract whatever truth there may be in these two positions without falling into either excess.

Faith and Good Faith. We can now see that there is an immense gulf between "good faith" and faith itself. This gulf is unbridgeable if we depend upon natural forces alone. Good faith, that is to say, good-will, has no real content. It is simply a good disposition of the heart. Faith, on the contrary, because it is adherence to God's Word, is an assent to an ensemble of revealed and defined truths in which the Word is refracted; without this the mind could understand nothing about God. Good faith can deceive itself and others also, for it sometimes happens that we do the wrong thing in good faith, either because our hearts are less pure than we think, or because our minds are poorly informed. But faith never deceives us at any time; it comes from God. It is the faith which justifies us and saves us, and not merely good faith.

However, a faith without good faith is without roots in the soul, and a believer who is willing to be in "bad faith" in believing would simply show that he does not really have the faith at all. He would not be a believer *because of God* Who is truth and Who reveals, but rather because of the ecclesiastical society, for example, to which he wishes to remain attached without being in agreement with it, or because of other motives which are neither true nor primary.

Christ and the Virgin. Christ did not possess the faith, but instead, from the moment of His conception, He possessed the vision of God. This was proper to Him in Whom we cannot distinguish a "human person" distinct from the "divine person" of the Son, Who was destined to "lead many sons to glory" (Heb. 2:10). Christ therefore did not suffer "in His faith." But the merit of faith was not absent from Calvary; it fell to Mary to suffer, in our name, for her faith. Christ, however, experienced abandonment and interior darkness. We should study Mat. 27:46, and explain this passage theologically, as far as this is possible.

Gifts of the Holy Spirit. Theology traditionally associates the gifts of understanding and knowledge with Faith. We should study this connection along with the corresponding gifts. There is a certain tradition, not lacking in rich content, which also ties the "gift of tears" to the gift of knowledge. Inversely, we should study the meaning of the "sin against the Holy Spirit" (Mat. 12:31; Mk. 3:29; Lk. 12:10; Heb. 10:26; I Jn. 5:16; etc.). The Theology of blasphemy.

Typology, sociology, ethnology of the faith; mission and propagation. Among the by-paths that can prolong our exploration or study of the faith, we must mention the following:

Typology of the faith. A more profound study of the types of faith at different age levels. The faith of the child (psychology, bases, characters, indispensable content), the faith of the adolescent boy and girl, and of the young man and woman, the faith of elderly people, married couples, etc. Nor should we neglect to study the faith at different stages in the history of the people of God (this is the classical and important theme): the faith of Abraham, of Moses, David, Jeremias and Isaias, John the Baptist. The faith of Adam.

Sociology of the faith. The faith in different classes of society. Psychology and content of the faith of workmen, peasants, middle-class people, city-dwellers, etc. The faith and the different professions —the faith of the physician, the philosopher, the historian, the manual worker. The faith of converts: the converted Jew and the converted Protestant, etc.

Ethnology of the faith. The faith of primitive man and of modern man. The faith of medieval man. The faith of the Oriental and the

Occidental. The faith of the Bretons and of the people of southern France. Faith and languages. Can the language in which the message of faith is communicated have any influence upon the interior attitudes and behavior of the believer?

Mission and propagation of the faith. How is the faith to be communicated to children? Role of parents. Role of catechists. Role of formulas used (on this point one should consult the indispensable works of Mme. Marie Fargues, especially the *Tests Collectifs de catéchisme,* published by Editions du Cerf, 1951, and those of the Abbé Colomb, professor at the Catholic Institute of Lyons). Pedagogical methods adapted to different ages. Merits and demerits of the binomial system comprising the family-and-parochial-school or the family-and-public-school, in the education of the faith. (Among other works on this subject, one could read L. Guittard's *L'évolution religieuse des adolescents,* Paris, Spes, 1952). Religious education of adults: problems of preaching, liturgical ceremonies, books; also the problem of the homogeneity of culture between clergy and laity. Propagation of the faith in mission territories. Touchstones of the faith in different religions. Translations of the message; symbols to invent or assume. Faith and indigenous mentalities. How shall the faith assimilate the new world visions, new philosophies and new humanism that it meets in today's world? Faith and expressions of the faith outside Greco-Latin culture.

Mission and tolerance. In this chapter we considered the matter of tolerance in our study of the attitude of the Church toward unbelief. What is the Christian's attitude? Should the man who possesses the truth of the faith be tolerant towards those who do not possess it and who may actually be disseminating error? Or should he be intolerant? When should the Christian profess his faith in a public manner? Must he sometimes be "importunate" (II Tim. 4:2). Re-read the Gospels and discover the theological principles which govern the Christian in his relations with the non-Christian. On this subject one could read A. M. Dubarle's article, *"Faut-il-brûler les hérétiques?"* in *La Vie Intellectuelle,* Jan. 1952, pp. 5–34.

Principles and definitions. To fix our minds upon the essential principles which govern theological argumentation, we have here compiled lapidary statements of St. Thomas Aquinas.

"Cujuslibet cognoscitivi habitus objectum duo habet; scilicet id quod materialiter cognoscitur, quod est sicut materiale objectum; et id per quod cognoscitur, quod est formalis ratio objecti." The object of every *habitus* which enables us to "know" has two aspects: *the thing* that is materially known, and *that which* makes it possible for the object to be known, which is its formal reason. In matters of faith, the formal reason is the *primary Truth*, that is to say, we adhere to the truths of faith *because they are revealed by God* Who is the primary Truth, and in the measure that these truths are revealed by God. The material object is also the *primary Truth*, in the sense that everything which we must believe is *either God Himself or that which disposes us for the enjoyment of God*. (Just as the object of medical science is health because medical science is not concerned with anything except in reference to health.)

"Fidei objectum per se est id per quod homo beatus efficitur." It is the essential (material) object of the faith that effects man's blessedness.

"Illa per se pertinent ad fidem quorum visione in vita aeterna perfruemur, et per quae ducemur ad vitam aeternam": The things that pertain essentially to the faith are those which will satisfy the mind and which we shall enjoy in eternal life. These are the things that are now leading us toward eternal life.

"Credere autem non potest aliquis, nisi ei veritas quam credat proponatur": No one can believe unless the truth which he believes is first proposed to him.

On the propositions of faith:

"Actus autem credentis non terminatur ad enuntiabile sed ad rem": The act of the believer does not terminate with the proposition but with the reality.

"Credibilia fidei christianae dicuntur per articulos distingui inquantum in quasdam partes dividuntur habentes aliquam coaptationem ad invicem": The things which the Christian faith presents for belief are divided into articles (of faith), that is to say, into parts having a certain order between them (and a certain "articulation").

"Ita se habent in doctrina fidei articuli fidei, sicut principia per se nota in doctrina quae per rationem naturalem habetur": In teaching the faith the articles of faith have the same role as principles that are self-evident in the teaching that is done in the name of natural reason.

"Omnes articuli fidei implicite continentur in aliquibus primis credibilibus, scilicet ut credatur Deus esse et providentiam habere circa hominum salutem secundum illud ad Hebr. 11:6; Accedentem ad Deum oportet credere quia est, et quod inquiren tibus se re-munerator sit": All the articles of faith are implicitly contained in certain primary things which we must believe, that is to say, every-thing is summarized in our belief that God exists and that He pro-vides providentially for the salvation of men. This is clearly stated in Hebrews 11:6—"For he who comes to God must believe that God exists and is a rewarder to those who seek him."

"Etsi non habuerunt fidem explicitam, habuerunt tamen fidem implicitam in divina providentia, credentes Deum esse liberatorem hominum secundum modos sibi placitos, et secundum quod aliqui-bus veritatem cognoscentibus Spiritus revelasset, secundum illud Job 35:11": (If there are pagans to whom no revelation was made, and who, consequently), did not have explicit faith, they neverthe-less possessed implicit faith in divine providence, through the rev-elation which the Holy Spirit gives to those who know the truth, that God is the liberator of men according to the means that are pleasing to Him. Is it not in the Book of Job that we find the pas-sage which tells us, "It is He Who makes us more prudent than wild beasts, and wiser than the birds of the air."

"Omnibus articulis fidei inhaeret fides propter unum medium, scilicet propter Veritatem primam propositam nobis in Scripturis secundum doctrinam Ecclesiae intelligentis sane": The believer ad-heres to all the articles of faith by virtue of a unique motive: The primary Truth which is proposed to us in the Scriptures as under-stood according to the teaching of the Church which has a sound understanding of them.

The respective roles of intelligence and volition in faith.

"Veritus prima ad voluntatem refertur, secundum quod habet rationem finis." Whenever the primary Truth is presented as an end, it concerns the Will.

"Actus fidei actus est intellectus determinati ad unum ex imperio voluntatis. Sic ergo actus fidei habet ordinem et ad objectum volun-tatis, quod est bonum et finis; et ad objectum intellectus, quod est verum": The act of faith is an act of the intelligence which makes a definite choice under the influence of the will. In this way the act of faith is in harmony with the object of the will which is the good and the end, and with the object of the intelligence which is the true.

"Veritas prima est finis omnium desideriorum et actionum nostrarum": The primary Truth is the end of all our desires and of all our acts.

"Assensus hic accipitur pro actu intellectus secundum quod a voluntate determinatur ad unum": The assent of faith should be understood as an act of the intelligence influenced by the will to make a positive choice.

(The grace of faith:) "Fides quantum ad assensum, qui est principalis actus fidei est a Deo interius movente per gratiam": The assent of faith—which is the principal act of the faith—comes from God, Who sets our will in motion interiorly by His grace.

"Fides non habet inquisitionem rationis naturalis demonstrantis id quod creditur. Habet tamen inquisitionem quandam eorum per quae inducitur homo ad credendum": The faith is not compatible with the quest of natural reason which seeks to demonstrate whatever is believed; the faith, nevertheless, supposes a certain inquiry regarding those things which can lead a man to believe (for example, when we want to know for sure that it was God Who said a particular thing and that it was confirmed by miracles).

"Primum principium purificationis cordis est fides, quo purificatur impuritas erroris": The first principle of the purification of the heart is the faith which purifies us from the impurity of error.

"Fides est necessaria tamquam principium spiritualis vitae": The faith is necessary as the very principle of the spiritual life.

BIBLIOGRAPHY [1]

1° *Sources.*

   a) Écriture

E. Walter, *Glaube, Hoffnung und Liebe im neuen Testament,* Fribourg, 1940.
P. Antoine, art. *Foi,* dans *Suppl. dict. Bible,* t. II, 1938, c. 276-310.
E. Tobac, *Le problème de la justification dans saint Paul,* 2ᵉ éd., Gembloux, 1941.
J. Huby, *La connaissance de foi dans saint Jean* (appendice au *Discours de Jésus après la Cène*), Paris 1932, pp. 146-191.
J. Dupont, *Gnosis, La connaissance religieuse dans les épîtres de saint Paul,* Louvain-Paris, 1949.
A. Schlatter, *Der Glaube im N. T.,* 4ᵉ édit., Stuttgart, 1927.

[1] Publisher's note. As a general policy throughout this volume, the bibliography of the French edition, when there is one, is printed first, followed by a supplementary one in English supplied by the translators.

b) Magistère ecclésiastique.

Trois Conciles ont dogmatisé sur la Foi: le concile d'Orange en 529, le concile de Trente et le concile du Vatican. Les définitions conciliaires ne visent pas à donner une dogmatique complète du mystère ou même d'un de ses aspects; elles rappellent la foi orthodoxe dans une conjoncture précise de controverse ou d'erreur. C'est ainsi — en ce qui concerne la foi, — que les conciles d'Orange et de Trente se situent dans un climat de foi de conversion: celui d'Orange pour affirmer que la conversion est grâce, celui de Trente pour mettre au point la conception luthérienne de la justification; tandis que le concile du Vatican, faisant face aux erreurs du rationnalisme et de l'adogmatisme modernes, traite de la foi comme adhésion intellectuelle. Il faut prendre l'ensemble de ces trois conciles pour avoir la pensée de l'Église.

Concile d'Orange:

Texte dans Mansi (tome VIII, 712 B sqq.), reproduit pour l'essentiel dans Denzinger 174-201.

Études:

E. Amann, art. *Semipélagiens,* dans D. Th. C., XIV, c. 1796-1850.

Roger Aubert, *Le problème de l'acte de foi. Données traditionnelles et résultats des controverses récentes,* 2° éd., Louvain, 1950.

Concile de Trente:

Décret *De Justificatione,* Session VI, en date du 13 janvier 1547.

Texte dans Mansi (tome XXXIII, 33 A ssq.), reproduit dans Denzinger 792a-843.

Études de F. Cavallera, dans B. L. E., 1945, pp. 54-64; 1949, pp. 65-76, 146-168 et de R. Aubert, *op. cit.,* pp. 73-87.

Concile du Vatican:

Session III, Constitution dogmatique *De Fide Catholica,* en date du 24 avril 1870.

Texte dans Mansi (tomes L-LIII), reproduit pour l'essentiel dans Denz. 1781-1821.

Études:

A. Vacant, *Études théologiques sur les Constitutions du Concile du Vatican,* Paris 1895, 2 vol.

R. Aubert, *op. cit.,* pp. 131-219.

R. Aubert, *Le Pontificat de Pie IX,* Bloud et Gay, 1952.

On trouvera dans le Rituel pour le baptême des adultes la réflexion vécue de l'Église sur la réalité de la foi chrétienne.

2° *Ouvrages généraux.*

Saint Thomas d'Aquin, II *Sent.,* d. 26-28. — III *Sent.,* d. 23-25. — I C. g. 6; III C. g. 40, 152, 154. — *De Verit.,* XIV. — Ia IIae, 62, 113. — IIa IIae, 1-16. — *Quodl.,* II, 6; VI, 2. — *Com. in Jo, passim.*

R. Aubert, *op. cit.,* (ouvrage fondamental pour l'histoire de la théologie de la foi).

R. Bernard, traduction et commentaire de IIa-IIae 1-16, 2 vol. Éd. Rev. des Jeunes, 1940, 1942.

Scheeben, art. *Glaube,* dans le *Kirchenlexikon,* t. 5, Fribourg, 1888.

J. Mouroux, *Je Crois en Toi; structure personnelle de la foi,* Paris, Éd. de la Revue des J., 1949.

M.-L. Guérard des Lauriers, *Dimensions de la foi,* 2 tomes, Éd. du Cerf, 1952 (Analyses spéculatives très approfondies).

3° *Travaux de détail.*

Section I

XXX, *Abraham, Père des croyants,* Paris, Éd. du Cerf, 1952.

J'ai rencontré le Dieu vivant. Témoignages avec deux études sur la conversion, par M. Nédoncelle et René Girault, Paris, Éd. Rev. des Jeunes, 1951.

J. Huby, *La conversion,* Beauchesne, 1919.

M. T.-L. Penido, *La conscience religieuse. Essai systématique suivi d'illustrations,* Paris, Téqui, 1935.

R. Guardini, *Vie de la foi,* Paris, Éd. Rev. des Jeunes, 1951.

G. Siegmund, *Psychologie des Gottesglaubens,* Münster, 1937.

G. Marcel, *Du refus à l'invocation,* Paris, 1940; *Etre et Avoir,* Aubier, 1935.

G. Bardy, *La conversion au christianisme durant les premiers siècles,* Paris, Aubier, 1949.

Section II

Pascal, *Pensées.*

A. Gardeil, *Crédibilité et apologétique,* 3ᵉ éd., Paris, Gabalda, 1928.

P. Rousselot, *Les yeux de la foi,* dans R. S. R., 1910, pp. 241-259; 444-475.

G. Brunhes, *La foi et sa justification rationnelle,* Paris, Bloud, 1928.

J. Levie, *Sous les yeux de l'incroyant,* 2ᵉ édit., Paris, Desclée de Br., 1946.

J. Leclercq, *Le problème de la foi dans les milieux intellectuels du XXᵉ siècle.* 2ᵉ édit., Paris, Casterman, 1950.

E. Masure, *La grand'route apologétique,* 2ᵉ édit., Paris, Beauchesne, 1939.

La Bonnardière, *Devoir de croire et sincérité intellectuelle,* Paris, Aubier, 1949.

A. Forest, *Les moments de la conversion,* dans *Études Philosophiques,* 1950, pp. 43-53.

XXX, *Foi en Jésus-Christ et monde d'aujourd'hui,* Semaine des Intellectuels Catholiques, 1949, Paris, Éd. de Flore.

Ch. Journet, *La naissance de la foi,* Fribourg (Suisse), 1951.

M. Nédoncelle, *La philosophie religieuse de John-Henry Newman,* Strasbourg, 1946.

H. Walgrave, *Newman's verantiheording van het geloof in de Kerk,* Anvers, 1946.

H. de Lubac, *De la connaissance de Dieu,* 2ᵉ éd., Paris, 1948.

P. Ortegat, *Intuition et Religion,* Louvain-Paris, 1947.

Section III

Th. Soiron, *Glaube, Hoffnung, Liebe,* Ratisbonne, 1934.

A.-M. Hunter, *Un Seigneur, une Église, un Salut,* Paris, Delachaux, 1950.

Lumière et Vie: Cahier 2, *Le Symbole des Apôtres* (fév. 1952); Cahier 6, *L'Église et la Bible* (oct. 1952).

L.-M. Dewailly, *Jésus-Christ, Parole de Dieu*, Paris, Éd. du Cerf, 1945.

M.-E. Boismard, *La connaissance de Dieu dans l'Alliance nouvelle d'après la 1ʳᵉ épître de saint Jean*, R. B., 1949, pp. 365-391.

H. Rahner, *Eine Theologie der Verkündigung*, Fribourg-Br., 1939.

J.-A. Jungmann, *Die Frohbotschaft und unsere Glaubensverkündigung*, Ratisbonne, 1939.

F.-X. Arnold, *Dienst am Glauben*, Fribourg-Br., 1948.

M.-D. Chenu, *La psychologie de la foi dans la théologie du XIIIᵉ siècle*, dans *Études d'hist. litt. et doct. du XIIIᵉ s.*, 2ᵉ série, Paris-Ottawa, 1932; *Position de la Théologie*, R. S. P. Th. 1935; pp. 232-257.

J. De Wolf, *La justification de la foi chez saint Thomas d'Aquin et le Père Rousselot*, Desclée de Br., 1946.

A. Brien, *Éducation et développement de la foi suivant les âges de la vie*, dans les *Cahiers du Clergé rural*, n° 133 (déc. 1951), pp. 449-466; n° 134 (Janv. 1952), pp. 1-19.

Lumen Vitae, Revue internationale de la formation religieuse, 27, rue de Spa, Bruxelles (La meilleure revue concernant les problèmes d'éducation de la foi).

XXX., *La foi des Jeunes*, Éd. Amitié étudiante, Louvain, 1949.

Section IV

A. Charue, *L'incrédulité des Juifs dans le nouveau Testament*, Gembloux, 1929.

M.-J. Congar, *Une conclusion théologique à l'enquête sur les raisons de l'incroyance*, dans Vie Int., 1935, pp. 214-249.

L. Brunschvig, *De la vraie et de la fausse conversion*, Alcan, 1937 (La philosophie de l'incroyance).

J. Malègue, *Vertu de foi et péché d'incroyance*, dans *Pénombres*, Paris, 1939.

A. Rousseaux, *La crise spirituelle de 1700 à 1900*, dans *Cahiers de Neuilly*, 15, pp. 1-19.

P. Charles, *Les raisons de l'incroyance*, N. R. T., 1946, 2, pp. 129-145.

L'incroyance des croyants, cahier de *Jeunesse de l'Église*, n° 6, 1946.

P. de Ménasce, *Causes permanentes et causes actuelles de l'incroyance*, dans *Nova et Vetera*, 1940, 4, pp. 423-440.

P. Claeys-Bouuaert, *Tous les athées sont-ils coupables?* dans *N. R. Th.*, 1921, pp. 179 ssq.

G.-B. Guzzetti, *La perdita della Fede nei Catholici*, Venegono, 1940. VIII, pp. 50-58 (sur la foi morte).

XXX. *Unité chrétienne et tolérance religieuse*, Paris, Éd. Temps Présent, 1950.

XXX. *Tolérance et Communauté humaine; Chrétiens dans un monde divisé*, Paris, Casterman, 1952.

L. Capéran, *Le problème du salut des infidèles*, Toulouse, 1934.

J. Maritain, *Neuf leçons sur les notions premières de la philosophie morale*, Paris, Téqui, 1950.

O. Karrer, *Le sentiment religieux dans l'humanité et le christianisme*, Lethielleux, 1936.

Van der Leeuw, *La religion dans son essence et dans ses manifestations*, Payot,

R. Caillois, *L'homme et le sacré*, Leroux, 1939.

Max Scheler, *Vom Ewigen in Menschen*, Leipzig, 1921.

H. Bergson, *Les deux sources de la morale et de la religion*, Alcan, 1932.

M. Blondel, *L'action* (1893), Alcan, 1950.

J. Valéty, *Le dernier péché du croyant,* dans *R. S. R.,* 1928, t. VIII, pp. 50-58 (Sur la foi morte).

BIBLIOGRAPHY

St. Augustine, *Faith, Hope, and Charity,* Westminster, Md., The Newman Press, 1947.
Brunhes, Gabriel, *Faith and Its Rational Justification,* St. Louis, Herder, 1931.
D'Arcy, C., *The Nature of Belief,* London, 1937.
—————— *Belief and Reason,* London, Burns, Oates, 1946.
Davis, Henry, S.J., *Moral and Pastoral Theology,* Vol. I, ch. 3, London, Sheed and Ward, 1941.
Dawson, Christopher, *Progress and Religion,* New York, Longmans, Green and Co., 1929.
Heenan, John C., *The Faith Makes Sense,* New York, Sheed and Ward, 1948.
McHugh, John A., O.P., and Callan, Charles J., O.P., *Moral Theology, A Complete Course,* Vol. I, pp. 272-400, New York, Joseph Wagner, Inc., 1929.
Newman, John H., *Grammar of Assent,* London, 1870.
Sheedy, Charles E., C.S.C., *The Christian Virtues,* pp. 73-98, Notre Dame, Ind., University of Notre Dame Press, 1949.
Toth, Thiamer, *Belief in God,* St. Louis, B. Herder Book Co., 1946.

Arnold, F., "Act of Faith, a Personal Commitment," *Lumen,* 5: 251-255, Apr '50.
Callaghan, C. J., "Faith and Reason," *Catholic Mind,* 45: 92-97, Feb '47.
Carpenter, H. J., "Reason and Faith," *Blackfriars,* 12: 135-146, Mar. '31.
Connell, F. J., "Need of Knowledge of Faith," *American Ecclesiastical Review,* 126: 193-203, Mar '52.
De Letter, P. S. J., "Faith and Apologetics," *Irish Ecclesiastical Record,* 82: 310-321, Nov '54.
D'Eypernon, F. T., S.J., "Faith, Man's Communion with God," *Lumen,* 9: 182-192, Je '54.
Forest, J., "Meaning of Faith: the Scholastics vs. the non-Scholastics," *Thomist,* 6: 147-162, Je '54.
Hoare, F. R., "Darkness of Faith," *Dublin Review,* 191: 105-116 (July, 1932) and 192: 92-104, Ja '33.
Horgan, J. D., "Newman on Faith and Reason," *Studies,* 42: 132-150, Je '53.
McNabb, V., "Faith and Reason," *Blackfriars,* 13: 327-332, Je '32.
Martindale, C. C., "Mystery of Unbelief," *Month,* 183: 165-169, Mar '47.
Mulhern, P. F., "Rejection and Protection of Faith," *Thomist,* 3: 33-44, Ja '41.
—————— "Dogma and Intellectual Freedom," *American Ecclesiastical Review,* 123: 443-451, D '50.
Murray, J. C., "Root of Faith: the Doctrine of M. J. Scheeben," *Theological Studies,* 9: 20-46, Mar '48.
Parente, P., "Function of Natural Reason in Eliciting the Act of Faith," *Theology Digest,* 1: 157-160, Autumn '53.
Ring, G. C., "Motive and Freedom in the Act of Faith," *Theological Studies,* 6: 147-162, Je '45.
"Problems of God and Intellectual Unbelievers," *Lumen,* 7: 367-372, S '52.

Chapter II

HOPE

by B. Olivier, O.P.

FIRST PART: The Revelation of Hope

Introduction: Psychological Analysis of Hope

I. THE OLD TESTAMENT

    1. The climate of hope
    2. The object of hope seen through its successive types
    3. The motive of hope

II. THE NEW TESTAMENT

    A. The synoptic gospels
        1. The new hope
        2. The present reign of God
        3. The eschatological reign of God
        4. The object of Christian hope

    B. Saint Paul
        1. The foundation of hope is faith
        2. The object of hope: glory or participation in the Kingdom
        3. The motive of hope: the promise
        4. The importance of hope

    C. Saint John

SECOND PART: The Elaboration of a Theology of Hope

I. REVELATION OF HOPE AND THEOLOGY OF HOPE

II. PRINCIPAL STAGES IN THE DEVELOPMENT OF THE DOCTRINE OF HOPE

    1. Millenarianism
    2. The influence of Origen

Chapter II

HOPE

First Part

THE REVELATION OF HOPE

Introduction: Psychological Analysis of Hope

Every Christian knows that hope is one of the three theological virtues. It is created in the soul by Almighty God together with grace and all the gifts that accompany it. Hope makes it possible for us to perform certain interior acts that are definitely decisive and of vital importance for the Christian. These acts have God directly as their object. It is by Revelation that we know the real nature of hope and its exact dimensions. And we must turn to Scripture primarily if we wish to have any real understanding of hope.

When God speaks to men, proclaiming His mystery to them, He uses terms that are accessible to them, and has recourse to ideas they understand. When God reveals charity, He awakens within us that idea of love that is well-known to all of us. When He reveals hope, we know that this virtue has something in common with the feeling of hope that fills our daily life. We must therefore begin with a brief analysis of human hope in order to fully grasp the meaning of the hope that is revealed.[1]

Hope, like every "passion," is basically emotional. It is a movement of the appetite toward some good thing that is offered to us. Whenever anything desirable is before us, there is an instinctive movement of love within us because the object is quite literally lovable. This is the immediate and primary reaction of the appetite with regard to everything lovable. But love is the seed of a whole lifetime of passionate desire. Almost from the start it seeks to conquer and will not be satisfied until the beloved is possessed. Consequently, the whole affective life is situated somewhere between loving desire at the beginning and the joy of possession at the end.

But it is not always possible to pass directly from desire to pos-

[1] A very rich, and very personal, phenomenological study, on the subject of hope, may be found in G. Marcel's *Homo Viator*.

session. Perhaps the beloved does not belong to us, or at least not yet. Then there will be longing desire between love and perfect joy. With the whole strength of our hearts we yearn for the object of our love; we strive for possession.

But suppose that some obstacle arises between desire and fulfillment. The outcome is perhaps uncertain and success will be difficult. We are reminded of the legends that told of dragons to be slain before the brave knight could marry the princess of his dreams. The obstacle surrounds desire with a certain element of uncertainty. Is final conquest really possible? In such moments the pressure of desire drives us toward the goal in spite of everything, and it generates a fighting courage in our hearts. St. Bonaventure called this a "sublimation of the soul." There is a struggle before us, an assault to be made, and success depends upon the means at our disposal. It is at this point that hope will rise within us or despair will overwhelm us.

It is a powerful movement that carries us toward the beloved object, but if its conquest seems impossible because we lack the necessary means of attainment, there follows the terrible abandonment of all the heart's courage, and a dark despair that is all the greater if the desire was especially strong and definite. For a while our whole being longs for possession of someone or something beloved, and suddenly we know for certain that we shall never be able to make this dream come true. It may happen, however, in spite of all the difficulties and the uncertainty that persists until the very end, that we have the assurance of eventual success because we are certain of efficacious help; then hope rises in the heart and carries us through all the difficulties, developing within us a profound confidence that is determined and patient. We see that the decisive element in hope is the efficacy of the means we employ and the help on which we rely.

We can characterize the man who hopes in the following ways:

1. He is a man who loves, and when he is separated from the object of his love, his whole being yearns for that object with deep desire. This desire gives him a feeling of real poverty and feeds upon itself. The satisfied man, however, or the man who thinks that he is satisfied, no longer desires anything. He is content, sated, and has the mentality of the wealthy. For this very reason he is as far removed from hope as anyone can possibly be. The man who desires nothing cannot hope for anything. But the man who has measured the emptiness within himself, and knows the aching void of unful-

filled expectation and spiritual loneliness, will be aware of his poverty and wholly ready for hope.

2. The man who hopes is entirely oriented toward the future. His perfect joy is neither in the present nor the past; it is still to come. His joy is found only in the possession of the good that he desires. All his wishes are centered in the moment of possession. He is an expectant man, but his expectation is fervent and active. Unlike the satisfied man, he is not enclosed within his happiness or his contentment, for the best of himself has not yet appeared. He lives for the future. And that is perhaps the truest characteristic of those who are young in heart.

3. Up to this point the man of hope is like the man of desire. But obstacles will distinguish between them. For in hope there is a tension which clashes with the difficulty. The man who hopes is not satisfied with contemplation of his goal. He struggles against the obstacle that separates him from it. He is in a state of continuous struggle. But he is certain that he will win. Even in the midst of uncertainty stemming from the difficulties confronting him, the basis of his certainty is the efficacy of the arms in his possession, although these may have come from outside himself. This is the essential and rather paradoxical characteristic of hope.

There is a sure and basic confidence which, however, is fringed with uncertainty. If there were no danger of failure, there would be no real hope but only a serene and quiet expectation and the simple acceptance of necessary delay. The whole strength of hope, and all its potential confidence, is therefore based upon the "means" of overcoming the obstacle. It is the quality of the means which will determine the measure of our confidence and the particular quality of our hope.

If we begin with this elementary notion, we can then consider the typical characteristics of hope in Revelation.

I. The Old Testament

1. THE CLIMATE OF HOPE

The history of Israel, as a whole, is an incarnation of hope. It does not resemble the history of any other people, for it has a character that is unique.

Israel was born with a call, a particular vocation. Even before it was constituted as a nation, a definite purpose was assigned to it. Its existence was not justified by an appeal to past tradition, for Israel is probably the only nation whose entire purpose of existence was to be found in the future. Its history began with a divine choice, for God had His idea which He wanted to realize in and through this nation in the course of a long evolution. For that reason He marked this people with the seal of vocation and oriented the original clan, and eventually the growing nation, toward the goal which He alone knew. This goal was made known to the people very gradually, and it required the long patience of divine pedagogy to reveal the true meaning of its destiny to the Israelite nation. Everything was certainly contained implicitly in God's original promise to Abraham, but the divine plan that was hidden through so many centuries was not revealed until the proper time. Like a blind man, Israel had to make its way toward a goal never imagined, or perhaps, more like a short-sighted man, impatiently eager, who cannot see farther than the very next step. God took this nation as He found it. He did not propose the true and essential hope all at once. Instead, He offered that hope in fragments. He made this people advance from one desire to another, from one hope to another, toward the object of the true hope. And the entire Old Testament is the history of that forward advance of a nation that knew that it was called, guided and sustained by Almighty God. It is the history of that immense aspiration which, as soon as it was gratified, immediately soared towards new objectives, and through these in the course of time the definitive object of hope finally appeared as the Reign of God in the Messianic Era.

This characteristic attitude of hope is apparent at the very beginning of Israel's life in the vocation of Abraham. God entered into this man's life and drew him apart from his environment to fashion him into the instrument of His purpose. Almost immediately God made a covenant with him in terms of a promise: "And I will make of thee a great nation, and I will bless thee, and magnify thy name, and thou shalt be blessed" (Gen. 12:2). This promise was renewed in a more solemn manner: "Look up to heaven and number the stars, if thou canst. . . . So shall thy seed be" (Gen. 15:5). Abraham accepted the divine word and believed with that faith which made him a righteous man. In the same moment he entered into the movement of hope.

It was the initiative of God that made a new man of Abraham. Separated from his clan and far away from his homeland, he was now facing the future uniquely. He had become the man of the Covenant and the Promise. The word of Yahweh had indicated a blessing whose force of attraction was powerful, for it was a blessing that Abraham really desired. We know that the assurance of a numerous posterity was very precious to all ancient peoples. Abraham did not yet have a clear idea of everything implicit in the immediate promise, but it was the beginning of the confident expectation which still abides in the hearts of all Christians.

He did not yet have the object of his desire, nor did he have the slightest visible assurance, for Sarah, his wife, was sterile. Human contingencies often seem to make possible happiness inaccessible. This is the kind of obstacle that can come between desire and possession. In such circumstances man can only have recourse to the word of God. If we are willing to wait for the promised blessing, and even willing to strive for its attainment, we are then making a total commitment of ourselves to God Who made the promise. Hope is not possible unless it is anchored unconditionally in Him Who is faithful to His promise. The elements which constitute the simplest act of hope have this vital complexity.

The sacrifice of Isaac was a trial which gave the father of all believers an occasion to prove his unshaken faith and also the strength of his hope confronted by the impossible and the absurd. For good reason he is the father of all who hope. In him the whole history of the Jewish people was already summed up, for they were the people who "journeyed toward the promise."

2. THE OBJECT OF HOPE SEEN THROUGH ITS SUCCESSIVE TYPES

1. The *initial promise* was meant precisely for the *posterity of Abraham*. But it was set forth in terms which suggest a scope that greatly exceeded the extent of a simple descendence that one man might hope for. "And I will make of thee a great nation, and I will bless thee, and magnify thy name, and thou shalt be blessed. I will bless them that bless thee, and curse them that curse thee, and IN THEE shall all the kindred of the earth be blessed" (Gen. 12:2-3). The object of the first promise therefore contains in embryo the whole development of the history of salvation. The first-fruits, the most immediate, were not long delayed. Each in his turn, Isaac and Jacob were confirmed in the same expectation, and from the time of Jacob the sacred writer could take pleasure in naming a posterity

that was already impressive and was destined to become the family tree of the twelve tribes of Israel.

2. A *second particular object* was soon associated with the first. This was the Promised Land. The combination of these two objects of hope was sufficient to evoke the great aspiration of the first Israelites.

"And the Lord appeared to Abram and said to him: To thy seed will I give this land" (Gen. 12:7). "I AM, and my covenant is with thee, and thou shalt be a father of many nations. Neither shall thy name be called any more Abram: but thou shalt be called Abraham: because I have made thee a father of many nations. And I will make thee increase exceedingly, and I will make nations of thee, and kings shall come out of thee. And I will establish my covenant between me and thee, and between thy seed after thee in their generations, by a perpetual covenant: to be a God to thee, and to thy seed after thee. And I will give to thee, and to thy seed, the land of thy sojournment, all the land of Chanaan for a perpetual possession, and I will be their God" (Gen. 17:4-8).

The most memorable events in the ancient history of Israel are simply the great steps in the realization of this promise. These events were the exodus from Egypt, the passage through the Red Sea, the crossing of the Desert, and finally the crossing of the Jordan and the progressive conquest of the Chanaanite cities.

Yahweh faithfully accomplished everything He had promised. The recognition of this fact could only strengthen the confidence placed in His word. It was in their living memory of the Promise that the little handful of people found courage to face superior armies and powerful nations in the defense of their land. And in defending the land originally promised and finally possessed, the people of Israel were conscious of the protection of the Promise.

However, once they were established, like a man who has "arrived," the nation dared to become self-dependent and attributed its successes to its own efforts. There was still expectation of the marvelous destiny that had once been promised, but the nation forgot the humility and the feeling of poverty and need which must always be characteristic of real hope. Israel was waiting for the Day of the Lord which was conceived as a dazzling manifestation of God's predilection for this particular nation, and as a time of superiority over all other peoples. But the prophets, one after the other, came to cast their reproaches and warnings in the face of the guilty populace. The Day of the Lord would be a terrible day for Israel because it would be judged according to its sins. The catastrophe of the Babylonian Exile was the final climax of the long series of chastisements.

3. And then, from the depths of utter ruin, hope was born again. All of this was foretold. It was God Who was striking them, and they needed only to repent and He would hear them again. *A new object* was proposed for their expectation: deliverance, salvation, *the return to their homeland.* The voices of the prophets revived their courage.

And I will gather together the remnant of my flock, out of all the lands into which I have cast them out: and I will make them return to their own fields, and they shall increase and be multiplied.

And I will set up pastors over them, and they shall feed them: they shall fear no more, and they shall not be dismayed: and none shall be wanting of their number, saith the Lord.

Behold, the days come, saith the Lord, and I will raise up to David a just branch: and a king shall reign, and shall be wise: and shall execute judgment and justice in the earth.

In those days shall Juda be saved, and Israel shall dwell confidently: and this is the name that they shall call him: The Lord our just one.

Therefore behold the days come, saith the Lord, and they shall say no more: The Lord liveth, who brought up the children of Israel out of the land of Egypt:

But the Lord liveth, who hath brought out, and brought hither the seed of the house of Israel from the land of the north, and out of all the lands, to which I had cast them forth: and they shall dwell in their own land. (Jer. 23:3-8).

The Second Isaias and Ezechiel also rejoiced to describe the return to the recovered homeland, the restoration of the Temple's worship, and the new city (cf. Is. 40, 41, 44, 45; Ez. 36, 40).

4. Finally there appears with growing urgency *the ultimate object* that was proposed to the hope of Israel: *the Messianic Era.* It is not easy to retrace in a precise way the line of development of the messianic idea among the Hebrews. This idea was extremely complex and one could say that it especially resembles a mosaic pattern of juxtaposed images.

The mysterious event had already been proclaimed by the blessing of Abraham, and by the blessing of Jacob's sons when Juda was distinguished from his brothers. It was made more exact with David. But this was only an outline. It was in the time of the writer Prophets that the messianic idea acquired capital importance.

Before the exile it was particularly the *first* Isaias who made himself the herald of the marvelous era, the prophet of the Messiah. His messianic texts are among the best known; all of us are familiar with the sign of the Virgin or the prophecy concerning Emmanuel (chapter 7), and the following text which is found in the Christmas liturgy:

The people that walked in darkness, have seen a great light: to them that dwelt in the region of the shadow of death, light is risen.

. . . FOR A CHILD IS BORN to us, and a son is given to us, and the government is upon his shoulder: and his name shall be called, Wonderful, Counsellor, God the Mighty, the Father of the world to come, the Prince of Peace. His empire shall be multiplied, and there shall be no end of peace: he shall sit upon the throne of David, and upon his kingdom; to establish it and strengthen it with judgment and with justice, from henceforth and for ever: (Is. 9:2-7).

The peace and prosperity of this blessed era are described with remarkable lyricism:

The wolf shall dwell with the lamb: and the leopard shall lie down with the kid: the calf and the lion, and the sheep shall abide together, and a little child shall lead them.

The calf and the bear shall feed: their young ones shall rest together: and the lion shall eat straw like the ox. And the sucking child shall play on the hole of the asp: and the weaned child shall thrust his hand into the den of the basilisk. (Is. 11:6-9).

The announcement of the Messianic reign is often included with references to the return from exile. The events are presented in a perspective that makes it very difficult to distinguish between the different objectives. Generally it seems as though the return to Jerusalem must coincide with the establishment of the final Reign of Yahweh (Jer. 30 and 31). Sometimes these texts refer to the realization of the eschatological kingdom which is identified with the "last days" (Ez. 38-39; the Second Isaias 41 and other chapters).

After the return to Jerusalem, the fulfillment of the promises was still delayed in spite of the restoration and reconstruction of the temple. They had not yet attained to that glorious and final reign of universal peace, abundance and happiness. The voice of the prophets was heard again, vying with one another in proclaiming the nearness of the kingdom of God. This was the great cry which was to resound through the later centuries, and with this proclamation John the Baptist inaugurated the New Testament.

How did the Hebrews conceive of this messianic era? It is difficult for us to answer this question because the Hebrews themselves did not have a very precise idea regarding it. Roughly, we can distinguish three elements. The prophets proclaimed the imminence of the Day of Yahweh. This would certainly be a very important event, but the idea remained quite vague. Most descriptions make it a day of terror. The Day of Yahweh would be a terrible day of sorrow rather than joy. And yet it would finally be a blessing to Israel, or at least to the little "remnant" saved from the destruction (Aggeus, Zacharias, Abdias).[2]

The Day of Yahweh would mark the establishment of the Kingdom of God. But on this point again the witnesses do not perfectly agree. Will the inauguration of this Reign occur with the sudden destruction of all things, or will it come at the end of a normal and peaceful evolution? In the judgment of M. J. Lagrange,[3] most texts suggest that the founding of the Kingdom will be a passage from a reign *de jure* to a reign *de facto*. In His own right God has always been the ruler of Israel first, and then of all other nations. His reign will consist essentially of the universal recognition of this divine right. And then the new era will begin, bringing peace and happiness, and Israel will finally occupy among the world's nations that position of eminence assured by the divine predilection. However, if we refer to the texts that belong to apocalyptic literature, including the Book of Daniel among the canonical writings, the whole perspective is changed.[4] The establishment of the Kingdom is here described as a sudden and final breaking-point in the normal and foreseeable unfolding of history, and as the general destruction that will mark the end of time. In a setting of this kind, the Kingdom of God very definitely acquires an eschatological character, and God's royal power is exercised essentially over the elect in a new world.

Finally, it is the *Messias* who is the person chosen by Yahweh to be the divine instrument in the establishment of this Kingdom. Generally we see Him as a wise, powerful and glorious king. He is to come forth from the line of David, assuring the ancient royal dynasty

[2] It seems that we can compare this "Day of Yahweh" in the Jewish mentality with the "Great Night" that dominates the Communist mystique.

[3] M. J. Lagrange, *Le Règne de Dieu dans l'Ancien Testament,* in the *Revue Biblique,* 1908, pp. 36-61.

[4] The apocalyptic style—one of the styles in Biblical literature—is notably characterized by an orientation that is definitely eschatological (claiming to predict the events of the last days) with an esoteric aspect. This was developed principally in apocryphal literature.

a lasting splendor. Micheas even designated Bethlehem as the place of His birth. Only Isaias foretells the sufferings and sacrifice of the Servant (chap. 53), but this aspect of the Messias, which was so untraditional and disturbing, was left in shadow. The image that prevailed was the one that best answered to the aspirations of a people who were still very down-to-earth and materialist; and this could only be the image of a king full of glory who establishes a kingdom of abundance and prosperity.

The expectation of the whole nation was turned toward that blessed period. Everyone hoped to see its appearance; everyone wanted to belong to the generation favored more than all others. Happy are those who will see this time of glory with their own eyes! It was therefore a *common and national hope* whose object was most often the messianic era conceived in terms of history and time. Many generations would perhaps still come and go before the inauguration of the Kingdom, but if they do not have the joy of living in the messianic era, their portion is nevertheless the hope and expectation of the kingdom, for they belong to the people of the Promises.

Now we understand why *purely individual hope* took second place.[5] For the promises were addressed to the People of God corporately, and to that people only.

However, the problem of *personal retribution* confronted the Jews. It was far from being solved in earlier times. Most often it was a wholly material prosperity that the righteous man expected as the reward of his virtue. He thought of this reward in terms of granaries abundantly filled and an old age marked with deference and consideration. He awaited this blessing with such absolute confidence that in his eyes the tribulations of other men necessarily indicated a state of sinfulness. This was the argument of the Book of Job. There was a rather vague idea of the hereafter, called Sheol, situated in the depths of the earth. The idea of happiness in a future life following the resurrection of the body did not appear until very late. Isaias was the witness of this hope:

[5] It is evident that this "collective" hope really existed only in the hearts of individuals, and in this sense one can call it individual, in the same way that the idea of the community only exists in the consciousness of individuals. But the object of this hope had a definitely communal character. It was not so much a personal happiness that was expected with certain confidence, but rather a fulfillment of the destiny of the chosen people by the coming of the messianic Kingdom of God.

Thy dead men shall live, my slain shall rise again:
awake, and give praise, ye that dwell in the dust:
for thy dew is the dew of the light: (Is. 26:19).

It is especially the Book of Machabees (second century before
Christ) which gives forceful expression to the expectation of the resurrection.[6] But they did not ordinarily perceive the direct connection
between that future life which was to be the recompense of personal
merit, and the messianic era that was the object of the promise. The
two objectives seem entirely different. It is only apocalyptic literature
that conceives of the kingdom of God as the exercise of divine royalty over a kingdom of the hereafter in which the resurrected righteous
men will share. (See Daniel 12:1 and other texts.) Faith in an immortal life beginning with the resurrection was not nearly as universal
as faith in the coming of the Messias. And if this latter faith was
common to everyone, although in different forms, it is also true that
even in the time of Christ the Sadducees, who were especially recruited
among the high priests, always denied the resurrection.

It is easy to see what a great distance remained to be covered. The
coming of Jesus was necessary, fulfilling the message of the prophets
and the oracles, in order that the true and spiritual meaning of the
Promise might be disengaged from its prosaic and very materialist
shell.

We have outlined the successive steps that mark Israel's progress
toward the great messianic expectation. In the light of Christ's revelation it is apparent that the objects proposed one after the other to the
longings of the Hebrew people were part of a complete plan in which
the realization of the divine purpose was interwoven. It was the Spirit
of God that tirelessly pursued this task. God used various enticements
to lead the people of Israel. He directed these rude men through aspirations that were meaningful to them, toward that high goal that was
to become the supreme object of their desire. All these temporal and
immediate blessings, which one by one set the people in motion, made
them go forward expectantly by keeping them in suspense, from one
step to another, toward the true hope. In the same way that David
and Cyrus can be considered types and figures that foretold the coming of the Messias, so likewise the innumerable descendants assured

[6] See the Second Book, chapter 7 (the account of the martyrdom of the
seven brothers and their mother, who affirmed their faith in the resurrection,
one after the other) and chapter 12 (in which we see Judas Machabeus
gathering funds for an expiatory sacrifice in behalf of the dead soldiers: "a
beautiful and noble action inspired by the thought of the resurrection!").

to Abraham, and the Promised Land and Return to Jerusalem, were landmarks in the journey toward the essential objective always apparent in the background: the great messianic expectation.

3. THE MOTIVE OF HOPE

What is the basis of the Old Testament hope? Unquestionably, as we have already seen, it was based upon faith more than anything else. It was faith alone that made it possible for hope to be born. But there are other bases that are more specific.

The theophanies, originally very numerous, and especially that of Sinai, profoundly established the sense of the absolute transcendence of Yahweh in the minds of the people, and gave them a clear idea of His sovereign omnipotence. This was accomplished through the sacred terror which the manifestation of God always produced. He was the only Lord, the Holy One, the Awful One. No other power could prevail against Him. "He does whatever He wills." On the other hand, while His omnipotence definitely separates Him from all created beings, He does not want to withdraw into an inaccessible domain but instead He comes forth into the life of men. He chooses Israel for His people and enters into a covenant with this people. He binds Himself to them with ties of love. Almighty God now also shows Himself as the Father whose goodness is infinite. He has an incomparable tenderness for Israel:

Can a woman forget her infant, so as not to have pity on the son of her womb? and if she should forget, yet will not I forget thee.

Behold, I have graven thee in my hands (Is. 49:15-16).

These are the profound reasons for the hope of this people. Conscious of their weakness and their impotence, they could only depend upon God with all of their being. They expected all things from God, as a free gift, for they knew the infinite power of Yahweh and His special goodness toward themselves. It was this absolute confidence in Yahweh, based upon His omnipotence and His infinite goodness, that inspired David's numerous songs that are among the most beautiful ever known. It was this essential element of hope, an immovable confidence and trust, that found magnificent expression in the whole Book of Psalms.

The Lord is my shepherd: I want for nothing;
In green pastures he makes me lie down.
He leads me to waters where I may rest;
He gives refreshment to my soul . . . (Ps. 22:1-2).

The Lord is my light and my salvation: whom shall I fear?
The Lord is the fortress of my life: of whom shall I be in dread?
. . . If a camp be pitched against me, my heart shall not fear;
If a war should arise against me, I will be confident (Ps. 26:1,3).

But the power and goodness of God still did not allow the people
to hope with absolute certainty for any particular blessing. This power
and goodness were the basis of a hope that was more or less undefined.
We cannot expect anything from God unless He has agreed to give it
to us and has made His promise to us. It was therefore the formal
promise of God which was the immediate motive of Israel's hope.

This is certainly apparent throughout the entire Old Testament.
Yahweh invoked both His promise and His fidelity to His given word:
"I will . . . fulfill the oath which I swore to Abraham thy father"
(Gen. 26:3).[7] In his discourses Moses often recalls to mind that only
the promise of Yahweh could be the foundation of the nation's hope,
and not the merits of Israel, the "stiff-necked people."[8] And when
the prophets, in their turn, renewed the song of hope in the midst of
imprecations and threats, they always referred to the divine promise
and to God's faithfulness to Himself:

For my name's sake I will remove my wrath far off: and for my praise I
will bridle thee, lest thou shouldst perish (Is. 48:9).
Surely Ephraim is an honourable son to me, surely he is a tender child: for
since I spoke of him, I will still remember him (Jer. 31:20).

The assured and precise foundation of the hope of the chosen people
was the promise of God and His faithfulness that was confirmed by
His many interventions in behalf of Israel. He saved them by "His
powerful, outstretched arm."

This was the great movement, briefly outlined, that was dependent
upon God alone and led the people of Israel in their quest, from the
beginning to the end of the Old Testament. This was a hope that was
still groping its way in search of its true object, but God was guiding
it along the paths which He had foreseen. According to the Epistle
to the Hebrews it will only find its fulfillment in Christ's revelation,
for the new law has brought us to a better hope (Heb. 7:11).

II. The New Testament

A. The Synoptic Gospels

The word ἐλπίς, which means hope, is not found in the Synoptic
Gospels. This fact may seem very strange at first. But we must keep

[7] Also see Gen. 17:1; 28:13-15; 48:3-4; etc.
[8] See Deut. 7:8; 8:1; 9:5, 9, 26-29; etc.

in mind that the idea of hope is expressed simultaneously with the idea of faith in the word πίστις (the faith). In the Synoptics, in fact, faith is almost always accompanied by this feeling of confidence and of absolute abandonment to God which we associate with the notion of hope. And furthermore, faith properly has a direct connection with hope. For if we believe in Jesus, we recognize Him primarily as the envoy of God, the Messias Himself. This acknowledges Him as the object of the Jewish people's expectation, and as the realization, in His own person, of the great hope of the Old Testament.

Consequently, even if there is no mention of hope in the Synoptic Gospels, the reality is nevertheless abundantly expressed.

1. THE NEW HOPE

Jesus makes His appearance as the Messias. He brings the age-long expectation to an end. Does this mean that there will no longer be any hope? On the contrary, hope finds its perfect form; there is now a "better hope." Christ had come to establish the Kingdom of God that everyone was expecting. But people were mistaken regarding the real nature of the kingdom. This is not surprising, however, for Jesus Himself called the Kingdom of God a "mystery" (Mk. 4:11; Mat. 13:11; Lk. 8:10). He had to proceed with patience in His efforts to correct the traditional conception, and He could not easily accomplish this purpose. The idea of a temporal and material kingdom was solidly established. People wanted to make Him their king after the first multiplication of the loaves. Later, in the eyes of the people the triumphal entry of Palm Sunday acquired the aspect of a march upon Jerusalem, and on the very eve of the Ascension one of the disciples even asked, "Lord, wilt thou at this time restore the kingdom to Israel?" (Acts, 1:6).

Jesus therefore had to make His disciples as well as the people, understand that He had come to establish the Kingdom of God indeed, but that it would be a *spiritual* kingdom. From the time of the Sermon on the Mount, the requirements mentioned for entrance into the kingdom firmly emphasized its spiritual character. The Beatitudes are untenable paradoxes for anyone thinking in terms of a material kingdom.[9] In this way Christ followed the line of hope of the Old

[9] According to the logic of the messianic conception in the Old Testament, we would expect very different "beatitudes" (the word *blessed* had a messianic resonance for the Jews, and was applied especially to those who would have the good fortune to be alive in the Messiah's time). Blessed are the valiant

Testament while also bringing it to perfect development. The Kingdom of God as a spiritual reality is presented in two aspects: it is simultaneously *contemporary,* earthly, being realized in historical time, and *eschatological,* heavenly, kingdom of the hereafter.[10]

2. THE PRESENT REIGN OF GOD

When Jesus first began to preach, He took up the theme of St. John the Baptist and the later prophets: "The kingdom of God is at hand" (Mt. 4:17; Mk. 1:15). But soon the transition was marked. At Nazareth, commenting upon the passage in Isaias, "The Spirit of the Lord is upon me because He has anointed me to proclaim the gospel to the poor," Jesus declared, "today is this Scripture fulfilled before you" (Lk. 4:16 et al.). And later He proclaimed, "The kingdom of God has come upon you" (Mt. 12:28; Lk. 11:20), "For behold, the kingdom of God is within you" (Lk. 17:20).

But this Kingdom was not established in its perfect state all in one moment. It had made its appearance, but it had to grow and develop. Most of the parables on the Kingdom insist upon this point: the parable of the seed which is the only one to grow (Mk. 4:26), the parable of the mustard-seed (Mt. 13:31; Mk. 4:30; Lk. 13:18, and finally the parable of the leaven in the dough (Mt. 13:33; Lk. 13:20).

Furthermore, the present condition of the kingdom almost necessarily implies a state of imperfection. The worst and the best are side by side, as we learned from the parable of the chaff mixed with the good wheat (Mt. 13:24) and in the story of the net that caught both the good and the bad fish (Mt. 13:47). Christ warns us that these disparate elements will be mixed together for as long as the earthly phase of the Kingdom continues. It is only at the "end of the world" that the final elimination will take place. Consequently, the present and temporal Kingdom will find its normal fulfillment in the eschatological Kingdom at the end of time.

---

warriors, blessed are the clever politicians, etc. But Christ proclaimed, "Blessed are the poor, blessed are the clean of heart, blessed are those who suffer. . . ."

[10] The expression which is translated Kingdom of God is in reality ambivalent. It means a Reign as well as a Kingdom. The Synoptic authors use it obviously in both senses. Sometimes they refer to a kingdom with its organization and hierarchy, and at other times they mean an interior reign that is hardly visible. Matthew speaks of the kingdom "of the heavens" rather than use the divine name.

3. THE ESCHATOLOGICAL REIGN OF GOD

The perfect Reign or Kingdom to be inaugurated at the end of historical time is described in various images. The evangelists compare it to an eternal feast in which the elect will enjoy the company of the holy patriarchs (Mt. 8:11; Lk. 13:29). They will shine like the stars (Mt. 13:43), live like the angels of God (Mt. 22:30). This final Reign will be the fulfillment of the Reign that was begun in this present world, but there must be a total destruction of the old before the new universe can become a reality. It is a pre-existing Kingdom, prepared for the elect at the very moment of creation (Mt. 25:34), which must finally come to take the place of the present Kingdom. Its establishment will be marked by the Second Coming,[11] that is to say, the return of the Son of Man who will come in power and glory to carry out the universal judgment (Mt. 25:31; Mk. 13:26; Lk. 21:25).

The date of this event is uncertain. If we take certain texts literally, we could assume that it is quite near (Mt. 16:28; Mk. 9:1; Lk. 9:27). But no one knows what moment God has chosen (Mt. 24:36; Mk. 13:32). That is why we must watch and be ready, having the loins girded and the lamp lighted, as we are told in the parable of the master who returns (Lk. 12:35) and in the parable of the ten virgins (Lk. 21:34).

The new Kingdom will be the Kingdom of the elect who have risen from the dead, for the Second Coming will be accompanied by the resurrection of the body (Mt. 22:23; Mk. 12:18; Lk. 20:27). All of this indicates quite clearly that the eschatological kingdom is conceived according to the apocalyptic tradition.

The Reign or Kingdom appears as a reality whose collective and social character is strongly emphasized. The very expression "Reign of God" or "Kingdom of Heaven" forbids placing the essential stress upon the aspect of strictly personal happiness. Before all else, in the perspective of the Gospels as well as in the Old Testament, the kingdom is to be a happy and perfect community governed by God. But certainly each individual has his personal place in this Kingdom. He must become an integral part of this community.

Man must desire and seek eternal life above everything else. He must prefer it more than all other things and sacrifice all the rest for

---

[11] The word *parousia* means "presence" or "coming" or "arrival." In the New Testament it has the technical meaning of the glorious return of Christ at the end of the world; this is its only meaning in our days.

its sake, if necessary, even his eye or his hand (Mt. 18:8; Mk. 9:43). This eternal life seems to be bound up with the Second Coming. For it is in the moment of Our Lord's return at the time of the judgment that man will truly enter into possession of life. It is then that Christ will gather together His elect, separating them from the evil persons and assign them to their places (Mt. 25:31; Lk. 14:13).

Eternal life, which ought to be the aspiration of all men, is essentially and entirely a sharing in the eschatological Kingdom which the return of Christ will inaugurate. It is the "possession" of the Kingdom: "Come, blessed of my Father, take possession of the kingdom prepared for you from the foundation of the world" (Mt. 25:34). The blessed life in the hereafter is therefore generally associated with the idea of the end of time and the Second Coming. However, several texts allude to a participation in the blessed life before the eschatological events. This is apparent in the parable of poor Lazarus which refers to "Abraham's bosom" as the abode of righteous souls before the resurrection, and we may recall Jesus' promise to the Good Thief, "Today thou shalt be with me in paradise." It seems, however, that this state is transitory, for if eternal life is an entry into possession of the perfect kingdom, it is normal that it be established at the end of time. And this idea is very consistent with the mentality of the Jews who apparently did not conceive of an eternity transcending time, as we do, but imagined it in terms of time prolonging itself into the infinite, which was called the "age" of the future, limited only in its origin which must coincide with the Second Coming when the "present age" is finally over.[12]

The Kingdom is prepared by God; it is a gift which proceeds from the pure goodness of God. But it is nevertheless a reward, and in this

---

[12] According to the Protestant theologian, O. Cullmann, in his excellent work, *Christ et le temps,* our present conception of an eternity utterly different from time can be attributed to the Greek philosophers and was not known to the Jews or the New Testament authors. These authors thought of eternity as endless time, for eternity and time were expressed by only one word: *eon.*

In a strictly temporal sense, the *eon* always designates:

1. the present time ("the present age") limited at its origin by creation and at its end by the end of the world;

2. time that preceded the creation and which was unlimited if one looks backward into the past (this could be called an eternity).

3. the time that will begin at the end of the world and will have no finish. This is the *"eon to come,"* the "future age." Eternal life in the other world, mentioned in the Gospel, is that eternity which will begin at the end of the present *eon.*

sense, it must be merited. Even the earthly Kingdom is not open to everyone. There are conditions to fulfill. These conditions are set forth in the Sermon on the Mount. And on the Last Day there will be accounts to render (as in the parable of the talents in Mt. 25:14, and the parable of the gold pieces in Lk. 19:11). If the social aspect is emphasized, it must also be remembered that personal commitment is necessary. Entry into the perfect kingdom is the recompense for individual merit (Mt. 5:12, 19:20; Mk. 10:21; Lk. 18:22). Therefore, if our hope for the future life must depend upon the free disposition of God and the formal promise of Jesus, it cannot be a purely passive and complacent expectation. We must conquer the Kingdom in some way or other, and become worthy of it personally.

4. THE OBJECT OF CHRISTIAN HOPE

We now see how Christ came to perfect the hope of the Old Testament. This testament had ended with the expectation of the Messianic Era. But the conception of the Reign to be inaugurated by the Messias had to be rectified, or rather extricated from its material shell. Jesus applied Himself to this task. He appeared and declared that He was the Messias, and He taught that He had come to found the kingdom of their hope. He said that the kingdom had already begun and was even then among them, but they were not to deceive themselves about it, for it was a spiritual kingdom. It was simultaneously a reign that operates within the hearts of men, and an organized kingdom with its visible hierarchy: Peter, the Apostles, the laws and sacraments. This kingdom was the Church. It must develop and extend over all the earth, but it will not find its perfection until the Last Day, at the Second Coming, when the Son of Man returns in glory. The final Kingdom will then be established, following the present Kingdom which is only its seed and preparation. And Jesus declared that man's hope should not end with the coming of the Messias, and the foundation of the kingdom, but from that moment it should be enlarged and directed toward the fulfillment of the Kingdom, and its plenitude for all eternity.

Such is the new character of Christian hope which was to follow the expectation of the people of Israel. The object of this new hope was no longer to be the establishment of the Messianic kingdom, for the kingdom had now come. It existed in their midst. Christians would now hope for the fulfillment and universality of this Kingdom. But this fulfillment of the divine plan and final flowering of the Kingdom would be concurrent with a definite event: the Second Coming. Consequently, all the aspirations of the new people of God are directed toward the *return of the Lord*. All our hope points toward this event.

With the essential object of hope we must also mention other objects that could be called "minor" and which were expressly proposed by Jesus, related however to the principal object. First of all there is the material subsistence which God will assure to the faithful. Not one of them will lack anything necessary:

> Consider the ravens: they neither sow nor reap, they have neither storeroom nor barn; yet God feeds them. . . . See how the lilies grow; they neither toil nor spin, yet I say to you that not even Solomon in all his glory was arrayed like one of these (Lk. 12:22 ff.).

All our efforts must be directed toward attainment of the Kingdom, and all the rest, including material subsistence and even earthly joys, will be added unto us; nor will we ever have to be concerned about such things, for it is God who gives them to us. Furthermore, Christ promised His permanent help to His Church for as long as the present age shall last (Mt. 28:20). Finally there is the gift of the Holy Spirit, but we can hardly call this a "minor" object, for it has such an important place in the life of the Kingdom.

With absolute confidence we can expect the help of the Holy Spirit from our heavenly Father, especially in times of persecution (Mt. 10:19; Mk. 13:11; Lk. 11:13, 12:11). It is He Who will give Christians the strength to be witnesses of the Gospel. Matthew's text ends with the promise of the assistance of Christ, but Luke's Gospel closes with the proclaiming of the gift of the Holy Spirit. And the Book of Acts especially emphasizes the place of the Holy Spirit in the life of the early Christian community—truly taking the place of the Risen Christ Who had ascended to heaven, and manifestly presiding over the great activity of the Kingdom of God on earth, the Church.

B. Saint Paul

1. THE FOUNDATION OF HOPE IS FAITH

According to St. Paul, faith is the necessary foundation of hope. The very idea of hope requires faith as its principle. As a matter of fact, hope can only be directed toward a good that we do not yet possess or which we do not see; therefore, such a good must first be an object of faith. On the other hand, it is the imperfect condition of faith in which we have knowledge without visible evidence, which makes hope possible and gives birth to it: "For in hope were we saved. But hope that is seen is not hope. For how can a man hope for what he sees?" (Rom. 8:24).

The *Epistle to the Hebrews* sums up the relationship between faith and hope in a lapidary formula which expresses this unity very well: "Now faith is the substance of things to be hoped for" (11:1). According to the *Epistle to the Romans*, the example of Abraham was the classical illustration of this unity. In Abraham faith and hope were combined in a way that serves as a model for all believers: "Abraham hoping against hope believed, so that he became the father of many nations, according to what was said, 'So shall thy offspring be.' And without weakening in faith, he considered his own deadened body (for he was almost a hundred years old) and the deadened womb of Sara; and yet in view of the promise of God, he did not waver through unbelief but was strengthened in faith, giving glory to God, being fully aware that whatever God has promised he is able also to perform" (Rom. 4:18-21).

2. THE OBJECT OF HOPE: GLORY OR PARTICIPATION IN THE KINGDOM

Christians have a real vocation to hope, for they are all called by God to one and the same hope (Eph. 1:18). And this common hope is both a sign and an element of their unity, in the same way as the one baptism, the one faith, the one Lord, the one Body and the one Spirit (Eph. 4:4). What then is the object of hope?

We must realize first of all that hope does not pertain primarily to the present life. "If with this life only in view we have had hope in Christ, we are of all men the most to be pitied" (I Cor. 15:19). For the object of hope is salvation, eternal life, glory. These are the terms that St. Paul uses most frequently, and it seems that he preferred the last word. These three words clearly express the same material reality considered under a particular aspect, and in the eyes of the Apostle, it seems that *glory* exactly defines the object of hope.

Above all else it is the glory of God which we must hope for and await, or more exactly, the manifestation of the glory of God and of our Savior Jesus Christ (Rom. 5:2; Titus 2:13). But it is our own glory also: "that glory which shall be made known in us" and that "weight of glory" compared with which the afflictions of this present age are nothing (Rom. 8:18; II Cor. 4:7, 3:17; Col. 1:27).

Our own glory, in fact, is simply our participation in the glory of

Christ. It is the manifestation of the divine glory itself within us (Rom. 8:17; Eph. 2:4; Col. 3:4; II Thess. 2:13). And this glory which we are called to share will not be a passing glory in us, like the fleeting glow on the face of Moses following his conversations with Yahweh. On the contrary, it is a glory of divine essence, permanent and immortal, which is truly eternal life (Rom. 2:7; II Cor. 3:7-18). And Paul multiplies expressions to define it. He calls it the manifestation of the sons of God, the glorious liberty of the sons of God and their perfect adoption (Rom. 8:19-23).

This object of our hope (glory, eternal life, salvation) is the heritage which God promised to Abraham. It is the *Kingdom of God* specifically which is mentioned in the Synoptic gospels, for the idea of the heritage was transmitted under the form of the Kingdom. For this reason Paul used parallel expressions having the same meaning when he spoke of inheriting eternal life (Titus 3:7) or of inheriting glory (Eph. 1:14, 1:18), or most often, of inheriting the Kingdom of God (I Cor. 6:9-10; Gal. 5:21; Eph. 5:5; etc.). We even find in the same sentence two expressions that are obviously identical in meaning; for example, he tells of inheriting the Kingdom of God and of inheriting incorruptibility (I Cor. 15:50). We cannot doubt that St. Paul thought of glory, salvation, eternal life and the Kingdom of God as different names for the same object of the Promise.

In the writings of Paul the Kingdom of God has a definitely eschatological character. Its identification with incorruptibility and eternal glory indicate this clearly. Furthermore, it is sometimes expressly named the "heavenly kingdom of God" (II Tim. 4:18), and is therefore bound up, in this respect also, with the end of time and the Second Coming. The *return of the Lord* is a concrete, precise event. It embraces the whole field of hope and combines all the elements of its object. For it is this event which must mark the fulfillment of the Kingdom, the total realization of the Promise.

Therefore, the return of Christ is presented as the specific object of our expectation under the different names the Apostle uses to designate this object. Most often it is the "second coming" or the "day of the Lord"; sometimes it is the "epiphany" or the "apocalypse" (I Cor. 1:7; I Thess. 1:9; Phil. 3:20; Titus 2:13; Heb. 9:28; etc.). Confirming this idea, the second epistle of Peter not only insists upon the expectation of the Day of the Lord, but asks the faithful to "hasten" its coming (II Pet. 3:12). In apostolic times the second coming seemed imminent, and Paul had to warn the Thessalonians against untimely interpretations. Peter felt that he could explain the prolongation of the fulfillment of the Promise by invoking the divine patience which granted a delay for the sake of repentance (I Thess. 5:1-2; II Thess. 2:1-12; II Pet. 3).

St. Paul liked to describe all the events that are to mark the coming of Christ; the preliminary signs, the resurrection, the apparition of Christ, the judgment, and finally the consummation of all that exists. It would be outside our scope to spend any time on these descriptions because we are considering the Second Coming only under its aspect as the object of hope. The resurrection, abundantly proved (especially I Cor. 15), is a condition for entrance into the eternal kingdom, for it will mark, for the elect at least, their everlasting union with Christ (I Cor. 15; I Thess. 4:16-17), for the body will have become incorruptible, glorious, full of strength and spiritual (I Cor. 15:35-50). However, the fate of souls before the resurrection does not seem to have preoccupied St. Paul. He hardly mentions it, and refers to these souls as having "fallen asleep" (I Cor. 15:15-20; I Thess. 4:13-15). There are two reasons that easily explain this preterition, both of which have their place in the conception of hope. First, if the Second Coming was near, as everyone thought, the importance of the transition period was very limited; furthermore, in the habitual perspective of Holy Scripture, the future of the individual is neither separate nor separable from the common salvation and destiny of the people of God considered corporately.

Finally, after Christ has pronounced judgment, the consummation of all things will take place. Our Lord's return will be His definitive victory over all His enemies. After His triumph over sin and the Prince of this world, He still had to vanquish death, the ancient adversary. But this had been accomplished. The work of the Savior has been achieved. He can leave the Kingdom and the dominion of all things in the hands of His Father (I Cor. 15:24-28). This will be the end of this "age," the end of the present world, but according to Peter it will also be the beginning of another world, the "new heaven and new earth" (I Cor. 1:8; II Cor. 1:13-14; II Pet. 3:10).

It is therefore Christ's return which is concretely the end and object of Christian hope, since it is the event which brings to that hope everything that was awaited. At the same time, this hope is marked by a dual characteristic.

Primarily it is centered upon a fact, an historic event which is destined to occur some particular day in the course of time. That is why, quite naturally, it has an element of tension which carries us through time, by our provisional desire, in order that we may attain to that future event. It is by this tension toward a future of which it is certain that hope becomes the great source of Christian action, the fount of patience and courage through all of life's trials. The man who hopes is like the runner in the stadium who keeps his eyes fixed upon the goal of the race and the crown of the winner (Rom. 5:3, 8:17; I Cor. 9:24-27; II Cor. 4:16-18).

Secondly, the object of hope is a fact which seems to be of essential interest to the people of God collectively. A hope aiming at happiness that is formally individual and without any explicit relationship with the Christian community is not what is intended here or anywhere else in the Bible. For St. Paul, salvation is not only for the people of God in general, but is a universal salvation. It is the whole of creation that awaits deliverance, "for we know that all creation groans and travails in pain until now" (Rom. 8:22), yearning for that day when it will also find its state of glory.

An important point concerning the movement of hope remains to be considered. That object, which, by definition, will not be attained until the future, is nevertheless already present in a mysterious manner. For we must not suppose that hope must necessarily compel us to acquire a perspective that is exclusively eschatological, as if the central event of the history of salvation must still take place. It has already been accomplished. This event was the work of Christ who obtained salvation for us. But this first coming of Christ requires His second coming, beyond the unfolding of time, as the crowning of the work of salvation which Christ fully achieved and which comes to men in the life of the Church.

In our present condition it is hope that enables us to have some foretaste of our future glory. It allows us to be glorified in this present time through our certainty of final glorification, for we know that hope is sure and does not deceive (Rom. 5:1-5). This is the general principle: through hope we possess eternal blessings, imperfectly but in a real way nevertheless. And in this way we participate in the glory of God. The God whom we shall see face to face in glory is seen even now, but as in a mirror (I Cor. 13:12). We ourselves are mirrors of the divine glory, called to be completely assimilated in the image that we reflect (II Cor. 3:14-18)[13] especially if we now possess salvation through the grace of Christ.

Salvation is the anticipated possession of eternal life. It is in hope that we are saved (Rom. 5:17 should especially be studied). We cannot over-emphasize the resonance of immediate actuality of this word saying, "it is in hope," for even though the consummation of our salvation is still to come, "we are saved" in this present time; we already have our salvation.

We do not need to wait until the resurrection to receive the first-fruits of our salvation. For while we await the time of our full likeness to the Risen Christ, we have already truly entered into the life of the resurrection; we are clothed with the Risen Christ (Rom. 6:3).

This anticipated possession of the object of hope makes eschatology itself already present. The eschatological times have begun. The indubitable sign is the gift of the Holy Spirit that was given to us. For the Holy Spirit which we possess is the proof, the beginning, the earnest of the future heritage that will consist in the full and final redemption (Rom. 8:23; II Cor. 1:22, 5:5; Eph. 1:13). And Peter, in his discourse of Pentecost, shows that the diffusion of the Spirit is the sign of the Last Days, announced by Joel (Acts 2:16). This is the new Christian conception of time. With Christ we have entered into a new era. The era to come, the future and everlasting age is already here.[14]

The signs of the future age, and the last days, are found to have occurred already, but the presence of sin, which is one of the signs of the era preceding the Second Coming, still continues. This means that with Christ we possess the essential thing now: salvation and eternal life, and yet the Second Coming is still the event that will mark the final transformation of the Kingdom.

3. THE MOTIVE OF HOPE: THE PROMISE

According to Paul the Christian hope depends entirely upon the *Promise*, or more exactly, it depends upon the promise made by God at the beginning and also upon the absolute fidelity of God to His Word: "Let us hold fast the confession of our hope without wavering, for he who has given the promise is faithful" (Heb. 10:23; also I Cor. 1:9; I Thess. 5:24; II Tim. 2:13; Titus 1:2; Heb. 6:13-20). We

[13] See on this point L. Cerfaux, *La théologie de l'Église suivant saint Paul,* "Unam Sanctam," Paris, Éd. du Cerf, 1942, p. 70.

[14] Doubtless we must note with O. Cullmann (*op. cit.*) that this is rather a new division of time, a bipartite division (the time before Christ and the time after Christ) centered upon the fact of Christ, which is superimposed upon the ancient tripartite division without destroying it (the triple eon).

must associate this idea with one of the great currents of Pauline doctrine. The Christian community, destined to become the *Ecclesia*, had become, after the Jewish rejection, the true people of God, the Israel of God. It is therefore this community that takes the place of the people of the Old Testament and inherits all their privileges. One of the most essential of these privileges was the oath sworn to Abraham, the Promise which God made to the patriarch and his descendants. And Paul interprets the initial promise in a sense that largely surpasses the history of the people of the Old Law. The descendant to whom the heritage was promised was really Christ (Rom. 4:12-16; Gal. 3:14-24). For this reason the glory and eternal life which come to us through Christ constitute the true heritage, the real object of the initial promise, and are identified with the Kingdom.

The force of the Promise as the motive of hope is further strengthened by the fact that we already possess the first proofs of its realization. The divine promise has already begun to produce fruit. We now have salvation through grace, and therefore, we have the assurance of our future glory. All of this comes to us through Christ and from Christ alone. All that we wait for, and all of our hope, must come from Him. It is Christ Who saves us; it is He Who gives us the new life. It was He who first rose from the dead as the beginning of our resurrection. And Christ is the mediator of the new Covenant (Rom. 5 and Heb. 9). Consequently it is Christ who is the great foundation of our hope. St. Paul refers to "Christ our hope" (I Tim. 1:4), and he means especially the Risen Christ.

The promise which God made and which was realized in Christ is part of a divine plan, a mysterious purpose hidden through many centuries, by which God in His wisdom and goodness ordered all things for His elect. At the beginning we therefore find the free disposition of God, His sovereign and gratuitous purpose (Eph. 1:3-12).

If all of this is sufficient foundation for our hope, we know however that hope requires an active and efficacious participation by ourselves. Everything has been prepared for us; salvation was obtained for us by Christ, but we must still enter into the perspectives of God and become integrated into Christ. If we hope to share His glory, we must participate in His Life and His sufferings.

4. THE IMPORTANCE OF HOPE

It is hardly necessary to emphasize again the important place of hope in the life of a Christian. Let us simply remember that Paul habitually refers to hope along with faith and charity. For him it was a trilogy that characterizes the Christian life in the present age (I Cor. 13:13; Col. 1:5; I Thess. 1:3, 5:8; Heb. 10:22). It belongs only to Christians, for other men are without hope or they possess an evil hope (Eph. 2:12; I Thess. 4:13). Together with faith and charity, hope is therefore the specific sign of the disciple of Christ.

C. Saint John

In all of his writings St. John hardly mentions hope at all. Consequently, it is unlikely that we would find any new elements in him. But he affirms, nevertheless, more than any other sacred writer, even more than St. Paul, the profound unity that exists between the life that Christ gives to us in this present time and the eternal life which will begin with the resurrection. We find phrases like the following, frequently juxtaposed: "he that believes in me will *have* eternal life," and "he who eats my flesh and drinks my blood *has* life everlasting and I will raise him up on the last day"; "he who hears my word has eternal life and is not subject to judgment, but *has passed* from death to life" and "he who believes *has* eternal life" (see especially chapters 5 and 6). Obviously, according to John the life of eternity has already begun and we have entered with Christ into the "world to come."

But it is the *Apocalypse* which, without mentioning the word, is the most beautiful and most lively illustration of hope.

It describes the struggles which the Church must face, the assault of all the enemies of Christ and the Christian name, which will finally culminate in the triumph of the Lamb. And those who have been faithful unto the end will share in His triumph. The whole history of the Church, which seems singularly tragic in this dramatic abridgement, tends toward that final apotheosis, and the *Apocalypse* could be summed up in this way: the attacks of the forces of evil can never prevail against the constancy and the steadfast expectation of the Church which aspires to the Reign of Christ, and the final triumph will occur at the appointed time. All the immense aspiration of the Christian people will be fulfilled by the apparition of a new heaven and a new earth, and the New Jerusalem will appear as a bride adorned with her spouse. And then hope will have finished its course; it will possess its object and will be absorbed in total joy: "And I heard a loud voice from the throne saying,

> Behold the dwelling of God with men,
>   and he will dwell with them,
> And they will be his people,
>   and God himself will be with them as their
>   God.
> And God will wipe away every tear from their eyes.
> And death shall be no more;
>   neither shall there be mourning, nor crying
>   nor pain any more,
> For the former things have passed away." (21:3-4).

The book ends expressly with the cry of hope, calling for the return of the Lord. "And the Spirit and the bride say, Come! And let him who hears say, Come! And let him who thirsts come; and he who wishes, let him receive the water of life freely. . . . Amen! Come, Lord Jesus!" (22:17, 20).

Second Part

THE ELABORATION OF A THEOLOGY OF HOPE

I. Revelation of Hope
and Theology of Hope

When we turn directly from the study of hope in Holy Scripture to a modern theological treatise, or to the doctrines of the great doctors of the Middle Ages, which amounts to the same thing, we notice a very definite change of perspective.

According to Scripture, hope is a forward movement, in absolute confidence based upon the divine Promise, toward the Kingdom of God. In the New Testament this kingdom is seen as something already begun, imperfect in its present phase, and destined to be transformed at the end of time into a perfect and eternal kingdom. There is one event that sums up the object of this hope in a very concrete way: the return of Christ, with its glorious consequences, the general resurrection and the entry into the final kingdom.

If we turn to a theological treatise, however, we shall find the object of hope presented in terms of "eternal happiness," that is to say, the possession of God, the supreme end. Such a change of perspective must certainly astonish us, and we notice immediately the substitution of an abstract term for a wide variety of notions that are much more concrete and more descriptive: the glorious kingdom as we find it described in the New Testament.

Here we see the profound difference that distinguishes theology from revelation. There is nothing metaphysical about revelation. It is the proposition which God makes to men concerning the "mystery of salvation." Intended for men, it is made to them in assimilable human terms, but these terms are used to express the inexpressible. Furthermore, intended for all men, the revelation of the mystery is proposed through the interpretation of a people whose racial identity is plainly evident, and whose ethnic, cultural and historic characteristics are clearly marked. Therefore, it enters into a human reality that is very concrete. Theology, however, is the inquiry and reflection of the mind, illumined by the faith, upon the revealed object. Consequently, it must discern the "intelligible values" in the object of hope, in a conceptualization and reasoning process imposed by the condition of the human mind, while obeying the impervious requirement of the intelligence which demands logic and unity in all things. It is therefore in the very nature of theology, and in its exigencies, to find in the center of the object of hope the essential principle around which all the elements are organized. And this principle will be discovered in the real and personal possession of God Himself, in the vision of God face to face. This is what theology considers as the essential thing beneath the biblical images of the "Kingdom," based upon the only texts which lift a corner of the curtain revealing the blessed life: "We see now through a mirror in an obscure manner, but then face to face. Now I know in part, but then I shall know even as I have been known" (I Cor. 13:12); "Beloved, now we are the children of God, and it has not yet appeared what we shall be. We know that, when he appears, we shall be like to him for we shall see him just as he is" (I Jn. 3:2). It is this supreme act of perfect union with God which constitutes the happiness of man. We now see why there is no real divergence, even if the vocabulary and perhaps the emphasis are different, as also the methods and nature, and therefore the evolution which we observe here is quite normal.

Yet, we may wonder if our theology has not tended toward exaggeration in its necessary distinction from revelation, as a result of certain factual and historic conditions. Perhaps it has been fashioned and developed under a metaphysical form as a kind of "wisdom" rather than a "doctrine of salvation." The case of hope seems to us quite characteristic in this respect. We need only single out two points, already mentioned, in which the conception of hope seems to have undergone a certain hardening.

Horizontal Hope and Vertical Hope

In the New Testament we have seen how hope was directed toward an event, a precise fact, which synthesized the whole object of the expectation of the people of God. Hope was therefore definitely "oriented." Time played an important part in all this, for hope carried the Christian through the course of temporal events in the direction of a particular moment, a special day. We may use a picturesque expression of Gabriel Marcel and say that it was like seeing through time. In its very movement it integrated the flow of time. And if the expected Kingdom was in reality a transcendent and preexisting Kingdom, it would nevertheless be attained only at the end of time's duration, the end of this present "age." This explains the real yearning for time's end which was characteristic of hope. And this is what is meant by *horizontal* hope.

This characteristic is not very apparent in our usual conception of hope. Most often the eschatological aspect is even eliminated from our treatises on hope. We are told that its object is the possession of God as our happiness. Stripped and diminished in this way, the object is transposed outside the temporal movement of hope and conceived in a syle that is definitely metaphysical. Doubtless it keeps all its richness for a philosophical mind, and even conserves its future character (for the possession of happiness is delayed as long as hope endures) but the movement of hope now points upward to become *vertical*. In fact, the object is presented less as an event than as a metaphysical object. It exists in the present, and we can attain to it immediately by a theological act; this is not an act that essentially passes through time but which transcends the natural order. It is to be feared that Christian hope might then keep the soul in quiet tranquility and assurance which would make it immobile, to the detriment of the continuous concern for vigilance and of readiness to face struggle with the mentality of a conquerer. It runs the risk, as often occurs, of being reduced to a kind of lazy certitude, without ardor. There is the conviction that we shall possess Paradise when the time finally comes, but of course "at the latest possible time"!

Community Hope and Individual Hope

Scriptural reference to the Reign or the Kingdom also insisted upon the communal character of the object of hope. Even eternal life as the recompense of personal acts was not considered apart from a direct connection with the community. We are reunited with Christ and all the elect at Judgment Day, and we remain with Him in His eternal kingdom. Our own destiny cannot be realized separately, for we enter into possession of the heritage with all the people of God.

As soon as we have isolated the vision of the divine essence as an essential reality of eternal life, an act that is eminently personal and individual, it is inevitable that the communal aspect should be given a complementary role. We then place a whole series of "complements" of beatitude alongside the principal object. These complements include the company of the elect, the sight of the Risen Christ and the resurrection of our own bodies. But the close identification of the Christian with the great divine family in its struggles and its glory is then almost forgotten.

Obviously this presents an extremely simplified distortion which Christians who are familiar with the Bible are certain to detect in modern manuals of theology.

II. Principal Stages in the Development of the Doctrine of Hope

Hope itself was certainly not a major object of theoretical study among the first Christian thinkers or the Fathers of the Church.[15] Even St. Augustine, for all his prolixity, only devoted a few chapters to hope in the hundred and nineteen chapters of his *Enchiridion de fide, spe et caritate.*

However, one of the most debated questions pertained to the Second Coming as the object of hope: and notably, its date and the conception of the eschatological kingdom.[16]

The primitive community made the Return of Christ the precise object of its expectation, associating eternal life with the Second Coming. The *Didache* bears witness to this fact expressly.

And yet experience revealed that the Second Coming was not

[15] See Tixeront, *Histoire des dogmes dans l'antiquité chrétienne,* 2 vols. Paris, Gabalda; R. Draguet, Histoire du dogme catholique, Paris, Albin Michel, 1941, from whom these notes are taken.

[16] Since it is impossible within the limits of such a succinct work to study the whole historical evolution of a doctrine, we must be satisfied to point out the principal stages in the development of this particular point. In the 3rd section will be found a few comments concerning the different positions of Jansenism and Quietism, touching upon the relationship between hope and love.

going to happen in the immediate future, and consequently the question of the state of souls between death and resurrection acquired a great importance. But the idea of an early return of Our Lord, and its association with the true eternal life, was so anchored in minds that it took several centuries before the problem of immediate happiness after death could be solved.

If we disregard the gnostics, Marcionites and Docetists (who deny the resurrection and the Second Coming) and restrict ourselves to Christian traditions, we can distinguish three great stages that led up to the theological systematization of the Middle Ages.

1. MILLENARIANISM

This is an evolved form of the expectation of the Second Coming which developed especially in the second and third centuries. This theory claims that Christ will return to establish a kingdom on earth that will endure for a thousand years, in which the resurrected elect will participate. Their reward will only be provisional, however, and after these thousand years the end of the world will take place and the judgment and final retribution will then occur.

This error is derived from the ancient Jewish conceptions of the temporal reign of the Messias and claims to find authority in certain passages of the Apocalypse.

St. Irenaeus adopted this theory. It became widespread in Egypt and Tertullian propagated this idea in Africa. But from the beginning it had found determined adversaries among large numbers of Christians. Origen and his disciples fought it. But we find it reappearing every so often in the course of the centuries like a kind of utopian dream that recurs in times of crisis.

2. THE INFLUENCE OF ORIGEN

A second period is marked by the name and influence of Origen. It was Clement of Alexandria, the "Christian gnostic," who opened the way for his disciple to study eschatological questions. Origen taught that the future life consists in the plenitude of revelation, the fulness of light. However, when righteous men die, before entering into heaven they must pass through paradise, a subterranean place where they undergo the purification of baptism by fire. Those who have nothing to expiate pass through without suffering. Then they rise from sphere to sphere, always becoming more and more purified, and they progress in the light until they are finally united with

Christ. The body rises in new matter and perfect form. Origen also taught the apocatastasis, i.e., the final restoration of all intelligent creatures to the friendship of God, including even the damned and the demons who had been purified by fire.

These theories, and especially apocatastasis, seduced the minds of men like St. Gregory of Nyssa (394), and the influence of Origen made itself felt among many of the Fathers.

The Latin Fathers of the 3rd and 4th centuries gave us several conceptions of the state of souls after death. Most of them taught that the Second Coming was imminent. Many of them thought that between death and judgment there is an intermediate state in which the elect have only the beginnings of beatitude, and the damned have a foretaste of their chastisement (these ideas are found, for instance, in the writings of Tertullian, St. Hippolytus in the 3rd century, and even St. Ambrose at the end of the 4th century). At the General Judgment, neither the righteous nor the impious will be judged because their fate will have already been determined. Only those sinners will be examined who were in need of purification after death (see St. Hilary, Zenon, St. Jerome and St. Ambrose). In 543, Pope Vigilius condemned the position of Origen and especially the theory of the perfect nature of risen bodies (spherical and ethereal bodies), and the apocatastasis, thereby affirming indirectly the eternity of hell.

It was not until St. Augustine's time that the authority of Origen was entirely supplanted. In his turn the authority of the Doctor of Hippo widely dominated all theological reflection until the Renaissance of the 12th century, and continued to influence theology all through the Middle Ages.

3. ST. AUGUSTINE

St. Augustine had accepted Millenarianism at first, but finally he rejected it emphatically. He believed that souls receive their reward or punishment immediately after death, but not in full measure until the resurrection. But can there be any vision of God while the soul awaits the resurrection of the body? St. Augustine does not affirm this except in the case of martyrs.

At the resurrection the flesh will remain flesh and will not become a spirit; it will be a "spiritual flesh." The pains of hell are everlasting (every trace of Origen's doctrine has been eliminated) and he conceives of a purification for certain sins (i.e. purgatory). Beatitude consists of the vision of God, face to face, but Augustine confesses his inability to decide whether the elect will see God with their material eyes or not.

Concerning the intuitive vision of God, the Greek Fathers of the same period were less firm. And among the Latins, Pope John XXII at a much later time expressed the opinion, retracted before his death, that the elect must wait until the general judgment to have the vision of the divine essence. In 1336, his successor Benedict XII defined the doctrine that the souls of the elect that are entirely pure have immediate vision of the divine essence, face to face.

The intermediate state of purgatory was doctrinally formed by gradual process. This doctrine was based upon the scriptural "fire that purifies" and the ancient practise of praying for the dead. This dogma was defined by the Council of Florence (1438) and was reaffirmed by the Council of Trent (1545–1563).

It may be said that eschatology found its definitive form with St. Augustine.

4. THE SCHOLASTIC THEOLOGIANS

These few comments are sufficient to show that the definition of the object of hope in its essentials was not clarified until after long reflection. But as soon as the righteous soul's immediate possession of God was affirmed, the importance of the Second Coming was somehow diminished. Desire for the resurrection became secondary, for the essential thing was assured from the first instant of the Beatific Vision. Furthermore, the final glory of the Church, the kingdom of God, another element associated with the Second Coming, seems almost eliminated from hope.

This latter fact can be imputed, partially at least, to a phrase of St. Augustine. The consequence of this doctrine weighed heavily upon the doctrine of hope during the whole medieval era.[17] In fact, according to Augustine hope can only be directed toward a *personal* good. It would seem that this does away with communal hope, and with the idea of each individual belonging to the People of God. For we must remember that it was to this people, collectively, that the heritage was promised, and the individual could only hope for the Church's glory in the measure that he found his own happiness in that glory.

[17] See P. Charles, *"Spes Christi,"* in *Nouvelle Revue Théologique,* 1937, pp. 1057-1075.

Moreover, the strongly metaphysical character of scholastic theology, which tried to find the "necessary reasons" for all things, as far as this was possible, was obliged to reduce to secondary importance in the rational organization of the object of hope the significance of an event (that is to say, a contingent fact) like the Second Coming.

Fortunately, while adopting and justifying Augustinian opinion, St. Thomas reintegrated the communal aspect into the object of hope. As a matter of fact, if hope can only desire personal blessings when left to its own movement, the same cannot be said about hope that is imbued with charity. For charity identifies us with those whom we love and makes us desire their welfare as though it were our own. Therefore, in the same aspiration of our hearts it permits us to hope for our own welfare and the well-being of all those to whom charity unites us.

Perhaps someone will object that this restores the idea of communal hope through subterfuge and by way of the "back-door." However, in reality, hope that is separated from charity is not perfect hope, and certainly not the rich hope that we read about in the New Testament. But we must still emphasize the significance of the return of Christ as an event. In the following chapter these points will be stressed.

Third Part

THEOLOGICAL ANALYSIS OF HOPE

I. Hope—A Theological Virtue

According to the famous definition of St. Anselm, the theologian's task consists in the use of his reason, illumined by the light of faith, "to seek for an understanding of his faith." He must try to justify the presence in supernatural life of that hope which is revealed in Scripture and also the capital importance which St. Paul attributes to it in associating hope with faith and charity. A great principle that is just as valid in theology as in philosophy tells us that "beings must not be multiplied without necessity." Theology must therefore show the need for such a virtue. This can be done by establishing the principles of supernatural life upon the model of the organization of human, natural life.

On the natural level man is endowed by nature with all the necessary principles to manage his human life very well. His intelligence enables him to know *truth,* not only speculative truth which is the pure object of intellectual contemplation but also the truth which must govern the conduct of his practical life. His will, which is wholly dynamic by nature, impels him toward the *good.* But the will is a blind faculty. It does not see or know, for that is not its purpose. It loves and desires; it wills and moves. As soon as it is in the presence of the good, it recognizes its own object instinctively. But this object is presented to the will by the intelligence which alone can see. All of man's life, which consists in a quest for happiness and joy, is therefore governed by these two principles: intelligence and will. The intelligence discovers the good which is the final end of man's life and proposes it to the will, and the will rushes forth in pursuit of the end.

But finally God intervenes to reveal to man a destiny which surpasses all human understanding, to tell man that he is created, in reality, for a happiness which is far beyond the reach of a human will.

Man must no longer strive to realize a merely human destiny, but also his destiny as a son of God.

From the moment that God raises man to this level of supernatural destiny which completely transcends the capacities of nature, the human principles that are sufficient for the conduct of human life become inadequate and impotent. Since man is made for God, and for a supernatural end, God must give him new principles that are supernatural.

We see why faith is necessary, for it is the light which raises the mind, capable of knowing truth, to the level of supernatural truth: God Himself and the whole mystery of the divine life of man. And the faith (supernatural "intelligence") fulfills its function as the illuminator of the will. It presents to the will this unimaginable happiness that is unsuspected and inaccessible. The faith does not reveal to man a system of truths that are merely theoretical or a wisdom that is purely intellectual. It reveals the mystery of salvation which concerns the whole destiny of this son of God and all his activity.

The will, which is a power of love, desire and conquest, suddenly finds itself confronting the supreme good before which its own forces leave it quite impotent. The will also must be raised and enlarged to the dimensions of infinite beatitude. It must be adapted to its new function and made capable of loving, desiring and conquering God Himself in divine intimacy.

This is the function of the two virtues of charity and hope. Charity places the human will in harmony with the supreme good which is God, as faith put the mind in harmony with infinite truth. But the absolute disproportion which separates the will from infinite beatitude presents a difficulty. Can man really obtain this good which seems infinitely desirable to the will as the supreme and unique end of his life? Isn't such happiness beyond our attainment? Is it really possible to reach such a goal? Or is it perhaps only an unrealizable dream, a utopia? We may well wonder how man, so puny and weak, can possibly expect this happiness and even "hope" for it. And that is the word for it, and the very purpose of the virtue of hope. For it is this virtue which, founded upon the formal promise of God and His omnipotence and goodness, will impel man to conquer the supreme happiness, the possession of God, in a great effort that is wholly confident. Indeed, this happiness is accessible because it is God Himself Who will give Himself to man for man's happiness.

In seeking the place of hope in the supernatural organism we discover at the same time its quality as a virtue and particularly as a theological virtue. The characteristic of virtue which makes all the acts which proceed from it good, is surely its harmony with the very rule of human behavior. And certainly God is the supreme rule. Hope is a virtue more profound than any other, except faith and charity, for it is truly theological. Not only is it infused by God alone into the soul, like every supernatural virtue, and not only does it finally bring to God some part of human activity as does every real virtue, but it has God directly for its object. Whatever hope expects to receive, it looks to God as its only help and only "means," and whatever it expects and hopes for is nothing less than God Himself, possessed for all eternity.

II. The Dual Object of Hope

1. THE "MOTIVE" OF HOPE.

In regard to hope reference is commonly made to its *motive* as distinguished from its *object*. By motive (*motivum* is that which moves us) we mean, in general, several elements which are quite disparate, for example the promise and the faithfulness of God, His goodness or His omnipotence.

But it seems useful to point out that the use of the word "motive" can be confusing. For our part, with St. Thomas we prefer to speak of the dual object of hope. There is the material object, that is to say, *that which* hope attains, and the formal object which is the *means* by which hope attains it, or the *basis* of hope.[18]

We may restrict the use of the word "motive" to designate that which moves us to hope, or that which makes hope possible a priori and justifies it exteriorly. This motive would consequently be the end of a "judgment of hopefulness," meaning that hope is possible and reasonable; but this would lead only to the beginnings of theological hope just as the judgment of credibility justifies the act of faith, as far as possible, while yet remaining exterior to faith.

This motive of hope is the divine promise, implying the faithfulness of God to His word as a necessary correlation. It is this alone which permits man to have the possession of God within the range of his desire. Without this divine Promise supernatural hope is not only impossible, but it is even inconceivable. Beatitude is an absolutely free gift. There is no way that we could desire it, even legitimately, unless we have the certainty that God offers it to us.

We see that we are not yet considering hope in the real meaning of the term. We are only at the preface, concerned about the exterior motive. It is faith which, revealing God's purpose to us, provides this motive. That is the reason for the statement that faith is definitely the foundation of hope.

But hope that is justified a priori by an extrinsic reason requires that we refer to the *formal* object rather than the *material* object if we are to have any understanding of what hope really is. This vocabulary has the great advantage of enabling us to perceive the unity of the act of hope in the two phases of its movement. For the dual object does not destroy the unity of hope. On the contrary, it assures this unity. There is not one act of hope terminating in God as the "means" or as the cause-of-our-beatitude, and another act terminating in God-our-beatitude. There is only one and the same act which is directed toward God-as-the-only-means and which also gives us that which terminates the act of hope: God-infinite-beatitude.

These are the two elements which must necessarily constitute the movement of hope. We know that faith presents exactly the same

[18] We could compare hope to a lever whose formal object would be the point of support.

phenomenon. In faith we adhere to God-as-Primary-Truth (formal object) in order to attain to the material object which is the revealed truth. It is uniquely this adherence of the mind to God-the-Infinite-Truth which enables us to accept the truth of that which is revealed. Here again it is impossible to separate these two aspects without destroying faith.

The same thing occurs with regard to hope. We cannot separate the dual object. If we want to attain to divine beatitude without reference to God-as-the-only-means, we destroy hope. It would also be destructive if we turned to God-as-the-only-means in order to will anything other than divine beatitude. This is the nature of the unity of hope in the dual object which we must now examine.

2. THE MATERIAL OBJECT: THAT WHICH WE HOPE FOR

Scripture presents this object to us as a reality that is extremely rich and complex. It was the desire for unity and clarity that is forever tormenting the mind that very naturally impelled theologians to determine the element that is the exact and essential object of hope in the Kingdom of Hope that is promised to Christians. The same problem arose in regard to matters of faith; and in this respect, among all the truths revealed in Holy Scripture, they were able to set forth the essential truths in a body of doctrinal articles. In regard to hope, of course, the task was simpler. All the images that describe the Kingdom of God in its perfect state show it as perfect happiness for men. Paul and John refer explicitly to the vision of God, face to face. In this concept we immediately recognize the essential reality of the Kingdom of God which is the possession of God in immediate vision and in the closest and most absolute union.

The psychological analysis of hope shows that this emotion is fundamental to love and desire (i.e., covetous love, as we shall see later in this chapter).[19] This means that hope is an impulse toward an object that is loved and desired. Whatever is good in itself will

[19] Gabriel Marcel, in his phenomenology of hope, departs on several points from the traditional analysis of this notion. He fears especially "a tragic confusion of hope with desire" which leads us not to recognize that "hope is linked to an inter-subjectivity," and therefore can only have a communitarian character through which it distinguishes itself from desire, and goes beyond it (see *Homo Viator*, chapters: "Esquisse d'une phénoménologie et d'une métaphysique de l'espérance" and "Structure de l'espérance," in *Dieu Vivant*, no. 19, 1951, p. 73-80).

arouse our love and desire. Therefore, it is precisely under its formal aspect of goodness or happiness that we must conceive of the object of hope. And this object appears as the supreme beatitude when we consider the supreme, complete, and unique hope of the man who is engaged in the adventurous pursuit of his supernatural destiny. For this reason theologians commonly designate the object of hope as eternal beatitude rather than its equivalent, the Kingdom of God. Therefore, if we sacrifice the more concrete scriptural term, which is also more complex, in preferring the more philosophical concept of the supreme good, the reality expressed is nevertheless exactly the same.

It is necessary, however, to make a distinction. St. Augustine's opinion that one can only hope for one's self, is philosophically exact. Desire is by nature a movement of the affective appetite which can only have a personal good for its end, and this must be the particular good of the person who desires. The same may be said in regard to hope. I can really hope for nothing but my own welfare. And yet, this gives us a feeling of being in contradiction to Scripture. But that is because the hope that is mentioned in Scripture is obviously the hope that is impregnated with charity, compelling me to break the chains of my purely individual destiny in order that I may unite myself to the whole people of the sons of God. To proceed in an orderly way we shall then distinguish between the object of hope when left to its own movement and the object of hope transformed by charity.

(a) *The Object of Hope Left to Itself*

Our object of hope, considered in itself, is the Kingdom of God, eternal life and glory in so far as these constitute our beatitude. In this respect we would have to re-consider the subject of beatitude. This can be exactly described as "God-possessed." It is therefore at the same time God Himself in His infinite reality (objective aspect) and the act by which we enter into possession of God (subjective aspect). Once again we must preserve perfect unity. Beatitude is essentially God, the highest good, but not considered purely as a good *per se*. It cannot be the highest good except in the measure that it is related to the subject. The object of hope can then be defined as God-the-Supreme-Good in so far as He is my beatitude.

This beatitude is essentially realized in the vision of the divine essence. For it is the vision, perfect knowledge, which brings God to us, and this vision, which is an act of possession, conveys the joy of possession as its immediate and necessary corollary. In this respect, the participation of the body is not absolutely necessary to the very essence of beatitude, since the act of the spirit which assures it can be accomplished without the body. However, to be complete and fulfilled, beatitude must penetrate the whole of man, and fill all his being. Man is not a pure spirit. He is spirit and matter, soul and body. That is why the resurrection of the body and its participation in the state of glory will complete our beatitude. It will not be increased in intensity but in extension, by inclusion of the body. We must also add the complement of essential beatitude which the company of the elect will constitute. The friendship of the saints is in fact an element of the happiness of heaven. It is a part of our beatitude, and therefore of the material object of hope.

But in the very movement by which hope is directed toward beatitude there is an inclusion in its object of everything which leads to this goal. We depend upon God for attainment to eternal life through Him, and therefore we look to Him at the same time for all the necessary means to reach this end. Consequently, everything which leads to the realization of our supernatural destiny normally enters into the range of hope.

It is primarily the whole domain of grace which is the beginning of eternal life: the increase of sanctifying grace and the virtues, the actual graces, forgiveness of sin and remission of punishment. This domain is the indispensable means and necessary condition of beatitude.

Next, it is the gift of temporal goods, in the measure that they are capable of leading us to eternal life; they constitute "all these things" which have been promised to us additionally. We see that the object of hope is in fact the same as the object of prayer. Quite accurately prayer has been called "the interpreter of hope."

(b) *The Object of Hope Informed by Charity*

The preceding comments concerning the material object only pertain to *my* personal beatitude. In the movement of hope alone, I can only will *my own* good. Doubtless, the good of another person can be the object of my desire and hope as such, but only in the measure in which they are also a good for myself, and to the degree that they are compatible with my own happiness.

To really hope for any good that is no longer for myself but for someone else instead, I must in some way be willing, desiring and hoping in his place, as if I were the other person. It is necessary that I completely embrace his particular cause and that I identify myself with the other person to such an extent that I become entirely one with him. It is love that achieves this kind of unity. Love ensures the union of the lover and the beloved. It is the subject-object synthesis which is the equivalent of the subject-object synthesis at the affective level which we find in knowledge.

This unity of love can be achieved in two ways:

1. The union is beneficial to the subject, the lover. This is concupiscent love, rather selfish because the object serves exclusively to enrich the subject who claims everything for himself. It is his own pleasure and comfort that the subject desires. In this way, and for this reason, a man will love good wine and travel and everything that is "useful" or simply "agreeable."

2. The union is beneficial to the object, the beloved person or thing, and when this is the case, the subject takes the object as his end, and as the value toward which his whole being is oriented. This is unselfish, disinterested love, comparable to the love of benevolence or friendship. The subject desires the well-being of the object. This is love in its perfect state; it is this kind of love that constitutes charity.

However, it is "self-centered" love which is the foundation of hope. We shall consider this point again, but we should now recognize that love, even in its perfect state, cannot abstract the first aspect entirely. When I love another person for himself, in a selfless, disinterested way, I find my personal perfection and my own joy in that love.

By its very nature, and necessarily, hope produces the first kind of love, the "imperfect" kind. Left to itself, hope does not generally produce the perfect kind of love. It is charity which will accomplish this, and by the union which it establishes between myself and another person, it will enable me to hope for the happiness of the other person to the extent that it is really *his* happiness, as if it were my very own.

By being filled with charity hope is enlarged to will the happiness of others, and in this enlargement hope finds the plenitude of its object. We can therefore restore this breadth, this "catholic" and cosmic dimension to hope in the manner of Holy Scripture.

The Christian was not created to hope all alone in his little corner.

He is by nature a son of God, bound to God and to all his brethren by divine charity. If the necessities of analysis require that we distinguish in hope that which comes to it by its own movement, and that which is given to it by charity, we should however guard against destruction of the reality itself. True hope is the hope of the true Christian whose very life is charity. He will not therefore be hoping only for his own happiness and his personal inclusion in the Kingdom. He will desire and await and hope for the perfect fulfillment of the divine plan, the coming of the final Reign of God.

The eschatological dimension (and more concretely the Second Coming) therefore finds its place, and rightly so, in the object of hope. It is included in that object for various reasons, simultaneously as the object of individual hope and also as the object of hope that is sustained by charity.

The coming of the Lord, the inauguration of the perfect Kingdom, considered in the course of time as the event that is the aspiration and expectation of the whole Christian people, is based primarily upon individual hope in so far as it implies our resurrection. In this respect, it is the necessary complement of beatitude assured by the vision of God. And to the extent that it marks the gathering of all the elect around Christ in His glory, it is still a part of "individual" beatitude. It is our assurance that we shall finally be with our friends in heaven.

The Second Coming especially completes the divine work and proclaims the triumph of Christ and of His Church, the salvation of the world and of the predestined. We are striving for all of these things here below, for they are things that we desire with all our strength, not merely for our own advantage but for the glory of God, and because of our love for God and for our fellow-men. In this sense the Second Coming is not the object of hope when hope is left to its own movement, but is rather the object of hope informed by charity.

It is therefore at this point that the great *event* (the return of Our Lord) is inserted into the complete formulation of the object of hope. Everything which constitutes the particular and necessary object of hope sustained by charity is connected, in its realization, with a very definite fact: the Second Coming. It is this event which is the concrete and historical objective toward which hope is ever leading.

Through charity the glory of God and the eternal happiness of our brethren have become the objects that are dearest to our hearts. It is because of charity that our hope extends to them. We will the glory of God and the salvation of other men; we desire these things and wait for them with all the zeal and confidence that we put into hope for our own beatitude.

Just as individual hope included in its object not only the end but also the necessary means for attainment, so likewise the hope of the Christian, who thinks and lives and acts in full consciousness of his incorporation in the Church, includes through charity the development of the Kingdom in its earthly phase along with the final glory of the Kingdom of God. The Christian has an absolute confidence in the invincible strength of the Church in the strife and struggle here below. He has the conviction, itself based upon the divine promise and dependent upon the active presence of the Holy Spirit, that the Church will pursue its course unfailingly in spite of the assaults of the world, and even in spite of the weakness of its members, until the final triumph. This is the message of the Apocalypse. And we know that hope has been the great source of true Christian optimism during the whole history of Christianity. However, this is not a vague feeling that "everything will happen for the best," [20] but the infallible certainty that the Kingdom of God is being built and will remain standing through all the persecutions.

3. THE FORMAL OBJECT, OR THE BASIS OF HOPE

The formula of the act of hope which the Church proposes to Christians requires that they name as their "motive" either the promise of God and His faithfulness, or in its more complete expression, both the promise and the divine attributes which are implicit, "Because Thou art infinitely good to us, omnipotent and faithful in Thy promises" (New Catechism of Belgium).

On the subject of the real motive of hope, theologians have different opinions. We need only recall the distinction that was made between the motive and the formal object. We must now discern the exact formal object, i.e., that which precisely constitutes the "means" on which hope depends for the attainment of its goal. Without any doubt, it can only be God. But we must determine what it may be in God that properly constitutes this means.

There are some who believe that it is only the goodness of God

[20] See the contrast which Gabriel Marcel develops between hope and optimism (*Homo Viator,* in the chapter, "Esquisse . . .").

(Duns Scotus and Suarez, for example, who insist upon the aspect of desire which is found in hope). According to others, it is the "divine assistance" or more exactly God as the auxiliary omnipotence (St. Thomas, St. Bonaventure, Vasquez, and most of the theologians of the Thomist school). There are still others who say that it is God considered both as our highest good and as auxiliary omnipotence. This latter system is obviously a kind of synthesis of the two preceding ideas and seems to claim the authority of Cajetan and Bannez (Ripalda, and the Jesuit theologians in general). Finally, there are a few not wanting to omit anything whatever,[21] who mention the omnipotence, the goodness and the faithfulness of God. (St. Alphonsus, Tanquerey).

All of these theories are subdivided again and they can hardly be discussed, one by one, at this time. We know that the promise is generally considered as the exterior and preliminary motive. And to understand the interior motive, or more particularly the formal object, we must remember the nature of the movement of hope. It is not merely a desire (the aspect of goodness or well-being which is primary in the object). Beyond desire, it becomes an expectation, fully confident, of an object whose possession is nevertheless still somewhat uncertain. The whole force of hope must therefore be concentrated in order to overcome the initial uncertainty. Its entire potential confidence is found in that "affective conviction" that it will attain to its object because it depends wholly upon Him Who alone can make its realization possible.

Hope therefore hopes for God because it hopes *in* God, and because it places in His hands the whole reason for its confidence. He alone is sufficiently powerful to lead our hope to its high goal, the possession of its object. It seems therefore certain that within the movement of hope it is the omnipotence of God, made available to ourselves, which assures perfect confidence and guarantees its efficacy. It is precisely the omnipotence of God that is given to assist us; this is the meaning of divine assistance or auxiliary omnipotence.

In any case one thing is certain. It is God alone Who is capable of giving Himself to us. Hope takes refuge in Him.

But just as God, acting according to the fulness of His infinite perfection which extends through all creation, enables His creatures to become in their turn the causes of other beings, in like manner

---

[21] There is an exposé and a critique of the different systems in the article *Espérance* (S. Harent) in *Dictionnaire de Théologie Catholique*.

He accords to certain beings the dignity of becoming foundations of hope. Doubtless they have this dignity only in an indirect manner and as the instruments of God, deriving from God Himself whatever efficacy they possess, but we can truly hope *in* them also.

In the highest degree there is the humanity of Christ assumed by the Word in the work of redemption. But there is also the whole life of the Church: grace and the sacraments, the gifts of God. Men themselves are called to cooperate effectively with salvation and to prepare for the coming of the glorious Kingdom. The saints in heaven, with the Virgin Mary at their head, and the men on earth whom God has placed in our way to be His collaborators are all truly the foundations of our hope by virtue of God's disposition, and we can put our hope *in* them also for good reason.

It is in this perspective that our own merits intervene in the formal object, in the cause of our hope. We certainly cannot glory in our own personal merits while forgetting that they also are a free gift of God, but we must recognize in them that effect of the mercy of God which leads us toward eternal glory. In this way we really collaborate with God in the work of our blessed destiny.

4. THE AUTHENTIC MEANING OF CHRISTIAN HOPE

We have discerned the material object of hope and the means on which it depends (formal object); we can now put together the elements of authentic Christian hope wholly penetrated by divine charity.

Hope is placed between faith and charity, for it is a kind of connecting link between these two other theological virtues. It is closely related to faith, for in the manner of faith it is oriented toward an object that is still absent. Faith is unseeing, and fulfills a provisional function, an expectative function that prepares us for the vision before which faith will be effaced. Likewise, hope awaits the possession of the desired object that is still deferred. It is directed toward complete possession, and when that point is reached, it will be dissolved. But it resembles charity in that it is not essentially a kind of knowledge, as faith is, but a movement of the will, a power of love, desire and joy. That is why it leads the soul quite naturally toward charity which is pure love. This will be further explained.

However, hope must take faith and charity for granted in order to be authentic and perfect. Here we find the mystery of the complex relations between the virtues, or rather the mystery of the admirable unity which can be attained only through multiple approximations. Faith provides hope with its object; for it is through faith primarily that man is placed in the presence of God, expectantly. Hope can move toward Him by its own original movement once it is based upon this knowledge of the God of love and joy. Similarly, hope supposes charity. But it keeps a relative autonomy, and hope can exist without charity, at least fundamentally, although we have already noted the need for a penetration by charity if hope is to find its fulness and increase its virtualities.

Here then is the Christian enlightened by faith and placed in the presence of God who offers Himself as the supreme good, the object infinitely capable of fulfilling all the yearnings of man. The Christian had already loved God, for true faith is not found unless there is a movement of love. And now he begins to desire Him, not as in some utopian dream or with hopeless longing, but with the whole strength of his soul that was made to see God he yearns for this supreme blessing. However, this is not yet hope, for hope is beyond desire even if it takes desire for granted. But God Himself has given His word. He has promised man an eternal and blessed union with Himself in the glorious Kingdom. The man who believes in God and loves God as his highest good, needs only to commit himself absolutely to God and depend upon God utterly and absolutely. Then he can be fearless and profoundly confident in the certainty of victory. He trusts in God for all that he hopes for, and he knows that God is not only the concrete satisfaction of his thirst for happiness, but that He is infinitely lovable for His own sake, infinitely worthy of an absolute love that is wholly selfless. He has now entered fully into charity. And at the same time his hope is enlarged to its greatest limits. Through charity his will is identified with the Will of God. He loves and wills all that God wills. But he is still on his earthly pilgrimage, and the work of God is not complete. It is this fulfillment that is the object of his hope.

Dependent upon the divine promise, and entering into the profoundest insights of Almighty God through charity, he identifies his will with the Will of God and loves and desires the well-being of his fellow-men as much as he desires his own. He now trusts God completely and with certainty he waits the fulfillment in glory of the whole divine work at the end of his long struggle, sustained and assisted by the grace of God. He proceeds joyfully, with haste, toward the crowning of God's work in his own life first, and the cry of

his hope echoes that of St. Paul, "cupio dissolvi et esse cum Christo"
—I long for death in order that I may be with Christ. But he also
walks in the joy of charity and of fraternal unity with all the sons of
God toward that glorious day of the final victory of Christ, the abso-
lute reign of God over a re-created universe. In a word, he proceeds
with his head held high and his face radiant, toward the day of
Our Lord's return, and the cry of his hope is that of the Apocalypse:
"Come, Lord Jesus!"

III. Hope and Charity

Faith, hope and charity constitute the trilogy of the theological
virtues. Faith provides an object of hope—without this, no hope
would be possible. The relations between hope and charity, however,
are less simple, for these two virtues are nearer one another, and
more similar also. They are both virtues of the will, and both are a
kind of love, even a love of God.

It is precisely on this point which draws them together that they
will now be distinguished.

1. THE LOVE IN HOPE AND THE LOVE THAT IS CHARITY

We have already noted the difference. The love that is found as
the basis of hope is an "interested" love, a concupiscent love. But
charitable love is selfless and benevolent. In hope's love we want our
own good, our personal happiness, and we desire and love all other
things insofar as they pertain to our own happiness. But in charity
we love God for His own sake and we do not confuse Him with
anything else. This very love is its own reward.

It is significant that love does not occupy such an important place
in hope as in charity. There is love in the elements of hope, but
love for a good that we do not possess and which consequently
awakens the desire for possession. It is a love for some good thing
whose conquest is fraught with difficulty that cannot be overcome
unless we commit ourselves to the divine power from which we
derive our absolute confidence. All these elements are necessary in
the constitution of hope. On the other hand, charity does not require
love as one of its elements, for charity is the essence of love. It makes
an abstraction of the possession or non-possession of its object. The
charity which we have for God in this life will not change essentially

when we see Him face to face. But hope will disappear. It will no longer have any reason for existence.

Moreover, the difference between these two kinds of love would be enough to make a definite distinction between hope and charity. Hope's love is self-centered, it seeks its own happiness. In this respect it is imperfect. But we must make an effort to understand these terms.

Hope's love, like the love of charity, is *supernatural*. Man can only love God as his beatitude and as the blessing that fulfills all his expectation of happiness, provided that this blessing be revealed to him and that he, himself, is made capable of loving and desiring God by a supernatural virtue. When we say that this love is imperfect, we must not forget that it is nevertheless perfectly supernatural.

Hope's love is *imperfect*. Indeed, it is imperfect when compared with the love of charity which is the perfect and complete form of love. This does not mean that it is love in any imperfect sense, or a love that has some inherent defect. Such a love is *legitimate* and, furthermore, it is necessary.

On this point many errors have resulted from the effort to correct and purify hope, but such effort has only succeeded in destroying hope itself. The Church has reacted vigorously by affirming the legitimacy of this "interested" love. Condemning the Lutheran doctrine, the Council of Trent affirmed:

> If anyone says that the righteous man commits sin when he performs a good work in the hope of eternal reward, let him be anathema. (Sess. VI, Can. 31, *Denz.*, 841).

Jansenius and his disciples (notably Quesnel) did not admit the legitimacy of the movement of hope toward beatitude unless it was sustained by the disinterested love of charity. According to them, it would not be legitimate to love or desire God as the constituent of our beatitude:

> Whoever serves God in the hope of eternal reward, if he does not have charity, sins every time that he acts with the purpose of attaining to that beatitude. (Proposition condemned by Alexander VIII, *Denz.*, 1303).

At the end of the seventeenth century, Molinos, the father of Quietism, taught that it is unworthy of perfect souls to keep the least measure of self-love in their hope. But Pope Innocent XI expressly condemned this proposition of Molinos by name:

Whoever has given his free-will to God must have no concern about any-thing, neither of hell nor of paradise; he should desire neither his perfection nor the virtues, neither sanctity nor his own salvation. He should expurgate his hope of all such desire. (*Denz.,* 1232).

Fenelon, espousing the cause of "pure love," claims that among perfect souls hope is just as disinterested as charity itself. Numerous propositions, extracted from his *Explications des Maximes des Saints sur la Vie Intérieure,* published in Paris in 1697, were condemned by Pope Innocent XII in 1699. For example: "There is an habitual state of love for God which is pure charity without any element of selfish motivation. Neither the fear of punishment nor the desire for reward have any place in such love. One no longer loves God in order to win merit or to find one's own perfection or happiness in that love . . . ; perfect hope is the disinterested desire for the prom-ises . . ." (*Denz.,* 1327, 1337).

In condemning these theories, the Church has only protected the nature of the virtue of hope. She affirms the legitimacy of "inter-ested" love. This does not mean that man should use God as a means at the service of his thirst for happiness. This would lower God and use Him for an end that is inferior to Himself. Such an intention would make love illegitimate. If we love God as our beatitude, we are making God the ultimate end of our life, orienting all our activity toward God and choosing Him as the supreme goal of our existence. This relates us, in all that we are, to God as our highest good and only value.

Charity will have its effect upon hope in order to give it a new per-fection. Not by substituting its own love for that of hope, because then it would destroy hope itself. Charity respects the nature of hope. It does not deprive hope of its object or divert its act. But together with hope's love it develops the other aspect of love, its supreme and perfect aspect.

Hope and charity therefore concur in developing the dual aspect which we see in love. Furthermore, charity dilates the object of hope to its ultimate dimensions. It leads man beyond exclusive concern for his personal salvation and lifts him above the quest for his own happiness. It identifies him with God and his neighbor, by the unity of affection, in such a way that the purpose of God as such and the good of his neighbor likewise, are introduced into the object of hope.

The man who loves God and his neighbor with charitable love that is complete and selfless, is concerned about his neighbor's happiness by the same movement which impels him to seek his own. Properly speaking, he cannot hope for God's happiness, because this is not an object in the future nor is it opposed by any obstacle, but hopes for the perfect manifestation of the glory of God in the final triumph of Christ and His Church. He truly hopes for the happiness of his neighbor and his eternal salvation beyond the vicissitudes of this present world. It is therefore charity which, by impregnating hope, lifts it to its state of plenitude. Far from destroying or supplanting it, charity brings it a new expansion and fulfills and perfects it.

St. Francis de Sales expresses this thought most wonderfully:

> We do not draw God unto ourselves, nor into our service, but we join ourselves to Him as our final happiness. . . . When we love God as our sovereign good we do not bring Him down to ourselves but bring ourselves to Him; we are not His end . . . but He is ours; He does not belong to us, but we belong to Him: He does not depend on us, but we depend on Him. (*Traité de l'amour de Dieu,* II, ch. 18).

That is why such love is not only legitimate but also necessary. The essential duty of man, inscribed in his nature as a rational and free being, is to strive in all his actions toward attainment of his final end, beatitude. It is this willing of the final end which dominates the whole moral life. Man must find his happiness in God alone. And precisely, hope's love is simply that love of God as our beatitude and as the final end of man's life. It is therefore a matter of movement toward that necessary point in such direction that disinterested love will be unable to destroy the "interested" aspect when love attains to its perfect state as charitable love, whereby man will love God and make a pure gift of himself. For it will remain true that this God Whom he loves for His infinite perfection will always be the beatitude of man, the final end of his life, and the only one who can satisfy that desire for happiness which is natural to man.

2. HOPE INFORMED BY CHARITY

Somehow we feel that the love which discovers God as the infinite good cannot be satisfied with this self-centered motivation. In the presence of the One who is supreme beauty, perfection and goodness, love must develop into a contemplation that is full of joy, and make the absolute gift of self in which there will no longer be the least self-seeking. Hope's love therefore leads to charity. There is a call to a more noble love, the love of God without conditions. Only then can love realize the full richness of its nature.

Hope can exist without charity, but it would then be a "dead virtue," and so would faith. If it remains alone and does not lead to charity, it limits the development of love whose entire internal strength tends toward the satisfaction of hope's highest aspirations.

IV. Hope, the Virtue of *Homo Viator*

"And now there remains faith, hope, and charity, these three: but the greatest of these is charity" (I Cor. 13:13). Faith and hope are the virtues of those who are journeying toward the God Whom they still do not see or possess; these are the "viatores"; but charity is everlasting.

The structure of hope makes it an exclusive virtue of "homo viator." The damned do not hope because eternal punishment, according to its very nature, makes it certain that nothing will ever be able to lessen the implacable rigor. Dante was a good theologian when he wrote the terrible warning at the beginning of his *Inferno:* "Abandon hope all ye who enter here." Hate and absolute despair are the fate of all who are damned.

The blessed souls in heaven no longer have true theological hope, for they now possess what they had been awaiting. They see God, and they have the perfect joy of being united to Him without fear of ever losing Him. However, they still have the desire and expectation of the resurrection of the body which will be the complement of their beatitude. But because they possess God, they have the absolute certainty that all the rest will come in its own time and as an infallible consequence.[22]

They are no longer subject to the law of those who live in fervent confidence but whose weakness leaves them exposed to the risks of failure. In this respect hope is characteristic of the "homo viator." It is composed of certainty and uncertainty at the same time, of firmness and solid conviction, but also of anxiety which continues until the last day. Popular wisdom tells us, "While there is life there is hope." We can also say, "While there is life there is nothing but hope." For as long as a man lives in this world, he can only have

[22] The question of hope in Christ and in the saints is the subject of a certain controversy among theologians. Let us point out an interesting study of P. Charles, "Spes Christi," in the *Nouvelle Revue théologique,* 1934 and 1937.

the hope of happiness, and not absolute certainty. This is the destiny of our human condition.

In the full measure in which it depends upon God, hope is infallible; in this sense there is no risk to be feared. And this is the source of our certainty. However, "certainty" should not be understood in its intellectual sense. This term properly belongs to the domain of knowledge, and it is only by analogy that we can apply it to the affective domain. The certainty of hope is more exactly an "affective conviction," an assurance of certainty founded entirely upon the power and the infallible faithfulness of God.

But there is still a margin of uncertainty in hope—and this is an element of its essence—a risk of unfulfillment. But this is a necessary aspect. We do not hope for anything that we are absolutely certain to obtain; we merely wait for it. There is only the quiet assurance of future possession, and we do not find that tension of the will, or that "sharp awareness of the soul" in the difficult conquest of an object that may elude our grasp. When Luther taught that man was saved only by the absolute assurance of his own salvation, which would be an unconditional certainty wholly derived from the superabundant justice of Christ, he was quite faithful to his principles, for not only did he deny the least freedom of the will but he also completely falsified the nature of hope. For hope can only be composed of a fervent "certainty" in which there must always persist a certain inquietude (*in-quies*). As long as hope has not fully attained to the possession of its object the soul cannot enjoy perfect rest, for possession will make hope disappear. *Inquietum est cor nostrum, donec requiescat in te,* said St. Augustine, "Our hearts are restless until they rest in Thee."

This uncertainty does not come from God, but from ourselves, our weakness and our inconstancy. We are not absolutely certain of our final perseverance. The Council of Trent declared explicitly:

> We cannot say that the righteous should be persuaded without the least doubt that they are justified . . . as if any doubt on this point was a doubt against the divine promises and the efficacy of the death and resurrection of Christ. For if we cannot, without impiety, doubt the mercy of God or the merits of Christ or the efficacious virtue of the sacrament, we can however fear the lack of grace when we consider ourselves or our infirmity and our indifference, for no one can know with the infallible certainty of faith that he is in grace with God (Session VI, ch. 9, *Denz.,* 802).

The gift of final perseverance especially cannot be the object of absolute certainty.

As for the gift of perseverance, of which it was written: "He that perseveres unto the end shall be saved" (Mt. 10:22; 24:13), let no one promise himself anything whatever with absolute certainty, although all men should place steadfast hope in divine help (Sess. VI, ch. 13, *Denz.,* 806).

And on this point a canon expressly defines:

If anyone claims to have absolute and infallible certainty of obtaining the great gift of final perseverance, unless by virtue of a particular revelation, let him be anathema (Sess. VI, canon 16, *Denz.,* 826).

In spite of the efficacy of divine grace, man endowed with liberty remains a being who is essentially weak and always ready to transgress. This is the tragedy of our human condition. All the anxiety and uncertainty that subsist in hope are derived from this condition. As long as man is not established in eternal life through the vision of God, he remains capable of sinning. The certainty of his hope comes from God; the uncertainty comes from himself.

This is certainly the condition of "homo viator," yearning for God in the most fervent and steadfast way, and also the most infallible, as long as God alone is desired, but the most fragile with regard to human weakness.

This last point enables us to perceive hope in its profound nature and original character. It reveals to us the irreplaceable role of hope in the pursuit of our destiny. Those who put their trust only in themselves, or who seek for the meaning of human destiny only in the free play of a free-will that is so easily weakened, and those who will only follow the "roads of freedom" by refusing, a priori, all transcendent help can only arrive at despair. The state of tension between the thirst for happiness and its impossible assuagement by the mere forces of human freedom attains to a culminating point. All of human effort is led into an impasse, and is all the more desperate because the effort was utterly sincere and lucid. And we cannot fail to taste the bitterness of Albert Camus' line in *Caligula:* "Men die and they are not happy."

All atheistic existentialism of our time sounds infinitely despairing. We need this experience of a world without hope to understand the preponderant place of hope in the Christian conception of destiny. We also are aware that man will more easily be a vile creature than a hero if he is left entirely to his own resources. We too have experienced the profound misery of humanity in our own cowardice and betrayals, as well as in our numerous attempts which end in abortive failures.

But in spite of everything, we know that our hope endures and we are sure that our hope is not a deception. We have the certainty that it will lead us to our goal, for we know that we were made for a supernatural and marvelous destiny, the possession of God Himself. We put our trust in God alone, for God does not betray or deceive us. That is why hope directs all our efforts and sustains us in our struggles; hope gives us the courage to endure anything and strengthens the will in that fervent impetus that will lead us unfailingly to eternal happiness if we do not interfere with the grace of God.

V. Sins Against Hope

"In medio stat virtus"—virtue determines the correct measure of all things. In its origins sin is always a lack of proportion. We sin against a virtue according as we depart from the golden mean, either by excess or by default. Can we say that the theological virtues also have a golden mean to be observed? In reality, they transcend all human measurements, for they have God for their object and He is infinite. With regard to the object, therefore, we are never in danger of excess. We can never believe or hope in God as much as we should. Nor will we ever love Him as much as He deserves to be loved. "The measure of the love of God," says St. Bernard, "is to love Him without measure."

And yet, these virtues are practised by ourselves, although we find ourselves in a highly determined condition. We have our limitations and our human nature is governed by laws. In this respect we can speak of measure. Our hope must respect the limitations of our human condition. It must keep to the golden mean between insufficiency and excess. It would be insufficient if we did not attain to the hope that is our vocation; and it would be excessive if we claimed the ability to go beyond the limits of the hope that is allowed to us.

We have now recognized the two sins of despair and presumption.

1. DESPAIR

This is not the place to make a phenomenological study of despair. We must be satisfied with a succinct concept of the sin of despair.

We must not confuse despair with certain attitudes or feelings to which this tragic grievousness is wrongly attributed. Despair is not pessimism which some men affect or really experience in their consideration of the events of the world or of their own lives. Nor is it the simple discouragement which sometimes haunts even the best men in times of hardship. It does not consist of a lack of enthusiasm or the mere relaxation of confident fervor, nor in the anguish that is even apparent in the saints themselves when they compare their imperfection with the infinite grandeur of God.

Despair, like every sin, is a conscious act, fully deliberate. It is the voluntary refusal of happiness, the consummated break with beatitude. This does not necessarily mean that the despairing man no longer desires happiness. On the contrary, he continues to aspire to happiness because of the forces within himself that demand his attention. But he has the definite belief that he will never be able to attain the happiness for which he yearns, and this is the interior torment of the despairing man.

Despair has therefore the character of irremediable surrender and abandonment. The man who despairs is denying God and refusing His goodness, His omnipotence and His love. It is a rejection of the supernatural destiny which God offers to man. Scripture gives us examples of despair, beginning with Cain who cried out, "My punishment is too great to be endured" and who lost himself in solitude. It tells us of Judas who despaired of receiving pardon and hanged himself.

It could be objected that despair is impossible unless there is a preliminary loss of faith. For is it not faith that enables us to believe in the love of God and in His infinite goodness, His forgiveness and His assistance? And if man believes in Him, how could he ever despair? In reality, faith can subsist in a soul that has given way to despair. Certainly despair implies a false judgment regarding the mercy of God, but this judgment can leave one's faith intact. The despairing man can really believe that God is infinitely good and that He desires the salvation of all mankind, and will forgive sins (such a judgment is derived from faith), but when he turns to the practical judgment that concerns his personal case, his logic weakens and he puts himself outside the destiny of believers. He refuses to apply the infinite goodness of God to himself; he turns aside and falls back exclusively on his powerless misery. This is the tragedy of sterile faith, and it is the cruel lack of logic of a faith that is not "alive."

Who can doubt that despair is one of the most serious sins? Is it not an injury to the most precious gifts that God has provided for the happiness of men: His power, His goodness, the infinite merits of Christ which cover every sin? Per se, the refusal to believe and hatred for God are more serious, the former being directly opposed to divine truth and the latter responding to God's love with hatred, but despair is perhaps of all sins the most dangerous and most terrible psychologically. The despairing man has nothing left for support, because anything that could give value or enjoyment to life is wholly destroyed.

There only remains the feeling of complete failure and the irremediable loss of the most powerful motivation in human activity: the sense of happiness. That is why we see in experience that despair logically leads to suicide when the despairing man, giving way to the ultimate and most monstrous aberration, seeks for the nothingness that he will never find.

2. PRESUMPTION

Presumption is the very opposite of despair. But we perceive the malice of this fault less clearly. Yet it directly contradicts hope because it makes for an immoderate movement toward beatitude. Presumption is an inordinate act of the will which claims to attain to a goal that lies beyond the limits assigned by God. It is often born of pride which is the father of all immoderate sentiment.

This excess can become apparent in two principal ways. In its first aspect, presumption impels man to will the attainment of beatitude without any reference to God, by reliance upon his own strength. Man is so foolishly confident of his own power and worth and excellence that he claims the ability to lay hold of his predestined happiness by his own will. But when he does this he blocks every passage toward the goal that he is pursuing.

The other aspect of presumption is more serious. It is a malignant deformation of trust in God. It does not refuse the help of God. On the contrary, it expects unreasonable and impossible things. The presumptuous man expects everything from God without doing anything himself; he claims that he can obtain from God the fruit of the promises without submitting to the required conditions. This is one of the major errors of Luther's teaching which deforms trust in God and goes so far as to demand the recompense of heaven for the predestined no matter what their vices and licentiousness may be. "Pecca fortiter sed crede fortius." Such is the presumption of those who believe that God is too "good" to punish sin, forgetting that the goodness of God is intrinsically a condemnation of evil, and such is the claim of obtaining forgiveness without repentance.

St. Thomas sees a sin against the Holy Spirit in this presumption.

VI. The Gift of Fear

A complete theological study of hope should culminate in the mystical methods in which this virtue holds an important place. But we shall limit ourselves to an outline of the spiritual movement in which it engages the soul and where we shall doubtless see the highest dimension of theological hope. It is from the angle of the gift of fear that we shall discover the mystical range of hope.

1. FEAR AND HOPE

Since the theological Summas of the Middle Ages, it has been customary to identify the seven gifts of the Holy Spirit with the various virtues. As a matter of fact, the bond which unites them to one another is not always very rigorous and the concern for symmetry seems to have been preponderant. The theological virtues are well presented, and the attribution of the gifts seems to respect a real relationship. The gifts of intelligence and knowledge are related to faith and the gift of wisdom is attributed to charity. Finally the gift of the fear of God is related to hope.[23]

Fear and hope unquestionably are closely related. They are complementary movements.

Even among the passions, fear and hope are in some way parallel. Based upon the same principle, the irascible appetite, their movements are symmetrical although in opposite directions (or: toward opposite objectives). Hope is directed toward a good that we expect with assurance, but it nevertheless implies anxiety, the "fear" of missing our mark. Fear, however, has for its object some evil that we dread but which we "hope" to escape. We see how these two acts are complementary. We always have some fear that we will not get what we hope for, and we always hope to avoid whatever makes us afraid.

[23] On the question of linking the gifts to the theological virtues, and particularly the gift of fear to that of hope, St. Thomas Aquinas himself changed his view. In his first writings he did not attribute any gift to theological virtues, but linked the gift of fear to the moral virtue of temperance (*Sentences*); later he introduced a reference to hope (*Summa,* Id), finally he attributed principally the gift of fear of the Lord to hope (*Summa,* IIa).

This correlation between the emotional movements of hope and fear is found again between the virtue of hope and the gift of the fear of God when transposed into theological life.

We should be careful to keep in mind, first of all, the primordial place of hope in the Old Testament. For it is hope which certainly characterizes the sense of Israel's evolution in the most exact way. The whole history of this people is situated in the perspective of hope. They were a people journeying toward God who expected everything from God. If there is any idea which takes precedence in the spirituality of the Old Testament, it is the idea of the fear of God. It was this idea that expressed and summed up the totality of man's relationship with God and gave it distinction as an idea that was extremely valuable. The whole range of concepts is included —from the most instinctive holy fear to self-less love. This association of ideas was very significant. And if we examine the bases of this fear of God, we will discern above all else the sense of the absolute transcendence of God manifested principally in omnipotence. Beyond all doubt this was the essential principle of reverential fear. And we know precisely that it is the divine omnipotence, which God has placed at our service, that is the formal foundation of hope. In other words, that which arouses our fear of God is also that which justifies and nourishes our hope in God.

But the connection will seem still closer to us if we examine the nature of the gift of fear a little more carefully.

2. THE GIFT OF FEAR

If it be true that fear has for its object some evil, how then can we speak of the fear of God, especially when it is a spiritual gift? How could God become an object of fear if He is the highest good in whom there is no evil at all? It is certainly true that the object of fear is evil, and in this sense God cannot really be feared. But fear quite normally goes beyond the evil, its direct object, and fastens upon the person from whom the evil may come. And God can be a source of evil or at least the occasion of some evil for man: whether it be the evil of the pain which our sins deserve, and which God inflicts upon us in His justice, or the evil of the sin itself which separates us from God, which is surely the greatest disaster.

We are only considering the fear which is capable of drawing us nearer to God and converting us to Him, for there can be a fear in man which separates him from God. And yet, if these two forms of fear which we have just mentioned are good and virtuous, the very different motives that inspire them will confer very dissimilar characters upon them.

If we think of God only as the avenger of sin, the One who has the power to chastise, the fear that we experience is then a *servile* fear. It is the fear of the servant or the slave trembling before the incorruptible master, the fright of the sinner before infallible justice. This kind of fear is salutary because it inspires the horror of sin, but it has very little nobility.

On the contrary, the sentiment which makes us fear the evil of sin because it separates us from God, our supreme good, has love for its source and is still an expression of love. This is *filial* fear; the fear of the child who is afraid of displeasing his father and who fears, above all else, the loss of his love. Saint Augustine called it *chaste fear,* like the fear of the wife who is afraid of being separated from the one she loves, of no longer meriting his esteem and tenderness. For her, this would be the greatest evil, for her whole life and happiness are found in her union with her husband.

It is easy to see that servile fear can hardly be favorable to hope. If our feeling for God is nothing more than the terror of a slave under menace, we cannot derive from this feeling the motives of a fully confident yearning for a loving Father who is ready to give us all things. Furthermore, this kind of fear is not a gift of the Holy Spirit. Only filial (or chaste) fear constitutes the gift of fear.

As a matter of fact, the gifts are special perfections which the Holy Spirit infuses into the soul and which render it fully docile to divine inspirations and wholly pliable in the hands of God. Reason is man's principle of activity, reflecting the divine intelligence, and the rule of action for the Christian is his reason enlightened by faith, divinized by grace. But God Himself intervenes directly in the life of His children to inspire, lead and encourage them.

The Holy Spirit is truly the interior guide of the Christian, his master of the spiritual life; he directs the attentive soul by His movements and by His superior reasons which reason does not know. For this to happen it is necessary that the soul be made sensitive to these suggestions, that it have antennae in touch with God so that the eyes are fixed upon Him at all times.

These dispositions of perfect docility are the gifts which realize them. And in the line of hope, it is the gift of fear which will complete and reinforce the theological movement. For filial fear can only impel the soul in a more absolute way toward Him whom it fears to lose. Filial fear is in some sense the negative form of hope.

In reality there are two movements in the gift of fear, and through these hope will culminate in mystical life.

1. The fear of separation from God. The whole life of the Christian strives for final union with God as its supreme end. To lose God forever is the irremediable failure, the ruin of our vocation to love and joy; it is tragedy. To lose God is hell. And it is sin which deprives us of God. That is why the movement of the gift of fear, into which enters the strength of charity's love, makes us hate and flee sin as the greatest of evils. But at the same time it projects us toward God. For in the presence of sin, and confronted with temptation and the mysterious fascination of evil, we feel our weakness profoundly. We are always at the mercy of an aberration, a moment of going astray. We feel that within ourselves nothing is really sure; there is no certainty of sanctity, nor any sure hope of salvation to be found within ourselves. For this can only come from God alone.

He alone is infinitely powerful. He alone is holy. He alone can keep us from evil and from ourselves. It is then that the fear which this separation from God inspires within us throws us upon Him unconditionally. There is no longer any possible place for the least presumption. We look to God for everything in total abandonment and infinite trust.

2. But the gift of fear is expressed in still another movement. It makes us afraid not only to be separated from God by sin, but also of trying to make ourselves equal to God—of comparing ourselves with Him, or considering ourselves as really something before Him. In a word, the gift of fear makes us aware of our "creaturely condition." And it is here that fear can be truly called *reverential*. It is the source of that interior reverence which nourishes the whole life of the virtue of religion. Even outside all eventuality of sin, we fear God and revere Him by fleeing with horror the idea of daring to compare ourselves with Him. And if the fear of separation must disappear in heaven, since we will there be united forever to God, and all sin will be impossible, this fear will however subsist in us as it exists in the angels. For it is essentially the fundamental attitude of the creature before the Creator: the creature's consciousness of its own nothingness and of the inaccessible majesty of God, expressed in infinite reverence.

The profound consciousness of our smallness before sovereign

Omnipotence, which doubtless constitutes the supreme act of the gift of fear, is precisely that which will drive the soul to the farthest limits of hope. For one must have the revelation of that infinite abyss which separates the Creator from His creature, the Holy God from the sinner-by-nature, in order to understand the prodigious character of the hope to which God calls us. When we have realized what God really is, with this feeling of holy fear, and when we have determined what we are, then only can we understand that we will never be able to throw ourselves upon God with confidence that is sufficiently absolute or sufficiently reckless. One must have penetrated to the very depths of that reverence to be able to advance to the limits of hope, or rather to understand that hope has no limit at all. Only the gift of fear can thus carry theological hope to that perfection which is manifested principally in those spiritual methods of the mystical life which the great saints have demonstrated: abandonment to God and spiritual childlikeness.

REFLECTIONS AND PERSPECTIVES

In the man who hopes there is a dual attitude which seems to be contradictory. There is a self-centered attitude because he is hoping for his own highest good, his very fulfillment, and for what he is unable not to desire. But there is also an attitude of total abandonment, because that which he is waiting for can only be procured for him by the gratuitous and merciful help of Providence. He can only conquer his good on condition that he must not pose as a conqueror; on the contrary he must be generously open to all the free and unforeseen advances of God. A sound theology should properly allow for these two attitudes. If we do not permit any "interest" in hope, we will then be falling into Quietism. And if we claim that happiness can be won without allowing for divine help, we would be tending toward Pelagianism.

How does this paradoxical act, which is both self-centered and self-giving, become psychologically inscribed in the will?

We should again look for this dual attitude of the soul in the Gospel and the epistles. Show that Pauline faith is wholly pregnant with confidence and hope of a future blessing. (And what a good!)

Show that the movement which comes forth from the soul toward beatitude is inseparable from the act by which the soul leans upon the "arm" of God who assists the soul. Show that there is really only one act of hope although it has a dual "object."

Hope and the Return of Christ. Is there a real hope in the soul of Christ in regard to the fulfillment of His Church? Is the edification of the Body of Christ an object of hope among the blessed souls until the Second Coming? In what sense can we say that the elect participate in the expectation of the Church?

Hope and Fear. Fear in the Bible. Show the importance of the fear of God in the Old and New Testaments. Portrait of the man who "fears God." Place of the fear of God among the virtues of the "righteous man" in the old and new Covenants.

Objects of hope and of fear. Can we say that hope is awakened in the soul when it considers the mercy of God, and that fear is born in the soul when it considers His justice? Explain in what sense this may be true.

The different fears. Distinguish and define the expressions of initial fear, worldly fear, servile fear, filial fear and chaste fear. Which are the fears that are contrary to the love of God and those which suppose it? Is it evil, and in what sense is it evil, to fear the punishment due to sin and to fear God in the measure that He is the author of that punishment? Can we define filial fear as a fear of offending God and of being separated from Him? In this case, how is it still applicable to the blessed souls? Make a psychological analysis of the slave's fear of his master, and the son's fear of his father, the wife's fear of her husband, and show how "servile fear," "filial fear," and "chaste fear" may also be found in the creature's relationship to his Creator. Is filial fear or chaste fear the best analogy? What is there in each of these that ought to be retained as particular and complementary? How are they associated with hope?

Fear and Religion. In what sense can we assimilate fear and religion? Is the essential element in religion the "tremendous," the awe of the soul before the greatness of God? Education of fear: how can we teach the fear of God to Christians? Excesses to be avoided, risks to be run. Is it legitimate to favor or nourish fear by means of a certain kind of church architecture, or by the atmosphere of the place, the play of lights and shadows, the requirements concerning the appearance and dress of the faithful? In what way does the fear of God add to simple respect? How can love lead to fear and fear lead to love? Is there any bond between fear and poverty of spirit?

Fear, anguish, anxiety and sadness. How can all these emotions also be Christian and be assumed by grace? In what way would this be impossible? Can momentary anguish be sanctifying? The case of

Blanche de la Force in the *"Dialogues des carmélites"* or *La dernière à l'échafaud*. Analyze the sin of sadness, despair and suicide. Show how sadness, fear and anguish that are truly Christian can be compatible with a certain peace and joy. Analyze this psychologically. Christian peace and tranquility. Distinguish and show in what way they are opposed. Education for peace. How can it be favored and expanded? Psychology of Christian peace. Compare the respective gravity of despair and presumption, or the tempting of God.

Gift of fear. Show what it is in the man who is justified, among the blessed souls in heaven, and in Christ. Its object. How it is related to the other gifts.

BIBLIOGRAPHIE

C. Spicq, *La révélation de l'espérance dans le nouveau Testament,* Avignon, Aubanel, 1931.

Saint Thomas d'Aquin, *L'espérance,* Trad. et notes de J. Le Tilly, Paris, Éd. de la Revue des J., 1929.

A.-M. Janvier, *Conférences de Notre-Dame,* Carême 1913, *L'espérance,* Paris, Lethielleux, 1913.

A.-D. Sertillanges, *Les vertus théologales. L'espérance,* Paris, Renouard, 1913.

Espoir humain et espérance chrétienne (Semaine des intellectuels catholiques), Paris, Éd. de Flore, 1951.

Il faut citer aussi, en littérature religieuse et en philosophie:

Ch. Péguy, *Le porche du mystère de la deuxième vertu,* Paris, N. R. F., 1929.

G. Marcel, *Homo viator,* surtout le chapitre "Esquisse d'une phénoménologie et d'une métaphysique de l'espérance," Paris, Aubier, 1944. Du même, "Structure de l'espérance," in *Dieu vivant, t.* 19, 1951, pp. 73-80.

BIBLIOGRAPHY

Davis, Henry, S.J., *Moral and Pastoral Theology,* Vol. I, Ch. 4. London, Sheed and Ward, 1941.

McHugh, John A., O.P., and Callan, Charles J., O.P., *Moral Theology, A Complete Course,* Vol. I, pp. 401-441. New York, Joseph Wagner, Inc., 1929.

Sheedy, Charles E., C.S.C., *The Christian Virtues,* pp. 99-110. Notre Dame, Ind., University of Notre Dame Press, 1949.

Coulon, W. M., "Certitude of Hope," *Thomist,* 10: 75-119, Ja-Apr '47.

De Letter, P., "Hope and Charity in St. Thomas," *Thomist,* 13: 325-352, Apr-Je '50.

Hofinger, J., S.J., "Christian Hope: Some Suggestions for a Catechesis," *Lumen,* 9: 387-397, S '54.

Kerns, V., "The Virtue of Hope," *Irish Ecclesiastical Record,* 79: 409-421, Je '53.

Lumberas, P., O.P., "Hope the Self-Seeker," *Cross and Crown,* 3: 174-189, Je '51.

McSorley, J., C.S.P., "Hope, the Forgotten Virtue," *Cross and Crown,* 2: 255-265, S '50.

Olivier, B., O.P., "The Meaning of Christian Hope," *Lumen,* 9: 373-386, S '54.

Chapter III

CHARITY

by B. Olivier, O.P.

FIRST PART: The Revelation of Charity

I. THE OLD TESTAMENT

1. God's love for men
2. The love of men for God
3. The love of neighbor

II. THE NEW TESTAMENT

The Vocabulary

A. The Doctrine of the *Agape* according to the Synoptics
1. The gratuity of divine love
2. The greatest commandment
3. The love of neighbor

B. The *Agape* according to St. Paul
1. The God of *agape*
2. "If any man does not love the Lord Jesus Christ, let him be anathema"
3. Fraternal charity
4. The preeminence of charity

C. The *Agape* according to St. John
1. God is love
2. Men are called to love
3. The unity of charity

SECOND PART: Outline of the Development of the Doctrine of Charity

I. THE PATRISTIC PERIOD

1. The Greek Fathers
2. The Latin Fathers: St. Augustine

3. The exterior activities of charity
   (a) Alms
   (b) The fraternal reprimand

V. SINS AGAINST CHARITY

1. Hatred
2. Sadness
3. Envy
4. Discord and its consequences
5. Scandal

VI. THE GIFT OF WISDOM

REFLECTIONS AND PERSPECTIVES

BIBLIOGRAPHY

Chapter III

CHARITY

First Part

THE REVELATION OF CHARITY

I. The Old Testament

The idea of loving, in its general sense, is expressed by the radical *aheb* from which is derived the substantive *ahabah*. This word, like the English word, includes various meanings ranging from the highest kind of love and the most pure to love that is carnal. Limiting ourselves to the domain that pertains to charity, we shall analyze the notion of love which may be considered according to three categories: God's love for men, man's love for God, and man's love for his fellow-men in accordance with God's Will.

1. GOD'S LOVE FOR MEN

God loves His people. This is one of the most fundamental truths that we find as early as the Pentateuch.

In the admirable discourses of Deuteronomy, the commentary on the Law and the primitive history of the Jewish people, this idea appears constantly: Yahweh loved the fathers of the nation of Israel. It was through love that He selected them and that He chose this people among all others to be "His people."

This love of God for men does not yet have a universal character. It was reserved for Israel alone. The other nations do not have any right to it, for they do not have the privilege of an alliance with Yahweh. By contrast, all the memorable events of Israel's history enable us to see in an indubitable way the divine predilection that watches over the destiny of the chosen people.

It was especially under the form of paternal love that God's love was manifested. Yahweh was the father of Israel. It was He who chose it, and He who formed it into a nation. It was He who truly brought it forth like a father engenders a son: "And thou shalt say to him: Thus saith the Lord: Israel is my son, my firstborn. I have said to thee: Let my son go. . . ." (Ex. 4:22).

Addressing Himself primarily to the nation as a whole, the divine paternity also reached to individuals within the nation. God was a father to every member of the nation. But the quality of a son of God required certain conditions and imposed requirements of sanctity. The sinful Israelite was still a son of God, but he was a rebellious son who did not deserve the privilege which he shared because he belonged to the nation. Yahweh was His father, but an angry father. Only the one who was righteous and holy could truly call himself a son of God (cf. Wis. 5:5).

This divine paternity was not merely a kind of official and juridical quality. Yahweh truly had a father's kindness and tenderness for His people. Among all the texts of the Prophets, there is the celebrated passage in Osee:

Because Israel was a child, and I loved him: and I called my son out of Egypt.

As they called them, they went away from before their face: they offered victims to Baalim, and sacrificed to idols.

And I was like a foster father to Ephraim, I carried them in my arms: and they knew not that I healed them.

I will draw them with the cords of Adam, with the bands of love: and I will be to them as one that taketh off the yoke on their jaws: and I put his meat to him that he might eat.

(Osee 11:1-4).

This passage doubtless gives us the most exact tone and the most habitual note of divine tenderness, the tenderness of a father who stoops down to his child to guide his steps, to feed him and protect him and cherish him.

But the love of God is sometimes presented in a setting of violence and passion, like a state of paroxysm that makes it resemble the love of a romantic lover or one who is jealous. It is then the outburst of a tenderness that requires a gift that is complete and undivided; it is the ardent complaint of a love that has been betrayed. One must read the parable of the two faithless sisters in Ezechiel (ch. 23), which expresses in striking images this power of divine tenderness and the violent clamor of a God thwarted in His love.

2. THE LOVE OF MEN FOR GOD

The precept of the love of God is not explicitly mentioned in the Decalogue. But it is like a principle that does not need to be expressed. Jesus summed up the whole law by this commandment: "Thou shalt love the Lord thy God with thy whole heart, and with thy whole soul, and with thy whole mind." Previously, in commenting upon the Law, Moses repeated this precept like a refrain:

> Hear, O Israel, the Lord our God is one Lord. Thou shalt love the Lord thy God with thy whole heart, and with thy whole soul, and with thy whole strength. . . . (Deut. 6:4-5).
>
> And now, Israel, what doth the Lord thy God require of thee, but that thou fear the Lord thy God, and walk in his ways, and love him, and serve the Lord thy God, with all thy heart, and with all thy soul. . . . (Deut. 10:12; cf. Deut. 11:1, 13, 22; 30:16, 20, etc.).

The precept of the love of God is therefore most certainly the first in the Law, or better, it is anterior to the Law; it is the Law's foundation. It is difficult to give rigorous acceptance to the antithesis of the Old and New Testaments in which some writers take pleasure in contrasting the God of fear and the God of love. A detailed analysis of the idea of fear, which is doubtless the essential characteristic of the relations between man and God in the Old Testament, shows that this idea also includes the notion of love.

Love for God should be concretely expressed by the exact observance of the law. The texts quoted above use the following expression as equivalents: to fear God, to love God, to keep His commandments, to walk in His ways. We find a characteristic echo of this in the long rumination of the Psalmist in Psalm 118. We must not conclude that love for God is nothing more than material faithfulness to the law. The Psalms notably insist upon the sentiment of trust and abandonment, and upon affectionate relations with God.

But love must prove itself by the conformity of man's will with the will of God, expressed in the Law. This is the great charter of the alliance concluded between Yahweh and His people, and it was the fidelity of Israel to this charter which guaranteed the perpetuity of the nation's affectionate relationship with Yahweh.

It is true that the idea of service and of meticulous observance often predominated in the Old Testament, readily transferring intimate and spontaneous submission of love to the background. The Prophets, especially, insisted upon the interior aspect of worship and upon the value of true and profound feelings that would imbue obedience to the law. They were therefore the artisans of a true evolution in the religion of Israel.

Often, in the texts of the Old Testament, love for Yahweh is presented as a means of assuring for oneself the divine protection and security and an abundance of blessings of all kinds. In this we must recognize the methods of divine pedagogy. Israel was a nation in the age of infancy whose progress toward a purer religion would be slow. It was necessary to educate this nation as one educates a child to whom is presented the alternative of punishment or reward in order to spur him forward in the way of goodness. He is still incapable of deciding for himself in favor of higher motives, or of understanding the value of the real motivation that governs his behavior. He will not be capable of this until he has attained to adulthood with the coming of Christ. In the same way we have seen hope pass through various stages that were quite commonplace before reaching its true object.

Christ had to take up the task of the Prophets in a certain manner and definitively reveal the true countenance of the love of God. He had to struggle against the legalistic conception which had come to prevail under the influence of the doctors of the law. Official religion, encumbered with casuistry in which the letter threatened to kill the spirit, aroused violent reactions.

3. THE LOVE OF NEIGHBOR

The "new" character of the commandment given by Christ, "Love one another," should not lead us into error. The precept of love for one's neighbor was very definitely inscribed in the ancient Law: "Thou shalt love thy neighbor as thyself" (Lev. 19:18).

Such love cannot remain at the level of abstract sentiment or mere theory. It must be manifested in daily life, especially through assistance accorded to one's neighbor in all circumstances. The particular laws of the Old Testament enumerate many cases in which a true Israelite must help his neighbor:

You shall not hurt a widow or an orphan. If you hurt them they will cry out to me, and I will hear their cry: And my rage shall be enkindled, and I will strike you with the sword, and your wives shall be widows, and your children fatherless. If thou lend money to any of my people that is poor, that dwelleth with thee, thou shalt not be hard upon them as an extortioner, nor oppress them with usuries. . . . (Ex. 22:22-25).

If thou meet thy enemy's ox or ass going astray, bring it back to him. If thou see the ass of him that hateth thee lie underneath his burden, thou shalt not pass by, but shalt lift him up with him (Ex. 23:4-5).

Thou shalt not hate thy brother in thy heart, but reprove him openly, lest thou incur sin through him. Seek not revenge, nor be mindful of the injury of thy citizens. Thou shalt love thy friend as thyself. I am the Lord. . . . (Lev. 19:17-18).

For the Israelite, his neighbor was essentially his compatriot, a member of his people, as the texts which we have just read clearly emphasize. His charity must be directed toward this neighbor. But this charity expressed in the precept does not have a universal character. Christ recalls this fact in order to show the sense of the commandment of the new law in a better way: "You have heard that it was said, 'Thou shalt love thy neighbor, and shalt hate thy enemy'. . ." (Mt. 5:43).

However, a particular precept extends love to "strangers," but such a clause seems to require justification. It was in remembrance of that period when Israel likewise experienced exile in a foreign land that the legislator required kindness toward men from outside.

Thou shalt not molest a stranger, nor afflict him: for yourselves also were strangers in the land of Egypt (Ex. 22:21).
Thou shalt not molest a stranger, for you know the hearts of strangers: for you also were strangers in the land of Egypt (Ex. 23:9).

The stranger who had a right to this kindness was the one who dwelt in the midst of Israel and was in some way admitted into the national community. A text in *Leviticus* specified this condition.

If a stranger dwell in your land, and abide among you, do not upbraid him: but let him be among you as one of the same country: and you shall love him as yourselves: for you were strangers in the land of Egypt (Lev. 19:33-34).

This shows us to what degree the idea of one's neighbor was still limited, and we can have a presentiment of the important evolution which Christ will effect in the conception of the love of others.

II. The New Testament

THE VOCABULARY

The vocabulary used by the New Testament to express charity is sufficient, by itself, to show the new orientation which Christ's revelation has given to the idea of love.

To translate the Hebrew terms, the Septuagint used three classic Greek words: ἐρᾶν, φιλεῖν, and ἀγαπᾶν, with a marked preference for the latter. Classical literature expressed voluntary and elective love especially by the verb ἀγαπᾶν. Ἐρᾶν designated passionate love and φιλεῖν signified the love of friendship. Ἀγαπᾶν was the least used of the three. The New Testament adopted this latter term and made frequent use of it. The substantive ἀγάπη owes its fortune to biblical literature. Although it was not unknown in classical literature, it was used very rarely and its meaning is uncertain.

It is therefore natural that when the authors of the New Testament had to express an original concept, they had recourse to these two words, ἀγαπᾶν and ἀγάπη, whose meaning was not too precise. Thereafter, in preference to any other term, these words were used to express the love of charity.

The Vulgate generally translates ἀγάπη by *caritas* or *dilectio* and the verb ἀγαπᾶν (no Latin verb corresponding to *caritas*) almost exclusively by *diligere*. It seems that the term *agape* was accepted as such in Latin and survived for a certain period, notably in the very concrete sense of a love feast (we still use the term in that way.) [1]

The choice of the word ἀγάπη by the writers of the New Testament therefore seems to indicate a definite intention: for a new thing they wanted to make use of a new word, or at least a word that was infrequent until then.

A. THE DOCTRINE OF THE *Agape* ACCORDING TO THE SYNOPTICS

To indicate more clearly the enrichment of the conception of love in relation to the Old Testament, we shall again turn our attention to the three divisions: the love of God, love for God and love for neighbor.

1. THE GRATUITY OF DIVINE LOVE

Israel had monopolized the love of Yahweh for its own advantage exclusively. Was it not the Lord Who had chosen His people among all other nations? Was He not bound to this people by His promises and by an indestructible alliance? To be a son of Israel was therefore to possess a strict right to the love of God. Such a conclusion was almost certainly bound to impose itself upon the mind of the Jews.

Furthermore, if we recall that the true Israelite, the real son of God, was the holy and righteous man (and we know how the official doctors understood this holiness in later times), we will readily understand that sinners, publicans and strangers were excluded from this privilege. It was the righteous, in the manner of the Pharisees,

[1] There are some very interesting remarks on this vocabulary in the work of H. Petre. *Caritas, Études sur le vocabulaire latin de la charité chrétienne,* "Specilegium Sacrum Lovaniense," Louvain, 1948.

and they alone, who could claim the right to Yahweh's love as descendants of Abraham.

This is doubtless one of the points at which Christ brought about the most ardent reaction against traditional conceptions. And yet Moses, from the very beginning, had insisted upon the gratuitous character of God's love: Israel had done nothing to merit this gift, on the contrary, its only response had been innumerable infidelities. We need only read chapter nine of Deuteronomy:

> Say not in thy heart . . .: For my justice hath the Lord brought me in to possess this land. . . . For it is not for thy justices, and the uprightness of thy heart. . . . Know therefore that the Lord thy God giveth thee not this excellent land in possession for thy justices, for thou art a very stiffnecked people. . . . Remember, and forget not how thou provokedst the Lord thy God . . . thou hast always strove against the Lord.

The Synoptics, in opposition to pharisaical claims, stressed the absolute gratuity of God's love, sometimes in a violent manner. This reaction seems to have been very definite after the preaching of John the Baptist. The official status of a son of Abraham of which the Jews were so proud was not sufficient to confer the right to God's love: "And do not think to say within yourselves, 'We have Abraham for our father,' declared John the Baptist, addressing the Pharisees and Sadducees; 'for I say to you that God is able out of these stones to raise up children to Abraham.' "

The attitude of Jesus, and His discourses and parables, proclaimed God's love for sinners to the great scandal of all who were formally "righteous." This was a real revolution. Christ took the opposite way from traditional opinion; He overturned the carefully established order.

The first Psalm sang of the happiness of the righteous and the punishment of sinners:

> Blessed is the man who hath not walked in the counsel of the ungodly, nor stood in the way of sinners. . . .

And yet here was Christ proclaiming, "For I have not come to call the just, but sinners." And all of His activity illustrated this astonishing statement. During His whole life He manifested a predilection for sinners and for the "poor" of all kinds.

He healed the sick, gave of His kindness everywhere, and placed the power of God at the service of all kinds of suffering, He generously dispensed these blessings without the least discrimination, requiring no proof of holiness whatever unless it be the act of faith which He required in His person. Moreover, He kept company with sinners and ate at their table; He risked the company of publicans and allowed Himself to be touched by a notoriously sinful woman. He refused to condemn the woman who was taken in adultery.

His parables accentuate still more this personal stand in showing that His conduct was very deliberate. The parable of the Lost Sheep for which the shepherd abandoned his flock arrives at this conclusion: "There will be joy in heaven over one sinner who repents, more than over ninety-nine just who have no need of repentance" (Lk. 15:3-7). The parable of the Prodigal Son witnesses to the untiring mercy of God for the sinner; and the joy of the father of a family at the return of the lost son contrasts with the bitterness and jealously of the eldest son, the "righteous" one (Lk. 15:11-32). The parable of the workers of the eleventh-hour, with its disconcerting lesson, gives perhaps the greatest enhancement to the absolute gratuity—far surpassing the limits of right and justice—of the divine gift (Mt. 20:1-16).

All of this demonstrates the free, spontaneous, gratuitous character of God's love which seems to be directed by preference to the most wretched souls.

Does this mean that the sinner has a value in God's eyes which the just man is lacking, or a real quality that attracts and justifies the divine predilection? May we infer from the attitudes and parables of Christ that the sinner is worth more than the just man before God? Certainly not, if we mean a positive value. An example quoted by St. Mark shows that Christ esteemed virtue above everything else. It was the example of the rich young man who could say, "Master, all these I have kept ever since I was a child," referring to the Commandments, and then the evangelist noted, "And Jesus, looking upon him, loved him" (Mk. 10:21).

But there is in the sinner a disposition to better understand the gratuity of divine love; he knows that by himself he has no right to anything. He expects everything from a gratuitous gift. The sentiment of personal righteousness opens the heart's door to pride, and encloses man within the satisfaction of his own excellence. The parable of the Pharisee and the Publican contrasts these two attitudes in order to teach a very definite lesson. But it is especially the solicitude for Christ for sinners that manifests the sovereign liberty of God in the gift of His love. This love is never motivated by the value of its object. There is nothing in man that could lay claim to that love, nothing that could demand that privilege as a right. The gift of God is perfectly free, the divine *agape* is gratuitous.

If it does not have a motive on the side of the object, we must not deduce that it does not have an end, that it does not have an effect, that it tends toward nothing. On the contrary, this gift is creative. It is love which brings God to men, which creates in them the dignity that they have in His eyes. If God loves men it is "that they might have life." St. John, especially, develops this idea and we shall come back to it at length.

2. THE GREATEST COMMANDMENT

Answering the question of a scribe, Jesus affirmed that the first and greatest of the commandments of the Law is the following: "And thou shalt love the lord thy God with thy whole heart, and with thy whole soul, and with thy whole mind, and with thy whole strength." And then He mentioned the second commandment, "Thou shalt love thy neighbor as thyself." He declared that in these two precepts the whole of the Law and the Prophets was summed up. And this love of man for God is expressed by the word *agape,* the same word that is used to designate God's love for men (Mt. 22:37; Mk. 12:30; Lk. 10:27).

Jesus Himself gave the most wonderful example of loving God above all else. The Synoptics make little mention of His intimacy with the Father, but His whole life appears as a perfect submission, full of love, to the will of God. His words in Gethsemane express it all quite completely: "Yet not what I will, but what thou willest." Before His eyes there was always the will of God which He must accomplish, that will which was manifested in the Scriptures. It was essential that the Scriptures be fulfilled even unto the ignominious death upon the cross. Nothing could turn Him away from that way of perfect obedience, and He rejected Peter's timid remonstrances, when the disciple wanted to turn Him away from this somber perspective, as a temptation of Satan (Mk. 8:31-33).

This absolute love for God was to be directed to His own person. Christ required this. He wanted men to love Him for Himself above everything else, with a love that surpassed the most legitimate and noble loves: "He who loves father or mother more than me is not worthy of me; and he who loves son or daughter more than me is not worthy of me" (Mt. 10:37). And even using a paradox to give greater force to His words, He gave this warning: "If anyone comes to me and does not hate his father and mother, and wife and children, and brothers and sisters, yes, and even his own life, he cannot be my disciple" (Lk. 14:26-27).

The absolute value and primordial importance of total charity for God and for the person of the Savior could hardly be affirmed with greater force and solemnity.

3. THE LOVE OF NEIGHBOR

When Jesus combined the precept of the love of neighbor with that of love for God in order to sum up the whole Law, He had not become an innovator. The proof is seen in the approval of the scribe who was listening to Him: "Well answered, Master, thou has said truly that he is one and that there is no other besides him; and that he should be loved with the whole heart, and with the whole understanding, and with the whole soul, and with one's whole strength; and that to love one's neighbor as oneself is a greater thing than all holocausts and sacrifices" (Mk. 12:32-33). But it was in the extension given to this love that Christ was making innovations.

You have heard that it was said, 'Thou shalt love thy neighbor, and shalt hate thy enemy.' But I say to you, love your enemies, do good to those who hate you, and pray for those who persecute and calumniate you, so that you may be children of your Father in heaven, who makes his sun to rise on the good and the evil, and sends rain on the just and the unjust. For if you love those that love you, what reward shall you have? Do not even the publicans do that? And if you salute your brethren only, what are you doing more than others? Do not even the Gentiles do that? You therefore are to be perfect, even as your heavenly Father is perfect (Mt. 5:43-48).

Saint Luke, in a parallel passage, adds:

Love your enemies, do good to those who hate you. Bless those who curse you, pray for those who calumniate you. And to him who strikes thee on the one cheek, offer the other also; and from him who takes away thy cloak, do not withhold thy tunic either. Give to everyone who asks of thee, and from him who takes away thy goods, ask no return (Lk. 6:27-30).

We now see that the conception of the *agape* for our neighbor here received an important complement. The character of *gratuity* is introduced into it. The *agape* was now to be extended to enemies. It cannot be restricted to a circle of family relations, or to those of one's nation, race or friends, in which we are sure of being paid in return. We must render good for evil, and be first in loving; it could be said that we must love without motive. Gratuity is therefore affirmed in the very object of *agape*. It must be affirmed, furthermore, in the manner of loving and the manner of giving, and this means that we must let ourselves be despoiled without complaint, and must give more than is demanded, with no hidden motive, and without the least self-seeking. Finally, the gratuity of this love for others is seen again in the motivation that must inspire it. We must seek to become like God; we must want to be perfect as God is perfect, showing ourselves to be true sons of God who dispenses His blessings without counting. We must want to be sons of the God who loves gratuitously.

The love of others is quite simply the imitation of the divine *agape*. (The texts of the Synoptics would not permit us to use the term participation in its strict sense.) But we already have a presentiment of St. John's idea: God is *agape* and the man who abides in *agape* abides in God and God abides in him (I Jn. 4:16).

Two terms are currently used to designate all those to whom *agape* should unite us. The terms are "brethren" and "neighbor."

The word brother, ἀδελφός, was certainly borrowed from the Jewish tradition. It seems that it was a Jewish custom to call each other "brother." It was an expression of their community of race and religion. St. Peter, in his first sermon, used the following terms as synonyms: Ἄνδρες Ἰουδαῖοι and ἄνδρες ἀδελφοί (Jewish Men and Men Brethren). We often see Christ conforming to this usage (Mt. 5:22-24; 7:3-4; 18:15-35; Lk. 6:41-42, etc.). In Matthew's text, already quoted, the word is used in its restricted, exclusive sense: "And if you salute your brethren only, what are you doing more than others?"

Jesus wanted His disciples to consider themselves as brethren. "But do not you be called 'Rabbi'; for one is your Master, and all you are brothers. And call no one on earth your father; for one is your Father, who is in heaven" (Mt. 23:8). The word "brother" in this text especially emphasizes the equality of all the disciples. The following verse leads us to seek the motive for this fraternity in the fact that they all have a common Father, the Father who is in heaven. But the context hardly permits us to discern a rigorous connection between the two ideas.

At least on one occasion Christ called men "His brethren" [2]—and

---

[2] It is difficult to say whether Christ applies this word to men in general or only to his disciples. According to L. Cerfaux (*La charité fraternelle et le retour du Christ*, Ephemerides Theologicae Lovanienses, 1928), it is a question here of the Christian community as opposed to the world.

in a text that reveals an important aspect of the fraternal *agape*. It is the famous description of the judgment of the good and the evil (Mt. 25:31-46). In this passage Jesus identified Himself with the least of His brethren and the lesson is quite clear. We must relieve and assist other men as if they were the Lord in person. We now see the unity of love for neighbor and of love for God—here it is Christ in His glorious state and in His capacity as the supreme judge, who identifies Himself with men—which St. John indicated with perfect clarity. We find a precise echo of this in the scene on the Damascus Road where Christ, speaking to Saul, the enemy of Christians, tells him, "I am Jesus, whom you are persecuting."

Our Lord elsewhere reveals ties of spiritual relationship which are of greater importance than those of blood. "Who is my mother and who are my brethren?" And stretching forth his hand towards his disciples he said, "Behold my mother and my brethren! For whoever does the will of my Father in heaven, he is my brother and sister and mother" (Mt. 12:48-50; cf. Mk. 3:31; Lk. 8:19-21). It is at the level of conformity to the will of God, that is to say, at the level of true love for God that the relations of essential kinship are established.

The term *neighbor* (ὁ πλησίον) is also inherited from Judaism. The Septuagint preferred this term in translating the Hebrew word that means "compatriot," the good Israelite, which contrasted with "stranger" or "Samaritan" in practice if not by right. For the Jew it was the man of his own race and nation who was, traditionally, his neighbor. It was to him alone that the duties of fraternity were due.

Christ broke with this conception in the parable of the Good Samaritan (Lk. 10:25-37). Wishing to have the meaning of the precept "Thou shalt love thy neighbor" given a more specific definition, a doctor of the Law asks, "And who is my neighbor?" Jesus contrasted the attitude of the priest, a levite, in regard to the wounded traveler and the Samaritan, an enemy of the Jews, who alone took care of the unfortunate man. And in His turn He concluded with a question: "Which of these . . . proved himself neighbor?" The answer which He gave to the doctor obviously modified the meaning which he had attached to the word "neighbor." Jesus gave this word an active sense: the one who shows himself to be a neighbor is the one who practices charity. The immediate lesson of the parable is that we must exercise mercy without regard to race or the quality of those who are in need.[3] But the example chosen by Our Lord gives this word "neighbor" a new extension which greatly surpasses the framework of the Jewish community.

Love for others considered as brethren, as neighbors, must be manifested in ways that are concrete, practical and efficacious. The Good Samaritan gave us a perfect example of this love. Several of the duties of charity are enumerated by the Synoptics. We must be merciful and avoid judging or condemning others.

> Be merciful, therefore, even as your Father is merciful. Do not judge, and you shall not be judged; do not condemn, and you shall not be condemned. Forgive, and you shall be forgiven; give, and it shall be given to you; good measure, pressed down, shaken together, running over, shall they pour into your lap. For with what measure you measure, it shall be measured to you. . . . (Lk. 6: 36-38).

We must forgive offenses against ourselves and practice fraternal correction:

> For if you forgive men their offenses, your heavenly Father will also forgive you your offenses. But if you do not forgive men, neither will your Father forgive you your offenses (Mt. 6:14-15). If thy brother sin, rebuke him; and if he repent, forgive him. And if seven times in the day he sin against thee, and seven times in the day turn back to thee saying, "I repent," forgive him (Lk. 17:3-4).

In all these texts we see that there is a very simple concrete rule, the great Golden Rule of charity for our neighbor: we must do unto others as we would have them do unto us. It is perhaps the most practical and down-to-earth formulation of this precept to say: we must love other men as we love ourselves.

B. THE *Agape* ACCORDING TO ST. PAUL

1. THE GOD OF *AGAPE*

In St. Paul, also, and perhaps even more than in the Synoptics, the whole movement of charity finds its origin in God's love for men. We now find ourselves confronting a fact which gives an original note to this conception of love. Paul is the man who had a personal experience, an experience of the sovereign gratuity of divine love, that was astonishing and indubitable. He fully lived the truth of Jesus' saying, "You have not chosen me, but I have chosen you."

Paul was a true Jew, a zealous pharisee formed in the school of the doctors of Israel, and a persecutor of the disciples of Christ.

---

[3] M. J. Lagrange, *Commentaire sur l'évangile de saint Luc* (on this passage).

And in a single moment, on the road to Damascus, grace had overwhelmed him. He felt in his soul and in his very body that God had given Himself freely. And that is why, in all Pauline theology of *agape,* the divine initiative is so justly emphasized.

If we do not find again in his writings the identification of God and *agape,* of which John was to be the herald, certain expressions have this tendency, however, as for instance this one: ὁ Θεὸς τῆς ἀγάπης—God is called "the God of *agape*" (II Cor. 13:11).

This love of God is especially manifested in that He gave us life, and He gave it to us through the supreme sacrifice of His Son.

> But God, who is rich in mercy, by reason of his very great love wherewith he has loved us even when we were dead by reason of our sins, brought us to life together with Christ (by grace you have been saved), and raised us up together, and seated us together in heaven in Christ Jesus, that he might show in the ages to come the overflowing riches of his grace in kindness towards us in Christ Jesus (Eph. 2:4-7).

The gift of God is therefore gratuitous, emanating from the free initiative of the Almighty, but it is meant for a very specific purpose: to give us life. The love of God is both gratuitous and efficacious.

The epistle to the Romans insists upon the great evidence of this love, the sacrifice of the Cross—a supreme gift which only the gratuitous character of divine *agape* could justify:

> For why did Christ, at the set time, die for the wicked when as yet we were weak? For scarcely in behalf of a just man does one die; yet perhaps one might bring himself to die for a good man. But God commands his charity toward us, because when as yet we were sinners, Christ died for us. . . . (Rom. 5:6-8).

This idea of the love of God being proved by the sacrifice of the Cross became the central theme of Paul's preaching.

It is from this divine charity that all charity proceeds. For the charity by which man, in his turn, will love is a gift which he receives from God. It is diffused within him by the Holy Spirit who is given to him (Rom. 5:5); it is a participation in the charity which is in God, for charity is the *agape* of the Holy Spirit (Rom. 15:30) to which the heart must be opened (II Thess. 2:10).

2. "IF ANY MAN DOES NOT LOVE THE LORD JESUS CHRIST, LET HIM BE ANATHEMA"

It has often been remarked that Paul does not refer to man's love for God very frequently in his letters. Anders Nygren in *Eros et*

Agape notes that the Apostle rarely uses the word *agape* to designate the activity of the Christian in relation to God, and on the faith of the witness of several Protestant commentators or scholars, he wonders if this word is understood by Paul at any time in the sense of love.

One thing is certain, and we shall touch on this point again, that Paul sums up the whole Law, not in the two juxtaposed commandments as was done by the Synoptics, but in the precept of love for neighbor alone. Furthermore, to nullify the theories of Nygren it is sufficient to read the texts in which the apostle, in a very clear sense,[4] speaks of *agape* towards God.

It is true that for St. Paul it was the acceptance of the mystery hidden from the beginning and revealed to the world by Jesus, which constitutes the essential response of man to the gift of God, that is to say, the mystery of faith (πίστις). But very often he associates love with this faith which is, in his eyes, the most fundamental attitude of the Christian before God. True faith cannot exist without charity (I Tim. 1:14; 2:15; II Tim. 1:14; I Tim. 1:3; 3:6). Faith operates through *agape* (Gal. 5:6).

And especially, we know the famous text in the first epistle to the Corinthians in which charity is placed above everything, even above faith, for faith without charity is nothing.

> If I should speak with the tongues of men and of angels, but do not have charity, I have become as sounding brass or a tinkling cymbal. And if I have prophecy and know all mysteries and all knowledge, and if I have all faith so as to remove mountains, yet do not have charity, I am nothing. And if I distribute all my goods to feed the poor, and if I deliver my body to be burned, yet do not have charity, it profits me nothing (I Cor. 13:1-3).

In this perspective we understand the exclamation, the categorical judgment which terminates the first epistle to the Corinthians: "If any man does not love the Lord Jesus Christ, let him be anathema" (16:22).

3. FRATERNAL CHARITY

Paul takes up in his turn the great commandment of love for our neighbor. He even gives it an extreme importance since he sums up the entire Law in this single commandment.

[4] Cf. among others: Rom. 8:28; I Cor. 2:9; I Cor. 8:3; Eph. 6:24. In all these texts; the love for God is expressed by the word *agapein*.

Owe no man anything except to love one another; for he who loves his neighbor has fulfilled the Law. For "Thou shalt not commit adultery; thou shalt not kill; thou shalt not steal; thou shalt not covet"; and if there is any other commandment, it is summed up in this saying, "Thou shalt love thy neighbor as thyself." Love does no evil to a neighbor. Love therefore is the fulfillment of the Law (Rom. 13:8-10).

This text is confirmed by a verse in the epistle to the Galatians (5:14): "For the whole Law is fulfilled in one word: Thou shalt love thy neighbor as thyself."

We could ask ourselves why St. Paul did not here mention the love of God. The context shows that it is a question of relations with our neighbor, and the apostle affirms that all the commandments pertaining to our neighbor (he does not mention any others) can be expressed in a very simple way: we must love one another. In the Christian order of things these precepts cannot be understood only as a duty of material and literal observance. They must be imbued with the great Christian *agape*. The love of God is certainly not excluded, for this love is taken for granted and is not at issue. St. Paul was only taking up the practical sign by which Christ wanted His disciples to be recognized: fraternal love.

It is by this love most particularly that the faithful will show themselves to be true imitators of God, and by this love that they will be conformed to divine holiness and will follow the example of their model and master, Jesus Christ.

Let all bitterness, and wrath, and indignation, and clamor, and reviling, be removed from you, along with all malice. On the contrary, be kind to one another, and merciful, generously forgiving one another, as also God in Christ has generously forgiven you. Be you, therefore, imitators of God, as very dear children and walk in love, as Christ also loved us and delivered himself up for us an offering and a sacrifice to God to ascend in fragrant odor (Eph. 4:31 and 5:2).

Within the scope of charity must be remembered the great idea of St. Paul on the unity of Christians with Christ and their union among themselves, for they are all members of a body of which He is the head. But the doctrine of the Mystical Body cannot be studied here.

4. THE PREEMINENCE OF CHARITY

Paul recommends the practice of all the virtues, but above everything else he places charity which is "the bond of perfection" (Col. 3:14)—and according to exegesis this means that it is the bond of all the virtues which constitute perfection, or better (according to

F. Prat), the bond which unites all Christians (the word "perfection" being considered as a genitive of apposition).

The hymn to charity which was quoted above (I Cor. 13) is a eulogy, full of poetic lyricism, concerning the absolute preponderance of charity. We must, says the apostle, aspire to charismatic gifts, especially the best of them, but there is one way which transcends all others: the way of *agape*. This appears surrounded by its court of virtues, the virtues which it produces and imbues. It is generally fraternal charity and all the virtues and acts which flow from it that are commonly recognized:

1. It is patient, 2. it is full of kindness, 3. it is not envious, 4. it does not boast, 5. it is not puffed up with pride, 6. it does nothing unseemly, 7. it does not seek its own advantage, 8. it does not become provoking, 9. it does not think evil (that is to say, it does not suspect others of evil intentions), 10. it takes no pleasure in injustice, 11. it rejoices with the truth, 12. it forgives everything, 13. it believes everything, 14. it hopes for everything (this does not refer to the theological virtues of faith and hope), 15. it endures everything (I Cor. 13:4-7).

Finally charity outweighs not only the gifts that are transitory (prophecy, tongues, knowledge) but it outweighs faith and hope which, likewise, will have an end. Only charity is eternal. "So there abide faith, hope and charity, these three; but the greatest of these is charity" (I Cor. 13:8-13).

C. THE *Agape* ACCORDING TO ST. JOHN

For good reason St. John has been called the apostle of love. His entire first epistle hardly mentions anything but *agape*. Furthermore, if we go through his gospel and his first epistle, we find the synthesis of everything that the Synoptics mentioned regarding charity. His reflection marks evident progress over the thought of the other evangelists and St. Paul. John constructed a true theology of *agape* in which the elements are linked and bound together perfectly. His doctrine is condensed in this page of his first epistle:

Beloved, let us love one another, for love is from God. And everyone who loves is born of God, and knows God. He who does not love does not know God; for God is love. In this has the love of God been shown in our case, that God has sent his only-begotten Son into the world that we may live through him. In this is the love, not that we have loved God, but that he has first loved us, and sent his Son a propitiation for our sins. Beloved, if God has so loved us, we also ought to love one another.

No one has even seen God. If we love one another, God abides in us and his love is perfected in us. In this we know that we abide in him and he in us, because he has given us of his Spirit. And we have seen, and do testify, that the Father has sent his Son to be Savior of the world. Whoever confesses that Jesus is the Son of God, God abides in him and he in God. And we have come to know, and have believed, the love that God has in our behalf. God is love, and he who abides in love abides in God, and God in him.

In this is love perfected with us, that we may have confidence in the day of judgment; because as he is, even so are we also in this world. There is no fear in love; but perfect love casts out fear, because fear brings punishment. And he who fears is not perfected in love. Let us therefore love, because God first loved us. If anyone says, "I love God," and hates his brother, he is a liar. For how can he who does not love his brother, whom he sees, love God, whom he does not see? And this commandment we have from him, that he who loves God should love his brother also (I Jn. 4:7-21).

In this passage are all the elements of the Johannine doctrine of *agape*. We shall try to recount the principal points with the help of this text and other passages taken from the writings of St. John. Two great ideas, it seems to us, dominate this doctrine:

1. God is love.
2. Men are called to participate in this love.

1. GOD IS LOVE

Ὁ Θεός ἀγάπη ἐστίν. This is the fundamental affirmation on which St. John's whole conception of *agape* is based. We saw that Paul spoke of the God of *agape*. John goes further, even to identification pure and simple: "God is *agape*." When we say *agape,* we are expressing the very nature of God.

1. God is Love primarily *in Himself*. It is His intimate life, His hidden nature. We know very little about this interior mystery of divinity if it be true that no one has ever seen God. And yet we perceive, through the character of Jesus, some reflections that enable us to surmise with more or less accuracy what this secret life may be.

The Father loves the Son. Christ stressed this truth: "The Father loves the Son, and has given all things into his hand" (Jn. 3:35). "For the Father loves the Son, and shows him all that he himself does" (Jn. 5:20). Notice the manner in which this love of the Father is manifested. He has no secrets from the Son; He admits Him into His complete intimacy. This is the same reason which Christ invoked to show His apostles that they are no longer servants but friends, because they share His secrets and His intimacy.

"Thou hast loved me before the creation of the world . . ." (Jn.

17:24); "As the Father has loved me, I also have loved you . . ." (Jn. 15:9); "in order that the love with which thou has loved me may be in them . . ." (Jn. 17:26); etc. We see that this is an eternal love which the Father has for the Son, beyond time, beyond creation. God *is* love.

As the Father loves the Son, so likewise the Son loves the Father, and He proclaims this not only to His disciples, but to the entire world: "That the world may know that I love the Father, and that I do as the Father has commanded me" (Jn. 14:31). This is the great sign, one of the two great signs, of love for God; conformity to His Will.

2. God is Love, "interiorly" first, in the intimacy of the divine Persons. But He is also love "exteriorly"; *God is Love for men.*

(a) Jesus gave His disciples the assurance that *the Father loves them:* "the Father himself loves you" (Jn. 16:27). This love is shown at its highest point in the supreme gift which God makes to men, the gift of His own Son. "For God so loved the world that he gave his only-begotten Son, that those who believe in him may not perish, but may have life everlasting" (Jn. 3:16). "In this has the love of God been shown in our case, that God has sent his only-begotten Son into the world that we may live through him" (I Jn. 4:9). This was the great work of God's love for us. He has given us His Son and through His Son He gives us eternal life.

This love of God is gratuitous; it is anterior to any love of ours. It is not a response, it is an initiative. "In this is the love, not that we have loved God, but that he has first loved us, and sent his Son a propitiation for our sins" (I Jn. 4:10). "And we have come to know . . . the love that God has in our behalf . . . God first loved us" (I Jn. 4:16, 19). This is a clear affirmation of the gratuitous predilection of God.

Certain texts seem to attribute a cause to the love of God. "But he who loves me will be loved by my Father . . ." (Jn. 14:21). "If anyone loves me, he will keep my word, and my Father will love him" (Jn. 14:23). "The Father himself loves you because you have loved me, and have believed that I came forth from God" (Jn. 16:27).

Of all the texts quoted up to this point, there are several ideas that should be retained because they bring out the harmony of the Johannine conception beneath an apparent contradiction of details. God, being Love, manifests Himself to men as love. He loves them first, freely and gratuitously. This initial love does not find and need not seek its justification or its motive in man. It is based upon the sovereign and free diffusion of the love that is in God which itself is God.

But this love is directed toward something precise. It is not diffused without purpose or without effect. It is not merely a blind emanation or a pure, instinctive radiation, indeliberate. The love of God is creative. It creates life in us. This is the purpose and the effect of the diffusion of divine life. It gives us eternal life. And this life is given in the supreme demonstration of God's love: the gift of His Son.

However, the eternal life which the gratuitous love of God creates in us still requires our personal cooperation. What is eternal life, as a matter of fact? It is "that they may know thee, the only true God, and him whom thou hast sent, Jesus Christ" (Jn. 17:3). This knowledge is a knowledge imbued with love. It is in this that our life as sons of God consists: "we are born of God," "we are called and we are truly sons of God," for "everyone who loves is born of God, and knows God. He who does not love does not know God; for God is love" (I Jn. 4:7-8). Eternal life is therefore to know God, and to know God is to love Him.

Consequently, the purpose of God's love coming toward us is to create eternal life within us, that is to say, Love itself. It makes us love in our turn; it makes us loving beings, diffusing love, in the likeness of God. That is why there must be a response of love on our part to the initiative of God Who loves us first. And to continue to enjoy God's love, we must, on our side, accept the effects of that love within us, that is to say, we must become lovers also: "Let us therefore love, because God first loved us" (I Jn. 4:19). And therefore, if we do not love God in our turn, or if we do not love Christ, it is because we are putting obstacles in the way of God's love for us. We are placing ourselves outside the love of God.

(b) The Father therefore loves men to the point of giving them His Son. But the *Son,* Himself, *also loves men.*

We have already seen this love associated with the Father's love: "But he who loves me will be loved by my Father, and I will love him" (Jn. 14:21). The end of John's Gospel abounds with evidence of Jesus' love for men. For it culminates in the supreme proof which Christ Himself declared, "Greater love than this no one has, that one lay down his life for his friends" (Jn. 15:13). As soon as the Last Supper is mentioned, the "disciple whom Jesus loved" stresses the meaning of the acts that are to take place: "Jesus, knowing that the hour had come for him to pass out of this world to the Father, having loved his own who were in the world, loved them to the end" (Jn. 13:1). And in the incomparable sermon after the Supper, Jesus let his tenderness overflow: "As the Father has loved me, I also have loved you . . ." (Jn. 15:9). "This is my commandment, that you love one another as I have loved you" (15:12).

We see how difficult it is to isolate a particular idea. The three themes are profoundly linked to one another: the love of the Father, the love of Christ, and the love of the disciples for one another. Jesus unites His love for His own to the love which the Father has for Him, to that very love which constitutes the intimate life of God: "as the Father has loved me." And the third idea completes the perfect unity of charity: "love one another as I have loved you."

The similarity of the love which exists between the Father and the Son and the love which binds the Son to men is denoted even more explicitly. The intimate love of God is shown in that the Father has no secrets from the Son, but gives Him all that He possesses. In the same way Christ's love for His own will be demonstrated. It is love extended to perfect intimacy, the love which deserves to be called *friendship*. "No longer do I call you servants, because the servant does not know what his master does. But I have called you friends, because all things that I have heard from my Father I have made known to you" (Jn. 15:15).

2. MEN ARE CALLED TO LOVE

The love which is in God and which God pours out upon men produces eternal life in them. And the eternal life which men possess, even now, is the knowledge of God which John identifies with love. To be sons of God and form the divine image within them, and to share in eternal life, men must therefore love in their turn; they must participate in the life of God's love. The true vocation of man consists in entering into the great movement of the *agape* of God.

In this *agape* man is therefore no longer only the object of God's love. He himself becomes a loving subject. He passes from passive love to active love. He loves in his turn.

This active love is itself a gift of God. It is the effect of the divine *agape* in man. It is God alone who gives life and makes men to be sons of God. It is He alone who gives *agape*. "For *agape* is from God. And everyone who loves is born of God" (I Jn. 4:7). But we must still accept this love which God creates within us. We must open our hearts to Him. The Pharisees refused to do this, and Jesus reproached them accordingly, "But I know that you have not the love of God in you" (Jn. 5:39-42). And since God first loved us, our own love can only be a response to His love (I Jn. 4:19).

How can man participate actively in *agape?* In two ways: by loving God and Christ, and by loving his fellow-men.

(a) *Love for God and for Christ*

St. John does not refer to the duty of loving God under the form of a precept. Instead of summing up the whole Law in a single commandment, he proceeds inversely: he shows that love for God must be proved by the observance of the commandments. "He who has my commandments and keeps them, he it is who loves me . . ." (Jn. 14:21).

It is therefore a matter of observing the law of Christ in love, as He also observed the commandments of the Father and always did what was pleasing to the Father. In this way love is truly proved and in this way men share in *agape* (cf. Jn. 15:10). A simple, material observance, exact and meticulous, inspired only by the sentiment of duty and the fear of divine justice would not be adequate. For "there is no fear in love; but perfect love casts out fear, because fear brings punishment. And he who fears is not perfected in love" (I Jn. 4:18). Furthermore, after Christ's remarks concerning the friendship into which He introduced His disciples, we cannot conceive of a system of relations based upon fear. There is only room for a love that is confident, intimate and complete. And the sublime dialogue with Peter after the Resurrection is evidence of this: "Simon, son of John, dost thou love me more than these do?" (Jn. 21:15).

It is therefore through fidelity to the commandments of Christ that men will prove their love for Him. Such is the great proof of that love. And among these commandments there is one to which Christ gave exceptional importance: the commandment to love our neighbor. This particular precept is derived from the Law, and therefore it is a part of the general proof in which true *agape* will be recognized. But its unique character and importance make of it another great proof of *agape* along with fidelity to the law.

(b) *Love for Others*

This is the commandment that is both ancient and new, the great sign whereby all men may recognize the disciples of Christ. "A new commandment I give you, that you love one another: that as I have love you, you also love one another. By this will all men know that you are my disciples, if you have love one for another" (Jn. 13:34-35). "This is my commandment, that you love one another as I have loved you" (Jn. 15:12). "These things I command you, that you may love one another" (Jn. 15:17). On no other point in the whole Gospel will we find such insistence. This is truly the legacy of Jesus; it is His commandment, the one to which He holds above everything else.

And St. John sees in this commandment the tangible proof, the one that can be verified, the one that does not deceive, of our sincerity in our love for God: "If anyone says, 'I love God' and hates his brother, he is a liar. For how can he who does not love his brother, whom he sees, love God, whom he does not see? And this commandment we have from him, that he who loves God should love his brother also" (I Jn. 4:20-21). There is therefore only one love by which we love both God and our fellow-men, and this is a single movement.

How must we understand the new character of this commandment? In a recent study (op cit.), L. Cerfaux sees in fraternal charity expressing itself in acts of assistance and mutual help, the virtue that is proper to the time that extends from Christ's departure to the Parousia. This is the characteristic virtue of the new era. Christians must prepare themselves for the return of the Lord in the practice of fraternal love, thereby separating themselves from the world which knows only hatred and which will pursue the fraternal community of Christians with its persecutions.

The love of neighbor is manifested in a concrete way following the example of Christ's love. Jesus proved His charity by giving His life for us. This was the supreme proof. In our turn we must be ready to give this same proof. "In this we have come to know his love, that he laid down his life for us; and we likewise ought to lay down our life for the brethren" (I Jn. 3:16). But we cannot be satisfied with perhaps a vain expectance of the occasion for such an act of love. On this side of the supreme proof, there are other proofs that should mark out our lives from day to day. Charity can find a thousand ways to prove itself: "He who has the goods of this world and sees his brother in need and closes his heart to him, how does the love of God abide in him? My dear children, let us not love in word, neither with the tongue, but in deed and in truth" (I Jn. 3:17-18).

In all things, finally, our love for our brethren will imitate Christ's love for us. "Love one another as I have loved you." Like the love of Jesus, who gave Himself not for the just, but for sinners, our love for neighbor must be a gratuitous love, a selfless love. Fraternal charity is not a means; it is an end. It is the fulfillment of the law. It is Christian perfection.

3. THE UNITY OF CHARITY

It has been possible to note how St. John took up in one way or another all the elements that we found in the Synoptics or St. Paul, to assemble them in a real synthesis. It is sufficient to recall the great statements of this doctrine to see the profound unity of charity.

God is Love. This was St. John's starting-point, which corresponds to the end of the movement which we found at its alluring beginning in St. Paul. The *agape* therefore defines the intimate nature of God. A few glances were given us into this secret life by the love which the Father and the Son have for each other.

This love which is in God and which itself is God is communicated to men. It is diffused through a gift that is absolutely free and gratuitous, through the supreme gift which God has made to the world: His own Son.

Divine life is creative within us. It gives us eternal life. And this eternal life which we possess even now, consists especially in loving in our turn: loving God and loving other men. In this way we have the life within us, and God abides in us and we in Him.

The love which has its origin in God is developed in several phases that are distinctly indicated by the text.

(a) My Father loved me with an eternal love (interior love in God).

(b) As my Father has loved me, I also have loved you (love of God taking men for its object, through the person of Christ, the supreme manifestation of God's love).

(c) As I have loved you, love one another (love in which we became active subjects and objects).

Each phase indicates an initiative that is sovereignly free; at the same time it implies reciprocity. For to the Father's love for the Son there responds the Son's love for the Father; to God's love and Christ's love for men, there responds the love of men for God and Christ; finally, the third phase clearly expresses reciprocity: "love one another."

This love in its various phases is *one*. The other forms of love take example from the interior love of God: *"as* my Father . . . ," *"as* I have loved you. . . ." And it is the same love that is communicated. First it takes men for its object and then communicates itself to them as a principle by which, in their turn, and in God's likeness, they will be able to love gratuitously.

That is why charity is the great factor in Christian unity: the fundamental unity of divine life, the unity of God with men, the unity of men together in God. Therefore, the great prayer of Jesus for unity concludes with that mention of the love which must accomplish it fully:

"In order that the love with which thou hast loved me may be in them, and I in them" (Jn. 17:26).

Second Part

OUTLINE OF THE DEVELOPMENT
OF THE DOCTRINE OF CHARITY

Charity is a value of capital importance in Christianity, and consequently we see why it was the object of numerous studies among the Fathers and also among the great theologians and the masters of the spiritual life. It is absolutely impossible, within the limits of a rapid study like this one, to give even a succinct idea of the entire history of the doctrine of charity. We must be satisfied with a few sketches of a very summary kind. And rather than hold to a monotonous nomenclature, we have preferred to select a few periods under which can be grouped the principal characteristics of this doctrine.

I. The Patristic Period

1. THE GREEK FATHERS

Among these Fathers we do not find any real treatise on charity. For this we must wait until St. Augustine and the medieval schools of theology.

The apostolic Fathers, the Apologists, and even the first speculative theologians limited themselves to commentaries upon Scripture.

CLEMENT OF ALEXANDRIA often mentions charity and his influence was exercised, after many centuries, upon a man like Fenelon in his conception of "pure love." In reaction against the heretical gnostics, he was the champion of a Christian gnosis which placed charity at the summit of the scale of perfection. For him Christians are divided into two categories: the simple Christians who are satisfied with a common faith, and the gnostics, that is to say, the perfect Christians, whose faith has been developed into gnosis.

To arrive at this perfection, and to attain to the state of the "accomplished man," one must go through the different "stages" marked by different motives of action: fear, faith and hope, in order finally to reach action by pure charity. For the perfect Christian, the gnostic, does not act through fear, nor by any desire for reward. He is only seeking gnosis, the knowledge of God wholly marked by charity. And Clement even writes,

> If by hypothesis one proposed to a gnostic to choose between the knowledge of God and his eternal salvation (on condition that these be separated, although these two things are absolutely identical), without any hesitation he would choose the knowledge of God, judging that he must desire for himself the state of a man who, beginning with faith, has raised himself to gnosis through charity (*Stroma*, IV, ch. 22).

Charity is bound up with gnosis which is the state of perfection. There are three elements in gnosis which Clement often combines. The first is impassibility (ἀπάθεια), the absolute mastery not only of irregular movements but of all the passions also, as well as sensibility itself. This impassibility reminds one of stoicism. The second element is none other than charity, the principle of the unification of all the faculties of the soul, which leads men unto the measure of the stature of Christ. Finally, the element which is most characteristic of Clement's doctrine, the gnosis; that is to say, that perfect knowledge which transcends simple faith and which, nourished by charity, introduces the Christian initiate to the contemplation of mysteries that are forbidden to the mass of the faithful.

Fraternal charity is described in *Stroma*, XI, chapter 9: the synthesis of everything which is according to reason, according to life and according to custom, or in a word, a community of life in which the other is "another myself." Clement attaches three virtues to charity which must accompany it. These are "hospitality," which attends to the welfare of strangers; "humanity," or fraternity towards those who share the same Spirit with us, which prompts us to be friendly to them with an intimate affection that is also efficacious; finally there is "dilection."

Among the Greek Fathers, the three greatest, who are doubtless Basil of Caesarea, his brother Gregory of Nazianzan, and John Chrysostom, were particularly preoccupied with the question of charity towards our neighbor, especially under the form of love of the poor. Witnesses of the misery suffered by people in the fourth century, they rose up, sometimes with violence, against the wealth and abuse of privilege of the possessing class. St. John Chrysostom is sometimes even depicted as a tribune publicly proclaiming the most burning social problems. In reality, like the two Cappadocians, he preached solicitude for the poor, in whom Christ Himself lives again, and detachment from material goods.

BASIL, to touch the heart of rich men more surely, described wretched poverty in the most sombre terms, and his description of a poor man reduced to selling his own children as slaves is almost haunting (Homily VI, 4). Acording to Basil, wealth is often a great obstacle to the exercise of charity. And while this virtue would seem to be easy for a rich man, it is in reality the one virtue to which he resigns himself with the greatest difficulty (Homily VII, 3).

GREGORY OF NAZIANZAN preached a sermon on "Love of the Poor" (Homily XIX). It is in a style that is full of rhetoric, but there is real eloquence in the way the orator, after contrasting the condition of the rich with that of the poor in clever imagery, refutes all the false arguments that the rich put forward to dispense themselves from the duty of charity. According to these arguments, the poor are in their wretched state through their own fault; the order of the world comes from God who knows what He is doing, etc. We see, from these few remarks, how well these homilies have kept their significance.

SAINT JOHN CHRYSOSTOM, when speaking of the poor, uses accents that are perhaps the most fiery of all his famous eloquence. He also violently criticized avarice, the abuse of wealth, and he preached true charity for one's neighbor, including not only material alms but also the gift of self. He wanted men to see that Christ Himself is truly in the person of the poor, and he put these words in Christ's mouth:

Certainly I could feed myself, but I prefer to go about begging, extending my hand before thy gate to be nourished by thee; it is for love of thee that I do this; I love thy table as thy friends love it; I rejoice to be admitted to it, and I declare thy praises to the whole world; I point to thee and tell all men that thou art the one who feeds me (Homily XVI, in *Epist. ad Rom.*).

Elsewhere he is even harsher, and also more persuasive:

What I have to say to you is saddening and horrible; however, I must say it. Put God at the same level as your slaves. You give freedom to your slaves in your wills. Liberate Christ from hunger, need, prison and nakedness. Oh! you shudder at my words.[5]

2. THE LATIN FATHERS: SAINT AUGUSTINE

Among the Latins, St. Augustine is often called the "doctor of charity." Perhaps no one wrote of God's love better than he. His theology, less objective and more passionate than the theology of St. Thomas, for example, reveals his personal soul on each page. Charity has a place of first importance in his writings. The order of the heart, in the sense that Pascal would use the term, is present in all Augustinian thought to such a degree that men refer to it as the "affective method."

St. Augustine did not devote long treatises to charity. The *Enchiridion de fide, spe et caritate* gives the lion's share to faith; only the final chapters, which are very short, pertain to charity. The treatise *De amicitia*, the *De diligendo Deo* which is a true treatise on the love of God, are attributed to St. Augustine, but they are the work of other authors. However, in most of his works, Augustine touches on charity, and as we know, under a lightly modified form, the famous saying in the Commentary on St. John, VII: "Ama et fac quod vis," love and do what thou wilt (the true Augustinian formula is: *Dilige et quod vis fac*).

According to the Bishop of Hippo, charity is Christian perfection: "Perfect charity is perfect justice" (*De natura et gratis,* ch. LXX, 84). The whole law is summed up in charity: in the love of God and neighbor. The *De diligendo Deo,* attributed to St. Augustine, exposes the method of charity.

How must we love God, and how must we love our neighbor. We must love God more than ourselves, and our neighbor as ourselves. We love God more than ourselves, if we prefer His commandments to our own will. As

[5] Homily, XVIII, in *Epist. ad Rom.*—These texts are cited according to the French translation of A. Puech, *Histoire de la littérature grecque chrétienne,* volume III, Paris, 1930, p. 500.

for our neighbor, we are not commanded to love him as much as ourselves, but as ourselves, that is to say, we must desire for him all the good that we must desire and will for ourselves, and above everything else eternal beatitude. We must help him reach this end through corporal and spiritual assistance in the measure in which reason requires it and in which our means will allow. . . . (*De diligendo Deo, ch. 1*).

True charity is a pure love, "chaste" according to St. Augustine, which loves God for Himself, to "enjoy" Him. For it is only the Trinity that we can truly enjoy (*De doctrina christiana,* chaps. 3-5).

St. Augustine contrasts the things that can be "enjoyed" with those that may be "used" (*frui* and *uti*). Creatures are only given to us for our use, in order to lead us to the supreme good which we shall enjoy.

The love of God must surpass all other affection. We must love God Who created us more than the father who engendered us, and love the Church which brought us into divine life more than the mother who brought us into the world (Sermon 344).

The perfection of charity cannot be attained in this present life. But we must progress constantly. Charity is active, it "cannot remain idle": "Always increase, march without halting, advance without respite, do not tarry on the way, do not retreat, don't wander from the route. The man who is not advancing is remaining where he was, and the man who comes back to the place he left is retreating" (Sermon 169). That is why the one who is on the road of progress can be called perfect (*De natura et gratia,* n. 15).

Absolute justice, through perfect charity, can only be fully realized when "we shall see God as He is, for then nothing can ever more be added to our charity when our faith will have become vision" (*De perfect, just. homin.,* ch. III).

St. Augustine, in this respect as in other domains of Christian thought, left his mark upon nearly the whole medieval era by his prestige and influence. Until the twelfth century, the genre that prevailed was that of the anthologies. But beginning with the twelfth century, there was an awakening of thought and birth of the lofty speculations of the mystics and the systems of the great scholastics.

II. Mystics and Scholastics of the Middle Ages

1. SAINT BERNARD

SAINT BERNARD, who is, with St. Augustine, the great singer of the love of God, made a study of charity most particularly in three of his works: the *Lettre à Guigues le Chartreaux* (Epist., XI), the treatise *De diligendo Deo* and the *Commentary on the Canticle of Canticles*. It is at the beginning of this treatise on the love of God that we find the formula that has become famous and whose second part was borrowed from Severus of Milève, the correspondent of St. Augustine: "Causa diligendi Deum, Deus est; modus, sine modo diligere," the reason for which we love God is God Himself; the measure of that love is to love without measure.

According to him, every man must love God, even if he does not know Christ. For if he is ignorant of Christ, the man at least knows himself and with his reason alone he sees that everything he possesses comes to him from God. The gifts of the body: it is through God that he subsists and sees and breathes; is it not God alone, who, according to Scripture, gives food to the body and makes His sun to shine upon the good and the evil, and His rain to fall upon the just and the unjust? And the gifts of the soul, by which man is made in the image and likeness of God (*De diligendo Deo*, ch. II).

The Christian has many more reasons for loving God, because he knows the goodness and mercy of God.

"What shall I render to the Lord, for all the things that he hath rendered to me?" (Ps. 115). In His first work (creation) He has given me myself; in the second, He has given Himself: and in giving Himself He has given me back to myself. Since I am a being who was given and redeemed (*datus, redditus*) I must give myself as the price of myself, and I must give myself doubly (*Ibid.*, ch. V).

It is especially the example of Christ, which the Christian has before his eyes, which makes this love easy: "He has given us His merits, He reserves Himself to be our reward, He gives Himself as nourishment to holy souls, He delivers Himself for the redemption of captive souls" (*Ibid.*, ch. VII).

In St. Bernard's very original conception, charity is developed in accordance with four phases. The first degree consists of the natural love which a man has for himself. This love is one of the four passions of man, along with fear, joy and sadness. It is a "carnal love" in which man loves himself for his own sake. Such a love becomes "social" when it is extended to others. And this again is a purely natural love. But God watches over nature and He makes man conscious of his weakness through salutary trials, and makes him seek a protector. Through grace, the instinctive love of self is therefore raised to the love of God. At this second degree, one loves God not

yet for Himself but for the blessings that are received from Him.
In turning to God in his necessities, man learns little by little to
know the divine goodness and to delight in it. Then he goes on to
the third degree. He loves God for Himself, because of His goodness. Finally the fourth degree marks the high point of charity: man
loves God uniquely for the sake of God, without any return upon
himself, and he only loves himself for the sake of God. In St. Bernard's opinion, it seems impossible for man to maintain himself
perfectly in this supreme degree during the whole course of his life.
Like St. Augustine, he thinks that this will be possible only in heaven
(*Ibid.,* chs. VIII, IX, X and XV).

In his *Commentary on the Canticle of Canticles,* the Abbot of
Clairvaux recognizes three stages in the ascension of mystical love.
In the first, love is sensible (*carnalis*) and is attached especially to
the humanity of Christ, constantly meditating upon the mysteries of
His mortal life. This is an "inferior" love, but Bernard describes it
with real predilection. As it becomes more perfect this love becomes
"reasonable," living by faith and repulsing all error. Finally it becomes "spiritual" love, attaching itself to God Himself in His divinity. It is only this spiritual love, extending beyond everything sensible, that can produce mystical union. But to reach this stage there
must be a call from God. And the soul that is chosen for this is
invited to a spiritual marriage; it becomes the spouse of Christ. It
then enters into the mystery of absolute union with Christ in which
it knows rapture and ecstasy.

2. SCHOLASTICISM

Along with this mystical fervor which was poured out with admirable lyricism and of which we have only quoted from one of
the witnesses, although the most famous, there was the nascent
scholasticism which brought its logic and its systematic rigor to
Christian thought.

Immediately, difficult problems arise. The nature of Charity is the
object of much research that is both fumbling and numerous. Is it
only an act, a movement of the soul, or is it a permanent reality?
PETER LOMBARD brought the principle of solution and was at
the origin of the conception of charity, and of virtue in general, as
"habitus." However, he laid a mortgage upon the theology of charity
by putting the mantle of his authority on the identification of char-

ity with the Holy Spirit. Even his own disciples reacted against this theory, but rather timidly.

Two questions were especially debated which contributed to the progress of the doctrine of charity. On the one hand there was the problem of the possibilities and limits of nature in regard to charity and supernatural merit, and, on the other hand, the problem of the implanting of charity in the natural love of God and self. These two questions cross-checked each other. After many hesitations, the light was reached. Natural love of God is not charity: their object is materially the same but is attained in a formally different manner. The object of charity is the God of mystery, revealed by faith. Only a supernatural virtue can attain it: faith for knowledge and charity for affection. But the charity that loves God with disinterested love is based upon the love of oneself, this aspect of "concupiscence" being inseparable from all love. Here we touch upon the very essence of love, which has stirred up many controversies and will doubtless always do so.

With Saint Thomas Aquinas the definition of charity as friendship with God was introduced into theology. This was a decision that constituted an essential stage in the elaboration of a doctrine of charity and which marked it in a definitive manner. Even in the Franciscan school, in which there is a definite tendency to emphasize the exclusively disinterested character of charity, even unto desiring one's own annihilation for the sake of divinity,[6] DUNS SCOTUS conceded that charity can be truly called a friendship, or more exactly, on account of the inequality which always subsists between God and man, a "super-friendship." A characteristic trait to be noted in this theologian is his identification of charity with sanctifying grace and, in spite of St. Bonaventure's opposition, this idea was perpetuated among Franciscan theologians.[7]

[6] Scot, *opus oxoniense,* III, d. 27; q. un. No. 13.
[7] In the limits of this kind of study we can only mention these most important phases in the evolution of the doctrine; it is not possible for us to study notably the theological foundations upon which the most celebrated schools of spirituality based themselves in their conception of charity.

Third Part

THEOLOGICAL ANALYSIS OF CHARITY

I. What Is Charity

1. THE DEFINITION OF CHARITY

Scripture has revealed to us the very rich nature of charity, and St. John notably gave us a well-ordered doctrine of it. Beginning with these scriptural data, and thanks to the reflection of the Fathers and the pioneers of theology, we are now able to investigate the nature of charity and define its contours and ramifications. And, doubtless, from the moment that we apply the mind to the study of a reality that is so mysterious, it is inevitable that we introduce into the analysis certain preferences. The light in which we consider the object conditions the image which we will make of it. This is the law of all human enterprise. What matters therefore is to use the best adapted and least deforming intellectual frameworks in order to encompass the reality. All that St. John tells us about charity seems to cite as its natural basis the definition of friendship which Aristotle put forth in his famous *Peri Philias*. Christ, in St. John, invites us to consider His love for us as a friendship: "I have called you friends." That is why St. Thomas Aquinas was not afraid of using Aristotle's philosophical analysis in his theology of charity. We shall see to what point the description which St. John makes of charity finds its exact expression in assuming, with the necessary transposition, the framework of friendship.

We shall therefore define charity as friendship with God and with all the children of God. And to justify and explain this definition, we shall recall the elements which constitute the idea of friendship and we shall show how this idea is the one in which charity, a supernatural reality, is best expressed.

2. THE IDEA OF FRIENDSHIP

(a) *Friendship is a love*

Friendship is a well defined species of love considered as a genus. It is not possible here to recount the whole metaphysics or the whole psychology of love. The passion of love was furthermore studied in the Treatise on human acts. It must be recognized that love, in its profound reality, continues to be a very mysterious thing for philosophers. We must be satisfied to recall the principal elements of this idea.

Love is the fundamental act of the affective faculty. It is the spontaneous reaction of the whole being expressing itself in its appetitive function in the presence of whatever attracts it, that is to say, the good. There are therefore two terms of counteraction: the object that is loved, or the good which acts upon the appetite as the final cause attracting to itself; and the living object, the man who, in his appetite, feels the attraction of the good and moves himself toward that end.

In the feeling which affects the subject in the presence of the good, we may distinguish various aspects, two sides. We shall keep their Latin names, as St. Thomas used them, because we lack a vernacular vocabulary that is precise and universally accepted.[8]

Love is essentially an *immutatio,* that is to say, a modification, a profound and original transformation of the appetite in the presence of its object. Before the good, before anything attractive, the affective powers become altered; they receive an impact, a break-up is produced within them, and they submit to the law of the object. Amorous language speaks of a "broken heart." It is exactly that. The appetite suffers; it is inwardly shocked and transformed by the object's force of attraction. This is the most general import of love. But in what does this transformation consist, and why is the heart broken? Here two ideas are necessary which form the two sides, ontological and psychological, of the movement of love.

It is first a *coaptatio.* If the heart is affected, it is because there is a mysterious affinity between itself and the object. The object produces a release, like an adaptation, in the appetite which can be compared to the one that governs a photographic lens. This adaptation can be described as a putting into unison, the realization of a perfect harmony in which is manifested the connaturality, the ontological relationship, not here at the psychological level but in the

[8] A more complete analysis can be found in two studies, the best without doubt on this subject: H. D. Simonin, *Autour de la solution thomiste du problème de l'amour,* Archives of the doctrinal and literary history of the Middle Ages, vol. VI, 1931; P. Rousselot, *Pour l'histoire du problème de l'amour au moyen-âge,* Beiträge zur Geschichte der Philosophie des Mittelalters, B. VI, Munster, 1908.

profound domain of being. This is the phenomenon which two beings perceive in a confusing way when, facing each other for the
first time, they have the feeling that they have always known each
other, and they feel that they were made for each other.

Complacentia, or amorous complaisance, is the psychological aspect of this ontological relationship. The mysterious affinity entering
into the sphere of consciousness produces in the heart this enjoyable
orientation towards the object. This side of love is one of the most
perceptible and most characteristic. The loving subject becomes
aware of all these forces within himself which were ready to be
aroused by the object. He takes pleasure in this object which enfolds
him with secret bands and he derives a profound joy from this. It
is not yet the joy of perfect possession, but it is the joy of anticipated
possession, the joy of a mysterious union proper to love.

Finally there remains a last movement: the *intentio* (from "intendere," to tend towards). If up to this point the appetite, namely the
initiative emanating from the object which attracts to itself and
arouses the appetite, has had a very passive role, to this attraction
now will respond the movement of the appetite which is set in motion in order to strive actively for the possession of the thing that
is loved. After having imposed its law, the object will, in its turn,
undergo the pursuit of the subject. The object therefore fully realizes
its nature as an end: it orients the activity of the subject towards
itself. It becomes the goal to be attained, the happiness to be conquered. The lover has set forth on his conquest and he will not rest
or find his joy until he has perfect possession.

Love has therefore, after all, a double countenance: it is both
passivity and activity. And its effect, or at least that towards which it
tends, is the total union of the lover and the beloved. This is the
subject-object synthesis. The two terms bound together through love
are only one thereafter; they are blended into unity. But this love is
in two stages. Love, by itself, produces the union of affection which
consists in a kind of affective possession which aspires to be changed
into real possession. This latter is realized by the effective union of
the subject with the object in its very substance. Love tends towards
this with all its desire, but by itself it is incapable of realizing it. It is
not enough, in fact, to love in order to be really in possession of the
object of one's love. But placed at the beginning of all movement of
affectivity, love will pursue its desire and call into its service all the

powers that will lead it straight to the definitive conquest of the beloved object. Only then will the appetite be able to rest in total joy.

(b) *Friendship Is a Benevolent Love*

Not every love can deserve the name of friendship. Only benevolent love can lay claim to it if it is also endowed with other qualities which we shall indicate.

We must recall the two species of love that were mentioned in the treatise on hope: concupiscent love and benevolent love. Concupiscent love is in reality the love of self in which the subject seeks essentially and deliberately his own good, his personal enrichment. His love does not stop at the beloved object as a value in itself; it only penetrates through the object in order to return to the subject. In this way men love wine, the dance, or valuable relations. In reality they are only loved for the pleasure or the usefulness that men find in them.

On the other hand, benevolent love is disinterested. It seeks not essentially the good of the one who loves but the good that is proper to the beloved object. This is the love which "wills the good"; the object is loved for itself. This is because the object appears as a value *per se,* worthy of being regarded and pursued as an end to which one relates oneself, and no longer as a simple means which the subject reclaims for himself. That is why such a dignity can only belong to a person. Only the person can be elevated to this dignity as an end of a personal being.

It is certainly evident that in loving this way, the subject finds his own perfection. Benevolent love is not a refusal which the subject opposes to all enrichment of his own worth. In seeking the good of the one that he loves, the subject grows himself, and finds his happiness even in self-sacrifice. For this aspect of "self-advancement" is inseparable from love. But only benevolent love can explain the sacrifice, for everything must be referred back to the object of one's love in order to love to the point of self-sacrifice. This is doubtless the purest manifestation of disinterested love. There is no greater love than to lay down one's life for those whom one loves.

(c) *Friendship Implies Reciprocity*

Benevolent love in itself is not yet friendship. The latter will not really exist unless there is reciprocity of love. In fact, friendship cannot be a one-way street. Two beings cannot truly be called friends if only one of them loves while the other is content to let himself be loved. The friend, says Aristotle quite excellently, must in his turn be a friend for his friend: *amicus amico amicus*. Friendship requires a certain equality in love, not an absolute equality, as for instance a kind of narrow levelling, but at least an equality that could be called proportional. Each of the two friends must love the other in the measure of his own ability and according to his condition.

We see that friendship is more than benevolent love which is itself much more than a concupiscent love. For disinterested love, in itself, does not necessarily call forth a response. It even seems that the absence of any responsive love makes its disinterested character appear still more noble. Is it not more perfect to give our love without expecting anything in return? This would be true if the motive of love were precisely this response. But such is not the case. Certainly, if nothing is expected in return, the one who loves shows his disinterestedness. But this does not tend to create in the beloved object that which is one of the most essential of the vital values: love itself. This is the good which a friend must especially want for his friend, so that he also may love in his turn, and be raised likewise to disinterested love. In sum, friendship is the conjunction of two disinterested loves. Reciprocity must be understood in this sense. If one desires a response, it is not because the gift of his love is fixed at this price, but because one desires to arouse benevolent love in the beloved being. Consequently, friendship is benevolent love carried to its highest requirements, even unto forming its own image in its object. And that is why, if friendship can only exist concretely in a subject, or more exactly in at least two loving subjects, it has in some way a value by itself and it could be said that it tends, at its limit, to become objectivized. In God alone, friendship realizes its full nature. By itself it is something existing; it is even a person. It is the Holy Spirit. Among men it does not attain to this existential richness, but it is really a society of persons, a community in which free beings are united by the most intimate personal ties.

(d) *Finally, Friendship Is Based upon a "Communion"*

We must correctly understand the meaning of this word: communion. In this respect, theologians give divergent interpretations. Some of them see in it only a "passive communion," that is to say, a similarity, while others insist upon an "active communion," or a pooling together. In fact, the latter includes the first and we believe that it is the true foundation of friendship.

Like all love, friendship is born of similitude. For love tends essentially to unity, and the perfect union of two beings is not possible if there does not exist between them that fundamental similarity which is already a beginning of unity. Two beings that are absolutely dissimilar cannot be united by love. And if it sometimes seems that a certain dissimilarity arouses love, in reality it does not create it but, as St. Thomas remarks, it only adds something piquant that reveals the force of the existing love to the consciousness.[9]

But beyond this "passive" communion which is resemblance, there is another which constitutes the nearest and most immediate foundation of friendship and which is, at the same time, the most proper act and expression of it. This is "active communion," or a sharing of everything, a sharing of the best. This is the reciprocal gift of wealth and above everything of intimacy. Aristotle saw two acts in this communion: the κοινωνία, or the sharing of what is materially possessed—and especially life in common, that permanent co-presence which permits continuous and personal exchanges of all the values of life. This communication of persons, the true communion of beings freely bound together, is the act of friendship, *par excellence*. Friendship here finds its nourishment and is constantly quickened in the ever-deepening discovery of this common treasure to which each of the friends brings his own share according to his measure.

All the strength of friendship and even its possibility rests upon this communion. Without this sharing of intimacy, and without this communication of personal life, there may exist certain forms of love but it will never be friendship.

3. CHARITY IS DIVINE FRIENDSHIP

(a) *Friendship with God*

We know through Revelation that charity (*agape*) is that love with which God loves us and which He has given us as a gift. God's very life—God is charity—coming forth from the heart of God to

[9] We cannot analyze here similarity as a source of love. On this subject precise information will be found in the study already quoted of H. D. Simonin, *op. cit.*

enter into us, charity makes us love God in our turn and love our neighbor with the same unique love. But among the numerous countenances of love, which will be the one that belongs to charity? It cannot be essentially a passionate love. God is a spiritual being who escapes from our senses; He does not directly affect our sensibility. If he solicits our affectivity, it is only in its spiritual part. Charity is spiritual love and not sentimentality; it is a love of the will and not of sensibility. And among the spiritual forms of love, we may affirm that charity is nothing less than friendship with God. But how is this unprecedented thing possible? How can the infinite distance between God and His creature be bridged to such a point? It can only be possible through a free gift of God. He alone can lift man to the level of His familiarity; He alone can create in man the basis for such exchanges.

We know that God has given man this *foundation* for the divine friendship. He communicates His own life to man, His own beatitude. He makes man a son of God, introducing him into the mystery of His intimacy. It is this life so communicated that makes friendship between man and God possible, for it is not sufficient that man be passive; he must bring his own share, and a divine share, to the common friendship. And since he has been made capable of a divine life similar to that of God, it is correct to define charity as a supernatural friendship with God and with all those who participate in the life of God.

We see immediately that this friendship can only come from the divine initiative. God alone can make it possible, for He alone can communicate to man this participation in His life which is the foundation of the charity-friendship. And if He does this, it is in an act that is sovereignly free in a gratuitous gift. It is the very nature of charity conceived as friendship that calls forth the affirmation of St. John: God has first loved us. And since the initial gift comes from God, man can only take his stand on the side of *reciprocity*. Since God has first loved us, we also must love God.

Let us specify how this communication of divine life permits true friendship with God. It is first a "passive communion," since it creates in man a resemblance to God. Man has become similar to God in a very special manner, through a similitude in his very being, and through that image of Himself which God creates in the soul. It is sanctifying grace that makes us true sons of God. But if, through grace, God makes man a being of divine race, if He communicates His life to him, it is to enable man to truly live by this life and to use it as the principle of his personal, vital acts. Grace is a new nature, that is to say, a principle of supernatural operations of knowledge and love which attain directly to God in His intimacy. In this way He gives man that "active communion," that sharing of all things in common, and that life-together, which is the immediate foundation of friendship. Thereafter they have a common treasure, a basis for reciprocal exchanges: the very life of God by which each lives.

Moreover, this is the proper effect of God's love for us. We find again the exact process of the *agape* described by St. John. God loves us first. But His love is creative. It creates the divine life within us and this divine life consists in loving God. Man receives this life in order to live actively by it and to make it the principle of his divine activity. It is the love with which God loves us which creates in us the love with which we love God: there is only one charity.

Consequently, founded upon God's communication of His divine life which becomes the patrimony common to God and to men and which creates reciprocity in man, friendship will be able to exist between man and God under the form of benevolent love. What God, in His charity, really wants is man's good, his true good— eternal life—and He gives it to him. What man wants for God in his reciprocal love is uniquely the good of God, and in a disinterested way. To love God for Himself is to desire that He be infinitely great, infinitely perfect; it is in a word what God wills: that God may be God. It is to will that He be recognized by all men as the only one who is Holy, the only Lord, the only Good. And not with the mental reservation of turning again to ourselves and our interests, but in the upsurge of our whole being towards God whom we desire and love uniquely for Himself.

It is unnecessary to specify that such charity can only be intrinsically supernatural. It rests wholly upon the gratuitous gift of God and upon the communication of divine life. It transports the heart of man beyond all human sentiment to the level of the very life of God.

What we have said up to this point shows sufficiently that charity cannot be reduced to a system of "platonic" relations with God or to a kind of respectful comradeship. God always remains the infinitely perfect; He does not stoop down to our measure but raises us to His level. Friendship with Him must be imbued with infinite respect and complete reverence. But it is a real intimacy, an unbeliev-able familiarity in which the friends share together everything that is most secret and most dear to themselves. It is the absolute gift, without reticences, of the friend to his friend, and is manifested primarily by oneness of will. When I love God, I have no other will than His: "It is no longer I who live, but Christ Who lives in me." And this friendship, if it is not under the influence of the pas-sions, may be passionate as we see it in the saints. It may reach such a degree of intensity that it overflows the spiritual faculties and transports the senses in its movement. It then annihilates everything that is not love, all that is not God, in order to attain to ecstasy. This is doubtless an extreme degree, but it is still in the range of charity.

(b) *Friendship with the Children of God*

Since Scripture reveals to us that charity is one, the *agape* which is in God is communicated to men in order to unite men to God and to unite men to one another. If charity is friendship between man and God, it must also be friendship between men themselves.

There is only one *foundation:* the communication of the divine life. In fraternal charity, everything still comes from God. For this is not human friendship; it is the friendship of the sons of God. To raise himself to the supernatural and divine love of his brothers, man's will, the power of spiritual love, must be lifted up to the divine life. And to realize a true, divine friendship between the sons of God, it is God who must provide the foundation: the divine life shared among men as a common patrimony. Through the effect of the gratuitous love of God, men belong to the same divine race and communicate in a supernatural resemblance. And this divine life is given to them in order that they may live by it together, and that they may have the exchanges of a real, divine intimacy between them. In this way charity's absolute unity is distinctly denoted, as St. John emphasized. The intimate life of God which is love—"as the Father has loved me"—is communicated to men—"I also have loved you"—and He gives it to them in order that it may be the principle of their love for one another—"love one another as I have loved you." We understand that it is God Himself who is the reason for loving our neighbor, for the raison-d'etre of supernatural friend-ship between men is their common participation in the life of God.

Beginning with this foundation, charity among men can be practised as a divine friendship. It will be a disinterested love, a *benevo-lent love*. Surpassing purely natural sympathies, and dominating in-stinctive antipathies, it makes us see other men as sons of God sharing the divine good with ourselves and called with us to the eternal society of the elect. The next man is no longer a stranger; he is our neighbor, our brother. He is a part of ourselves. United to him by this same divine life, we desire his good as we desire our own; in a vigorous way we love our neighbor as ourselves.

The good that we desire for him is especially the supreme good of the fullest possible participation in the divine life. We desire his essential good as a son of God. But he is a son of God who is still involved in the contingencies and necessities of life on earth. He is a son of God who remains a man with human needs. That is why charity must extend its concern to human needs if it is not to be illusory. There must be understanding of the mind and heart and moral and material assistance. The love of God gives men every-thing that is necessary to them on the human level as on the divine level—levels which must not be opposed absolutely, for it is the whole of human nature that is elevated to the divine dignity. And our charity must be similar to God's. Everything that contributes to the true good of our neighbor contributes to his greater participa-tion in divine life. There is not a material and practical charity as distinguished from a spiritual charity. There is only one charity which loves completely.

We have seen that friendship implies reciprocity. But can true charity be realized unless our neighbor, in his turn, loves us? Is this not an excessive requirement?

Let us first note that Our Lord's precept, addressed to everyone, in itself implies this requirement of reciprocity: "Love one another." If we must love our neighbor, he also must love us. Fraternal char-ity, which is the object of Jesus' special commandment, must be a reciprocal love.

Friendship-charity—this condition follows from its nature—can only be realized fully among the children of God, that is to say, those who really participate in divine life. In those who truly live their life as sons of God, the reciprocity of love is assured. And we see why, in the question of charity's objects, it may be said that we must have greater love for those who participate more fully in the life of God. This is the simple application of the principles of a friendship based upon the gift of God. But if charity, in its perfect

state, requires a reciprocal love, how shall we love sinners and
enemies in a charitable way, since in this case there is no love in
return? Can this charity still be defined as friendship?

Benevolent love which we must have for our enemies and all
those who are outside divine friendship must desire their good, and
especially their supernatural good. What we must desire for them
primarily is therefore their entry into the great family of the children
of God. Doubtless the foundation of a divine friendship does not
exist in them, or rather it does not presently exist. But every man,
whoever he may be, is potentially and by vocation a son of God;
he is called to really participate in the divine life, and this is sufficient to include him in our charity. This will not yet be fully or
actually a friendship with regard to him, but by nature it carries
within itself a call to fulfillment, to perfect friendship. It makes us
will our neighbor's good, and more especially his divine life which
is love. All true charity therefore tends to produce love in our neighbor, and notably the reciprocity of fraternal love. And it will not
attain its perfect effect or be completely achieved until our neighbor
will have entered in his turn into the movement of disinterested love.

We must not forget that many obstacles, due to our present condition, paralyse the exercise of perfect charity. Even towards God,
our charity confronts limits that it would like to pass over. We need
not speak of sin, to which our weakness exposes us. The power of
charity ought to be sufficient to keep us from it. But there are all
those conditions of our present state. We cannot live continually in
actual conversation with God. We must eat, sleep and attend to all
the humble duties which life imposes. Certainly each of these acts
can be inspired by love and be inbued with charity, but our hearts
are inevitably distracted from the Beloved. They cannot be occupied
exclusively with God, without interruption. And especially with respect to the perfect union with God, the total and definitive possession is delayed for as long as our earthly life endures. We shall
not possess God immediately or without veils until we reach the
glory of heaven. Perfect friendship with God will only be achieved
in its fulness in the future world.

The same may be said of our fraternal charity. The absence of
the foundation of divine friendship in our neighbor imposes a long
patience upon the desire of our charity, but we know that our desires before God are efficacious at the level of grace. There still
remain the contingencies of life which weigh heavily upon our super-

natural friendship: remoteness, incomprehension that is not even voluntary, the burdens of existence, our faults and those of others. It is only in the eternal society of the elect in which all the children of God will be gathered together, definitively and fully communing in the divine life, liberated from material obstacles and fixed in the perfection of the unique love, that the exercise of fraternal charity will attain its perfect fulfillment.

This is charity in its profound nature: supernatural friendship with God and with the children of God. All that is essential is contained in this definition. The questions which we must still consider are secondary questions. They can only be understood in the light of this bold idea which we can never repeat too often: God has loved us and has called us to friendship with Himself.

II. The Role of Charity in the Christian Life

A. Charity, the Supreme Virtue of the Christian

1. CHARITY IS THE MOST PERFECT VIRTUE

We have up to now considered charity as a friendship between God and man and between man and his neighbor. It must be said that charity is not an entitative reality that exists by itself. In God alone, as we have seen, it is such a reality: it is a divine Person. Created charity is a virtue which resides in man, more specifically in his spiritual, affective faculty, the will. It is a virtue of the will. It is under this aspect that we must now examine it.

All virtues have the function of making human acts intrinsically good. The role of the moral virtues is to make these acts conform with the rule of reason, the norm of the morality of action. In Christian life, of course, it is not a matter of reason left to its lone function as a natural norm, but of reason engaged in the work of grace and conforming perfectly to the supernatural norm of all activity: God as the ultimate and supernatural end.

By nature the theological virtues are even more virtuous than the moral virtues. For they directly touch the supreme rule. God is not only the end of their exercise but their proper object. Faith makes us believe in God and believe God. Hope makes us hope in God and hope for God. Charity makes us love God. If we add that it makes us love our neighbor, it is still for the sake of God and it is God Himself whom we love in other men.

And if, among all the virtues, faith, hope and charity have a particular excellence, it is charity that is preeminent among the theological virtues. The first two are bound up with the condition of the "homo viator"; they will cease with the actual state of man. In heaven the vision and total possession of God will put an end to faith and hope. But charity is eternal because it is the love of God which will not cease with the vision but find its perfect development. Moreover, if we only consider the actual state of these three virtues, we must recognize that charity has a superiority which is derived from its own structure. Faith and hope have God as their object, but only in so far as we obtain something from Him. Faith adheres to God in order to draw forth infallible knowledge from divine truth. Hope is dependent on God in order to obtain beatitude from Him, the possession of God. But charity, on the contrary, attains to God in a movement that is absolutely simple. It loves God only in order to love God. Its yearning is achieved and established in this very act. It loves God for His own sake and it abides in Him; it finds its rest in this love. It lays hold of God in a simple act—God for the sake of God. And since the perfection of a virtue is to attain to the rule of all good action, no virtue can be the rival of charity which takes possession of the supreme rule of action in an incomparable way.

2. CHARITY TRANSFIGURES ALL THE VIRTUES

The superiority of charity over all the virtues would be sufficient to indicate the preponderant role which it must play in the Christian's life. All the other virtues merely prepare the ground for charity in one way or another. They put order into the moral life or they make for adherence to God in knowledge and confident desire, but the whole edifice is crowned by this disinterested love of God. Aspire to all the virtues and all the superior gifts, recommended St. Paul, but seek especially charity. But the excellence of charity is still more evident in the influence which it exercises upon all the divisions of the moral life. Faith without charity is nothing, according to the witness of St. Paul; hope without charity is mutilated and dead. And we may go so far as to say that there is no true virtue, perfectly stable in its own nature, without charity.

Virtue, in fact, orders things to the good. We can speak of two kinds of goods: the essential supreme good, which is God, and the particular good limited to a determined domain. But even the latter has value only as a good in so far as it is itself related to the supreme good, if it is directly ordered to that good, or at least, does not contradict it. If I desire a thing that is good in itself but which, in the concrete circumstances, is in opposition to the ultimate end, this good is in reality a false good, empty of all real goodness. Particular goods are the object of different virtues. These virtues must produce good acts pursuing a particular good end (giving what is due to others, mastering our passions, etc.). And since these particular ends only derive their goodness from their conformity with the last end, it is necessary that the desire for the last end be firmly assured in order that these different virtues may be solidly established. There must be some other virtue which fixes man, in all his action, in regard to the supreme end. Charity is this virtue precisely. It is charity that establishes me in God and which makes me tend, through all my behavior, towards this final end of my life. It is charity which assures the seeking for God in everything.

Without charity, therefore, there can be particular virtues conducing to a particular good. Every act that is done outside of charity is not *ipso facto* a morally bad act. But such acts are lacking that substantial foundation of all virtuous activity which is the firm and ardent desire, in everything, for the supreme end: God. Only charity can assure this order, this stability of the virtues. Thus we see how it introduces its efficaciousness into the most secret workings of each virtue. Beyond their proper object and beyond their particular end, it makes the other virtues penetrate into the movement towards its own proper end. It passes quietly into the action of the virtues; it nourishes them interiorly and dilates them beyond the limits of their normal efficacy by making them tend, through their immediate end, to God Himself. Doubtless, it does not destroy the respective nature of each virtue in any way, for it respects the originality and autonomy of each; but to the particular virtue's essential orientation towards a limited proper object, it adds that new and incomparably richer orientation towards the supreme end.[10]

Therefore charity certainly appears not only as the principal virtue of the Christian, but as the bond and profoundest principle of unity of the whole virtuous life. It is exactly the "bond of the virtues," the "bond of perfection." When a Christian performs an act

[10] It is because it thus brings a new specification to each virtue in ordaining it to its end (the end being the principal specificator or "form" of moral acts) that it is said of charity that it is the "form" of all the virtues.

of temperance or obedience, he is also making an act of charity; he is then showing forth his love for God. Charity, the virtue that is aside from all others, penetrates all the virtues and raises and transforms them in order that they may be directed to the love of God.

We can now see the whole difference between simple humanism and Christian perfection. The man who only wants to be a complete man and reach the sound equilibrium of being concerned about the development of all his natural resources, is bound to practice all the moral virtues which, alone, can assure this human perfection. He will aim for perfect integrity in the scrupulous respect for everything that belongs properly to other men; and for strict justice, respect for the Supreme Being, filial piety and civic spirit, gratitude, affability, in the full mastery of his passions by temperance and strength of soul, and in a wise prudence that acts in good earnest. In this way he will be able to realize the ideal type of just man (but we know that even human perfection is hardly possible without the help of grace to heal the infirmities of our fallen nature).

For the Christian the ideal of perfection is very different: it is love. Doubtless love does not dispense him from a perfect integrity. On the contrary, charity will pursue its requirements in all the domains of the moral life, but it transforms the orientation of this ideal of justice because it relates everything to love. It is love that is the great value in life and all the rest is in the service of love. Perfection's point of equilibrium and its center of gravity is displaced, even its very meaning is transfigured. The ideal is no longer to be a perfect just man; it is to resemble God and be united to Him in the most intimate intercourse. A Francis of Assisi can hardly be presented as a perfect achievement of humanism; he is however an accomplished type of Christian perfection: he is the man who lives only for God.

Transporting all the moral virtues in its movement, charity elevates them to the point that they become principles of supernatural merit, for it is charity which is the true source of merit, and it is from charity that the other virtues hold their supernatural value. This is not the place to define the nature of merit. Let us simply remember that merit requires a double simultaneous principle: the relation of efficacy established by God alone between our virtuous acts and the eternal reward to which they truly give right thanks to divine liberality, and the use of our liberty: in fact only acts that are fully free can be rewarded. For this double reason, it is certainly charity which is the immediate principle of merit. It is charity that directs all our acts to the love of God and to the eternal possession of God, the fruit of love. Whether in the payment of our debts or in reprimanding our sensuality or in a movement of anger, charity makes of them acts of love for God and assures their explicit reference to God. If the love is disinterested, it still has the right to possession of the beloved. And on the other hand, as far as liberty is concerned, nothing is less forced than what is done through love. It is through their inclusion in the movement of charity that even the most humble acts of simple integrity become meritorious for eternal life.

3. BEYOND THE MORAL LIFE

If therefore charity entirely transfigures the exercise of the virtues, it far surpasses the whole moral life. As a matter of fact, the latter is still only the a-b-c of the Christian life. Doubtless, as we have just said, it is a divine life because it has been transformed by supernatural love, but it is beyond the properly moral domain that charity will deploy its most original resources. We must be prudent, temperate, just and courageous; in a word, we must practice all the virtues and we must practice them for the love of God. But once these moral bases have been assured (and it is charity itself which assures them perfectly) charity can then give full amplitude to its own life.

Here we pass over the frontier that separates the ascetical life from the mystical life. When it reigns as mistress, charity introduces us into the mysterious kingdom of the mystical life. Alas! too many Christians imagine that they have realized their vocation when they have reached the point of detachment from sin and are especially exercising the moral virtues. They resemble the man who, posesssing the rudiments of grammar, would imagine himself to be a poet. But the whole divine life in its highest and most characteristic exercise is still to be lived. It is now at least that charity will be able to display itself without reticence.

It is charity which will induce faith to go beyond the simple acceptance of revealed truths by the intelligence to examine with love and persistence the secrets of the beloved. Never again will faith be satisfied; it will want to know everything about this God who has shown Himself to faith "through an enigma." And hope, besides the new dimension which it acquires and which we have indicated in its regard, will become impatient to possess the One who has promised

Himself to it. There will be no rest for hope until time has been abolished and the long awaited Day appears. And especially charity will strive with all its strength towards that which is its supreme desire and accomplished act: total and indestructible union with the God of love. It knows that He will not be perfectly possessed until this life is over, but it also knows that it can attain to an unbelievable union even here below. It desires intimacy with God without reserve; it wants to lose itself in Him, and be wholly absorbed in His infinity, no longer having any other will than His, or other joys than are found in Him. It wants God, God alone and completely. And reaching the limit of what mortal flesh can bear of love, the soul discards the heavy companion which can no longer follow it. It is then thrown outside itself through the violence of its love; it experiences ecstasy.

At this point we are not able to say more. We must let the saints speak who have approached so near to the secrets of God.

B. Origin, Growth and Disappearance of Charity

1. Charity is a love (this is the act) and it is a virtue of love (permanent principle of action). Therefore its principle and place within us is the affective faculty, and more exactly that affective faculty which alone is capable of appreciating a spiritual good: the will.

But man cannot give himself charity. Based upon the communication by God of His own life, it absolutely transcends the natural order and all human powers. God alone can give it; it is the Holy Spirit who diffuses it in our hearts. We receive it in baptism with grace and all the infused virtues; it is given back to us after sin through the sacrament of penance, always through an effect of God's magnanimity. Consequently it follows that this gift, gratuitous and free, is not measured by the natural qualities of the subject who benefits from it. Doubtless certain dispositions of soul are required to welcome this gift, but these dispositions are themselves under the motion of grace; they are already the effects of grace, clearly distinct from natural capacities and talents.

2. Charity is not given once and for all and fixed in an unchangeable degree. It has its own life and therefore its progress and development. Scripture reveals to us the possibility of charity's growth. St. Paul wrote to the Ephesians: "Rather are we to practice the truth in love, and so grow up in all things in him who is the head,

Christ" (4:15). And to the Philippians: "And this I pray, that your charity may more and more abound" (1:9). The Council of Trent solemnly defined this truth (Session VI, canons 24 and 32).

This progress is perfectly proper to our condition of "viatores," travelers journeying towards God—the end of our earthly pilgrimage. It is especially charity which permits us to approach God progressively and to enter always more fully into His intimacy.

How is the increase of this infused virtue to be accomplished? It does not increase quantitatively as though a new portion of charity were added to the existing charity. Charity is one. Its progress will be marked by a deeper implanting in the soul and by a close possession of our power of affectation. Knowledge, for example, can grow not only in intensity, by a more acute penetration of truth, but also in quantity or extension, by reaching out to other objects and new domains. But charity, on the contrary, must attain to the totality of its object as soon as it exists or it will deny itself. But it will progress by increasing its fervor, by making itself more generous and by invading our whole being more completely. However, since it is infused in us by God alone, we cannot directly intensify our own charity ourselves. We can only obtain this growth from God. And we obtain it through the sacraments, especially the Eucharist which unites us to Christ in an incomparable manner, and through devout and persevering prayer. We also obtain it by way of merit. For our acts of charity (the acts that follow directly from charity and those which are produced by the other virtues which charity inspires and vivifies) give us the right, in the service of God, to an increase of our charity. Does this mean that every supernatural act *ipso facto* merits this increase? No, it does not. But they all prepare us for this, although the growth is only accorded by God when man is ready for a more fervent act of charity.

A comparison with the increase of naturally acquired habits can enlighten us here. The source and mode of growth will obviously be very different, for in the case of acquired habits, the repetition of the acts automatically engenders and develops the habit while for charity, as for all the infused virtues, it is God alone who gives the origin and the growth. But we can find three kinds of acts in charity as in the domain of the natural habits: a) successive acts of equal intensity, at least approximately; b) successive acts of decreasing intensity; c) successive acts of increasing intensity. The first only maintain the habit. Thus charity can remain uniform, always the same. The second, when pertaining to acquired habits, runs the risk of weakening the habit by leaving more activity to the forces which tend to destroy it. Consequently, charity can let its fervor diminish; it becomes less generous, less eager. And yet, contrary to natural habits, and because it comes from God, charity is not directly impaired by this slackening but obviously it has no tendency to growth. Finally, the most intense acts naturally reinforce an acquired virtue. They strengthen the will and favor the establishment of the virtue. Charity knows these impulses of a generosity which it had not yet attained. Circumstances, difficulties and temptations place charity in situations that make it surpass itself in order to be perfectly faithful. Then it bounds forward towards God with a new fervor.

Such are the different species in which one can classify the acts of charity. What is their effect with regard to its growth? Let us note that every act of charity has a real supernatural merit. But we are now seeking to know if every act of charity merits specifically an increase of the virtue of charity. We can sum up the solution of this problem very briefly as follows (this question is moreover the object of controversies which we cannot analyze). Every act of charity, whether equal to the degree possessed before, or whether "remittent," that is to say, of less intensity, merits an increase of charity and disposes to it. This was the declaration of the Council of Trent (Session VI, ch. 16), based on the text of Matthew, 10:42: "And whoever gives to one of these little ones but a cup of cold water to drink because he is a disciple, amen I say to you, he shall not lose his reward." But each act of charity does not merit an actual or immediate increase. This would only result from a more intense act which, inclined by the dispositions maintained in preceding acts, now effectvely realizes (always by way of merit) this increase which the whole life of charity desired and prepared for, even when it was sustaining the weight of ordinary routine.

And this increase can be pursued indefinitely; it has no limit. It embraces, in fact, the movement of the growth of grace which is its source. The latter being a participation, necessarily limited in a finite being, of the infinite divine life, cannot, by definition, attain to satiety. That is why the Christian can grow in charity indefinitely; at no moment of his life is he permitted to stop and say, "I have reached the summit." He must always keep in mind the counsel of Our Lord, "You therefore are to be perfect, even as your heavenly Father is perfect."

3. Just as charity can increase, it can also diminish and even disappear. It is not directly and automatically lessened by the infrequency of the acts, nor even by venial sin, for it is God who puts it into the soul and who maintains it there. However, infrequency creates a harmful disposition which can indirectly lead it to ruin, for human weakness is then felt more acutely and there is the risk of falling into serious sin.

The latter destroys all charity with a single blow. Faith and hope, for example, are not annihilated except by an act which is directly opposed to them (heresy or despair, to mention only these). They can continue to exist, but as imperfect virtues, in the soul that is in a state of sin. But any grave sin against any virtue whatever is directly opposed to charity because it substitutes another end for God whom charity makes us love above all else. It is the very negation of charity. There is absolute incompatibility between the rejection of God as our last end, in which sin consists, and that love of God for Himself above everything else.

III. The Object of Charity

Charity is one and its object is one. It is the love in supernatural friendship which unites us to God and makes us desire the divine good. But this good can be considered as being in God Himself and in all those who share in it. For we have seen that it is by reason of its proper nature that charity is founded upon God's communication of His intimate life and divine beatitude to men. Furthermore, to love God is to love what He loves and to will what He wills. It is to identify our will with His: *idem velle, idem nolle.* God desires not only His own good but also the good of all those whom He calls to His divine life. That is why the object of charity is one as charity itself is one. To love God and to love our neighbor is the same thing. We cannot love God charitably without extending that love to our neighbor, and we cannot love our neighbor charitably without desiring the divine good for him, with God and like God. Therefore God is the reason for loving our neighbor.

Without losing sight of this profound unity of charity, we must distinguish the particular objects.

1. THE PARTICULAR OBJECTS OF CHARITY

The first and essential object is God considered in Himself. From God charity will be extended to "everything that is of God."

(a) First of all with respect to *persons*. They are objects of charity inasmuch as they participate actually, or at least inasmuch as they are called to participate, in divine life.

1. *Charity for Oneself*

"Well ordered charity begins with oneself." This old popular saying is full of good sense and wisdom. We have defined charity as a friendship. But friendship supposes a multiplicity of persons. There must at least be two. If therefore it is legitimate and necessary that man love himself first and that he desire his own good (without which there is no other possible basis for love whatever), how can he love himself with charity?

We know that the supreme act of friendship is the perfect union of those who love each other; this is the unity to which love essentially tends. But what greater unity can be found than man's unity with himself? The union of friendship tends, in reality, to imitate and reproduce this fundamental unity of the person which remains the type and ideal of the perfect union. And that is why the golden rule of friendship is inspired by this typical unity: to love our neighbor as another self.

We can therefore love ourselves by way of charity and we can do it by wishing for ourselves what God wishes: the most total participation in divine life. Then we love ourselves truly as God, in God and for God.

2. *Our Neighbor in General*

If our neighbor is a son of God, his inclusion in the object of charity is obvious. It is with the same act of love that we love him and love God; and by our neighbor we must understand not only our human brethren but also the angels with whom we form the unique and great family of children of God. There would be many things to say and to learn from the experience of the saints in regard to this friendship with the angels and especially with our guardian angel who enters only rarely into the perspectives of our conscious charity.

3. *Even the Sinners*

They also have a right to our charity because they are capable of sharing in the gift of God. Doubtless they are not presently established in the divine life, but they are called to it as we are. God "does not want their death but that they should live" this life of children of God. This is the supreme good which we must desire for them with all our powers, but the sin which is in them must arouse our hatred for we must love men and detest the evil which is in them. If they identify themselves with evil in any way, they must then become the object of our hatred. Such is the case with demons.

4. *Even Our Enemies*

By enemies should be understood not those for whom we feel an instinctive aversion, but those who wish or do us harm. We cannot love them with charity in so far as they are our enemies, for this would be, on our part, to approve and love the evil. But we must love them because they are men and are therefore marked as we are by the vocation of children of God.

What degree of charity must we show them? The precept of charity for everyone obliges us to include them in our common charity. We cannot exclude them from our benevolence. But certain circumstances (cases of necessity, grave danger or vocational obligations) may require our particular, explicit and very personal charity in their regard. The perfection of charity, which goes beyond the minimum required by the precept, requires this special charity for our enemies even outside cases of necessity.

(b) *Certain things* themselves, other than persons, can and must be part of the object of our charity.

1. First of all it is *charity* as such. For we can love the love which we feel for someone, and take pleasure in it and find our joy in it. In friendship we love both the friend and the friendship which we have for him, and notably the good that we desire for him. We will therefore love in a charitable way the persons for whom we desire the supernatural good, but also we shall love this good in our neighbor, this divine life in him.

2. *Our own body* must be loved with charity. This is the condemnation of the absolute hatred of the carnal which always proceeds from the musty decay of Manicheism. The body is an integral part of our being; it is the servant and the partner of the soul. And the revelation of the future resurrection has taught us to esteem this creature of God for which a place will be made in the glory of the spiritual Kingdom.

We must love the body with charity and not with a purely instinctive or dissolute love. We must want to integrate the whole

bodily order within the life of supernatural love. It is here that asceticism finds its place in a sound Christian equilibrium, for the
body is marked, in our present condition, with the seal of concupiscence. While it ought to be an instrument of love, it easily becomes an occasion of sin, a permanent temptation. Asceticism and
particularly corporal penitence cannot therefore be an absolute
value; they are a means of integrating the whole of man within our
love, and they are the necessary exercise of an authentic charity.

3. Finally, nothing less than the *cosmic order* in its ensemble is
encompassed by our charity. We have said that we must love the
spiritual good of our neighbor, his participation in the divine life.
But even material goods can be the object of this charity as the
necessary assistants of the supernatural life. It cannot be said, certainly, that we bind ourselves by friendship or charity to irrational
beings, for only persons are worthy of that, but we love in them the
manifestation of God's glory and their usefulness to our neighbor.
In all things the Christian must be able to recognize and love God.

2. THE ORDER OF CHARITY

All these objects are not offered pell-mell to our love. There is an
order of charity, a hierarchy in its objects. And, as in every hierarchy, the elements will be classified and subordinated according to
their degree of proximity to the principle which governs the whole
series.

First of all there will be an *objective order* in which the objects
will be disposed one above the other according to their degree of
excellence. In this case the principle is God, the supreme object of
esteem and appreciation. He will be the object of charity, *par excellence*. Then the other beings will be esteemed and loved preferen-
tially, according to their proximity to God. Here, briefly, it is sanctity which must be the normative measure of our charity.

But along with this objective order in which everything is considered in its relationship to the principal object, God, who must be
esteemed and valued above every other good, there is a *subjective
order*. For love is a relation between two terms: the subject and the
object. The subject is also a principle of an order in which he will
command a whole hierarchy which could be called not one of esteem
or excellence but of affective intensity. This is doubtless a concession
to nature, but we know that the order of grace does not destroy the

natural order, but is built upon it. It is proximity to the loving subject that will govern this subjective hierarchy.

This dual principle is clear but its practical application presents
several difficulties. Moreover, we cannot measure with mathematical
precision the degree of charity that is suitable for everyone. For
charity is a living reality and it would be fruitless to encumber it with
meticulous calculations. It is good-will, an impulse of the heart established in grace, and not the work of a grocer.

1. *God* naturally has His place at the highest level. He must occupy the supreme degree in our esteem as in the intensity of our
love. We must love Him more than ourselves, and more than those
who are naturally dearest to us: "He who loves father or mother
more than me. . . ." For "God within me is more myself than I am."

2. We must love *ourselves* more than our neighbor. Let us understand this clearly: we are here comparing our spiritual being, our
soul, to that of our neighbor, and we must prefer our own spiritual
good to that of our neighbor. For, on the one hand, it is our common participation in the divine life which is the foundation of our
charity for our neighbor; and within ourselves the unity is absolute.
On the other hand, the natural movement inclines us to love ourselves first, quite normally and legitimately. There is no excessive
egotism in this, for we have the responsibility for our own destiny
before all else.

But we must love the spiritual good of others more than our material good. This is a question of excellence in fact and the spiritual
good ranks first. Even in the subjective order, our neighbor's soul
is nearer our soul than is our material body at the level of divine
friendship. In practice, the necessary preeminence is not always easy
to discern. Are we always bound to sacrifice our corporal life for
the soul of our neighbor? If every man has the duty of taking care
of his own life and health, he is not, on the contrary, directly responsible for the salvation of his neighbor except in certain extreme
cases, or if, by profession, he has the cure of souls. The spontaneous
sacrifice of life for the salvation of others derives from the perfection of charity rather than from the obligatory precept.

3. Finally, our love of neighbor has its *preferences* as Scripture
shows us (cf. I Tim. 5:8). This is quite normal. Charity does not
make man a kind of spiritual robot who distributes his love in equal
portions to every comer. We must love in God, for God and like
God. We know that God Himself has His preferences and He has

shown His predilection. Who would dare to claim to be loved by God as much as was the Virgin Mary? Our charity must therefore embrace the divine preferences. It must have greater esteem for those who are nearer to God, the saints. Furthermore, we are placed in the world, in the midst of a network of personal relations, of which each one has its original character with the beings who surround us (ties of kinship, particular affinities, social or spiritual functions). The intensity of our charity will vary according to the intimacy which unites us quite normally to our neighbor. If we desire a greater good for those who are worthy of it, it is quite natural that our love be more ardent and more earnest in regard to those who are nearest to us, even if they are further from God.

Charity will have its preferences even in Paradise, but there, each person being definitively established in his holiness, it is the objective order which will completely prevail, or rather the two orders will coincide. Charity will then have perfectly realized its essential order, and each of the elect will appear in the radiation of his divine splendor. The particular ties which the necessities of our earthly condition created will no longer be relevant: "they shall be like the angels in heaven." But the profound and holy affinities of this world will not disappear. The exchanges of the blessed life will remain marked by that very personal intimacy of lives that were united by an eternal divine friendship even while on earth.

IV. The Activities of Charity

We must still consider the acts by which charity is expressed and the fruits which it produces in the soul, and then the sins that are opposed to charity.

1. THE PROPER ACT OF CHARITY: TO LOVE

What is the act of charity par excellence? Charity is a divine friendship, a special relationship between the two terms: God and the Christian. It is a reality which personally engages each of these beings, one toward the other. Here we want to determine the manner in which the Christian must express his divine charity.

He loves and at the same time he is loved. We learn from St. John that the Christian can only love God with friendship because he is loved by God, but from man's point of view which of these two movements will constitute the proper act of his personal charity? Beyond doubt it is his active love. He cannot be satisfied with letting himself be loved by God, or with continually receiving while limiting himself to the praise of God's tireless generosity. He must love in his turn. Besides, we have seen that this is the characteristic effect of the love which God has for us; it is the fruit of its efficacy. And it is also the primordial requirement of true friendship. If one of the friends merely consents to being loved by the other, he does not have right to the name of friend, for he is lacking that indispensable reciprocity.

In our friendship with God, we know that the initiative comes from above. It is He Who first loved us. It is an act of charity to accept this love, but we would be raising obstacles to the divine love if we prevented it from producing its proper effect within us—that we should love God in our turn. The act of charity par excellence is therefore to love. To love in the great and small occasions. We must not want to reserve the manifestations of our charity for rare cases in which we would be driven to heroism. True love is impatient to show itself and it is often in the small things of every day that it is most needed. Does not love have a thousand turns and delicacies which make its smallest gestures priceless?

How must we love God? We have fully answered this question in our analysis of charity as friendship. We must love Him for Himself and above everything else, knowing well that we will never be able to love Him as much as He deserves. We desire His good, His glory, with all our strength and in everything. Charity makes us ready to give our life for God or to use it in His service in the course of our days. It makes us yearn with the whole strength of our soul for the most intimate union and the deepest identification that is possible with God. The summit of love is this fusion of our being with the being of God. It is this mystery of unity that cannot be expressed and for which the mystics have devised the most astonishing images. At the threshold of this mystery all words are surpassed and ideas are impotent. It is beyond telling, ineffable.

2. THE INTERIOR FRUITS OF CHARITY

We can only indicate briefly these fruits which charity produces in the soul without considering their profound nature or their multiple ramifications.

(a) *Joy*

It is primarily joy, that interior gladdening and spiritual rejoicing that is more subtle and more noble than pleasure, which is born in us by the possession of a beloved good, which we have desired and finally attained. And as the good which we desire by our charity is that of God and our neighbor, it is our awareness of their happiness which creates joy within us.

We rejoice that God is God; we praise His goodness and His glory, and we find our purest joy in the contemplation of His infinite perfections. But this joy is not yet absolute. For if on God's side the good is unfailing, we for our part always feel ourselves in exile and exposed to the sin that would deprive us of God. That is why there remains in the midst of our joy, as if to mark the imperfection of our present condition, that sadness at the delay imposed on our definitive union with God and that other sadness of knowing that we are not saints.

(b) *Peace*

Charity is the source of interior peace, that is to say, perfect unity within self. It is charity that achieves the unity of the soul. The latter is no longer torn to pieces by divergent and contradictory desires since all our affections are related to the supreme and unique object, God. Here again perfection is not accessible in this life, and the conquest of interior peace requires many efforts and many beginnings.

Charity is also the principle of true peace among men. It unifies the wills since its object is the good of others. It makes us desire what our neighbor essentially desires. If the reign of charity were achieved, there is no doubt that peace would be assured between men and between nations.

(c) *Mercy*

But it could be objected that all these fruits of charity suppose a world in which everything is perfect, where at least we would only meet with good will and physical and moral health. This is a utopian world, for evil exists and misery is established and encrusted among men. Must charity close its eyes in order to safeguard joy and interior peace? Not at all, for this would destroy charity. It is the good of our neighbor that charity is seeking. Suddenly it confronts his suffering and distress; then charity gives birth to mercy. This is the virtue of the compassionate heart which feels the pain that over-whelms our neighbor and which shares the pain with those who suffer. This is a very special virtue, distinct from charity but inspired by it, which introduces the reality of suffering into the movement of love. It is this virtue which makes us put St. Paul's counsel into prac-tice: "Rejoice with those who rejoice; weep with those who weep" (Rom. 12:15).

3. THE EXTERIOR ACTIVITIES OF CHARITY

If love impels us to will the good of those whom we love, it can-not be a theoretical and inefficacious sentiment; it cannot remain enclosed within the heart. The good that it desires must be effec-tively achieved. By charity we desire our neighbor's good and we do good to him.

Beneficence is therefore, in one way or another, the general ac-tivity in which charity will be able to expand in its practical exercise. This act can take many forms, among them we must indicate prin-cipally the *works of mercy*.

It is customary to distinguish the spiritual and corporal works of mercy. The corporal works: to feed the hungry, to give drink to the thirsty, to clothe the naked, to shelter the stranger, to visit the sick, to ransom captives and bury the dead. The spiritual works: to instruct the ignorant, to counsel the doubting, to console the afflicted, to correct faults, to forgive offenses, to bear with other men and to pray for everyone.

(a) *Alms*

At this point we must consider alms-giving, an evidence of mercy inspired by charity. We cannot go deeply into such an important problem in a few lines. Let us therefore simply indicate the great principles of the duty of alms-giving.

It is a grave obligation to give alms. St. Matthew's well known text (25:41, and ff.) describing the Last Judgment is an irrecusable witness for it: "For I was hungry, and you did not give me to eat." But how can we determine the conditions of this obligation?

The Christian is bound by charity to give his excess as alms, that is to say, whatever remains after his own needs are assured. Ob-viously it would be necessary to define exactly what these needs may be and where excess begins. But let us say only that we cannot here establish any universal norm. Each Christian must measure, in conscience and loyalty, what is necessary for himself and for those who are dependent upon him, not only for a strict subsistence, but according to his state of life and his social obligations. For this he must let himself be guided by the true meaning of charity and fraternal assistance. It is certain that a Christian who would want to be prepared for all possible eventualities through an excess of prudence, and who, for this reason, would deny having any excess, would fail in his duty of charity.

This excess must be given to the needy, that is to say, to those who cannot provide for an extreme or grave need without the help of others. But we cannot emphasize too greatly the quality of alms-giving. Most often it is the manner of giving that reveals true charity. Alms-giving must be imbued with love and thoughtfulness. It should truly be the act of a brother who helps his brethren.

(b) *The Fraternal Reprimand*

As we have rapidly examined the duty of alms-giving among the corporal works of mercy, let us add a word concerning a spiritual work of mercy: reprimands or better, fraternal correction.

This is a duty of charity and not merely a facultative gesture. Since charity obliges us to seek our neighbor's good, it requires that we be able to intervene, in good earnest and with love, to preserve our neighbor from the evil in which we see him sinking. "But if thy brother sin against thee, go and show him his fault, between thee and him alone. If he listen to thee, thou hast won thy brother" (Mt. 18:15).

However, we must not see in this precept an invitation to be forever moralizing. Here more than elsewhere a wise discernment is necessary. We must take into account the hope of success, the circumstances and dispositions, and act with the greatest considerateness. A smile and real affection make so many things acceptable! Fraternal reprimands must never aim at alleviating a soul possessed by untimely zeal, nor serve as an outlet for enervation. Its only purpose must be to serve the good of our neighbor.

V. Sins Against Charity

To charity and the virtues that flow from it are opposed certain vices which will be manifested by acts which go contrary to charity. We can classify them according to their relationship of contradiction with the various acts of charity which we have indicated. Hatred is opposed to love, the act of charity par excellence. Malignant sadness and envy are opposed to joy. And opposed to peace are all the forms of discord from interior disagreements to brawls and warfare; to acts of beneficence may be opposed the evil-doing and ill-will that are caused in general by injustice. We shall rapidly review these sins against charity, but we shall omit whatever actually belongs to the domain of justice, as for instance, warfare.

1. HATRED

Hating is the exact opposite of loving. It is therefore the sin which is the most directly opposed to charity. And as the object of charity is God and our neighbor, we will find this dual object exposed to hatred.

It seems almost impossible to hate God. One can only hate what is evil, or at least what is considered evil. How could God appear as an evil? Doubtless, for anyone who would see God as He is, the very essence of Love and Goodness, hate would be impossible; and even if a man considered only the effects of the divine action that are perceptible to us, it seems incredible that he could fall into this aberration since we know that everything that God wills and does can only be for our happiness.

Of course this sentiment is not born spontaneously. It witnesses to the paroxysm that may be reached by a will engaged in evil and stubbornly attached to its sin, for God is the One who forbids evil and who punishes it. When man sinks so deeply into sin that his will is completely drowned in it, then God is no longer anything but an enemy to him, the One whom he would like to destroy, and as charity is the summit of the whole supernatural life and also the source of every solid virtue, so likewise the hatred of God is the extreme point of the whole movement of sin and the principle which can impel man towards every monstrosity.

If hatred of God is the gravest of all sins, hatred of our neighbor can claim the same sad primacy among the sins that may be committed against our neighbor. From the material point of view, the evil which we really do to others is doubtless graver than this intimate sentiment of the soul, but the latter establishes the soul in a more profound and more permanent disorder which will normally find expression in evil-doing.

2. SADNESS

This is not the reasonable and legitimate sadness which we have seen mingled with joy for as long as our exile endures; on the contrary, this is an evil sadness that is directly opposed to joy. It is this sentiment that makes us grieve over a true good which, by depravity of the mind, we consider as an evil. Such is the sin of the man who finds the divine good depressing. Instead of finding his joy in it, exulting and rejoicing in the goodness of God, and in His mercy and glory, he only feels vexation and resents God for being so perfect. A feeling of this kind cannot fail to have the most serious repercussions upon the spiritual life, for it makes God and divine things distasteful.

Less grave however is the sadness felt by many Christians when they are inwardly aware of an attraction toward forbidden fruits. Their souls are divided between contradictory desires, the weight of the flesh and their weakness struggling against their aspirations toward the good. They experience a kind of weariness, a beginning of aversion in regard to spiritual things. But these are movements that do not yet engage the will. However, they must be resisted with strength and attentiveness, for this is the open road to distaste for God if we are not vigilant.

3. ENVY

Envy, which must not be confused with common jealousy or the taste for rivalry, is exactly the sadness that is felt when we contemplate our neighbor's good. The success of others, their qualities and their achievements appear to us as a personal injury, or an evil thing. Or else we rejoice when something harmful happens to them; we applaud their failures and we experience an evil joy because of their tribulations. This is because we have the idea that everything that raises others will lower ourselves. We see clearly that this attitude is directly opposed to charity which enables us to see our own good in the happiness of others and makes us find our joy in it.

Envy is then manifested by the following petty and disloyal attacks: accusations, evil gossip, disparagement, and malicious criticism. All these progeny show that envy is found at the source of many evils and that it is rightly counted among the capital sins.

4. DISCORD AND ITS CONSEQUENCES

To the peace of charity is opposed the discord which is followed by a whole series of after-effects: disputes, altercations, brawls, etc. While charity wants to achieve concord between men by placing in the first rank of their preoccupations the divine good in the love of which all wills communicate, discord, in its perfect malice, is the voluntary dissidence which deliberately breaks up this unity.

We must not liken this sin against charity to difference of opinion in which each man, actually pursuing the same essential end, personally judges the opportuness of the means. In itself, this divergence is in no way opposed to union in charity. But it could impair it if it foundered in obstinacy.

One form of discord that is particularly grave is the one that tears asunder the unity of the Church: *schism.* This has a direct bearing upon charity. It breaks the union in which all the members of the Body of Christ are bound together under the authority of the Sovereign Pontiff, and it renounces the communion of all the sons of God. Moreover, it often degenerates into heresy, as history proves, and even when the faith remains intact, charity has been destroyed.

A member of Christ has voluntarily withdrawn from the community; brothers have denied the divine fraternity. An obstinate blindness and a hardening pride against a demanding discipline caused the initial break and the gulf continues to widen.

5. SCANDAL

We know the severe condemnation which the Gospel pronounced against scandal: "Woe to the man through whom scandal does come!" Doubtless this was one of the sins, including hypocrisy, against which Christ rose up with the greatest violence. This is because scandal possesses a very special malice. Not satisfied with rejecting God and revolting against Him, the sinner now incites others, by his counsels and example, to turn away from God. And this is certainly a sin that is directly opposed to charity.

There is a distinction between active scandal, considered in the one who scandalizes—either direct, if the sin of others is willed, or indirect if the sin is only contemplated—and passive scandal, considered in the one who experiences it. The sin can therefore exist in both the one who lets himself be led into evil and the one who incites others to commit sin. But even if there is no real passive scandal, the active scandal persists and continues to be sinful because the force inciting to evil is not irresistible.

Normally, the man who is firmly attached to God does not let himself be turned away from the right way by the bad example or solicitations of others. But the weak are exposed to this, and they are at the mercy of temptations and the influence of other men. As for the "scandal of the Pharisees," it is not a real scandal but is only an evil pretext invoked hypocritically to justify sin.

Active scandal, if it be direct, voluntarily seeking the fall of others, is a grave fault in itself. It is opposed to charity and also to the virtue that is affected by the committed sin. It therefore has a double malice. Indirect active scandal, which does not expressly will the sin of others, but foresees and accepts it, is also guilty unless the act that is done with the risk of scandal is intrinsically good or at least indifferent, if it be related to an honest end and if there be a serious reason for doing it. In this case, if possible, one must act secretly in order to limit the possible harm of the act that must be done.

We must therefore, by charity, always think of the weakness of those who might judge us badly through ignorance or the failure to discern our purpose, and avoid the very appearance of evil as far as possible. In regard to the scandal of the pharisees, it is unnecessary to say that it should not trouble the consciences of Christians in any way.

VI. The Gift of Wisdom

Something more must be said about the gift of Wisdom which is attached to charity. We shall show primarily how this gift of the Holy Spirit maintains very close relations with charity.

The intellectual virtue of wisdom must be distinguished from the gift, but we can discover in the virtue several important indications. Of the two "virtues" of the speculative intellect, knowledge and wisdom, the first judges things in a highly determined domain (mathematics, psychology, etc.), by their first causes, in order to disclose their ultimate explanation; the second judges everything from the highest and most universal point of view. It is the deepest and most complete virtue of knowing.

We find this same character of universality in the gift of wisdom. It will judge all things: beings, events, etc., but according to a mode and under an aspect utterly superior to those of all human knowledge. This gift accorded by God to the intelligence pertains directly to the order of knowledge and not of affection; it is not however a purely intellectual penetration by the mind. It is a manner of seeing all things, similar to the way that God sees them, and the most excellent act of the gift of wisdom consists in judging divine things themselves.

The mode of this knowledge gives its specific character to wisdom. It judges divine things not by a knowledge acquired by study, nor by a passing illumination of the intelligence, but by a certain connaturality with the things of God, an interior experience and empirical taste of God and spiritual realities. By this gift we are raised to that summit from which God looks out upon the universe and judges all things; we think as God thinks; we feel what He feels, and we see everything through His eyes. We perceive and examine the truth according to a divine understanding which far surpasses all human knowledge. When men speak to us of spiritual realities and the mystery of God, we recognize and enjoy something in this which is familiar to us. We examine these things from within in the manner of habitudinarians.

Such knowledge proceeds more from the heart than from reason. The faith which raises the intelligence to the perception of divine truth is, however, always enveloped by veils; it reveals to us whatever the intelligence can grasp with divine help. But our familiarity with God makes us conjecture and feel the things that are more hidden in this unfolding mystery. Briefly, even in the domain of faith, we experience more things than we perceive.

We see immediately that this knowledge can only come from charity. It is a knowledge that is wholly penetrated by affection, an empirical knowledge, a grasping of the mystery through the intuitions of love. No intellectual effort, even when the mind is enlightened by faith, can lead us to this delightful understanding. This is par excellence the act of the gift of Wisdom: *sapit,* it is enjoyable. Only love, in its most intimate essence, can unite two beings in such a way as to give them this identical manner of seeing things, looking at everything and enjoying everything in a total communion and understanding each other merely by a hint. The Christian united to God through love finds Him everywhere. Everything speaks to him of the Beloved. He sees His hand and His presence in everything. He recognizes His goodness in all things, and guesses His intentions; he knows His ways and His tendernesses. In a word, he delights in mysteries which, without love, his mind would never have suspected.

Consequently, the gift of Wisdom seems to develop all his potentialities in the highest degrees of the mystical life.

REFLECTIONS AND PERSPECTIVES

*Biblical theology of charity. Agape in St. John and St. Paul. God
revealed as Agape. Revelation of Agape communicated to men.
Agape, foundation of all Christian doctrine. History of the theology
of Agape. Agape and charity. Christian fraternity.*

"Interested" and "Disinterested" Love. There is this dual movement in charity, but in another manner, which we have recognized
in hope. The love of charity, like all love, is "interested" in one respect, in the sense that if I truly love, it is at least radically and fundamentally an other self whom I find and whom I love. But the love
of charity is also, like all love of others, disinterested, for as long
as I love myself and seek myself, I don't really love the other person,
and how could I then love the wholly Other and truly give myself
to Him? The man who does not interiorly renounce all that he possesses and renounce himself also is not worthy of the Kingdom of
God. The self that finds and seeks itself in the love of God is the
spiritual and divine self for whose life the renunciation of the carnal
self and sometimes of the body itself, is necessary.

In reality, the words "interest" and "disinterest" are not the most
suitable to designate this double movement of love. It is better to
say that love is an upsurge, an outlet from self, an ecstasy (in the
etymological sense of the term), and that it also assures growth,
fulfillment and extension to the being who loves. No created being
attains to his end without love; this means that no created being
becomes his true self unless he emerges from self.

It is important to remember where the movement of love, which
is charity, is placed. If I love another self, that is to say, if the love
is based upon a similarity, it is the common reality in God and in
man on which man's love for God is founded. This common reality
is the gift which God makes to us of His life and His happiness. Our
love for God is founded upon *our communion in the same happiness*
(the same beatitude) *and the same life.*

Consequently we love with the same charitable love—or so we
ought to love—all those with whom we are led to communicate in
the same divine life, the same beatitude. The Christian rejoices that
God is happy with the same happiness that is reserved for him, and
that the angels and the elect share this same life. He rejoices to meet

here below those who love God and live profoundly in this life. There is nothing more precious for him to desire for others than to communicate this divine good which is truth, love, life and happiness.

Charity and divine Persons. Analyze the nuances of our love towards each of the divine Persons.

Charity and friendship. St. Thomas, and the theologians who follow him, define charity as a friendship and apply the Aristotelian categories of friendship to it. Is this definition entirely adequate? Does it mean that there cannot be any charity, properly speaking, unless there is a "neighbor" capable of friendship? For example, can the administrator of a society who only comes into contact with men on paper, love them through the mediation of the society which he serves—not one by one but collectively, with charity (even though there cannot be any *friendship* between a man and an administration)? Another example: the missionary touched by famine in India who will create and organize, for the benefit of the Hindus, new rice plantations on other lands. . . . In other words, does charity require us to keep the human contact that is necessary in the knowledge of others and which is taken for granted in every friendship? Can it be exercised by mediation (of a society or an administration)? Is charity more real if we give a glass of water to some poor man and bring it to him personally, than if we work in an office that seeks to provide water for all men? Can the transformation of structures be the object of charity? Is it not, on the contrary, a more real charity to know and love man as he really is, in his own life framework and in the always imperfect conjunction of the society to which he belongs, rather than to merely try to modify the way of life and to improve the general conditions of society? The theology of our "neighbor" and the theology of the "socius" (understood in the sense of an anonymous and unknown member of the society to which one belongs: compatriots, soldiers of the same army, administrators and employees of a corporation, taxpayers subject to the same taxation, clients of the same enterprise, etc.). Theology of the "common good."

Charity and joy. Does joy accompany every real charitable love? Do we always joyfully love whatever is loved voluntarily? In what does the sin of sadness consist? Joy and sadness in the mind. Joy and sadness in sensibility. Is it more perfect, from the viewpoint of the human act, that it be accompanied by joy? And inversely, if an act is not accompanied by any joy, is it imperfect by definition (not from the viewpoint of merit but from the viewpoint of the act considered in itself)? Joy and sin. Joy and the Cross.

The stages of charity. Describe and analyze the stages of charity according to spiritual writers. Is it legitimate to distinguish three stages: beginning, progressive, and perfect? The classical distinction of three stages of life: purgative, illuminative, unitive. Does this distinction mean the same thing? Show the differences. Is there a corresponding division of detachments, or of "nights"? Can we distinguish in the spiritual life a time when sin is avoided, and a time when there is progress in virtue, and a time when there is adherence to God? The theological and psychological justification of these stages. The growth of the love of God in the soul. Analyze and compare the *Itinerarium mentis ad Deum* of St. Bonaventure, the *Interior Castle* of St. Teresa of Avila, the *Ascent of Carmel* of St. John of the Cross, and the *Treatise on the Love of God* by St. Francis de Sales.

Charity and the divine will. How can we know the will of God? What is meant by the phrase: to do the will of God? Show that we do not always have to do that which God wills to happen, but that we must will that which God wants us to will (viz.: the mother of a man condemned to death must try to save her son, even if it is finally God's will that he undergo this punishment).

Charity and human loves. How does charity encompass every human love? Psychology of conjugal love when this love has become true charity; psychology of a mother's love for her baby, of a father's love for his children, of the adolescent's love for his parents, and of man's love for his profession, his country, etc., when charity inspires these loves.

Growth and education of love. What are the conflicts of tendencies and of loves which the child, the adolescent and the adult must overcome? How does he normally overcome them? What is the normal terminus of affective tendencies in the adult? Education of charity at different ages.

Natural love of God and charity: oppositions and relations.

Hierarchy of loves. Describe the duties that result from the hierarchy of human loves in some particular condition: those who must be loved more (children, spouse, parents, different neighbors, etc.); those who should be loved best.

Friendship and charity. Must all charity be a friendship (see above)? Must all friendship be a "charity"? What must friendship have in order that it may also be charity? Merit and demerit of human friendships. Friendship between man and woman (outside of marriage): particular conditions of a true friendship that does not harm any other love. "Friendship" between a priest and a philothea (a woman under spiritual direction). What should be thought of this text of an anonymous English mystic: "Friendship between a man and a woman is not forbidden. It can even be meritorious if they love in God and for God. . . Would not women consider themselves forsaken if they did not receive direction or help from men. . . They have great need of the counsels of virtuous men."

Charity and peace. What is the peace that charity gives? The peace of Christ and the peace of the world (Jn. 14:27). Peace of soul: true and false peace. Is Christian peace absolutely exclusive of all concern and anxiety?

Restless, scrupulous and anxious temperaments; "characteristics": how can peace be taught? Is peace the first good that we must desire for the soul?

The beatitude of peace (Mt. 5:9). Exegesis and theology.

Charity and mercy. What is mercy? Different forms of misfortune which call for mercy? Different mercies; which is the best?

In regard to such mercy (for example the mercy of instruction or of a sacrament), is it better for the soul to give it or receive it?

Beatitude of the merciful (Mt. 5:7). Exegesis and theology.

Charity and the Holy Spirit. Love that is "appropriate" to the Holy Spirit: basis of this appropriation in Scripture; meaning and scope of this appropriation.

Uncreated charity and created charity in the soul. Relations, ordering. How can it be said that the Holy Spirit acts in us by charity? Charity and gifts. How does charity bring with it all the gifts of the Holy Spirit? Theology of gifts, beginning with Isaias 11:2.

Charity and the fruits of the Holy Spirit (Gal. 5:22-23). Theology of the fruits of the Holy Spirit.

Charity and the new law. Charity and grace.

Charity and sacraments. The Eucharist, sacrament of charity, sacrament of the Church and of unity. How does the Eucharist express the unity of Christians and charity of the soul? How is it helpful to the unity of the Church, and how does it nourish the love of the soul?

Charity and the other sacraments. Charity and Penance: how should we make our "examination of conscience" and accuse ourselves; how should the soul be guided from the point of view of charity (rather than from the point of view of conformity to a law that is wholly exterior)? The sin of omission from the point of view of charity. Show that the requirements of vital dynamism which is inherent in charity may be incompatible with a morality of the law or of the precept or of "conscience." Charity and the priesthood (the priest, teacher and minister of charity). Charity and marriage: How is marriage a sacrament of charity of Christ and the Church?

The external acts of charity. Beneficence. Towards whom, primarily, should each Christian do good? What good should he procure? In what manner? *Hospitality.* Emphasize the texts relative to hospitality in the New Testament, and then in the Fathers, particularly St. Ambrose, St. Augustine, and St. John Chrysostom; analyze and comment upon Mt. 25:35-45, in particular. Mention the customs relative to hospitality in the traditions of different peoples and civilizations; compare these customs with those of the Bible. The "mystery" of the guest in the different religions other than the Jewish-Christian, in the Old Testament and finally in the New. How can hospitality be found and practised in a civilization of "the masses" in cities where the passing stranger is quite as anonymous and unknown as the native inhabitant? Is there a duty of "collective" hospitality (hospitality of a particular category of people, for example the Negroes in France, by another category of people, the French). *Almsgiving.* The duty of almsgiving; on what is this based? Show that the necessity of denying oneself and of giving from whatever one has, is more urgent than the necessity of helping any determined work; in this respect study Luke 12:16-21 and especially the parable in Luke 16:1-15; also analyze Luke 11:5-13; 14:12-14; 16:19-31; 21:1-4. Is everyone obliged to practise almsgiving? Why? What must each person give? Are the alms that are given directly to a poor man better than alms for a "good work"? Respective values of these two kinds of alms. Can money that is unjustly earned be distributed as alms? *Fraternal correction.* Is it a charity to want to correct the faults of our neighbor? See Luke 17:3-4; Matthew 18:21-22; 18:15-17; James 5:16. When and how should this be done? Correction of subordinates; the duties of correction of children by parents. Correction of our equals and superiors. Private and public correction: usage and discretion.

Sins against charity. Hatred. Its forms, its gravity. Hatred and resentment, hatred and aversion. Distinguish aversion of sensibility and hatred of the mind or the will. Can a sensible aversion for someone be compatible with a great charity? How? Is it normal that charitable love should not be accompanied by an accord of the sensibility? Can a Christian have hatred for anyone? How must he, or can he, understand the psalms of imprecation: Ps. 108; 17:38-43; 34; 51; 68:23-29; 136:7-9; etc. Hatred of evil, of the devil. The national enemy and the personal enemy (*hostis* and *inimicus*); theology of the "enemy" in the Old and New Testaments (cf. Mt. 5:43-44; Lk. 6:27, 35; Rom. 12:20); the "Enemy" in the New Testament (cf. Mt. 13:25, 28, and all the citations of Ps. 109:1-2; Mt. 22:44; Lk. 20:43; Acts 2:35; I Cor. 15:25; etc.). *Sadness.* The psychology of sadness, its causes, its gravity. Distinguish the sadness that is felt for having sinned and which engenders a deeper joy, and the sadness that comes from an exaggerated love of self. The evil which sadness creates in the soul, and the evil it does to our neighbor; the duty of cheerfulness (Mt. 6:18). *Envy* and *jealousy.* Distinction of these two sins. Their root. "Comparisons" of self and our neighbor which engender either envy or pride. Show that humility does not result from a comparison of self with one's neighbor but with God. The physical, biological, psychical and spiritual causes of feminine jealousy; temporal and spiritual remedies; means of the pastorate in dealing with jealousy. *Discord, disputes* and *blows;* the gravity of these sins. *Schism;* see the treatise on the Church. *War.* Wars of aggression, colonial warfare, wars of defense; are there any possible motives for a "just war"? Theology of obedience to the State; theology of the conscientious objector. The means of warfare: are not all the means of killing equally immoral? The morality of the means of warfare that are not directly deadly: camouflage, deceptive propaganda, lies, seduction, the corruption of the enemy's morals, etc. The responsibility of Christians in the struggle against war in peace time. Responsibilities of Christians in questions of rearmament or disarmament. Is the passive attitude of a man like Gandhi more naturally "Christian" than an offensive attitude? *Sedition, insurrection* and the *coup d'état.* Is it possible today to construct a theology of insurrection *in abstracto* and *in generali?* Can an act be condemned in principle and abstractly and yet find a kind of *post factum* justification? Affective and moral factors of "taking sides" and of political option.

The meaning of God and the sin of stupidity (the sin of wilful ignorance). The meaning of God which charity gives, particularly through the gift of wisdom. The theology of the gift of wisdom and of Christian wisdom. The sin of stupidity (wilful ignorance) understood as opposing itself to the understanding of God: slowness of spirit and the closing of the heart to the things of God. Causes and gravity of the sin of stupidity. Is disgust with God and divine things always a sin, and a grave sin? How can we maintain the taste for divine things in the soul? Study the word, the meaning and the properties of *wisdom* in the Bible. Portrait of a wise man according to the books of Wisdom and the New Testament.

Wisdom and contemplation. The role of charity in the act of contemplation and in the contemplative life. Affective knowledge and contemplation. Knowledge and charity in the "mystical" life.

BIBLIOGRAPHIE

Études philologiques, historiques, et textes:

Hélène Petre. *Caritas,* Étude sur le vocabulaire de la charité chrétienne ("Specilegium sacrum lovaniense"), Louvain, 1948 (Étude sur le complexe d'idées qui gravitent autour du précepte de la charité).

Anders Nygren, *Erôs et Agapè,* Paris, Aubier, t. 1, 1944; t. 2 et 3, 1952 (Ouvrage aujourd'hui classique d'un évêque luthérien suédois, que l'on devra lire avec discernement).

Parmi les éditions d'ouvrages patristiques, il faudrait citer de nombreux textes de saint Augustin: nous renverrons aux volumes publiés chez Desclée De Br. dans la coll. des *Œuvres de saint Augustin.* Nous citerons seulement, parmi les Pères grecs, Maxime le Confesseur, dont les *Centuries sur la charité* ont été publiées au Cerf, Coll. *Sources chrétiennes,* en 1943 (Intr. et trad. de J. Pegon).

Études théologiques:

Saint Thomas d'Aquin, *La Charité,* Tome 1, trad. et notes de H.-D. Noble; tome 2, trad. de J.-D. Folghera, notes de H.-D. Noble; Paris, Éd. de la Revue des J., 1936 et 1942.

H.-D. Noble, *L'amitié avec Dieu,* Paris, Desclée de Br., 1932.

R. Garrigou-Lagrange, *L'amour de Dieu et la Croix de Jésus,* t. 1, Juvisy, Éd. du Cerf, 1929; *Les trois âges de la vie intérieure,* Paris, Éd. du Cerf, 1938.

A. Lemonnyer, *Notre vie divine,* Paris, Éd. du Cerf, 1936.

A. Gardeil, *La vraie vie chrétienne,* Paris, Desclée, 1935.

M.-A. Janvier, *La charité, sa nature et son objet,* Carême de Notre-Dame, Paris, Lethielleux, 1914.

J. Périnelle, *Dieu est amour,* Paris, Éd. du Cerf, 1942.

Théologie particulière de la charité-amour du prochain:

En dehors des articles de dictionnaires et des nombreux commentaires bibliques (en particulier sur I Cor., 12 et 13), on lira:

Paul Philippe, *Le rôle de l'amitié dans la vie chrétienne,* Rome, Angelicum, 1938.
J. Guitton, *Essai sur l'amour humain,* Paris, Aubier, 1948.
Dom I. Van Houtryve, *L'amour du prochain selon saint François de Sales,* Paris, Vitte, 1945.
A.-M. Goichon, *Le pardon,* Paris, Éd. du Cerf, 1946.
L'Église, éducatrice de la charité, Actes du Congrès national de l'Union des œuvres à Lyon, Paris, Éd. de la rue de Fleurus, 1951.

BIBLIOGRAPHY

D'Arcy, M. C., S.J., *The Mind and Heart of Love,* New York, Henry Holt and Co., 1947.
Davis, Henry, S.J., *Moral and Pastoral Theology,* Vol. I, chs. 5-9, London, Sheed and Ward, 1941.
Falanga, J. J., *Charity, the Form of the Virtues according to St. Thomas,* Washington, D.C., 1949.
Farrell, Walter, O.P., *A Companion to the Summa,* Vol. III, pp. 61-116, New York, Sheed and Ward, 1940.
Garrigou-Lagrange, *The Love of God and the Cross of Jesus,* St. Louis, Herder, 1951.
———, *The Three Ages of the Interior Life,* St. Louis, Herder, 1948.
Sheedy, Charles E., C.S.C., *The Christian Virtues,* pp. 111-156, Notre Dame, Ind., University of Notre Dame Press, 1949.

Bayer, C., "Charity Developed in Its Exercise," *Lumen,* 9: 633-638, D '54.
Budde, G. J., "Christian Charity, Now and Always: the Fathers of the Church and Almsgiving," *American Ecclesiastical Review,* 85: 561-579, D '31.
De Letter, P., S.J., "Hope and Charity in St. Thomas," *Thomist,* 13: 204-248, Apr '50, and 13: 325-352, Jl '50.
———, "Perfect Contrition and Perfect Charity," *Theological Studies,* 7: 507-524, D '46.
Fox. S. F. D., "Charity and Justice," *Blackfriars,* 12: 412-416, Jl '31.
Hughes, D., "Dynamics of Christian Perfection," *Thomist,* 15: 247-288, Apr '52.
Jackman, A., "True Idea of Charity," *Catholic Mind,* 37: 597-603, Mar '39.
Kelly, G., "On the Duty of Loving the Neighbor, Especially Enemies," *Review for Religious,* 7: 299-312, N '48.
Kress, A. J., "Social Charity," *Catholic World,* 153: 569-573, Aug '41.
Phibbin, W. J., "Scholastic Teaching on the Nature of Charity," *Irish Ecclesiastical Record,* 42: 20-46, Jl '33.
"Precept of Charity Toward God," *American Ecclesiastical Review,* 89: 634-636, D '33.
Schneider, J., "Charity, Divine Friendship," *American Ecclesiastical Review,* 104: 481-491, Je '41.

THE CARDINAL VIRTUES

Faith, hope, and charity, which we have just been studying, belong directly to the vocabulary of the Gospel. The virtues of prudence, justice, fortitude and temperance, which we shall now consider, have come to us, at least in their systematic organization as the four cardinal virtues, from Hellenic morality. Once again the theologian must justify his borrowing from the philosophers.

There are three remarks to be made here.

1. Moral theology, which studies man in so far as he is the image of God, is meant to serve as a guide in all our actions. But there is more than one kind of guide. It is certain that the analyses of this theology would not greatly guide a child if anyone had the absurd idea of teaching them to him. It is equally certain that theology does not make the claim at any time that it can take the place, by a more reflective and analytical attitude, of the spontaneous and living attitude of the Christian who desires to "follow Christ." *The imitation of Christ,* because it consists of modeling oneself upon a living person, upon Him who is the Life and is our Life, is in fact alone capable of arousing the vital impulse before and after theological reflection. But Christ, who is our supreme guide, does not make the theologian's efforts useless. On the contrary, He gives them vitality. He does not prevent theology from being our guide in its own manner. Instead, He points out the way for it.

2. The believer, in the efforts of his intelligence—and especially, as we shall see, in the struggles of action and life—cannot continue an imitation of Christ without seeking the reasons and motivations. It is not his fault if his intelligence was made to see and if he is unsatisfied so long as he does not possess full light; the very nature of his intelligence makes this inevitable. And just as he desires to see God with all the strength of his being, so likewise he wants to know what the image of God may be and how he may become a perfect image of God. "You therefore are to be perfect, even as your heavenly Father is perfect"—by following Christ: Certainly the Christian wants all this. But he also wants to understand the nature of this perfection in his own action, and he wants to know what the following of Christ implies. What are the interior anima-

tions of the Master, and what are the qualities of the Christian who follows Christ? These are the questions which he will ask himself sooner or later. And these are the questions of moral theology.

Apart from the theological virtues, the New Testament doubtless provides us with certain lists of virtues. For instance, in his praise of charity, St. Paul wrote, "Charity is patient, is kind; charity does not envy, is not pretentious, is not puffed up, is not ambitious, is not self-seeking, is not provoked; thinks no evil, does not rejoice over wickedness, but rejoices with the truth; bears with all things, believes all things, hopes all things, endures all things" (I Cor. 13:4-8). Since God is Charity, we have there a spendid portrait of Jesus Christ who is the glory of the Father, and the theologian could take this catalogue of virtues as the framework of his reflections and analyses. And yet this would not be sufficient. It was not St. Paul's intention to provide an outline for the theologian, and it would betray his thought and betray the literary genre of this eulogy whose purpose was parenthetical to see in it a systematic organization of the Christian virtues. However fruitful the theologian's commentary may be, it will contain repetition and serious gaps.

Wherever we may seek in the New Testament, we will nowhere find a rational system in which everything pertaining to morality is gathered together and harmoniously arranged. And yet man can not dispense with this. He wants to know what he must do in every domain and every circumstance. The teaching of Christ is insufficient for him. Certainly not in the sense that Christ did not say enough in regard to what is necessary for salvation, but in the sense that all the domains of morality are not studied—far from it!—in the Gospel; the very circumstances in which various acts are presented perhaps give them a character of relativity which the theologian must at least be able to appreciate. It may also be said that the Christian, of any state of life and at any moment, may have recourse to the Holy Spirit who is within him. But this recourse to the Holy Spirit, however universally efficacious it may be in the moral life, is not an explanation. The theologian may appeal to Him, but this cannot satisfy all his own requirements.

Therefore the theologian, who not only seeks to understand the moral behavior of the creature who is "the image of God," but especially that which the creature *must* do, and the manner that is required for educating and guiding him, is led to build a kind of system—the simplest and most comprehensive that is possible—in which may be found in an orderly way all moral matters and in particular all the virtues. It is interesting to note that, as a matter of fact, the "moral systems" adopted by the various theologies that are current in the Church are of different inspiration and structure, and while the Church has certainly given its preference to one of them (the one that we are studying now), it has not, properly speaking, canonized a single one. This indicates to us the measure of relativity that is found in systematization which, in our turn, we are adopting for motives which once again are based upon our theological and metaphysical conception, and not upon our caprice. This measure of relativity is furthermore inherent in any theological work in which reason is always mingled with the datum of faith in order to classify it and understand it.

Our analysis now turns to Greek philosophy for its framework. This borrowing which requires a measure of relativity in theology, as we have already said, also implies a certain degree of risk: the possibility of contaminating our theology with rationalism. The theologian must be aware of this and know how to make the borrowed philosophical concepts more flexible, in view of his own synthesis, when required. Moreover, this should be quite natural, because the inspiration of each is radically different.

The excellent merits which we attribute to the organization of moral matters around the four cardinal virtues of which prudence is the principal axis and mover do not signify that theology must never make use of any other anthropology. Every study of man may assert its rights in this respect, and these rights should be judged according to the exactness of the conformity between the philosophical presentations and the human reality analyzed in them. As long as he remains firm in his faith and loyal to the letter and spirit of the Word of God, the theologian may be liberal in welcoming whatever is true and good and beautiful in all the wisdoms of the world.

3. Evangelical morality is a morality of love. The intention of the theologian is therefore to present an objective order of virtues and acts which correspond exactly to the dispositions and effects of love. Is this not a risk? But is it possible to make this kind of analysis of the love of a determined and living subject? Is it not always unpredictable? If St. Paul was careful to note that his "letter of recommendation," which encompassed all of his doctrine, was written not with ink and upon tablets of stone, but with the Spirit of the

Living God upon the hearts of men (cf. II Cor. 3:3), shall we not say the same about our morality? Let us consider an example:

It is not difficult for theology to show that we must not kill and that we must not kill ourselves "because this is contrary to the charity which man owes to his neighbor or to his own body which is the Temple of the Holy Spirit." And yet how many contrary examples are given to us! Abraham, the father of believers, was ready to sacrifice his own son, and the author of the epistle to the Hebrews praised his act (Heb. 11:17); Samson, who was counted among the righteous (Heb. 11:32), killed himself; Judith killed Holofernes, and how many others! Christ did not want the "twelve legions of angels" (Mt. 26:53), which He could have obtained through recourse to His Father, in order that He might not prevent the fulfillment of the Scriptures. St. Ignatius of Antioch, fearing that the beasts might not attack him, declared: "If they do not want to come to me, I shall do violence to them; I shall throw myself before them so that I may be devoured. Forgive me, little children, I know what is advantageous to myself." St. Gorgonius and his companion, imbued with a lively desire for martyrdom, begged the emperor to condemn them also: "Why do you only punish that man, since we deserve to be condemned with him?" St. Ambrose (Virg. 3:32-34), and likewise Eusebius (Eccl. Hist. 8:12) and St. John Chrysostom (De S. Pelagia, Nom. 1, 2) considered the virgins who escaped violation through suicide holy martyrs. And we could multiply these examples. St. Thomas wisely said, "It is not permitted to kill oneself unless by the authority of God or the instinct of the Holy Spirit (nisi vel auctoritate Dei, vel instinctu Spiritus Sancti, De decem praeceptis, De quinto praecepto legis)." These examples, in regard to the respect of the body (or regarding murder), could be extended to other virtues.

This leads us to determine the level at which our moral considerations are held and to appreciate their value.

When we try to present the qualities of the soul which necessarily correspond to love, either as dispositions or as effects, we shall not usually take into account that aspect of the human act which would now be called "the existential aspect" as opposed to its essential or formal aspect. An act that is insignificant in its essence (or in its materiality) may have great value if it is fraught with much love; an act that is materially sinful may be excused if it is done through complete ignorance of the evil and with a good intention that may even be virtuous—like the "indirect suicide" of Gorgonius and so many martyrs who voluntarily surrendered themselves—if it is done "by the authentic instinct of the Holy Spirit." An act of great value with respect to theology, like the solemn vow of religion whose merit is comparable with martyrdom, may have little importance if it is done without great love, without awareness of what it implies, or with no appreciation of what has been sacrificed, and for extrinsic motives which, although not sinful, are nevertheless secondary.

This necessary relativity of moral conclusions does not diminish its worth. It merely determines its scope. Theology is not here considering the degree of love which each Christian possesses, and which he may or may not put into each act of virtue; nor does it consider to what exceptions love may lead this or that person in the circumstances in which it pleases God to place men. But it does try to enumerate and define the embellishments, however dazzling, that interiorly adorn the souls of the saints. "And she has been permitted to clothe herself in fine linen, shining, bright. For the fine linen is the just deeds of the saints" (Apoc. 19:8).

It is useful for everyone who wishes to avoid deluding himself regarding his own love to refer from time to time to these norms which theology endeavors to establish. It is necessary for the teacher, if he desires to teach authentic love, to give training equally in the humble virtues whose role is to assure the conformity of love with all the powers of the soul. However, it would be dangerous if anyone were deceived regarding the exact scope of these references and judged all moral value by anything other than the love whose clear vision within each of us is finally reserved for Almighty God.

Chapter IV

PRUDENCE
by A. Raulin, O.P.

INTRODUCTION: Man is left to his own counsel.

REFLECTIONS AND PERSPECTIVES

BIBLIOGRAPHY

Chapter IV

PRUDENCE

Introduction: Man Is Left to His Own Counsel

"God made man from the beginning and left him in the hand of his own counsel" (Ecclus. 15:14). One of the essential aspects of man's condition is this "mastery" of his own life, definitely a limited mastery, but very real nonetheless. How is this privilege to be used if we are to use it well? This is the problem of prudence, as the very word implies. Let us not try to be more precise just now. An inquiry concerning the revealed data is necessary first. If we try to form a very elaborate concept at the start, we would run the risk of ignoring many rich scriptural ideas, and even if these do not adequately provide an exact notion of the "virtue of prudence," they are nevertheless the essential matter of this treatise; philosophical notions merely provide the outline.

And if it seems arbitrary to place our study after the theological virtues and before the other moral virtues, let us remember that the "conduct of our life" which has God for its end and not for its object, does not have the primary importance of the three theological virtues, but on the other hand, being the government of ourselves, it naturally precedes all the rest. Prudence is the first of the cardinal virtues.

1. PRUDENCE IN THE OLD TESTAMENT

The Bible does not contain any category of books that pertain specifically to morality. There is moral doctrine in the Pentateuch and in the Kings, the Psalms and the Prophets. But there are also the "sapiential" books which concern morality, although their principal characteristic is the particular aspect under which they consider everything. Their appeal is to the reflection of the reader, sometimes to his ordinary common sense or to his experience, at other times to his sense of the greatness of God and the vanity of created things, but always to his understanding. The word of the Psalmist will serve as an example:

I will instruct thee, and I will teach thee the way in which thou shouldst walk; I will counsel thee, keeping my eye fixed upon thee. Be not without understanding like the horse and the mule, whose spirit is controlled by bridle and bit, otherwise they come not near thee. (Ps. 31:809).

The sapiential books include *Proverbs, Job, Qoheleth* (called *Ecclesiastes*), *Sirach* (called *Ecclesiasticus*) and the book of *Wisdom*. To these books we would have to add certain texts drawn from other writings that are definitely sapiential, particularly some of the *Psalms* (1, 36, 48 among many others) and *Baruch* (3:9 to 4:4).

Obviously it is in the "sapiential" books, more than any others, that we will find indications relative to prudence. We will find the term in the Latin Vulgate (*prudentia*) or in the versions based upon the original texts. As a matter of fact, there is no Hebrew term that has been translated in a necessary or sufficient manner. Quite often it is the context that determines the exact translation. However, the important thing is that the idea is there. Whenever the sacred author refers to the ability to correctly discern what ought to be done, he is teaching prudence.

Sapiential literature is not the exclusive possession of the Jewish people. The wise men of Israel were the heirs and imitators of the wise men of Egypt and Babylonia. In regard to the lessons of experience and the choice of themes, they were even largely dependent upon their predecessors. We should not be surprised to discover that the most ancient sapiential texts in the Bible (the first nucleus of the book of Proverbs) present an ideal savior-faire that is very similar to the wisdom of the Egyptians and Babylonians. However, the monotheistic faith of the chosen people remained intact and, as might be expected, it determined the thought of the wise men of Israel in progressive degree. At the end of the curve will be found the identification of wisdom with the Law of Moses:

This is the book of the commandments of God, and the law, that is forever (Baruch, 4:1).

The question before us now—and it is essential in our study—is whether this text contains the true message of the Old Testament in regard to prudence. Were the most ancient texts, which did not make this identification, nothing more than primitive approximations that may be ignored once we have come upon the final formula: "True prudence is to observe the Law"?

In this discovery there is certainly a profound truth. We can have no safer guide than the One who created us. And if He has indicated our line of conduct, it would be senseless to seek elsewhere. The best government of ourselves is necessarily the one that brings us into conformity with the will of God. This is an acquired truth that nothing can ever undermine.

We know, however, that the law of Moses, although divine, was only transitory. Today our law is the law of the Gospel which is inscribed in our hearts. We know that if we are only concerned about the letter of the law we may well betray its spirit. Christ reproached the Pharisees for this often enough. Circumstances could make a literal application of a text in the law of Moses contrary to the actual will of the legislator. It was necessary to exercise judgment in each case. It was not the purpose of the Law to provide rules of conduct that would be adequate for all the circumstances of personal, family and political life. It was the mission of the Prophets to keep Israel in the line of its authentic tradition in the hour of great decisions. The Law did not take the place of prophetical teaching nor did it make it unnecessary to discern what had to be done in each particular case.

When Ecclesiastes tells us, "He that observeth the wind shall not sow: and he that considereth the clouds shall never reap" (11:4), teaching us that we must know how to put an end to our deliberations or never be able to act at all, he is not giving us a text of the Law. However, he does give us a rule of conduct that is extremely useful in our practical life. He is teaching us prudence.

It is remarkable that the wisdom of Israel is not satisfied to tell us: Thou hast received a Law; now apply it. But instead it is careful to give us principles of discernment in order that we may carry out any action satisfactorily. All the practical counsels, for example those that fill the book of Proverbs, are not merely preliminary outlines which the discovery of the Law would render useless; on the contrary, they orient us in a different and complementary direction. The highest wisdom is to conform ourselves in everything to the divine Wisdom, and the revealed Law does not dispense us from the lessons of experience and good sense. The counsels which the Bible gives us in this respect also come from the revealing God.

It would not be possible for us to set forth in detail all the counsels that are so abundant in the sapiential texts. We must limit ourselves to a consideration of the main lines.

Prudence is an aptitude, a savior-faire, but not an aptitude for doing evil (Ecclus. 19:19), although the word can have an evil connotation—prudence, i.e. wisdom that is of the earth (Bar. 3:23). Its foundation is the fear of Yahweh (Prov. 1:7). It knows its limits and is aware that "There is no wisdom, there is no prudence, there is no counsel against the Lord" (Prov. 21:30). And it warns us to distrust ourselves (Prov. 3:5).

How is prudence acquired? In three ways. First by prayer, as Solomon understood. Next by docility toward our parents, our teachers and experienced elders. There is no wisdom without docil-' ity. We must know how to accept a reprimand (Prov. 10:17). Even the king, whose need for prudence is all the greater because he exercises a higher command, must surround himself with counsellors and listen to their advice (Prov. 24:6). Finally, prudence is acquired by experience. It is in the name of experience that the rules of wise conduct were given to us, whether in the choice of a good wife, or our relations with her, the education of children, or our relationship with friends or with people of high station. Laziness is condemned because of its disastrous effects (Prov. 10:4-5 et passim). Likewise, there is a condemnation of anger (Prov. 14:17), the excessive love of wealth (Prov. 23:4-5) and all kinds of irregularities, whether personal or family or social. Work, mercy, purity, integrity, justice and kindness are, on the contrary, wise rules of conduct. A certain kind of prudence, in the sense of caution, is also necessary, and this lesson is drawn from harsh experience.

We must not always expect a moral judgment from these wise men. Their wisdom often consisted of the mere statement of a fact: "The rich ruleth over the poor; and the borrower is servant to him that lendeth" (Prov. 22:7). What does this mean? Was the author of the proverb indifferent about such a state of things? This seems hardly likely. More probably it was his intention to have his disciples themselves deduce the consequences from the stated fact. The disciple will not be formed until he is able to distinguish between good and evil by himself and make his own *summa* of personal experience. The Law calls us to obedience and wisdom calls us to docility, and here we find a nuance. The highest wisdom will be to live obediently to the Law while also forming ourselves in the school of experience.

2. PRUDENCE IN THE NEW TESTAMENT

The New Testament is the terminus and the fulfillment of the Old Testament in its totality. Our Lord did not only fulfill the Law, but He was also the consummation of the work of the Prophets and the greatest of the wise men of Israel. It should not therefore surprise us that He made constant appeal to the arguments of prudence. Such was the case, for example, in the closing phrases of the Sermon on the Mount:

Everyone therefore who hears these my words and acts upon them, shall be likened to a wise man who built his house on rock. And the rain fell, and the floods came, and the winds blew and beat against that house, but it did not fall, because it was founded on rock. And everyone who hears these my words and does not act upon them, shall be likened to a foolish man who built his house on sand. And the rain fell, and the floods came, and the winds blew and beat against that house, and it fell, and was utterly ruined (Mt. 7:24-27).

It is a direct appeal to prudence which Our Lord addresses to us when He says to His apostles: "Be therefore wise as serpents and guileless as doves" (Mt. 10:16). Similarly, when He counsels us to increase our talents (Mt. 25:14-30) or gives us the example of the man who calculates the cost before going on a journey, or the king who considers his chance of victory before going out to face the enemy (Lk. 14:28-32). We cannot cite everything, but the essential points are obvious now: the value of the Kingdom of God is of such greatness that it is a wise move if we give up everything to acquire it (the Hidden Treasure and the Pearl of Great Price). It is true prudence if we leave everything to follow Jesus.

The rules are not uniform; they depend upon the circumstances. Jesus sent away the man who had been a demoniac and who begged Our Lord to make him a disciple because it was now his particular mission to tell people in his own country everything that God had done for him (Lk. 8:38-39). On the other hand, it saddened Jesus when the rich young man did not have the courage to follow Him (Lk. 18:24). As long as Jesus was among the disciples, they did not need to fast, but the time would come when they would fast (Mt. 2:15).

However, two great rules seem to be imposed more particularly upon all men generally, and this is a dual rule of prudence: we must not trust in riches, and we must always be vigilant.

We must not put our trust in riches. Was that rich man prudent who was making plans after taking stock of his rich estate, while ignoring that his soul might be required of him that very night (Lk. 12:16-20)? Certainly not, because true prudence would be to sell everything one possessed and give the money to the poor: "Make for yourselves purses that do not grow old, a treasure unfailing in heaven, where neither thief draws near nor moth destroys" (Lk. 12:33). Even the crafty prudence of an unfaithful steward can be a lesson for the children of light. Let them make friends with their riches by giving them to the poor who are the friends of God. What investment in this world could ever compare with this security (Lk. 16:1-9)? Christian prudence meditates upon the birds of the sky and the lilies of the fields. Its rule is to seek the Kingdom of God and His justice; it knows that all the rest will be added unto it (Mt. 6:33).

Vigilance. This is one of the most frequent themes of the Gospel. Vigilance that was symbolized by the lighted lamp that must not only be kept burning but also carry its store of oil. Was it not this oil that distinguished the prudent virgins from the foolish virgins (Mt. 25)? How imprudent it was to fall asleep knowing that the master might return at any moment!

It is not only the Gospel in the New Testament that teaches us prudence. St. Paul echoes its teaching. He requires prudence in aspirants to the episcopate: a bishop must be able to govern his own house properly (I Tim. 3:4). Elderly women must be wise counsellors to the young (Tit. 2:4). The apostle writes to the Ephesians (5:15): "See to it therefore, brethren, that you walk with care: not as unwise but as wise," and to the Romans, "it is now the hour for us to rise from sleep" (13:11), and again, "be transformed in the newness of your mind, that you may discern what is the good and acceptable and perfect will of God" (12:2).

We may also quote St. Peter: "Be sober, be watchful!" (I Pet. 5:8), and the Apocalypse: "Therefore, if thou wilt not watch, I will come upon thee as a thief, and thou shalt not know at what hour I shall come upon thee" (3:3). Here we see in what sense Christian prudence is developed.

3. PRUDENCE IN THE LITURGY

It is hardly surprising that prudence is found less in the temporal cycle than in the sanctoral. It is even more remarkable that it is less apparent in the Proper than the Common of the Saints. This is because the manner in which he governs his life may well be characteristic of a saint, whereas he could not have the prerogative of having lived a good life. Depending upon the three theological virtues, and particularly on charity which is the essence of perfection, prudence is *par excellence* the *common trait* of all the saints. It is diverse in its realizations but one in its function.

Shall we consider the case of a martyr? The Gospel reminds us that if we seek to save our life we shall lose it and that a man cannot give anything in exchange for his soul. This means that martyrdom can be the only valid economy. Another gospel in the same Common reminds us that if we wish to follow Christ without being willing to renounce all else it is quite as foolish as to undertake the building of a tower without first calculating the cost. A text drawn from the book of Wisdom shows us the unbelievers who looked upon those who suffer persecution for the sake of justice as being madmen. But in the hour of judgment it is their turn to be confounded and to cry out, "We fools esteemed their life madness . . . but the way of the Lord we have not known" (Wis. 5:4, 7).

Shall we consider the case of a Confessor? "Let your loins be girded and your lamps lighted" says the gospel. Vigilance is especially your duty because you have a higher place in the Church (confessor pontiffs). "Who, dost thou think, is the faithful and prudent steward whom the master will set over his household to give them their ration of grain in due time"? Who indeed, if not the bishop who governs his flock with the prudence of the saints? The Parable of the Talents will be applied to him: And he who had received the five talents came and brought five other talents. Wisdom requires that we lay up treasure in heaven and not upon earth, and yet the hundredfold was promised even in this world to those who forsake all things to follow Christ. Happy is the man whose wealth would allow him to do evil but who masters himself and knows how to make good and prudent use of his possessions.

Shall we consider the case of a virgin? She is praised for having sold all that she owned in order to purchase the field where treasure was hidden. She is numbered with the prudent virgins who were ready at the right hour to go forth to meet the bride-groom. It will be remembered that St. Paul, like his master, wanted Christians to be free from vain cares, *sine sollicitudine*. Happy are those who have had the wisdom to acquire this liberty by their profession of virginity.

Finally, shall we consider the case of a woman who is first sanctified in marriage? Her eulogy is there before us. She is called the strong woman, virtuous and industrious who goes about her tasks with energy and prudence, as a woman "who knows what she is doing."

Christian prudence is set forth in the liturgy as the background in sanctity with these characteristics: the sacrifice of secondary possessions in order to obtain the essential blessings, freedom from vain preoccupations, the good use of money, foresight, circumspection, a liking for work, vigilance in awaiting the master's return.

4. THE ANCIENT PHILOSOPHERS AND THE FATHERS OF THE CHURCH

The enumeration of the four virtues which were later to be given the name "cardinal" was very ancient. It is found as far back as in Plato for whom it was "obvious" that the head of the State to be perfect must be wise, courageous, temperate and just (Rep. I, 4, 427 a). This enumeration was constantly maintained in the platonic and stoic tradition. We find it again among the Latins, for example in Cicero (*De inventione rhetorica*, I, II, c. 53). Moreover, a Father of the Church, like St. Ambrose, considered it as classical among both the Greeks and the Latins (*De Virginitate,* c. XVIII, P.L. 16, 303).

However, Ambrose was not willing to admit that it was of pagan origin. He insisted upon its scriptural origin, and in this respect, he appealed to the book of Wisdom which he believed could be properly attributed to Solomon (*De Paradiso,* c. XII, P.L. 14, 318). As a matter of fact, we find the following passage in that book on the subject of wisdom: "She teaches temperance, and prudence, and justice, and fortitude" (8:7). He also has recourse to an allegorical interpretation of chapter two of Genesis; the four rivers flowing forth from Paradise are the four virtues in question (*Ibid.* c. III, P.L. 14, 296). This exegesis was not new, however, for it can be found in Philo the Jew (1st century of our era), but it is a rather uncertain exegesis because Philo and St. Ambrose do not make the same virtues correspond to the same rivers. (Cf. Philon, *Commentaire des Lois,* I, I, XIX, ff.)

Whatever may be the position of St. Ambrose, we may say that the enumeration of the cardinal virtues is of philosophical origin, for the Wisdom attributed to Solomon was written about 100 B.C., and borrowed its enumeration from the philosophers.

Among the cardinal virtues, Plato gave preeminence to prudence. For the Socrates of the *Republic* this preeminence was an obvious matter which fits in very well with the moral intellectualism of Socratic thought. Prudence is a virtue of reason, a directive virtue. Just as fortitude is the proper virtue of warriors, prudence is the virtue of the "guardians," that is to say, the leaders of the City. It will be found wherever good counsel reigns. It is notable, however, that it only pertains to enterprises of general interest which coordinate all the activities of the City. Ability, however great in any particular domain, does not deserve to be called prudence.

Let us bypass for the moment the doctrine of Aristotle, rightly called the heir of platonic thought, which was so original precisely in regard to this subject. We will consider his doctrine again in connection with medieval theology when, for the first time, it was introduced into Christianity.

Cicero, like Plato, does not hesitate to assign the first place to prudence in the group of the four traditional virtues. He proposes a definition of prudence in these terms: "the science of things that are good, bad and indifferent"; in other words, its function is to inform us about the moral qualification of all things. Another interesting point is Cicero's comment that prudence must keep an eye upon the past (memory), and be attentive to the present (intelligence) and foresee the future (foresight).

Philo teaches us that there is prudence of one kind and prudence of another. Some people vulgarly call a man prudent who makes sophistic speeches and who is clever in expressing his ideas, but Moses knew that such a man was merely a lover of oratory and not really prudent at all. It is not in words but in deeds and in virtuous practices that prudence is found. In reality the only prudence that deserves to be called beautiful is the universal wisdom of God. Nevertheless there is a human virtue deserving of the name. This is the science of what ought to be done and what ought not be done. And this is the most estimable of the virtues of the soul for it is the one that pertains to the rational part, the head, while fortitude belongs to the heart and temperance to hunger and thirst (*Ibid.*).

With St. Ambrose, prudence becomes Christian and evangelical. It claims for its own the declarations of St. Paul on the folly of the cross which is wisdom according to God. The great examples of prudence may be found in the Bible and this study has greater worth than the most scholarly classifications (*De Officiis*, I, I, c. XXV, P.L. 16, 62). Do we desire to understand it well? Ambrose relates it to the blessing of tears. It consists of "weeping for the things that

are decayed and seeking those that are eternal, and of weeping for
the things of this world which struggle against one another in order
that we may seek the God of peace who has chosen the foolish of
this world to confound the wise" (*Ev. sec. Lucam,* I, 5, c. 66).
Without denying his biblical inspiration, Ambrose knew very well
how to make use of the philosophers. With all tradition he sees the
virtue of reason in prudence. He suggests its role to us when he
says that the prudent man is the one who acts in such a way that
he will never have anything to repent. And he insists strongly upon
the solidarity of the virtues. No one is really prudent unless he is
at the same time courageous, temperate and just, and no one is
really strong or temperate or just if he is not really prudent (*De
Officiis,* I, I, c. XXVII, P.L. 16, 65).

St. Augustine continues the tradition of St. Ambrose. He is familiar with Cicero and quotes him. The role of prudence among the
cardinal virtues will be the will to discern good and evil (*Enar. in
Psalm* 83, n. II, P.L. 15, 1739). He does not see an exact hierarchy of values, however. Do you give first place to temporal blessings? You will then be prudent if you seek such blessings and flee
from anything that troubles you in this world, but your prudence
will be carnal and St. Paul said that carnality is the enemy of God
(Rom. 8:7). Or do you give eternal blessings their true place, which
is the first place? Then you will be prudent in the measure that you
seek them and overcome all the obstacles that prevent their attainment.[1] St. Augustine likewise tried to show how the moral virtues
are bound up with charity and are like a translation or expression
of charity. Fortitude, for example, is love which endures all things
for the sake of the beloved. In the same way prudence is love discerning wisely the things that are favorable and those that are not
(*De moribus Eccles.,* c. XV, P.L., 32, 1322). Essentially therefore
it is a virtue of discernment which, in the service of love, discrim-
inates between the things that are of service and those that are
injurious.

St. Gregory the Great is a practical moralist. He knows the four
virtues, of course, and calls them the "principal" virtues; and if he is
somewhat uncertain about the right order of the three others, he
does not hesitate to put prudence in the first place.[2] As a Christian
moralist he knows that true prudence is not impressed by the ap-

---

[1] *Expos. quorundam propos. ex Epist. ad Rom.,* 49, P. L., 35, 2073.
[2] *In Ez.,* I, hom. 4, P. L., 76, 809; cf. *in Ez.,* II, hom., 10, P. L., 76, 1068.

parent successes of evil men (*Mor.,* I, 6, c. 6, P.L. 75, 733) and that it consists of the faithful practice of the virtues that are most essentially Christian, the virtues that seem to be folly in the eyes of the world: reconciling our words and our thoughts, never using crafty simulation, never rendering evil for evil, praying for those who speak ill of us, seeking poverty and renouncing possession, never resisting those who would rob us, turning the other cheek, and in a word, taking the Gospel seriously and putting it into practice (*Mor.,* I, 10, c. 29, P.L., 75, 947).

That which was striking to St. Gregory, following St. Ambrose, was the solidarity of the virtues. The four principal virtues are the four corners of the house. Not only must all of them be here, but their development must be harmonious: if one of them weakens, all will be weakened (*In Ez.,* II, hom., 10, P.L. 76, 1069). And St. Gregory gives us a fruitful exegesis of the teaching of Our Lord: Be therefore wise as serpents, and guileless as doves: "Some men are so simple that they do not know what is right. But the innocence of true simplicity is lost if we do not attain to the virtue of rectitude. For if this rectitude does not make them informed, simplicity will never suffice to keep them in innocence" (*Mor.,* I, I, c. 2, P.L., 75, 529). This stresses the importance of light and discernment in the moral life of the Christian. His prudence will be quite different from the wisdom of the world. It is inconceivable apart from simplicity, but the Christian's discernment must not for that reason be less sure or less intelligent.

5. ARISTOTLE AND SCHOLASTICISM

In the matter of prudence, as in so many other matters, it was the influence of Aristotle which, in the Middle Ages, gave a new impetus to theological elaboration. The sixth book of his *Nicomachean Ethics* renews the question.

It was primarily in relating it to the other virtues of the soul that Aristotle shows the true nature of prudence. Its domain, he tells us, is that of *acting* and not of *doing*—which distinguishes it from art. The work to be accomplished by prudence is not exterior to man like a work of art, but is instead a fine human act. And if we are to be able to speak of prudence we must not judge the act in terms of some particular end, but refer in the last analysis to the plenary end of man, "living a good life." Such a reference is not required of the artist or the artisan *as such.* Who is the most capable in the domain of art? The one who produces chefs-d'oeuvres at will but who can also produce very ugly things if he pleases, or the one who produces horrors of the same order while trying to do his very best? If prudence, assuredly, would here find what was to be expected, it is because it is a moral virtue, which art is not. We must judge with reference to the ultimate end of man.

Aristotle also points out that prudence is of the practical order and in this respect it is distinguished from scientific knowledge. It pertains to action. The domain of prudence is simply the one in which man can exercise his action, that is to say that it does not go beyond the domain of future contingents, which of course can be or not be, depending on whether we act in one way or another. Prudence must certainly refer to universal principles, but it could not properly function unless it were fully aware of concrete and particular reality. And if it were necessary to choose, Aristotle would not hesitate to prefer an acute and sure sense of the particular rather than theoretical knowledge. Consequently, in his opinion—perhaps based upon his own experience—young men can be learned but they are not, in the same degree, prudent because they lack experience.

Prudence is a rational virtue, which gives it a place apart among the moral virtues. Every human act requires the intervention of the practical reason and the faculties of appetite (will, passions). The act will not attain its perfection unless these different factors are maintained in the right way, which supposes a stable disposition, a virtue, in each faculty. The role of prudence is to assure the good functioning of reason at the point where it becomes involved in action. We must not fall into the intellectualist excesses of Socrates and say that all the virtues are prudence. But we must maintain that there is no true virtue without prudence.

However high prudence may be, it is not the supreme virtue of the soul. It would be this if man, whose life it governs, were the supreme reality. But since man is not the zenith of the universe, the wisdom which contemplates divine things is superior to prudence.

All these elements lead Aristotle to this definition of prudence: virtue of the practical reason governing human actions conformably with truth.

If by skill we designate that which consists in discovering and carrying out the means of arriving at its proper end (the task of practical reason) then prudence is the same kind of skill excepting that the desired end is the true and authentic goal of all human life.

Aristotle finds prudence not only in the life of the individual but also in domestic and political life (the prudence of the leader and prudence of the subject). He adds to prudence a virtue for rectifying the deliberation required for action (*eubulia*) and two others which assure the exactness of practical judgment (*synesis* and *gnome*).

The first witness that we have of the reading of book VI of *Nicomachean Ethics* by a medieval theologian is found in St. Albert the Great in a course later than his *Summa de Bono*. Previously we find only infiltrations of Aristotelian morality.[3]

St. Thomas Aquinas follows St. Albert; he has left us a commentary on the *Nicomachean Ethics,* and also elaborated a whole treatise on prudence in his *Summa Theologiae* (IIa, IIae, q. 47 to 56). St. Thomas often quotes the Bible, and utilizes Cicero, Macrobus, St. Augustine, St. Gregory, but the framework of his treatise is obviously Aristotelian. The notion of supernatural prudence gives this study its theological character, which raises the question of the gift of counsel.

After St. Thomas Aquinas, the subject is not further developed, not even by his commentators. The studies are grouped more and more around the notion of conscience. They continue to recognize prudence as the first of the cardinal virtues, but in fact they study it less and less. This is regrettable. The art of self-government does not consist merely of a series of judgments. It is important to accord it all the stability and all the continuity which only a *virtue* of the practical reason can provide.

6. NECESSITY OF A VIRTUE OF PRUDENCE

Every truly human action requires the concurrence of reason. Without reason the will is incapable of producing any act and without its intervention the passions are merely animal reactions. Now if the human will—and, dependently, the passions—are capable of good and of evil, then human reason is capable of truth and of falsehood. It is evident that human action cannot claim complete success if reason does not stay in the line of truth. Action is then quite as

[3] Cf. Lottin, *Les Débuts du traité de la prudence au moyen-âge.* Rech. Théol. anc. et médiév. IV (1932), pp. 252-283. Recension du Bulletin Thomiste, IV (1934), pp. 213, et ss.

evil as when the appetitive faculties do not maintain themselves in the line of their proper object, the good.

It is therefore necessary that reason be conformed to the rule of truth whenever it intervenes in action. But how shall this conformity be assured?

With regard to the general principles of morality, we have them in what the scholastics called "synderesis." Thanks to this, we judge that we must do good and avoid evil, and we know the great principles of the natural law and the terms of our duties. But is the rectitude of our intelligence engaged in action sufficiently assured? No, it is not. It is in concrete action that our destiny is worked out. The human person, permanent in its substance and unity, on the way of return to God, only progresses toward its goal by acts that are concrete, individual and singular, and by engagement in a constantly moving reality. God, the Good, and the True are unmoving, my soul is spiritual and incorruptible, and yet I find myself at all times in a given place and at a particular moment in time, and in particular circumstances. The act which will realize within myself the most faithful likeness of God or which will efface it, the act which will maintain myself in the axis of truth or turn me away from it, the act which is presently good or evil for myself is singular and intransmissible. It is the point of the river that I shall never touch twice. This concrete character of the act is what justifies the necessity of prudence.

This concrete character makes theoretical analysis of prudence difficult. An example will show this more clearly. My wife and I live with my mother, who is in my care. I know in a general way that I must do good. Furthermore, I know that this goodness will mean peace in my home. Blessed are the peacemakers, said Our Lord. In the present case the voice of nature would proclaim this to me if the Gospel had not declared it. I sincerely want peace; it is a profound disposition of my soul. I have no other passionate desire than this, and I am willing to make any sacrifice for it. But do I have all the required dispositions for a morally satisfactory action in my home? No, I do not, for it is in the details of daily living that I must work for the peace that I desire, and this will not be possible without a great deal of discernment, judgment, tact and psychology. I shall have to know when to be silent and when to speak, when to smile and how to steer a conversation. I must know how to avoid unfortunate situations by careful foresight; in a word, I shall need a whole group of qualities that derive from intelligence. Can it be said that all of this "ability" is irrelevant to morality, that my desire for peace is all that is necessary, and that it matters little if I proceed well or badly to assure this peace? Obviously this would be an error. Our morality must be realistic. We must act not only in harmony with the end pursued, but also in a manner that leads to the end effectively. If the peace is broken through no fault of my own, then certainly I may depend upon the justice of God Who knows and fathoms the heart, and my good intention will do instead of success. But when peace depends upon my own behavior—and who can deny that it does depend on myself in large measure?—it is my duty to act reasonably and intelligently. And if this condition is to occur more than once, it will be necessary that I be endowed with a stable disposition and with a deeply rooted aptitude for discerning concretely whatever will save the peace that is compromised or affirm it. I need the virtue of prudence.

7. THE NATURE OF THE VIRTUE OF PRUDENCE

It can be summed up in a word. Prudence is a virtue of the intelligence (the practical intelligence), but it supposes a rectified appetite (the will and the passions) and a stable attachment of my whole being to God.

1. Prudence has its seat in the *intelligence*. Consequently it is a matter of discerning and seeing the relation of a concrete reality to an aspiration that is universally valid. It is a question of judging a case and ordering an action. All these are the work of reason.

2. The seat of prudence is the *practical* intelligence. It is not a question of speculation, or of knowing for the sake of knowledge, but of knowing in order to act. May it be said that these are two kinds of intelligence quite opposed to each other, the speculative and the practical? Yes, on condition that we recognize that they do not exclude each other. The astrologer who falls into a well because he did not watch where he was going is the caricature of the scholar who is lacking the most elementary prudence. Neither the scholar nor the prudent man can be dispensed from considering both the universal and the particular. But the scholar is interested in the particular only because of the intelligibility which he finds there, and the prudent man is interested in the universal in order that he may better govern the particular.

Prudence is more practical than even the most practical science.

It is a virtue of the intelligence *in so far as the intelligence is effectively engaged in action.* The prudent man is not deliberating in his room; he is in movement toward a goal. It is because he is actually striving toward this goal that he deliberates, judges and undertakes. It is on the battlefield that we will find "military prudence." The author of a book on tactics, however oriented toward action his work may be, is not engaged in the action; he is not exercising prudence but science, a practical science if you will, but not prudence, because it culminates in a conclusion that must still be applied to *each* case. The prudent man, as such, can only be interested in a *single* case, the particular one in which he finds himself engaged. It is one thing for manuals of strategy to profit from the prudence exercised on the fields of battle; but it's something else to say that prudence greatly needs to be informed by manuals of strategy. It is a matter of two different kinds of mental activity.

3. During the whole course of its activity prudence is intimately bound up with the exercise of the appetitive faculties, the will and the passions. It does not give us the ends of our moral action by itself, but receives them from above. Primarily from synderesis, but also from the virtues of justice, fortitude and temperance, not to mention the theological virtues. Let us again consider the example in the preceding paragraph. Prudence does not make me will that my mother and my wife respect their respective rights for the sake of peace; this would be the role of justice. But prudence makes me search for the proper means of attaining that end and puts them to work. In a word, it forms my virtuous intention from day to day. It always depends upon that virtue as a motive that proposes the end and especially orients it towards itself. Inversely, prudence will appeal to the virtuous dispositions of the appetite to carry out its purposes, for example, it will appeal to patience, as in the case we have mentioned.

4. Prudence is a moral virtue; it is not a technique or an art. This is so because it is not limited to the pursuit of any end whatever, but rather an end which, even though it be particular, remains under the motivation of the authentic, ultimate end of man. There are people who have a capacity for causing trouble between the best of friends, and there are others who are able to reconcile enemies. Both have ability, but there is prudence only in the one who can promote harmony.

Art does not have this universality. It seeks its end which is not the end of mankind in general. That is why an artist may refuse to make use of his talent or damage his own work without loss of the art itself. But the prudent man cannot refuse to act prudently. Father Noble's excellent formula defines prudence as "morality at work, morality in action; if therefore it voluntarily undertook to order evil actions, it would no longer be morality; it would no longer be prudence" (S. Thomas d'Aquin, *Somme théologique,* édition of the Revue des jeunes, *La prudence,* Explanatory notes, p. 239). There is no rest for prudence; it can no more have respite from work than mankind from journeying towards its ultimate goal.

5. If we define prudence as a virtue, we are saying that is a stable disposition. It is perhaps surprising that there should be such stability when we have insisted upon the changing character of prudence which is adaptation to constantly changing concrete reality. Certainly prudence must always be inventive and original in order to fulfill its role; there are never two identical situations. But this does not diminish the stability of the virtue itself. The decisions themselves are infinitely variable, and they do not recognize a formula, but this does not prevent prudence from being strongly rooted in the soul. Sometimes we hear it said of a man that he is surprisingly quick at repartee; he is never caught off guard. This is a reference to a permanent trait of his character, even though this characteristic consists precisely in the constant originality of his repartee. Prudence is also a stable disposition for the most flexible adaptation.

6. Prudence could be called the virtue of the golden mean, which would correspond quite well to the idea that good sense commonly makes of it. But it would then be necessary to define the other moral virtues, fortitude and justice and temperance, as tending toward the golden mean in the domain that belongs properly to them. And they do tend that way in a general manner, but not precisely. It is prudence which will declare in each particular case: here is the golden mean. The virtuous instinct may be strong and sure, but it does not dispense from careful watchfulness and sound reflection.

8. NATURAL AND SUPERNATURAL PRUDENCE

We have seen that prudence has two poles—both essential to our idea of it. There is the reality that is concrete, daily and particular, and there is also the total and ultimate end of human life. It is the role of prudence to take into account the details and circumstances of every action, but at the same time it is not fully itself unless it refers all this contingent matter not merely to some particular end but to the end of human life.

It is this tension between two poles that opens a serious debate between the believer and the unbeliever. The believer will say that prudence supposes the state of grace, that is to say, thorough orientation toward the authentic, ultimate end of man, which is a supernatural end. If you build your whole life upon a high ideal, but purely natural, you are fatally committing an imprudence, the most serious imprudence of all: you are not taking ultimate reality into account. "For what does it profit a man, if he gain the whole world, but suffer the loss of his own soul?" Your reckoning, however excellent it may be, is false because your premise is false. Attribute as many qualities to yourself as you wish, but do not call yourself prudent. You may be successful in everything, but you lack the *only* success that matters. But the unbeliever replies: your "state of grace" hardly seems to be a guarantee of prudence; it would be easy to find examples of faithful believers who completely lack this practical intelligence and have none of that sense of concrete reality which you yourself have called the essential thing in the virtue of prudence. Therefore, according as we stress the concrete character of the exercise of prudence or emphasize the reference to the absolute, we are tempted to say that prudence is a natural virtue based upon experience, or a supernatural virtue whose destiny is bound up with that of the virtue of charity.

It is perhaps in this domain of prudence that the classical distinction between acquired virtues and infused virtues best appears in all its truth. There are two kinds of prudence: the one is acquired and the other is infused. And the full scope of prudence is not perfectly covered unless the two collaborate closely.

What is infused prudence without acquired prudence? An indispensable auxiliary of charity, an auxiliary without which man could not realize his eternal destiny. Its only concern is the direct concern for salvation. How is it born? How does it die? Its destiny is bound up with charity. All men in the state of grace, and they alone, possess it. What does it assure to us? That without which charity would not be living: the practical and habitual discernment in matters that pertain to our eternal destiny. If we were particularly lacking in judgment, initiative or discernment, its work would be, together with humility rightly understood, to make us seek help and counsel from those who are better endowed than we are. Even among young people who are well endowed but utterly inexperienced, it works in this way. It is found even in the soul endowed with grace but which does not have the use of reason (small children, the insane), but then it exists only in the habitual state, because it does not have any human acts to direct. But when this is said, is it really prudence? Absolutely, because it works concretely and effectively in leading us to salvation. However, it is not a plenary prudence: it does not confer universal discernment. It may leave whole areas of our practical intelligence untouched. And if, at the moment when accession to the state of grace introduces it into the soul, it comes up against strongly anchored habits of negligence, temerity, etc., or evil natural propensities, its task may be rendered extremely difficult. It does not have a direct hold upon deficiencies of that order. Consequently it requires the cooperation of acquired prudence.

What can be said now about this acquired prudence? Can it be found alone, without infused prudence? Yes, it can. For it is based upon good, native dispositions, good moral principles, virtuous inclinations, education, experience and the very repetition of its acts. Is it a real prudence? Yes, at least in one sense: if it is really something more than a kind of ability, and if it is based upon a moral ideal that is authentic even if imperfect, and applies this ideal to the concrete reality of life. But it is not real prudence in another sense, because it is seriously imperfect. It never achieves anything more than rectitude of the natural, moral order without meritorious efficacy and with no bearing upon eternal happiness. Fatally and finally it misses the goal.

The Christian is not meant to possess only the infused virtues or only the acquired virtues. He must make the one fruitful by means of the other. In action the directive element will be supernatural prudence. For it is this which holds the secret of the end. This alone can propose the principles that determine the virtuous golden mean. Often, in fact, this golden mean varies considerably according as we are governed by the Gospel or by reason alone in our discernment. The theologian need not be disturbed when he sees theology borrowing so frequently from the philosophers; the rule of our conduct is supernatural prudence and Christ is our only Master.

Acquired prudence nevertheless has a very important role. Our task is not finished when we have done everything possible to guard against the loss of our eternal salvation. It is not sufficient to keep ourselves from making fatal choices. We must still become perfect in judgment, counsel and act. We must be able to give wise counsel to our neighbor and make the Christian ideal effective in all the areas of life—in politics and the social order and the home, in legislation and customs. How can we succeed in this task without the education of prudence, or without using all the resources which nature places at our disposal, or unless we know how to make the best use of them? We need good habits and virtuous inclinations which infused prudence cannot assure without our cooperation. Unlike the supernatural virtues, natural prudence cannot be acquired all in one moment, but it does provide a solid and harmonious basis for their possession.

The Christian must therefore submit his life to the direction of infused prudence; it alone is real virtue since it is moved by charity and will govern him in a Christian way. But this does not dispense him from working for possession of a solid "acquired prudence" which is the auxiliary without which true virtue could not achieve the fulness of its prudential work.

9. CONNECTION OF THE VIRTUES

We have met with this theme in several Fathers of the Church, particularly in St. Ambrose and St. Gregory: the virtues hold together; they are undivided in their solidarity. This idea is also found in Aristotle who specified with his more elaborate philosophical technique that their solidarity is seen in prudence, for no virtue can be complete unless it is joined with prudence; and this latter virtue is not really itself unless accompanied by all the other virtues.

With the coming of grace into the soul, the connection of the virtues, far from becoming more slack, is made even closer; but then it is charity, the proper virtue of the last end, which assures the unity of the virtuous organism. Does this mean that prudence is no longer the central core of the other moral virtues? On the contrary, it keeps its role but it is assumed into a vaster ensemble. Man without grace built his virtuous edifice little by little by fortunate moral efforts, and it is prudence that directed the work. But grace brings the unity of a virtuous organism fully constituted at the very start, and in this case the first mover is charity. Infused prudence here keeps its eminent role of binding together the other moral virtues; it has the responsibility of assuring the supernatural government of oneself. Although constituted at the start, the virtuous organism must strive to acquire its functional perfection, and to accomplish this it follows the laws that are proper to its constitution, that is to say, charity directs the other virtues by the mediation of infused prudence which itself, in the exercise of its functions, constantly benefits from the help which is brought to it by acquired prudence. This latter prudence therefore becomes doubly subordinate, but it loses none of its dignity for it collaborates with the fulness of its means in a supernatural work that infinitely surpasses it.

10. DELIBERATION, JUDGMENT, AND THE BEGINNING OF ACTION

It has already been stated that prudence does not assign to us the ends of our moral life. It takes these for granted and its task is to assure their effective realization in the flux of the concrete. Therefore it takes possession of the human act at the moment when the will is efficiently striving toward the goal and deliberation begins.

In fact, it is very rare that a goal can only be attained in one particular way. And even if the means are unique, there will always be the modalities of their application which will be infinitely variable. This is why it is necessary for man to set out first of all in search of the possible means for satisfying his aspirations. But it is not enough to find the means; they must be qualified, and their advantages and disadvantages must be noted. The ins and outs must be discerned and the consequences must be foreseen. Briefly, the means must be visualized in order that we may see what they will in fact be concretely if we decide to carry them out.

When the means have been inventoried and qualified, nothing however has yet been accomplished. The problem even seems to be more complicated because the simplicity of our original desire has been superseded by an accumulation of possible solutions. This is when deliberation, properly called, intervenes, for it is simply the elaboration of the judgment. If everything depended upon the will alone, it would turn to any means at hand which reason proposed as efficacious. But reason must confront the proposed means in the light of the general laws of morality and also in view of the concrete case, and make a decision based upon the precise action that seems best to undertake. Multiplicity must be reduced to unity; certainly not to an indivisible unity, for each contemplated plan has its internal complexity, but to a unity of conception and execution.

When the definitive judgment has thus been made and the will has confirmed it by turning to the means that were judged best (this is the choice), it remains to order the action and command the faculties of execution. There is now a return from the unity of the choice to a new multiplicity of phases and executive details.

It is not necessary for us to return at this point to an analysis which was made in the chapter on human acts. Let us however recall the three acts which, being the work of the practical intelligence already fixed upon the desired end, pertain to the virtue of prudence; these acts are the counsel, the judgment and the precept (*imperium*). The human act requires the virtuous functioning of reason in these three phases of its activity in order to comply with all the requirements of goodness.

It should be noted that experience proves that those who are the most capable of producing a multiplicity of possible solutions from their practical sense are not necessarily the best endowed for the reabsorption of that multiplicity in the unity of a judgment that is well-founded and sure. Remarkably inventive, they are often unable to make decisions. On the other hand, some may be equipped with excellent judgment that accomplishes nothing but evil, or that completely fails to achieve what was however so well chosen. Such a person does not know how to begin.

It is very important to see these divergences in psychological types if we are to be successful in the complete and harmonious education of the virtue of prudence. To the three phases of the human act there correspond special prudential aptitudes which separately require cultivation. We must not disturb the equilibrium of a complete and harmonious action by an education that is too exclusive in one aspect or another. We must be trained to deliberate and to give good counsel, as also to judge concretely and practically. We must train ourselves to command, and first of all to command ourselves. Natural dispositions can help us in this more or less, but if they are deficient there must be additional training all the more systematic.

After Aristotle, authors have reserved for prudence the completion of the work, including the presiding over the start of the action and carrying out this action to successful conclusion. This is in fact the goal towards which counsel and judgment will tend. We will then assign to the rectitude of the deliberation an auxiliary virtue, organically one with prudence but distinct from it, the virtue of good counsel, the *eubulia,* in the Greek of Aristotle.

According to Aristotle, judgment will always require two virtues, one for ordinary cases (*synesis*), and the other for exceptional cases (*gnome*). In most cases a sound judgment is sufficient for discerning among several means the one that has the highest coefficient of morally sound efficacy. These are classic cases. They do not dispense from judgment, because being particular and concrete no formula can be adequate to settle them virtuously, but at least they agree with the ordinary principles of moral action. But it is not always so. It sometimes happens that we must discount accepted habits and subordinate rules in order to preserve the great laws of human action. It is not enough to have ordinary good moral sense if we wish to be in command of these situations. Another kind of prudence is necessary. This is quite apparent in military life. The primary rule of prudence in this domain is respect for discipline. It is within the limits of received commands that initiative is allowed. But prudence sometimes requires that a colonel act contrary to the formal order of a general. Many colonels, however, are incapable of such virtuous disobedience, although their judgment may be very sound. In the order of moral life the same principles hold true. Certain exceptional cases require another kind of judgment. It is again a virtue, attached to prudence and organically one with it, which assures the rectitude of such audacious decisions. Prudence is something quite different from the meaning that is commonly given to the term. It is now used in the sense of false prudence which never takes too great a risk and is always careful not to become involved. On the contrary, however, prudence is the virtue of initiative and responsibility.

11. THE QUALITIES THAT MAKE THE PRUDENT MAN

In modern language a "prudent" chauffeur is merely one who does not drive too fast. If prudence were no more than this, the qualities that it requires would be quite simple. As a matter of fact, the prudent man according to our definition, expressed in terms of automobile driving, is not the one who does not drive too fast, but he is a driver who drives well, and that is quite a different matter. Much finer qualities are needed in the prudent man. It is not sufficient that he moderate the speed; he must be capable of going fast, perhaps very fast when it is required, and yet know how to pull through situations that are most difficult.

In reality a human life is differently complex than an automobile ride, and consequently the prudence which presides over its conduct requires a whole ensemble of qualities. We must try to specify the essentials.

The first quality required is *experience,* or better still the aptitude for benefiting from acquired experience. It is a matter of ordering a contingent action. However, knowledge of the particular is not innate in man and furthermore, it cannot be deduced from a priori principles. No deduction will reveal to me the heredity of an orphan whom I am sheltering. Some knowledge can only be acquired by observation of facts. Do you wish to become a good master of novices? You will need experience with young people. It is only when you have counselled many of them that your direction will become really sound. You must let the facts speak for themselves and more important, you must pay heed to them. For there are old men who have learned nothing from life. They have lived a long time, but they have not known how to record the lessons of experience. If we know how to benefit from everything in which we have participated as actors or spectators, then we have learned one of the great secrets of prudence for the government of our own lives and for the direction of others.

Does this mean that experience is sufficient? No, it contributes powerfully to an accurate knowledge of the particular case and its interpretation, but if this knowledge is to be fruitful it must be based upon *firm principles.* There is no prudence without an understanding of the concrete, nor is there prudence without a course of conduct that is founded upon rules that are universally valid. If prudence is to be virtuous, it cannot be pure pragmatism. It must at least repose upon the natural law. Jewish Wisdom also had recourse to the Law. Christians find it in the new law that is inscribed in their hearts by the Holy Spirit who has been given to them.

It is equally of first importance—and this is one of the great themes of sapiential literature—that we should not put too much trust in our own prudence, but allow ourselves to be instructed with *docility* by those who know better than we: "Lean not upon thy own prudence" (Prov. 3:5). How many false steps young men would spare themselves if they were a little more willing to govern themselves according to the counsels of their elders! Not that they ought to be servile, but docile. And it is not only young people who are in need of counsel. Two heads are always better than one, and it is rare that a consultation does not make us attentive to some aspect of a problem which we had not taken into consideration. It would be easier for a mathematician to do without a teacher than for a man of action to dispense with advisers, for mathematics are purely rational while concrete action is made up of a thousand details and points of view which one man, by himself, however ingenious, would find it difficult to encompass.

The prudent man must also be endowed with *sure-sightedness,* that is to say, with the ability to grasp the situation as it really is. Taking counsel is not enough. Frequently we must act without having the time or the possibility for consulting anyone, and at such moments we must make a decision, often without delay. On the other hand, even if we are able to take counsel, we must inform our advisers and present the facts to them. In most cases their judgment will depend upon our presentation of the data of the problem. There is at least one point on which they are closely bound up with our estimation; this is our interior reaction, which is of capital importance. That is why it matters greatly that our vision be clear. In this domain our counselor cannot be substituted for ourselves. He can only help us. If our first perception is lacking in exactness, docility will most often avoid a catastrophe. But there is a great distance between this negative protection and an action that is truly prudent.

At the stage of personal deliberation, the most important qualities are a certain *fertile imagination* in practical matters—for we must know how to discover the possible means for attaining the end—and the ability *to weigh the pros and the cons* of the different solutions proposed. The accuracy of this judgment will depend very largely upon the *freedom of the soul* with regard to its passions. It is said that envy is a bad counselor, and this is certainly true, but it is not the only one. If the passions are not governed by reason, they impair the serenity needed by the mind for wise deliberation, and exercise an exterior pressure upon the decision and pervert it.

It is evident that the prudent man must have a sense of what may possibly happen, and this sense must be very acute. He must be endowed with *foresight.* The words prudence and foresight are one and the same. To be a good counselor it is not sufficient to have good principles, or to be able to see a situation realistically; one must also know how to snuff the wind and foresee the psychological reactions that the contemplated act will unleash and in what direction it will be carried out. It is in the future that the action will take place and in the future that it will leave its mark. An action that is good in itself may have deplorable consequences. It is a matter of foreseeing the effects before starting the cause in motion. But some will object that this is impossible because the future is hidden from us, and if anyone is able to see into the future it is because of a special talent that is not given to many. It is true that we do not know the future with certainty, and that is why Scripture tells us, "the thoughts of mortal men are . . . uncertain" (Wis. 9:14). But thanks to experience, we can manage to surmise it, and most of the time we need not act at random.

Among the events of all kinds, the future hides various dangers. The prudent man will pay special attention to these perils that lie in wait for us. He has foresight, and therefore he will take *precautions*. This is exactly what most men would call prudence, as was mentioned before. Without falling into this error which would deprive our virtue of its greatness, we must recognize that the world is quite full of traps of all kinds, and we must keep our eyes open. Everything must be done in moderation, but a good dose of precaution is never useless.

Finally, the prudent man must be *circumspect,* that is to say, he must be careful about the many little details and circumstances which, although they do not constitute the act, may profoundly modify its value. These are the circumstances of time, place, manner and everything else. It is an art to know how to take into consideration the modalities of the act that are worth our attention, and to brush aside the others. This is an art, and we must apply ourselves to master it.

We could extend each of these paragraphs indefinitely. The whole of human life would be included. All of our reading, every movie, every play and each experience of our lives could be crowded into this study. But the essential thing is not to be exhaustive in such matters but instead to encourage reflection.

12. THE SOCIAL FORMS OF PRUDENCE

We have been considering prudence primarily as the virtue of self-government. We are, after all, directly responsible for our own actions, but we know very well that our actions involve us in social complexes whose good, i.e. whose purpose, is not identical with our purely individual end.

We do not need to establish the idea of the "common good." It will be sufficient if we simply remember that the common good is something different from the sum total of particular goods. It has its own unity and its own forms. All men journeying toward their last end are dependent upon one another in the framework of various organizations in which some exercise authority and others are subordinate.

Whoever has responsibility in a social body receives, by this very fact, the mission to lead a group of his fellow-men, at least for some particular purpose. And if he must have a virtue in order to govern himself, it is all the more necessary that he have one to direct others.

Among social bodies there are two that particularly pertain to men in general, for they do not concern individuals in their capacities as technicians, scholars, or artisans, but in so far as they are men; these are the family and the State.

The common good of the family is not of a technical order. It pertains primarily to the life of man. Consequently it requires real prudence in members of the home. Parents must certainly possess various skills, for example, the ability to educate, and competent management of money, etc. But they require more than this. They must be able to play their part with prudence, since they are the determining factors of the total welfare of a natural cell, the family.

Merely individual good is here surpassed very broadly. A new virtue is needed, *family prudence*. It is difficult to conceive of a prudent father of a family who is unable to govern himself, but on the other hand it is easy to imagine a strong man who is capable of directing his personal life although unable to carry the responsibilities of the head of a family. This is another kind of prudence. Let us note, moreover, that if family prudence is found eminently in the father and mother, it is also found in the older children because of the role that has fallen to them. And we must also mention the youngest children because they have their part in the service of the common good of the family. Their prudence must be exercised in docility, respect, willingness and other virtues of this kind. And every educator can and must participate in the radiation of family prudence because he is the authentic representative of the authority of the parents.

In regard to the State we must give analogous consideration. Politics are not purely technical. The common good of the City concerns man in his totality. And moral values cannot be foreign to the public domain. Not only must those who govern be prudent, but they must possess this virtue in an eminent manner. Each one will exercise it under a particular aspect, according to the function that he exercises in the State. Those who are members of a consultative assembly must have the prudence of a good counselor. And those who enact the laws must excel in judgment and choice. Still others, having executive authority, must imbue their rule, the *imperium,* with prudence. Finally the citizens, and more especially in a democratic regime, must be endowed with that *political prudence* that will make good and useful citizens of them.

Apart from the family and the State, are there other groups who require a particular form of prudence in their leaders and members? We have already mentioned military prudence. And now we may want to turn our attention toward another social body, the Church. The Old Testament strongly emphasized the importance of prudence in a father, and perhaps even moreso in the leader of the people; the New Testament counsels us to require an eminent form of prudence in the bishop who is a leader of the new Israel (Lk. 12:41-44; cf. the pastoral epistles). This *episcopal prudence,* to which a special prudence in the faithful must correspond, makes for action that is in harmony with the whole body of the Church.

Certainly it is now evident that the higher our responsibility may be, the more perfect must be our prudence. We can never legitimately treat one of our fellow-men as a chess-board pawn or as a mere cog in a wheel. Man is a unit; we cannot touch a single fiber of his being without causing a wave to be transmitted through his whole person even unto his eternal destiny. As soon as we become responsible for one of our fellow-men, it is prudence instead of skill that becomes essential. Nor is it only individual prudence, since it is not our own destiny alone that is at stake, but social prudence. Is a distinct virtue necessary for each case? Certainly not; for what social relationship is there that does not come under one of the great kinds of prudence: political or domestic prudence? In the last analysis, can our fellow-man be anything other than a parent, a citizen or a brother in the faith?

13. VICES OPPOSED TO PRUDENCE

St. Augustine wrote, "There are not only vices opposed to each virtue in an obvious way, as temerity is opposed to prudence; there are also vices which, in a certain manner, are near the virtue and similar to it, certainly not in reality but by a deceptive appearance: opposed to prudence we find then not only temerity or imprudence but guile" (*Contra Julianum,* I, 4, c. III, P.L., 44, 748). In matters of prudence this division of vices is particularly well-founded. It is very preferable to a strict classification of vices of default and vices of excess. There is never an excess of prudence; there is only the caricature of it. We shall then consider vices that are manifestly contrary to prudence and the kinds of prudence that are false.

It is interesting to note first of all that these two kinds of vices ordinarily derive from different passions. There are the shortcomings, the passions that blind us and overshadow our reason in such a way that we are unable to reason; the practical reason capitulates in allowing itself to be paralyzed. This occurs when there is violent carnal desire or an explosion of anger. Other passions, more prudent, divert the practical reason for their own purposes. Far from paralyzing it, they make it fully contributory. Reason capitulates again, but this time in order to be at the service of the conqueror. Avarice and malice are passions that willingly make us industrious and inventive; they are without equal in attaining their end. "For the children of this world, in relation to their own generation, are more prudent than the children of light" (Lk. 16:8).

We shall first consider the vices that are obviously opposed to prudence. These are haste, thoughtlessness, negligence and inconstancy.

Deliberation is one of the essential phases of a reasonable act. This is what is forgotten by those who act with *haste,* without sufficient reflection. They have not taken counsel or become informed, nor have they considered the dangers to which they expose themselves unreasonably. The result is that they become involved before their decision is mature, and throw themselves head-first, literally precipitating themselves. It is only too evident that there is disorder in this procedure. Man being left in the hands of his own counsel owes it to himself only to act knowingly. However, the degree of haste should not be measured in terms of the rapidity of deliberation. Certain decisions must be made rapidly; excessive delay would not be virtuous. Some deliberations, on the other hand, may continue for months and still they do not permit the starting of an action that is exempt from haste. There are solutions that do not mature until after many years. But there are also minds that are more or less quick and it would be wrong to want to delay the decisions of those whose sure-sightedness is particularly sound. It is in respect to each particular case that we must determine the golden mean, for apart from this there can only be haste or culpable delay.

Thoughtlessness is very like haste and most often the two vices are bound up together. However, they are not identical. Haste skips over a rung and descends too quickly from general principles to the solution of the particular case. Thoughtlessness, for its part, intervenes at the moment of judgment. Whether practical reason has deliberated for a long time or not matters little in this case. It is possible that all the various solutions have been foreseen and that one has nevertheless delayed a great deal. In any case, at the moment of decision one fails to take into account an element of the problem that is essential or at least important. The judgment is not necessarily too hasty but its foundations are at any rate too narrow.

The two sins which we have just mentioned are inconceivable apart from a certain *negligence;* one may neglect to deliberate or to weigh all the factors needed in the balance of the judgment. Negligence is also the element of guilt in all imputable ignorance. It is the root of all the sins of omission. This explains its importance in the moral life of man. It intervenes at the point where there is a positive duty, but one takes no account of it or is uninformed about it or doesn't care; one's mind is elsewhere. Consequently, the duty is omitted. That which is missing is a strong desire for doing the right thing, which would have kept the attention alert. But the practical reason also carries its share of responsibility. Its functioning was vitiated. The vice of negligence is directly opposed to the urgent recommendation of the Gospel: "Watch!" The foolish virgins were negligent virgins; they ought to have procured oil for themselves.

Inconstancy aims at the effort itself. It halts an action that is under way without any valid motive, even though the action was maturely deliberated and satisfactorily chosen. As a matter of fact it is always born of another vice, particularly laziness, or a passion which, happening unexpectedly, canalizes all the available activity. It is important, however, to point it out, for there is a deficiency in the practical reason whenever it does not maintain its decisions once it has seen their necessity.

Can such sins and faults against prudence be mortal? Yes, if the good that has been taken away or obstructed or neglected is necessarily a matter of salvation. Or if they betray a certain contempt for God or His law. In other cases they are venial.

Prudences of a false kind are wholly different from the vices previously enumerated. Far from leaving the practical reason dormant, they make it contributory. The disorder then comes from the intrusion of an undue end, or from means that are perhaps well founded in the human sense but morally without value.

If it is a matter of disorder in regard to the end, we are then concerned with *prudence of the flesh*. It resembles the virtue of prudence like a sister, but is based upon a false hierarchy of values. Instead of putting eternal goods and temporal goods in their proper place, respectively, it accords too much consideration to goods that are inferior. Such prudence is clever, certainly, but it is in the service of an evil master. It will know many degrees. In certain cases it will be the very type of mortal sin organizing the whole of one's life in dependence upon a created good. St. Paul's saying may then be applied to it in all its force: "For the wisdom of the flesh is hostile to God, for it is not subject to the law of God, nor can it be" (Rom. 8:7). In other cases the evil will not be so profound. One may not respect the hierarchy of values as one should, but God is still one's last end. Too much value may be accorded some created good even though one does not make of it a supreme good. In this case the sin will be of the venial type. Let us note, however, that carnal prudence should not be confused with an ability of a purely temporal kind which, by itself would not be bound up with any hierachy of values; such would be the case in regard to professional competence. Such ability is a relative, human perfection to which the practical reason may give either a good or an evil orientation.

It is not always the end pursued which, being only an apparent good, perverts the working of prudence. The end can be perfectly good while the prudence is false. For there are illicit means which can pretend to be "good means." Don't people speak of "pious lies"? They have the appearance of goodness but they are "officious" lies. They do not really derive from authentic prudence but rather from its caricature. What shall this disorder be called? Should we call it guile? This word may lead us slightly astray, but nevertheless the meaning is clear. It is not sufficient to pursue an honest end and eliminate the means which are in flagrant contradiction with the rules of morality. We must also track down the hypocritical means which pose as virtuous and be rid of them.

We would be finished with our examination of the vices opposed to prudence if the Gospel did not warn us against a certain form of solicitude or anxiety which reveals a lack of confidence in the wholly paternal Providence of God. "Therefore I say to you, do not be anxious for your life, what you shall eat; nor yet for your body, what you shall put on . . . do not be anxious about tomorrow; for tomorrow will have anxieties of its own" (Mt. 6:25, 34). Is this carnal prudence? Yes, it is a form of it since the rule that can lead us back to the right way can be formulated as follows: "But seek first the kingdom of God and his justice, and all these things shall be given you besides." The danger would therefore be that we neglect the important matter of the Reign of God through our concern for earthly matters. We must not try to twist the letter of a text that is so clear by any explanations that are supposedly reasonable. At least we must make a precise statement of the central idea in this thought. How can we commit sin in our concern for the future and in our carefulness to assure ourselves the goods that are necessary for our subsistence and for that of our dependents?

We can commit sin by serving Mammon instead of making Mammon serve ourselves. We can sin by not according to our spiritual life the required solicitude, because our attention is concentrated elsewhere. And finally we commit sin when we remain anxious and without trust in Providence after we have done everything that depended upon ourselves. There are so many anxieties that are useless and which do nothing whatever to solve our problems; however, they deprive us of a precious freedom of mind which could be so useful to us! Nevertheless, the Lord did not give us the example of the birds of the sky and the lilies of the field to encourage us in idleness or improvidence. Our Lord saw the true hierarchy of values threatened by the excessive and wholly vain concern for temporal matters and the future. He cried out His warning, that is all. Along with the parable of the lilies and the birds there is also the story of the tower and the battle. We must be free of illicit anxieties, but we must also be provident.

14. THE CERTITUDE OF PRUDENCE

Prudence has the mission of assuring the rectitude of the government of ourselves by ourselves. Now that we are better informed about its requirements, resources and adversaries, we can ask ourselves: does it have the capacity for assuming this task, and are its determinations affected by a sufficient coefficient of certitude to permit our hoping that it will lead us to our last end?

At the level of nature alone (and it is at this level that we must make equitable judgment of the value of prudence that is wholly acquired), the last end remains quite indistinct. It is not the yes or no of admission to eternal happiness. Therefore it is quite difficult to measure the success of a life at this level. It is extremely relative.

We may however recognize that natural prudence alone is quite poorly equipped for leading anyone at all to this even imperfect happiness. How can a man constantly govern himself according to the requirements of the virtuous life by his own means alone? He will do his best and will have excellent achievements, but he will always remain very far from the ideal. How could he inform himself about all the dangers that threaten his virtue? There are so many that are unforeseen. How could he have the required sure-sightedness to carry out in a constantly changing concrete reality the great principles which he professes? Acquired prudence has its greatness, but if we want to judge it accurately, we must be very satisfied if its successes are merely passable. And moreover we are considering it without reference to the problem of salvation.

Supernatural prudence has a completely different role. It journeys toward eternal happiness, and makes us journey in that direction also, and toward a judgment that will be a yes or a no. It achieves its purpose if it safeguards the flame of charity, and loses it if that flame is extinguished forever. It was conceived for this work. Children and simple folk, because of supernatural prudence, display astonishing wisdom. Its successes are not illusory. And yet it remains the virtue of man, that limited being, and has its seat in his practical reason. Grace certainly raises nature higher, but it does not suppress the unforeseen surprises of the concrete. Even supernatural prudence may therefore be understood in the sense of these words from the book of Wisdom, "For the thoughts of mortal men are fearful, and our counsels uncertain" (9:14). Certainly we must not despise the solidity of a judgment founded upon natural and supernatural experience or docility to the counsels of wise men and the law of God. Such a judgment possesses all the certitude that may be expected of a human judgment, and this certitude may be perfectly sufficient for virtuous living. It remains true, however, that whatever may happen, this prudence is quite inadequate to bring us safely into port. And it is at this point that the role of a new element appears in our supernatural organism: the gift of counsel. We must say a few words about this gift in concluding this section.

15. THE GIFT OF COUNSEL

A well-equipped modern ship must have something more than a captain and pilot to direct its course; it takes on board a radio to obtain the directions and messages that come from shore from time to time. This is a passive role, but very useful in the navigating of the ship. And the soul that is in the state of grace, along with the virtues by which it is actively directed, also possesses its receptive antenna, that is to say, a disposition to receive the directions of God. There are situations in which even supernatural prudence would not provide sufficient help. Our Lord Himself indicated this when He said to His Apostles, "But when they deliver you up, do not be anxious how or what you are to speak; for what you are to speak will be given you in that hour. For it is not you who are speaking, but the Spirit of your Father who speaks through you" (Mt. 10:19-20). This is the intervention of the gift of counsel. The study of this gift is part of the general theology of gifts. Like the others it belongs to the state of grace, always being one with charity. And like the others it is characterized by the mode of passivity which it introduces into the soul. It must be said in regard to this, and regarding the others also, that it leaves intact the freedom of man, for God always fully respects the nature of the beings whom He moves and governs. It is the domain to which it appertains, the domain of prudence, which gives proper character to the gift of counsel. For this reason it is the natural crowning of our whole study.

REFLECTIONS AND PERSPECTIVES

The word and the reality of prudence. There is an immense gulf between, on the one hand, our term prudence in the meaning commonly given this word today, and on the other hand, the reality which we are now studying under this very name of prudence.

It is the fate of important words, even those that are most important, of a civilization or culture, to become devaluated. A few of these may be mentioned: *economy,* which originally meant the organization of a house, the administration of a business, or the divine purpose of salvation, has come to mean a kind of avarice. *Politics,* the science or art of governing peoples, now has the meaning of foxiness. The *apostolate,* which means the sending by God of His messengers to men, now sometimes signifies a kind of propaganda or conquest, even profane. Likewise, *prudence,* the human virtue par excellence, the great and beautiful virtue whose praise echoes through all the books of the Bible, has often come to mean, in our time, a fearful precaution, or the calculating of the miser or the "housewife," or the fear of taking a risk.

The prudence that we are considering, however, is quite the opposite. It is the virtue of initiative and responsibility, the virtue of human risk, the virtue which is above all the moral virtues because it is the virtue that governs human behavior. It is the axis of all morality, and we could not possibly exaggerate its importance.

Doubtless faith, hope and charity *inspire* and measure it interiorly. But faith, hope and charity themselves are enhanced by it in their exterior acts: the martyr who decides to risk his life by making an exterior profession of faith before a godless government is making a splendid act of prudence; the brevity or length of the prayers which a Christian chooses to address to God may be attributed to his prudence, or even simply the time that he decides to give to God each day; the exterior act of charity, however generous it may be, may lose its value if it is obtrusive, indiscreet, that is to say, imprudent: at the least, love failed to apply intelligence to the act, and to act intelligently.

Man was created by God in His own image, that is to say, with intelligence and volition, and endowed with a certain autonomy, capable of governing himself. The prudence by which man "governs himself" is the first of the cardinal virtues, cardinal par excellence.

Prudence and the Examination of Conscience. How does it happen therefore that prudence has such little place in the Christian's examination of conscience? Or in the exhortations of spiritual directors? Each of us should exercise reflection in order that we may put our lives under the sign of authentic prudence, that is to say, under the sign of *intelligent* behavior, inspired by faith, hope and charity.

The man who fails to apply his intelligence to all his acts is lacking in charity. The best that a man has to offer is not so much his money or his exterior goods but rather his intelligence. The vices opposed to prudence: thoughtlessness, haste, inconstancy, negligence, etc., are finally due to a lack of charity.

Prudence and improvidence. It is not necessary to oppose one to the other, or to choose one in favor of the other. There is the parable of the lilies and the fields, but there is also the parable of the tower and the parable of the battle (Lk. 14:28-33). In the psalms there is the verse *In manus tuas commendo spiritum meum,* and there is the verse *Anima mea in manibus meis semper.* Human behavior that has no place for trust in God, or for religious improvidence, or for sleep, would be imprudent. But human behavior that is forever seeking recourse to God in order to make up for its own negligence and improvidence would be equally imprudent. Wise improvidence must itself be foreseen, chosen and ordered; in this way it is equally prudent.

Prudence and obedience. Prudence is the virtue of the adult man, but who is adult? Maturity of the soul is a goal to which we have never perfectly attained, and towards which we must always strive. However wonderful it may be, man sometimes finds it painful "to be left in the hands of his own counsel." It weighs heavily upon him to have to govern himself or to decide for himself. He would like to give someone else the responsibility. And it happens that a Christian may feel himself liberated and satisfied when he has found a superior who unburdens him of all reflection and all responsibility, leaving him only the leisure to obey. This is the problem of *spiritual direction,* and it is also the problem of *religious obedience.*

Spiritual direction is not intended to make or keep minors in a state of minority but to educate future adults. The spiritual director is not a superior but a guide, and the spiritual son does not owe him obedience but docility. The son is asking counsel from him, not a command. It does not go contrary to prudence to ask counsel for the governing of one's life, because as a matter of fact prudence, which must be informed, must be provided with counsel, and nothing is better than the word of a virtuous, experienced man who fears God and is filled with the Holy Spirit. It then remains for the directed person to make a final decision and to act in his own name, taking into account everything that has been said to him and with respect for the spiritual worth of the director. Doubtless there are cases when the director cannot be judged or when it is best to obey simply. But obedience that is pure and simple is then only prudent because it is provisional: a necessary stage preceding a greater maturity.

Religious obedience presents a more complex problem. It is not true that those who fear the responsibilities of life are ordinarily attracted to the religious state. Many do not enter religious life because they have a weak character and lack strength to choose it. Many who do not fear the responsibilities have, for this very reason, assumed the responsibility of giving their whole life to the Lord in the religious life. The obedience of the religious, moreover, does not require that he abdicate his intelligence or make no further use of prudence. On the contrary, a generous obedience demands that one give himself completely, including his intelligence: either in order that the intelligence may make all that is required understandable and enable him to do everything satisfactorily, which is the ordinary case, or that it may allow him to distinguish the true from the false, the good from the evil, in the received command, and discern what ought to be carried out and what should not. Man commands an animal with his hand, by pushing or striking him; but he commands another man by his word, because he is addressing the other man's intelligence, which, within himself, commands everything. Finally, if it be true that certain monastic spirituality insists upon the "minor" state of religious with respect to the Father Abbot, this state of minority to be acquired is quite similar to that of "the spiritual child-likeness" that is so often recommended by the Gospel. And if it be true that the Gospel requires that we become again like little children, this means, as St. Paul explains it, that we must "not become children in mind, but in malice be children" (I Cor. 14:20). "We have not been encouraged," says St. Leo, "to return to the games of childhood or to its imperfect beginnings, but to take from that state the things that are even becoming to mature age: that our passions and emotions may pass quickly, and the return to peace be made promptly, that we may not remember offenses or have any desire for advancement or status, that we should love the common life and find equality entirely natural" (Sermon 37). On religious obedience, one may read *L'obéissance et la religieuse d'aujourd'hui,* Editions du Cerf, Paris, 1951, and *Enfance et maturité spirituelles,* in *La Vie Spirituelle,* Oct. 1951.

But the problem of spiritual direction raises other questions. It is not only the directed man—or more often the directed woman—who would like to be able to be relieved of heavy spiritual responsibilities. Sometimes it is the guide, himself, who has recourse to the ready-made formulae of casuistry in order that he may always be on the safe side. Casuistry may render services. Ordinarily it presents solutions that are both general enough to cover current practice and concrete enough, however, to take the place of an adequate and final answer in each case requiring decision. But who cannot see that it is a kind of guess? What doctor could heal his patients if he never repeated anything but the formulas of a book? A fortiori the spiritual physician who treats sicknesses that are differently complex, multiple and detailed, and cases that are always personal. Casuistry can offer examples, but it is dangerous to use it without discernment, and its use is all the more perilous because it is the easy prey of guides who are lacking precisely in discernment and sound doctrine.

The whole theology of spiritual direction must still be worked out. Work projects: The history of spiritual direction from the first Fathers of the Desert until the 16th century, and from the 16th century to the present day. The necessity and role of spiritual direction in the economy of the Church's life and in the economy of each Christian's life. Is the direction of conscience necessarily a privilege of the priesthood? The role of the staretz in the Orient. The direction given by "mystics." The preparation of priests for spiritual direction. Individual direction and collective direction. The role of parents in relation to their children, and of a husband in regard to his wife? The priest and spiritual direction of married women. The matter of spiritual direction; cases in which it seems particularly necessary: detachment from sin, advancement in extraordinary ways, great desires for perfection mingled with an unconscious self-love and futile attachments, etc. The subject of spiritual direction: the choice of the director, docility and clear-sightedness, the good use of direction. On all these subjects one may consult the following studies, among others: *Prudence chrétienne,* Editions du Cerf, Paris, 1948, passim, particularly Philippeau, *Prudence et obéissance,* and J. M. Perrin, *La direction spirituelle.* One may also read with discernment, H. Sauvage, *La direction des femmes, in Supplément de la Vie spirituelle,* May, 1952.

Direction and counsel. The theology of the gift of counsel.

The Morality of Prudence and the morality of conscience, duty, casuistry and law. Evaluate from the viewpoint of the morality of prudence, which alone permits man to "personalize" himself, the morality of conscience (static morality), and duty (duty is imposed from outside ourselves, while the good, which is desired by every being, is imposed interiorly and is capable of giving life and dynamism to morality), and evaluate the morality of the law (only prudence is able to give interior and human value to anything that is an exterior command), etc.

Prudence, intelligence and knowledge. If prudence, the virtue of intelligence, is necessary in every virtuous act, in what measure is it necessary to be intelligent in order to be virtuous? To what degree can there be sin through lack of intelligence? The measure of the lack of charity in the lack of intelligence? Criticize the theory that presents morality as a matter of intelligence, showing the pros and the cons.

Does good moral behavior require a share of knowledge? Knowledge of theology, morality, experiences? Which ones? Give examples. Analyze the sin of ignorance, its causes, its gravity, its excuses. The responsibilities of different educators: parents, teachers, the State (through the law).

Is the communication of moral knowledge sufficient for a sound education in prudence? If the prudential act consists in an effort of intelligence to discover or create the suitable, rational order in each action, how can prudential intelligence be developed in others? Criticize the education which aims at making obedient subjects without concern that they be made "prudent." Inversely, criticize the education that is limited to the conveying of knowledge or the effort to develop the mind, without training in practical decisions which are the most characteristic acts of a noble prudence. The need for knowledge of the faith in the prudent man. Show the connection between the theological virtues and Christian prudence.

Is the knowledge of self necessary for moral behavior? In what measure? Self-knowledge and temperament, character. Psychoanalysis: usefulness of the subject's point of view, and of the director; the dangers.

The discernment of spirits: signification, history, theology. The virtue of discretion (in the original meaning of the term which signified discernment, proportion): show the role of this virtue in religious rules, particularly its capital role in the Rule of St. Benedict.

Domestic prudence. Necessary knowledge (in morality) for the foundation of a home, and for the education of children. Knowledge of the other sex in one and the other spouse. Knowledge of child-rearing in the future mother? The education of the parents. The mistakes "of ignorance" in the conduct of the home. Lack of considerateness. Elaborate a theology of the home, following a theology of the "sacrament" of marriage.

Political prudence, or "Politics." What are politics? Read the *Politics* of Aristotle and the commentary of St. Thomas Aquinas. Show that politics are more than a science or an art, and that they are really a kind of "prudence." The end of politics: the happiness of man? On this subject see *Prudence chrétienne,* previously cited.

The science that is necessary in politics. History, experiences, psychology, the science of government, jurisprudence, and laws, etc. Does the Church have a "social doctrine" or a "political doctrine"?

The history of these doctrines in theology. The principles of political theology. Foundations in Scripture.

The theology of means in politics. Laws, propaganda, power.

The division of powers: legislative, judicial, executive. Merits and demerits of the division of powers, or of their combination in a single head.

The question of the "best political regime" from the point of view of political morality.

The political education of the citizens. Is it necessary and useful? Who should give it? How?

The domain of Political power. How far does it extend? The question of the public school and the private school. Childhood. Homes. The unions. The relations of the Church and State; the nomination of bishops; national ceremonies (viz.: national funerals) in the Church. What are the best relations of Church and State? Separation, subordination (of the Church or the State?), or union of the two?

National and international politics: moral principles.

Special prudences. Pastoral prudence. The conduct of churches, direction of souls. See the chapter on the "States."

Prudence in labor unions. Prudence of the heads of industry, of the union official, etc. Determination of the purpose of the business concern, of the labor union, etc. See the chapter on "Justice."

Military prudence. Prudence of the leader. Responsibilities, formation. Prudence and obedience of the soldiers. Prudence and evangelical charity.

Prudence in the youth movements. Formation of the "leaders."

(Review the Reflections and Perspectives of chapter VI, Vol. III, and chapter V, Vol. IV.)

BIBLIOGRAPHIE

Théologie biblique de la prudence:

C. Spicq, *La vertu de prudence dans l'Ancien Testament,* in *Revue biblique,* XLII (1933), pp. 187-210.

H. Duesberg, *Les scribes inspirés,* Paris, 1938-39.

A.-M. Dubarle, *Les sages d'Israël,* Paris, Éd. du Cerf, 1946.

Et d'une façon générale les commentaires des livres sapientiaux de l'ancien Testament (le souvenir que le terme biblique de sagesse est souvent synonyme de ce que nous appelons ici prudence). On se reportera aussi avec profit aux éditions des livres sapientiaux dans la *Bible de Jérusalem* dont les introductions, les tables et les index sont particulièrement bien faits et pratiques.

Histoire du traité et théologie de la prudence:

Saint Thomas d'Aquin, *La prudence,* 2ᵉ éd., Trad. et notes par Th. Deman, Paris, Éd. de la Revue des J., 1949 (Ce livre de 556 pages donne le texte de saint Thomas et la traduction dans les 245 premières pages; c'est dire que les notes explicatives et les renseignements techniques sont abondants. Ils sont aussi particulièrement excellents).

A.-M. Henry, Th. Deman, etc., *Prudence chrétienne,* Coll. *Cahiers de la vie spirituelle,* Paris, Éd. du Cerf, 1948, 216 pages (D'un abord plus facile que le volume précédent, plus pratique aussi, et présentant bien l'ensemble de la doctrine. Important chapitre à la fin sur la politique (prudence politique).

A. Gardeil, *La vraie vie chrétienne,* Paris, Desclée De Br., 1935 (Lire la partie intitulée: "Le gouvernement personnel et surnaturel de soi-même," pp. 99-189).

O. Lottin, *Les débuts du traité de la prudence au moyen-âge,* in "Recherches de théologie ancienne et médiévale," IV (1932), pp. 270-293.

Isabelle Rivière, *Sur le devoir d'imprévoyance,* Paris, Éd. du Cerf, 1933 (Vive réaction, au nom de l'Évangile, contre la fausse prudence qu'est la prudence bourgeoise).

Sur la politique (prudence politique) on lira avec profit:

Ch. Journet, *Exigences chrétiennes en politique,* Fribourg (Suisse), Lib. Univ., 1946.

E. Mounier, *Les certitudes difficiles. L'itinéraire politique,* Paris, Éd. du Seuil, 1951.

H. Sacher et O. von Nell-Breuning, *Gesellschaftliche Ordnungssysteme* (*Wörterbuch der Politik*), Freiburg, Herder, 1951.

P. Janet, *Histoire de la science politique et ses rapports avec la morale,* Paris, Éd. Alcan, 1903.

J. Maritain, *Du régime temporel et de la liberté* (Coll. *Questions disputées*), Paris, Desclée De Br., 1933.

BIBLIOGRAPHY

Davis, Henry, S.J., *Moral and Pastoral Theology,* Vol. I, pp. 259 ff. London, Sheed and Ward, 1941.

Farrell, Walter, O.P., *A Companion to the Summa,* Vol. III, pp. 141-164. New York, Sheed and Ward, 1940.

McHugh, John A., O.P., and Callan, Charles J., O.P., *Moral Theology, A Complete Course,* Volume II, pp. 1-29.

Sheedy, Charles E., C.S.C., *The Christian Virtues,* pp. 157-168. Notre Dame, Ind., University of Notre Dame Press, 1949.

Connery, J. R., S.J., "Prudence and Morality," *Theological Studies,* 13: 564-582, D '52.

Gebhard, W. A., "The Intellectual Virtue of Prudence," *Thomist,* 8: 413-456, Oct '45.

Muntsch, A., "Prudence a Necessary Virtue," *Review for Religious,* 8: 82-85, Mar '49.

Steinmueller, J. E., "Holiness and the Cardinal Virtues," *Homiletic and Pastoral Review,* 51: 39-44, Oct '50.

Chapter V

JUSTICE

THEOLOGICAL POSITION OF THE TREATISE ON JUSTICE,
  by A. Girard

CONCERNING JUSTICE PROPERLY SO-CALLED,
  by J. Tonneau

THE TYPES OF JUSTICE, by L. Lachance

REFLECTIONS AND PERSPECTIVES

BIBLIOGRAPHY

Chapter V

JUSTICE

THEOLOGICAL POSITION OF THE TREATISE ON JUSTICE

Theological Position of the Treatise on Justice

Before undertaking a "treatise on Justice" in this Introduction to Theology, we must be on guard against a temptation to which certain authors who have written about this virtue seem to have yielded. Often such a study has been conducted as if it were something that pertained more to the law, or alas, to casuistry, than to theology. Certainly nothing is more difficult than to avoid continually laying oneself open to such criticism. There are many chapters in our books of morality which could be written quite as well by a jurist or a casuist as by a theologian, especially those in which there is a study of contracts, or of offences against justice and the reparations that are then called for, or even abstract notions of law or domain and the various modes of acquiring possessions. Each writer sheds his own light on the subject, from his particular point of view. But who cannot see how much the perspective will differ in regard to the same material, and how different the results will be, even when the writers hold identical positions.

It is therefore necessary to indicate the theological position at the start of this treatise. We will then have the advantage of giving cohesion to all the infinitely small details, to all the grains of sand which, for lack of an appropriate connection, could slip out of the hands of anyone who wished to catch hold of them.

1. ORDER OF THE ULTIMATE END

In the order of the "return," a theme which will be found in all morality, variously orchestrated, passing into each of the parts of the choir and all the tones of the scale, the motif that must be emphasized most of all is the order of the ultimate end.

A frequent confusion makes of moral theology a science of the acts of the will. But the import is much stronger and more complete if we envisage the moral order as the order of the end. Then everything takes the same direction, everything is polarized towards a superior unity, in which are integrated the thousand elements which consideration of the human will alone would not permit uniting into a coherent and directed whole. Our morality is certainly the study of voluntary acts. But we do not want it to be called voluntarist. The good and the end, the perfect good and the last end, are all one. Our morality will therefore be a morality of the end. That is why the orderly contemplation of the multiplicity of human acts and of their principles begins with the contemplation of the end to which, in the movement towards God, the rational creature must tend. It is a matter of "realizing" within us the image of the Trinity in a full manner, which is perfected according to our "processions" of intelligence and love. We must freely fashion this divine resemblance, according to which and in view of which we have been created. A theological view of justice must begin with this complete outlook.

2. JUSTICE IN GOD

The theologian judges things in relation to God. By considering for a moment the divine attribute of justice, we shall conceive what our own justice ought to be. This is the plan which Bossuet indicates for us (*Sermon sur la justice:* Rameaux 1666; first point):

> If I wanted to go back to the principle, I should have to tell you that it is in God primarily that justice is found, and that it is from this high origin that it is diffused among men. In this respect it would be easy for me to show you that God, being sovereignly just, governs the world in general and mankind in particular, by an eternal justice, and that it is this immutable attachment to His own laws which, in the midst of infinite agitations and changes in nature, accounts for a self-sustaining spirit of uniformity and equality in the universe. Next, we should see how justice flows into us from this celestial source to make one of the most beautiful features of the divine resemblance in our souls, and from this we should conclude that we ought to imitate this constant uniformity of divine justice by a firm and inviolable love of equity and the laws.

It is not necessary now to comment upon justice in God, since the subject is studied elsewhere. (Cf. Treatise on the One God by

R. P. Paissac, Vol. II, chap II.) Let us only recall that the biblical texts in which "justice" is incontestably attributed to God should not be understood as the justice of equality (or commutative) but only as proportioned justice (distributive). The first is hardly inclusive in the relationships of God with His creature. It only pertains to equals, and in regard to material things, but God is still the first generous giver of the goods of grace and of nature. The Apostle asks, "Or who has first given to him, that recompense should be made to him"? (Rom. 11:35). And in the recompense accorded to our supernatural merits, St. Augustine noted (Letter 194, 5, 19; P.L. vol. 33, 880) that these merits come only from grace, and in rewarding them God is crowning His own gifts. In regard to distributive justice, it is perfect in God, and is superior to the justice which determines in us the division of goods, rewards and punishment. Every being receives what is necessary to play his part in the universal harmony; and spiritual beings themselves are assured of the supernatural help sufficient to achieve their salvation. The rewards are distributed superabundantly, according to the measure of our charity; the punishments are proportionate, although inferior, to the evil we have done. And this justice in God is one with His infinite mercy. These two attributes, says the Psalmist, hasten toward each other to exchange a loving kiss (Ps. 84:11).

3. JUSTICE AND JUSTIFICATION

But another problem solicits our attention. Apart from the texts to which we have just alluded, there are others which designate the justice of man. Sometimes the Bible gives this word the precise signification of a virtue which consists in rendering to others what is their due; at other times it indicates justice in a very general sense, that is, the practice of the virtues by which man is acceptable to God. Sometimes this word has the meaning of the life brought to men by the Savior, accompanied by our obedience to Him.

How should a highly spiritual meaning be drawn from a passage which is semantic in a juridical sense?

The Hebrew word which designates justice comes from a root which means "to be right," as opposed to anything that is devious: "to go straight to the end" without any deviation in one's course. In Greek and in Latin this word also indicates conformity to the law. But while justice is a social virtue in the classical languages (the "piety" which comprises the duties towards the gods), for the Israelite it is a religious virtue. The law, for him, is identified with the will which God has made known to us. A person is just when, in his general conduct, he conforms to the divine will. A thing is just if it corresponds to the will of God manifested in the Torah. It is only metaphorically that men speak of a just weight, a just balance, or just measure, conforming to the normal standard. (Cf. Prat. *Theology of St. Paul,* vol. II, p. 362.)

A theology based upon Scripture cannot therefore remain insensible to the fact that perfection in the Old Testament is described in terms of justice. We know that the Old Testament sometimes presents the moral life under the image of love: Osee used this plan first, but we see that it was rather late. However, in a habitual manner, the ideal of perfection was an ideal of conformity to an external law. Christ also spoke of justice in terms of a vocabulary to which His contemporaries were accustomed, but He gave a different meaning to the word. The crossing point between these two definitions would certainly be Matthew's text: "For I say to you that unless your justice exceeds that of the Scribes and Pharisees, you shall not enter the kingdom of heaven" (Mt. 5:20). This certainly pertains to an interior justice, the completion of the old justice, which goes down to the depths of the heart and does not stop with visible gestures and attitudes. The examples which Jesus gave men make this very clear.

If therefore perfection in the New Testament is called "justice," let us not forget that it is no longer a justification by the law but by faith and grace. Or rather, the New Testament is a new law for us, a law of grace, interior and spiritual, and we will be justified, not by a merely legal and forensic declaration, as the 16th century Reformers desired, but by grace and charity diffused in our hearts by the Holy Spirit. (Cf. Council of Trent, sess. VI, canon 11.)

Justification According to St. Paul

It is the whole doctrine of justification by living faith that we wish to express here. To say it briefly, since treatises on faith and grace touch on the matter, the words "holiness" and "justice" are practically synonymous in St. Paul. By baptism the new man is created according to God "in justice and holiness" (Eph. 4:24); in other places the order of these words is reversed (I Cor. 1:30; 6:11). And if faith justifies, we continue nevertheless in the extension of the ancient law, but in a perspective that is infinitely more enlarged, since it permits us to see, even now, and obscurely, the shadow of the divine object in all its dimensions.

For St. Paul, justice is understood in the Hebrew sense which we defined above, especially when he speaks of the justice of God (in the subjective sense of a divine attribute, or in the causative sense as a quality caused in man by God). But Paul, who thought as a Semite, wrote in Greek; he could not fail to give the words "just, justice" the social meaning which they signify in that language. Furthermore, the will of God requires that man live with his fellow-men in the respect of their rights; the Decalogue formally prescribes this. This is so certain that in the most frequent meaning of justice brought by Christ who re-created us, we feel the effect of the justice, a cardinal virtue, which is not absent from the Bible, but which the scholastics have systematized by using the data of Greek philosophy. It is easy to derive the principles of a special morality from the Gospel and from St. Paul; and the vast synthesis of this morality has been constructed in the encyclicals of recent Popes.

At this point therefore we cross-check our first idea that, by the study of the virtue of justice, we are not placing ourselves on any other terrain than that of Scripture, and that we are not considering any ethical system whatever, no matter how superior, but rather a complete and true theology. By the observation of our social duties we remain very definitely in the order of return which leads us to God through Christ.

Faith is opposed to the Law, not with an absolute opposition, as white is opposed to black, but it is rather the difference between a completed status and its rough model, or between the stained-glass window flooded with light and its dim copy on paper. The Gospel is called the new Law.

We have just contemplated in God the supreme analogy of our virtue of justice, and we have indicated the theological relations between our treatise and the justice of Scripture. But let us go further now. How by the practice of our virtue, are we centered in the moral order of the return to our last end? And why, in this return, does charity, a social virtue if there ever was one, require a further rectification of our will by justice?

4. NECESSITY OF JUSTICE IN OUR MORAL LIFE

When we speak of justice, we think too often of the juridical order; we see an ensemble of rights and duties codified by texts, in

which a magisterial or authoritative interpretation defines the outlines, thereby indicating the limits of our obligations in a rigorous
way. Though we fall seldom into the error mentioned above of only
considering the will as a moral faculty, this whole order of justice
is practically excluded from the ordering of our activity towards the
last end. Justice is then no more than an ensemble of positive prescriptions which derive their value only from external force that can
compel our obedience. From this there results, among the lesser disadvantages which this position entails, the "not seen, not caught"
attitude: the fear of the policeman as the only norm of morality, the
justification of the laws that are "purely penal," infractions of which
require payment of the anticipated penalty without in any way en-
gaging the conscience.

It is then forgotten that the greatest part of human activity is exercised in the social domain and that it is by the exercise of our
social functions that we really work within the sense of our supernatural destiny.

There is hardly any need to insist upon the "social" side of man.
To lead his life he needs many things which he cannot obtain by his
own efforts alone. To attain his natural end, he is a member of a
family and a nation, and today this word has a meaning that is being
constantly enlarged. To realize his supernatural end, he sustains himself in an organism of the same order, the Church. This social life
imposes necessities and laws upon him which, by the very fact that
they contribute to his reaching his end, enter into the moral order.
And they make it necessary, in order that they may be observed
cheerfully, and with facility and certainty, that good and habitual
disposition of the will be fostered towards the common good or the
particular good of the beings with whom we live—which is called
justice.

But the point of view of the theologian must be strongly indicated
here; and it is higher than that of the moralist. Ethics is found at
the natural level, that of acquired virtue; but the justice with which
we are concerned is infused virtue, the supernatural virtue, deposited
in our soul at the same time as charity. By this virtue the perfection
of the natural order is assured within us in our relations as Christians with other men. Let us here note an important point; it is not
any kind of human right that infused justice will make us respect,
but rather the right of others to eternal life. And because eternal life

represents a fulfillment of the whole being in God, the Christian, more than anyone, is careful not to frustrate other men's rights in regard to their personality, dignity and needs. The rights to food, life, work, political liberty, family liberty, the education of children by their parents; and especially the right to truth, which is so fundamental for the Christian, and to instruction in spiritual things are rights which he respects more than anyone else. Even where these rights do not exist, the Christian wants to establish them.

How far above preoccupations with simple, human honesty we are! And yet this simple honesty is so beautiful that Aristotle declared that it shines like a star of primary greatness in the sky of the virtues! We shall "accomplish every justice" not only to develop within us the virtue of an Aristides (to whom his contemporaries had given the beautiful surname, "the Just," before condemning him by ostracism) but by finding our inspiration in that superior role which God quietly imposes upon us when He abides in our souls: to lead us to eternity more than to satisfy temporal rules, in view of heavenly happiness more than the felicity of this present world, and to imitate God more than to conform ourselves to human laws.

Justice and Charity

However, a difficulty arises. We place justice in the will and we have just established its necessity for the complete realization of the human order. But why does the theologian have to consider this virtue of justice which, even infused, is so highly surpassed by charity? By charity, do we not desire for our fellow-man the superior good, God, who transcends all other goods?

Here is precisely one of the essential differences between justice and charity.[1] Charity is fundamentally a friendship of love, and friendship achieves such a blending of two friends that my friend is another myself. I love him as if he were myself, and the good which I desire for him is "my" good. My friend is simply my neighbor, if I transpose the friendship in charity. Do we not use the term "next of kin" when we refer to those in whom there circulates the same

[1] Without insisting on this distinction still more basic which treats of the object of the two virtues: charity desires God Himself, loved for Himself, and through the neighbor, for the same reason that makes the Divine Persons love Themselves, among Themselves. Justice has for object the rights of others, a created good different from God.

blood as in ourselves? The Old Testament's "Diliges proximum sicut teipsum" (Lev. 19:18), and the comment which Jesus added to it (Mt. 5:43) "et odio habebis inimicum tuum," are understood in a tribal perspective.[2] But in the Gospel, our neighbor is not only a brother, the son of the same father, or descendant of the same ancestor, but every man in whom is realized, or can be realized, the dignity of a son of God. Every man is therefore my neighbor, even if he be the Samaritan hated by the faithful Jew, and must be loved by me as I love myself.

The same cannot be said of justice. For this concerns man towards whom it is exercised essentially as by an "other," opposed to one self, with an opposition which however does not imply any hostility, since one owes justice even to one's enemy. It is based upon a relationship of otherness and not of identity. Its object is the right done to others, rendered in equality. And one of the degrees of distinction between the virtues attached to justice is precisely the quality of this right: legally, it lays the foundation of the principal virtue of justice; morally, it serves as a basis for more of the "social" virtues. Even "religion" will be opposed to charity in its consideration of God not as the friend whose life is communicated to us, but as the Supreme Being to whom the creature presents with fear and trembling the homages that are necessarily unequal to His infinite majesty.

5. CONCLUSION

We have considered justice as the participation, within us, of an attribute of God. Then we have distinguished in Scripture the various meanings of this word and their relations. We have next shown the necessity of such a disposition of soul to reach our end; finally we have distinguished it from charity. Consequently this study enters with full right into a theological construction.

We are not jurists, satisfied to draw from the texts all their consequence, but who are not concerned about their adaptation to a superior moral law, and who would leave to one side, for positive law, the "agrapta nomina" of which Antigone, before her uncle Creon, attested the infrangibility (Sophocles, *Antigone,* v. 454).

Nor are we casuists, careful above all to minimize obligations and,

[2] Leviticus speaks of a brother of the same race.

by a meticulous proportioning of various opinions, to relieve consciences of troublesome duties. We want to be theologians who order all human activity, private or social, in the perspective of supernatural destiny. And in order that social acts may also tend towards their end, they must be governed and directed by the virtue of justice. We shall not forget, in the variety of determinations that will follow, this properly theological viewpoint, thanks to which the treatise is placed in its true perspective.

CONCERNING JUSTICE PROPERLY SO-CALLED

I. RIGHT OR THE JUST, THE OBJECT OF JUSTICE

1. Determination of the Object
   - A. The place of Right
   - B. Description of Right
   - C. Constitution of the Object

2. Division of the Object
   - A. Right in its Varieties
     - (a) Natural Right
     - (b) Positive Right
       - Divine Right
       - Human Right
       - The "Jus Gentium"
   - B. Right in its Reductions
     - (a) Reduction by default of a legal obligation
     - (b) Reduction by default of strict adjustment
   - C. Right in its Counterfeits

II. CONCERNING JUSTICE AND INJUSTICE

1. Definition of the habitus of justice and of injustice
   - A. On the virtue of justice
   - B. On the vice of injustice

2. Structure of the habitus of justice and of injustice
   - A. The matter of the habitus of justice and of injustice
     - (a) The domain of relations with our neighbors
     - (b) The external operations
     - (c) The golden mean, the objective of justice
     - (d) Formal division in matters of justice
       - General and legal justice
       - Particular justice

B. The "subject" of the habitus of justice and of injustice
  (a) Review of ideas that are supposed to be known
  (b) The will, subject of justice
     Possibility of a habitus in the will
     Points of view of justice and the will
3. Moral signification of the habitus of justice and of injustice
  A. The greatness of justice
  B. The gravity of injustice

III. JUDGMENT, THE ACT OF JUSTICE

1. What is judgment
2. Is it permitted to judge?
3. The conditions of good judgment
  A. The rash judgment, or judgment vitiated for lack of truth according to the order of prudent reason
     Psychological origin of rash judgment
     Gravity of rash judgment
     How shall we avoid rash judgment?
  B. The legality of judgment
    (a) Legality of judgment in regard to natural right
    (b) Legality of judgment in regard to positive right
    (c) Beyond the written laws
  C. The quality of the judge

Concerning Justice Properly So-called

We are studying the phenomenon of justice in its purest and simplest meaning, in such manner that we may recognize it later and be better able to judge it when it is presented in its varieties and particularities. It is a good method that consists of passing from the simple to the complex, from the pure to the mixed, from one to many or to a fraction.

This study of pure justice introduces three sections:
1. concerning the right or the just, the object of justice;
2. concerning justice in itself and injustice;
3. concerning judgment, that is to say the act of doing justice or doing the right.

But before beginning this first chapter, it is fitting to stop briefly to consider the necessity of entering upon the treatise on justice by consideration of the right.

Introduction: The consideration of right is necessarily primary.

The study of justice must begin with a question concerning right, the object of justice. Often we study the virtuous habitus and we observe its attitude for itself; this leads to the act, for we see it exercised and from this we are led to the object which is realized in and by the act. A very enlightening example: the treatise on prudence in St. Thomas, in which the study of the object is made almost by allusion, without there being any question devoted to it or even an explicit article. In fact prudence shapes its object in the midst of action, by gradual process, according to its needs. Like the gladiator of the ancient proverb, "in harena capit consilium," not only is the counsel arrived at immediately, but it is while acting that one judges and decides what ought to be done, here and now, in view of circumstances which are constantly changing.

The treatise on faith puts us on the trail. The first consideration which is presented in this study is that of the object. This object, *primary truth,* imposes itself. It does not depend upon the habitus in any way, but has its own consistency, its constitution; it is a given fact, it exists, it can be analyzed.

There is an analogous reason here. The object of justice, the *jus* or *justum,* exists in itself, in an inalterable independence. There is something *positive,* which seems to consist precisely in a definite relationship with others, and not with the acting subject. If the debt is so much, that is the amount which the just man pays. The intensity of his justice is of no importance in determining the amount of his commitment. He will not have to pay more because he is more just. Better yet, not only is there no necessary connection between the virtue of justice and right, but there is not even any connection between the just act and right. One can offend against right without being unjust and even without acting unjustly, as one can realize or respect right without being just and without acting justly. For each of the other moral virtues there is a solidarity between the work and the act of the virtue. If, without making an act of temperance I abstain in fact or restrict myself (i.e. by necessity), this abstinence or these restrictions have no value whatever as a work of temperance. On the contrary, the work of justice is perfectly defined without reference to the virtue or the just act of the acting subject. The rectitude which we expect from a just deed is constituted by the reference of that deed to others, abstraction being made of the reference to the acting subject. A deed is called just because it exactly corresponds to something else to which it is referred, for example, the payment of a wage due for service rendered. Today this objective manner of approach to justice seems to be taken for granted. Modern philosophers and jurists are rather inclined to exaggerate this objectivity, treating the juridical order as a *reality to be done.* Justice then finds itself reduced to a technique. But there was some merit and originality in St. Thomas' definite extrication of his conclusion: Right is the object of justice.

Under the name of justice, in fact, tradition understood a reality less commonplace and less specific. And this resulted from a general conception of the four cardinal virtues which was too vague.

According to the Fathers, and even according to the philosophers, these virtues merited the epithet of cardinal because of their generality, and because they are found at the basis of every virtue, as so many elementary conditions and fundamental features required in every reasonable activity. Every human virtue has an element of knowledge, of rational discernment. This is the portion of prudence which resides in the part of the soul which is rational by essence. To act virtuously is therefore to maintain oneself with firmness in the line of reason, whatever may be the assaults of passion or the difficulties of action. This firmness is the work of fortitude. It is also a matter of curbing impulsive actions and outbursts of passion in order to conserve rational proportions; this is the work of temperance. Finally justice distinguishes itself in every virtuous activity, since we always see the virtuous man correctly accomplish his duty, no matter what he does, and always meet his obligations in every matter even as he always maintains a proper attitude and treats all persons and all things as he ought. Briefly the necessary elements of all virtuous behavior are prudent discernment, a just conscientiousness, firmness and moderation.

St. Thomas' critique of this tradition is a model of lucidity and precision. He remarks that such a way of distinguishing the four cardinal virtues is ineffective. It results in distinguishing prudence, the virtue of rational discernment, from the undivided group of the three other virtues. For prudence perfects reason itself, while the others only require a participation of reason applied to the passions and operations. (This critique is significant, and we could easily discover the psychological theories which it touches indirectly.) But this conception leaves justice, fortitude and temperance indistinct; these are virtues of that part of the soul which is only rational by participation, or by its subjection to the other. In fact, every moral virtue is primarily an habitus; it is not therefore surprising that we discover firmness in it. Next it is a virtue, and consequently there follows the obvious idea of rectitude, correction and the exact accomplishment of what ought to be done. Finally, this virtue is moral, i.e., rationally specified and for that reason all virtuous activity in us carries within itself that measure which reason gives. In this respect we could certainly distinguish fortitude, justice and temperance if it were possible to separate habitus, virtue and morality in all this. But it is the same moral virtue which is at once morality, virtue and habitus; we should therefore always and everywhere have the same virtue presenting a formality of justice, fortitude or temperance according to the points of view.

To distinguish the four cardinal virtues effectively we must find the means of attributing to each, in its own right, one of these fundamental characters which are found in every virtue. For example, in what circumstance does fortitude merit the privilege and in a certain manner the monopoly of firmness? When does justice merit that of rectitude?

To be a cardinal virtue fortitude must not limit itself to that firmness which is common to every habitus, but show a typical firmness which is revealed in a predicament in a specific domain: in the face of mortal dangers. Certainly fortitude is necessary everywhere. Under the attraction of tempting delights, if there is a lack of firmness, a man will yield, give ground or quit his post. Nevertheless, more than pleasures, it is our fears which are likely to make us lack firmness, or make us fall and retreat; and since we are seeking the object that is characteristic of a cardinal virtue, let us say that the domain in which we can most clearly show our firmness will be when there are dangers of death. The really strong man, the one who possesses the cardinal fortitude, is the one who does not lose countenance and who remains unshaken before the imminent danger of death.

We could reason in the same way regarding temperance. Certain fears, it is true, can make us perform immoderate acts or make us go beyond reasonable limits. However, experience proves that the attraction of pleasures is sovereignly efficacious in this respect and, above all, the attraction of pleasures relative to the sense of touch, the pleasures of the flesh. We shall therefore speak of temperance when we are able to maintain proportion in this domain.

The same reasoning is applicable to justice. The domain in which typical rectitude is revealed along with the most exact and most rigorous correction is that of juridical relations. It is for this reason that the virtue of justice has right for its object. Three important consequences follow from this: in this juridical domain it is a matter of rectifying operations rather than passions. It is in the will that cardinal justice resides. Finally, and especially, justice and injustice involve other people, the other man as such. All these features are required at the very outset, because cardinal justice pertains to the most purely characteristic domain of the just. Doubtless other virtues, religion for example, will outweigh the cardinal virtue of justice and other cardinal virtues in certain respects. Nevertheless, from a technical point of view, for a moralist concerned about an exact classification, justice, like each of the other cardinal virtues in its own domain, possesses an incontestable superiority. It considers what is purest and most complete in regard to the just deed. Whatever may be their beauty, and in some points their superiority, the other virtues comparable to justice never pertain exclusively to the just deed in reduction or in similitude.

The cardinal virtue of justice, in so far as it is a distinct virtue, has right for its proper matter.

I. Right or the Just, the Object of Justice

1. DETERMINATION OF THE OBJECT

A. *The Place of Right*

Let us try to place right in relation to the idea which we already know.

St. Isidore defined law as a "species of right." This formula is not displeasing to practitioners of law, for it is normal for them to consider the law as a source of right and consequently to discern in right certain elements that belong to legitimate or legal right, as contrasted with other parts of law (contractual or common, for example). But for the philosopher of law, as basically for the theologian, notwithstanding all the respect that is due to Isidore, this definition of the law as a species of right is erroneous. Right does not consist in the law, not even partially. Law is not right, properly speaking, but rather the rule or expression of right.

Let us compare the artistic process and the legislative process. The artisan conceives the idea of the work to be done. This idea serves as a rule or a law in his art (habitus) and in his artistic operations. It is not possible to confuse the idea with the art, nor with the work either. But the idea finds its expression in oral or written formulas, nevertheless. These are the prescripts or the rules of the art in question. Similarly, in general every voluntary agent conceives the idea, giving himself a representation of what he intends to do and of the system of means which he plans to employ for this purpose. This idea is expressed in words, if such should be the case, or in writing, or by still other signs, but there is a difference between the formula that states the rule for making a work of art and that which declares the rule for acting well. The first only implies a practical knowledge; it *declares* how one should proceed *if one wants to realize* a particular artistic effect, but it does not decide anything about the effective exercise, the actual operation of the art. In other words, it is not the musical art that tells the artist if he should sing, and it is not the art that tells the architect whether or not to build a house, etc. On the contrary, the moral formula is stated in regard to the fact of effective exercise itself. It constitutes a practical judgment, and even a precept if it has attained its perfect differentiation. It is to this that prudence, the moral virtue of the practical reason, tends.

This review of ideas permits us to place law and right in an exact manner. If it is a question not of any kind of reason, but of a political reason, for example, that of a prince who is acting in his capacity as prince, this reason, qualified by the virtue of political prudence, conceives and formulates the idea, the practical plan of the complex activities which the common good requires. We are not here referring to those purely speculative conceptions to which any philosopher or publicist may let himself be drawn with impunity, or which may preoccupy a statesman in his moments of recreation. We are speaking precisely of practical conceptions, that is to say, conceptions involved in the efficacious and realizing movement of a political prudence animated in the order of the exercise by the influx of the moral virtues (notably justice), in a subject who is otherwise endowed with effective powers.

These conceptions, wholly practical as they are, must not be confused with the reality of the common good nor with the reality of the ways and means, nor the operations and relations which concur or which lead to the common good. But these conceptions, when they have reached their maturity, and when they are fully differentiated, take the imperative form of a practical commandment. They do not declare what ought to be done if one desires some particular effect; they tell us what must be done in a practical way, here and now.

On the other hand, nothing exists in the social world unless it is communicated by signs. That is why the ultimate differentiation of the commandment requires a recognizable, perceptible and intelligible formulation for political prudence. It is this authentic formulation (and once again authentic in order to be efficacious and to exist socially) which constitutes the law in the philosophical meaning of the term.

St. Thomas, it is true, seems to adopt a more restricted definition of law when he writes: law is the prudential rule when it is promulgated. In reality, he introduces a positive condition of contingent order into the definition of the law which is bound up with historical categories and with Roman and modern conceptions of law. But the philosopher cannot forget that many civilizations and prosperous societies have attributed and still attribute the force of law to custom. This is because acts themselves, under certain conditions, have

an expressive value; they are at least as symbolical of the commanding reason as spoken or written words. The pure conception of law
therefore includes an authentic and efficacious promulgation, but
the forms of this promulgation vary according to the communities
to be governed, and according to the nature of the rules to be promulgated and the circumstances.

Therefore law (legal enactment) is not the idea, but the imperative expression of the idea which the head of the State's reason
makes of the civic order.

But in regard to right, this idea and the order itself are another
matter. The idea that is made of the order is more or less exact,
more or less subtle. This depends a great deal on the prudential
habitus and the knowledge that is at the head of the State's disposal.
And this constitutes a qualification for him. But the order itself and
its perfection are elsewhere, even though the quality of the head of
the State is not indifferent to it.

The distinction must be clearly perceived. It is not sufficient to
ascertain the obvious distinction which is established between a previously *given* order (the natural order, traditions, or a lastingly
established social order) and the idea which the legislator who is
preparing to superimpose a new positive order, fully constructed,
makes of it. For example, consider any established, traditional order
in matters of property; the legislator's idea of this order, which will
be more or less exact, will inspire legislation pertaining to chattels
and rents. This goes without saying. But we must try to discern, in
the legislative act itself, both the idea, which is the representation
of a positive juridical order which is imperatively formulated in law
(a specific legal enactment), and the juridical order itself.

The idea is a disposing *quality,* affecting the practical intelligence
of the legislator. But the political order itself is not a quality; it is a
complex of relationships between human persons diversely qualified,
who are endowed with various and correlative powers, acting in
different ways upon one another or acting diversely upon certain
things in regard to certain other persons. The remarkable thing in
matters of justice is that one discovers in this objective order of
relations an objective field of morality. This order is in fact itself
objectively qualified. It has a way of establishing itself, and of enduring and evolving, which qualifies it humanly and which is not
purely and simply the moral reflection, good or evil, of human actions, reactions and intentions, of which for one part it is the effect.

Here we have a new duty for the honest man to consider: the respect for, or the reestablishment of that order, which we call "right," in whatever is there expressive of moral meaning.

In summary: Political prudence is the virtue that is capable of formulating the law which expresses right.

B. *Description of Right*

(a) Right refers primarily to the things themselves. Things (as opposed to persons) are the object of right (as opposed to the subjects of right). This object can be a deed, whether voluntary or not, or an act, or an abstention, or it can be a material thing considered as the object of an act, the matter of the deed, etc. For example, if I am a seller, I consider the payment as my right; and likewise I shall consider as my right the number of monetary units contractually stipulated as the selling price, that is to say, the matter of the payment. The payment, and indirectly the money or the delivered merchandise, are inscribed in the juridical order as far as they establish men in relations of right.

(b) The science which teaches us what is "right" is also called law. It is in this sense that men say: to learn or to teach law, to study law. This is a scientific habitus, that is to say, a quality of the first species.[3]

(c) The French term "droit" is also used in the sense of a right (human right, civil right), and more precisely in modern terminology the term connotes subjective right, to designate the power or faculty which men possess (i.e., which is socially recognized and sanctioned) to perform certain acts or to hold property. There are also the right to vote, the right of usage, etc. In less technical language, there are certain freedoms which are also called rights, these are freedom to work, freedom of the press, etc. These freedoms or these subjective rights consist of faculties, powers; *they are qualities of the second species.*

(d) In Latin, the expression "in jure" occasionally and originally designates a phase of the procedure (first phase of the trial, in which the parties appear before the magistrate and establish the action before him; then the action is recognized, the formula is drawn up, and the parties next appear before the judge or the arbiter who pro-

---

[3] The "quality," in the philosophical meaning of the word, comprises four species: 1) The disposition or habitus, 2) The power or the impotence, 3) The "passion," 4) The figure.

nounces his decision by a yes or a no, the phase "in judicio.")
Sometimes, and notably in the period of the late Empire, the expression "in jure" refers to the locality of the functionary who is responsible for both the instruction and the judgment (extra ordinem procedure).

(e) Finally men give the name of right to the rule which governs the just activity, which governs an activity that conforms to right. This rule is actually identified with the law, but it is the law conceived less as the expression of right than as the measure of juridical actions, less as a rule that is regulated than as a regulating rule. In other words, it is the law in its active, rectifyng action, a kind of exemplary form to which actions are conformed, or which brings out the incorrectness of contrary acts. In this sense men act outside the law or bend before the law. Right is then conceived as a product of reason, a proposition, a practical judgment, an exemplary of juridical action.

There are doubtless other meanings of the word right.

A general division will begin to introduce us into the constitution of right.

(a) There is, roughly, a wide meaning. Whatever is correct is right; right corresponds to all moral rectitude, to virtuous righteousness in the ensemble of behavior. This is a general conformity to the order, to the rule. In Christian language the just man and justice require perfection in all relations.

(b) Then there is a strict meaning. Virtuous rectitude specified by right is characterized by the fact that it is established in relations with others. This feature is essential and constitutive. It is this point that we must examine thoroughly if we want to know the inmost constitution of right.

C. *Constitution of the Object*

The argumentation can be re-stated very concisely in the following syllogism:

It is the proper object of justice to regulate relations with our neighbors.

But right is the order of relations with our neighbors.

Therefore right is the proper object of justice.

But this severe statement does not say a great deal. What really matters is to grasp the full scope of the terms. If there is rectitude in every virtue, it is well known that rectitude in matters of justice is determined by a certain correspondence, a certain decorum, and by an adjustment in regard to other men; however other virtuous rectitude is determined by a correspondence, decorum and adjustment of the subject within himself, in relation to himself, of his action in relation to his powers, and of his powers between themselves, etc. There is a great difference between these two rectitudes. Properly speaking, there is no adjustment possible between any but distinct beings; when we speak of correspondence, decorum and adjustment with oneself, we are speaking metaphorically.

That is why rectitude in matters of justice does not require any particular subjective attitude in the acting subject. It is entirely a matter of objective rectitude; the object is something which is presented in itself and which has value in itself. This reality, independent of the subject, is right, i.e., it is the just.

An act of temperance is an act done with temperance—I do not say with an habitus of temperance, but at least with a rational measure of temperance. And there is this kind of rectitude in temperance precisely because the act is done in a temperate way. The same cannot be said in regard to justice. An act of justice is not just in this way. Juridical rectitude is in some way exterior to it; it resides in a certain independent reality to which the act of justice directs the doing of the act as action, whatever may be the manner. The act is what it is; it turns out as it may and certainly we do not say that its performance is morally indifferent. It may be quite important morally and humanly. Nevertheless, it will be perfectly just if it conduces to that term in which right essentially consists. Let us meditate this very bold text of St. Thomas: "Men say that a thing is just, that is to say, having all the rectitude of justice, that to which the act of justice conduces, without even considering the manner in which the subject accomplishes it, whereas, on the contrary, for the other virtues it is the manner in which the subject acts which determines the rectitude of his act" (IIa IIae, q. 57, a. 1). With the other virtues, the manner alone matters; it is this which constitutes the virtuous rectitude. In matters of justice, strictly speaking, the manner does not count; the only thing that really matters is not even the effect of the act but the term, a certain state of fact to which one tends, voluntarily or not, willingly or unwillingly, and which has, in itself, the value of right. It is in the very situation that the constitutive elements of the just deed and of right are found.

Therefore, at the risk of reducing justice to its metaphorical meaning, we must allow that its object is that ensemble of relations in which our rectitude is established in regard to other men. But it is not impossible to see these relations a little more closely.

The question is one of an order of relations. Let us take the idea of the relative, not in the manner of the complacent individual or the "blasé" for whom all impressions are equivalent and superficial. On the contrary, let us make every effort, through an informed and perspicacious realism, to lay hold of certain more tenuous values of being.

In relationship there are two aspects to consider. Like every "accident," [4] the relationship *inheres,* as we say, in a subject; without this it does not exist. But this *relationship* is formally constituted by a *"reference,"* a correspondence. We know however that the *relationship* is only presented in some predicaments that are capable of establishing a *relationship* by putting a subject in relation to another thing. It is certain that the *substance* does not establish any relationship, nor, by itself, the *quality.* On the contrary, the *quantity* offers the occasion of comparison and correspondence. Likewise, the *active* and *passive power,* the act of acting or of suffering, naturally establishes the subject in relation to something other than himself. Other predicates (the place, the site, the when) derive from relations rather than establishing them.

1. From the *existential* point of view, the *relation* in which right consists is created by the disposing act of reason, exercised under the realizing impulse of the will and the moral virtues or more precisely by the consecutive decision in the choice. If the juridical order conceived by a mind does not arrive at this degree of realization, it is as though it did not exist. It is chimerical, utopian, adorned perhaps, like the legendary dream, with the rarest qualities, but remaining in the limbo of the possible.

2. In itself, in its formal, specific reality, the relation of right described so far as an adjustment includes analytically the two ideas, closely connected, of equality and alterity. It is obviously equality which is first derived from the concept of *jus:* this is the type of the perfect and of the pure adjustment. But the analysis of equality leads necessarily to the idea of alterity between the two equal terms at the same time that it specifies this alterity.

[4] "Accident" is used here as a philosophical term. In a given subject we distinguish: its *substance,* that which it is, and its *accidents:* its quantity, its location, its relations, etc. Substance and accidents are the "predicates" of being.

(a) Equality entails alterity:

In fact, every kind of inequality can be traced to a relationship of dependence and domination; one of the two terms is the cause of the other under some relationship, and that is why the latter has within itself something of the first. Or else both proceeding from the same principle of being, the one participates in the principle more than the other. By this very fact, the latter depends upon the one which, participating more fully, realizes more perfectly the common character and causes the imperfect participations, at least in virtue of example. In all order, the perfect is the cause of the imperfect, and the more perfect is the cause of the less perfect. We can therefore say that there is a necessary connection between equality and alterity. The terms "others" owe nothing to each other, for otherwise they would necessarily be unequal, and we have excluded this by hypothesis.

(b) We were saying that equality specifies alterity. We could conceive of this alterity as a pure heterogeneity. But this would be an error. Note that the word *alter* does not mean *alius*. *Alter* is the second of a couple, it is the term of a binary relationship. And it is true that the relation of right implies a common belonging to the same order on the part of equals. Certainly there is no participation in each other; this would be inequality. But there is equal participation of the one and the other in a same principle of being: without this there would be no common feature in the one or the other, which is the basis of their relationship of equality. And without this, we could no longer say that they are equals, nor even refer to them as *others,* for when we speak of the *one* and of the *other,* it is still a way of uniting them and of conceiving of them in correlation, as though included within the same circle and participating in the same form.

That is why the perfect notion of right, the perfect relationship of justice, is confirmed between two persons who are equally subject to the same prince: "ambo sub uno principe." In this case the prince only represents the principle of unity, the measure or the basis of the relation of equality.

Other people are not therefore strangers; the alterity which characterizes justice suggests that there exists between some men and other men a certain previous community in which they are equals, as equally participating in a same form and therefore as equally subject to a transcendent principle of unity.

It seems that the same is true in those relations of the quantitative order which are called numerical, or inequality. Quantities can only equal themselves or adjust themselves, or put themselves into relationship, because they are definitively amenable to one and the same principle of being which measures them: the principle of unity. But while unity, in this sense, is not a number, being the principle of the number, the community which we discover in the principle of relations "ad alterum" is not one of right. It is a metajuridical reality whose dispositions will not be without influence upon right, exactly as the terrain on which one builds entails certain consequences for the arrangement of the house. We shall see an application of this in the types of right "in reduction."

2. DIVISION OF THE OBJECT

What has just been said concerning the constitution of the object should be helpful to us now. For we must find a formal principle of division of right, a principle drawn "ex visceribus subjecti," as men say. According to this requirement, we distinguish as many juridical orders as there are proper foundations to support a specific type of egalitarian relation. This means that there are as many juridical orders, and as many formal divisions of right, as there are courts of last appeal (of "princes"),[5] of sovereign reasons determining distinct types of egalitarian adjustments.

This allows us to exclude a wholly material division of the juridical domain at the very start. There are all kinds of professional categories in a state that is under a single highest tribunal; these are responsible for fulfilling the various tasks that are needed in a State that is rather complex. For example there are the magistrates, the military officials, the clergy and the merchants. There are as many kinds of relations as there are individual categories or corporations. There are professional hierarchies, and in each of these orders there is a juridical adjustment. All the merchants are amenable to the code of commerce; the soldiers are subject to the military code. The magistrates are classified according to certain regulations (codified or not) which are also concerned with the organization of the courts. Finally, the clergy have their own charter, for example under the regulations of a concordat. These are distinctions which are very

---

[5] We use the word "prince" in the rather metaphysical sense, including all possible forms of government, whenever it is a question of government as the basis of any given society.

important in practice. And yet they are not essential juridical distinctions in so far as they only represent a kind of material division into compartments in the heart of a total civic conception, expressed and realized by the reason or pattern of one and the same "prince." This makes for only one formal juridical order, proceeding from a single principle, a single political government, in spite of the complications and the diversity of the regulations, modeled upon the complexity and diversity of the social relationships which the idea of the prince must regulate.

In this way, corporation law, formulated and authoritatively imposed upon professional men by the "prince," is put into its place in the laws of the State. It would be a different matter if it were recognized that organized professions have the competence to regulate themselves, which supposes, within the professions, a proper authority, under the control of the State, conceiving and governing the corporate order. We know that the syndicalist thesis claims this relative autonomy for corporations; in this sense, syndicalism and state socialism exclude each other as juridical pluralism is opposed to totalitarianism.

In this manner the separation of Church and State transforms the juridical status of the clergy under the concordat: thereafter ecclesiastical right is formally distinguished from the civil right as belonging to another sovereign tribunal. We can imagine an analogous separation of military right from civil right in the hypothesis in which the organization and use of armed force would be subject to a tribunal that was superior or exterior to the States.

It is fitting here to hold fast to the formal divisions of the right, divisions that are based upon a distinction of principle—we could even say on a distinction of "princes." We must seek thoughts and reasons, conceiving by themselves and for themselves imperative juridical orders.

The application of the formal principle of division brings us face to face with juridical orders that are not only distinct but unequal. There are several real sources of right, but the right which emanates from them is not univocal. We can, roughly speaking, place these authentic, analogous or equivocal rights under three headings:

Right in its varieties
Right in its reductions
Right in its counterfeits

A. *Right in Its Varieties*

(a) Natural Right

There is an order established by the very reason of the originator. The One who created natures conceived them intelligently and constituted them according to the idea that He wanted to make of them. Their coming into being, their development and their completion was in some way wholly inscribed beforehand in the realizing thought of the Creator. This is a genuine and imperative order. When creatures conform to this conception freely or necessarily, we may say that they conform to the law of their nature. On the other hand, if they break away from the law of their own nature, either freely or accidentally, we may say that their activity is incorrect; it is a "sin."

The first characteristic of this natural right is obvious. It is not laid down by man; it is given with one's nature. This is what distinguishes natural right from positive right, conceived and realized by human design.

Secondly, this natural right does not admit of any dispensation. A dispensation would amount to an inconceivable modification applied to the essential concept of created beings.

For the same reason, natural right is immutable and invariable in essential matters in all times and all places for any particular nature. Doubtless, on the basis of a nature that is essentially stable, variations may be added to this nature by freedom, chance or circumstances that are variable. And this explains certain relative diversities which make the pure concept of natural right more flexible. Nevertheless, these variations can only be secondary, adding something to natural right while taking nothing essential from it.

These observations are traditionally attributed to natural right. It is fitting to remark in this respect that men generally speak of natural right in very broad terms. Can we apply to natural right the precise definition of right which we have been considering up to this point?

There is first of all a great difference to be established between natural right relative to non-rational creatures and the same right as it pertains to rational natures. The order of natures, in both cases, was conceived by a single idea, the sovereign concept of the Creator. But this order is not imposed in both cases as a rational order. It is shared differently.

Let us be careful to note that it is not only a difference of promulgation; this difference really exists. As opposed to the Stoics who considered the cosmos as a great being animated by a unique *logos,* thereby making all creatures participate in greater or lesser degree in the same reason, we admit that irrational creatures receive the impression of the divine concept through their submission to the eternal law, although under the form of blind, natural instinct. This law therefore is not properly promulgated, that is to say, it is not presented as a legal imperative. On the contrary, rational creatures receive an impression of eternal law which has the force of promulgation properly so called, although they receive this natural inclination in the manner of a rational principle that is evident in the practical order, and as imperative as it is immediate. This human participation of the eternal law presents itself thus with the character of a law, as the rational expression of a practical order, while the formula of a divine concept in regard to inanimate beings only has the nature of law in the thought of God, or partially in the minds of those who read *in Verbo,* or spell out some elements of eternal law in nature.

But this difference of promulgation only serves to point out an objective difference. It is the order itself, in reality, which differs in quality, when we pass from irrational to rational creatures. In the world of primary things, we may say that there is no order that is proper to them. To see an order in them we must see a mind hovering over them, first the mind which creates them with their order, and then the minds which see them in their order. In themselves and by themselves, they remain inanimate things, with the relations of things and the contiguities and sequences of things. Their activities, considered in themselves, are the simple behavior of things, in some way mechanical. They bear their order as a blind man carries a light, in the service of someone who sees. It surpasses them. Their order is not made by them, nor for them. Properly speaking, in them there is only an occasion offered to minds to realize an order or to discover an order. It is for this reason that nature is uninterested in individuals, but is uniquely concerned about the species. What really matters is not so much the perfection of beings but the specific function played by them, in a universe conceived by a mind, in the service and for the perfection of other minds.

On the other hand, in the world of rational creatures there is an immanent order. These natures are spiritual enough to reflect upon themselves, to be masters of themselves in recognizing their essential order, and to accept it as true and real in the act which makes them intelligibly present to themselves. Spirituality alone authorizes this possession of self. And it is very certain that in man an entire non-spiritual part escapes this possession, remaining opaque, immersed in the material order of the universe. From this point of view man is acted upon like the rest; the principles of his behavior do not obtain the force of law within himself but in the creative mind, and the internal relations of his parts (caloric, luminous, chemical changes, weight, etc.) do not have in themselves, but only with regard to minds, any force of law or correct adjustment or just disposal.

But the reason of man, considered as a nature, requires more. The order of this rational nature is definitely a *given* order: the author of natures conceived and realized it. But while it is placed in lower natures without their awareness, in such a way that they cannot receive it as an order, being limited to experiencing it as a blind instinct led by a transcendent mind, it is given to spiritual natures by way of intelligible presentation. And this means that these spiritual natures are first given to themselves, while things are given to minds. Consequently, rational natures truly realize their proper condition only by *accepting* this basic order which specifies them, and in assuming it while also taking possession of themselves. It is therefore in their own eyes that the basic order of these natures obtains the value of right, correction and just disposition; this value is inherent to it. It characterizes it essentially as an order of rational natures. If it were not presented, by itself, as a rational decision, it would constitute not a rational nature, but any nature whatever which bears the divine concept without having the secret of it, a nature opaque to itself, transparent only to minds and not entering into a rational order except in the measure in which minds assume it from outside as a useful ingredient.

In brief, the natural order is only imposed as an order of right in rational natures alone.

But we must now be even more specific. This natural order of rational creatures is not necessarily juridical in the strict sense. And in fact, we must keep in mind that men speak very often of natural right in a metaphorical sense. From what has been said, it follows that one can conceive of natural right as the rational order inscribed in these natures by their Creator and one may suppose that they perceive this by the very fact that they enter intelligently into possession of self or that they are present to themselves, as is fitting for such natures.

But how many things are comprised in this rational order! In reality it is a question of first principles of the practical reason, which govern the initial activities, and which animate the least and farthest practical conclusions. To be able to give this order the juridical quality, it is necessary to restrict the extension to the domain of relations of men to each other.

We see that we are far from the too acceptable definition proposed by Ulpian: "Natural right is that which nature teaches to all animals," not only because it establishes the law in the midst of irrational natures, but because its content is too jumbled: [6] "The union of the husband and wife which we call marriage, the procreation of children, education." Ulpian tended to identify right with general integrity.[7] There is the same equivocation in Paul, the great jurisconsult.[8] For Gaius, there are two kinds of right: civil right, proper to each state, and right which he calls *jus gentium,* but which he identifies with natural reason and in which we recognize in fact natural right.[9] By insisting upon the clause "that which natural reason constitutes between all men," which does not seem to be an arbitrary interpretation, we can admit the coincidence of this definition with that of Aristotle summarized by St. Thomas: political right (i.e., the ensemble of social relations) is distinguished as physical right (naturale) and positive right (positivum). But it must be noted that positive right does not continue to be bound up with legal right, for the customs allowed in each state, endowed with force and juridical sanctions, constitute an authentic positive right; or if we prefer, we may consent, with St. Thomas, to extend the idea of law beyond the written texts.

Whatever may be said about these divergences, which are in large part verbal, nature teaches man all kinds of rational rules which only express metaphorical right: integrity, moral correctness in its fundamental principles.

Among these rules of natural right, the only ones that should be retained as rules of right properly so-called (let us not say as rules of positive right) are those which pertain to our relations with other men. Therefore, of the three precepts of right enumerated by Ulpian,

[6] Ulp., lib. I. Institutionum, D., I, I, De Justitia et Jure, I, #3.
[7] Ulp., lib. I Regularum, D., I, I, De Just. et Jure, 10, #1.
[8] Paul, lib. 14 ad Sab., D., I, I, De Just. et Jure, 11.
[9] Gaius, lib. I Institutionum, D. De Justitia et Jure, 9.

we shall retain the last two: "alterum non laedere, suum cuique tribuere": do not harm anyone; give to each one what is due to him.

(b) Positive Right

This is what Aristotle called legal right and which he described in that manner to contrast it with natural right. Whatever pertains to legal right can indifferently be the one or the other before being promulgated. It is neither the one or the other until after promulgation.

Actually, natural right is also a positive right, for after all it depended and always depends upon the divine free will to promulgate this law in the hearts of created natures. But it is easy to see that our statement brings out the difference between a right which, for ourselves, is found to be given before hand and which we only accept intelligently and the right which we see originating, increasing and disappearing in our societies, according to the desire of our reason.

In any case, it is again a question of a genuine right. It is an order, imperatively conceived and promulgated, concerning relations with others. And this positive right, as we have already indicated, is distinguished in as many kinds as there are distinct reasons concerned with the effective conception and realization of such juridical ordinances.

Divine Right

Curiously, we here find God as the positive legislator. In a certain sense, dear to ancient theologians and decretists, we may call natural right divine. Is not God the author of natures?

However, let us look at the matter more closely. What is "divine right"? Not only a right which has God for its author (otherwise natural right would certainly be divine right, as the ancients thought), but right which is promulgated by the laws of God: "Jus divinum dicitur quod divinitus promulgatur." In this respect this right is definitely opposed to natural right which has God for its author, but which is promulgated to us in and through our very nature.

The difference of promulgation introduces an essential difference between the *laws,* at least from the viewpoint of the subjects; for it is promulgation which effectively applies the legal formula to the executors, as "the usus activus" effectively applies the given order to the powers moved by the will. But this difference of promulgation does not necessarily entail an essential difference in right, for once again the latter is not constituted, but only formulated, by the promulgated law. Therefore, there is most certainly a divine law, since juridical precepts have been expressly formulated by God. It remains to be seen what may be the proper consistence of divine right which finds its formulation in the divine law.

The right promulgated by God concerns two categories of precepts, for God is both the author of natures and the head of a religious society. To find the right place for the first category of precepts within natural right, we believe that we must exclude them from divine right properly so-called, while also recognizing that they are the object of a positive divine law at the same time as natural law.

In fact, the juridical order which they constitute depends on the will and the thought of the Creator, and this order has attained its full juridical differentiation, since it is perfectly formulated and promulgated in the heart of rational natures. It is true, however, that the rational rectitude of this natural order is unapparent to the majority of men. But this does not deprive it of any of its value as right, but rather proves the usefulness of a more explicit legal formulation. Consequently, we see the usefulness and moral necessity of another legislation and a second promulgation (the Decalogue).

This pedagogical role is perfectly proper to the law whose object is not to constitute right but to instruct men, giving them a practical instruction which is not limited to theoretical formulation but makes for execution by the executory force attached to the precepts, and by the attraction of rewards and the threat of punishments also.

Moreover, it is obvious that the divine laws are constitutive of religious societies, and God only promulgates them through the intermediate agency of socially qualified organs: patriarchs, prophets, especially Moses and Christ. In any case, the divine laws fulfill a pedagogical function like all laws. Among all the social signs and symbols intended for the religious education of the peoples, the divine law, the practical and imperative formula of right which must govern such societies, is presented as the most intelligible and most effective sign.

From all this it follows that the precepts of natural right summarized and promulgated by the divine law (the Decalogue, the prohibition of adultery, etc.) remain substantially precepts of natural right and we therefore conclude that divine right does not include them formally. This right is therefore essentially a positive right. (It regulates the judiciary, ceremonial and sacramental acts.)

Human Right

Man is a legislator. Human reason, when socially qualified to conceive and regulate an order of relations between men, is a legislative reason.

A legislator announces generally the right which he has enjoined. Consequently, there are as many human juridical orders as there are specifically distinct orders of relations. Each rationally regulated sphere of relations provides a distinct kind of right. All right, in this sense, is social; right is the rational form of social relationships. It is the soul of human societies: ubi societas, ibi jus—Where there is society, there is right.

It is a question of a human, positive right, an equilibrium fixed by the reason of man. Public right, in the modern sense, is a right that pertains to a public object. It has this new implication that society, considered as a juridical person, is interested in this equilibrium, and is, so to speak, explicitly or implicitly a party to the contract, because public interests are at stake. This supposes that the State has affirmed its moral personality, which was the case in ancient Rome, as also in France increasingly since the fourteenth century, but which was not the case under a feudal regime in which the relationships now considered as amenable to public right (government, finance, taxes, war) were then relationships of private right and of patrimonial character, based upon ties contracted between persons. However, it is no less true that these relationships of private right, independently of individual arrangements between private persons, were also governed by general customs, statutes and traditional rules, derived from religious morality, holy books and Roman laws interpreted more or less correctly, and from judiciary precedents.

The "jus gentium"

It is better not to translate this expression which has a technical value. In fact, the notion of the "right of nations" is quite different. It translates the Latin expression "jus inter gentes," used for the first time by Vitoria and designates the external, positive right of sovereign States between themselves. This is international right with its division into *private* or *public* international right, according as the rules which have always been the object of treaties between States concern the relations between individuals under the jurisdiction of various States (marriages, nationality, naturalization, extradition, etc.) or the relations between the persons which are the States themselves. This conception of international right is modern: in the sixteenth century Vitoria and Suarez, in the seventeenth century Grotius, Pufendorf, and Leibnitz, and in the eighteenth century Vattel, were the founders of it.

The jus gentium is a datum wholly different. This expression, in ancient authors, whether philosophers or jurisconsults, is linked to the destiny of the jus naturale. We may recall the extension given by Ulpian to the latter: "quod natura omnia animalia docuit." This is an attractive philosophical insight, but not very useful to the practitioner. On the contrary, to the extent that conquests, wealth and commerce put Rome into relations with foreign peoples, there was revealed the existence and the interest of a natural right common to men and proper to human beings alone, whatever may be the case with animal nature.

Cicero points out that nature, in everything concerning man, establishes a human right. (I. Cic., *De fin. bon. et mal.,* 3, 20, 67.) He does not call this natural right or civil right; he seeks for an intermediate formula: "quasi civile jus." Since nature seems to blend men into a kind of vast city, the properly natural right of men is a quasi civil right. Just as the "gentes" federated as a Roman people provided a civil right for themselves, it seems that nature, by federating the "gentes universi," that is, all the peoples of the world, gives them the "jus gentium" as their civil right. Cicero discerns, in the right of foreign peoples, these two parts: a right of nature, the "jus gentium," and the laws that are proper to each state (Cic., *De officiis,* 3, 5, 23).

Gaius, as a practitioner, ignores the natural right extended to animals. He speaks of the jus gentium, constituted by the ratio naturalis, "quasi quo jure omnes gentes utuntur" (Gaius, lib., I, Instit., D., I, I, de Justit. et Jure, 9).

He groups together the prescriptions distributed by Ulpian between natural right and the jus gentium. For according as they take natural right into consideration or not, the authors are inclined to exclude from the jus gentium, or introduce into it, certain fundamental rules which are absolutely indispensable to human reason as natural first principles.

It is more instructive to establish an organic link between natural right and the jus gentium.

Natural right expresses a rectitude which manifests itself as an immediate evidence, by itself and without previous reasoning. Then, beginning with these natural juridical principles, the processes of reason culminate in conclusions whose connection with the principles is sound enough and clear enough for all men to be generally imbued with them. These reasoning processes consist in discovering proprieties and adjustments which have juridical value *because there ensues* a situation consistent with natural right. For example, natural right does not require that some particular field belong to some particular, private owner, but if the *private property* contributes to the establishment of peaceful relations and to the efficacious exploitation of material goods, in this respect and indirectly it is connected with natural right.

In brief, it seems fitting to maintain the jus gentium in the category of human positive right, since these prescriptions, however generalized and persistent they may be, are definitely the work of human reason. These are immediate and quasi inevitable conclusions, but they are only *conclusions* of natural right.

Because they are conclusions obtained by a rational development, the prescriptions of the jus gentium do not enjoy the absolute infallibility and universality of natural right properly so called. They are not derived solely from nature. There are practical necessities, common prejudices, social institutions and uncriticized traditions which influence the rational development and sometimes incline it, on some particular points, in a direction that is contrary to natural right. For instance, slavery was a part of the "jus gentium" for a long time in the civilized world (Cf. Institut, Justin., I, 2, De jure naturali et gentium et civili, 2).

But because these conclusions are general and immediate, and because, on the whole, they can only be logically derived from natural right or determine it in a useful way, and, furthermore, because they take value as principles for a great many other particular juridical conclusions, we willingly associate them with natural right. We say that they belong to natural right, but we distinguish two zones (or more) in the latter: primary natural right, which corresponds to the immediate *data* of human nature in juridical matters, and secondary natural right, which groups the first great conclusions inferred *positively* by the common reason of the people and which corresponds to the *jus gentium*.

B. *Right in Its Reductions* (See IIa IIae, q. 57, a. 4)

We must now consider ordered social relations in which order does not attain to perfect juridical differentiation. This imperfection, in comparison with "political right" which is right properly so-called, can proceed from two sources, or more precisely, results from the deficiency of two sources of right.

(a) Reduction by default of a legal obligation

It is the existential perfection which is deficient. By private convention or by custom, a certain relationship, a certain order of relations is received (an order of proprieties, worldly obligations, payments of debts of honor) as correct. But this order is not put into existence with the efficacious rigor or the imperative character of right. And this inefficacy, in our opinion, is imputable to the weakness of a realizing will; the latter did not want or did not feel obligated to engage itself dynamically in this realization.

Let us consider an obvious and revealing sign of this voluntary default. One cannot act in pursuit of a claim against a partner who is lacking in manners or who forgets to pay a debt of honor. What shall we infer from this? That, more profoundly, no will, neither that of the "prince" nor that of the contracting parties, intends to take into account this order of relations or efficaciously assure its existence; on the contrary, it is admitted, or men pretend to admit that the partner *owes it to himself* to fulfill his obligations, but that one does not stoop, or even think of demanding the execution of it. In other words, for the quasi-creditor these are things which must not count, and which neither add nor detract anything from the consistence of his being or his patrimony. He is above all that. Whatever he receives, and he has perhaps been waiting for it anxiously, he refuses to consider as his property or as accruing to him. The payment will be discreet (an empty envelope), and as far as possible the payment will be offered unobtrusively, under the pretext of giving a gratuity (a tip). It will leave no trace that may be checked (secret funds).

In short, this fine order of social relations is supposed to be considered with detachment, as if it had sprung into being quite spontaneously and no one was responsible for it. Thus the debt (legal) is not assured because no will affirms itself as the effective creditor, that is, as pursuing the obtainment of his own property in the efficacious realization of this order. Every debt disappears if the creditor consents to it; but in this domain it seems that the creditor gives his consent always and a priori.

We discover here, advanced in the domain of social relations, the extreme point of metaphorical right. There is in fact a purely moral rectitude in question, sometimes even factitious, but a rectitude which is confirmed in a particular domain and by actions that are very similar to right properly so called. This will allow the attachment to cardinal justice of moral virtues which are not concerned with an object that is properly due, but which treat it as though it were due. These virtues are closer to justice than metaphorical justice, but nevertheless they do not attain to the purity of justice properly so called.

(b) Reduction by default of strict adjustment

This time the order of relations certainly exists. It is vigorously and imperatively set in motion by the interested and sovereign will or wills, but in itself, in its essential consistence, it does not express the strictly egalitarian equilibrium of right properly so-called. We have remarked in fact that the egalitarian equilibrium gradually disappears as the alterity between the terms of the legal relation is attenuated. The inequality signifies the dependence of one term in relation to the other, the smaller belonging to the greater.

St. Thomas after Aristotle and in the same spirit, studies three cases of this unequal right: the right of the master and the slave, the right of the father and the son, the right of the husband and the wife (jus dominativum, jus paternum, jus uxorium).

The slave, as such, is an integral part of the patrimony; he is in the master's service as a living instrument.

The son prolongs the father, the race and the individual being of the father: "filius est aliquid patris quia quodammodo est pars ejus." The son is a part of the paternal being who has arrived at a proper subsistence, but who, in the eyes of the ancients, continued to belong to the father, as a homogenous part of his being, and not, like the slave, as an instrument. Here again, alterity is lacking, and by this very fact the proper notion of equality. Therefore, there is no right properly so-called between the master and the slave, or between the father and the son. In his relations with the son or with the slave, the father or the master only deals with himself.

It will be said that all this is true if we consider in the son and in the slave this precise formality of a son or a slave. But isn't this formality a legal convention hypostatized by a misuse of abstractions? In reality, it is a question of two men confronting each other: the son and the slave are men, equal in nature to the father and the master. Consequently there is a strict right between them.

Yes! But it is precisely because we are considering these persons very concretely that we are led to shape a special right for them, in some way made to measure. If we take things abstractly, here is how we would proceed: the son as a son, a pure term of paternal generation, and the slave as a slave, a pure instrument of the master, have no right. But the son and the slave, as men, have right equal to the right of the father or the master. Here we have a concrete situation wholly disregarded. There are very characteristic social relations which do not receive any proper juridical form. But let us take things more concretely. We are considering distinct persons, subjects of right, characterized by a situation of dependence and inequality in their mutual relations. Therefore the *true* right which concerns them will be a specially defined right, corresponding to their determined situation, a paternal right and a dominative right.

The case of a husband and wife is a little different. The right which governs their relations is nearer to strict right without being confused with it. For the wife is not an instrument in the service of the husband. In this respect, we must remember the progress achieved since ancient times, for among the ancients the wife was truly an instrument, not of pleasure for pleasure-seekers, but an instrument in the service of the family institution. Her rank in the family was inferior, she was placed "loco filiae." On the other hand, it is evident that the wife is not, like the son, an extension of the husband's being, a prolonging of his person, the adornment of his vanity or the living symbol of his power. The man and the woman are both equally perfect in their specific being; human nature is the common measure and fundamental unity equally shared by the one and the other. It is by the father that the son, and by the master that the slave, accede to the specific dignity of free and rational beings; their dependence follows from this. But this is not the case with the husband and wife who are equals in their being. The woman owes nothing to her husband in this respect.

Moreover, as husband and wife, they are united on a basis of equality. They have contracted marriage on the basis of an absolute equality and in full liberty. Together they have founded a common institution; this is not the home of the husband. It is their home jointly. They give themselves and belong equally to the family institution, by the same right. Therefore, marriage as such, the conjugal life, is still a common measure, a fundamental unity, equally shared by the two spouses and in regard to which they are strictly equals, "ambo sub uno principe," both under the same principle: the principle of unity which human nature constitutes, and the principle which the household itself constitutes.

What therefore is the source of the inequality? What kind of belonging attaches the wife to the husband in a marriage which both have contracted and in which they live associated upon a basis of perfect equality?

The difference between them, which is the source of their inequality, is of a functional order. The very unity of the household requires the unity of the conjugal activities, and that is why there is a natural hierarchy in this society. The equality of being and of dignity of the husband and wife remains intact. But there is a hierarchy between them, therefore a dependence and a belonging at the level of common activity. While the son's belonging to the father is in some way entitative (the very being of the son is derived from the father), the wife is dependent upon her husband uniquely in that which concerns the *direction of her activity* in view of the common conjugal welfare. Outside of this functional authority, there is perfect equality between the associates. Regardless of what is sometimes said to the contrary, it is not the husband who gives his wife the dignity of a spouse, as if the wife entered the husband's home or family by the husband's grace. In reality, the husband and the wife together establish their common household. And this basic equality subsists during the entire conjugal life. The one and the other are equally responsible in regard to each other; their duties and their rights are rigorously equal. The inequality of the spouses is expressed in a functional hierarchy, a kind of practical arrangement, which permits a happy division of functions and a fruitful unity of purpose and of action in the fulfillment of the common tasks. It is this functional hierarchy which establishes marital authority (the ancients called it marital *power*). From this there follows a reduction of right between the husband and wife.

C. *Right in Its Counterfeits*

This time it is a question of an adulterated order, cut off from its ordering principle in spite of its well-regulated appearance. The apparent order perhaps offers an admirably adjusted equilibrium, and the effects are imposing. But its basis is ruinous; it inclines to falsehood.

This is the case with certain regulative systems which cannot insert themselves into the universal structure of the order, although they may satisfy certain partial requirements of life in society, as sophistical conclusions can solve immediate problems without being able to be justified in relation to the universal first principles of the speculative reason.

We know that the prescriptions of "secondary natural right" can be mingled with errors; so much the more in the details of particular positive rights can there be found, and almost inevitably will be found, badly deduced prescriptions, and solutions that are apparently efficacious but really contrary to primary natural right. There is a specious sophism somewhere, a fault in the rational development (e.g., laws regulating divorce, the charter of the maffia, the constitution of a tyrannical government, etc.).

II. Concerning Justice and Injustice

I. DEFINITION OF THE HABITUS OF JUSTICE AND OF INJUSTICE

A. *On the Virtue of Justice*

How shall we define the virtue of justice? Since every virtue is the principle of a good act, a virtue is necessarily defined by the good act which is relative to the proper matter of this virtue.

We already know, and we shall see more clearly, that justice considers that which pertains to our neighbors as its proper matter. Therefore Ulpian is right in designating the act of justice in reference to that which is properly the matter and the object of this virtue: "jus suum unicuique tribuens," the act which gives to each man his due. And in this definition we have what we would call the *specific difference*.

Let us understand these words correctly: *jus suum unicuique tribuens*. This requital can be made in two ways:

(a) by way of decision and direction: in this sense the "prince," or the judge whom he delegates, is specially the subject of it or the responsible author. It is he who is just, in this manner, when he states the law and orders its realization, and pursues its execution, if necessary by ways of constraint.

(b) by way of execution: in this sense, once the law is clearly recognized, the subordinates must pay off their obligations; they can be the subjects of this virtue of justice, finding themselves actively qualified by it.

But, since it is a question of virtue, and not only of an act, let us also mention the *generic conditions* for lack of which no activity, in any matter whatever, could be virtuous; that is to say, first the requirements of voluntariness (requirements of knowledge, choice and intention), and next the requirements, properly so called, of the habitus (stability). Stability that is in some sense objective: we want to render to others that which belongs to them, in all circumstances, always. And subjective stability: we always desire this, without exception.

B. *On the Vice of Injustice*

Aristotle remarks that there must be two distinct and contrary habitus to the principle of the just act and to the principle of the unjust act. For the situation is not the same in that which concerns the sciences and powers and that which concerns the habitus. The science of law instructs us in both what is just and what is unjust. But the virtuous habitus of justice cannot make us commit an unjust act. There is a habitus of injustice in the principle of unjust acts, contrary to the habitus of justice. And in the matter of relations with our neighbors we shall define injustice by the act that is contrary to the just act. This unjust act has the technical name "injustificatio," that is to say an actual and active injustice.

We may proceed with the elaboration of a definition of injustice beginning with *"injustificatio"* exactly as we defined justice beginning with *jus suum cuique tribuens.* We would arrive at a formula of this kind: injustice is the habitus by which a man, according to a constant and determined will, does not give to each man his due.

The *specific* element of the definition, the proper act, is the *injustificatio,* that is to say the fact of not rendering to each one (or to anyone) his due.

But here likewise are the *generic* conditions required if this activity is to be genuinely vicious. On the one hand there are the general requirements of voluntariness. There is no injustificatio properly so-called, but only an accidental injustificatio, if the agent does not intend it.

It is certainly an unjust deed that one is doing, but properly speaking one is not doing it; in some way it is done materially. Thus a disturbance, or a perfectly unjust state of things, may happen unexpectedly, without there being any formal *injustificatio* anywhere; this is owing to the proper and exterior consistence of the just or unjust object. On the other hand, without an intemperate intention, there is no intemperance, neither material nor formal; the eventual organic disorders, without this intention, do not have the sense of intemperance.

Like other generic elements of the definition, we must in second place determine the proper conditions of every habitus, for lack of which there will perhaps be *injustificatio,* but not the vice of injustice.

Man can in fact yield to *injustificatio* quite consciously under the influence of very diverse interior principles. Anger can lead him to strike, wound or kill other men; concupiscence can lead him to steal the property of others, or to offend the honor and violate the rights of a husband, etc. We are then confronting a passionate man whom anger or intemperance are moving to unjust actions; but we cannot infer the habitus of injustice from these unjust actions. On the contrary, when the agent takes pleasure in deliberately injuring other men, his action then proceeds from the habitus of injustice; only the latter can produce this deliberate, firm and stable will of *injustificatio.*

It goes without saying that such perversity of the will is quite rare. It is not, thank God, within the capacity of just anybody. It supposes the vice of injustice. Most men who commit formal injustices are not formally unjust. It is under the influence of a passion, generally concupiscence or fear, and not under the influence of "injustice," that they ordinarily commit injustice.

2. STRUCTURE OF THE HABITUS OF JUSTICE AND OF INJUSTICE

After having roughly considered the notions of justice and injustice, we must analyze more exactly these habitus. We can do this suitably by studying their *matter* and their *subject,* each in its turn.

We know what these two headings designate when it is a question of habitus. Under the title of *matter* we consider the formal object of a virtue, that is to say the proper domain rectified by justice, and, more precisely, the kind of rectification which is properly fitting to this domain. Under the title of *subject,* on the other hand, intervenes the cause, in some way material, of the habitus, the power which must be qualified, whether the habitus be just or unjust; and, more exactly, the potential indetermination, the "characteristic disposability" which calls up a habitus to determine and dispose this power according to this line.

A. *The Matter of the Habitus of Justice and of Injustice*

The fundamental idea is not new. It is the idea of relationship to our neighbor, ad alterum. We shall be satisfied to express everything that is found to be implicit in this mother-idea. Because it is a question in matters of justice and injustice of our relations with other men, it follows:

1. that these habitus properly concern our external operations;
2. that their measure is objective;
3. that the habitus is formally divided with regard to the diversity of the term "other."

(a) The Domain of Relations With Our Neighbors

The general idea of justice implying that of equality and adjustment, it is by essence that justice possesses this character of being in reference to our neighbor, for equality with oneself is unthinkable. There is no equality of one being except with another being.

We could declare ourselves satisfied with a relative alterity, permitting a kind of equality or adjustment: for example, in the midst of a living organism, the adaptation of one function to the rhythm of another function as when the heart precipitates or decreases its movement in order to adjust itself to the more or less considerable exercise of other members. In this, in fact, there is a sufficient plurality to establish a certain equality which establishes itself between various principles of movements. There is a real adjustment in this. Doubtless the justice of which we speak is a moral matter, and we can agree to reserve the name of justice for the moral domain, for in this domain again, as in a harmonious microcosm, there are all kinds of realities, actions, powers, habitus and rational rules between which law and justice would reign.

Let us not reject this conception absolutely. There is in fact a relationship between alterity and justice that is so essential that there is a place for justice wherever alterity exists; but in return and for the same reason, if alterity is only apparent or metaphorical, there is only place for a semblance or an image of justice.

Certainly in the moral universe as in the physical universe, there are all kinds of active principles which are opposed according to a genuine alterity and therefore may be adapted to one another effectively. But in the view of the moralist, the moral virtue of justice need not be preoccupied with all the types of adaptation which may be met with. For the only active principles which morality takes directly into consideration are the principles of human action. In fact it is always a question of governing human acts. The other movements, whether spiritual or corporal, of which man is the center, the term or the origin, are directly of interest to the philosopher, the physician or the naturalist. They do not concern the moralist, unless indirectly, when they are in some way assumed in a human act.

Therefore justice, as a moral virtue, does not recognize any real alterity except between the only principles capable of acting, in the technical and strong sense of this word which involves reason and liberty.

Justice therefore requires an alterity, a distinction of persons, since it is the man and not merely one of his organs or powers which acts, properly speaking. And we must carefully note that between one man and another the required alterity, as the basis of a just equilibrium or an unjust lack of balance, definitively rests upon that which opposes them as free and voluntary subjects by making them different principles of action.

This remark introduces a consequence which at first seems strange, but which is of great practical import and is easily explained. The will of the partners plays a great role in the exchanges of justice. Since men are distinguished as *others* in that they are distinct persons, and since they distinguish themselves as persons by their own will, it follows that not only is it impossible to be just or unjust in regard to oneself, but also that *one can neither act unjustly without willing it nor suffer unjustly by consenting to it*. As a matter of fact, anyone who provokes an unjust deed *against the self* without willing it is not acting in this respect; he does not oppose himself, as a distinct agent, to another agent; his will, the principle of his action, does not rise up against another will.

In order that we may clearly understand this truth, let us take an example. During the course of a game, someone wounds one of his partners, involuntarily. But he is not guilty of any imprudence or negligence. We say that this deed, the injury in itself, does not pose any question of justice. We see that the wills were unanimous when it was a question of playing together, and they continue to be unanimous, for the awkward player himself agrees with all his companions and with the victim in deploring the accident. There is still no matter of justice or injustice. And things would remain there, if by chance the blow which might have been fatal had not caused any wound or damage. On the other hand, even if all real injury had been avoided, the blow itself would have created a juridical situation if its author had wanted, directly or indirectly, rightly or wrongly, to inflict it, whether by just revenge, by malice or by culpable negligence.

Of course, in our example, the question of justice comes up immediately, not because of the injury itself, which is involuntary by hypothesis, but because of its consequences. The latter in effect raise a question of interest, in the etymological sense (*inter est,* one is divided thereupon), between the debtor and the creditor, between the involuntary injurer and the victim. This is because the situation is thereafter modified in such a way that the two wills are necessarily opposed. However, nobody accuses the first man of being the author of an unjust aggression. It is not on this point that there is opposition between them. But until there is reparation for the damage done, they are confronting an *unequal situation* which does not depend upon the victim (who is involuntary in this respect) but which depends, in its actual existence, and in its duration, upon the involuntary injurer. The latter did not *act* when he wounded the other, and that is why he is not guilty of any aggression, but he *acts* thereafter for as long as this unequal situation which occurred by his deed continues to subsist by his will, against the will of others.

Here again is a practical application of the same principle. It is said that the lightness of the matter diminishes the gravity of the injustice: in itself, however, injustice is a grave sin, because it is harmful to the welfare of other men—directly opposed to charity. If an injustice is to be only venial, it must be denatured and must be diminished in its genus. This is what happens when we presume that the victim of an injustice in some trivial matter does not consider himself to be injured, and that he cannot reasonably claim to press his rights in all their rigor in such a matter, and briefly, that he accepts the occurrence. For example, if someone takes an apple in the garden of another man, this does not of course prevent the gardener from giving harsh looks, or even inflicting punishment upon the trespasser. But any man of good sense will consider that there was no formal injustice in this action, because no reasonable will should seriously attach itself to these trifles as though they were his own good, to the point of putting himself in a relationship of alterity to another reasonable will in a matter of this kind.

(b) The external operations

It is a well-established truth that justice, unlike the other moral virtues, has for its object the rectification of the operations and not the passions.

Doubtless the passions are also operations, but what distinguishes them in the eyes of morality, to the point of making them worthy of another name, is the singular manner in which man finds himself affected by them. Moreover, these operations which are called passions are not enclosed within the interior of the subject. They also break forth and express themselves in external acts. But such operations are of interest to morality precisely because a man's manner of being, when he yields to them, is suitable or unsuitable for a reasonable subject.

If, however, we neglect this affective side, the external operations remain subject to two kinds of possible rules: to the rules of art, in so far as they tend to fabrication (*facere*); and to rules of law and justice, according as we apply them to our relations with other men. As justice governs this domain of relations with other men, its object is definitely external operations.

But we shall not be surprised to see justice meeting with other moral virtues that govern the passions, or even with technical rules, in external operations; for external operation interests justice in the measure in which it is directed to our neighbor, but it can also affect any other habitus to the degree in which it flows from these interior principles. In this way the external operation which consists in selling a piece of property may combine, for instance, three kinds of habitus affecting the realization of this act: one or several types of habitus that are purely artistic or technical, because the operation involves the drawing up of a deed in good and due form which a man must know how to prepare correctly; and one or several types of virtuous habitus governing the passions, for example liberality, since the interested party must dominate his attachment to money if he does not want to be inwardly hindered in accomplishing this external act, like those excessively avid merchants who cannot make up their minds to conclude a transaction; and finally justice, in order that the transaction may establish a just balance between the object sold and the price, and respect the rights of the seller as well as the buyer.

In a certain sense there are even movements of joy and sadness which proceed from the exercise of the virtue of justice and which are considered, in the opinion of Aristotle and St. Thomas, as secondary ends of justice. In this respect justice is comparable to the other moral virtues. It is pleasant to exercise it when one possesses it, and one suffers to see it thwarted. But it is one thing for a virtue to produce these consequent joys or sadnesses, and another thing to have the rectification of the passions as the object.

In matters of justice, therefore, it is a question of the external operations which concern our neighbor, and which make us enter into communication with other men. We see under what angle the external realities intervene as the object of justice, not in themselves, nor insofar as they please or displease us, nor in the degree that they are useful to us, but insofar as they are for us the occasion and matter of an adjustment with our neighbor. Strictly speaking, the virtue of justice makes the virtuous man competent in the application of external realities (acts, material goods, even words) and in communications or relations with other men.

And even among all the ways of applying these external realities "for our neighbor," there are some that enjoy an unquestionable priority. These are the actions by which we distinguish and measure these external realities in one way or another. The fundamental operation in our relations ad alterum consists in effect in distinguishing and establishing the mine and thine, that which is due to each of us. All the rest depends upon this fundamental activity, not only in matters of justice however, because every other communication supposes that this exact and previous discernment is complete (the fact of paying one's debts, for example, supposes that one has distinguished his own property from that of other men); but also in matters of other virtues which adopt the mode "for our neighbor" as in matters of justice (like liberality). This fundamental discernment is the first postulate of justice and it maintains itself as a light in the heart of all just activity.

(c) The Golden Mean, the objective of justice

Every virtue consists of a *medium rationis,* a mean imposed by reason; the very notion of moral virtue implies in effect a conformity to right reason and it is this conformity to the rational order which formally constitutes the goodness of the moral virtue. The mean in question is proposed by reason in every moral virtue by way of a measure and specifying form.

But the rational order, the norm of virtuous perfection, takes a different form when it is a question of external passions or operations. In the first case, the human measure is established only by the acting subject's conformity to reason, for the passions, as such, are only good or bad in so far as they affect this subject well or badly and are humanly fitting for him or not. When, on the contrary, we consider the operations as such, we are not concerned with their subjective reaction upon the agent, or the light which they throw upon his inner morality, but we appreciate their rectitude as human operations according as they are adjusted or not to our neighbor.

This latter feature is considerable. The only operations that are truly characterized in a moral way in their external reality are the operations that have some bearing upon our neighbor. The external operations can be limited to the handling and the useful or acceptable application of external things, but then, these operations have no moral character. They are neither good nor bad in themselves, but uniquely in relation to their author and to his intentions and his emotional and habitual behavior. The relation to things does not provide the operations with any moral object or any principle of moral differentiation whether of goodness or of evil. The operations which only bear upon things, therefore, differentiate themselves with reference to the reason of their author: *medium rationis.* A particular expense may not be appropriate for me, if I am poor; but it is suitable for someone who is richer. Some kind of food, in a particular quantity, and in certain circumstances, is suitable or unsuitable for me, according to what I am and what I want. We cannot say that any expense or any food is suitable or reasonable in itself, without reference to the person of the subject.

But when the operations affect our neighbor, reason perceives in their external reality a specifying moral object, good or bad, according as these operations attain or do not attain a just measure, independent of the subject, or of his intentions, his manner of being, or his action. This is a certain adjustment of the *res* (operation, or the thing carried out) which imposes itself from outside as morally good or evil, and as conformable or not to the rational order: *medium rei.*

Certainly the *medium rei* is *also* a *medium rationis*. But in the case of the passions or the operations which do not concern our neighbor, we will only expect rational rectitude in the subject. Whereas justice recognizes a kind of moral goodness or malice in the presence or absence of a certain external proportion between the operation and our neighbor. That is why justice does not seek its medium, its point of equilibrium, or its measure of perfection, in the dispositions or the intentions of the subject, but in the external state of things whose consistence, the manner of being, by itself, and objectively, agrees or disagrees with the moral and rational order.

It is certainly a question of a *medium,* a *mean*. Not that justice itself is located at equal distance between two contrary vices, like liberality between prodigality and avarice. All the virtues do not consist *essentially* in a golden mean. But all consist *causaliter in medio,* or in other words, they all have the effect of efficaciously establishing a golden mean, each in its own domain.

Justice strives to achieve and safeguard this golden mean in the reality by the external operation. Let us examine well its consistence and how it tends to guarantee to *each man his own good.*

The matter of justice is the external operation, in so far as it corresponds duly to our neighbor, whether by itself or by the thing that it carries out. We do not yet ask ourselves in the name of what rules this correspondence is established, or how it happens that such a quantity of something belongs to any particular person while a larger or smaller quantity corresponds to some other person. We only keep in mind that in all cases justice guarantees the share of each man, and that is why the *mean* of justice is formally found at the exact point of correspondence between the external thing and the external person. This standard establishes itself objectively between one more and one less; it therefore constitutes a definite objective mean.

To determine this standard, that is to say the measure of external reality exactly corresponding to each person, is to determine what is due to each. Therefore the proper act of justice is to render to each his own, to rectify the operations in regard to our neighbor according to this gauge, the exact measure of what is proportioned to him.

It is easy to explain, by analogy with commercial relations in which justice is exercised first and commonly, why we extend the terms of gain and loss to the whole domain of relations of justice, in order to designate the more and the less between which the medium of justice is established.

(d) Formal division in matters of justice

Until now we have considered justice *in the proper sense* (which excludes metaphorical justice), but in the whole extent of its domain *for our neighbor*. Now, the proper matter of justice, its external operation which consists in rendering to others their due, permits the introduction of a formal division into this domain. This division includes legal or general justice on the one hand, and particular justice on the other hand. It is this division which must be explained now.

Its origin is ancient. Aristotle proceeding according to his customary method, which consists in seeking in current language for the starting-point of his philosophical analyses, states that men commonly speak of two types of just and unjust men (*Eth.*, E. 2, 112q to 31ff).

First there is the unjust man, the "paranomos," who acts against the laws; next there is the man who is "pleonektes" and "anisos," that is to say, who wants too much (of good) and not enough (of pain). It must therefore be admitted inversely that there are two types of just men: the "nomimos" and the "isos."

Thereupon, Aristotle reasons: since the nomimos, by conforming to the law, is just, this is never to doubt that legal things are in some way just things: τα νόμιμά ἐστιν πως δίκαια. Now law tends to the common welfare, it has bearing upon everything that is required for this welfare and for its conditions, its integral elements and its guarantees. This is so true that we can qualify as just, in this first sense, everything that produces, nurtures and guarantees this welfare and its elements for the community. This is the *legal just*. It extends to all kinds of virtuous acts: acts of fortitude, as when the law commands us to remain at our post in spite of danger; acts of temperance, when it forbids debauchery and intoxication; acts of moderation, when it prohibits cruelties and injuries. This remark allows Aristotle to identify this (legal) justice in some way with every virtue, and it is in this sense that the Philosopher, apparently, and many of his commentators, in any case, understand the epithet *general,* accorded to this virtue of legal justice. St. Thomas thoroughly examined this idea.

But Aristotle is led to describe a particular justice: τὴν ἐν μέρει ἀρετῆς δικαιοσύνην. Here is how he does this. Just as particular virtues (fortitude, temperance, moderation, etc.) subsist under legal justice, a universal virtue, there must also subsist a particular kind of justice, defined not in relation to law (as legal) but defined as a virtue of equality. Everything that is unequal is illegal, but, as we have seen, everything illegal is not unequal, since the illegal comprises acts of cowardice, intemperance, hatred, anger, etc., besides the acts that are tainted with inequality.

St. Thomas, after St. Albert, takes up this Aristotelian division and improves it, not only in itself but also by inserting it into his own synthesis of the virtues.

General or legal justice

There is no doubt about the Aristotelian origin of this concept. Does this mean that the concept of general justice was transmitted from the Philosopher to the Angelic Doctor without any alteration? No, indeed. This virtue of general justice was adapted to the Thomist "climate" and inserted into a synthesis of the virtuous life. Since then, by the continuity of the terms, there has been a genuine evolution of the ideas and an enrichment of the doctrine.

Let us also be on guard against other anachronisms. The word law does not express in the English of the twentieth century what was signified by the word lex for the Christian of the thirteenth century. What then shall we say about the expression: legal justice? Both in Latin and in English the epithet "general" is endowed with a whole range of meanings; but let us not take sides too readily, especially because in the Thomist system of the virtues there is a technical manner of understanding this generality which does not coincide exactly with that of Aristotle. Finally, when we see St. Thomas speak of the *bonum commune,* let us not hasten to identify this notion with the *common good* dear to the social morality of our time, for this very conception of a social morality is modern; and the problems that it discusses are modern. And certainly the representations and conceptions that it brings to mind are also modern. When St. Thomas declares that general or legal justice has the *bonum commune* for its object, he has in mind something wholly different from this modern proposal: the common good is the object of social justice.

To be clear, we are determined to set aside quite deliberately any (or at least conscious) preoccupation with modern problems and conceptions. For the moment we shall be unaware of social justice, of which St. Thomas does not breathe a word.[10]

According to Aristotle, as we have seen, legal justice is general because it is pure virtue. This teaching was only too well understood in the Christian moral tradition; it was still prevalent when St. Thomas, led by the requirements of his psychology of the virtues, took it up on his own account by interpreting it in an original manner.

Here, in three stages, is his argumentation:

1. Let us remember that justice orders man in relation to other men (understand a real *other,* and not a metaphorical other), and that the just man can enter into relations with another man in two ways: first with another man considered as a particular individual, in his singularity; secondly, with another man considered "in communi." What is the meaning of this expression: "ad alium *in communi* (consideratum)"?

The rest of the text says simply: "in this sense that to serve the community is to serve all men comprised in that community." In this we must not, apparently, be in a hurry to discover the affirmation of a justice in regard to the whole, considered as a juridical person distinct from the sum of its members. The analogy of the whole and of the part will only intervene in the second stage of the demonstration. For the moment, whatever may be the case with the metaphysical nature of the collective being, the text invites us to think that the other (*alius,* in the masculine gender, which cannot designate a sociological entity) is always a human being. The reflection remains at a radical and formal level in which it is clear that there is definitely no justice except in regard to man. This said, there still are the following considerations.

(a) Sometimes we consider the other man in his singularity, that is to say, absolutely, making abstraction of his community ties. Such a schematic and simplifying consideration imposes itself in daily juridical relations for the convenience of transactions. Thus in mat-

[10] The signification that we are giving in what follows to the expression *common good* is that of *bonum commune* of St. Thomas.

ters of sale, men deal with every client who presents himself without concern about his family situation, his social position or his honorary titles, etc. Normally, at any rate, this is the case. In other words, we abstract the other man from his social environment.

(b) Sometimes there is occasion to consider the other man, no longer divested abstractly, but with his community relationships, involved in a social order in which he finds himself concretely endowed with qualities, and with a dignity and a kind of new density. We are then dealing not just with another man, but with another man socially situated, whether it be a prince, a father of a family, the head of a business, a wage-earner, a clerk or a soldier. The determination of the qualities which justice takes into consideration depends nevertheless upon very contingent sociological representations, according to the times, the environment and also the matters that are treated.

2. Let us now show that when justice, properly so called, orders us to our neighbor *in communi,* that is to say to the other man considered in his sociological determinations, it merits the qualifying term of general. It is only here that the analogy of the whole and of the part intervenes legitimately to provide a medium of demonstration. The other (it is therefore always a question of another man) considered in his community ties is in effect comparable to a part in a whole. Now every perfection whatsoever of the part belongs to the whole. There is therefore no good of the part which does not contribute to the perfection of the whole. This analogy reveals that there is no virtue, nor any human perfection, in ourselves or in other men, which does not provide an occasion of adjustment towards our neighbor, that is to say, which does not establish a relationship of justice properly so called. Nothing, by hypothesis, being excluded from the whole, we see that acts of each kind of virtue can belong to justice in so far as the latter orders us to our neighbor *in communi.* In this respect, justice is rightly called general.

Let us specify that justice towards the other man *in communi* is not the only virtue which, according to St. Thomas, is general. Charity is general also. Moreover, inversely, there are several vices, called capital, which are general in their own way, being leaders that command and entail a whole series of other vices and sins that follow upon them, in some way serving as a final cause of these satellites. St. Thomas strives to classify the case of general justice by giving a rank, a proper essence, to this virtue that is called total, "tota virtus, omnis virtus." He explains in what way it is general, but at the same time he insists much upon the fact that it is a special virtue in itself, with its own matter, its formal object, and that it must no longer tower over all the virtuous categories without distinction, as was customary in many traditional theologies.

For there are two ways for a being to merit the epithet of general. According to the first sense, a thing is general if it can be attributed (in the strong sense, implying subjective identity) to several; thus animality is a genus which can be attributed to several species: man, horse, etc. In this case there is essential identity between that which is general and that in relation to which it is general. The genus enters into the definition of the species. We must affirm the genus of each species. The general being that to which it extends, we can attribute it to the species.

On the other hand, according to the other sense, the general is not that to which it extends in a general way, but it exercises a general influence upon that to which it extends. Thus the sun extends its influence upon the whole physical world; it is everywhere *generally* by its luminous, calorific and other influence. But it is not everywhere otherwise; it does not identify itself with any of the beings influenced by itself.

The same may be said about general justice. It is not general by way of identification with all the other virtues. From this point of view, which is specific, general justice is a virtue among others, a special virtue defined by a special object in a proper matter. Doubtless this object is no other than the "common good," but properly this object is particular to it. General or legal justice is a perfectly defined virtue, whose essence is specified by its special object which is the *bonum commune*. As a negative cliché the doctrine is the same in regard to injustice *illegalis:* it is a special vice, defined by its formal opposition to the common good which it despises. It does not limit itself to inflicting actual harm upon the common welfare, as happens with every sin, but it orders the other vicious activities in defiance of the common good.

We therefore surmise that general justice (or injustice) can be connected in different ways with the other virtues (or vices). We can imagine a just man, who loves the common good, who finds in his general justice the lever of a diverse virtuous activity, especially in matters of external operations, but also, and more radically, in matters of internal emotional behavior, the latter being rectified all at once because its rectification must facilitate the rectification of the external operations, and because it constitutes, in itself, an integral element of the common good. Inversely, an unjust man, who formally despises the common good, finds in this general injustice the motivation for many other vicious external acts and internal emotional disorders, which also are considered as injustice and as a source of injustice.

Such is the formal connection. The dominating virtue gives its species to the acts of the dominated virtues in an authentic manner. Deliberate fornication, with the intention of doing harm to the common welfare, is a formal act of general injustice rather than intemperance.

From another point of view, we may consider a virtuous life that is complex and diversified: the good exercise of these virtues, especially by reason of the external operations that follow, but also in itself, orders to the common good even if the author does not formally have this intention. In this there is a material connection, certainly efficacious and frequent. A public order, at least approximate, comes forth almost spontaneously from the exercise of private virtues, even if on the whole the agents are not concerned about this superior result. But this time their acts are not specifically and formally acts of general justice. It is in this way, on the other hand, that public disorder is introduced, without any thought given to the matter, through the disorder consented to by private morals.

3. There remains only to justify the epithet of legal accorded to this virtue. It is understood that general justice is a special virtue which is formally defined by the object which rightly presents itself for consideration: the common good. St. Thomas here remarks laconically: "And since it is the role of law to orient us towards the common good, this justice, called general, is called legal justice; it is by this in effect that man corresponds to the law which orders the acts of all the virtues to the common good" (IIa IIae, 58, 5, c.). But let us not see a simple verbal rapprochement, a play on words, at the basis of this explanation. A whole doctrine is involved here, with reference to the treatise on laws and to the treatise on prudence, and in the treatise on justice with reference to the question of "epikeia."

We know that the ideo-dynamic mechanism of the human act, with its incessant conjugation of a rational specification and a voluntary exercise (see chap. I, vol. III), is translated, in the virtuous order, by an analogous conjugation between prudential activity and the activity of any moral virtue. While the dynamism of the moral virtue (for example, the appetite of the "good to render to our neighbor") successively *realizes* the vc'untary phases of the virtuous act: *consensus electio, usus activus;* the prudential order rationally *specifies* this moral activity by the successive phases of the *consilium,* the *judicium,* and the *imperium.*

Being a question of the common good, let us specify that we are referring to political prudence and general justice.

Now the law (I do not say in its very diverse technical formulation, but in its essence of decision expressed by reason) is precisely the expression, by the prudent political reason, of a general principle of practical action, in view of the common good. Considered in its essence, the law is nothing else but this.[11]

Legislative (or ruling) Prudence calls forth an appetite from the voluntary side, virtuously rectified in regard to the common good by general justice. Law, being a rational formula, emanates substantially from reason; it is a work of reason and prudence. But of a reason and prudence that are dynamically animated by a *just* political will. Thus the law is the common work of the virtues of prudence and general justice. From the point of view of specification and of rational direction, it is a matter of prudence. From the point of view of its execution, it is a matter of general justice (not only the execution of the law that is drafted and promulgated, but of everything which must be carried out from the very first, with a view of enacting a just law to be realized, for this legislative formulation is also human activity).

At this point three remarks are necessary:

(a) These political virtues should be found in all those who constitute the community: in the head of the community by his principal status (I was about to say princely); and in the subjects—by

---

[11] Naturally we must rid ourselves of a vulgar conception of law, less attentive to the substance of this act than to its external forms and to the guarantees of procedure with which it is surrounded. Often men give the name of law to simple acts of governmental political authority (viz., a law giving approval to a treaty or a contract, a law erecting a public establishment, a law of amnesty; in France, in 1926, an "administrative Fund of national defense bonds, and of industrial exploitation of tobacco, and of amortization of the public debt" was instituted by a law, and even by a constitutional law. Such language has no philosophical meaning whatever).

secondary and ministerial status. For example, when political prudence belongs to the head, it is specially called "ruling" or "legislative"; the generic name of political prudence is sufficient to define that of subordinates.

(b) We must also note that political prudence and general justice, whatever may be the excellence of their legislative activity, have a much vaster scope than this latter activity. Law is only a universal formula, a general principle of action, and everyone knows that this general formula does not apply to all concrete circumstances. When laws are stated, it is still necessary to proceed to "action"; how many laws have remained a dead letter for lack of civic virtues of justice or prudence in their application! And on the other hand, the legal texts have many loop-holes which omit from their general prescriptions a large number of details which neither can nor should be determined by laws. Here the field is open for certain virtues connected with prudence and general justice.

Completing the directive role of legislative prudence, specially in those exceptional circumstances which are beyond the scope of legal conjectures, St. Thomas recognizes a "eugnomosyna" with a view of prudent judgment in such circumstances, while political prudence governs the judgment in normal circumstances.

Likewise with regard to general justice. If there are no laws, or even contrary to the text of a law, the good citizen has the duty of acting in such and such a way in exceptional circumstances by the virtue of equity; the latter is apparently identified with the "eugnomosyna," with the reservation that this exceptional judgment is attributable to prudence from the point of view of direction, and to justice from the point of view of the exercise. In this case there is spontaneous recognition and payment of a debt of justice which the laws do not formulate.

There is moreover a trace of mild hesitation with regard to the precise definition of equity or "epikeia." And this depends upon the extension that is given to the notion of legal justice. If we say that the latter's unique object is conformity to legislative texts or prescriptions, equity, at the heart of justice taken as a whole, constitutes a part which is distinguished from legal justice and is superior to it. But if we give, as ought to be done, the full signification to legal justice—a conformity to the law both as to the letter and with regard to the legislator's intention which is the better part of it—then equity constitutes the highest point at the heart of legal justice.

Legal justice should not in fact be defined by obedience to the law, but by a relationship to the common good, the latter being at once the object of general justice and the end envisaged by the law. Therefore the just man, by legal justice, is less concerned about obedience to the law, or even the presumed intentions of the legislator, than fostering the common good, in which he agrees with the legislator, identifies himself with him, and is in accord with the law. With his love for the common good, he has at heart the very principle of the law.

(c) Finally, if the law, in the precise and juridical meaning of the word, does not regulate all political life, we must not believe that political life properly so called constitutes the sole domain of prudence and general justice either. In reality, wherever there is a community of men, whether it is a question of limited groups within a political society, or federations comprising several cities with a view of a common end and action, there is matter for regulation according to what is called political prudence and legal justice, independently of any city or any civic law. Here again, it is proper to make our modern conception of social life more flexible by repudiating fetishistic worship of the State and the written law. It is good to return to the medieval perspective of a juridico-social pluralism, extremely complex and various, with a multitude of communities enjoying particularist rights, according to the local customs, personal statutes, and contracted engagements. This multiplicity of unequal and various social relations was obviously bound to favor education and the exercise of the most subtle virtuous nuances in matters of political prudence and legal justice.

Particular Justice

Legal justice is all virtue, not by substituting itself for all the virtues, but by ordering certain acts of these special virtues to the common good. General justice therefore needs particular virtues for ordering to the common good, virtues which only have particular goods as their object.

Now, if the rational order established in our passions offers a fruitful source of particular goods which the concupiscible and irascible virtues take as their object immediately, there is in our external operations, in the measure in which they establish a relationship with another individual, a domain to govern virtuously. In this domain, there can only be a question of a virtue of justice and it is immediately a matter of particular goods, of good that concerns individuals. Far from taking its place, general justice requires particular justice, for it matters greatly to the common good, envisaged immediately by legal justice, that relations to other men and between individuals, should be governed immediately by a special virtue, particular justice.

There is a specific difference between these two justices, due to their respective objects: the reason of the common good is one thing, and the reason of the particular good is something else, as the idea of the whole is different from the idea of the part.

Let us note, however, that particular justice which immediately orders man in relation to the good of another, exercises, in its own way, a certain *general* influence upon other virtues of the subject— even in matters of passions. This is because justice is located in the will, the universal motivating power of the soul. And also because the passions, accidentally, can affect relations with our neighbor, especially by their manifestations and the external reactions which they call forth.

However this relative generality of particular justice is not comparable to that of legal justice. We know that the latter has right of control directly upon the life of the passions; doubtless it affects first and foremost the external operations of which the passions are the principle, because the common good is also first affected by these external manifestations. But the passions in themselves, insofar as they affect for good or evil a subject who is a member of the community and whose good belongs to the good of the whole, concern general justice. Particular justice does not enjoy the same privilege.

B. *The "Subject" of the Habitus of Justice and of Injustice*

The question of the "subject" is far from being an idle question or a matter of curiosity. It is necessary to know the proper and immediate "subject" of a habitus in order to know the structure of that habitus. The habitus is only comprehensible in respect to certain necessities which it must satisfy in the subject. To know these necessities, these particularities of the subject, is already to understand the role, the life and the effects of the habitus.

Justice is an operative habitus. It does not reside in the essence of the soul to qualify it; it directly qualifies a power, the will, as the power of action. In other words, man is qualified by the habitus, not purely and simply in order to act—the power provides for this—but in order to act in a certain manner.

(a) Review of ideas that are supposed to be known.[12]

The habitus is a quality of the first species. We must know what a quality is. It is true that it is not possible to give a definition of quality. But quality is in effect that by which we are qualified. And there is no vicious circle in this, for this manner of expressing oneself, besides being inevitable, is sufficiently enlightening. In the concrete we understand what it means to be qualified. Qualification is an accident which disposes, determines and orders in a certain way.

This accidental determination can affect the subject at the quantitative level in a manner which, in short, is very superficial by establishing a certain order between its quantitative parts, distinct and external in relation to one another. Nor should we understand the word "establishing" as an efficient causality; it is not quality which realizes such an order, but quality is a manner of being, that of the subject determined by this quantitative order.

In a more penetrating manner, quality can affect the subject by making it susceptible to the influence of outside causes, that is to say, to suffering.

Qualification can go so far as to make the subject capable of acting, in a given sense.

Finally there are qualities which give the subject a certain manner of being in himself, a manner of conduct and of self-restraint, considering what he is naturally.

These are the different species of qualities classified properly in a progressive order or an order of invention. In reality, according to the order of exposition, we must give the first place to the qualities which affect the subject in himself, in relation to his nature. Next come the qualities which affect the subject, no longer directly in what he is *secundum naturam,* but according to a certain character proceeding more or less dierctly from his nature. Consequently the order is: his action, his suffering, his quantity. Thus we find our·selves confronting four species of qualities traditionally known:

First species: the habitus and the disposition.

Second species: the power and the impotence.

Third species: the "passion" and the "qualitas passibilis."

---

[12] Cf. The simple and clear synthesis of H. D. Gardeil, *Initiation à la philosophie de Saint Thomas Aquin,* Paris, Éd. du Cerf, 1952. On the species of qualities, cf. volume IV, *Métaphysique,* pp. 102-103.

Fourth species: the form and the figure.

In the first species, we distinguish the habitus from the simple disposition; for the habitus possesses over the simple disposition the advantage of a natural stability, that is to say a stability which is not only or necessarily de facto, but which is de jure, because, in spite of accidental weaknesses, its causes are naturally stable. Such for example is the difference between science, based upon a demonstration, and opinion which rests upon probabilities.

If we take into account the difference in the subjects qualified by the habitus, we find ourselves facing another distinction, between entitative habitus and operative habitus. But we must not allow ourselves to transform the latter into qualities of the second species. But sometimes the reality, the qualified nature, is an essence; in this case, the habitus disposes it to be itself and in itself in a certain manner which affects its nature, and therefore in a good or evil manner. Sometimes the qualified reality is itself a power, that is to say a reality whose whole being is in some way tending and oriented towards action. We must then get a clear idea of the qualification which results from it for this power. No new way is opened by the habitus for action, but the habitus qualifies the power in what it is in itself, that is to say in its very movement, since it is this fruitful generosity which constitutes the reality of the power. By the habitus the power will then find itself qualified to proceed to the act, not in any manner whatever and just as it is, but in a certain manner in relation to its own nature as a power. It is for this reason that these habitus are called operative; not that they are absolutely principles of operations, but they qualify a being in its operative movement itself, and therefore they are principles of operative qualification, or preferably principles of the qualified operation in so far as it is qualified.

The habitus does not therefore give the power to proceed to the act; it supposes this power in the nature or the faculty, but if there is habitus, it means that this power preserved a share of indetermination, fulfilled precisely by this qualification. For want of such an indetermination (a necessity in a power that is wholly passive; full determination of a nature which is pure act and which is no longer susceptible to anything) there would be no place for a habitus.

The terrain of choice, the ideal subject for the habitus, includes the natures or faculties which participate in the freedom of the rational order, at least in that which concerns objects that are not absolute; it requires a potential indetermination of the nature or the power. This means that the will is a privileged candidate.

(b) The Will, Subject of Justice

Possibility of a Habitus in the Will

There is no need of a habitus to dispose the will to pursue the good to which it is ordered by nature. It is in fact the very definition of the will to be a tendency, an appetite of this good. Nothing can dispose it towards this, because it is so disposed by itself. This good to which the will does not need to be disposed, is the good which appears such and which is presented as such by the light of reason. For the will to be disposed by habitus to a good of reason, there must be a particularity presented to which the will is not by nature inclined.

This, in effect, is what happens. It is not a question of a will in itself; every will is the will of a subject. Therefore when we say that the will is inclined by nature to pursue the good which is proportioned to it, we are taking a short-cut which must not be allowed to trick us. In reality, the will (of a subject) is naturally inclined to the good which the reason (of the subject) presents as proportioned to the subject. And we then conceive of the eventuality of an hiatus between the good presented by the reason and the voluntary appetite of such a subject. The good can in fact exceed the natural span of the appetite in two ways: specifically and individually. From the specific point of view, the subject can find himself confronting a good that is excessive in relation to the limits of his nature; his will won't be found to be naturally disposed, by itself, to accede to such a good. It will have to be raised and disposed to this supernatural good (charity). From the individual point of view, finally, it may happen that a good that is natural to man, presented as a good by the natural reason, exceeds the natural and spontaneous aspirations of the will; for the latter is naturally opened to the good of the subject, but awaits a determination, an additional disposition in regard to the good of reason which is not the individual good of the subject. From this follows the necessity and possibility in the will of a habitus in regard to the *good of our neighbor*, even if this *good of our neighbor* is also a *good of reason*. Thus the virtues which have as their object the good of our neighbor: justice, liberality, etc., perfect the will.

Points of View of Justice and the Will

What we know about justice allows us to affirm that this virtue is not concerned with governing an act of knowledge. It aims at accomplishing a righteous operation. One is not just when one knows, but when one does something just. Therefore, justice can only reside in a power defined by a practical object, that is to say in an appetitive power, since the appetite is the immediate principle of practical activity.

But of what appetite is it a question? There are two of them: the sensible appetite, corresponding to a sensible apprehension and divided consequently into the irascible and the concupiscible; the will, which is the appetite corresponding to the rational knowledge. The conditions of the just act provide the decisive argument: to give others their due can only depend upon a rational apprehension, for it is a question of perceiving an intelligible, not sensible, relationship between other men and their good, the rational belonging of a good to a person. The will is only directed towards this object as a consequence of a comparison effected by the reason. Justice therefore resides in the will.

Consequently, justice, residing in the will, is admirably placed for extending its empire over all the operations which are under the dependence of the will, as soon as they affect the good of our neighbor. This generality for a long while made men believe that justice resides in the soul, quite entirely. This is not necessary, rather through the will does justice govern all the parts of the soul.

3. MORAL SIGNIFICATION OF THE HABITUS OF JUSTICE AND INJUSTICE

The Greatness of Justice

Aristotle already sang the praises of justice: If we consider general justice, it shines among all the moral virtues with a brilliance that is especially ardent because its object, the common good, is endowed with a character that is almost divine, transcending all individual goods in their singularity in order to express them in their very order. Neither the morning star nor the evening star can be compared in beauty with justice.

Shall we say that religion itself is inferior to legal justice Expressed in these terms, the question is odious. One does not draw up a prize-list of the virtues as for a classification of excellence. The virtues are not entities that are more or less great, or more or less highly placed on some imaginary scale. The virtues are habitus, that is to say, they are qualities disposing the moral subject in one order of activity or another, conformably with his rational nature.

The only question which arises here is tantamount to asking ourselves in what order our notions of justice and religion or the other virtues are classified. Put in this way, we must definitely say that the notion of legal justice is comprehensive in relation to the notion of religion; legal justice includes the virtue of religion in its perfect comprehension, for legal justice would be incomplete and halting if it did not govern us precisely in that which concerns the greater other, the one who is other in a transcendent manner, and whose good is precisely the more general, and the more widely common. Let us not speak needlessly about an inferiority of religion, for religion obviously constitutes the highest part of legal justice. Thus the iron of the javelin is only a part of the javelin, but it is the most precious part; all the rest is made for it and has value because of it. Without religion, legal justice would be discrowned, like a disarmed javelin.

If we consider particular justice, we shall admire its perfections also. First of all the perfection of residing in the will—and this perfection does not only consist in the platonic privilege of belonging to the noblest part of the soul. Positive privileges follow from this, since by the will the empire of justice will extend into all parts of the soul. There is also the perfection of seeking the good of our neighbor. It is more noble to achieve and defend the good of our neighbor than to be preoccupied with our particular good. And it is a sign of greater activity and greater efficacy to extend our action further.

Doubtless, the act of liberality possesses a singular perfection in what it presents spontaneously and with largesse. But liberality itself rests upon respect for the relations of particular justice, and the beneficiaries of liberality can only be limited in number, while justice is directed to everyone. As for legal justice, in considering the common good, it opens to virtue a vaster field and still wider perspectives than does liberality. For the latter, in its very act, only tends toward the good and to the moral elegance of the generous man.

Religion surpasses particular justice in virtuous perfection because the divine eminence, its sovereign alterity, cannot constitute a particular good. When we say particular we mean partial, therefore balanced by other parts; this comparison is injurious and inadmissible when it is a question of the sovereign par excellence. Therefore religion, the eminent part of general justice, can only dominate all the other parts of justice, and notably particular justice, whether commutative or distributive.

There can be no question of comparing the theological virtues with justice, not even with general justice. The theological virtues make us perform acts that are more than human and they surpass in perfection the most beautiful human virtues, that is to say the moral virtues.

The limit between the two domains is perhaps the virtue of mercy. This virtue can be considered, and this is its current meaning as a moral virtue; in that case it is a virtue residing in the concupiscible, with the effect of governing the sadness which the misery of our neighbor causes in every reasonable man. It is then inferior to legal justice, which can decide to do something about it. But mercy can also be considered as an act of the will, governed by the reason, by which we abhor efficaciously the misery of our neighbor, which requires that we have the will to deliver him from it effectively. By this act, we participate in the merciful activity of God Himself whose property it is, so to speak. To relieve the suffering in their misery is the deed of Him Who is truly superior; it is an act that is eminently fitting to God. This raises us above justice, as also above the strictly human virtues.

B. *The Gravity of Injustice*

In itself injustice is a grave sin, mortal by its nature. This is understandable. The gravity of a sin, or a vice, arises from the opposition in which it places us in regard to the principle of the divine life within us: charity. Now, in matters of injustice, there is no doubt that the opposition is direct and inevitable between this vice and charity. There is absolute contradiction between the movement of charity which prompts us to will and perform the good of our brethren and the movement of injustice which consists in depriving our neighbor of his good. By injuring our neighbor by injustice, we infallibly do harm to our own brother.

This conclusion is strictly true only when there is formal injustice. Furthermore, we can commit formal and mortal acts of injustice without however being possessed of the habitus of injustice.

But the doctrine is so solid that the slightness of the matter itself does not attenuate, properly speaking, the gravity of the injustice. The slightness of the matter only permits one to make one's escape from the field of injustice by the established and reasonable presumption of our neighbor's acquiescence: "Volenti non fit injuria."

III. Judgment, the Act of Justice

Here we find ourselves confronting the word "judgment," but let us not have the logician's reflex for whom judgment is simply the conclusion, the work of the second operation of the mind, the assembling of a certain number of simple ideas, and affirming, in this ideal unity, the real unity of these elements, joined together in existence as they are in judgment. This would not be false, assuredly. But we prefer another way, humbler and closer to experience.

1. WHAT IS JUDGMENT?

Judgment is properly that which is done by the judge in the performance of his functions, which implies, in the primitive and strict sense, the determination of that which is just and right.

From this follows a wider meaning in which judgment signifies the right judgment in all things, whether speculative or practical. To determine that which is or that which ought to be, is in effect to judge.

It is notable that the act of judging is taken into particular consideration in speculative (logical) matters because judgment gives a conclusion which is a good in itself—the good pursued by the speculative activity of the reason. In practical matters, on the other hand, we do not ordinarily consider the judgment in itself. We discover it when we analyze the process of the virtuous act, but as the judgment of the temperate or courageous man has value only in view of the act of temperance or of fortitude, it is not studied for its own sake.

On the contrary, for social reasons and for reasons pertaining to the very nature of justice, the act of judgment, in matters of justice, has enough consistence and distinct objectivity to be considered in itself.

Social reasons: there are persons whose function is to judge. There are regulations, places and times devoted to judgments. The judgments are surrounded with pomp and form which make of them events of social life, charged with signification and heavy with consequences.

Reasons pertaining to the nature of justice: the formal object of the other moral virtues is constituted in each case and for each individual case according to the concrete judgment of the virtuous man, resulting in a conclusion which has value only for himself and for the present case; but the *medium rei* which is for the just man to define and achieve, is measured objectively, by the application of stable and universal principles of which the just man is not the master, and which in no way reflect the singular dispositions of the subject, but which, in return, necessarily affect the relations with other men. Consequently, the judgment in matters of justice has everything necessary to be considered as an act of justice, in itself.

Certainly however, the pronounced judgment must still be executed in order that justice be done. But precisely in this respect is manifested the profound difference of judgment in matters of justice and judgment in matters of fortitude and temperance. When just judgment is pronounced, it only needs to be carried out; as a judgment, it is perfect. The execution in no way modifies its tenor; the *medium rei* is attained and defined. There remains only the duty of exact conformity to it. The reason of the executor, in the course of execution, has no bar upon the content of the judgment. On the contrary, the very conclusion of the judgment of fortitude or temperance is always malleable, revisable and adaptable up to the last moment of execution, by the will of the virtuous man; or rather, the judgment is made by gradual process during the action. It is not really decisive until the moment in which the action itself is produced, for the truth of this singular judgment is continually related to its agreement with the virtuous appetite.

Furthermore, in matters of justice, as experience shows clearly, before any formality of execution, the judgment constitutes a genuine act of justice or injustice, by itself and according to the cases. And by itself the sentence modifies, according to the law or against the law, the relations of the subject with other men. The execution will perhaps result in materializing this effect and entailing consequences which, in their turn, will produce new juridical relations. But prior to any course of execution, the sentence already constitutes

an act of justice or injustice, a genuine external operation efficaciously modifying the relations to *other men,* a genuine act of disposition in regard to certain goods. And it would be easy to show that
justice is more formally affected by this external operation which
consists in defining the juridical relations, and in deciding for instance the line of a boundary between two properties, than by the
material operations which are based upon this definition and which
carry it out, such as the entering into possession and the material
exploitation of the domain at first defined. For the external operation
which formally constitutes the matter of justice is that which formally measures our relations to other men, and therefore, more than
the usage, as such, of the goods, it is first and foremost their distinction and their division. The very usage of the good of other men is
just or unjust according as it expresses materially a true or false
definition of this good of other men.

Let us therefore conclude that judgment is properly an act of justice, and that among all the acts of justice it is the principal act,
that from which all the others proceed, and that which gives all the
others their soul, their form of justice—all the others affecting justice only in the measure in which they imply an explicit judgment
or one whose meaning is taken for granted.

To specify the origin of this act, it is sufficient to have recourse
to the doctrine of the virtues. Every virtuous judgment requires two
connected principles (at least), which expressly recall the two ideo-
motive principles of the human act. A virtue of the *reason* is necessary to pronounce this judgment, for the pronouncement of a sentence, the expression of a practical order, can only emanate from
reason. And a virtue of the intellectual or sensible appetite is necessary, disposing the subject from the dynamic point of view, without
which the subject would not be competent to judge according to the
virtuous ideal; he would not be effectively inclined thereto.

According to this dynamic point of view, the judgment of the
courageous man is connected with his virtue of fortitude, and the
judgment of the temperate man is connected with his virtue of temperance. Likewise, judgment in matters of justice, to be virtuous,
requires in the man who is judging an inclination of the appetite in
that regard, that is to say the virtue of justice.

But in any case, whether it is a question of fortitude or temperance or justice, virtuous judgment does not emanate from these
virtues immediately, as from their near source; these virtues cannot

depart from their role which is to incline the appetite. Virtuous judgment emanates immediately from prudence, and precisely from that part of prudence which is called "synesis" and which is defined as "bene judicativa," that is to say as charged precisely with the elaboration of good judgments.

It follows from this that in a given society, one is more or less qualified to judge and more or less capable of doing so, according as one participates more or less in the virtues of (legal) justice and (political) prudence. These virtues are found, as a principal qualification in the one who precides over the general welfare. They are found as a subordinate and ministerial qualification in the subjects. The prince is qualified to judge, with an imperative authority. Other men participate in the judgment, make it their own, in the measure in which they adhere to it and in which they carry out the sentence.

2. IS IT PERMITTED TO JUDGE?

A beautiful Christian tradition, solidly supported by scriptural texts, leads us to think that we must never judge. Here are its principal arguments: "Do not judge, that you may not be judged" (Mt. 7:1). Let us note, however, that in this verse the sense of judging is unfavorable; judging is here equivalent to condemning. It belongs to the Master to judge us, since we are all His servants. "Who art thou to judge another's servant? To his own lord he stands or falls" (Rom. 14:4). Furthermore, being sinners, it is not for us to judge other men and convict them of sin: "Wherefore, thou art inexcusable, O man, whoever thou art who judgest. For wherein thou judgest another, thou dost condemn thyself. For thou who judgest dost the same things thyself" (Rom. 2:1).

Let us therefore see in what sense judgment is an act of justice. This is the time to make our definition of judgment explicit: it is necessary that judgment should result from an inclination of justice; it is necessary that it be expressed by prudent reason, and finally it is necessary that it be the deed of a competent authority in some given society. Let us therefore exclude:

(a) unrighteous judgment, that is to say a judgment which goes contrary to the inclination of justice by violating the rectitude of the law;

(b) usurped judgment, pronounced by someone who is unqualified for this;

(c) rash judgment, which concludes without prudent reason, on the basis of slight and insufficient evidence, beginning with simple suspicions or conjectures.

It is important to see clearly that this doctrine is formal. Men no longer commonly have the sense of justice in sufficiently vivid manner to perceive this. They believe that unrighteous judgment goes contrary to justice, and the two other conditions seem negligible. Or rather, in that which concerns rash judgment, they are hypnotized by the unfortunate consequences of certain rash judgments which decide falsely and which have unjust consequences for our neighbor. In reality, whether rash judgment falls justly or falsely, and whether or not it has unfortunate and unjust consequences for our neighbor, it is primarily in its rashness that it is unjust. Likewise, in regard to usurped justice, it is the very act of pronouncing without mandate or quality which constitutes an injustice.

(1) The precept "nolite judicare," in its absolute tenor, is therefore too rigorous: it must be interpreted. Our Lord does not forbid the act of justice, but vicious judgments, whether the judgments be vitiated by "temerity" (St. Augustine), or for lack of competence, as for example when they pertain to objects which God reserves to Himself for judgment (the future, the mysteries of the Faith, the secrets of the heart, etc.), or finally for lack of the virtuous inclination of justice.

(2) It must however be maintained that man is sometimes competent in certain matters. God is not the only judge, for He has constituted man, in certain respects, with the qualification of a minister of divine judgments. When he judges in these conditions man pronounces just judgments: "Judge that which is just . . . because it is the judgment of God" (Deut. 1:16-17).

(3) Our condition as sinners should not prevent us, if such should be the case, from performing this act of justice which is judgment. St. Paul's statement (Rom. 2:1) does not mean that man, in all cases, does wrong in judging, or that he should be condemned on this account when he condemns in other men a misdeed of which he has been guilty himself. He means that by condemning other men, the sinner ipso facto recognizes himself and declares himself guilty.

3. THE CONDITIONS OF GOOD JUDGMENT

In this will be found again the three requirements of every just judgment: the virtuous inclination of justice, the truth of prudent reason, and competent authority.

A. The *rash judgment* or judgment vitiated for lack of truth according to the order of prudent reason.

Let us not forget in what the vice of rashness (temerity) consists formally, in regard to a judgment. It is neither the tenor of the sentence nor the consequences of its execution which we consider as unjust; they may or may not be so. We examine the process of the judgment, its manner, its origin, and we perceive that it suffers from a vice that is in some way constitutional to such a degree that this act, instead of being an act of justice treating our neighbor as ought to be done, is an unjust outrage against our neighbor. We suppose that it is admitted that obviously the judgment as such, independently of its consequences, constitutes an operation toward our neighbor, affecting and modifying effectively the relations with our neighbor, the relations of law. Otherwise by this incorrect way of judging, we would become guilty of moral faults (accepted error, negligence, etc.) but we would not formally offend against justice.

From the point of view of justice, it is proper to distinguish several kinds of judgment; all do not affect our neighbor equally. There is first of all judgment in justice, by the judge, with its indisputable force as a thing judged in regard to everyone. The judgment expressed by an individual has its existential value; it modifies juridical relations in a real measure, but its social reality is less. Therefore, if it be vitiated, it is less grave. Finally judgment that is wholly inward and is not externally expressed enters reductively into the domain of justice, like an imperfect species of judgment. It is thus that sin, in the highest degree, is the mortal sin; we study venial sin by comparison with the latter. It is thus also that the malice of an interior act is measured in relation to the external act; the desire for fornication derives its malice from the external act of fornication, etc. It is no less true that the secondary kinds of injustice present an authentic malice of injustice, like the desire for an excess of drink presents an authentic malice of intemperance. That which can be admitted is that, generally, by their nature, and except for accidental complication, interior judgments are more readily venial.

These precautions taken, the conclusion is simple; rash judgment constitutes an error against justice.

Let us be careful not to contrast rash judgment with a conclusion that is scientifically demonstrated. Judgment, in matters of justice, can only be an opinion, that is to say a judgment of probability.

The judge gives an opinion. For the sentence envisages individual and contingent cases in question. It is a matter of knowing, if yes or no, X or Y has done this or that, on such a day, in the presence of such a witness, etc. The solution can never be demonstrated in the scientific and logical sense of the word. It would be vain to examine the essence of X or Y; one would never discover in them an analytical requirement necessarily leading to such a conclusion. The judge's sentence must be and can only be probable, presumed to be true, and for this it is sufficient if it has the quality of probable. This is all the certainty that can be expected, in a contingent matter, from these kinds of judgment concerning human actions.

The laws of correct judgment will therefore be those of the likely and the probable. We are not for this reason reduced to the arbitrary. There is a logic of the probable. We do not reach a judgment (conclusion) of opinion, or probable judgment except from probable premises, that is to say from opinions that are immediately probable, which are the declarations of common sense, or the "reasons," that is to say the general propositions commonly received and admitted by reason of their probability or likelihood. The conclusions (mediate opinions) are only probable by the probability of the premises (immediate opinions which have the role of probable proofs). A judgment which does not rest upon these probable bases or which does not proceed from them with likelihood could not express a probable opinion. This hazarded opinion could not reasonably play the role of the true, not being probable in the technical and strong sense of the term.

Such is the vice of rash judgment or the "judgment of suspicion." Cicero, who vulgarized Aristotle's doctrine of the *Topics,* and also distorted it, here provides the following definition of suspicion: the suspicion constitutes an opinion of evil which proceeds from slight evidence. This definition seems to identify the suspicion with a *judgment* of opinion which would have the fault of imputing some discredit to our neighbor without relying upon anything other than slight evidence, too slight to be probable, and which would not deserve to play the part of truth. But opinion and suspicion are two different notions. Let us briefly recall what the judgment of opinion really is.

Science and intelligence have the truly necessary as their object. They are distinctive in that scientific judgment results in a certain conclusion by way of demonstration, while the intelligence procures from undemonstrated propositions, from an immediate necessity, the principles known by themselves, necessary from an evident necessity.

The object of opinion is the contingent truth which can be or not be. It is futile and contradictory in this domain to lay claim to any scientifically demonstrated evidence or conclusion. The very nature of the object, being contingent, is opposed to it. However, judgments of opinion also comprise immediate propositions and mediate propositions or conclusions. We may pass from one to the other by way of a syllogism, not demonstrative but dialectical. This syllogism, quite like the other, may be vitiated and thus lead to error, but if correctly conducted it gives all the certainty suitable in the matter.

It is clear that opinion can not conclude from necessary proofs as a starting point. And on the other hand, any conclusion, even in a matter of opinion, needs proper and immediate principles, which cannot be extended and multiplied indefinitely under pain of never reaching a conclusion in a probable manner.

The judgments of opinion, in matters of contingent truth, are therefore distinguished analogically into immediate and mediates, as in a necessary matter there are evident propositions and demonstrated propositions. And just as the light of evidences animates and affirms the truth of the conclusions by the way of the demonstrative syllogism, so also, in matters of opinion, by way of the dialectical syllogism, the probability of the immediate judgments of opinion is communicated to the mediate judgments or conclusions. The certitude of these propositions is called probability.

It is essential to note that opinion, with its probability, implies an adhesion of the mind, a judgment. Doubt on the contrary leaves the mind in suspense, and thereby excludes probability. For many modern theologians, as for the layman, probability does not imply this adhesion to a choice, that is to say a judgment, but signifies the more or less of appearance which militates in favor of a concurrent solution or several of them. It is said, for example, that the opposite solutions of an alternative present or do not present the same degree of probability. As long as one speaks in this way, one remains obviously in doubt and there is no probability at all, in the technical sense. Probability supposes, in effect, an opinion, not only eventual and possible, but actual, that is to say the adhesion of the mind to a *probable* proposition, likened to the true and held to be true. By deciding not to adhere to the proposition as yet, it is clear that one would refuse to liken it to the true, and one would effectively consider it as improbable. It is in fact probability which defines and specifies opinion.

But if two contradictory propositions can be arrayed with a few favorable appearances, at the same time and for the same mind, they cannot, assuredly, here and now, be probable for the same mind and be accepted as true. The probability of the one excludes that of the other; the probable would not be probable if it were not, in the domain of opinion, quite as exclusive of contradiction as is demonstrated truth in the domain of science. If the probability of a conclusion allowed that of its opposite to subsist against all probability, this probability would have no resemblance to truth; it would not have the right to call itself probability and there would not be any opinion.

These ideas being supposedly known, we see without difficulty by what vitiated mechanism of the dialectical syllogism one obtains a "judgment of suspicion" instead of a probable corrupt judgment.

Certainly not every suspicion is to be rejected. Suspicion has its role to play in the formation of the judgment of opinion; it is the sound reaction of the reason awakened by certain unfavorable indications. One remains in doubt, but these indications weigh heavily upon the scale of balance. It tends to produce an unfavorable opinion in the mind if nothing counterbalances such evidence. But as long as one remains at that point, there is no judgment; the sin is slight, if there be any sin. But in what exactly does it consist? This disorder consists in the excessive influence exercised upon our mind by evidence that is too slight (everything is relative) in relation to the effect produced, which is nothing less than the doubt that is cast upon or maintained against the goodness of our neighbor.

Assuredly, there would also be disorder if we obstinately closed our eyes; we must be able to have doubt about someone when reasonable evidence calls for it. But suspicion is vicious when the weight of unfavorable evidence does not reasonably justify even simple doubt; and such suspicion is not without injustice, because it implies a contempt for the person of our neighbor. If in fact we esteemed that person as we should, we would not suspect him or be doubtful about him on trifling evidence. In this respect the imprudent suspicion is properly *rash:* temerity indicating contempt for the rule of action rather than the precipitancy of an emotional impulse. One would not be taking the matter seriously because of one's contempt for the person it affects.

The disorder is aggravated and achieved when, from this first degree of suspicion (doubt) one passes to the second degree which consists less in a suspicion than in a "judgment of suspicion," that is to say a judgment based upon suspicion. In this case, there is a judgment, an opinion, that is to say a determined adhesion to a conclusion held to be probable, likely, resembling the true (this is all one). The vice of imprudence which disorders this judgment (second act of prudence) can result quite simply from the rash haste with which one accepted the above-mentioned suspicions in the preceding phase of the *consilium-consensus;* but the vice of imprudence can also force itself through more precisely in the judgment itself: one may have no illusion about the triviality of the assembled evidence, but the eyes are closed to its trivial nature, as to the contrary evidence also, and one proceeds *thoughtlessly* to the judgment. This species of imprudence in the phase of judgment is called inconsiderateness. Rash precipitancy of the *consilium-consensus* would already be sufficient to explain the defect of the judgment that follows. But even after a correct counsel, there may still be an incorrect judgment on account of a rash inconsiderateness. Why rash? Because one has contempt for the data assembled in counsel, or one neglects to pay attention to such data which would permit a correct judgment. Now, to admit such contempt or such negligence when it is a question of forming an unfavorable opinion about our neighbor includes a harmful contempt in regard to the person of our neighbor. The proper malice of the rash judgment is there—not because one has a bad opinion of his neighbor, but rather because one's bad opinion of someone, so slightly founded, is harmful to him. To judge him with this unconstraint is to maltreat him unjustly.

Psychological Origin of Rash Judgment

Let us first note that, as the proper injustice of rash judgment does not consist in the harmful consequences of this judgment, neither does it consist in the irregularity of the affectivity which occasioned the formation and permitted the expression of this same judgment. And this even pertains to the hypothesis in which it is precisely from an irregularity opposed to justice that rash judgment originates. Injustice, like other disorders, can produce an injustice, but it is in itself that we must judge the latter when we qualify it as an injustice. For if the injustice can originate from other sources than injustice, the injustice in its turn can produce other vicious effects than that of injustice.

To understand the psychological origin of this kind of injustice which constitutes rash judgment, let us recall that the moral virtues are connected in prudence. The means that are considered and compared in the prudential counsel present themselves each with its attractive side, its value, according to the more or less fervent complaisance and inclination with which the will, unequally disposed to these various means according to its virtuous or vicious habitus, tests them, applies itself to them, and reconciles itself with them in the *consensus*. Elements of judgment, for example certain unfavorable indications, will pass wholly unperceived in the counsel, or will seem negligible, if the will is not affected by any agreement with them. In this way a word or a gesture of equivocal meaning is admitted by very chaste ears or eyes without any problem and understood simply in its natural and obvious sense, with no unpleasant innuendo. On the contrary, however, the least unfavorable sign, if the will finds its own consonance in it and delights in it and consents to it, is then in some way magnified by it and has the chance to weigh heavily in the counsel. It is in this way, to continue the preceding example, that the conversation quickly becomes intolerable when one speaks to vulgar or perverse persons who perceive in the most simple remarks a thousand innuendoes of which one would never have thought. As a harmony of sound waves brings out the resonance and amplifies it, the consensus gives worth, in the counsel, to the elements which arouse complaisance and receive the consent of the appetite.

For this reason, and because of the consent of their corrupt appetite, evil men readily suspect evil. Where there is only an unfavorable indication that is too tenuous to be reasonably taken into consideration, or even where there is no unfavorable indication whatever in the mind of the virtuous man, the vicious person clearly sees a notable indication, sufficient to establish a suspicion, perhaps even an opinion, that is to say an unfavorable judgment. His personal malice makes him easily admit, as self-evident, and as expected and discounted, the malice of other men. If he is a thief, he believes that everybody is a thief. If he lies, he does not trust the statements of anyone. If he is corrupt, he does not believe in anyone's virtue.

That is also why we readily suspect those whom we do not like. For us they are evil men; we *must* find, it is natural that we should find evil in them. On their part, the least appearance, the slightest equivocation, seems to us deserving of unfavorable interpretation. If we feel contempt for them, we never fail to discover abysses of turpitude in them and in their acts. If we hate them, we find a thousand odious attributes in them. If we are angry with them, their deeds and gestures frequently seem harmful to ourselves and call for a just punishment; if we envy them, everything that comes their way seems to be an undeserved and intolerable favor.

We see without difficulty how these perverse dispositions of the appetite provoke and reinforce suspicions and rash judgments. Without confusing the malice of these affective dispositions with the malice of injustice of the rash judgment, we can account for the rational error of the counsel and of the judgment in this moral atmosphere. There follows an unjust opinion concerning our neighbor, a judgment that is so rash that it is equivalent to treating our neighbor with an unjust contempt.

Aristotle adds that old age also makes men suspicious. But the case is wholly different this time. Or rather, we must make distinctions.

Old people, of course, are not perfect; they are even inclined to certain faults which, without being proper to them, are nevertheless familiar to them. Old men, for example, are often unfeeling and avaricious. These vices make them quick to judge or suspect other people unfavorably, either by imputing their own vices to them, or because they despise in others the obstacle which is contrary to their senile passions. Thus callous old men believe that everybody is as hard as they are; the avaricious do not believe in the disinterestedness of youth, or else they despise a child who is considered to be a prodigy, or a sick person considered as a useless mouth to feed and an occasion of expense, etc. In all this, we find the two above-mentioned sources of rash judgment: the malice of the subject, and evil sentiments in regard to our neighbor. But this is not proper to old people, and it does not teach us anything new.

On the other hand, however, old people have the advantage of a long experience, and it is said that this experience makes them suspicious. They have often suffered the effects of human malice, and have experienced it within themselves; they hardly have any more illusions. This experience, far from being an obstacle to the sound exercise of prudence, contributes to it effectively. In the phase of counsel, if docility is eminently fitting to young men without personal experience, memory is the unquestionable portion of old people. Far from being an imprudent vice, memory constitutes a resource, an integral part of prudence. Suspicion, in the very degree that it proceeds from a long experience, tends to probable certitude and deviates from rashness. That is why it is necessary to make special provision for this source of unfavorable judgment which is not in itself a source of "judgment of suspicion" and which becomes so only by accident, especially by the disastrous and corrupting influence of evil sentiments.

Gravity of Rash Judgment

When we want to weigh the gravity of a rash judgment, it is proper to take into account three points of valuation.

(a) first of all the triviality of the indications which establish the suspicion and on which the rash judgment is based. This is the formal point of view, for the unjust temerity of the judgment is formally constituted by the slightness of the alleged motives in a matter in which the good of our neighbor is involved. It is for this reason that suspicions, when they originate in an experienced mind and tend to be identified with a probable certitude, diminish the unjust malice of the rash judgment in the same proportion.

(b) In the second place the more or less external character of the rash judgment intervenes; as a matter of justice or injustice, the judgment has greater existential reality and juridical efficacy because it is more exteriorized. There is a certain order of gravity, related to the external realism of the action, for the operation affects other men and justice in so far as it is external. Consequently we may conclude that the circumstances in which the rash judgment was expressed will modify the gravity of the injustice in the measure in which they affect its publicity: number of witnesses, private letter or public newspaper, etc.

(c) finally we must also take into account the more or less considerable gravity of the evil that is rashly suspected in our neighbor or which is thoughtlessly imputed to him. It even seems that many rash judgments originate in the immoderate exaggeration of a real evil, which was not imprudent or rash to suspect in our neighbor, by generalizing the matter without legitimate cause: for example, because someone was seen one day in slightly tipsy condition, some people will conclude that the man is a drunkard, etc. Justice requires that simple indications of equal weight should lead us less effectively to doubt our neighbor or to judge him unfavorably in serious matters than in slight matters. It is more difficult for the virtuous appetite to receive these indications, consent to them, and agree with them when they imply the loss of a greater good for our neighbor. This resistance is the work of the virtuous habitus of justice which makes us love the good of our neighbor, and consequently makes the idea that we could impair that good almost unbearable. The more just we are, the more cautious we will be when the good of our neighbor is at stake, and all the more so because it is a matter of a greater good.

How Shall We Avoid Rash Judgment?

Rash judgment is an unjust way of emerging from doubt. But there is a way which is correct and which imposes itself when one can neither continue in doubt nor acquire a probable certitude. It consists in favorably interpreting the doubtful situation.

Obviously, the question does not arise if one can acquire a probable knowledge that is sufficient for judging without temerity. In this case, provided that one judges according to the laws and that one is qualified to do this, the judgment is virtuous; it is an act of justice.

It also happens that one may remain in doubt without disadvantage. But this requires that the judgment should not be required by an obligation of law or honesty, and it is also necessary that the doubt by itself should not be harmful.

If the doubt were so unreasonable that it became harmful, one would be obliged to be rid of it purely and simply. It would not be necessary to formulate a new judgment, but one would leave things as they were and would hold to one's anterior opinions, over which, hypothetically, nothing has been able to make reasonable doubt prevail.

But if the doubt is established, and is therefore unharmful, and if nothing compels judgment, it is wise to remain in doubt as long as one has not reached probable certitude. More especially because by leaving the mind in suspense one can nevertheless provide for the necessities of the action thanks to *interpretation "by supposition."* The latter formally dispenses us from judging as good or as evil in a determined manner; perhaps it does not even necessarily imply the existence of a real doubt, but as a measure of safety, *one supposes* the worst in order to guard against it more effectively. For example, I do not judge passers-by in any way; I do not even question their honesty, but I lock my door when I leave home, nevertheless.

Note that certain precautions could become injurious: if they were directed against certain persons in particular without cause, or if they were publicized as exceptional, or if, in one way or another, they acquired the signification of a harmful doubt or so much the more if they seemed like a rash judgment. Practically, it is the circumstances, the social customs, the environment, the type of education and personal tact which, by determining the signification of these precautions, also establish their just limit.

Let us therefore suppose that the doubt is reasonably established and that we are not obliged to neglect it; let us also suppose that we must put an end to this doubt by a judgment. Finally, let us suppose that, in spite of our diligence, we do not arrive at any probability. In these conditions, the doubt must be ended by an interpretation that is favorable to our neighbor.

The principle is already known: the sole fact of lightly accepting an opinion that is unfavorable to someone is to be lacking in justice towards him, even if, perchance, the opinion is found to be in accord with the truth. It is not being judged unfavorably that is disloyal and harmful to our neighbor, but being judged with thoughtlessness and harmful temerity. Nobody can inflict this injustice upon his neighbor; if we judge someone unfavorably, it must always be for cogent reasons. Furthermore, when we judge someone and have not reached any certain conclusion, we are obliged to avoid the unfavorable decision, that is to say that we must allow the favorable decision to put an end to the doubt.

But is it possible to reconcile this thesis with the absolute rights of truth?

To admit absolutely that one must always interpret doubtful cases on the good side is to condemn oneself to be in error most often, if it be true, as experience proves and as Scripture affirms, that the number of fools is infinite and that most men are inclined to evil. Intellectual correctness seems to forbid us this favorable prejudice; at the very least it imposes impartiality upon us. The answer to this objection must find support in the idea of just judgment. However, in the judgment that we make about anything, the goodness or the evil of this act is not considered from the point of view of the thing that is judged; it matters little to the latter what the judgment we make may be. It is only the good or the evil of the person who is judging that is at stake; it is for himself that the judgment is good if it be true, and is bad if it be false. That is why the effort of everyone, when judging anything, must tend simply to judging things as they are.

On the other hand, when the judgment concerns a person, it is from the point of view of the person who is judged that one must place himself above all, in order to call him good or evil. This judgment is an act which, by itself and by its consequences, pertains to our neighbor, affecting him effectually. It is good or evil first of all for our neighbor according to the favorable or unfavorable tenor of the sentence.

Certainly, the truth or falsity of the judgment that affects persons constitutes a real good or real evil for the mind which judges. Persons can be treated as an object of knowledge; the law of this knowledge will be to attain the true always or as often as possible. But it becomes injurious when we only consider persons as objects, as the instrument or occasion of intellectual gain for the subject who observes them and who judges them, without taking into consideration the wrong that one can do them by treating them in this way. This contempt for the repercussions of our action upon the good or the evil of our neighbor is not without an unjust contempt in regard to his person.

Therefore the observer of things and events acts well in the measure in which he approaches the true. But the just man who deals with his fellow men sees first of all the good of his neighbor which must not be harmed unjustly. Now then, to judge our neighbor unfavorably, when we have no probable certitude, is to harm him unjustly. Therefore, the just man, in such a conjuncture, will judge other men with favor, even if he must for this reason renounce some eventual personal advantage: the reputation of being a penetrating psychologist, the joy of delivering a cruel word, the satisfaction of seeing his presentiments realized, or the intellectual joy of holding faster to the truth.

Let us insist upon this. With this favorable bias, one must deliberately accept the risk of error and in fact there is reason to think that a man may thus be mistaken more often than with the unfavorable prejudice. But one is therefore doing harm to himself. St. Thomas admits that a bias of interpreting doubts on the good side *may* lead us into error in the majority of cases. In the world of men this disillusioning concession is doubtless justified by experience. But after all, it matters little: the truth of the thesis is not identical with a statistical comparison. It is better to be mistaken most of the time by one's good opinion of people who do not deserve it, than to be right most often while paying for this advantage at the price of an injustice. There is no parity whatever between the two situations. In the second case (the unfavorable interpretation) one has the *chance* to light upon some speculative truth, which is a good for the mind, a good which is relative and secondary however, even from the purely intellectual point of view, since it is only a question of individual and contingent truths. On the other hand one inevitably falls into a practical error which makes an attempt against a necessary truth, against a total human good, the truth of our relations with our neighbor, since one deliberately commits the error of treating his neighbor as a thing.

On the contrary, in the first situation, by the favorable interpretation of the doubt, one does not accept any error, neither theoretical or practical, in a positive way. It is immoral to deliberately welcome an error, even if it be of a theoretical kind; but it is precisely at this point that one does not accept the error, but rather, one exposes himself to the *risk* of error. But it is reasonable to run this risk, for firstly one has a proportionate motive, which is to avoid the injustice of a judgment rashly brought against our neighbor in an unfavorable manner, and secondly the evil which one risks is not so grave. The error of fact committed in the favorable judgment of persons who are really unworthy does not entail any harm that is so formidable for the person who is thus mistaken that he must envisage everything absolutely rather than expose himself to this risk of error. Such an error, in fact, does not indicate any intellectual vice, or impair any essential good of the intelligence, for the truth or the error of these contingent and individual matters hardly depends upon intellectual vigor or the correctness of rational efforts. When one is mistaken, there is no need to feel distressed about it; and when one has the fortune to be right, there is no reason to glorify oneself beyond measure.

This error of fact, mediocre even from the point of view of pure intelligence, is in no way comparable to the truth that one obtains at the practical level by a favorable interpretation of doubt in which the rectitude of the prudential reason is fittingly animated by a virtuous instinct of justice.

B. *The Legality of Judgment*

To pronounce a judgment is quite simply to determine what is just. But this judgment is in no way arbitrary on the part of the judge. He must find the just measure wherever it is and apply it where it is necessary.

We know that the just deed proceeds from two sources: the natural right and positive right. The judge must therefore inspire his sentence with natural right as well as positive right.

But both natural and positive right find expression in legal prescriptions, in one way or another. On the other hand, however, the whole of right cannot be expressed in the law. Three questions therefore arise:

(a) Legality of Judgment in Regard to Natural Right

Here, the law is limited to the declaration of the prescriptions of the natural right. It does not bring them essential juridical force, but this declaration has a proper pedagogical effect. The law can neither extend nor restrain the scope of the prescriptions of natural right. Finally, the law itself only has worth if it conforms to the natural right.

(b) Legality of Judgment in Regard to Positive Right

The judge could not be satisfied to be right in regard to the natural right. At this point there is an intervention of the rules that are found to be studied for themselves in juridical science and technique. This does not affect morality except indirectly. One is obligated to know the rules of the profession that one exercises; a judge who takes his place in the court-room without knowing these rules and who limits himself to dealing out his sentences merely in good faith is committing an injustice.

The course of this interpretation is roughly as follows: to know what the legislator has said, and what he meant; to know what he intended to achieve, and finally to verify the positive legality as compared with the natural right. We must not here forget that positive legality does not coincide with the written law at all points.

(c) Beyond the Written Laws

The best written laws cannot foresee everything. It is then necessary to adapt their prescriptions with equity to concrete situations that are more or less analogous but which the laws have not regulated. This is done by extending the interpretation of positive right and in reasoning by analogy, a contrario, a pari, a fortiori, etc.

In repressive matters positive right prescribes this rule: No punishment without law. And this must be understood in the strictest sense. One can only punish in the precise cases which have been foreseen by a text. More specifically, it is not only the punishment but the crime which supposes a previous law: No crime without law. Such is the principle of the legality of punishments and of offenses, formulated for example in article 4 of the French Penal Code: "No contravention, no offense, no crime may be punished by penalties which were not pronounced by the law before they were committed."

In the older systems of Law, on the other hand, the principle of arbitrary imposition of punishments was allowed, and this gave much more power to the judges. The modern rule [13] is justified, and imposes itself even inwardly upon conscience, because it guarantees individual liberty against the abuses of repression and because it corresponds to the equilibrium desired today between the different powers. However, it is no less true that the application of this rule sometimes entails disadvantages; a judge, convinced that he is dealing with a criminal, cannot condemn him if no legal text previous to the infraction foresees or sanctions it.

There is moreover a political justice which is not subject to this rule or to these positive forms. The existence of this justice, perfectly legitimate, is not without disadvantage either, when those who exercise it are lacking in the political virtues of justice and prudence.

On the contrary, in civil matters positive right prescribes that the judge must pronounce a sentence at whatever cost: "The judge who shall refuse to pronounce judgment under pretext of the silence, obscurity or insufficiency of the law, may be prosecuted as guilty of a denial of justice" (French Code Civil, 4).[14] It is here a question of defining the respective rights of two parties and bringing them to an agreement: if there is no legal text, the judge will make his pronouncement according to his conscience, by arguing from principles of reason and right, which amounts to borrowing from unwritten laws the solutions which the written laws cannot impose.

[13] *Nulla poena sine lege*—no punishment without specific (positive) legal provision.

[14] In the Common Law such "gaps" are bridged by "reasoning by analogy." However, courts may refuse to do so.

C. *The Quality of the Judge*

Let us here recall the doctrine of judgment which was studied above. The judgment that is in question in matters of justice, the true judgment which constitutes an operation affecting our neighbor and defining his rights, is not merely a true conclusion derived from speculative principles by a good mind. It also constitutes an application, a practical exercise. The separation which we customarily admit between the legislative, judicial and executive powers could here lead us into error if we erected it into a truth of principle instead of leaving it at the level of technical arrangements.

In reality, political activity is analyzed like any other human activity, in two component elements: the specifying representation and the motion of exercise. These two elements do not constitute two distinct kinds of action proceeding from two distinct categories of agents; neither of the two is conceivable, nor exists without the other. Together these two, really and indissolubly allied, account for all activity.

Judgment, understood in its strong and primitive sense as an operation directed to our neighbor or as an act of justice, implies these two elements. The work of prudent reason, it is substantially a declaration of practical truth, but in this respect it is what is material in this action. The formal element is the appetitive impulse which animates this work of reason and gives it effective force, which jurists call coercive or executive force. This element is provided for the judgment by the moving will, itself virtuously animated by justice.

This analysis puts us in the way of solution. In a given society it isn't just any reason or just any will that is qualified to judge legitimately, or to draw up the law. This comparison is formal and we may say that it is worth a reason. The adequate author of a judgment is one who holds legislative authority; he alone, by principal qualification, rationally orders according to his political prudence and effectively moves the life of the community in view of its welfare, according to his virtues and his political knowledge and art. It is he who, promulgating the laws, lays down the general principles of social activity. It is he again who for the same reason derives and exercises directly or indirectly the practical conclusions of the legal principles in the concrete. A prince who is content to formulate excellent principles is merely outlining his political task; if he is virtuous, that is to say prudent and just as a politician, he will proceed to the *usus,* i.e. the application. Obviously he is not required to do everything in person, but he must know that his authority, if not his own hand, must be everywhere. The common welfare is at stake.

That is why the one who judges without having authority (personal and ordinary, or at least delegated) is incapable of pronouncing a real judgment that is effective and authentically accepted in the community. Certainly, in a private capacity he can formulate a true conclusion, if he knows the law and the facts of the case and if he is motivated by right intentions. But in the very measure in which he claims to give effective worth to his conclusion, i.e., the executory force of the judgment, he commits an injustice. He is unduly exercising a motion upon persons, upon members of the social body who are not dependent on him. In a sound society, this infringement is hardly dangerous, for the unqualified man does not possess the material means to impose his claim. But we can easily imagine a society less well organized, in which certain "potentes" would have the means of carrying out their sentence by money, force, cunning or the fear which they inspire. Doing this, they would ruin the legal order and the social order within it, which is the essential good of the community. There is the *same injustice* in the imposition of a so-called law that is not decreed by the public authority, and the imposition of a judicial sentence by one's private authority.

TYPES OF JUSTICE

Types of Justice

1. THE TYPES OF JUSTICE

Justice is not a unique virtue. From legal justice, a virtue of universal radiation, to particular kinds of justice, there is only analogy; and between these latter there is only a distant resemblance. This supposes that the idea of law which is logically anterior to that of justice, is itself extremely elastic.

In the sphere of natural morality, there is no duty more profound or more universal than the one which legal justice has the mission to perform. Its object, the common good, is primary. It is the most imperious motive whose influence man can experience. It confers on both justice and law their character of first principles, and it is the function of justice and law to foster this common good. Distributive justice stabilizes the contributions of the social whole in relation to its parts: the citizens. It assigns to each person his proper share of the advantages of the community life. The measure which it sanctions is therefore proportional, keeping in mind social situations, legal statutes, services rendered to society, sacrifices made for the common good. It attains to "rectitude" when the honors and the responsibilities are distributed in equation with the merits and with competence.

A very common error consists in confusing distribution with division, and in making the latter enter into the orbit of distributive justice. However, the operations by which division is established are for the most part operations of a private order: inheritance, gifts, personal initiatives, contracts, discoveries, occupation, etc. These operations are subject to the high surveillance of the civil authority, but are not part of its functions.

Commutative justice, finally, regulates the daily relations of individuals among themselves not less than those of private institutions between themselves or with individuals. It is ordered to the safeguard of the proper good, and the equality which it establishes is arithmetical. In this kind of justice prestation is equal to counterprestation. However, this does not mean that no account is taken of the quality of persons and services when this equality is established. Thus, for instance, reparation will be greater in the case of insult to a dignitary than if one is lacking in respect for a simple citizen. The exchanges of commutative justice consist in a usage of external realities: things, persons, or even works. A usage of things when, for example, one takes from or renders to someone the object which belongs to him; a usage of persons when one commits an injustice against the very person of a man by striking him or injuring him, or else when one expresses external marks of respect for him; finally, a usage of works if someone, by just rights, demands a service from another man or renders it to him. If therefore we take as the matter of one or the other justice everything of which the usage is an external operation, distributive justice and commutative justice have the same matter, for things may be either withdrawn from a common whole for distribution to private persons or exchanged from one to the other. There is also a certain distribution and a certain exchange of laborious tasks. But if, in each of these two kinds of justice, we take as matter the principal acts themselves by which we make use of persons, things or works, we must distinguish two matters, for distributive justice regulates division and commutative justice regulates exchanges between two individuals.

Of all these exchanges, some are involuntary, others voluntary. They are involuntary when someone uses the thing or the person of someone else against his will: the thing if someone takes the property of another man; the person if someone attacks or strikes or insults or defames his neighbor, or if someone sins against someone else by committing adultery with that person's spouse, or by beguiling his servant in order to steal him from him. All this can be done either secretly or in broad daylight and by violence. The exchanges are called voluntary when someone voluntarily transfers his property to another person. If the thing is transferred gratuitously, as in a donation, this transmission is not an act of justice, but an act of liberality. The voluntary transfer of a property only concerns justice in the measure in which it raises a question of debt. This can happen in three ways: (1) someone simply transfers his property to another person in compensation for the other person's property: this is the case in transactions of purchase and sale. (2) Someone cedes his property to another person by granting him the use of the thing, upon condition that the grantee return it: if this usage is granted gratuitously, it is called usufruct in regard to everything that can produce a profit; or it is called a loan or advance with respect to anything that is incapable of producing a profit. If this usage is not gratuitous, the transfer is called a rental or a lease. (3) Someone entrusts a property with the intention of taking it back, and not for the purpose of use, but for conservation, as in a "warehouse"; or for the purpose of posting bond, as when one puts his property in pawn, or posts "bail" for another person.

In all acts of this kind, voluntary or involuntary, the just mean is determined in the same way: the legality of the compensation. That is why all these actions proceed from a single kind of justice: commutative justice.

When these three forms of justice are flourishing in a society, its existence is well-ordered.

2. JUDICIARY FUNCTIONS

A. *The Function of a Judge*

At the very center of the State's institutions of judiciary order is found that of the judges. It dominates all the others and makes them final. In this, more than in the others, the authority, prestige and coercive force of the State is incarnated. The judge, in effect, is not a private person but a public person. He speaks and decides in the name of the community and according to official information, that is to say information that is taken from the documents of indictment. He must make an abstraction of any relations he may have had with the accused. He is obliged to lay aside his friendships, his aversions, his personal interests and his political preferences. In a word, he must be aware that he can only legitimately judge other men in the name of the community and by virtue of a mandate granted by the community.

For it appertains to the community to make the laws and to apply them. This privilege has devolved upon it by its very nature, since it is the experienced order of law, which is its soul, its being, its immanent common good. Its very conservation requires that it be the community which exercises justice and the determination and application of sanctions.

The proper act of the judge is the judgment, and the judgment has bearing upon the object of justice: the law. Is not the very name of the judge, *judex,* derived from *jus dicens,* meaning the one who declares the law? According to the saying of the Psalmist—justitia convertatur in judicium (Ps. 93:15)—"Until justice be turned into judgment." He formulates the law concretely: he defines and determines it.

For this purpose he must possess certain professional qualifications and try to find his general directions in the law. "Men may discuss the institution of temporal laws," says St. Augustine, "but when they are definitively instituted, it is not permitted to judges to judge them, but only to judge according to them." The judge, moreover, must be filled with a great love of justice. A theoretical and abstract knowledge of the law is not sufficient; the law on which he must make his pronouncement is a concrete law, immersed in a whole multitude of contingencies and circumstances. The knowledge which he must possess is also that which proceeds from connaturality, sympathy and acquired virtue.

In the tragic case in which the human law is contrary to the Natural Law, the judge must refrain from judging. It still happens that human laws, either by reason of their technical imperfection or because of their general or universal character, are incapable of covering the infinite variety of individual situations. The legislator who is conscientious in fostering the common welfare, only considers the "general case." It may then happen that the mechanical application of the law will lead to injustice. In this case the judge would be ill advised to rely upon the letter of the law. He would expose himself to a betrayal of the purpose for which the law was instituted. To remedy the deficiencies of the text in regard to particular cases, he must have recourse to general juridical rules, and consider the intention of the legislator and the principles of equity. "No reason of law nor any cult of justice," says Justinian, "can allow measures wisely taken in view of their usefulness to men, to be construed to their detriment and to a treatment that is too severe, as the result of an interpretation that is too strict."

Another case is that of doubt: doubt *de jure* and doubt *de facto*. De jure doubt results from the law's obscurity or from its excessive consciseness. Then the judge, who cannot refuse to pronounce a judgment, has the faculty of turning to the more general principles of the law, and to the authorities and the customs, and to elaborate a jurisprudence which has the possibility of becoming law. The sentence of the judge has the value of law and institutes the law. In "de facto" doubts, which concern the guilt of the subject, if it is necessary for the judge to take sides, it is not essential that he refuse to give the accused the benefit of the doubt. In Natural Law—and the Gospel, as we have already mentioned, this outlook is imposed upon us—contrary to the position of several modern legislative systems, the accused must be presumed to be virtuous and innocent. His perversity must be demonstrated. If it be a grave fault for a judge to let himself be influenced by his political passions, his sentiments, or by pressures and gifts, it is also a sin to condemn anyone upon simple suspicion, or in not letting the accused person benefit from the insufficiency of proofs. St. Ambrose (in Ps. 18, serm. 20) said that "the good judge does nothing of himself, but he pronounces according to the statutes and the law." He is a public person, a representative of authority, and only has the mandate to pronounce upon public matters, attested by proofs and depositions of official character. As a delegate of society, he can only rely upon the elements that are found in the accused person's record, and conform to the established procedure and the forms required by the statutes and the usages of the tribunals.

If the judge is juridically incapable of dismissing the proofs and invalidating the testimony, he is obliged to judge according to the juridical truth, according to that which results from the official data. He must condemn, even if private information inclines him to think that he is making a mistake. There would in fact be serious disadvantages in acting otherwise. This would introduce arbitrary procedure into the exercise of justice, and subjectivism, which would make for scandal. A judgment that was contrary to all the depositions and all the evidence would ruin the authority and prestige of the tribunals in the opinion of the public. People would lose confidence in an institution that is necessary for the conservation of public order and the common welfare. Every objection vanishes before these considerations. The judge who pronounces an erroneous judgment according to the official data does not make himself a party to the lies and deceptions of the witnesses. He cannot incur any share of their responsibility.

Lastly, the judge cannot pardon or acquit the guilty person by his own authority. It is his duty to reestablish equality between the two parties, the accuser and the accused. This is the very purpose of the trial. And this requires that he make the consequences of an injustice fall upon the accused, and that he accord to the plaintiff the reparations to which he is entitled. Sanctions have their justification in the social order. If, by error, he delivers an unjust judgment and does harm to one of the parties, he is obliged to make reparation as soon as he has recognized his error provided such reparation is possible.

B. *The Parties*

The judge has the duty of pronouncing just sentences, that is to say, the duty of defining and determining the law. By this alone he satisfies the purposes of the judiciary function of the State. All those who take part in the trial must help him to attain this end: to define and determine the law.

The trial aims at reestablishing equality between two parties: the plaintiff and the defendant in trials of civil matters; and in those which are of criminal order, the accuser and the accused. It is therefore important to specify what are the duties of these parties in natural justice, for if the external form of these duties is subject to the conditions of positive law—whether ecclesiastical or civil—the moral substance, itself, remains identical with it.

In civil matters, the defendant, if he realizes that he is in the wrong, does not have, as is commonly believed, the right to withdraw into silence and still less to lie. If he is interrogated according to the procedural forms, he is obligated in conscience to admit his wrong. If by false or simply equivocal answers he leads the judge into error and induces him to make an unjust judgment, harmful to the other party, he is obliged to make amends for his injustice. The purpose of judiciary institutions is not to sanction the perverse wills of certain individuals to an escape from their obligations, but to safeguard the rights of every citizen.

In criminal matters let us examine the case of the accuser and the accused.

(a) *The accuser.* The accusation, in our modern societies, has become the object of a public service, depending on the public prosecutor or the minister of justice, in such manner that the accuser, whose duty is to seek and compile information and place it in the files, as also to denounce the guilty person, is in fact a public body. However, as he will have to collect the elements of the evidence from individuals, the latter are not completely relieved of their obligations or their responsibilities.

Let us specify, first of all, that for an indictment to be licit, on the part of an individual or that of the police force, it is indispensable that it be made in view of the public interest. If a fault is of strictly private order, it only concerns God. It does not need to be denounced to the authorities. The knowledge which we may have about some evil can only, therefore, in justice and in charity, be divulged for the benefit of the common welfare. "To reveal secrets to the detriment of a person," says St. Thomas, "is assuredly to act against fidelity; but such is not the case any longer when this revelation is made in view of the common good, which is always preferable to the good of an individual. Therefore it is never permitted to become a party to a secret that is prejudicial to the common good." Penalties, in fact, do not have an absolute character in this world; they are not ordered to the sanctioning of faults in such manner that the satisfaction is complete. They are only proper to safeguarding the order, security and peace of society.

Finally, in order that there may be an obligation in conscience to make an accusation, it is necessary that one be capable of providing the evidence of the facts set forth. If one is incapable of establishing it by honest proceedings, the obligation in regard to the common good gives way. How many unjust proceedings we could mention here! How many false investigations conducted by the police with the purpose of deluding the public and concealing the person who is really guilty! This kind of thing is a serious deficiency of justice, granted that society has a strict right to see guilty men punished, and nobody has the right to rouse suspicion imputable to innocent men by means of feigned investigations. It is equally immoral and forbidden to make use of means that are intrinsically dishonest on the pretext that they are efficient. The end does not justify the means. The efficient means are only legitimate if they are honest.

The accusers, especially if they are public persons, have the obligation to preserve the common good, and to this end they must discover and denounce all criminals. But this is not the case with the guilty men themselves.

(b) *The accused.* Justice doubtless imposes upon the accused the duty of telling the truth if he is the person who is really guilty and if he is interrogated by the judge in good and due form. The judge, being the legitimate representative of authority, has a strict right to obedience. However, because such a total submission calls for heroism in so far as it implies submission to the penalty, human laws have provided for another kind of procedure. They have arranged the order of the trial in such a way that the guilty man is released from the obligation of confessing his fault and the establishment of the proof is exclusively the responsibility of the accusers. The accused therefore has the opportunity, without incurring guilt, of escaping from human punishment, provided that he make no appeal to falsehood or calumny in order to exonerate himself. He may even lodge an appeal, after condemnation, granted that he is obliged to obtain permission for it from a superior authority which decides if the motives which he alleges are valid and if his appeal is admissible.

C. *The Witnesses*

After the judge and the parties, the trial allows for witnesses and lawyers.

The witness is not always required to give evidence. If his information pertains to a private fault, holding but little detriment for the public good, it is better for him not to divulge it. If, on the contrary, it pertains to a fault which does injury to the public good, a distinction must be made. If the accused is guilty and if the witness is summoned by the judge and conformably with the prescriptions of the law, he is then obliged in conscience to give evidence. He cannot refuse to do this without failing both in obedience and in the duty which devolves upon him to do his part in the maintenance of the public order. If the accused, unable to establish the proof of his innocence, is threatened with an unjust punishment and undeserved dishonor, the witness is obliged to go to his defense by his own will and to testify in his favor. To be silent at such a time when one could denounce the error is to give approval to the false accuser and to make a compact with him. It is obvious that the witnesses who, knowingly and by deliberate purpose, give false testimony and induce the judge to pronounce an erroneous judgment, are themselves the causes of injustice, guilty of perjury and obliged in conscience to make amends for the wrong which they have done to the person against whom they have given false evidence.

Testimonies are not all of equal value. This depends upon the qualifications and the dispositions of the witness. The testimony of criminals, thieves, perjurers, etc., is subject to caution. It can only be accepted with circumspection. Similarly, for reasons that pertain more to the order of psychological incapacity than to the moral order, the testimony of children and near relatives, and that of persons who are dependent upon the accused or susceptible to his influence. Their testimony runs the risk of being deficient in objectivity if not in sincerity. It is for the judge and the lawyer on the opposite side to distinguish the psychological and moral motives and to delimit the value of the depositions.

D. *The Lawyers*

Neither is the lawyer exempt from the rules of justice and morality as some people are too often inclined to think. It is not lawful for him to use any means whatever or to aim only at winning the case.

First of all, if it be his function to defend the accused, he still does not have the obligation to identify himself with him and to espouse his interests unconditionally. He is not the proxy of his client, but his assistant, his counsellor and protector. He does not represent him before the court, but defends him. It would, however, be pushing disinterestedness too far if we thought that he could enjoy the objectivity and impartiality of the judge and the witness. St. Thomas says, "The judge and the witness have impartial relations with the parties opposing each other; the judge is obliged to render a just sentence and the witness must make a juridical deposition; they regard both parties with an eye that is equally serene. The lawyer, on the contrary, defends the cause of one party uniquely. His very role places him in the necessity of showing himself partial."

This partiality is limited by the fact that he is not, once again, the proxy of his client; it is limited especially because he is a semi-public person, accredited by society and by his profession, responsible for the good administration of justice. He is a part of institutions: those of the bar, and of the court. He must not therefore have uniquely in view the claims of his client, but also the interests of justice and of society.

From this responsibility his duties are derived. His primary duty is that of competence. The good exercise of justice and the interest of the client both require that he have a profound knowledge of the law, of jurisprudence and of procedure, and that he be capable of extricating from the records all the facts and circumstances that are capable of making the defendant's claims prevail; and finally, that he be able to connect them with the principles of the law and prepare a speech for the defense that is suitable for the enlightenment and persuasion of the judge. If he is not qualified, and if he shows himself to be negligent in the accomplishment of his professional duties, he is doing an injury to justice.

Since he is in a certain measure in the service of society and is bound by the general rules of morality, the lawyer cannot accept any case whatever. It cannot be said of him, as it is written, "Thou helpest the ungodly" (II Par. 19:2). It is forbidden to cooperate in evil, either by counselling it or by help·ng to do it, or by consenting to it in some way; to counsel and countenance evil is in fact almost the same thing as to do it. Therefore the lawyer cannot knowingly gain a victory in an unjust cause. If he makes himself guilty of this, he is sinning gravely and is obliged to make amends for the harm that he has caused to the party on the opposite side. By virtue of the same principles, if it happens that in the course of a trial, a case which he first believed to be good is revealed to be evil, it is his duty to abandon it. At the very least he must counsel his client to enter into a settlement with the other party, without however confiding to him the motives which impelled him to withdraw.

Does this mean that only honest people have a right to the services of a lawyer? Certainly not. There is often a margin between the claims of the plaintiff and the requirements of the law. If the accused is deprived of the counsel and assistance of a lawyer, he would find himself in a condition inferior to that of his adversary and exposed to incurring a penalty which would exceed his wrong deed. The guilty party always has the right to assurance that the trial which he is undergoing will be conducted according to the forms of the law. He also has the right to require that the exactness of the facts alleged by the opposite party and especially the interpretation which the latter puts upon them shall be verified. Finally, it is legitimate for him to try to diminish the severity of the penalty by calling attention to the extenuating circumstances: thoughtlessness, inexperience, inadvertence, youth, poverty, etc. These are so many motives which allow the lawyer to lend his support to an evil case, but which could not authorize him to gain a victory at any price. Furthermore, the use of illicit means is never permitted, even in support of a good case.

"The lawyer," says St. Augustine (Epistle 153), "has the right to require payment for his services." He has a right to his fees. The services that he renders are useful to both individuals and society; it is therefore proper that he be compensated for them. It is permitted to him, as to every citizen, to aspire to live from the exercise of his profession. It is even his right to require compensation that is proportionate to the dignity of his career. However, he must not go beyond certain limits. The social position of the client, the nature of the services rendered, the amount of work involved and the customs of the country contribute to the determination of the reasonable and therefore the virtuous norm. If he deviates from these rules, there will be abuse and injustice.

3. THE DEMANDS OF LEGAL JUSTICE

Legal justice takes its measure upon the laws and aims at the insertion of the individual and of associations into the political society in such a way that the material and spiritual welfare of the nation will be achieved. Its supreme rule being the common good, its sphere of influence extends to everybody: both those who govern and those who are governed. It regulates those who govern both in their relation to the common good and in their relations with foreign nations, as well as their relations with their own subjects.

A. *Those Who Govern and the Common Good*

General justice, while it must be cultivated by all the citizens, must be the eminent quality of those who govern; it belongs to them in a very particular way, in the manner of an architectonical art, as the ancients said. It rectifies their will; it inspires them with love for the good which it is their proper function to foster. It especially inspires them with the firm and constant will to take the measures that are capable of assuring its achievement. Therefore they are more guilty when they deviate from it.

1. Granted that it is principally by the laws that those who govern exercise their authority in government and assure the establishment of the social good, it is above everything else by legislating that they are in danger of acting contrarily to the general directions of justice and therefore in danger of sinning. This is what happens every time laws are made which contravene the prescriptions of Natural Law and almost every time that they deviate from constitutional law. Those who govern are not dispensed from conforming their acts to the imperatives of the law promulgated by the Author of nature and they are rarely invested with a power that places them above the constitution. Their jurisdiction is limited to the making of laws that are in conformity with Natural Law and the constitutional law.

2. They sin again if they refuse to comply with the requirements of the common good. In antiquity, tyranny and despotism consisted

in exploiting the people for personal ends. In our days, they take another form: they consist in legislating and governing with a view of party interests or those of a political caste. This is a more subtle but not less serious corruption of the highest and most beautiful of the virtues.

3. The division of responsibilities and taxes that are necessary for the public administration and the maintenance of the common good also gives those who govern the occasion to exercise justice or injustice. The law creates among the citizens a whole order of obligations towards society. This order must be rational, that is to say conceived according to the principles of *proportional equality*. It must not favor one class to the detriment of another. It is necessary that the sacrifices which it imposes on each person be proportioned to his social conditions, his profession, his legal status, and to the advantages which he derives from the benefits of the common life. Fiscal laws which would make the costs of public administration fall upon humble people, the agricultural and working classes for example, would be unjust. Their author would transgress the rules of social justice which demand that those who benefit most from the organization should have the greater obligation of defraying its cost.

B. *International Relations*

Those who govern, because they represent the nation, also have the responsibility of determining the relations of their country with foreign States, both in time of peace and in time of war. This kind of obligation results from the solidarity of nations, for they are parts of a whole whose unity, order, peace and welfare react upon their own existence. The nations have at the same time their proper rights and duties and their common rights and duties. The rule which must preside over the establishment of these relations is therefore always justice, that which guards the respective rights of each of the nations and that which aims at the international common good.

The technical means of delimiting these rights and their usage are agreements, treaties and international conventions. In the course of the last few centuries, a whole system of legislation has been elaborated with the purpose of arranging the relations of the States between themselves and of fostering an international order. Unfortunately, it has been warped on many occasions. Instead of serving to promote the truly common good of all the nations, it has only served to glorify force, to consecrate success, and to subordinate the small nations to the interests of a few hegemonies. And in the measure in which it has deviated from its purpose, it has been irrational, immoral and unjust.

In the cases of differences between two States, the normal procedure would have been to present the case to a superior tribunal, invested with the authority of the universal society of all the nations. This has been done when the points in dispute were of minor importance. But for more serious claims, recourse to arbitration has been impossible. For lack of a technique sufficiently to the point on the part of the League of Nations or the United Nations Organization, and also for lack of a judicious philosophy of sovereignty on the part of the States, the only practical means available to the nations that were vexed has been to become a law unto themselves. They made up for the absence of international authority by a "declaration of war" which the theologian, most of the time, would have little reluctance to judge immoral.

C. Those Who Govern and Those Who Are Governed

(a) Duties of Those Who Govern

Those who govern have other duties in regard to the governed. They must maintain the properly civil order.

Those who govern, as was said previously, must take the initiative in establishing tribunals, in naming judges and in watching over the good administration of justice in order that everyone may be assured of the peaceful enjoyment of his rights. The judges determine and define in the name of the supreme authority, but conformably with the just claims of everyone.

There still are many exchanges between private associations and individuals in which the government does not have the initiative, but over which it possesses a duty of surveillance and a right of control: donations, sales, purchases, rental contracts, wages, testamentary wills and the rest.

It must be understood that each social organism possesses a proper economy and particular ends, and that both, being distinct from those of the government, do not enter directly into its sphere of influence. We must also remember that the nation, as a civil society, is presented under two aspects. First, it can be regarded as a society having its specific nature, a proper structure and physiognomy, which definitely distinguish it from other forms of society. And as such, it enjoys characteristic functions which adapt it effectively to the pursuit of the common good; it can, through the intervention of appropriate services, legislate, govern, administer and exercise justice. Secondly, it must be considered as a primary and perfect society. It possesses, in effect, these two characteristics which are attached to its very essence. And then, by virtue of the principle of philosophy which says that that which is first in an order envelops by its imperative and finalizing influence everything which is contained under that order, civil society must make fruitful and supervise from above the activities of all the individuals and all the private associations which are formed within its bosom. This is necessary, granted that its own purpose, the common good, is composed of all the particular goods and their harmonious arrangement. If the individuals and the private associations were left to their own arbitrary control, there would be disorder.

It follows from these principles that those who govern have the responsibility of watching over the physical and moral security of the individual; and of protecting the family, controlling the *division* of goods by laws governing inheritances, contracts, work and all the operations of the social and economic life. If they fail in this respect, they make themselves responsible for the evils which result from a bad division of powers and property.

(b) Duties of Subjects

Legal justice, we said, is the eminent quality of those who govern. It is also that of the governed, under another form. It inclines them to submit themselves to the laws; it makes them collaborate for the common good and for the development of the social order. And this raises the problem of moral force in human laws.

The principle is clear. Every law, if it is rational, is good; it obliges inwardly in conscience.

If it is to be rational, as we have already specified, it is necessary that it proceed from legitimate authority and that it aim at fostering the common good, the true good, the one which imposes itself in the eyes of reason. It is also necessary that it make the basic division of sacrifices and responsibilities according to proportional equality, i.e. in relation to the juridical status of the citizens and the advantages which they derive from the organization of the life of society.

Authority may not be legitimately constituted, and then it is not authority: it has neither competence nor jurisdiction nor power to bind consciences. However, if there is no legitimately constituted authority, and if the order and the peace are maintained, and the national patrimony is respected, it would be difficult to refuse one's submission, even if only provisional, without being deficient in legal justice. Passive resistance, which is always licit when it is a question of unjust laws, may not always be licit when power is usurped. Does this not entail the deterioration of the national good?

The common good can have the aspect of public utilities and of services destined to the maintenance of collective security. It is then established by the appropriation of taxes, the establishment of military service, etc. The tax-payer who would refuse the obligation of paying his taxes through contempt for the common good, would sin against justice. Submission to the fiscal and military laws only obliges in conscience in the measure in which the common good, civil and national, is directly or indirectly affected. And this, of course, is not always easy to discern and determine.

The common good is also materialized under the form of unity, order and peace. These are so many goods that the members of the community possess corporately. Against them there are the protesting disparagers of the régime, the promoters of dissensions, the violently seditious and the virtual seditious, that is to say those who, owing allegiance to a foreign power surreptitiously strive to undermine the institutions of the country. Their injustice is grave, and borders on that of treason. St. Thomas, comparing sedition with brawling, writes: "It is obvious that sedition goes counter to justice and the common good. It is therefore in general a mortal sin, and all the more grave because the common good to which it is detrimental is more noble than the private good to which the brawl is opposed."

4. THE ECONOMY OF DISTRIBUTION

We have already drawn attention to the danger of confusing distribution and division, and upon the misunderstandings which this confusion can ocasion. Thus, the legal status and social condition of the citizen are not necessarily the result of distribution; they usually proceed from personal initiative or from birthrights. There are also serious disadvantages in considering order, security, peace, and the general state of prosperity as "distributed" goods. Those who enjoy these goods do not benefit from them personally to the exclusion of other men, but in common with them and corporately. The distributed good is on the contrary a good which, granted to a citizen, is then appropriated by him, belonging to him thereafter in an exclusive and inalienable manner. This explains why distributive justice is considered as a particular virtue which envisages the establishment of the individual good.

Even more than legal justice, distributive justice is the special portion of those who govern. To foster the common good, consequently, the efforts of everyone are useful and necessary, while for the establishment of a judicious and equitable distribution of goods the clear-sightedness and the justice of the superior are especially necessary. Moreover, the only one who can distribute that which is common is the one who has the disposition of it, together with its keeping and its administration. That is why the exercise of this form of justice is reserved for those who preside over the destinies of the nation.

What are the goods that are capable of being distributed? St. Thomas replies: "Justice has external operations for its object, namely, the distribution and the exchange which consists in the *usage* of certain external realities: things, persons and services. A usage of things, when for instance, one takes from or gives to someone an object which belongs to him; of persons when one commits an injustice against the very person of a man by striking him or injuring him, or else when one gives marks of respect to him; of services, finally, when by right, one requires work of someone or provides him with it. If therefore we take as the matter of both justices, the realities themselves of which the putting to contribution is a usage, distributive and commutative justice have the same matter: for things can be withdrawn from the common property and distributed to individuals, or exchanged from one to the other. There is equally a certain distribution and compensation of tasks. But if we take as the matter, in each of these two kinds of justice, the principal *acts* themselves, by which we make use of persons, things and services, we must distinguish two matters, for distributive justice directs the distribution while commutative justice regulates the exhanges between two persons" (IIa IIae, q. 6, a. 3).

Distributive justice therefore pertains to the same goods as commutative justice: it is only related to the common good in order to obtain the matter for distribution. That which it attributes to each person is of the order of individual advantages.

Let us here note that apart from the goods that are properly distributed, there are the goods that man acquires from the fact of his insertion into a society, which he would not have if he were not part of a whole. Such are all the goods of society, the goods which all men enjoy corporately. They are usually called common goods. They are not distributed collectively, but are possessed in that way.

There are also all the rights of the citizen as such, equal rights, determined by the constitution or the régime, and recognized in each of the members of the society. They imply the rights of man and constitute the basic and common legal status; they establish the power of the citizen, his juridical capacity. They are anterior to the distribution and are attributed by virtue of the Natural Law and the constitutional law. And if this attribution is bad, it is not those who govern who are unjust, rather the constitution is defective. All men must demand the rectification of the statutes, for these rights are due in justice.

Finally there are the gratuities, the offices, honors and benefices that the governing authorities grant to deserving citizens in the name of the community. These particular goods are properly distributed. They can be ordered above all to the personal betterment of the individual; such are gratuities and honorary titles. Or they can be considered especially with a view of the betterment of society; such are the public mandates and functions, with the honors and material advantages that are connected with them.

The rule of distributive justice is that superiors must conform their administration to the dignity of the individuals. They must avoid being "respecters of persons." They are only authorized to grant honors, favors and rewards to those who have merited them from society, either by a long career of service, or by the honor which they have themselves reflected upon it. To be just, every distribution must have a cause. Favoritism in regard to relatives, friends and partisans undermines confidence, foments disorder and constitutes an evil. It unjustly deprives deserving citizens of a mark of gratitude and a pecuniary advantage to which they have right.

The functions that are granted to certain citizens for the administration of public affairs and the promotion of the common good of the nation can only be attributed to those who offer guarantees of honesty, and who have the competence and qualifications to fulfill them. Without these, personal preference and a double injustice would ensue: towards the individuals who are suited for civil positions and who lay claim to them, and toward society which has the right to require that the public affairs be well administered.

These principles are not only valid for civil society; they are valid for the religious society and for every form of society.

In the course of recent years theologians have argued vigorously whether injustice, in matters of legal and distributive justice, makes restitution obligatory.

If we understand restitution in the strict sense, it is not only compulsory in cases in which one must *return* that which one has taken or destroyed, but in the wider sense of *reparation* there can be no doubt that every justice obliges in conscience to make amends in the very measure in which it has injured the rights of individuals or society.

The obligation to make amends becomes more urgent if someone has promised an office or a benefice to a candidate who merits it on the basis of examination or competition. The success of the candidate then creates a right in his favor. We must not say that those who have not succeeded have paid the same costs and incurred the same expenses as the successful candidate, for they do not find themselves to be in the juridical position of the one who, by succeeding, has fulfilled the conditions of the tacit contract between himself and the collator of the benefices. Here we find ourselves confronting a compenetration of distributive and commutative justice. The obligation to make amends is accordingly reinforced.

5. JUSTICE AND INJUSTICE OF ACTION

Persons, in the hierarchical whole that constitutes the city, may be either simple citizens or office-holding personages: either private persons or "public" persons.

A. *Justice or Injustice Toward a "Public" Person*

"Public" persons enjoy a particular excellence and ascendancy: their greatness and their prestige are esteemed not because of what they are by birth, but in terms of the reality which they represent and the dignity in which they participate. They symbolize God, fatherland and society as a whole. They enjoy prerogatives which belong to themselves personally, although they are granted to them because of their status as public persons. Their rank establishes relations between themselves and the other members of the community which are not between equals but between a superior and an inferior.

These relations affect commutative justice, since in this form of justice social rank is often taken into account: for example, when it is necessary to determine the extent of services rendered or affronts received. However, in their entirety the duties of the citizen towards those who hold office or authority are not connected with those of strict justice whose function is to render to each man his due, according to a certain equality or proportion. The virtues that are connected with justice without realizing the perfect idea of it determine these kinds of obligations.[15]

B. *Wrongs that Can Be Done to a Neighbor*

From private person to private person there are voluntary exchanges and involuntary exchanges. The first can be made either by action or by word. The whole economy of these exchanges is assured by one and the same virtue: commutative justice. When an individual's will is resolved to render to each man his due, he respects the persons of his fellow-men as well as everything that pertains to them. Commerce, or at least the communication with other men, can be greatly diversified in its elements, but the measure to be kept is always the same; it is arithmetical equality. Everywhere and always, it is a matter of respecting the possessions of other men in their integrity. And, need we say it again, a single virtue suffices.

The situation is not the same when one is lacking in justice. There are many ways of failing in this virtue and of doing harm to our neighbor. When we examine them we shall better understand, by way of contrast, the primordial role which communicative justice plays in the life of society.

(a) Among the wrongs that one can do against his neighbor, the most serious is the one which consists in making an attempt against his life: this is the question of *voluntary homicide*—by murder, assassination or any other violent means.

But are there not certain cases when it is legitimate and even praise-worthy to kill? Is the right to life absolutely inviolable?

The good of life is the first and most radical of all goods; it is the support of all the others. Man has a right to it that is established in nature, an absolute right. Therefore it is written, "Thou shalt not put the innocent and just man to death." For man is a person, endowed with intelligence and freedom; he is capable of rising to the knowledge of the Absolute and of undertaking the quest for God. Furthermore, he has the image of the holy Trinity engraved within him. He exists therefore for his own sake, and in some way finds his

[15] See the chapters on religion and the "social virtues."

justification within himself. He has his own proper destiny, a destiny whose realization is entrusted to him. He is a subject with rights, and in particular the basic right which is the principle of all the others, the right to life. To take this from him without cause is to violate his right and impair the work of God; it is even a violation of the rights of God, Who, alone, is the master of life and of death. We can briefly judge the gravity of homicide by the following reflections: the murderer injures a person who is deserving instead of his esteem and his love; he does harm to someone who is worthy of recompense; he deprives society of an industrious citizen and an honorable man; he shows great contempt for the rights of God and the duties of charity.

In our modern societies homicide has acquired unsuspected proportions. Without mentioning the systematic putting to death of civil prisoners, prisoners of war and hostages, mention must be made of infanticide, abortion, euthanasia, painless execution of the feeble-minded, the sick, abnormal people, the insane and the dying. All these executions are violations of the rights of the person and the rights of God.

(b) Obviously we must set aside *accidental homicide*. An accident is involuntary by definition, and like anything that is the effect of chance, it remains outside the intentions and decisions of the will. It is not taken into account when it is a question of determining the responsibility and guilt. And yet it happens that the accidental is not completely involuntary. Thus, when someone deliberately commits an illicit, guilty act which he could and should omit, if this act entails the death of an innocent man, he is responsible for the consequences of his act to the very degree that he could and should have foreseen them. Anyone who strikes a pregnant woman, for example, would find it difficult to be relieved of responsibility if the child dies as a result. The case is almost the same when one neglects to provide men with the care that is necessary for their life. If the vigilance and the precautions which could and should have been provided are missing, the author incurs responsibility and guilt, and again in the very measure in which there was carelessness. Such, for example, would be the case with an employer who was not concerned about the health and life of his employees.

Another case of involuntary homicide is the one that results from *legitimate defense* against an aggressor. It is a question, in the case in point, of an act from which two effects may result: namely, the saving of one's own life and the death of the aggressor. The action is licit, since the person who was attacked wants to protect his own life. However, this would not be so if he planned to kill in order to defend himself, when he could do otherwise; the homicide would then be directly willed.

(c) If homicide is immoral and anti-social, what must be said about the putting to death of traitors, murderers, the seditious and certain criminals?

No one, first of all, maintains that the *death penalty* is necessary and obligatory. A given system of penal law may, by reason of the particular mentality of the people, exclude the death penalty and be rational and effective nevertheless. But this is not the real question at issue. Our present problem is to know if punishment can include permission to put a guilty man to death.

The answer to this question involves a whole philosophy of penal law. We might as well say that the answer has not been unanimous.

Rousseau and his disciples, starting from the hypothesis of a state of nature anterior to that of society, date back the origins of society to an agreement, a social contract. In this contract the individual will have reserved his basic liberty as well as his right to life. What is more serious, however, is that this right is assumed to be absolute, natural and therefore inviolable. Consequently, the State, which only has the powers granted to it by its citizens, could not have the right to inflict the death penalty. This argument has the same worth as its premises. But it is false to say that man is not sociable by nature. Moreover, the Natural Law is not only individual; it is also social. Society possesses, as fully as the individual, certain rights that flow from its nature. And when they are infringed by those of the family and those of the individual, sound reason requires that it be the latter which yield, granted that they are inferior and that whatever is inferior can never prevail against that which is superior.

Followers of the materialist and determinist school of thought, which was initiated by the Italian, Lombroso, and which is greatly in vogue among a certain category of psychoanalysts, consider the criminal as a man who is abnormal, sick and irresponsible. There could no longer be a question of punishment if such is the case. The only reasonable line of conduct for society is to guard against the dangers which the evil-doer causes. It is incontestable that there are more irresponsible persons among public offenders than is commonly believed. And since it is less a matter of punishing the crime than the criminal, it is necessary to set up a preliminary inquiry for the purpose of examining the mental dispositions of the accused. But to conclude that there are no longer any criminals is to stretch the point unjustifiably.

After all, there is no lack of optimistic theorists who claim that there is no cause to punish criminals: they are people who are more to be pitied than blamed. It would be better to try to re-educate and rehabilitate them. It is indubitable, of course, that many criminals are capable of being improved and put back on the right road, but as they do not all have favorable dispositions, this rehabilitation can only be accomplished when they have served their sentence. The punishment, moreover, as we shall see, is not primarily ordered for the amendment of the guilty person.

This question is subject to argument. Those who say that it is legitimate to condemn certain public offenders to death, in particular murderers, assassins, and traitors, argue in the following way.

To begin with, assassins have fallen from their dignity as persons. They have debased themselves to the level of the beast by their contempt for the light of reason and by giving in to their brutal instincts. The man who exempts himself from the directives of justice and law, thought Aristotle, is worse than a ferocious beast; he is more malevolent.

Society, which establishes and maintains the public order, and is the appointed guardian of the common good, has the right, established in nature and required by the primacy of its end, to repress disorders and extirpate disturbing elements. The individual may sacrifice an infected part of his body to save his life and the body's health; why should not the State, whose mission and end are superior to those of the individual, have the right to amputate a member in order to prevent the contamination and corruption of the whole social body? Is not the whole greater than any of its parts? The death penalty, moreover, is not only an instrument of legitimate defense; it aims at punishing or avenging contempt for authority and the public order. It has the value of a preventive medicine and possesses an exemplary virtue. It intimidates the weak and helps them overcome their temptations. Consequently society has the right to have recourse to it if it decides that such punishment is appropriate. It is not this punishment which is a vestige of barbarism, but the crimes which it wants to repress.

Obviously the death penalty can only be inflicted after a trial in good and due form. No one, by his own authority, can take the initiative to execute an offender. "Whoever," says St. Augustine (*De civ. Dei*, libr. I), "without official mandate shall kill an offender, will be condemned for homicide, and so much the more because he did not fear to arrogate to himself a right which God had not given him." And St. Thomas says, "Just as the removal of a limb is a matter for the physician to whom one has entrusted the body's health, so likewise is the care of the common good entrusted to the holders of public authority. It is for them alone to decide upon the execution of evil-doers."

(d) The question of homicide entails that of suicide and that of the duel. *Suicide* is not a violation of commutative justice; it rather goes against one's duties towards oneself as well as against the rights of society and those of God.

Everyone owes love to himself. And this love is natural, innate. It is the spontaneous expression of the most profound law of being, that of self-preservation. By virtue of this law engraved in the very depths of our substance, every being instinctively and stubbornly resists anything that militates against his existence. The man who, by his reason, becomes aware of this instinct, will see in it the expression of his Creator's will, and cannot act against it without erring and sinning against both the light of his reason and the most imperious law of his carnal being. "For no one ever hated his own flesh," says the Apostle. The danger would rather be that one might yield too readily to instinct and go beyond moderation in loving the body.

Suicide is also an act against society. The individual owes himself to the whole from which he came forth, and to which he is bound by a multitude of spiritual ties. He cannot make an attempt against his own existence without becoming guilty of injustice towards society. If everyone who experienced tribulation and discouragement put an end to life, it would be the ruin of humanity.

Suicide especially goes against the rights of God. God is the absolute master of life. It is He Who gives it and it is He Who takes it back; it is He Who "makes us live and die." Consequently, anyone who takes it upon himself to decide that it is time to put an end to his days is like a man who arrogates to himself the right to judge a case that is not subject to his jurisdiction. He usurps the rights of God, to Whom alone it appertains to determine life and death. It must not be alleged that man is his own master, and that he can dispose of his being as he pleases. The mastery which was conceded to man over himself does not pertain to his nature, his individuality or his birth. All of this eludes the control of his free-will. He has never had any dominion over his being. He has had neither the privilege of accepting nor the right of refusing his birth, nor has he obtained them during the course of his life. One only has control over the things that are the fruit of the will. This mastery is therefore uniquely related to the use that is made of one's life, the development of one's resources and the attainment of one's ends. No one has any right over his body, except that of making good use of it.

(e) The *duel* could not be legitimate in Christian morality either. It is always unjust and evil. It is malicious because it participates in both homicide and suicide. The duelists both expose themselves to the danger of death and both arrogate to themselves a right over life which can only belong to God and to His representatives.

(f) Without going so far as to deprive him of life, one can still harm his neighbor in his person by violence and incarceration. *Blows and wounds* can be inflicted either during a fight or as a measure of punishment. In fights the one who, under the impulse of hatred or anger, starts up against another man and beats him unmercifully, can hardly escape from a sin against justice and charity. The situation is different, of course, in regard to anyone who is defending himself, provided that he does not put any hatred into his defense.

The *correction of children is necessary*. (Cf. in particular Prov. 13:24; 19:18; 22:15; 23:13-14; 29:15-17). They need to be reproved and punished. It is not unjust for parents to spank them, if they believe that the children deserve it, granted that they have the authority in their home. However, they must use their power with moderation and discretion, for fear of aggravating the children. The continual sentiment of fear, and too frequent threatening with the rod produce bad results in the formation of personality. And if it happens that the parents are carried away by passion, going beyond moderation, they are lacking in justice and charity.

(g) *Incarceration* was frequent in antiquity and men often were inclined to practise it in defiance of justice. However, it is not necessarily unjust. It represents a licit form of chastisement. St. Thomas justifies it in these terms: "Corporal goods are made into a hierarchy in the following manner: firstly, the substantial integrity of the body —we do harm to it by death or mutilation; next, the gratification and appeasement of the senses, to which are opposed the blows that are received or any painful sensation; finally, the movement and use of the limbs which are hindered by enchainment, imprisonment or any other mode of detention. To put anyone into prison or deny him his liberty in any way is forbidden if it is not in conformity with justice, either as a punishment or as a preventive measure against certain dangers."

Such are the principal duties which flow from commutative justice in regard to the person of our neighbor.

6. JUSTICE AND INJUSTICE OF SPEECH

The person derives a singular excellence and dignity from his reason. Consequently, a person has a right to the exceptional treatment which commutative justice accords.

To better understand what is required in this new ensemble of duties, let us try once again to state the ways of failing in these duties. First of all we shall mention outrage.

(a) An *outrage* (contumely) is a kind of affront. It is a sin of the tongue, especially consisting in injurious words, although it can materialize itself in attitudes and gestures which speak louder than words. An outrage is allied to, but not identical with, an insult, reproach, opprobrium, jesting, and abusive language, as to any verbal expression that is likely to provoke shame and humiliation. It is the opposite of respect and veneration.

St. Gregory (Mor. lib. 31, cap. 17) states that an outrage is derived from anger: and this is accurate. If, in fact, it can proceed from other sources, it is most often from this passion that it results. An angry man seeks to gratify his vengeance; by what swifter weapon could he do this than by hurling an outrage in the face of the person who is its object? "The angry man," observes Aristotle, "seeks revenge openly."

The outrage, abusive language, and insults can admit of a grave omission of justice and charity. This depends on the intention and feelings of the one who utters them. If he has the will to attack the honor of the person to whom he addresses them, he commits a sin analogous to rapine or theft, for the just man shows no less attachment to his honor than to his material goods. If, on the other hand, the abusive words are meant for his reproof and correction, they may not be outrages, properly speaking. They do not then entail any sin against justice.

Finally, the gravity of the outrage does not only depend upon the intention of the one who utters it; it also depends on the character of the person to whom it is addressed, and on the number of witnesses. Joking and teasing, for instance, cannot constitute serious sins.

(b) Another way of harming our neighbor, but this time by attacking not his personal excellence but his reputation and the good opinion which he enjoys, is defamation.

Defamation is one of the most common and most frequent ways of failing in justice and charity. One is not embarrassed to tear his neighbor to pieces. And there is nothing new about this. The Apostle James said, "If anyone does not offend in word, he is a perfect man" (3:2). Defamation is the daughter of envy. It results from the fact that men cannot easily tolerate the consideration and esteem enjoyed by their fellow-men. It can be defined as "the disparagemen of the reputation of our neighbor, without the knowledge of the person affected."

It is distinguished from outrage by the fact that it is committed without the knowledge of the person whom it wants to harm. It is further distinguished in that it does not directly injure the honor but the reputation of our neighbor. Outrage disgraces by showing the little respect that one has for the outraged person. It is openly and in his presence that the offensive remarks are made. Defamation, on the contrary, is committed in the absence of the defamed person and indicates more fear than contempt. It is not therefore the honor, but the reputation that it attacks directly. It seeks to ruin reputation surreptitiously and clandestinely.

St. Thomas enumerates four direct ways and two indirect ways to injure the reputation of our neighbor: we may attribute false wrongs to him, or we exaggerate his real sins, we reveal that which is secret, or we ascribe evil intentions to his good actions; and, indirectly, we may deny the good that he does, or we multiply our concealments maliciously.

St. Paul says of defamers that they are "hateful to God" (Rom. 1:30). This is because reputation is a more precious good than temporal treasures and it is serious to rob a man of it. It is a direct attack upon charity and consequently, by its nature it is a mortal sin, except in cases in which it results from levity of mind. And even when it results from levity of mind it can still be serious if the remarks that are made gravely harm our neighbor. Compared with homicide, adultery, outrage and theft, it is generally less serious than the first three, but more serious than the last. Thus it is written in the book of Proverbs: "A good name is better than great riches" (22:1).

There may also be an infringement of justice by listening to the remarks of a disparager. If by obvious complaisance we approve, encourage, or even provoke such remarks, we are sinning no less than he. If, on the contrary, we only approve in an indirect way, that is to say if by human deference we do not disavow or rectify his infamous remarks while we are in a position to do so, we are less at fault, unless however we are obliged by duty to protest, or when the lack of disapproval does not entail disastrous consequences. Human deference is not a virtuous motive. It is not sufficient, in every circumstance, to change a serious fault into a slight fault.

(c) We have seen how one can make an attempt upon the honor or the reputation of a man. One can also injure that other spiritual good which he possesses: friendship. This is the sin of *dissension*.

Sowers of dissension are like defamers; they spread their injurious remarks in a furtive way to destroy, no longer reputation, but concord, harmony, esteem, and the communion of thought and sentiment that exists between husband and wife, relatives, and friends in general. They try to stir up minds against one another and to bring about the rupture of the most precious ties. They use defamation and duplicity, employing different speech according to whether it is a question of one party or the other. Their stigmas bring about loss of affection and discord.

Holy Scripture is not gentle toward this kind of perfidy: "The whisperer," it tells us, "and the double tongued is accursed" (Ecclus. 28:15), and again, it says that there is "an evil mark of disgrace upon the double tongued, but to the whisperer hatred, and enmity, and reproach" (Ecclus. 5:15-17. Cf. Prov. 16:28; 17:4; 18:6; 20:17; 26:20-28; 30:10).

Effectively, dissension is worse than outrage or defamation. The damage which it causes is greater, for friendship is the best of all external goods. "Friendship," said Aristotle, "is preferable to honors. It is worth more to be loved than to be honored." Holy Scripture itself affirms that "Nothing can be compared to a faithful friend" (Ecclus. 6:15; Cf. Prov. 15:17; 17:9; 17:17; 18:19, 24, etc.).

(d) Mockery and cursing are joined to the injustices of speech already mentioned.

Mockery is almost synonymous with raillery, derision and malevolent joking. It consists in not taking someone's afflictions seriously, and in taking advantage of his shortcomings to make him seem ridiculous and cover him with humiliation. It is distinguished from outrage, defamation and dissension by the very intention of the person who makes a weapon of it. He wants to make the person whom he is addressing lose face and do away with his confidence in his integrity, throwing him into shame and confusion.

To judge the gravity of mockery, we must consider two things: the misfortune or the deficiency which one finds amusing and laughable, and the person whom one is mocking. If the mocker is joking about a misfortune or a deficiency that is of small importance there is no serious sin. If, on the contrary, it is the person whom he wishes to make seem ridiculous, by affecting not to take the person's suffering seriously, his mockery implies a certain contempt for his fellow-man which is sinful. There is nothing more effective than ridicule to paralyze the efforts of men of good will.

Cursing constitutes another kind of abuse of speech. It consists in calling down evil upon someone and in wishing it to him. It is not necessarily illicit. It sometimes happens that justice fulminates the anathema, by way of chastisement, against the evil-doer with a view of making him aware of the gravity of his condition. But this is an exception of which the individual cannot take advantage. To will the misfortune of our neighbor is directly contrary to justice and charity. Leviticus declared long ago: "He that curseth his father, or mother, dying let him die" (20:9). The gravity of cursing is measured by the nature of the evil that is wished and the sentiment which inspires it.

7. MAN AND MATERIAL GOODS

A. *Domination and Property*

Recognizing the importance of material goods in life, we must define the laws which govern their use. We lay down as a principle that man enjoys a natural domination over the material goods of the universe. The definition of domination will throw some light upon this principle.

The term *domination* has a more extended sense than the words possession and property. It refers to the person himself who dominates, and to his inclinations, his habits, his acts, his works and possessions. Its object is everything that falls under the ascendency of freedom. Only persons are able to exercise mastery over themselves and over everything that is attached to their personality. The subject of domination is only the person, for he alone enjoys reason and freedom. Beings that act by mechanical necessity cannot be masters of their works. "We are masters," says Saint Thomas, "of things submitted to our free-will; we dominate them."

Domination therefore supposes a power of usage, that is to say, a power of disposing with a view of usage. However, domination does not consist in this power, but in the relationship which it establishes. This relationship is of the kind that exists between the mover and the movable. The mover is that reality which is able to move; the master—the "dominus"—is one who is capable of disposing anything that is subject to his domination with a view of a usage and an end.

It is thanks to our possibility of reflection, of examining our acts, that we can enter into the exercise of domination. By reflection we enter into possession of our acts: we are masters of them. We dispose of them with a view of usages and of ends. Through the medium of our acts we enter into possession of our habits, our inclinations and ourselves. And we always enter into possession of material goods through the instrumentality of our acts. Domination, obviously, is a multiform idea.

We said that man enjoys a natural domination over the things of nature. Being a "person" he consequently enjoys a superiority over things, a sovereignty over them, and therefore a power of usage in relation to them. The ontological status of a person entails a privileged juridical status.

Man holds this power from God, who is the sovereign dominator, having made everything by His liberty. Human domination, on the other hand, is only relative to usage. Man is only master of things because he can (and must) make a rational and free usage of them. God, on the contrary, is master of things, not only because He can govern them and make them *serve* the manifestation of His glory and His goodness, but because He created them. His domination is therefore more basic. It pertains to being itself. God is the master of its conservation and transformation. Man is made in the image of the Holy Trinity; he participates as a free cause in providence and in its government; he is capable of ordering things to usages and ends. He is naturally made to make use not only of his powers and of his body but of the physical universe which prolongs in some way the microcosm which he constitutes by birth. Things themselves, moreover, establish this power which man has over them. They are consequently ordered to man as to their extrinsic end and their fulfillment. The imperfect exists for the perfect; it is subordinate to the latter by its very nature. Man is, by right of birth, the dominator not only of his acts but of the universe.

This possession of the universe, included in domination, is not a theoretical possession, only possible or virtual. It is on the contrary a real and actual possession, although general, undetermined, and common. By virtue of his ontological status as a person, man is really master, really *dominus*. He has really received the powers of thinking, speaking, contriving, willing and possessing.

This possession is the *principle and end* of all the historic forms of possession, of all the possible systems of property. If the person were not the end of things, if he did not have by nature a right to possession of them, he would yield to violence every time that he tried to appropriate them and use them for his own benefit. Economic systems suppose, as a postulate, that man has the right to enjoy the goods of the earth, their whole raison d'être being to enable man to enjoy life more. A disposition of property which resulted in an irrational usage, and which would have the consequence of reducing a considerable portion of humanity to famine, would be radically unjust. It would fail in its *essential end* which is to foster a better usage, a better division and a better enjoyment of material goods.

Because it is general, undetermined and common, human possession needs to be determined and specified by the will of man. It has in fact been determined by the conventions, customs, usages and juridical forms to which the peoples have submitted their life. Like all other rights, the right of possession has evolved, sometimes for the better and sometimes for the worse, according to the value of the constitutions in which it has been incorporated. Its destiny has depended upon the doctrines which inspired the societies that regulated it.

Not only man, but human society enjoys the right of domination. It possesses a determined territory through the medium of the citizens who are its immediate owners. This type of domination is based upon the fact that the supreme authority has jurisdiction over the nation's subjects and consequently, that it enjoys the right to govern from above their exchanges and the just division of their possessions;

this supposes a certain domination of the latter. Society's power over persons is extended to that which prolongs them, that is to say to their possessions. This is what is called "superior domination."

This superior domination imposes on the government the duty to defend the possessions of its subjects; and on the part of the latter, the duty to contribute to the expenses which devolve upon the State for the maintenance of internal and external security (the payment of taxes, military service, etc.). Superior domination is derived from Natural Law: it finds support in the very essence of civil society, considered as *primary society,* just as the division or distribution of property, whether productive or not; that is to say, the passage from common possession to that of groups and individuals, is based upon Natural Law, at least by secondary derivation.

The division of property, which confers on individuals or groups of individuals the power to acquire, manage, exploit and transfer it, is a condition that is so indispensable to the common prosperity, to good order and peace, that reason immediately perceives that it imposes itself as a primordial measure. This second type of natural law, spontaneously deduced from the primary ends of the common life, is what ancient authors called the *law of nations.* Nothing in nature, considered absolutely, indicates that property should or should not be distributed. However, division has been the work of the natural use of reason and liberty, which, in the long run, have established the customs, conventions, and the historic laws or rights which are related to it. Occupation, regulation, concession, legacy, purchase, sale, law and the rest have been admitted as technical processes.

The use of reason and liberty has therefore taught man what advantage he could derive from these indetermined powers which are his will, his intelligence, his hand, his lingual aptitude, and his natural gifts. It has likewise taught him that his domination, wholly general, needed to be determined under the form of collective or individual appropriation. This seemed necessary to him, first of all for better economic output, granted that everyone gives more attentive and more indefatigable care to whatever belongs to himself alone than to anything that belongs to all men or to several. Next, for better order in the administration of property. Since normally each man turns toward the kind of exploitation which his aptitudes, tastes and family traditions denote for him, confusion and incompetence are consequently found to be most often eliminated by the very play of freedom, natural inclinations and economic possibilities. Finally, for the maintenance of peace, since individual property avoids at least one kind of quarrel: the kind which arise between those who possess everything in common and indivisibly. In a word, individual possession (or possession by a determined group) of the matter and means of production seems more capable of assuring economic and social well-being.

The division of property, as we have said, does not necessarily result in private property; collective possession can also be its result. In antiquity, the territories granted in common to tribes, patriarchal families, clans and brotherhoods, offer so many forms of collective possessions. Property that is collectively owned by communities, co-operatives, companies, business firms, still provides an example in our day. We may go further, however; for as a matter of fact, new forms of collective possession have been contrived. Some men have extolled the pure and simple nationalization of a large portion of the economic life. Others only propose those intermediate kinds of nationalization which are the State administrations, the service organizations, and societies of mixed economy. Still others work for the establishment of cooperative administrations or tripartite administrations, assured simultaneously by the State, the worker and the consumer. The question then arises concerning the legitimacy of these forms of possession.

The State governs. It has the obligation of using all the means at its disposal in order that property may be in the service of the common good. And, if the very powerful means at its disposal prove incapable of preventing the exploitation and unjust treatment of the workers, it is authorized to have recourse to the radical measure of expropriation. Nevertheless, the latter does not inevitably entail nationalization. It is possible to entrust the administration of certain basic industries to the public without having recourse to pure and simple nationalization with its ordinary sequel of abuses: contrivances of politicians, red tape, negligence, despotism of civil servants, irresponsibility at every stage, and mechanization of work and of life. Cooperative units, cooperative administrations, and even tripartite administrations, enjoying full administrative, financial and commercial responsibility and with the obligation to be an organized and economically profitable business, capable of supporting the fiscal costs and of meeting competition in both the domestic and foreign markets, are frequently more capable than State monopolies in remedying abuses, satisfying the workers' need for emancipation and in safeguarding the person's privileges of freedom and responsibility.

We established above that man has a real power over the goods of this world and that this power has been determined by their division and distribution. Man therefore enjoys a power over the portion of property which has fallen to him. Exercising this power, man in some way tightens the bonds between himself and the thing possessed. The latter is no longer merely something which *may be utilized* by him, but becomes a *possession,* a prolonging of his personality, a projection of himself externally, a kind of acquired "organ," although still separate from himself.

This intimacy of the relationship between man and the things which he has made his own is easily understood if we recall that the person is master of his acts, and that he acts freely upon external things and envelops them or penetrates them with his energies in order to transform them and make them fruitful. It is not only by virtue of his native dignity as a person, but also because his goods are effectively the bearers of something of himself, because they participate in his own liberty that man becomes *master* of what he possesses. Between himself and his goods, there is established that kind of *natural* relation which binds the cause to the effect.

But this is not all. The human individual is a maker. This means that he is capable of animating his efforts with intentions, dreams, ideas, plans and rationality. Everything he makes bears the effigy and mark of that which haunts his reason. His works are the incarnation of a purpose, a practical, working idea. It is not sufficient that they be the effects of freedom; they must also be the reflections of reason, the answers to his dreams, and the creations of his thought. And we easily understand that after such a communion with the soul of their master, things are bound to him by a natural relationship of belonging. Consequently, the transmission of goods has always been considered as of Natural Law, at least of that secondary Natural Law which has been defined. Children are the continuators of their parents, their flesh and blood, the trustees of their ideal of life and of the traditions in which that ideal is incarnated. It is self-evident that the goods in which this personality is inlaid have naturally fallen to them.

Private property consolidates the family and stabilizes it, not only in the present but even in the future, and establishes the continuity of the generations. Like the traditions of which it is the material support, it perpetuates habits of industry, generosity and foresight. It is also a guarantee of security in freedom and dignity. It permits man to save something in provision against hard times and the years of old age, and to shelter his family from ordeals and poverty.

Foresight, careful saving, the ambition to improve his condition, the pleasure of doing favors for his relatives and friends, the desire to make new friends and to enlarge his influence, and the sound ambition to relieve the poor, are so many sentiments which can contribute to the fulfillment of personality. Private property makes all these joys possible.

We have already noted that "human" property is the principle and the end of every arrangement of collective and private property. Material goods have been given to humanity to permit provision for its needs in such manner that production and distribution are found to be subordinate to consumption. If therefore certain goods are attributed to certain individuals for a better management and better exploitation, it does not follow that produced goods can be distributed in the same way. Aristotle and St. Thomas, although in favor of the division of goods and appropriation, do not hesitate to affirm that property finds its ultimate finality in the common good. The goods of the earth must be sufficient to satisfy the needs of the nation, and thanks to the facility of communications and transportation, they must be sufficient for the needs of all humanity.

The order is therefore as follows: the immediate end of production is the welfare of the individual and his family; the final end is the welfare of the human community. This is an application of the principle which requires that personal ownership should never be the final end, but an intermediate end, subordinate to the common good.

By what techniques can private goods be made common? By all types of commercial operations, the equitable compensation of services, equitable taxation and just redistribution of tax money, the transformation of the revenue from certain taxes into public assistance, but also and perhaps especially by the virtues of liberality, beneficence, mercy and the generalized fulfillment of the precepts of justice and charity.

B. *Theft and Restitution*

Theft, the secret usurpation of the possessions of our neighbor, is different from pillage which is accomplished by means of recourse to violence. But both are done against the will of the possessor. Pillage is more serious than theft, because it combines outrage with the harm that is caused.

When there is a determined will to harm our neighbor, theft can be serious, even if there is slightness of matter. But even petty thefts, if they are repeated often, may constitute a grave matter, because they cause serious harm to our neighbor. However, not every theft necessarily entails a serious lack of justice if the matter can be considered unimportant.

To seize the property of another man in case of necessity is not a theft, however. This is the exercise of a natural right. In case of necessity, all things are common; the right to life precedes that of property; "human" property precedes appropriation by distribution. "The goods which some men possess superabundantly," says St. Thomas, "are owed, by Natural Law, to the feeding of the poor." The order of legal justice, no less than that of charity, requires that the goods of the earth should provide for the needs of men.

The counterpart of theft is *restitution*. It consists in re-establishing someone in the possession and enjoyment of his property. It is an act of commutative justice.

Just as respect for justice is necessarily a matter of salvation, so also is restitution. Sin cannot be pardoned unless one has the intention of escaping from it by the re-establishment of the law, by restitution. If there is always a duty to make restitution, there is not however a serious obligation to accomplish this duty except when there has been a serious sin against justice.

Restitution, like injustice itself, is capable of having diverse forms. If it is a matter of theft, plunder, receiving stolen goods, restitution is perfect as soon as the stolen thing has been returned to its owner. The sinner only needs to expiate his sin or undergo the penalty inflicted by the judge, if he has been brought into court. If it is a question of damages or wrongs caused to one's neighbor in matters of commutative justice, that is to say in his possessions, his person or his honor, one must then make reparation in the measure in which this is possible. One may make compensation for the evil that was done either by a payment of money or by restoring honors, recanting, making apologies, or by nullifying the sense of one's remarks, and so forth. Damage in matters of distributive justice may be of two kinds. They result when someone unduly brings about the removal of a man from his position, his benefices or his privileges;

or on the contrary, when one prevents someone from obtaining certain advantages or certain goods. In both cases, one must make reparation in so far as possible.

Restitution must only be made to the party who has the right to it. Otherwise the due is not rendered, the equality is not re-established and the law remains infringed. If the beneficiary is completely unknown, and if inquiries to find him have failed, one may make restitution in another way, for example by giving alms for his salvation. If he is dead, restitution must be made to his heir who is accounted to constitute only one person with him. If he is very far away, one must send him his property, or if the latter cannot be easily transported, it must be left in a safe place after having informed the interested party about it.

Property that is granted by virtue of generosity and the obligingness of the owner, such as loans, must be returned by the recipient. If they were stolen, he must consider that it was by a gratuitous obligingness and for his own use that they were accorded to him. It is for him to sustain the detriment caused by their loss. The case of deposits, however, is not the same, because it is the depositary who renders service. He is obligated to return the article entrusted to him; however, if it has been stolen, lost or destroyed, he is not bound to make restitution unless there was negligence and guilt on his part.

Finally, let us specify that accomplices are collectively obliged to make restitution, and that restitution, in itself, does not allow delay. Just as it is a sin against justice to seize the property of our neighbor, it is also sinful to retain it unduly. The owner has a right to his property and to its usufruct.

C. *Commercial Transactions*

In the limited and closed economy of antiquity, material goods circulated but little. Exchanges were made immediately, from one individual to another. Only luxury objects and rare products needed to be imported through the intermediary services of merchants. In our days, however, nearly every product becomes a kind of "merchandise." Except for farmers, almost no producer consumes what he produces. And it is sometimes necessary that he find a market for his surplus production at the other end of the earth. This resulted in the development of commerce and the need for middlemen of all kinds to assure the circulation of the goods.

Commerce therefore appears, in our complex world, as a function that is necessary for the circulation of goods and the satisfaction of man's essential or artificial needs. And, considering the conditioning exercised by the "economic" upon the "spiritual," it concurs in the divine and human well-being.

In our day there is no longer any doubt concerning the usefulness of commerce. But we may wonder if the quest for profit is not the supreme motive. Many merchants only see in their occupation a source of income. And yet the primary and essential end of the person who fulfills a function must be associated with the very end of that function and not with his personal advantage. Commerce is first of all a public service. The primary end of commerce is to correctly render this service.

The merchant certainly has the right to live from his work. But profit can only be the end or motive of the business-man if it is subordinate to the very end of commerce, that is to say to the social welfare.

The two legitimate ends of commerce are therefore: social service which is the intrinsic end of commerce, and profit. In what conditions are the commercial operations themselves legitimate? This is the question of the just price.

The just price.

The just price is not necessarily the one on which the contracting parties have finally come to terms. A price is not called just because it has brought free men to a point of agreement and has marked the terms of a sale or a purchase. The price, which is commonly expressed in monetary terms, is the indication of its value. Price and value are related to each other. The just price is the one which is equal to the economic value of an object; the unjust price is one which is below or above it.

But the idea of economic value is complex. It is based upon the degree of usefulness of the objects, but it also depends immediately upon their power of exchange, and the latter is found, either on the buyer's side or the seller's side, conditioned by several factors that are difficult to appraise.

On the buyer's side, it is necessary to consider the "desirability," which does not always correspond to the necessity or the usefulness of the object. For example, water, which is more necessary than diamonds, does not enjoy the same degree of "desirability." This suggests that the rarity or the abundance of a product can make it more or less desirable. Rarity therefore enters into the accounting in the appraisal of the value of an object, on condition however that it be real and is not artificially produced by monopolies cornering the markets. Rarity, however, does not justify an unbridled rise in prices, for one does not sell the buyer what he requires for himself. We must also consider the purchasing power of the consumer. Thus, it is permitted to realize better profits on luxury articles than on things that are necessary for the maintenance of life. The buyers of these two kinds of merchandise do not generally enjoy the same wealth.

From the seller's side, we must consider the cost, the profit and the risks. The cost of merchandise itself depends upon elements either invariable—the factory, machinery and amortization of the investment, or variable—the primary matter, of which the conditions of extraction are subject to change, the costs of transportation, the work incorporated in the manufactured object which is remunerated in relation to the social conditions of various countries and the index number of the cost of living, and all the other costs relative to the marketing of the product.

To whom does it appertain to determine the just price? What is its arbiter? Ancient authors answered that this devolved upon the "common estimate." They meant by this that commerce is subject to social regulations which are objective and independent of the will of the two individuals. Competition, if it is honest and free, can also succeed to a certain degree in moderating profits and in making prices vary according to the requirements of the conditions of production and consumption. But this raises the question of free competition which we shall not broach here. It seems incontestable in our days that it is impossible, without the help of the public power, to determine the equitable character of prices.

In summary, commerce is a social institution. The end and the rules of commerce are not individual, but social. Its operations are just when they are realized in conformity with this end and these rules.

We have noted in passing that one of the elements of the cost consists in the amortization of the investment. This is because, since the coming of heavy industry and big business, money is invested in the form of capital and becomes one of the elements of production. In ancient economy money was only a means of exchange; in modern economy it is also an instrument of production. And as the accumulation of capital is achieved by the mobilization of savings, money is no longer amassed only to be spent for consumable products, but also for deposit, investment and lending.

The attitude of the Church, which saw in lending at interest a form of usury, has not changed. But there has been a change in the principal and secondary uses of money. Money can in effect be considered as the symbol and measure of the value and, therefore, as a medium of exchange; this is its original and essential role. And considered from this angle, it has no productive virtue. But it can still be considered in its secondary uses, by the specialist in coins, for example, who views it as an *objet d'art* or a collector's item. Such is also the aspect under which it is regarded when men see in it an instrument of production. Not that it is productive in itself in the hands of someone who accumulates it for an investment, but once it is in the hands of the borrower or the entrepreneur, it permits the procurement of the primary matter and the labor. Thanks to nature and to the labor of man, money then ceases to be sterile. It acquires a usefulness analogically assimilable to that of a tool and it can be lent, like any tool. We may say with St. Thomas: *qui habet pecuniam . . . habet lucrum in virtute.* Money is virtually lucrative, that is to say that it is at least capable of being rented. From a means of exchange it becomes an object of exchange; the rate of interest is changed into a rental price, a form of income. The lender associates himself with the exploiter and shares his profits as well as his risks. That is why he has the right to claim a share of the profit as something that belongs to him.

REFLECTIONS AND PERSPECTIVES

A first reflection imposes itself concerning the *extent* of justice. It has been said that justice affects all the external operations which puts me into relationship, proximately or remotely, with someone other than myself. In other words, everything that I do, and which another person sees, hears or perceives, pertains to justice in one way or another. Thus the theology of justice includes social morality, political morality, international morality, economic morality and business morality, the morality of the Court House (morality of Judgments and trials), the morality of property, of Social Security, of Public Assistance, etc. Aristotle was right in giving a royal and sovereign character to justice and in considering the just man as one who accomplishes every virtue.

But if the domain of justice is so extended, how are we going to distinguish the other cardinal virtues, or even more the theological virtues which are quite as capable of commanding "external acts"? For anyone who can exactly formulate it, the answer to this question will have the advantage of determining the role of every virtue in any human act, and of making it comprehensible.

Let us say first of all that the same external act may pertain to different virtues, according as it is considered under one relationship or another. An external profession of faith, for example, is very obviously an act of faith, but it is also an act of religion and therefore, in a certain measure (as is explained in the following chapter) an act of justice; this can also be an act of truth, if it is a question of not lying in public, or not concealing the truth from our neighbor, and this act also pertains to justice, in another but very real manner (see chapter VII).

Adultery may certainly be first of all a sin of intemperance, but it cannot fail to be, at the same time, a sin of injustice, because it is an attack against the rights of the husband. The same may be said of rape, kidnaping, incest, in which the sin of injustice is doubtless still more serious. Inversely, if the relations between Christian husbands and wives are primarily and essentially acts of love and conjugal charity, they are also acts of fidelity, that is to say, in a certain measure, acts of justice. Thus, it is easy to show that every external act, which puts one into relations with one's neighbor, even if it affects other virtues, also concerns justice, even an imperfect justice if "our neighbor" is not an equal, or if the terms of the communication with our neighbor are not stipulated in the law.

Having said this, we must specify what are the "formal objects" of the virtues other than justice. We shall see further on that fortitude and temperance have as their object the putting of a measure of reason, that is to say a measure of order, into the passions; fortitude puts man in position to overcome the almost instinctive repugnance of the sensibility and the affections before the perils of death, either by anticipating the obstacle if necessary, or by remaining standing without taking to flight or without withdrawing if reason commands it; temperance, on the other hand, puts man in position to avoid being carried along by the passions of the "concupiscible" whose tendency is to lead him farther than is proper. It is therefore easy to distinguish that which pertains on one side to fortitude and temperance, and on the other side to justice, which only governs pure will. But it is equally certain that man rarely performs acts of "pure will," and that the act of justice ordinarily demands a certain fortitude (for example magnanimity), and a certain temperance (for example kindness, clemency, modesty); this fact indicates once again that the existential act is always complex, composed of various diverse elements which pertain to several virtues. However, the act will be practically qualified by the *intention* of the one who performs it. Rape is ordinarily a sin against temperance; it will especially be a sacrilege, a sin against religion, if the sinner's intention is to attack God in the person of a nun, for example.

We do not need to insist upon the distinction between justice and prudence which are not in the same "genus": justice has for its "subject" the will, prudence the reason. Prudence intervenes in every virtuous act in order to give it the measure of reason; the binomial prudence-justice is in every human act as inseparable as the binomial intelligence-will, and for the same reasons.

Finally the distinction of justice from the theological virtues is equally evident in itself. These virtues have the privilege of having God Himself for their object, to whom we adhere, by faith, because He enables us to know the Truth; to whom we hold fast by hope, because He alone is capable of making us truly good; to whom we attach ourselves by charity for His own sake. Therefore their perfection does not reside in a reasonable "mean" but on the contrary in a perpetual surpassing of every tendency. It is not possible to be too greatly attached to God. The theological virtues, associating us with God who is the end of our life, are the Christian inspirers of all the virtues. Charity, which is the greatest of the three, is the mother and "form" of every true virtue.

And yet, that which is theoretically simple often seems complex and difficult in practical life. How many "charitable" people do we not see who are apparently but little concerned with justice. It has even been remarked that it was a quite common tendency of certain "mystical" persons to exclude justice from their lives. But charity, if it be true, must inspire justice; it never dispenses from it. Failure to consider the right to recompense, the regulations of social security, the laws of the just wage, the trade union laws, etc., under pretext of being amenable to a higher law, which is the law of charity, is to deceive oneself. Charity desires the good of our neighbor; it cannot avoid wanting, before all else, "to render to each man his due." It is even in the nature and in the line of certain charities to be transmuted into justices; for "it is to give for good when we give the recipient a *right* over the gift. To be a gift for good, the gift will tend to transform itself into an institution and will lose the character of a gift. The gift for good does not require thanking, for if the gift of him who loves his brothers with charity should be the most costly, it must be the least costly for the one to whom it is given" (Jean Thomas, o.p., *Amour du prochain et éco-nomie*, in a volume on *L'amour du prochain*, Ed. du Cerf, 1953). And yet, for all that, nothing should prevent the acts of strict justice, which the Christian is obliged to perform, from being done in charity, with the greatest love to which, as a Christian, he aspires. Charity puts kindness and flexibility (we dare not say "unction," for this word is often taken amiss) into the exchanges of justice, in which the partners are opposed, each in his own right, more than they are united; it appertains precisely to charity to unite them, while respecting the rights of the other, and thus to transform "society" (in the purely juridical sense) little by little into a human "community" of friendship.

Positive laws. The principles which determine and define natural and positive laws, and the "jus gentium," have been presented in this chapter. It remains for theology, which aims at being practical, to consider the details of certain positive laws, either to outline them completely if they pertain to the laws of God or the Church, or to better understand them in their inspiration and sources, and thus permit a greater fidelity, or to consider them theologically and denounce the "legal" which is not always moral.

The Commandments of God. Origins of the commandments of God; sources of the sacred writer (cf. H. Cazelles, *Études sur le code de l'alliance*, Paris, Letouzey et Ané, 1946). The Decalogue in Revelation, the commandments as "Words of God": cf. M. E. Boismard, *La Bible, Parole de Dieu et Révélation;* a very fine study which appeared in *Lumière et Vie*, Oct. 1952, pp. 13 to 26. History of the literary editing and of the two recensions (Ex. 20:1-17 and Deut. 5:6-18). History and theology of the promulgation (cf. Ex. 19:9, 19; Deut. 5:2-5); must we distinguish promulgation and putting into writing? How must we understand the statement that God Himself wrote the tables of the Law (Ex. 31:18; 32:15 ff.; 34:1; Deut. 4:13; 5:22, 9:10); compare and contrast the biblical conception of the Word to the Koranic conception of the suras, "descended" at Mecca or Medina (cf. on this subject G. Abd-el-Jalil, *Aspects intérieurs de l'Islam,* Paris, Ed. du Seuil, 1949, pp. 17 ff). History of the tables and stones of the Law in the history of Israel, particularly in the sapiential literature and the psalms (cf. Ps. 118). Place and role of the Decalogue in the New Testament (Mt. 19:17; Mk. 10:19; Lk. 8:20; Mt. 19:17 ff.; Rom. 13:9; Jas. 2:11; etc.); in the Church, for the instruction of the faithful (translations; variations of the classification of the precepts; importance of the Decalogue since St. Augustine); it seems, in fact, that before St. Augustine there was little mention of the Decalogue in speaking to the faithful. In the Gospel, said St. Ambrose, we have a better knowledge of our duties: cf. on this subject Dom Froger, in *Le huitième jour,* Paris, Ed. du Cerf, 1947, pp. 519 ff.; the Decalogue, an outline for examinations of conscience (merits and demerits of this process which makes us consider sin primarily as a disobedience to an external law, and not as a personal failure in goodness and love). Details of the commandments of God. Relations and oppositions in respect to the contemporary religions of the Exodus (cf. Cazelles, op. cit.). Relations between the Decalogue and Natural Law. The precept of the Sabbath. Origins of the Sabbath (Babylonia?); Biblical raisons-d'être for the observance of the Sabbath (Ex. 34:21; Ex. 23:12; Deut. 5:12-15; Ex. 31:13-18; Ex. 35:2-4; the chronology of these texts); history of the promulgation of the Sabbath: cf. Ex. 16:22-30; Num. 15:32-36; Neh. 13:15-22; Num. 38:9; Lev. 23:3); the Sabbath among the first Christians; the Christian transposition of the Sabbath to the "day following the Sabbath": Sunday (cf. *Le huitième jour,* op. cit.).

Commandments of the Church. (Cf. A. Villien, *Histoire des Commandments de l'Église,* Paris, Lecoffre, 1936). Origin, history. The obligation of attendance at Sunday Mass; origin, history and content of the precept. Abstinence from "servile work"; signification, content of the precept (cf. Mgr. Michaud, *Les oeuvres serviles,* in *Le jour du Seigneur,* Paris, Laffont, 1948, pp. 199-239). The precepts of Fasting and Abstinence; origin, content, dispensation, theological signification. The precepts of yearly Confession and Communion. Origin, signification. Can a fervent Christian life be limited to obedience to these precepts? What is the "age of reason" starting from which the 3rd and 4th commandments are obligatory? History of the determinations of the "age of reason." (It is especially notable that in the 13th century the "age of reason" was still compared to the "age of puberty." Cf. St. Thomas Aquinas, IIa IIae, 189, 5). What knowledge of Christian doctrine is necessary and sufficient for First Communion? Upon whom does the instruction devolve? What is the meaning of "Easter Communion"? Duration of the liturgical paschal season and of the canonical paschal season when the precept may still be fulfilled. May we distinguish the letter and the spirit of the precept in this respect? Compare the precept with Jn. 6:53. Money for support of the Church. Biblical foundations of the precept: Mt. 10:10; Lk. 10-7; I Cor. 9:9-14; I Tim. 5:18; can Deut. 18:1-8 be invoked in favor of this precept?

Canon Law. Its source, its content. Theological signification and scope. Cf. *Theology Library,* Vol. I, chap. 4, by Fr. Bouchet.

Civil Law. For a profound understanding and correct analysis of contemporary laws, the study of the ancient sources of Roman Law is best. 1. In the age of the "Compendiums": the *Gregorian Code* (295) and the *Hermogenian Code* (323) so named for the jurisconsults who assembled the imperial laws in these codes; the Theodosian Code (438); the *Novelles* and the *Constitutiones Sirmondianae; the Code of Justinian* (529), the *Digest* or *Pandeucte* (533) and the *Institutes* of Justinian (533). To these compendiums must be added three private collections: the *Epitome Juliani* (554), the *Anthenticum,* and the *Greek Collection.* 2. Next comes the period of the commentaries: we need only mention Jean le Teutonique and the *Glose ordinaire* (Bologna, 1215); Huguccio and the *Summa super Decretis* (Bologna, 488); Guy de Baisio and the *Rosarium* on the decree of Gratian (1300); Vincent the Spaniard and the commentary on the decretals of Gregory IX (beginning of the 13th century); the *Summa aurea* of Henry of Susa on the decretals of Gregory IX (before 1253). 3. Without going further with our investigation, it would be fitting to indicate the influence on civil law of the "Barbarian" laws: Burgundian, Visigothic, Salic, Ripuarian; the laws of the Lombards, Thuringians, Saxons, Frisians, etc.

The first theological doctrines on justice. Let us simply mention the names of the most illustrious authors: St. Thomas Aquinas (*Commentaries* on the books of Aristotle, and IIa, IIae, q. 57-122). Francis of Vitoria, O.P., bachelor in 1516, then doctor of the faculty of Theology of Paris in 1522, professor at Valladolid from

1523 to 1526, then at Salamanca from 1526 to 1546. (*Commentaries* on the *Summa Theologiae; Relectiones* containing the *De Potestate civili,* the *De Potestate Ecclesiae relectio prior* and the *De Potestate Ecclesiae relectio posterior,* the *De Potestate Ecclesiae et Concilii,* the *De Indis* and the *De jure belli,* 1539). Vitoria is considered as the founder of international law. Dominic de Soto, by turns professor at Salamanca and confessor to Charles XV (*De justitia et jure* published in 1553–1554).

The basic philosophical doctrines of theological treatises on justice. We shall only mention those which are set forth in Plato's *Republic,* Aristotle's *Ethics* and *Politics* and Cicero's *Treatise on Laws.*

Morality and social doctrines. Does the Church have a social doctrine? an economic doctrine? Biblical and theological foundations; encyclicals which refer to them. Can the Church accommodate herself to all social doctrines (limits of this accommodation)?

Merits and demerits of a "Catholic political party"; of temporal organizations with Catholic labels.

Church and State. Define the proper powers of the Church and those of the State in Church-State relations. Can the State legislate in religious matters (forbidding certain cults, certain gatherings, certain practices, processions, sermons; order certain kinds of worship such as military funerals in church; compel priests to fulfill certain obligations toward the nation (military service), or toward the political régime (fidelity to republicanism) or toward a particular cause ("the peace movement")?

Questions of social or political morality. Theology of *property.* Biblical foundations of the law of property (cf. Étienne Gilson, *Un gomor de manne,* in *La Vie intellectuelle,* Nov., 1946, pp. 6-19; and A. Feuillet, *Les riches intendants du Christ,* Lk. 16:1-13, in *Recherches de science religieuse,* Jan., March, 1947, pp. 30-54. Other articles could be mentioned which, however, are easily found in reference books and manuals; we limit ourselves to these two studies which are particularly suggestive). How can we account for private property in Christianity? It seems worth while for theology to hold to an argument put forth in the documents of the magisterium according to which the right to property is necessary as based upon the requirements of the human family: an institution founded by God, which can only safeguard its divinely endowed autonomy by family property.

Theology of *authority* and of *political obedience*. What is a legitimate authority? What is a legitimate government? To what point
is one obliged to obey legitimate authority? The theology of conscientious objection and of disobedience to abusive political power.
In what measure can a government ignore public opinion? Can it
"form" and "direct" opinion by the press, radio, television, publicity, and all the means at its disposal? What is the government's
role in an election? Is it always better for it to abstain (either from
directing opinion or from counselling, informing and instructing)?
What is a "democracy of free men"? Can a democracy be properly
called a democracy in which men freely elect but are incapable
either of informing themselves or exercising judgment (lack of culture)? Is it correct to consider all the citizens of a nation as equals?
Can the law establish a hierarchical difference between some men
and others (for example, in giving the right to vote)? Between men
and women? Between those who have fulfilled their military service
and those who have not served in the armed forces? Between the
illiterate and those who have been successful in some examination?
Between those who pay a certain amount of taxes and those who
pay less (viz: the qualifying basis of the right to vote under Louis-
Philippe)? In a word, if the citizenry of a country is defined by the
condition of liberty, does the government have the power to decide
whether a man is humanly an "adult" or whether he is still humanly
a "minor"? By what criteria? Does the law which gives the right to
vote to men and women starting with age 21, without any distinction
of culture, wealth or social responsibilities, constitute a sufficient
approximation to justice? Does the State itself have the duty to instruct the citizens and train them for their civic responsibilities? Or
should it merely create free organisms for civic training? Is instruction, in a general way, a strict *right* of the citizen? What is the "will
of the people"? How shall we define it? Can we in justice distinguish
major peoples and "minor peoples"? In the name of what criteria?
What is a nation (distinguish between "people" and "nation")?
Can a nation with definite frontiers only admit a single "people"
within its territory, or a single race, or at least make a distinction
between peoples and peoples? On the basis of what criteria can we
consider that an invading "people" is an "occupant" or that it is one
of the "national" peoples: for example, can we distinguish, in this
respect, among the inhabitants of France, the descendants of the
Greeks, the Latins, the Franks, the Teutons, the Bretons, the Nor-

mans, etc.? May we distinguish among the inhabitants of North Africa the descendants of the Berbers, the Kabyles, etc., and the descendants of the Romans, Arabs, the French, Italians, and Spaniards? Among the inhabitants of South Africa may we distinguish between the Boers and the Negros, etc.? Can a nation lay claim to the rights which it used to have in the past (for example, in a territory which it has lost)? What is the criterion of the "continuity" of rights of a nation (viz. continuity of rights between the France of Hugh Capet and the France of today, now that there is neither identity of territories nor identity of political régimes)?

Morality of *taxes*. Rights and duties of the State; the limits of its rights. Rights and duties of the tax-payer. Can he escape from part of his taxes under pretext of not using certain public services (airports, public schools of the State, etc.)? In a country where fiscal fraud is quite generalized on certain points, must the tax-payer make his declarations according to the written rule or according to custom? The moral nature of fiscal fraud, and of fraud in matters of customs.

Morality of public *tolerance*. Should the State forbid by law every public offense against truth (for example in the Press), and every social fault? Primacy of liberty or primacy of truth? Tolerance or intolerance? May a Christian who has political responsibilities in certain circumstances encourage or promulgate a law creating "licensed brothels"? Can a law "tolerate" evil customs? Can the laws "overlook" certain public shortcomings?

The sin of *omission* in matters of justice or charity. How shall we determine it? Its gravity. Can or should the law punish certain faults of omission (viz., not helping some person in danger), and certain abstentions (viz., not voting)?

Abortion. Is abortion always a sin? Can the law allow and regulate it? Can the physician perform an abortion that is requested of him? Show how abortion is opposed to charity and to the institution of the family.

Morality in *examinations* and *competitions* (Medicine, Administration, etc.). Can the "recommendation," on the part of the student, on the part of the professors, be justified? In what way, and in what circumstances? (Viz. recruitment half by competition, half by co-optation.)

Questions of international morality. What is "national sovereignty"? Foundations and relativity of this sovereignty (from the

point of view of history and from the point of view of the Gospel).
When may it be said that there is an impairment of national sov-
erignty? Legitimacy of a defensive war? Does a nation have rights
and duties in regard to other nations? May a nation colonize another nation or another territory? In the name of what principles?
Rights and duties of a protecting nation and of a nation taken into
protectorship or under mandate? Must the "war criminal" always
be punished? By what tribunal? In the name of what authority? Is it
just to seek for war criminals only among the members of the enemy
nation? Is the "reprisal" just? In what measure can the term "collective responsibility" be allowed in justice? For example can we
consider all the "occupants" of a country as equivalently responsible
for the crime of invasion? Until what moment, if it is universally
recognized that beginning from a certain time they are assimilated
by the country (viz. Franks, Normans, etc., into "France"; Turks
into "Turkey," etc.)? Organization of the nations. May an organization of nations in justice refuse to admit a nation into its midst?
Can it establish a hierarchy among the nations? Can it judge nations which are not federated with it? Division of property. Does a
country with a high "national income" have duties towards under-
nourished nations or those which are simply less rich than itself?
Does a nation in which human culture is quite wide-spread have
duties towards uncivilized peoples: the sending of technicians? professors? physicians? cultural missions? Must the Church, through
her missionaries, undertake all these efforts for the instruction and
development of mankind as long as the civil organisms fail to do so?

Morality of trials and judgments. Do men have the right to make
an accused person "confess" if he does not wish to say anything?
Are the following procedures legitimate: blows, fear, degradation,
Penthotal, Acetone, etc.? Can they be justified? May the judge ask
the accused to make his "self-accusation," his public confession,
either orally or in writing? Or to disgrace himself publicly? Can
public opinion constitute an offense (an offense of opinion)? Does
opinion have limits beyond which the law may intervene? In an
"offense" not foreseen by the law, who has authority to judge? Who
has the capacity to determine the Natural Law when it is evidently
unpublished? (Trials of Nuremberg, Japan?) A judgment in which
the judge, the accusers, lawyers, and witnesses were all of the same
party, or the same side (judgments of "collaborators" by members
of the Resistance) would be considered just or unjust? Legitimacy

of punishments: blows, injuries, certain prisons, concentration camps; legitimacy of penal time? What are the duties of a government even towards the condemned? What are the "experiments" which it does not have the right to perform?

Theology of labor (of the world of labor). Rights of directors, technicians, inventors. Rights of the workers. Rights of Capital. Duties of all these. Moral value of liberalism, of managerialism. Social security of the workers: do they have a *right* to "security" (which kind?), to gratuitous care, education and housing? Trade unions. When may one decide that there is a duty to form a union? or a duty not to form one? Should a Christian always join with Christians, or is it sometimes preferable for him to unite with non-Christians for the defense of temporal interests? or the defense of liberties?

Morality of business and of economic exchanges. We shall here limit ourselves to asking the following three questions:

1. Is business uniquely a matter of justice or also of charity? In commerce, is it always a matter of a paying and a paying back in kind, that is to say, is it always a question of an exchange in which one gives as much as the other? Consider for example: the Marshall Plan (nothing in exchange); the act of a patron who establishes a university by a gratuitous gift; the fact that I pay taxes for the maintenance of highways although I do not have an automobile. In the economy are there no other elements than what is owing which ought morally to be considered?

2. Are all economic structures compatible with morality, or are certain structures incompatible? Are the feudal régime, the capitalist régime and the socialist régime all equally compatible with morality, the only question being that men act differently in each? A régime of integral organized planning (authoritarian attribution of all goods, including consumer goods) would, or would not be compatible with Christian morality? Inversely, is a completely capitalist régime, in which each person makes the race for the greatest monetary gain, compatible with Christian morality? Among economic and even political régimes, which one is compatible with Christian morality? Which is more or less favorable?

3. What is an illicit profit? What is a theft? Such a question did not have much meaning formerly, but in the present conjuncture it has become a burning question.

That which, in effect, characterizes the structures of today is "imperfect competition." Merchandise of various kinds, equal by nature, is differentiated: there is no real competition between the macaroni of one brand and the very similar macaroni of another brand, or between the case that bears one label and the case that bears another, etc., because one firm or one brand makes the weight of its advertising and of its monopolizing power weigh upon its products. In this hypothesis, actually frequent, of a monopoly or a cartel, there is no longer any "free competition."

The hypothesis of free competition was in effect the following: There is a very large number of manufacturers (or merchants) and not any of them can foresee what is going to happen—prices go up, and everyone sells; prices go down, and everyone waits. But no one can have a direct influence upon prices. It is obvious that this hypothesis no longer works for a firm like Péchiney, for instance, which by itself could radically change the French aluminum market by increasing its production considerably. To the degree that a company has acquired some economic monopoly, it is capable of influencing the market unilaterally. Competition cannot be defined or judged outside the network of relations, forces and powers in which it is involved.

It is evident that a monopoly of power may entail an increase of profit which is not necessarily justified by the risk and the labor of the entrepreneur, but by his simple *power*, because there is no equal competitor (Coca-Cola in the U.S.A., the Azaitbatsus in Japan). This raises the question of the "transfers" (of money or merchandise) therefore: a man (or a firm) acquires the power of arrogating to himself automobiles, lands, buildings, numerous employees, not because he has rendered greater public services, but because he is *powerful*. Theology ought to examine the moral nature of these "transfers," which are justified by some and considered as "thefts" by others, although they do not enter into the ancient categories of theft.

Example: A great enterprise makes enormous profits. Will it distribute them as a bonus over wages? or as supplementary shares to the stockholders? The directors decide (partly to escape taxation) to construct a sumptuous administration building and to acquire another enterprise. Do the directors have the right to arrogate to themselves the profits of this new enterprise acquired with money which normally ought to have been distributed? However, there was no "theft" in this, and the operation is legal.

Another example, likewise similar. The self-financing of the enterprise. It is certain that business enterprises should only count upon their own investments when there is no other credit. But to what point is this self-financing legitimate? Is there not an unjust transfer when all the excess profits of the business go constantly into new investments and the wage-earners and stockholders receive nothing additional? Don't the latter deserve something, *at least in charity* if not in strict justice? And is there still full justice when the good of charity is no longer respected? Is it not more just, for example, to construct apartments for the workers than sumptuous buildings for the administration?

Consequence: the transformation of the structures, the fruit of this imperfect competition, means that the redistribution of credit is no longer done normally. If we want our investments always to produce a profit, we would end by ruining our neighbor. If, for example, the United States only gave money to those who can pay interest, Europe would ruin itself and would no longer exist economically. (The goods of production most often elude the reach of the people who have the greatest need of them.) If the United States therefore gives money gratuitously to Europeans or Asiatics, it is because the mechanism of automatic equilibrium no longer functions. Distribution must be made in a different way; the present tendency is to give gratuitous credit (Colin Clarck). The interest of the capital consequently is not imposed; this is a mode of redistribution which is essentially a function of a determined structure. It seems that men are returning more and more, mutatis mutandis, to the ancient position of the Church on usury.

Beyond all these problems, in business, as in industry and politics, it would be necessary to envisage a theology of human risk. A business leader, for example, is not dispensed from having audacity, or from risking a fortune in an expansion or in new enterprises, because he must have primary concern for the human problems involved, and for the housing of his workers and the "justice" of his uses of money. To make a leap forward is sometimes the only way of assuring a better solution of human problems, although it is always a risk. Elaborate a theology of risk based on the film "The Sound Barrier."

We shall not give any bibliography on these problems of economic morality whose data are in full evolution. Specialists will derive advantage from consulting the Institut des Sciences Économiques Appliquées (ISEA, 35, bul. des Capucines, Paris IIe) directed by M. François Perroux, which does not neglect to consider the human, and therefore moral incidence of economic problems.

Complete these *Reflections* by those which were made after the chapters on *Law*, Volume III, and *Prudence*, Volume IV.

BIBLIOGRAPHIE

Sur le droit et la vertu de justice:

Saint Thomas d'Aquin, *La justice,* Tome 1, trad. de M.-S. Gillet, notes de J.-T. Delos, tome 2, trad. et notes de C. Spicq; tome 3, trad. et notes de C. Spicq; Paris, Éd. de la Revue des J., 1932, 1934, 1935.

G. Renard, *Le droit, la justice et la volonté,* Paris, Tenin, 1924.—*Le droit, la logique et le bon sens,* ibid., 1925.—*Le droit, l'ordre et la raison,* ibid., 1927.

L. Lachance, *Le concept de droit selon Aristote et saint Thomas d'Aquin,* Ottawa, Éd. du Lévrier, 1948.

Th. Delos, *La théorie de l'institution,* Paris, Arch. de l'hist. du droit et de sociologie juridique, 1931.

M.-S. Gillet, *Conscience chrétienne et justice sociale,* Paris, 1922.

O. Lottin, *Le droit naturel chez saint Thomas d'Aquin et ses prédécesseurs,* Bruges, Beyaert, 1931.

"Doctrine sociale" de l'Église.

C. Rutten, *La doctrine sociale de l'Église,* Juvisy, Éd. du Cerf, 1932.

A. Lemonnyer, J. Tonneau, R. Troude, *Précis de sociologie,* Marseille, Publiroc, 1934.

B. Welty, *Herders Sozialkatechismus. Ein Worteruch der katholischen Sozialethik in Frage und Antwort,* Fribourg, Herder, 1951.

R. Linhardt, *Die Sozialprinzipien des hl. Thomas von Aquin,* Fribourg, 1932.

R. Geysen, *Bibliographie internationale de droit social, droit du travail,* Bruxelles, Éd. Érasme, 1950.

Sur la politique: P. Janet, *Histoire de la science politique dans ses rapports avec la morale,* T. 1 et 2, Paris, Alcan, 1903.

F.-M. Stratmann, *Jésus-Christ et l'État,* trad. P. Lorson, Tournai, Castermann, 1952.

M. Defourny, *Aristote, Études sur la "Politique",* Paris, Beauchesne, 1932.

Propriété, travail, doctrines économiques.

G. Renard, *Propriété privée et propriété humaine,* Paris, 1925 (reproduit dans *La théorie de l'Institution, essai d'ontologie juridique,* Paris, Recueil Sirey, 1930).

Ch. Calippe, *Le caractère social de la propriété d'après la tradition judéo-chrétienne,* in *Semaine sociale de France,* 6e session (Bordeaux) 1909, pp. 99 ss.

J. Maritain, *Du régime temporel des biens et de la liberté,* Paris, Descl. de Br., 1933.

C. Spicq, *L'aumône, obligation de justice ou de charité?* in *Mélanges Mandonnet,* I, Paris, Vrin, 1930, pp. 245-264.

Sur la propriété, on lira surtout le très bel article *Propriété,* de J. Tonneau, Art. *Propriété et Salaire* dans le *Dictionnaire de théologie catholique.*

J. Haessle, *Le travail,* Trad. E. Borne et P. Linn, Paris, Desclée De Br., 1933.

X.-Z. Caracciolo, *Essai d'un code chrétien du travail.* Textes pontificaux disposés sous forme de code, Beyrouth, Impr. cath., 1950.

M. Rocha, *Travail et salaire à travers la scolastique,* Paris, Desclée De Br., 1933.

J. Tonneau, H. Denis, etc. *Travail et salaire,* Paris, Éd. du Cerf, 1943.

G. Friedmann, *Problèmes humains du machinisme industriel,* Paris, N. R. F.

V. Brants, *Esquisse des théories économiques proposées par les écrivains des XIIe et XIVe s.,* Paris, Lecoffre, 1895.

D. Villey, *Petite histoire des doctrines économiques,* Paris, P. U. F.

R. Gonnard, *Histoire des doctrines économiques de Platon à Quesnay,* Paris, Lib. Valois, 1928.

R. Gonnard, *Histoire des doctrines économiques,* Paris, Libr. gén. de droit et de jurisprudence, 1947.

A. Dauphin-Meunier, *La doctrine économique de l'Église,* Paris, Nouv., Éd. lat., 1950.

F. Perroux, *De l'avarice des nations à une économie du genre humain* (Remarquable étude, in *La Vie Intellectuelle,* Nov. 1952, pp. 5-35).

A. Sandoz, *La notion de juste prix,* in *Revue thomiste,* XLV (1939), pp. 285-305.

É. Janssens, *Le juste prix, Liège.*

H. Garnier, *L'idée de juste prix chez les théologiens et les canonistes du moyen-âge,* Paris, 1900.

P. Boven, *Le prix normal,* Paris, Payot, 1924.

A. Lamarche, *La justice et le prêt à intérêt,* Coll. *Études rel.,* Liège.

Respect de l'honneur, de la réputation. de la vie d'autrui.

A. Gay, *L'honneur, sa place dans la morale,* Fribourg (Suisse), Impr. S. Paul, 1913.

A.-M. de Sobradillo, *La procréation et la stérilisation au point de vue du droit naturel,* Paris, 1932.

Nous renvoyons également, sans les citer ici, aux articles de dictionnaires et de revues (spécialement ceux des *Cahiers Laënnec*)

BIBLIOGRAPHY

Bernard, George C., C.S.C., *The Morality of Prizefighting.* Washington, C.U. Press, 1952.

Cornell, Francis J., C.SS.R., *Morals in Politics and Professions.* Westminster, Md., The Newman Bookshop, 1946.

Cronin, John F., S.S., *Catholic Social Principles.* Milwaukee, The Bruce Publishing Company, 1950.

Davis, Henry, S.J., *Moral and Pastoral Theology,* Vol. III, pp. 141-199, 255-409. London, Sheed and Ward, 1941.

Demant, V. A., *Theology of Society.* London, Faber and Faber, 1947.

————, *The Just Price. An Outline of the Medieval Doctrine and an Examination of Its Possible Equivalent Today.* London, St. Christ. Mov. Press, 1930.

Dorszynski, Julius A., *Catholic Teaching About the Morality of Falsehood.* Washington, C.U. Press, 1948.

Fanfani, Amintore, *Catholicism, Protestantism, and Capitalism.* New York, Sheed and Ward, Inc., 1935.

Farrell, Walter, O.P., *A Companion to the Summa,* Vol. III, pp. 165-246, 303-356. New York, Sheed and Ward, 1940.

Gilson, Etienne, *The Church Speaks to the Modern World: The Social Teachings of Leo XIII.* Garden City, N. Y., Doubleday & Company, Inc. (Image Books), 1954.

Glover, William K., S.M., *Artificial Insemination among Human Beings.* Washington, C.U. Press, 1948.

Hughes, Philip, *The Popes' New Order.* New York, The Macmillan Company, 1944.

McDonald, William J., *The Social Value of Property according to St. Thomas Aquinas.* Washington, C.U. Press, 1939.

McHugh, John A., O.P., and Callan, Charles J., O.P., *Moral Theology, A Complete Course,* Vol. II, pp. 30-276, 402-464. New York, Joseph Wagner, Inc., 1930.

McLean, Donald A., *The Morality of the Strike.* New York, P. J. Kenedy & Sons, 1921.

Miller, Raymond J., C.SS.R., *Forty Years After: Pius XI and the Social Order.* St. Paul, Radio Replies Press, 1947.

Regan, Robert E., O.S.A., *Professional Secrecy in the Light of Moral Principles.* Washington, Augustinian Press, 1943.

Ryan, John A., *Distributive Justice.* New York, The Macmillan Company, 1922.

Ryan, John A., and Husslein, Joseph, S.J., *The Church and Labor.* New York, The Macmillan Company, 1920.

Sheedy, Charles E., C.S.C., *The Christian Virtues,* pp. 169-250. Notre Dame, Ind., University of Notre Dame Press, 1949.

Suhard, Card. Emmanuel, *The Church Today.* Chicago, Fides Publishers Association, 1953.

Sullivan, Joseph V., *Catholic Teaching on the Morality of Euthanasia.* Washington, C.U. Press, 1949.

Toner, Jerome L., *The Closed Shop.* Washington, American Council on Public Affairs, 1942.

Crane, P., S.J., "Commutative Justice, Social Justice, and the Family Living Wage," *Christus Rex,* 8:131-137, Apr '54.

Cronin, John F., S.S., "The Message of *Quadragesimo Anno* Today," *Social Order,* 6:2-12, Ja '56.

Farrell, Walter, O.P., "No Place For Rain: Is our society subsisting without either the vice of injustice or the virtue of justice?" *Thomist,* 12:397-424, Oct '49.

Fitzpatrick, J. P., S.J., "Encyclicals and the United States," *Catholic Mind,* 53:1-12, Ja '55.

Kirk, Russell, "Social Justice and Mass Culture," *Review of Politics,* 438-451, Oct '54.

Newman, J., "Theology of Social Action," *Irish Theological Quarterly,* 22:31-48, Ja '55.

Regan, Robert E., O.S.A., and McCartney, John T., "Professional Secrecy and Privileged Communications," *Catholic Lawyer,* 3-14, Ja '56.

Wright, Bishop John J., "Crime and Punishment," *Catholic Mind,* 47:193-199, Apr '49.

Chapter VI

THE VIRTUE OF RELIGION

by A. I. Mennessier, O.P.

Chapter VI

THE VIRTUE OF RELIGION

1. RELIGION, A MORAL VIRTUE

It may seem strange that the study of the virtue whose object is to govern our relations with God should not come until after the very human virtue of justice. But this order, traditional since St. Thomas Aquinas, is meant to indicate, not the rank of this virtue, for in reality it is the most eminent of all the moral virtues, but the kind of duties and the nature of the obligation which it implies. Relatively to God it is certainly a form of justice. And the Hellenistic and Ciceronian origin of such a classification matters little, after all.[1] It is significant that in placing religion among the moral virtues and in the wake of justice, St. Thomas and the subsequent theological tradition emphasize important psychological features. Certainly our relations with God, in the supernatural order, are established primarily by the theological virtues. In the light of faith we depend upon God in order to attain the supreme good which He is Himself and for whom our hope yearns; better yet, by charity we enter into friendly companionship with the divine Persons, and our whole life is led by this movement of love. But we must still measure ourselves, creatures that we are, with this God, who, by introducing us into the mystery of His own life, only increases our dependence upon Him. St. Augustine spoke of the worship which we render by faith, hope and charity. This means that faith completely enlightens us in regard to our duties as creatures, and that the filial movement of love which turns us toward God makes us render them with greater perfection. This also means that the theological acts themselves not only will inspire the homage which we render to God, but will be a matter of choice for it. In fact, the theological virtues and the virtue of religion will always mingle their activities whenever it is a question of our relations with God. If we specify the various motives of these virtues, it is because this distinction is not useless for this self-culture in which the virtuous life consists. The distinguishing of the virtues corresponds not only to the various mo-

[1] Cf. D.T.C., art. *Religion* (vertu de), col. 2, 307.

tivations of our different duties, but also, and perhaps especially, to special reactions in the cultivation of ourselves. To understand that our relations with God imply not only the reception of primary truth in our minds, and the confident longing of our desire and fervent spontaneity of love, but likewise the judicious rectification of a moral virtue, is to assure their genuine equilibrium. A debt intervenes here which it is our duty to pay.

2. OUR DEBT TOWARD GOD

If it is now a matter of justice, we must agree, however, that it does not consist in rendering the equivalent of what we have received. There can be no equalization of the debt incurred: *Quid retribuam Domino pro omnibus quae retribuit mihi? . . .* We have received everything from Him, even our being. This kind of justice is one which is achieved relatively to persons whose beneficence implies for us a dependent situation. The good turn establishes the debt. But the "adjustment" consists in recognizing the superiority which such gifts imply in regard to ourselves. The first duty is then one of respect, of which the marks are measured by the excellence denoted by the influence that was beneficial to us. But this homage implies a practical subjection also, which places us under the orders and in the service of this beneficent superiority. St. Thomas Aquinas who principally analyzes these duties in speaking of virtues which govern our relations with parents and those who govern us, sums them up in these two words: *Reverentia et obsequium* (cf. IIa IIae, q. 102, a. 2), reverence and service.

Therefore, we need only measure the excellence of the divine blessings which establish our debt in order to understand the unique character of the respect and submission which we must show toward God. It is indeed this "singular respect" of which Bérulle speaks, and which sees in God the transcendence of the very Being, the source of our existence. God is the Creator, and He is also the Lord. He governs this universe which He created. This divine dominion over the creature participates in the creative transcendence. From this follows a submission, a will to enter into the insights of God, which doubtless will be found in every moral virtue but which it will appertain to the virtue of religion to realize the fundamental disposition within us.

As we are in perpetual emanation from God and dependence upon Him, writes Bérulle, let us be in perpetual elevation and relation to Him. . . . This is the right use of the soul which binds itself voluntarily to God by the exercise of piety; but it is necessarily bound to God by the condition of its being and by the effects of the power which God is constantly exercising upon it.

Established upon these essential, divine gifts which are the existence and government of the universe, our debt of religion is measured not only by the creative transcendence and the sovereign authority of Providence, but also and especially by the gratuitousness of the love which is thus exercised in our regard. Supernatural Revelation, by revealing to us the secret of this love of God for His creature only therefore motivates our religious debt in a more complete and more perfect way, while also encouraging the response of our charity. As a supernatural virtue, religion will then appear to us, before all else, under the aspects of an act of thanksgiving. *Ante omnia gratias agite,* says St. Paul. And the bond of charity, the theological virtue, and of religion will appear very close. It is thus, moreover, with the bonds of love and justice in the virtue of filial devotion. Whether it beholds in God His creative paternity, or that paternity of adoption in which the first is completed and perfected, it requires first of all that we render love for love. But it also demands that, becoming aware of the transcendence of the creative and redemptive love, we unite the respect of our adoration and the homage of our filial submission to the spontaneous impulse of our hearts. Our duties as creatures continue even unto the call to intimacy with the divine Persons. Let us even say that they have increased through the revelation of the "exceeding great love" of which St. Paul speaks. Our impotence to equal God's love for us naturally finds expression in adoration.

But this will also enable us to better understand how our religion is dependent upon the religion of Christ. The Bérullian school liked to see in Him "the mediator of our religion" (Olier). But let us simply say that if the virtue of religion has all the features of filial devotion, it is in Christ's soul that it will find its perfect example. Our whole supernatural life is a participation in His filial life. But in His holy Humanity, Our Lord had more than all others, in coming to pay our debt, the sense of the rights of God. These words of the Gospel: *"Pater Juste—Pater Sancte"* have an immense depth for our religious meditation. Our prayers and our devotion must be joined to His prayer and His sacrifice.

3. THE SENSE OF THE DIVINE TRANSCENDENCE

What we have just said regarding the religious attitude of respect and service which our situation as creatures before God makes binding, must be completed by a brief analysis of the particular sentiment which it will appertain to the virtue of religion to cultivate and utilize: the sense of the sacred, the instinct of reverence which is evoked in those who have an insight of the majesty of God.

Modern religious psychology has been very attentive to it, sometimes making it the essence of religious sentiment, or the original starting-point of religion itself. From the studies of a Rudolph Otto, for example, we can at least lay hold of certain features of psychological description. In the face of the *"mysterium tremendum"* which is, according to Otto, with the *"fascinosum"* the first aspect of the category of the sacred, there awakens within man what he calls the "awareness of being a creature." "Kreaturgefühl." The "reverentia" which a St. Thomas Aquinas describes is definitely this awareness of the creature before the inimitable transcendence *"quando in consideratione tantae altitudinis homo in propriam resilit parvitatem"* (III Sent., d. 34, 9, 3, a. q. 4). An act of this kind, which his theology attributes to the gift of fear in its purest form, continues even in the beatific vision of God. "There will always remain an act of man beholding God as inimitable (*arduum*—But how shall we translate this word? An infinite distance, he will say elsewhere. . . . God Himself possessed in the vision remains the inaccessible, the wholly Other . . .). Fear will therefore disappear in so far as it is a dread of possible separation, but will remain in the act of admiring and revering this *arduum,* which is what happens when, considering such loftiness, one huddles trembling in one's own littleness . . ." In the very soul of Christ our theology recognizes the presence of this reverential sentiment of which the Old Testament is full. The nearness of God rouses it. Familiarity with Him should not eliminate it. If, in Christian psychology, another gift of the Holy Spirit, *piety,* seems at first to emphasize the feeling of a tender intimacy (*dulcis et devotus affectus ad Patrem*) it is always a question of a respectful tenderness. It is the proper act of the gift of piety to "revere God in a filial sentiment." But, on the other hand, this very fear to which is attributed this great respect for God which we mentioned above, bears the name of filial fear—or better still, to designate the tenderness of an instinctive reverence which remains in the highest divine intimacy, it is called with St. Augustine *"Timor castus . . .* a wife's modesty" (IIa IIae, q. 19, a. 11).

It remains that this sentiment of the holiness of God, of His authority as a creator and as Providence, will be the very basis of this

Does not this Mussulman with his humble and suppliant gesture remind us of those "strangers" whom our Lord met: the Roman and pagan centurion about whom He said: "Amen I say to you, I have not found such great faith in Israel" (Mt. 8:10); the pagan woman of the Syro-Phoenician race: to whom He said: "O woman, great is thy faith! Let it be done to thee as thou wilt" (Mt. 15:28).

In these attitudes of adoration, the methods of recollection and prayer which these different religions command, we must not be afraid to appreciate what is good and to recognize that sometimes our piety expresses itself with less religion: we whose faith has received everything! How is it that in our assemblies of the faithful ordinarily so quiet, so passive and distracting, we recoil to the point of shame from positions of prayer? From the beginning it was not so.

An Arab in prayer: one of the gestures of "calat" (ritual prayer).

psychology which the virtue of religion must develop within us, in order that the homage which it induces us to render to God may not be a vain formalism. Our debt is measured by the transcendent eminence of the One who is Being itself and the first love. We must have an ardent feeling in order that our attitude may be truly that of a creature. "The whole external worship of God," says St. Thomas Aquinas, "is principally ordered to foster in man reverence toward God." "*Totus exterior cultus Dei, ad hoc praecipue ordinatur ut homines Deum in reverentiam habeant*" (Ia IIae, q. 102, a. 4). We shall return to this subject a little further on by showing the role attributed to the sacred in worship, and the religious usage which we make of this sentiment of the holiness of God in great acts like the vow, the oath, the adjuration. We must first describe the great interior acts which are proper to the virtue of religion: devotion and prayer.

4. THE ESSENTIAL ACT OF THE VIRTUE OF RELIGION

It is the *devotio*, which our English (vernacular) word devotion translates very badly, which has acquired in current spiritual language a meaning quite different from what it had in the strong theology of the Middle Ages.

"Devotio," says St. Thomas, "comes from *devovere*, and *devoti* designates those who, in some way, consecrate their own person to God in a total subjection." Devotion is not therefore here understood as a simple taste for the things of God, but as the profoundest and most absolute homage of the creature to his Creator. In the face of God, we can only surrender ourselves, and becoming aware of our belonging to Him, at the foundation of being, we must deliberately yield our will to Him. It is the whole man who thus gives himself to God, for the will is man completely. "Willingness," "Attachment," the Bérullians will say. Some will likewise say "Abandonment" in the sense which Bossuet at least gives to this word when he writes, "O my God, help me find that act, so vast, so simple, which commits all that I am to You, which unites me to all that You are . . . This is the act of abandonment. This act commits the whole man to God." Thomist theology, by using the word devotion, intends to emphasize still more strongly perhaps the character of a voluntary gift, of the active and determined submission of such an act, and its aspect of religious homage. St. Thomas defines it admirably in a few words: *habere promptam voluntatem*, to have one's will in readiness for everything that concerns the honor of God. Devotion is therefore the generator of all the ulterior acts by which "the honor and service of God" will be accomplished on our part, itself already being the homage of our will. These very acts, whether they are acts of worship properly so called, or acts of the other moral virtues inspired by religion, will only have religious meaning through this devotion. They will also receive from it that quality of "promptitude" which we here make a specific feature and a kind of property of devotion. Profound psychology: *promptus* comes from *promere*, to push forward, and this expresses very well the attitude of anyone who, conscious of owing everything to God, holds himself in readiness to answer "Present!" as soon as the divine glory is at stake. But this "promptitude" especially expresses the totality of the homage which the will makes of itself to God.

Nothing must hinder this profundity when, for example, it is a question of a choice of means, the movement of the will. God desires it without reserve. But this availability itself communicates a kind of eagerness, a nuance of joyful cheerfulness in the subsequent acts to which the divine service is related. In noting this joyful aspect of devotion, which likewise pertains to the great motives of faith which inspire it, and to the hope and charity which sustain it, our theology seems to have indicated one of the features of Christian worship. And when Christ made the Eucharist the center of our worship, did He not at the same time make it the legacy of His joy?

5. PRAYER

If devotion, understood as we have defined it, realizes the essential attitude of religion, subjacent to all the other religious acts which it inspires, prayer then appears as a great spiritual act in which the dependence of the soul in regard to creative Providence is expressed in a fundamental way. In our theology we understand it formally as the prayer of petition. To consider it as an act of the virtue of religion is to give it all its greatness, as we shall see.

In truth, several definitions of Christian prayer are given. The most common: an elevation of the soul to God, *elevatio mentis*, describes in its entirety a spiritual act in which the activity of the theological virtues seems at first to have more place than the virtue of religion properly so called. Whenever we specify that in this elevation toward God our desire is expressed and our petition is formulated, the latter certainly seems at first to be inspired by these same theological virtues. Faith lifts our soul toward God, our desire rises toward Him like an appeal of our charity which hope sustains. But we have previously said that the virtue of religion cannot therefore fail to be exercised as soon as we enter into relations with God. And it then appears that this conversation with Him, which is prayer, will only find the right tone by attaching itself to this virtue which places us before God in the position of creatures. Furthermore, the prayer of petition will appear as an essential act of the creature recognizing his dependence and making acknowledgment to God of the service which he owes Him.

To understand this fully, we must place ourselves in the grandiose perspectives in which St. Thomas places himself when he treats of prayer, the act of a reasonable creature, associated as a secondary providence with the primary Providence of God, and subordinating himself to His eternal designs in order to contribute, in this very way, to their realization. Prayer, we then say, is an act of the practical reason. Understand by this statement that we make use, in our petition, of that faculty which makes for our nobility, giving us mastery over ourselves and power to govern our action. When we have done this, we recognize its limits and we declare ourselves dependent upon an order of sovereign realizations which is wholly dependent on the divine omnipotence and wisdom. But prayer, the token of our dependence, and the homage of the creature, becomes therefore, by the efficacy which God accords to it, the instrument of our will in serving His glory and in cooperating with the designs of His wisdom.

Our prayers obtain, consequently, that which eternal Providence, the source of all order in the world, has decided to realize by means of them. These great considerations which endeavor to throw some light on the mystery of the efficacy of prayer, by showing how this human process interposed into the providential plan, also brings to light the religious quality of such an act.

Homage, as we have said, of the secondary providence which we are, to the primary Providence, prayer first of all requires that we be conscious not only of our limitations and our needs—this is only a starting-point—but concerned about the accomplishment, beyond our own acts and by means of them, of the eternal issues which are the work of God. "The pure beggar does not pray," wrote Henri Bremond, intending by this remark to designate what he called the theocentric nature of prayer. And certainly the order of petitions in the Our Father is definitely this one, as all the commentators have noted.

Prayer likewise, bringing us into harmony with the providential order, must keep an exact appreciation of the latter, in regard to created means. The virtue of religion must here prevent us from tempting God. The tempting of God is, according to our theology, a sin against religion because it disregards the order of divine wisdom which requires that secondary causes should be in their proper place. Prayer is one of them. But it does not take the place of action. It prolongs it at the point where action fails. And doubtless it should accompany it also even when we are masters of our achievements. This is because there is always, in reality, an exceeding of our powers in the humblest of our actions. Each of our acts is interposed in a design of totality of which God is the master. It is described in the eternal in which it has its final issue. The truly religious soul is conscious of this. This point of insertion of the most personal direction of our life into the sovereign design of God is prayer. All the more so as the essential object of Christian prayer, according to St. Augustine, is the *vita beata*. Everything tends toward this, and nothing finally is obtained unless it leads us toward it.

It is within the same perspectives that the intercession of the saints is understood. Whoever prays, by joining with the order of the eternal wisdom, at the same time enters into harmony with a whole spiritual universe. The prayer of the saints, who have entered into eternity, appears to theologians as one of the great active forces which lead the world towards this blessed goal where they have already arrived. The prayer of the saints prolongs our own, or better still, it is our prayer which should find support in theirs: an act of "*dulia*" on our part, in regard to the homage which we thus render to their glory and to the beneficent influence which their eminent charity deserves. But it is an act of *religion* in reference to the requirement of a prayer which, rising toward God, is harmonized with the whole universe that He governs. However secret prayer may be, it is never a purely individual act, being by its very nature a surpassing of ourselves. It is, within us, to echo the saying of St. Paul, that call, that groaning of the whole of creation bringing forth its eternity.

Therefore Christian prayer will finally appear to us as a participation in the prayer of Christ, the center of the redeemed universe.

6. EXTERNAL WORSHIP

It is the whole man who owes himself to God, and what is more, man in the midst of the created universe. If the totality of religious homage is expressed in this offering of the will which is *devotion*, and if *prayer* itself subjects us, in our appeal to God, to the providential order which governs the universe, these are however wholly interior and spiritual acts which call for external realizations in which the whole human being, and the created goods at his disposal, take part. But we must measure the meaning and the role of these external steps exactly.

First of all we will note that the intention of homage and service which the virtue of religion will communicate to our other moral activities will be the truest manifestation of our will to render what is owing to God. A primary moral virtue, religion exercises its influence (*imperium*) even upon our most profane acts by referring them to God. It therefore places its own motivation in the immediate service of charity, in which our entire virtuous life finds its orientation and the principle of its merit. The virtue of religion then, according to St. Thomas Aquinas, has the countenance of a virtue of holiness, that is to say that it utilizes our awareness of the rights of God over us, and of the holiness of His being, in order to lead us to a greater effort of detachment, and of stability in our orientation toward Him. This is realized in typical fashion in the religious state in which, by means of the vows, it is the whole of life that is committed to God and ordered to His service. The meaning of our obligations toward God, the renewing our our availability in regard to His will through the act of devotion, should likewise help to bring about a growing ascendancy of charity in the common Christian life. It is in this sense that the act of any moral virtue exercised through a motive of religion is rendered more meritorious by it, according to the usual teaching of theologians.

The rites and external manifestations of worship are not therefore in any way the principal matter for the virtue of religion. However, they constitute acts which are proper to it (*actus eliciti*), and even if they are required, as we shall say, by our very nature, they only have meaning in the measure in which, serving as an expression of interior religion described above—devotion and prayer—they help in its fulfillment.

The need for external worship in which the gestures of the body and the realities of the created universe have their part, does not mean that material creatures themselves have in any sense a kind of debt of religion which it is for man to make them accomplish. This is a very imaginative view of things, but I mention it because it is met with. It is also a very materialistic view which a sound theology is bound to dispel. It is the rational creature who is subject to the duties of religion in regard to God. The whole creation belongs to God essentially and completely. No human act can add anything to it. But the free will of man, itself, must submit itself to its Creator, and it is in our minds that this extrinsic glory of God is achieved, which is realized in the consciousness of His glory and the approbation of His wisdom. *Clara notitia cum laude.* If a sensible cult is required, it is because the incarnate spirit which man is, is dependent on the sensible in which he finds all his knowledge, and in which he finds signs and symbols capable of expressing his profound soul. Religion demands that we render homage to God. It will be rendered in man's manner. But it is not God whom these ritual gestures and material offerings directly concern. Yahweh, according to the prophets of the Old Testament, did not take delight in the victims which were offered to Him. He desires contrite and humble hearts. And it is man's heart which, in these external manifestations of worship, is led to the religious sentiment by the expression which is thus given to it. The gesture sustains the sentiment and develops it by exteriorizing it. The symbol specifies the thought which is formulated by it, and helps to fix it and sometime to awaken it. There is therefore, in sum, in the external worship of religion a double relation: the one with God to whom is directed the total homage, which, finally, consists in the free submission of our mind, and the other with man himself, in whom the hierarchy of the spiritual and the sensible is established, according to an order which is related to his own nature.

This is first of all to confer an essential value of signs upon the sensible realities which enter into the worship of God.

We do all of this for ourselves, in order that, through these sensible works, our intention may be directed toward God and kindle our feelings. At the same time, we confess in this way that God is the author of our soul and of our body, offering Him spiritual and corporal homage. That is why it is not astonishing that heretics who have denied that God was the creator of our body have condemned corporal homage in divine worship. This also shows that they forget their human nature, judging that sensible representation is not necessary for them in order to attain to knowledge and to an interior feeling. It is however a fact of experience . . . (*Cont. Gent.,* bk. 3, ch. 119).

It will be the mark of a well ordered cult if its symbols are chosen with care, both as to their evocative value in regard to divine realities which arouse the religious sentiment, and their educational value in regard to the latter. Faith will here be the rule. The divine institution guaranteed to the liturgical laws of the Old Testament that rectitude in which was so strongly affirmed the transcendent holiness of God along with His unicity. The Church, under the new covenant, has authority to determine liturgical institutions and approve the private devotions which are lawful for the faithful to use.

As for the very measure of exteriorization that a cult must have which is essentially meant to foster the spiritual union of man with his God, it is one of the aspects of the moral virtue of religion to lead to its prudent determination.

If it is a question of private worship, the personal, spiritual need will be the law. A great relativity will here appear in the external practices of devotion. But a minimum will always be safeguarded if we want to prevent religious sentiment from losing itself in vagueness and indefiniteness.

With regard to public worship, it is necessary that it have external form, being a social act. The external rites will here affirm the collective duty, but they will be determined by the collectivity itself and by its spiritual needs.

7. BODY, VOICE AND CHANT

When we begin the detailing of the great aspects according to which sensible realities enter into the worship of God, the traditional order of theologians is the following, also made manifest by St. Thomas Aquinas in the prologue to question 84 of IIa IIae: "Adoration, in which the body lends itself to the veneration of God—the acts in which we offer some thing taken from external realities—acts in which divine things come into our usage."

By the term *adoration* we understand, differently from modern spiritual language which uses this word to designate interior reverence for God, the act of prostration of the body which expresses it. "Corporal signs of humility, which awaken in our heart the sentiment of submission which we owe to God, being natural for us to approach to the intelligible through the sensible" (IIa IIae, q. 84, a. 2). The liturgy thus expresses all the nuances of veneration through gestures which range from simple bowing of the head to complete prostration. Genuflection and kneeling are the most common among us, and the kiss likewise. But the posture of the body which remains standing is also a religious gesture of prayer. The orientation of the body likewise acquires meaning in our liturgies. It is not fruitless to Christian piety that, in public worship, the faithful should be attentive to the common attitudes which the liturgy suggests to them, and to the meaning which it associates with them. With regard to private piety, it can only gain by this discipline of the body which perhaps was better known in former times. A certain respect for God, and of the very prayer which we direct to Him, is here at stake. Note that this corporal aspect of worship is likewise motivated by the penitential character which may be associated with our religious homage.

To these considerations on the role of the body in our acts of religion, let us add a few remarks on vocal prayer. More than in any other, it is in this act that the close bond of the body and spirit is manifested in our relations with God. The expression of our desire, a petition which, while striving to rejoin the providential order states the appropriate requests of our human initiatives—the prayer, however unspecified it may be—is stated precisely. But where then is the exact boundary between "mental" and "vocal" prayer? As a matter of fact, we consider as vocal prayer properly so called that in which the movement of the lips intervenes, a pronunciation, even in low voice. And this minimum is required in certain obligatory prayers, such as the breviary of clerics. We therefore find the principle of the application of our body to divine worship, very specifically. But at the same time is posed the moral problem of the attention required in order that such prayer may have all its religious value. Classically, attention to the words themselves is required as a minimum—and by this we understand that it is to manifest a religious intention if we are careful about the wholly external correctness of an act of worship. But we likewise notice that to pay attention to the meaning of the pronounced formulas entails a greater religious value and, what is more, the attention must be directed toward God Himself, the recipient of this homage. In any case, consequently, interior prayer is preponderant, and the external formulation is wholly relative to it.

St. Thomas Aquinas distinguishes from prayer properly so called, whether formulated by the lips or not, what he calls vocal praise. We are less accustomed to make a distinction between prayer and praise. Formally, praise consists in proclaiming the greatness of God, and in stating His great attributes. And certainly, there is first of all a wholly interior praise which consists in divine contemplation. It results quite simply in silence, for God is in Himself beyond all praise. But this is a term, and the same requirement of formulation is found again for ourselves who only have access to the spiritual through the sensible, and of external enunciation in order that the divine glory may be extended. We will formulate the divine praise, St. Thomas explains, with much acuteness, by proclaiming the divine names. To name God is to praise Him, for humanly praise consists in showing someone that we appreciate what he is doing. But, on the other hand, we only "name" God by reason of His works, for He is, in Himself, the unutterable, beyond every name. Human speech thus assembles everything that is intelligible in the created universe in order to honor God therewith, and it is this created universe which gives us indications of the Creator. This is the great homage which speech renders to God and which unquestionably gives it a distinctive place in worship. It is speech itself which finally gives intelligible meaning to all the external symbols of which a liturgy is formed.

The chant is joined to speech. This is because the religious attitude is not made of pure intelligence only but also of affective reactions with which sensibility must be in agreement and which it can assist, but with all the discretion which it owes itself and, according to St. Thomas Aquinas, without being at the expense of intelligibility. "If one is devoted to the chant," he wrote, "for the enjoyment found in it, the soul is distracted and cannot be attentive to the meaning of the words . . . If, on the contrary, one chants with devotion, one meditates more attentively on what is being said. Consequently one pauses longer over the same objects; and, furthermore, as St. Augustine says, 'all the sentiments of our soul find modulations in chanting which adapt themselves to their various nuances and, by a secret harmony, make them vibrate.' This is also true for the hearers. And even if they do not understand what is being chanted, they know nevertheless that divine praise is the reason for these chants, and this is sufficient to awaken their devotion."

We may say the same thing about music in all its forms—while noting however, in this respect, that the sensible manifestations of the religious sentiment may admit of various aspects. If it is a question of liturgy properly so called, it seems that the intelligible meaning ought to outweigh emotion.

God does not sing to us, He speaks to us: He addresses Himself to our mind; it is with our conscious soul that He reckons first of all, and through it He establishes the relation; the soul itself must respond. We are nearer to God with a well meditated psalm, or a verse inscribed in the heart, than when we are soothed by no matter what music.[2]

But the expression which we give to our interior life can be presented as a free effusion, an overflowing of the soul which invites all

[2] A. D. Sertillanges, *Prière et musique,* in *Vie Int.,* vol. 7, p. 137.

the sensible powers to chant the homage of the heart. It is no longer a question here of merely directing our soul to God—and of offering a liturgical text—but of expressing, for the joy of expressing. A certain magnificence of worship is here the expression of an overflowing interior richness. Music is its distinctive means, and will therefore be all the more religious to the degree that it is simply music.

8. THE ACTS OF OFFERING: THE SACRIFICE

The offering is again a spontaneous human symbol of homage. Every cult is familiar with it, and it is normal, consequently, that in presenting to God the material goods which we use, we declare our acknowledgment that we have received all of them from Him.

The difficulty begins when it is a question of defining that which makes an offering a sacrifice. For the latter is in fact the act of divine worship, par excellence. The importance given to it in Christianity in which our redemption is accomplished through the sacrifice of Christ, which is the center of eucharistic worship, has claimed the very special attention of theologians.

The history of religions is first of all laid under contribution. The sacrifice of firstfruits appears in the most primitive civilizations as a religious act which, setting apart some portion of the fruits of the earth or the game of the hunt to be offered to the Supreme Being, expresses dependence in regard to the dispenser of all blessings. Subsequently, in the great polytheistic religions, the bloody sacrifices become typical of the homage rendered to the divinity. But it was among the Semites that bloody rites acquired the greatest emphasis. The Mosaic ritual describes the four great kinds of sacrifices: the holocaust, the unbloody sacrifice, the sacrifice of communion, and expiatory sacrifices. The various purposes of the sacrificial rite are here disclosed: adoration, thanksgiving, a desire for union and intimacy, expiation and reparation for sin, and petition. But the symbolism of blood appears to be the most essential. Blood is a sacred thing preeminently. The principle of life is in the blood. Coming from God, it can only be rendered to Him alone. Therefore, to shed blood takes on a religious significance by itself, but also admirably expresses the desire for expiation, the offered victim being substituted for the life of sinful man whom it redeems.

Furthermore, blood is likewise symbolical of a contracted covenant. By bringing it to the altar, men manifest their desire for union with

God. Yahweh Himself contracted a covenant with His people in the form of human covenants: the shed blood, the shared victim.

The sacrifice of Christ on Calvary itself will be a sacrifice of blood, the God-Man's homage to the infinitely holy Father of life, a propitiation for all humanity, and a sign of the renewed covenant according to the very words of the Savior when, at the Last Supper, He presented the eucharistic cup to His own.

Does it follow that we must seek for the essence of the sacrifice in a destruction of the victim and by this act distinguish it from a simple offering? Not necessarily. Theories of sacrifices which make it consist in a *destruction* are not satisfying and do not even correspond to the true symbolism of the rites which the history of religions clearly shows us.

> This does not seem to correspond to the profound essence of human religion nor to the sacrifice of what it is the expression. Neither the sentiment of sin nor adoration itself will make man destroy the being which he has received, as though it were the best way to honor the divine being. On the contrary, his profoundest impulse will be to attest that he holds this being from the Creator and to offer it, by desire, intention and efficacious will to Him who is his supreme end as He is his first principle. . . . Man's sacrifice will not be an act of destruction violently separating the creature from the Creator, but an act of oblation or donation which makes him enter into an intimate communion with Him. (Lepin, *La Messe et nous*, p. 74.)

In any case, we must have a definition of sacrifice which is also in accord with the rites that do not have any destruction of the thing that is offered, as is the case, for example, in the offering of firstfruits.

A sound philosophy of sacrifice will recall to mind that the rite— for it is here a question of the sacrifice properly so called—is an act of external worship and that it therefore enters into the category of signs. The problem is therefore exactly as follows: sacrifice being an act signifying homage rendered to God, in what does its proper signification consist, and for what reason is it required? It seems therefore that we must say quite simply that property of sacrifice is to bear in itself a signification of homage that is exclusively latrial, that is to say reserved for the divinity:

> When we externally signify our inward feelings of respect, we give certain marks of reverence to exalted creatures, and this goes as far as adoration (understood in the sense of prostration). But there is one thing which we reserve absolutely for God, and this is sacrifice. . . . Who ever had the idea, says St. Augustine, of offering a sacrifice to a being whom he did not know, think or imagine to be God? (IIa IIae, q. 84, a. 1).

Sacrifice then appears as preeminently the sacred rite, that is to say reserved for God, and this is the great requirement of such an act.

To strengthen within us, through sensible means, the idea of the transcendence of God over all things, says St. Thomas, we must give Him tokens of respect that are entirely distinctive, *per hoc quod aliquid ei separatim exhibemus. . . .* Among other religious acts, the sacrifice itself has something special: tokens of honor, such as genuflection, prostrations and others of this kind can be rendered to men; the intention we place in them makes the difference. But sacrifice is that which men have always reserved for God or for whatever they held to be such. (III *Cont. Gent.,* ch. 120).

It seems therefore that we can define sacrifice very formally by the idea of an essentially sacred action, that is to say determined in its symbolism as being reserved for divinity. *Sacrum facere.* This does not merely signify that we are consecrating what is being offered to God, but that this offering itself enters into the constitution of a rite which is the sacrifice, that is to say a sacred action. A text of St. Thomas defining sacrifice must again be quoted here:

There is sacrifice properly so called, he writes, when the things that are offered to God are the subject of an action as was the putting to death of animals, or as is the breaking, manducation and blessing of the bread. The very name of sacrifice indicates this: to do something sacred. (IIa IIae, q. 85, a. 3, ad. 3).

Sacrifice therefore appears to us as a *symbolical donation or oblation with a signification that is essentially latrial* (cf. D.T.C., art. *Sacrifice,* col. 677).

But what is the origin of this signification itself? "The determination of the symbols is a matter of human convention," St. Thomas affirms again, "the determination of the sacrifices is of human or divine institution" (IIa, IIae, q. 85, a. 1, ad. 1).

Subjacent to this institutional determination, there are certainly spontaneous reactions of human psychology. To offer God (*ob-ferre*) our external goods in acknowledgment of our dependence upon Him is in any case naturally essential to sacrifice. It is also essential that the manner of offering give evidence of homage reserved for God alone. It is here that the institutional determination will intervene, but in relying again upon the symbolism more or less spontaneously recognized as being able to have a sacred character. Thus, as we have already indicated, among the Semites the effusion of blood, the symbol of life, belonged only to God. It is for the history of religions, for psychology and for exegesis to find all the symbolisms which the human being has been able to express in the act of worship that is the most important and the most obviously synthetic of all his duties toward God. When, in revealed religion, God Himself determines by what rites He wants to be specially honored, through the mediation of those who speak in His name, the sacrificial institution appears, like the very history of revelation, with the features of a divine pedagogy which orients rites commonly received in human religions toward the service of the true God. "All of these usages partly common to all the nomadic or non-nomadic Semites were known to Moses and accepted on the part of God (M. J. Lagrange, in *Rev. Bibl.*, 1901, p. 615).

With regard to the sacrifice of Christ on Calvary, it appears at the summit of all religion of humanity as the act that is the most manifestly expressive of the rights of God and of His holiness, and is it not the most expressive sign of the extent of our duties toward Him? To whom therefore could the blood of Christ be offered if not to God, His Father? Let us especially note that Christ wanted to make of this offering a sacrifice properly so called. Not merely a sacrifice in the broad sense, as when we speak of making a sacrifice of our life. The act of Calvary becomes the essential rite of the new covenant. The sacramental sacrifice instituted at the Last Supper expresses it, as the rites of the ancient Law signified it by anticipation. The death of Christ was the fulfillment of these great rites of the Old Law.

We have defined sacrifice as the act which essentially signifies latrial homage. Needless to say, this act of virtue of religion is enriched by all the finalities which it knows. If the exercises of the virtue of religion, as was said before, is inseparable from that of the great supernatural virtues which inspires it, this central act of external worship will be pre-eminently the point of convergence of all the interior richness of our supernatural psychology. This is the source of the classical definitions of sacrifice: *opus factum ut sancta societate Deo inhereamus—aliquid factum in honorem Deo proprio debitum ad eum placandum.* To be united to God, to obtain His pardon and His graces, to manifest our love for Him, all these great intentions will animate our homage. The sacrifice of Christ will then appear once again as the unique and decisive sacrifice of humanity, by reason of the infinite charity which inspires it.

9. THE SACRED

We have defined sacrifice by seeing in it the sacred action in which is sensibly manifested the homage due to God. It is important to insist briefly upon this idea of the *sacred*. St. Thomas sees it a specialization for use in worship, intended to symbolize the unique respect owing to God.

Human sentiment, he writes, is natural in this respect that common things, not distinguished from others, are the object of less respect. . . . That is why it was necessary that special eras, a special locality, special instruments and special ministers be ordered for the worship of God, in such manner that the minds of men should thereby be led to a greater respect for Him. (Ia IIae, q. 102, a. 4).

The reserved character of everything that pertains to divine worship will therefore be the principal means of inducing this religious veneration. Around the sacrifice, the act that is pre-eminently reserved for God, the whole order of the sacred will be organized in the cult: notably the consecration of the persons and the objects of the cult.

This throws light upon the notion of a sacrament, at least in what it has in common with the Old and the New Law. If we take this idea in all its generality, we shall find that it recalls two aspects: preparation for the act of worship and participation in the worship itself, in the sacred things. Under the first aspect, it is a matter of conferring or receiving a holiness from the cult which makes us fit for the exercise of the cult. The consecratory rites of the Old Testament, and the Christian sacraments conferring a character are of this type. Likewise the legal purifications of the Old Law to which corresponds, in the Christian cult, that spiritual purification provided by the sacrament of Penance. With regard to the aspect of participation in holy things, its type is found in the sacred meals which accompany the sacrifices. Their religious meaning is obvious. The symbolism of covenant with the divinity already contained in the sacrifice is completed by them. But just as the offering manifests our submission to God, it is still to declare ourselves dependent when we receive something from Him.

Such is the aspect, properly pertaining to worship, of sacraments in general. With regard to Christian sacraments, their "holiness" is related first of all to the grace of Christ which they communicate to us by signifying His mystery of death and of life. It is through their relation to the holy Humanity of the Savior, the source of grace, that they are defined. But we must not, for this reason, forget their signification which is properly religious and a matter of worship. The dispositions of the virtue of religion are essential to the reception of the graces which they bestow upon us. And it is by not forgetting their devotional aspect that we particularly understand the role of sacramental characters, and the double aspect of the Eucharist, a sacrament of the body offered in sacrifice and received in communion.

It is good to remember that consecrations in worship remain in the order of signs, proper to external worship. The consecrated object is signified as being reserved for the worship of God. If the sacramentalism proper to Christian worship is even extended to objects, it is in terms of the religious symbolism which is thus given to them. Intended to lead us to sentiments of religious veneration of which our worship is the manifestation, they will be its instruments, according to St. Thomas, in the manner in which sacraments properly so called are the instruments of grace. This is an aspect of sacramentals which is perhaps too little perceived.

10. VOWS

A vow is defined as a promise made to God. Therefore it is primarily comprised within the religious category of the offering. To promise is to offer by anticipation. By only considering this aspect, we shall already see the role of the virtue of religion. It will require that the homage be worthy of God. The acts of virtue will provide the matter of the vow. And as it is a question of putting oneself under obligation, it must then be within our power and we must not be already bounden by it. This is the meaning of the adage: *votum est de meliori bono*.

But the virtue of religion intervenes again to characterize the very quality of the obligation incurred. To promise is to give certain rights to the recipient of the promise; it is to bind oneself to him by giving one's word. Every promise obliges: a debt of fidelity of which the necessities of social life establish at the human level the obligatory demand. In the case of the vow, this requirement is transposed to the transcendent level of our relations to God; it is therefore an obligation directed to the absolute. It is through religion that the obligation will be fulfilled.

We must especially see the religious value of the very act which we perform when we promise something to God. The external acts of religion—and the vow is one of them—are an homage signifying our dependence on God. By the vow it is our very freedom which we declare dependent, by binding it to Him. We offer not only that which we promise, but in the very act of promising we give something of our freedom. This religious homage is obviously at its maximum when it is a question of the vows of religion by which we completely give away our freedom by making the gift of our whole life to God. Therefore the religious state is comparable, in significative value, to that of the sacrifice or even the holocaust. But every vow, however partial its object may be, bears within itself this offering of freedom to the Creator.

Theology also points out the advantages of the vow. Not only by ordering toward God the acts of virtue which one promises to perform for Him does one give them an intention of homage which increases their merit, but, subjectively, the will becomes fixed and stabilized in its good intentions. Does the spontaneity of a will which claims to keep more fervor by remaining free always have the value of the seriousness and intensity of a will which is bound to God? After all, we will recall that vows are ranged among the external acts of the virtues of religion. It is therefore with them as with the acts of external worship: their usage is relative to the usefulness which one can personally derive from them.

The cessation of the obligation of the vow can occur by annulment, dispensation or commutation.

The annulment of the vow is the act of anyone who has governing power over the will of the person who made the vow, or over the matter of the vow. The latter is directly annulled in the first case, and indirectly in the second. Direct annulment may, for example, be the act of a father in regard to his minor children, or of religious superiors for their subordinates in regard to the private vows which they have made after their religious profession. With regard to indirect annulment, it is the act, for instance, of a husband and wife who may mutually annul the vows which infringe upon their respective rights, even if they were made before marriage.

Dispensation is a very different matter. It is the act of an authority which declares, in God's name, that the bond has ceased to obligate. It implies the power of jurisdiction and requires a just motive in order to be valid.

Dispensation from all public vows, perpetual or temporary, and

pronounced in the Institutes approved by the Holy See, is actually
reserved to the Sovereign Pontiff. This includes private vows, for
example the vow of perfect and perpetual chastity, and of entrance
into a religious order of solemn vows. This reservation, moreover,
only has bearing upon vows that have perfection of matter and of
mode. Dispensation from vows of virginity, temporary chastity, celibacy and entrance into a religious community of simple vows, is not
therefore reserved to the Holy See. Likewise vows that are pronounced in a conditional manner or under the influence of fear,
however slight, or pronounced before the age of 18.

Bishops or prelates having analogous jurisdiction may dispense
not only from other unreserved vows, but even from the above-
mentioned private vows in cases of urgent necessity. Regular confessors who have the powers of the Mendicant Orders may dispense
from all unreserved vows and from the vow of chastity in urgent
cases. Ordinary confessors only have these powers by virtue of particular indults or in a Jubilee year.

The commutation of the vow, that is to say the replacing of the
promised work by another one, may be made, when there is no question of reserved vows, by the person who has made the vow, provided that the substituted work be better or equivalent; if this is not
the case he must have recourse to anyone who has the power to
dispense.

11. THE SENSE OF THE SACRED AND SOCIAL LIFE

It is under this general title that we may range the triple chapter
which St. Thomas consecrates to those great acts of the virtue of
religion which are the oath, the adjuration and praise. In reality
they are combined by him under the theme of the usage of the
divine name. And this is a great religious philosophy. To name
God is to evoke His presence and rouse the greatest sentiment of
sacred respect which must inspire our entire life. We have already
mentioned the praise of God and the public acknowledgment which
we owe Him for the greatest of His works. But the oath and adjuration introduce the divine presence into the very midst of our secular
life, in all our social relations. We therefore use the divine name
"by way of the oath, to confirm our own words, by way of adjuration to induce others to do something." Let us briefly examine these
two acts.

(a) *The Oath*

This is an appeal to divine witness, with a view of convincing others of the truth of our statements. Not that we expect an external manifestation of divine power which would come to confirm our spoken word. However, we rely upon His eternal justice, and we find support, in fact, in the great awareness of God which those who believe in Him must have. In this sense the oath is a great religious act. It is a testimonial which we render to God, primary Truth, who knows the most secret intentions and whom we cannot deceive. It is especially a recognition of His quality as the guarantor of moral values on which all human, social life is based. The oath has therefore a social value as homage, which our laicized societies unfortunately reject.

By reason of its matter, the oath is distinguished as an oath of assertion and an oath of promise. The latter obligates one to fulfill the promise especially because of the appeal to divine witness. The latter does not only guarantee the actual sincerity of the one who promises, but also the obligation which he intends to incur by his promise. Canon law specifies (Can. 1316-1321) the conditions of obligation and annulment of the promissory oath. Its beneficiary may release from it. The same powers of annulment, dispensation and commutation of which mention was made in regard to the vow are exercised in regard to the oath.

Traditional moral qualities, which moreover are mentioned in canon law, and which are required for the oath, are the conditions of judgment, justice and truth. This therefore implies not only that the divine guarantee be invoked in just and true matters, but with judgment, that is to say "an oath is not to be taken lightly, but for a necessary reason and with discernment" (St. Thomas). It is proper to insist upon this great respect that is due the oath, which can only keep all its religious import through a prudent reserve. If we multiply oaths or use them in matters of little importance, we would be failing in this religious sense on which the efficacy of the oath is based, or at least we would be weakening it.

(b) *The Adjuration*

This is likewise a religious act of singular greatness, if it is properly understood. It consists in imposing something in God's name, that is to say in appealing to the very motive of the virtue of religion in order to obligate. It is obvious that such procedure supposes a serious reason and great circumspection. But when we have said this, it implies a conception of the divine basis of authority which legitimates it. If all human authority remains limited, however, within the bounds of its competence and its scope, it is nevertheless a real participation in the authority of God who is its foundation. Its legitimate orders obligate in conscience and therefore it may, in order to manifest the urgency of this obligation more vigorously, formulate it "in God's name." Just as the oath proclaimed God as the guarantor of the moral values of fidelity without which no human society is possible, the adjuration declares Him to be the source of all authority.

In fact, the most typical case of adjuration certainly seems to be, in the case of religious obedience, the "formal precept" whose conditions are moreover generally specified and limited by the Constitutions that are concerned about the elimination of all personal authoritarianism. After all, it is already a question of obligations with religious value. But in these, the superior commanding *"in virtute spiritus sancti et sanctae obedientiae"* does not make direct appeal to his own authority, but to the very authority of God.

The adjuration is likewise presented under another form, which is no longer that of commandment but of request. It accompanies the request made to God, when our prayer evokes His great attributes as a motive for granting them. But, when we address our fellowmen, adjuration consists in appealing to their religious sentiments in order to obtain from them whatever we are imploring.

It is still another form of adjuration to address demons in order to constrain them in God's name. We do not have natural power over them, and therefore we can only make use of the divine name. Exorcisms intended to drive out a demon in cases of possession can only be undertaken under conditions that are strictly determined by ecclesiastical authority.

12. SINS AGAINST RELIGION

The traditional classification places sins against the virtue of religion in two great series, according to *excess* or *default*. It is thus that faults contrary to a moral virtue are generally classified, and the virtue of religion, as we have said, is a moral virtue. We shall therefore have on the one hand the vices of *superstition,* and on the other hand those of *irreligion.* It is well understood, of course, that it is not in relation to essentials that there can be any excess in religion. One can never have too much devotion. But the external acts can be inclined to it, and especially that deviation which diverts to irrelevant ends or addresses divine worship to unauthorized recipients. Theological tradition will therefore classify the various kinds of *superstition* as follows:

1. *Adulterations of the worship* of the true God.

2. *Idolatry,* which directs this worship to others than God.

3. *Divination,* which seeks to satisfy a curiosity that is foreign to divine worship by means of superstitious practices.

4. *Superstitious practices* which are attached to vain observances and turned aside from a real religious meaning.

With regard to the vices of *irreligion,* they will be enumerated according as they imply a direct irreverance toward God or only toward holy things; the *tempting of God and perjury* for the first case; *sacrilege* and *simony* for the second.

Acts extremely varied are thus combined under this general title of superstition and irreligion. It will be fitting, in all the cases, to judge them morally with reference to an exact idea of the relations of man and God. In this way will appear, notably, the opposition to the virtue of religion of superstitious observances or divinatory processes which, at first sight, may seem to have nothing in common with religious worship. This will be made clearer by a brief exposition of these various abuses.

13. IDOLATRY. FALSE WORSHIP AND EXCESSIVE WORSHIP OF GOD

Illicit worship, the adulteration of the worship of the true God, or, as the last scholastics said, *cultus vitiosus veri nominis,* is deceived about the manner of honoring the true God, about the *objectum formale quod* of the worship to offer Him; the worship of false gods—*cultus falsi nominis,* is chiefly deceived in regard to its recipient, the *objectum cui.* The Fathers of the Church called this second species more simply idolatry. It is this religion of false gods which must be placed before devotional superstitions, the more so because it was for this that the name of superstition was reserved during the first centuries of the Church. Idolatry is the absolute type of superstition, and, historically, the archtype of all the other kinds. By its mistaken direction, the idolatrous worship through the logic of the error is also mistaken in the expression of divine worship. But it is by borrowing or copying these aberrations of pagans that the false worship and excessive worship of the true God will originate.[3]

[3] Sejourne, D.T.C., art. *Superstition,* col. 2771.

Concerning idolatry itself we cannot here enter into an historical exposition of its various forms. It formally consists in rendering supreme and absolute worship to something other than the only true God.

This general definition itself covers two forms of idolatry: the one, which corresponds to popular conception of ancient paganism, sees in the image itself the term of divine worship, and confuses God with the *idol* which is the representation of Him. The other, less crude, distinguishes the divinity from his image. This double aspect is perfectly summed up in a text of St. Augustine cited by St. Thomas: "Anything is superstitious which has been instituted by men relatively to the making and the worship of idols, or with the purpose of honoring as God the creature or some part of the created world." [4]

Theology, with the whole Christian tradition, points out the extreme seriousness of the sin of idolatry.

If sins against God are the most serious of all, there is one which is supremely serious: to render divine honors to a creature. Whoever does this sets up another God in the world and infringes upon the sovereignty of His dominion (IIa IIae, q. 94, a. 3).

But our theology especially inquires into the origin of such a religious deviation. Certainly, on this subject, the contribution of the history of religions and of religious psychology is most important. We will note, however, that for the Catholic theologian the principle of a chronological anteriority for primitive monotheism must be safeguarded. This dogmatic solution being reserved, "the entire field may be opened to the most various hypotheses to explain the origin of idolatry; Catholic dogma will not receive any impairment (on condition however that the scientific explanation should not intend to exclude the theological explanation of the moral evil of idolatry)" (A. Michel, art. Idolâtrie, D.T.C., col. 616).

We must distinguish two elements in idolatrous acts, writes A. Michel (art. cit., col. 622)—and this is also the conclusion of the fine works of Fr. Lagrange, Mgr. Le Roy, and Fr. Condamin: the one, which I should willingly call the formal element, the persistence of the transcendent idea of God, independent of naturistic theories and whose origin is anterior to the appearance of idolatry on the earth, an idea which specifically makes *divine* worship rendered to beings who are unworthy of it, to be a deformation and a guilty corruption of the latrial act reserved for God alone; the other, the material element of idolatry (the only one mentioned in the hypotheses put

[4] Saint Augustine, *De doctrina Christiana*, 11, 20.

forth by rationalist scholars), which is the choice made by man under one of the psychological influences, analyzed by historians of religions, and under the original influence of a moral kind which the lack of balance introduced into human nature by sin represents, of objects unworthy of divine worship.

We must here point out how greatly the reflections of a St. Thomas Aquinas on this subject continue to be most enlightening in their traditional simplicity. If the problem, in his opinion, is not that of the origin of religion but of its deviations, it does not merely begin with the revealed fact of primitive monotheism. This is because religious bearing, expressing itself in worship, appears to him as one of the most essential inclinations of human nature *"Quodam naturali instinctu se obligatum sentit Deo ut suo modo reverentiam et impendat"* (IIa IIae, q. 85, a. 1). The human sources of idolatry are then summed up under three principal headings: natural ignorance, source of errors about divinity combined with a double disorder of an emotional kind: the latter pertains first of all to the intrusion of feelings whose vivacity communicates an absolute appearance to their objects. The danger of putting them in the place of God is great if it is a question of feelings which, by their very structure, are of the religious type, like those in which veneration and love are mingled. St. Thomas sees in them the origin of the idolatrous worship of the dead. Modern idolatries of the race, the nation, etc., would doubtless be of this type.

The other source of disorder is indicated in these terms: *homo naturaliter de representatione delectatur.* The attraction of the sensible, in all its forms, but particularly the danger of delighting in what Bergson calls "the mind's propensity for fabulosity."

Adulterations of the worship of the true God recall in their turn two kinds of superstitions: false worship and merely excessive worship in which the external practices take precedence over spiritual religion. The problem arose at the very origin of Christianity; the Mosaic observances had become obsolete; and more especially the pagan usages had been definitely repudiated by St. Paul. Subsequent theological systematization, by insisting upon the significative value of the external elements of worship, especially see in the superstition which is attached to the worship of the true God, an error in the matter of signs: whether the latter are, by themselves, unadapted to the Christian religion (i.e., outmoded rites of the Old Law, or pagan usages), or whether the vagueness of the symbols contains the risk of error for anyone who uses them. This shows the importance of the liturgical prescriptions of the Church, and of their wise interpretation and of necessary conformity to these rites.

With regard to superfluous worship, this is how St. Thomas explains it:

> Anything that is not proportioned to the end will be excessive. What is the end? To render glory to God and submit ourselves to Him. If therefore we intermingle in our worship such things as may be, of their own nature, unrelated to the glory of God and incapable of raising our mind to Him, or of restraining and moderating the desires of the flesh, and ways of acting which deviate from the institutions of God and of the Church or are contrary to commonly accepted custom, must all be held as excessive and superstitious: these things pertain only to externals and have no relation to the interior worship of God. (IIa IIae, q. 93, a. 2).

These excesses may be particularly evident in the private *devotions* with which some of the faithful encumber themselves. The Church often intervenes with a certain rigor to forbid devotions which may have not only a false object (for example, the penitent Heart of Our Lord), but even merely a needless one. She requires the greatest circumspection relatively to new initiatives, notably apparitions, revelations, prophecies and miracles. The spiritual fruits of certain manifestations of popular piety do not themselves exclude deviations whose danger may be great because of the scandal produced among unbelievers.

14. "VAIN OBSERVANCES" AND DIVINATION

The superstitious practices which we are now considering, and which range from more or less magical practices to the more inoffensive superstitions of daily life, are so traditional that the catalog which the Middle Ages made of them remains unchanged.

The various modes of divination are still in use; with regard to "vain observances," St. Thomas classified them in this way: *"ars notoria,"* methods for acquiring knowledge without effort, with which are associated all illuminisms; practices intended to exercise a physical influence, with which are associated all the "magical" means and all forms of sorcery; superstitions of omens concerning good or evil fortune; finally the use of amulets.

In what way are these various practices contrary to the virtue of religion? It is here that moral judgment must be exercised together with considerable openmindedness concerning the natural facts and the scientific study which may be made of them, and at the same time there must be considerable exigency relative to the religious deviations which the "occultisms" of all kinds generally entail.

Traditional theology sees in divinatory or magical processes an impairment of the virtue of religion, in the measure in which one expects to acquire from these means a knowledge or a power of acting that belong only to God. The danger then appears of collusion with evil spirits of whom Catholic dogma affirms the existence, either because they really intervene, or simply because the exercised act is a more or less implicit appeal for their intervention. St. Thomas Aquinas, who had a highly spiritual concept of demons, definitely notes moreover that the latter's intervention consists principally in imprisoning in error the impresssionable creature who so easily lets himself be tempted by these more or less mysterious practices, in which there is no need for supernatural effects in order that, for the most part, the disordered imagination suffice for the most unlikely distortions of religious sentiment. This is the great danger of occultism. By the sense of the mysterious which it develops, it provides a kind of diminished religion for many, in which astonishing credulities base their reasoning upon a few real facts which, for its own part, metaphysics tries to classify scientifically.

Thus we believe that it is finally a work of religious purification if we endeavor to observe this kind of facts with all the objectivity that is possible, in order that, stripped of that halo of pseudo-religious mystery which surrounds them, they may appear in their real tenor as natural phenomena, verifiable by scientific observation, even if they are not always explicable.

In this matter, the works of Doctor Osty concerning the facts of lucidity (metagnosticism), or mediums producing physical effects (telekinesis, etc. . .) seem to be one of the most efficacious eliminations of the fantasies of spiritualistic interpretation and the charlatanism which often accompanies it.

Concerning divination, it is notable that medieval theology was particularly interested in astrology and in the process of drawing lots. This is because one of the great problems which St. Thomas had to solve was that of the defense of human freedom in the face of cosmic determinism of which the Arabian commentators of Aristotle made themselves the propagators. Consequently, he was careful to measure the domain in which the influence of the stars may be exercised, in order to safeguard the spiritual autonomy of free will. When this reservation has been made, it is lawful for scientific astrology to endeavor to discern this kind of influence. With regard to the drawing of lots which appealed to chance to decide upon a practical determination, St. Thomas had no difficulty in showing that it may be a legitimate usage on condition that there be certain prudent caution, and a true religious sense of Providence.

If he had been informed about the natural character of metaphysical lucidity, would he have allowed consultation with mediums or clairvoyants? Certainly not without warning of the danger, which we pointed out above, of slipping into a curiosity about the future that would be harmful to the true religious sense, and into a vain credulity. After all, the objective examination of the results of clairvoyance shows, at the merely natural level, that not only is the domain of information obtainable from it very limited, but that there is constant danger of accepting an erroneous interpretation, the subconscious desires of the consultant being one of the preponderant sources of the observations of the "seer" or of the interpretation which he gives to what he perceives.

15. THE VICES OF IRRELIGION

Irreverence toward God directly, and irreverence toward God by the profanation of holy things: such is the general classification in which our theology sums up these sins, which no longer only have the external aspect of an undue proliferation in divine worship, or of a deviation from religious sentiment in inferior forms, but which denote a real absence of the sense of the sacred.

The *tempting of God* is mentioned first of all. We have already indicated the sense in regard to prayer. To expect from God, in an imprudent and often presumptuous way, an intervention which does not respect the normal order of His Providence, is to disregard the latter, and therefore wrong the divine Wisdom. To tempt God is properly speaking to put Him on trial, and to expect a miracle in order to be certain of His power. This doubt is a disrespect. However, even outside formal doubt, Cajetan remarks that the tempting of God may simply consist "in a disdain for secondary causes, which is not justified by any necessity or utility."

Perjury also appears to be one of those acts which indicate a profound absence of the sense of God. To take Him as the witness of a lie is to wrong His sovereign truth. Let us note again here that the truth of the oath does not merely consist in expressing oneself sincerely at the moment of swearing, but in the case of promissory oath, in fulfilling what one has sworn to do. There is an opinion which states the matter as follows:

The person who does not fulfill what he has sworn, in all sincerity, to do is not making God the witness of a lie, if he had the intention of fulfilling it at the moment of making the promise. He simply gives evidence of inconstancy and infidelity, in a matter which he had promised under the authority of God; he therefore commits an irreverence toward God, but its seriousness or slightly sinful nature is in proportion to that of the inconstancy or infidelity.[5]

It seems that St. Thomas would be more exacting, for he understands that the sworn promise engages the honor of God, in whose name it was made, although the obligation of the vow contracted toward God Himself is still more strict.

16. THE PROFANATION OF THE SACRED

It is still the sovereign respect which we owe to God which is injured by irreverence toward anything which, being dedicated to His worship, receives a sacred character from it. This is what we call sacrilege. But the irreverence, in this case, is measured by the more or less sacred character of these realities. Therefore a distinction is commonly made between sacrilege toward persons, places or holy things. Moral theology strives to appraise this more or less sacred quality of them all, and also to distinguish the different aspects according to which wrong may be done to them.

With regard to *persons,* the sacred character belongs to the clerical state or to Religious, and to the making of the public vow of chastity.

Sacrilege, in regard to them, will result:

(a) from violence, for which canon law provides special punishments of excommunication, variable according to the dignity of the outraged clerics.

(b) from the encroachment of jurisdiction in regard to clerics enjoying the privilege of the forum.

(c) from the sin of sensual vice.

The profanation of a sacred thing is called a *"real" sacrilege.* This pertains to sacred things either by virtue of divine institution, like the sacraments, or by virtue of a consecration or blessing, such as vestments and sacred vessels, the objects of worship; by reason of what they represent, like the holy images, relics, etc.; because of

[5] Merkelbach, *Theologia moralis,* II. *De Religione,* a. 3, n. 750.

their purpose, like the property that is intended for the use of worship or for the needs of the Church.

Finally, the *local sacrilege* consists in the violation of a sacred place, which supposes that the latter, blessed or consecrated according to the rites of the Church, is meant for ceremonies of worship (churches, oratories) or for the burial of the faithful (a cemetery). Profanation of a sacred place makes necessary the "reconciliation" of the holiness of the place by a special ceremony. Canon law specifies the acts that are capable of profaning a church: they are the crime of homicide, an observable and gravely sinful shedding of blood, "an impious or sordid usage," and finally the burial of an infidel or an excommunicated person. (Cf. can. 1172.)

17. SIMONY

At the end of a long history, which begins with the *Acts of the Apostles,* in which we see Simon Magus offer money to the Apostles in order to obtain the power of giving the Spirit (Acts 8:18), this is how present Canon Law juridically specifies the conditions of simony, which, in certain periods such as the eleventh or the fifteenth centuries, caused so many ravages in the Church.

Canon 727, section 1. The deliberate will to buy or sell an intrinsically spiritual thing for a temporal price, for example sacraments, ecclesiastical jurisdiction, consecration, indulgences, etc. . . . or a temporal thing in such relation to a spiritual thing that the first can in no way be realized without the other, for example an ecclesiastical benefice, etc., or when the spiritual thing becomes the object, even partially, of the contract, for example consecration during the sale of a consecrated chalice, is simony in divine law.

Section 2. To exchange temporal goods attached to spiritual things, for spiritual goods, or even for temporal goods if this is forbidden by the Church because of a danger of irreverence toward spiritual things, constitutes simony in ecclesiastical law.

The following canons specify the conditions of sale and of purchase, of exchange, and of more or less tacit agreements; the ecclesiastical punishments which affect simoniacs; cases likewise in which there is no simony: as when the spiritual good is not properly the object of the temporal contract, but its occasion, in conditions that are legitimated by law or custom, or when, in the case of the sale of a consecrated object, for example, the price only takes the material value into account.

The moralist must here simply judge the nature of this sin as opposed to the virtue of religion. For this reason, simony is commonly

ranged among the "real sacrileges," that is to say, the profanation
of holy things. But we will note the emphasis here placed not only
upon the idea of the sacred, but upon that of the spiritual realities
which the whole life of the Church involves.

This is what gives a very particular character to simony. The definition of sacrilege is dominated by the thought of the sovereign
respect due to God through everything which is connected with Him.
In this respect, we insist upon the need for awareness of the supernatural mission of the Church. The latter is the continuator of Christ,
the depository of His grace. This places us at the very start of a
transcendent level wherein all human bargaining must cease. An essential aspect of the virtue of religion is thus brought out, not only
in the appreciation of the transcendence of God the creator, but of
His Paternity, the source of that spiritual grace in Christ which permits us to unite ourselves to Him in a filial worship. The great idea
of the gratuity of the divine gifts is thus at the beginning of a religion which makes us, with the reference that is proper to our creaturely state, render thanks to the Father from whom comes every
perfect gift.

REFLECTIONS AND PERSPECTIVES

Man, placed before God, and concerned about having true relations with Him, finds himself torn between two demands: on the
one hand, God is transcendent, and how could man attain to him,
or how could man fail to find Him universally in everything that he
does? On the other hand, God has given everything to man and
everything that man is comes from Him; how then could man refuse to pay Him the particular homage of his gratitude and his
submission? On the one hand, man must offer everything to God:
his thoughts, his deeds, his smallest acts, his possessions, the earth
and the whole universe, but on the other hand, this universal offering would debase the offering itself if man did not separate something from it to make of it a select portion reserved for God. On the
one hand, there is no distinction between profane and sacred; everything belongs to God and is returning to God, but on the other
hand, there can be no religious education nor any religious life possible if something, at least, is not set apart to be visibly and sensibly
offered to God. On the one hand, man is spirit and returns everything to God, inwardly, of all that he is, and on the other hand, man
is spirit and body; he is the priest of the material universe, and can

only offer it externally and visibly in a partial way: religion is not a theological but a moral virtue; its object is not God but the *worship* which we *owe* to God.

This fruitful tension poses the problem of the *sacred*. What is the sacred? How does it happen that "rational" man of Western Civilization has so greatly lost the sense of the sacred while the latter is still so vital in all "primitive" religions? Isn't the sense of the sacred of all "primitives" the real truth? Concerning the *sacred* in general, read Dom Gaillard, in *Le huitième jour,* pp. 528-530 (*La Vie Spirituelle,* April 1947); *La Maison-Dieu,* n. 17, *Le sens actuel du sacré,* passim; A. G. Martimore, *Le sens du sacré,* in *La Maison-Dieu,* n. 25, pp. 47-74; Y. Congar, *Théologie de l'Eglise, maison du peuple de Dieu,* in *L'art sacré,* Aug. Sept., 1947, pp. 205-220. This theology of the sacred, so important today, must be detailed under a variety of headings:

Religious education. The education of children: how to give them the religious sense? True and false postures; postures which are suitable for a particular age and not before. What words to use, and words to proscribe. Religious education through the Bible. Cf. Lubienska de Lenval, *L'éducation du sens religieux,* Paris, Spes, 1946; M. Fargues, *Introduction des enfants de neuf ans au catéchisme,* Desclée de Br. (1937). The religious formation of adults: an immense problem; we shall limit ourselves to referring to the résumé of the conferences of Chevetogne, 1950, by Abbé Ch. Moeller, and in particular his presentation of "Predication et Catéchèse," in Irenikon, vol. XXIV, 3rd quarter, 1951, 313-343.

The liturgy (from two Greek words meaning *public office*) is preeminently the place of the sacred. On this subject see *Theology Library,* volume I, pp. 81-127. Special mention is also made of the liturgical review, *Worship,* and the work of the Liturgical Press, St. John's Abbey, of the Liturgical Summer School, University of Notre Dame, and of the National Liturgical Week.

Our liturgy, as indeed our whole religion, was inaugurated at the Last Supper, when Our Savior instituted the Eucharist which is at the center of our worship and of all our ceremonies. But the Last Supper, in which the firstfruits of our religion were constituted, is itself a consecration of the ancient paschal festival. We cannot therefore understand our liturgy or its developments unless we first study its prefigurations and in some way its provisional outlines in the Old Covenant. On all this, see especially Dom Gregory Dik, *The Shape of the Liturgy,* Westminster, Dacre Press (1945); J. A. Jungmann, *Missarum solemnia,* Paris, Aubier, volume 1, 1951; volume 2, 1952; volume 3 to be published; many articles by Fathers Bouyer, Chenu, Congar, Roguet, Dalmais, Daniélou; and those by Dom L. Beauduin, Dom O. Rousseau, Dom J. Leclercq; and by Mgr. Chevrot, and Fathers MM. Guardini, Parsch, Martimort, Philippeau, Chirat, etc., in *La Maison-Dieu, La Vie Spirituelle,* the German, Austrian, Belgian liturgical reviews, the books and collections of the European liturgical movements. One will find in them many essays on the theology of the liturgy which is still to be undertaken. Also see the collective work, *Liturgia,* published by Bloud and Gay, in 1947, which we have cited once and for all.

The definition of the Christian liturgy. The liturgies; their origins, developments, characteristic features, the reason for their multiplicity. Limits of the liturgy: where does the liturgy stop, and where do the "paraliturgies," devotions, private prayers, etc. begin? Characteristics of the liturgy, its value as a theological source, its role as the expression or education of the faith. Is the liturgy a matter for "initiates"? Or is it just as valuable for the formation and instruction of non-Christians? Origins, meaning, and actuality of the distinction: the liturgy of the catechumens and the liturgy of the faithful. The liturgical offices: their origins, composition and theological content. The liturgy as a sacred play: comparison of the Christian liturgy with the liturgies and "mysteries" of the pagans. Liturgy and emotions: is the liturgy a generator of joy, sadness, peace, fear, awe? The difference between liturgies of ancient and modern composition. Liturgy and daily life: the borrowings of the liturgy from the customs and ceremonies of ordinary life, from the usages of the Roman Empire, or even from ancient religions; influence of the liturgy upon secular life; by what means, and in what manner? Liturgy and sacraments (See *Sacraments* in volume VI of this work). Liturgy and "mysteries"; the origin and evolution of the word "mystery"; the theology of mystery, and of mysticism (Cf. Bouyer, *Mystique, essai sur l'histoire d'un mot,* in *Supplément de la Vie Spirituelle,* May, 1949, and *Mysterion,* in the same review, Nov., 1952).

Sacrifice and Priesthood. The theology of sacrifice. Must the Christian theology of sacrifice begin with the sacrifices practiced in all human religions in order to explain the sacrificial value of the act of Calvary, or beginning with this act alone in order to analyze all the elements and implications of the Christian sacrifice? The theology of the Last Supper, the Crucifixion, the Eucharist, understood as "sacrifices." On this subject, see the following, among many other studies: Ch. V. Heris, *Le mystère du Christ,* Paris, Editions de la Revue des Jeunes, 1928; De La Taille, *Mysterium fidei,* Paris, 1921, and the same author's résumé in *Esquisse du mystère de la foi;* M. Lepin, *L'idée du sacrifice de la messe d'après les théologiens depuis les origines jusqu'à nos jours,* Paris, Beauchesne, 1932, and a few chapters in Bouyer, *Le mystère pascal; La messe et sa caté-chèse* (coll. *Lex Orandi*).

The sacrifice of Christ and our own sacrifices. The sacrifice of the Church, the sacrifice of the faithful. Their meaning and theology.

The priesthood. The priesthood during the course of time (cf. P. Gordon, *Le sacerdoce à travers les âges,* Paris, La Colombe, 1950; M. Gorce and R. Mortier, *Histoire générale des religions,* volume 1, Paris, Libr. Quillet; Em. Lesimple, *Le pressentiment chrétien dans les religions anciennes,* Paris, A. Maisonneuve, 1942; Mircea Eliade, *Traité d'histoire des religions,* Paris, Payot, 1949). The priesthood in the ancient covenant, the priesthood of Christ, and the priest-hood of Christians (cf. *Theology Library,* volumes V and VI).

Liturgy of the divine office. The different "offices" of the Church. On what bases were they originally constituted? The spirit of their composition and elements. The theology of the divine offices: con-tinual prayer, perfect prayer, the prayer of those who watch with Christ. On all this, see A. M. Henry, *Pour une meilleure intelligence de l'office,* in *Lauda Jerusalem Dominum* (*La Vie Spirituelle,* Jan., 1947). What is the meaning of "the office, the *official* prayer of the Church"? The origins and scope of this phrase. Show in what way (1) the baptized, (2) clerics and (3) Religious, are deputed to the divine office. The "hours" of the divine office: the number of "hours" in the different liturgies; in the East, in the West, and in the ancient offices of the Western canons, and among the monks, etc. (on this subject see Martimort, *Les offices du dimanche soir,* in *Le jour du Seigneur,* Paris, Laffont, 1948, pp. 245ss); appraise the value of the number seven adopted as the number of "hours" in contemporary Western liturgies; origins of the hours, their theological meaning. The psalms; appraise the pedagogical and theological value of the psalms for the religious culture of Christians; how does it happen that the Church finds in them the most beautiful part of her prayer? The use of psalms in the Church, the Christian meaning of the Israelites' petitions, of the imprecations and the expectation of Israel, etc. The antiphons, the responses; their origins, usage, pedagogical and theological value in the structure of the offices. The readings. The Old Testament origins, the usages mentioned in the New Testament, the theological importance of the reading of holy books, the sermons of the Fathers, the lives of the martyrs, for the culture of Christians. Origins of the short lessons, the capitularies. Ancient and modern acceptations. Office and tradition the real signification of all the elements of the divine office in the conjuncture of a monastery or a basilica from the fourth to the sixth centuries; present signification; possible adaptations, or those that are desirable? On this, see *Le trésor de l'ffice divin; vers une reforme du bréviare,* in *La Maison-Dieu,* n. 21 and *Explications sur l'office et sur la manière de le dire,* in the *Bréviaire des fidèles,* Paris, Labergerie, 1951. "Traditional" value of the disposition of the psalms during the week in the Roman, Ambrosian, and monastic breviaries; and of the application of certain psalms to certain feasts, and certain hours, in the Eastern and Western liturgies.

Symbolism. "The sacraments find their matter in the elements of the material universe, water, oil, bread, wine, fire, light, etc.; what is more, they are constituted by and in typical human activities: bathing, meals, gestures of the hands." The symbolical architecture is therefore developed on two levels: "on the historical level, in which the mystery of Christ, and of His life, His death, and His resurrection, is represented by the efficacious inter-play of words and gestures, unfolding from the essential symbolical action to the allegorical refinements; and on the level of nature, which also has a symbolical dimension, in the water which purifies, in the ointment which strengthens, in the meal which restores, rejoices, and creates the community, in the fire which enlightens, warms and burns. The altar cloth will be quite simply the tablecloth which covers and adorns the table where we are going to eat: a detail which enlarges the great symbol of the Supper, in a sound figuration; the cloth is also the shroud of Christ in the tomb: allegorical evocation of the mystery that is again present through the liturgical rite. And so forth." (M. D. Chenu, *Les sacrements dans l'économie chrétienne,* in *La Maison-Dieu,* n. 30, pp. 15-16.)

Study the symbolical signification of sacraments in history: what every sacrament signified in the past (in the life of Christ prefigured and proclaimed by the history of Israel), and in the present (in the life of the Church and that of the soul which receives the sac-

The great novelty of Christianity is to have detached worship from all relationship to a determined place. There is no longer in our religion a sacred woods or a grotto of mysteries; or any "black stone" which participates in some divine privilege, or a mountain which has the monopoly of bringing us closer to God. The true sanctuary of God is neither on Gerizim nor in Jerusalem, but everywhere that His adorers *in spirit and in truth* may be found (Jn. 4:23).

The first abode of Christians, after their community had to leave the synagogue, was the house of one or another of them. It is by a paradox, which only the conservatism of all human society explains, that the civil basilica, which accepted the new religion, imposed on the Church the fundamental features of its own construction for many centuries: the rectangular form of the basic plan, the apse in a half-circle at the rear, divisions into several naves which certain Greco-Roman interiors already possessed, timber-work ceiling, a tile roof with two slopes, etc. Even the atrium which is in the front of the Roman dwelling and the central basin remain in the plan of the primitive sanctuaries which we know: St. Peter's of the Vatican, St. Paul-Outside-the-Walls, and the Nativity in Bethlehem. When the atrium disappeared, the basin passed into the interior and formed the holy water font in which the faithful "purify" themselves on entering. Without touching it, the Church therefore little by little transformed the purpose of the atrium, the court-yard of the Church, which in many places became the privileged place for burials, the "paradise" of the baptized.

The interior arrangement of the furnishings and even the choice of the latter were hardly determined during apostolic times. It was the usages which fixed, little by little, these arrangements, according to the places and the customs, and quite variously. It seems that originally the center of the church was the bishop's throne, or that of the elder; then it was the altar.

We would find this same indetermination at the beginning in the liturgical language and vestments which the Church used, in most of her rites—at least apart from the fundamental rites which Tradition received from the Lord Himself or from His apostles, and which the sacred writers of the Church established in the Holy Scriptures.

The Church is open to all peoples, all customs are good . . . and she is open to all that is true and sound in all religions: this is the way that Pope St. Gregory directed the monk Augustine, sending him into England, and ordering him to "baptize" the pagan temples by sacrificing to the true God; it is thus that certain of our churches are simply former Mosques, as at Cordova, or former synagogues, like Santa Maria la Bianca in Toledo. To make of the Church a "chapel," even if it be Latin, is to close the door to all men who are not of Latin stock or Latin culture; it is to sin against catholicity.

This charming little church of Pskov which we show here to take the Western reader away from his usual environment and open his mind to the catholicity of Christian "styles" is an example of that flexibility of the Church which adapts itself to all peoples; or what is more important, the Church does not have to adapt herself to any place, for she is everywhere like the Spirit of God.

(Church of Pskov, Russia, 1156)

rament), eschatologically. The same study for the sacramentals, the blessings, the liturgy of the divine office, etc. Study the symbolical meaning of the elements: water, oil, etc.; of the gestures: bath, meal, etc.; of the words and the postures. Original meanings of these elements and their present signification (for example, the water of Baptism).

Symbolism and vision of the world. Study of the symbolical language in terms of the world-outlook of each period. Show, for example, that water was charged with a particular symbolism when men conceived of the universe according to the trilogy of Water-Earth-Heaven (or Underworld-Earth-Heaven), the (flat) earth resting upon the waters, imposing certain limits upon them, and supporting, by its highest points, the firmament and the overhead-waters. The permanent value of certain natural symbols; new symbols resulting from modern man's vision of the world, their usage in everyday life and in poetry, their possible utilization in the religious life. On ancient symbolism, read for example Fr. Lundberg, *La typologie baptismale dans l'ancienne Église,* Upsall, 1949, and H. Riesenfeld, *Jesus transfiguré,* Copenhagen. On problems of theology and liturgy posed by the modern system of symbols for the sacraments, cf. in particular *La Maison-Dieu,* n. 22: "Permanent value of symbolism."

The symbolism of the heart, of the loins, of the head, the face, and the hands; of bread and wine, of water and fire, of oil and ointment, of the north, the east, the west, the wind, the gates, etc., in the Bible and in the Liturgy. Cf. in particular *Lexique biblique et liturgique,* in *Bréviaire des fidèles,* Paris, Labergerie, 1951.

The word. Theology of the Word of God, and of preaching. Economy of the word in Revelation, in the apostolate (or missions), in the liturgy, in the gift of faith, and in the sacraments. How can the Word of God acquire human form?

On all this, read the very fine and concise book of L. M. Dewailly, *Jésus-Christ, Parole de Dieu,* Paris, Editions du Cerf, 1945. Also see, J. Leclercq, *Le sermon, acte liturgique,* in *La Maison-Dieu,* n. 8, pp. 27-46, and C. Moeller, *Théologie de la Parole et oecuménisme,* in Irenikon, volume XXIV, 3rd quarter, 1951.

The sacred books and the liturgical books. Economy of Scripture in Revelation and the apostolate. Theology of the Bible and Biblical Theology. (Cf. *Theology Library,* volume I).

Liturgical books: their origins, the composition of the sacramentary, of the Epistolary, the Gospelary, the Collectarium, etc., the

Hymnal, the Lectionary, etc. Origins of the combined books, the Missal, the Breviary, etc. Scope and religious value of the "rubrics."

The worship rendered to the holy book in the different liturgies. The kissing of the Missal. Its origin and meaning.

The creeds of faith. Their origins and history. Influence of the conciliar formulas on the development of the liturgy. (Cf. the *Credo* of Nicea, and the *Credo* of Constantinople.)

Liturgical languages. Is there a need for sacred languages in the Church? Do they serve any purpose or provide any advantage?

Origins of the different liturgical languages, their usage, their evolution. Secular languages and sacred languages: the theology of languages. Cf. Bardy, *La question des langues dans l'Église ancienne,* Paris, Beauchesne, 1948; *La Maison-Dieu,* n. 11, passim; *La question du latin,* in *La Vie Spirituelle,* Jan., 1947; Chéry, *Le français, langue liturgique?* Paris, Éditions du Cerf, 1951. Liturgical Latin and secular Latin: cf. The works and studies of C. Mohrmann.

Reserved words. The name of Yahweh, the name of Jesus; theology of names (cf. *Le nom de Jésus* in *La Vie Spirituelle,* Jan., 1951). Ancient words conserved in liturgical language and Christian vocabulary: from Hebrew (amen, alleluia, etc.), from Greek (Kyrie eleison, charism, baptism, etc.).

Sacred seasons. The ages of the world. The theory of the six ages in the Fathers of the Church. (Commentaries on the parable of the Workers of the Eleventh Hour). The secular time and Christian time. Cf. Cullmann, *Christ et le temps,* Delachaux et Niestlé, 1948, and critique of Th. G. Chifflot, in *La Maison-Dieu,* 1948, n. 13, pp. 26 ff. Theology of time. Theology of the religious times of history. (How many should we distinguish?) Sacred time and secular time.

The Christian feasts. Theology of Easter (cf. Bouyer, *Le mystère pascal,* Paris. Éditions du Cerf, 1945) and theology of Christian feasts. The hierachy of the feasts. (On Christmas, cf. E. Flicoteaux Avent, Noël, Epiphanie, Paris, Éditions du Cerf, 1941.) The liturgical calendar, the liturgical cycles, their meaning. Prefiguration of the feasts in the Old Testament. Feasts of the saints, meaning of the veneration of saints; theology of the veneration rendered to saints according to the Liturgy.

Sunday. Origins, theological signification. Sabbath and Sunday. Sunday and the Mass. Sunday and rest. Cf. *Le huitième jour,* Paris,

Éditions du Cerf, 1947, and *Le jour du Seigneur,* Paris, Laffont, 1948.

The hours of the day. The hours consecrated to prayer in the East and in the West. Ancient and modern signification of the "hours" of Western liturgies (Prime, Tierce, etc). The hour of the Mass in the ancient Church. Cf. Jungmann, *Missarum solemnia,* op. cit., volume I.

Day and night, the East and the West. Symbolism in the Old Testament, in the Church. Signification of oriental Churches, and the import of this signification in Christianity. The day, its determination (from evening to evening) in the Jewish world; the importance of this determination of the "holy year."

Sacred places. Comment on Jn. 4:20-23. In what sense should we understand that there are reserved or sacred places in Christianity?

The Christian church. Signification and theology of the dedication and the consecration. The hierarchy of places within the interior of the church: the altar, sanctuary, pulpit, baptistry, etc. Origins and signification of the Ikonostasis among the Eastern Christians. On the mystery of the altar, cf. *La Maison-Dieu,* n. 29. Likewise cf. Jungmann, *op. cit.*

The most privileged places. The holy places. The holy cities (Jerusalem and Rome); hierarchy, theological signification of "the holy city," in Christianity. The cathedrals, basilicas, high-places, the "memoriae," etc.; their origins and signification.

Places of pilgrimage, and the pilgrimage in Chrisitan economy (cf. F. Louvel, *Projet pour un pèlerinage,* in *La Maison-Dieu,* n. 7, pp. 126-136: a remarkable essay on a theology of pilgrimage). Importance of the pilgrimage in Christian tradition and practice.

Sacred furnishings and vestments. Altar, pulpit, statuary, pictures, chandeliers, sacred vessels, monstrance, etc. The origins and hierarchy of the "sacred" between these different furnishings or instruments, and the reasons for this hierarchy.

The priestly liturgical vestments. Cf. Jungmann, *op. cit.,* volume I. The clothing of the priest in secular life: why must the priest wear distinctive clothing in daily life? Compare and give the reasons for the decision of Pope Celestine I in 428: "Discernenda plebe vel ceteris sumus doctrina, non veste; conversatione, non habitu; mentis puritate, non cultu." (Letter to the Bishops of Gaul): We priests must be distinguished from the faithful people not by our vestment but by the profession and teaching of the faith; not by our clothing, but by good morals; not by the cult of external things but by purity of mind. Contemporary canonical decisions. History of priestly attire in the Western and Eastern Churches. Symbolism of white and of black in the sacerdotal vestment of the Middle Ages. To what degree should a Christian priest be a "separated person" and show this separation by his behavior, his clothing, and the customs of his life? The basis of this doctrine in the New Testament.

The habits of Religious (cf. *The Rule of Saint Benedictine,* ch. 55: the primitive Benedictine habit does not differ from that of the common people of the place); the habits of Nuns. Origins, evolutions, and signification. Origins and signification of the religious enclosure.

The clothing of the faithful. The "white garments" of the newly baptized during the week *in albis.* Origins, signification, and present heritage. The clothing of women; why the traditional veil? Comment on I Cor. 11:2-16. Cf. Gertrude Von le Fort, *Eternal Woman,* New York, Sheed & Ward, 1956. Present import of this tradition. Clothing of penitents, formerly, and of First Communicants today, etc.

Biblical studies on the vestments of priests in the ancient covenant, its significations in that time and for the future. Christianity's borrowings from Jewish customs, and from the traditions of pagan religions in furnishings and vestments. Why must there be special vestments in a Christian system? The signification.

Sacred chant and music. Cf. *Theology Library,* Volume I.

Sacred gestures and practices. The gestures of prayer. Are there specifically Christian gestures and postures? Gestures of the Mass, of the Office: signification, pedagogical import. The gestures of the priest. The gestures of the faithful (The "circumstantes," that is to say, should not the faithful, when attending Mass, be standing with their hands raised? Cf. Jungmann, *op. cit.* pp. 292 ff.). Prayer on one's knees, its late origins. Prayer and prostration, or while bowing. The gestures of adoration, of penance, etc. Pedagogical import. The religious education of children and Christian gestures. Human gestures that are types in the Bible and the liturgy. *The bath.* Ancient practice and multiple significations of the baptismal bath (cf. Per Lundberg, *op. cit.*). The nuptial bath; comment on Eph. 5:25-27; the nuptial bath of the Church in the liturgies of the Epiphany (cf. Dom O. Casel, *Le bain nuptial de l'Église,* in *Dieu vivant,* n.

4, pp. 43-49). Purifications in the Old Testament; borrowings from or imitations of foreign religions; ritual purifications of the Old Covenant and spiritual purifications of the New; usages of holy water; compare the rites of the purification of women in childbirth in the Old Testament and the blessing accorded to the mother in the Church. *The meal.* The meal in the Old Covenant; its sacred character; the prayers of the meal. The eucharist, the "agapes," the Christian meals; blessings and thanksgivings; fasting (cf. Dom Mazé, *Liturgie et pénitence,* and Dom J. Leclercq, *Prière, Jeûne, et aumône,* in *l'Église et le pécheur,* Paris, Éditions du Cerf, 1948, pp. 203 ss, and 226-228). Dancing and choreography, in the Bible, in the liturgy (cf. Dom J. Leclercq, *La vie parfaite,* Paris, Brepols, 1948, pp. 33-34), and in regional Christian customs. Processions; their Christian signification. *Funerals;* the Wake with the corpse, the interment; the rites and their Christian signification. The resurrection in the liturgy for the dead; prayers for the dead; prayer for the souls in Purgatory. Indulgences (cf. L. M. Dewailly, *Les Indulgences,* in *La communion des saints,* Paris, Éditions du Cerf, 1945).

Exorcisms in the sacraments, the blessings, consecrations and dedications. Theology of the action of demons upon man, the human body, and upon inanimate things and places. Cf. Bouyer (volume 2 of this work) and, practically, H. Dénécheau, *Contre les mauvais esprits et les maléfices,* obtainable from the author, Nueil-sur-Layon (M.-et-L.), 1952.

States of life that are considered "sacred." The priest; his subsistence: should the priest live from the altar, or work with his hands? The history of traditions on this subject; the theology of sacerdotal poverty. The mass stipends; origins, theology; how may we offer "mass stipends" so that they may have a religious meaning and avoid all simony? Virginity; is there a sacred character of virginity in the Christian system? In what circumstances? Maternity: the blessing of fertility in the Old Covenant; and in the New. The "consecration" of the husband and wife through the sacrament of matrimony. (See volume VI, Matrimony.) The nuptial blessing. The "sacred persons" in Christian economy. Study the word *saints* in St. Paul (cf. Rom. 1:7; 16:2; I Cor. 1:2; 14:33; etc.). On the laity, cf. Congar, *Jalons pour une théologie du laïcat,* Éditions du Cerf, 1953.

Sacred art. Icons; the theology of the icon. Is there an art that is specifically Christian? Is there a sacred art in the Latin Church? In what sense? On the East, see particularly the articles of C. J. Dumont and of P. Evdokimov, in *La Vie Spirituelle,* Jan., 1950. On the West, consult the review *L'art sacré,* passim.

Painting, architecture, statuary, glass-work, imagery, etc. Comparative religious signification and value of the styles according to periods and places. Comparisons with the religious art of other religions and with secular arts. Theology of sacred art (its authors, its purpose, its place in the economy of salvation).

Asceticism and devotions. Ascetical means in use in the churches and according to periods. Cf. Dom Stolz, *L'ascèse chrétienne,* Amay, 1948, and especially from the point of view of contemporary psychology, the pamphlet *L'ascèse chrétienne et l'homme contemporain* by a group of theologians and psychiatrists, Paris, Éditions du Cerf, 1951.

Devotions. The Way of the Cross, the Rosary, the Nine Fridays, novenas, etc. Theological value of each. Comparison of these devotions with liturgical acts, viz.: the ceremony of the Exultet on Holy Saturday.

Techniques and methods of prayer. Methods of prayer according to the different schools: monastic, Dominican, Franciscan, Carmelite, Ignatian, etc. Theological and pedagogical value. Cf. *L'oraison,* Coll. *Cahiers de la Vie Spirituelle,* Paris, Éditions du Cerf, 1947 (containing an important bibliography). The theme of the desert in tradition. Religious value of silence.

The techniques. The "prayer of Jesus." Hesychasm and prayer in the Name of Jesus. Cf. in particular *La prière de Jesus,* by a monk of the Eastern Church, Chevetogne, 1951; *Writings from the philokalia on prayer of the heart,* Faber and Faber, 1951; *Récits d'un pèlerin russe,* translated by J. Gauvain, in *Cahiers du Rhône,* (1943); the article *La dévotion au nom de Jésus dans l'Eglise d'Orient,* in *La Vie Spirituelle,* Jan., 1952. The doctrine of Gregory Palamas and the techniques of prayers: value and criticism. Compare this with the discretion of Saint Teresa in the *Interior Castle.*

Techniques in other religions. Yoga. (Cf. *La Vie Spirituelle,* Aug.-Sept., 1952, pp. 193-195), the Dhikr (the prayer to Allah, of the Moslems), the Nembutsu of the Buddhists. Borrowings and possible imitations in Christianity? Scope and limits of these techniques.

Modern techniques in the churches. Utilization of modern techniques in churches: the electric light replacing the oil lamp in the sanctuary, electric bells, electric organs, loud-speakers, synthetic candles, artificial flowers, etc. Possibilities and dangers of these techniques from the point of view of natural symbolisms, and of the sacred that is connected with them. Comparative value.

Possibilities in foreign religions. Must the missionary reject everything pertaining to the pagan (or Jewish, or Mohammedan) religion of the men to whom he is addressing himself.

Words. The words which already have a religious character (pagan, Hebrew, or Mohammedan). May these words be assumed into Christian speech? Which words? In what circumstances? Study the words of Judaism which the first Christians had refused to conserve: "hiereus" (the "priesthood" attributed to the heads of Churches and to the elders), altar, etc. Show, on the other hand, all the Greek or Aramaic words, impregnated with religious culture, which Christianity spontaneously inherited. The translation of Christian religious words into the different Mediterranean languages in the first centuries: translation or transcription? May we translate words like Holy Spirit, Apostle, Baptism, Blessed Virgin (among peoples who do not know virginity, etc.)? On all this, cf. A. M. Henry, *Les missions et les langues* in *La Vie Spirituelle,* Nov., 1951, pp. 415-149, and in a general way the bulletins of the *Cercle Rerum Ecclesiae* (61, rue Madame, Paris, VIᵉ), and on a particular case, L. Bouyer, *Mysterion,* in *Suppl. de la V. Sp.,* Nov., 1952. The symbols. Can the missionary use symbols that are already imbued with foreign religion and foreign signification? Study the different religious symbolisms of Christianity imported from other religions and assimilated; for instance in the Bible itself (viz., the symbolisms of the serpent, the dragon, and the moon, cf. Apoc. 12:1, etc.). Cf. on this subject, Mircéa Eliade, *Traité d'histoire des religions, op. cit.* However, read this with discernment.

Sacred art. May the Church, to its own advantage, use the architecture, sculpture, painting and furnishings of strange religions? On what conditions? Mention a few Christian churches which are ancient pagan temples (in Rome), or ancient synagogues, ancient Mosques (in the south of Spain), etc. On this subject see the very fine issue of l'*Art Sacré,* (March-April, 1951): *Le douloureux problème des arts missionnaires.*

The wisdoms. On the utilization of the foreign Wisdoms in the Bible, cf. A. M. Dubarle, *Les sages d'Israël,* Paris, Éditions du Cerf, 1947, pp. 254 ff.: J. Daniélou, *La sagesse et la folie,* in the *Bulletin du Cercle Saint-Jean-Baptiste,* July, 1952. (See the review in *La Vie Spirituelle,* Oct., 1952, pp. 310-311). Cf. the introductions to the sapiential books of the *Bible de Jérusalem.* Utilization of the Wisdoms in Christianity.

Philosophies and theologies. Cite philosophers and theologians, (Moses Maimonides, the Arabian theologians of the 12th and 13th centuries) utilized in Christian theology; mention certain "theses" accepted in Christian theology. Conditions for assimilation of a philosophy into Christianity.

The rites. The quarrel over the Chinese rites. The history and theology of the case.

BIBLIOGRAPHIE

Saint Thomas d'Aquin, *La religion,* Tomes 1 et 2, Trad. et notes de I. Mennessier, Paris, Éd. de la Revue des J., 1932 et 1934.
A.-J. Festugière, *La sainteté,* Paris, 1942.

Sur la liturgie (Une initiation pratique et simple est celle de D. Perrot, *Sous la tente de Dieu,* Tardy, 1949), nous renvoyons à la bibliographie de notre tome 1 pp. 123-124. On trouvera dans l'ouvrage cité *Liturgia* (Paris, Bloud et Gay, 1930) une bibliographie abondante à toutes les fins de chapitres. On mettra à jour ces listes d'ouvrages en suivant les publications du *Centre de Pastorale liturgique* (*La Maison-Dieu,* revue trimestrielle; la collection *Lex orandi,* etc.) et les études des grands liturgists actuels: B. Fisher, J.-A. Jungmann, R. Guardini, en Allemagne; C. Mohrmann aux Pays-Bas; Dom L. Baudin, Dom Capelle, etc. en Belgique, etc. (*L'anné liturgique,* de Dom Guéranger est actuellement en cours de réédition chez Desclée de Br.).

Sur le sacrifice, on se reportera au chapitre sur la messe (Tome IV).

Nous citerons seulement les ouvrages suivants sur la prière (belles prières, méthodes et manières de prier, etc.):

Paul Philippe, A. Journet, etc. *L'oraison,* Coll. *Cahiers de la Vie spirituelle,* Paris, Éd. du Cerf, 1947. On trouvera au terme de ce cahier une excellente bibliographie mise en ordre et présentée par le P. L.-M. Dewailly.
A. Hamman, *Prières des premiers chrétiens,* Paris, A. Fayard, 1952.
Le P. Hamman a présenté ici les plus beaux textes de la littérature eucologique primitive.
Voir aussi G. Bardy, *La vie spirituelle d'après les pères des trois premiers siècles,* Paris, Bloud et Gay.
Saint Anselme, *Méditations et prières,* Coll. *Pax,* Paris, Desclée De Br.
Saint Thomas d'Aquin, *Prières,* Paris, Art catholique.
Les belles prières de sainte Mechtilde et de sainte Gertrude, Coll. *Pax,* Paris, Desclée De Br.
Sainte Catherine de Sienne, *Oraisons.*
Savonarole, *Dernières méditations,* Fribourg (Suisse).

Bossuet, *Méditations sur l'Évangile et Élévations sur les mystères,* Paris, Garnier.

Bossuet, *Méthode courte et facile pour faire l'oraison en foi,* Paris, Art. cathol.

J. et R. Maritain, *De la vie d'oraison,* Paris, Art. cathol.

D. Joret, *Recueillements,* Paris, Desclée De Br.

Mgr Guerry, *Vers le Père,* Paris, Desclée De Br.

Dom Lehodey, *Les voies d'oraison mentale,* Paris, Gabalda.

P. de Maumigny, *Pratique de l'oraison mentale,* Paris, Beauchesne (2 vol.).

Dom G. Belorgey, *Sous le regard de Dieu,* Lyon-Paris, Éd. de l'Abeille.

Dom G. Belorgey, *La pratique de l'oraison mentale,* Paris, Éd. du Cerf (2 vol.).

R. de Langeac, *Conseils aux âmes d'oraison,* Paris, Lethielleux, 1931. (Ces conseils, très denses, sont édités aussi en appendice de *Virgo fidelis,* du même auteur).

J. Gautier, *Pour ma vie intérieure,* Paris, Desclée De Br. Abrégé de J. Tanquerey, *Précis de théologie ascétique et mystique* (à l'usage des clercs).

Marie-Eugène de l'Enfant-Jésus, *Les oraisons des débutants,* Tarascon (Carmel).

P.-Th. Dehau, *Des fleuves d'eau vive,* Lyon-Paris, Éd. de l'Abeille.

Dom E. Vandeur, *O mon Dieu, Trinité que j'adore,* Maredsous. Élévations sur la prière de sœur Élisabeth de la Trinité.

R. P. Pinard de la Boulaye, *L'oraison mentale à la portée de tous,* Paris, Albin Michel.

R. Plus, *Dieu en nous,* Toulouse, Apost. de la prière.

Dom Vonier, *La nouvelle et éternelle alliance,* Paris, Desclée De Br.

Dom Vonier, *Christianus,* Paris, Éd. du Cerf.

A.-D. Sertillanges, *Recuieillement, Affinités, Devoirs,* 3 ouvrages publiés chez Aubier (Paris).

P. Charles, *La prière de toutes les heures.*

G. Brillet, *La vie intérieure de Jésus; Jésus parmi les hommes,* Paris, Desclée De Br.

M.-V. Bernadot, *De l'Eucharistie à la Trinité,* Paris, Éd. du Cerf.

J. Périnelle, *Comment faire oraison,* Paris, Éd. du Cerf.

Bède Frost, *La prière chrétienne,* Paris, Éd. du Cerf.

R. Guardini, *Initiation à la prière,* Trad. J. Minery, Paris, Alsatia, 1951.

Sur l'office divin, citons pour mémoire les *bréviaires* romain, monastique, dominicain, franciscain, carme, etc., dont on trouvera une édition soit chez les éditeurs pontificaux des différents pays, soit aux maisons généralices des différentes Ordres. Parmi les traductions françaises du bréviaire romain, il faut citer actuellement:

Hugueny-Roguet, *Le bréviaire romain,* Paris, Éd. Labergerie. Les Éditions Labergerie ont également publié en 1951 *Le diurnal du bréviaire romain, latin et français.*

Heures du jour du bréviaire romain en latin-français, Paris-Tournai, Desclée S. Jean.

Il faut également citer deux bréviaires pour fidèles:

Bréviaire des fidèles (A.-M. Henry), Paris, Éd. Labergerie. Entièrement en français (1344 pp.).

Livre d'heures, latin-français (En-Calcat). Ouvrage de 2.320 pages dont 743 en latin. (Cet ouvrage, done une édition existe aussi en 2 volumes, ne contient pas les évangiles, mais seulement les références aux évangiles qui doivent donc nécessairement accompagner le *Livre d'heures*).

Parmi les petits offices de la Sainte Vierge:

Petit office de la Sainte Vierge, Paris-Tournai, Desclée S. Jean.

Petit office de la Sainte Vierge, rite dominicain, Paris, Éd. du Cerf.

Office de la Bienheureuse Vierge Marie selon le rite des Frères prêcheurs, Paris, Lethielleux, 1931.

Terminons cette liste d' "offices" en mentionnant le très beau livre de prières "pour tous les jours de l'année et pour toutes les étapes de la vie," admirablement composé avec des textes de la Sainte Écriture, de la Liturgie, des Écrits des Pères de l'Église, des grand écrivains ecclésiastiques de tous les siècles. Le livre qui s'intitule *Groot Gebendenbœk* (Éd. Spectrum à Utrecht, Pays-Bas) n'a pas son correspondant en français. Particulièrement bien illustré, l'ouvrage comporte 1.672 pages sur papier bible.

Compléter cette bibliographie par celle du chapitre XVIII (La vie contemplative).

A propos des religions païennes, lire *La valeur des religions païennes,* Québec, L'union miss. du clergé.

BIBLIOGRAPHY

Bernadot, M. V., O.P., *From Holy Communion to the Blessed Trinity,* London, Sands and Co., 1934.

Davis, Henry, S.J., *Moral and Pastoral Theology,* Vol. III, pp. 2-68, London, Sheed and Ward, 1941.

Farrell, Walter, O.P., *A Companion to the Summa,* Vol. III, pp. 247-302, New York, Sheed and Ward, 1940.

Howell, Clifford, S.J., *Of Sacraments and Sacrifice,* Collegeville, Minn., The Liturgical Press, 1952.

McHugh, John A., O.P., and Callan, Charles J., O.P., *Moral Theology, A Complete Course,* Vol. II, pp. 277-401, New York, Joseph Wagner Inc., 1930.

Miller, John H., C.S.C., *The Relationship Between Liturgical and Private Prayer,* Trier, 1955.

Plus, Raoul, S.J., *God Within Us,* New York, P. J. Kenedy and Sons, 1929.

Sheedy, Charles E., C.S.C., *The Christian Virtues,* pp. 259-288, Notre Dame, Ind., University of Notre Dame, Press, 1949.

Vonier, Anscar, O.S.B., *The New and Eternal Covenant,* New York, Benziger Brothers, 1930.

Kaiser, A. F., C.PP.S., "Liturgy, Enthusiasm, and Heresy," *Priest,* 10:31-39, Ja '54.

Martindale, C. C., S.J., "Private and Liturgical Devotions," *Worship,* 27:120-124, Feb '53.

Mullahy, B. I., C.S.C., "Spirit of Poverty," *Worship,* 28:224-232, Apr '54.
Rock, A., "Liturgy, Theology, and the Church of God," *American Ecclesiastical Review,* 128:426-437, Je '53.
Roguet, A. M., O.P., "Theology of the Liturgical Assembly," *Worship,* 28:129-138, Feb '54.
Schmidt, H., S.J., "Problem of Language in Liturgy," *Worship,* 26:276-292; 342-349, May, Je '52.
Vitry, E., O.S.B., "Music and Prayer," *Orate Fratres,* 25:549-558, Oct '51.

Chapter VII

THE SOCIAL VIRTUES

by M. J. Gerlaud, O.P.

1. Man, a social being
2. The organism of the virtues in the apostolic teaching
3. Theological classification of the social virtues
4. The virtues of veneration
   - (a) Filial piety
   - (b) Patriotic piety
   - (c) Deference
   - (d) Obedience
5. The virtues of civility
   - (a) Gratitude
   - (b) Vengeance
   - (c) Truth and its opposite vices: lying and indiscretion
   - (d) Courtesy
   - (e) Liberality
   - (f) Extra-legal equity
6. The gift of piety

REFLECTIONS AND PERSPECTIVES

BIBLIOGRAPHY

Chapter VII

THE SOCIAL VIRTUES

1. MAN, A SOCIAL BEING

It is the property of virtue to perfect the movement of our natural inclinations within us, by submitting them to the order of reason. It is therefore normal that the activities of the Christian in his community life be thus perfected. The object of our study is now the totality of those virtues, related to justice, which with the latter and with charity, spiritualize our *social* behavior.

Is it fitting to underline the major importance of such virtues? Philosophers, in emulation of one another, repeat that man is essentially a social being; the Gospel and the whole Word of God teach us that the Christian is a member of a body to such a degree that his salvation is quite as communal as it is personal. For the Christian there is no opposition between the divine community of which he is a member through grace, and the earthly community to which he belongs by right of birth. The latter, for him, is like the sacrament of the former. Faithfulness to his fraternal duties in the city is the sign—and it is an integral part—of his faithfulness to the demands of the Kingdom of God: "Amen I say to you, as long as you did it for one of these, the least of my brethren, you did it for me" (Mt. 25:40). The theologian does not abandon these perspectives when, ordering his moral learning, he classifies the virtues which regulate the psychology of the social Christian and gives them a secondary place under the principal virtue of justice. To claim that these virtues do not correspond to the whole definition of justice is in no way to minimize their vital value; and to qualify them as virtues that are "attached" to justice is not to say that they are "minor" virtues.

In this study we shall learn, primarily, as is fitting for a theologian, from the Word of God, in order that we may know the psychology of the social Christian in its elementary principles. With St. Thomas we shall attempt a classification of the social virtues, and we shall consider each of them briefly, lingering a little longer over some particular problems that are more perplexing.

446

2. THE ORGANISM OF THE VIRTUES IN THE APOSTOLIC TEACHING

In Pauline teaching the theological trio occupies an incontestable place. Nevertheless the three virtues of faith, hope and charity are not sufficient to divinize all the behavior of the baptized person. In Paul's epistles, like those of the other apostles, we find them accompanied by a whole retinue of other virtues which sanctify the daily activities of the Christian. The hymn to charity (I Cor. 13:4-8) shows it to us as a queen, surrounded by fifteen other virtues, and Paul could have continued his enumeration. We see the evidence for this in the many virtues which the Apostle recommends for the observance of the recipients of his epistles.

Some of the virtues bear characteristics that are rather individual; for example, humility. Most of them, however, pertain to social behavior. This should not surprise us, for the Christian is essentially a social being: "because through him (Christ) we both have access in one Spirit to the Father. Therefore, you are now no longer strangers and foreigners, but you are citizens with the saints and members of God's household" (Eph. 2:18, 19).

Paul does not hold fast to vague exhortations; the Christian's activity in the city is of such importance for the Kingdom of God that with Peter and James he touched upon all the details and the happenings of social life.

The basic fact which dominates the whole apostolic teaching is therefore the community of life of all Christians in Christ: "For just as in one body we have many members, yet all the members have not the same function, so we, the many, are one body in Christ but severally members one of another" (Rom. 12:4-6). All the baptized will relentlessly avoid anything that would be capable of ruining this spiritual solidarity, and first of all *lying:* "Wherefore, put away lying and *speak truth* each one with his neighbor, *because we are members of one another*" (Eph. 4:25). There is no faithfulness possible without light; "Walk, then, as children of light (for the fruit of the light is in all goodness and justice and truth)" (*ibid.* 5:8-9).

In that paschal light which banishes all hypocrisy from charity (Rom. 12:9)—charity "rejoices with the truth" (I Cor. 13:6)—with infinite degrees elementary justice, together with charity, regulates all the relations which bind together the many sons of God in unity;

they honor one another reciprocally (Rom. 12:10; I Peter 2:17), and they are at one another's service (Gal. 5:13-14), open-hearted to the needs of their brothers even to the point of working in order that they may share with anyone who is in poverty (Eph. 4:28); therefore they must defend themselves against that "root of all evils" (I Tim. 6:10), which is the love of money: "Charge the rich of this world not to be proud, or to trust in the uncertainty of riches, but in God, who provides all things in abundance for our enjoyment. Let them do good and be rich in good works, giving readily, sharing with others, and thus providing for themselves a good foundation against the life to come, in order that they may lay hold on the true life" (ibid. 6:17-20). They should open their homes as well as their hearts: "Share the needs of the saints, practising hospitality" (Rom. 12:13; I Pet. 4:10). Is not every generous act a sowing that promises a proportionate harvest? (II Cor. 2:6-12).

This ardent love for one another, this charity which "covers a multitude of sins" (I Pet. 4:8) rejects all connivance with evil. No more than their Father, the sons will not tolerate evil. There are holy angers whose source is love, the love which stands erect against evil, avenges goodness and order against its bites. How delicate is this feeling of efficacious disgust in the presence of evil in a man who is constantly waylaid by egoism and only too ready for low revenge: "Be angry and do not sin . . . do not give place to the devil" (Eph. 4:26). It is not a question of opposing one disorder against another disorder: "Let all bitterness, and wrath, and indignation, and clamor, and reviling, be removed from you, along with all malice" (ibid. 31). This legitimate anger, quickened by fraternal love, is a reaction of health against that sickness of sin which, in the life of one of its members, compromises that of the whole body: "And if anyone does not obey our word by this letter, note that man and do not associate with him, that he may be put to shame. Yet do not regard him as an enemy, but admonish him as a brother" (II Thess. 3:14-15). With modesty and kindness, each one, according to circumstances, will perform this spiritual alms-giving which is fraternal correction." "Let us not become desirous of vainglory, provoking one another, envying one another. Brethren, even if a person is caught doing something wrong, you who are spiritual instruct such a one in a spirit of meekness, considering thyself, lest thou also be tempted" (Gal. 5:26, 6:1)

Briefly, the baptized who live under the government of the Spirit will refrain from "works of the flesh" which, together with "libertinism, impurity and debauchery" are "enmities, contentions, jealousies, anger, quarrels, factions, parties, envies," and they will produce that "fruit of the spirit" which, with charity, joy and patience, are "kindness, goodness, faith, modesty, continency" (Gal. 5:19-24).

To these duties which characterize the relations of individuals between themselves, the apostolic teaching adds others which define the Christian's behavior toward the group or the collectivity of which he is a member.

The family, the basic unit of society, deserves special mention. Paul explains this in both his epistles to the Colossians (3:18, 4:2) and to the Ephesians (5:22, 6:10). In all of these there is the same concern for unity and order, without which there can be no health for a living organism. This order necessarily implies a hierarchy between the members of the family, a head who commands, and subjects who obey; however, they remain equally removed from dictatorship, slavery and demagogy. This is a subtle relationship in which the distinction of rank and of duties finds its counter-weight in the enthusiasm of all the members for unity under the impulses of love. Fraternal love already calls all the baptized to such a reciprocal service that in all humility they may be *subject* one to another (I Pet. 5:5); the very particular sentiments of the wife in regard to her husband will maintain her *a fortiori* in a loving submission to him: "Be subject to one another in the fear of Christ. Let wives be subject to their husbands as to the Lord" (Eph. 5:21-22). The husband does not inherit the power of an Arabian chief; in his turn he must serve his wife even to the point of sacrificing himself for her: "Husbands, love your wives, just as Christ also loved the Church, and delivered himself up for her" (*ibid.* 25).

And here is a completely different shade of meaning in the commandment of obedience as it pertains to parents and children: "Children, obey your parents in the Lord, for that is right. 'Honor thy father and thy mother'—such is the first commandment with a promise—'that it may be well with thee, and that thou mayest be long-lived upon the earth," (*ibid.* 6:1-3). However, not all rights are granted to parents over their children: "And you, fathers, do not provoke your children to anger, but rear them in the discipline and admonition of the Lord" (*ibid.* 6:4); how revolutionary was this formula in a time when the rights of the "paterfamilias" were almost unlimited!

Finally, in another relationship in which love also reigns, there are the mutual duties of masters and slaves. The letter to Philemon concerning his slave Onesimus set forth these general directions:

> "Slaves, obey your masters according to the flesh, with fear and trembling in the sincerity of your heart, as you would Christ: not serving to the eye as pleasers of men, but as slaves of Christ, doing the will of God from your heart, giving your service with good will as to the Lord and not to men, in the knowledge that whatever good each does, the same he will receive back from the Lord, whether he is slave or freeman.
>
> And you, masters, do the same towards them, and give up threatening, knowing that their Lord who is also your Lord is in heaven, and that with him there is no respect of persons" (*ibid.* 6:5-10).

In this passage Paul is respecting the social order of his time; he does not condemn slavery in spite of its defects, but he throws leaven into the lump, and little by little this leaven will accomplish its work and the basic fraternity and equality of men between themselves will be confirmed more fully. Such fraternity and equality, however, will not suppress the diversity of functions nor any hierarchy among men in the human community, nor in the family community either; there will always be commanders and subjects. But the faithfulness of all of them to their task, whether they command or obey, is judged in relation to the common good of which all of them are equally the servants; all men, masters and slaves, employers and employees, are under the jurisdiction of the same Master, in the diversity of their functions; they are members of the same body, grouped together under Christ, their only head.

This same doctrine governs the relations of citizens with the state and its leaders:

> "Be subject to every human creature for God's sake, whether to the king as supreme, or to governors as sent through him for vengeance on evildoers and for the praise of the good. . . . Live as freemen, yet not using your freedom as a cloak for malice but as servants of God. Honor all men; love the brotherhood; fear God; honor the king" (I Pet. 2:13-18).

Paul, of course, would have wished that the Corinthians, who were litigious to excess, would settle their differences among themselves: "Do you not know that we shall judge angels? How much more worldly things!" (I Cor. 6:3). This does not mean that he was slighting the jurisdiction of public magistrates, even if they were pagans, but he wanted to avoid the scandal of discord between brothers and call to mind the requirements of the fraternal community: "it is altogether a defect in you that you have lawsuits one with another" *(ibid.* 7). Therefore, he does not contradict himself in the epistle to the

Romans when, perhaps because of his admiration for Roman power, he good-naturedly outlines the duties of a Christian toward the civil power which he briefly summed up in his letter to Titus (3:1): "Admonish them to be subject to princes and authorities." All power comes from God, and power that exists *de facto* is from God: "Let everyone be subject to the higher authorities, for there exists no authority except from God, and those who exist have been appointed by God. Therefore he who resists the authority resists the ordinance of God" (Rom. 13:1-3). Furthermore, the power is exercised in the name of God; the prince is "the minister of God," whether it is a question of good to be fostered or of evil to be repressed (*ibid*. 3-5). From this we may conclude that obedience is not a matter of fear of punishment, but a matter of conscience.

The state is an image of the family of God; the governors are the "ministers of God," and in that measure, the "servants of God" owe them interior obedience, the obedience of free men which is ultimately amenable to God alone; for the same reason, they owe them the honor which is coupled with fear: "Render to all men whatever is their due: . . . fear to whom fear is due; honor to whom honor is due" (*ibid*. 7). These sentiments of the soul command the external deeds which are forms of service on the temporal level: "Render to all men whatever is their due; tribute to whom tribute is due; taxes to whom taxes are due" (*ibid*.), as on the spiritual level: "I urge therefore, first of all, that supplications, prayers, intercessions and thanksgivings be made for all men; for kings, and for all in high positions (I Tim. 2:1-2).

This obedience, this respect and honor, is particularly required of baptized persons in regard to the heads of their church or the brethren who deserve consideration because of their singular devotion to the Christian community: "Now I beseech you, brethren—you know that the household of Stephanas and of Fortunatus are the first-fruits of Achaia, and have devoted themselves to the service of the saints— to such as these do you also be subject, and to every helper and worker" (I Cor. 16:15-16). Paul takes pleasure in insisting upon these delicate sentiments, which are the blossoms of charity quite as fully as of justice. To the Corinthians he recommends respect for his very young disciple Timothy: "Now if Timothy comes, see that he be with you without fear, for he works the work of the Lord just as I do. Therefore, let no one despise him" (*ibid*. 10-11). He will praise them in his second letter for their deference and their submission in regard to Titus whom he had sent to them to perform a difficult mission (II

Cor. 7:13-16). As he understands it, the responsibility of *presbyters* is such that after having been the object of a very prudent discernment before the imposition of hands, they are deserving of the consideration of the community in the fulfillment of their task: "Let the presbyters who rule well be held worthy of double honor, especially those who labor in the word and in teaching" (I Tim. 5:17), but all this honor is not meant to relegate these deserving men to isolation; therefore the brethren should show them a particular affection: "Now we beseech you, brethren, to appreciate those who labor among you, and who are over you in the Lord and admonish you. Esteem them with a more abundant love on account of their work" (I Thess. 5:12-13). With another shade of meaning, the epistle to the Hebrews takes up this same them: "Obey your superiors and be subject to them, for they keep watch as having to render an account of your souls; so that they may do this with joy, and not with grief, for that would not be expedient for you. Pray for us" (Heb. 13:17-19).

These few notes concerning the social virtues of the Christian according to the teaching of the apostles, are already sufficient to bring out the evangelical concept of the "Kingdom of God" with its double aspect, earthly and heavenly. Christians are its citizens; they hold various ranks in the kingdom according to the duties that are entrusted to them, but they live in the unity of their calling:

> I therefore . . . . exhort you to walk in a manner worthy of the calling with which you were called, with all humility and meekness, with patience, bearing with one another in love, careful to preserve the unity of the Spirit in the bond of peace: one body and one Spirit, even as you were called in one hope of your calling; one Lord, one faith, one Baptism; one God and Father of all, who is above all, and throughout all, and in us all (Eph. 4:1-7).

Filial and fraternal love is the law of the Kingdom; its forms are many and various according to the conditions of the vital exchanges between the Kingdom's servants: filial piety, esteem, respect, honor, obedience, liberality, fortitude in the presence of evil, compassion and forgiveness, all being blossoms of the unique stalk of charity which the unique Spirit nourishes: "But above all these things have charity, which is the bond of perfection" (Col. 3:14).

3. THEOLOGICAL CLASSIFICATION OF THE SOCIAL VIRTUES

Charity is the first of the social virtues; it unites the members of the Christian community to one another and to Christ, their head.

This solidarity is manifested in its elementary degree by *justice* thanks to which each member respects the rights of the others: "The man who loves someone renders him his due spontaneously and with joy, and even adds something more for him quite generously" (III *Cont. Gent.*, ch. 128).

The property of justice is to render to each one his due in such a way that *whatever is given should be equal to what is owed*. But this justice, in the pure state, is insufficient to regulate all the social behavior of the Christian: therefore apostolic teaching enumerated, in addition to justice and charity, a large number of virtues which, without being confused with these, are like overtones. And for its own part does not experience show us various ways of paying our debts, just as there are various kinds of debts. We may recognize our debt to another person and we acknowledge it even when we admit the impossibility of liquidating it; to claim otherwise would even be to deny the debt; for example, in his filial piety the child recognizes the extent of his debt to his parents, but at the same time he confesses his inability to pay it; the height of justice would then be to humbly confess insolvency.

On the other hand, not all debts contracted by men among themselves correspond to the notion of debt in the same way; the debt of a buyer to the seller is one thing, and the debt of fidelity which requires every man to tell the truth to his neighbor is something else; and it is still another kind of debt, and how very subtle, that requires each person to make life pleasant for his neighbor. In the first case, we spoke of debt in the strong sense, as a "legal" debt, since among men the law is the external rule of their obligations; in the other cases, the debt is only "moral." If a man does not acknowledge this, he dishonors himself; he is no longer a complete man or an "honorable" man. In the presence of pure justice we therefore meet with other forms of virtues which participate in some measure in the idea of justice without realizing it fully; either the debt is never completely liquidated, or else it is not a debt in the strict meaning of the term. The first series of these virtues have fortunately been named *virtues of veneration and of reverence*, and the second series were given a generic name, the *virtues of civility*.[1]

St. Thomas devotes forty questions of his IIa IIae to the study of these various virtues (Questions 80 to 120). Faithful to the principle

[1] Trad. de la *Som. Théol.*, édit. de la Revue des Jeunes: R. P. Bernard, *La vertu*, Renseignements techniques, pp. 435 et ss.

which he derived from Aristotle, of studying each virtue according to its subject, he presents the virtue in its positive being, and then in its opposite vice. From this is derived the following outline for the study which interests us:

A. The Virtue of Veneration and Reverence
    I. Filial piety
    II. Deferences
        1. respect
        2. obedience
            Its opposite vice: disobedience.
B. The Virtues of Civility
    I. Gratitude
        Its opposite vice: ingratitude
    II. Vengeance
    III. Truth
        Its opposite vices:
        1. lying
        2. simulation and hypocrisy
        3. kinds of falsehood:
            (a) boasting or bragging
            (b) false humility.
    IV. Courtesy
        Its opposite vices:
        1. flattery
        2. the spirit of contradiction (quarreling).
    V. Liberality
        Its opposite vices:
        1. avarice
        2. prodigality.

To direct his line of thought, the Angelic Doctor quite obviously learned from ancient stoicism, represented by Cicero in his *First Rhetoric*. However, he did not remain confined within the framework of the six virtues named by the Roman moralist: religion, piety, gratitude, "vengeance," consideration, truth. He borrows courtesy from the Neo-Platonist philosopher, Macrobus, and liberality from Andronicus, the Peripatetic. He likes to quote other masters, Aristotle primarily, or Seneca, especially in regard to gratitude.

In this recourse to various masters of human morals, the Doctor is not yielding to any caprice. He is the theologian who is obliged to explain the Word of God. He inquires among the philosophers, as among the "saints," and is free to present the result of his research and his thorough investigations in an arrangement which is proper to himself. Nor is he taken in by his arrangement of moral learning. Was he not careful, in broaching the second part of his moral work, to inform us concerning his thought on this precise point; following the Stoics, he will group the moral virtues under the four cardinal virtues, but such a reduction is not absolute: *aliae virtutes morales omnes* aliqualiter *reducuntur ad virtutes cardinales*. The more so as, on the subject of each cardinal virtue he will study all the virtues which *in any way whatever*—"qualitercumque"—are related to it, and their opposite vices. "In this way—and this is important for a doctrinal synthesis intended for beginners—nothing that pertains to the moral order will have been neglected." [2]

Three other questions terminate the general treatise on justice, one of them on *extra-legal equity,* the second on the *gift of piety,* and the third on the *precepts of justice,* such as they are given to us in Scripture.

In the thought of St. Thomas, the first of these questions, whose subject is *extra-legal equity,* overlaps both those devoted to the virtues connected with justice and also the general treatise on justice: like Aristotle, he explains that equity is a part of justice, but it also surpasses it, and consequently it surpasses the limits of the outline. In regard to the question of which the gift of piety is the object, it gives the whole treatise its profound meaning: the justice of the Christian is a filial and fraternal justice; it summons us to make the ascent to the queen of the virtues, charity itself. It also delivers us from that error which would consist in settling upon an analysis which kills, and in considering the moral world, and in the particular case, community life, as a game of patience, composed of detachable pieces, fortunately grouped together again. The true moralist, after this analysis which is fruitful for a better knowledge of all the resources of nature and grace, must take up again the proper synthesis of the life which is animated by the breath of the Spirit, and find the *Unity* which is not

[2] Prologue of the IIa IIae. In the *Sentences* (III Sent., dist. XXXIII, q. 3, a. 4), Saint Thomas presents six classifications of the virtues connected with justice, borrowed from various philosophers. His personal position is not in full accord with that of the *Summa Theologiae:* thus, he considers as *subjective* parts of justice certain virtues which, in the other, he will call *potential virtues,* namely: deference, obedience, vengeance, and truth in one respect.

confusion, the perfect Oneness of God in the many-faceted participation that is realized by the sons of God.

4. THE VIRTUE OF VENERATION

The term "piety" designates primarily a sentiment of love and respect for God; it is synonymous with "religion." *Piety* governs all worship which is directed to the Divinity, and rules over the principle of our entire life and its evolutions. God, in His sovereign liberality, allows His creatures to participate in His causality, and to become in some way an object of worship. Thus we speak of "filial piety" and of "patriotic piety" to express our veneration for our parents and our country—both of these being secondary principles of our being and of its growth.

(a) *Filial Piety*

Our *filial piety* is directed first of all to our father and mother from whom we receive our life and, through education, the formation of our soul: "Thou shalt honor thy father and thy mother," says Scripture in many places. Filial devotion is also directed to all the members of the family who share their life and in whom, consequently, we find them again.

It has therefore many nuances according as it pertains to our brothers and sisters, our grand-parents or more distant relatives. It also affects conjugal love in that the husband and wife, while striving for a growing intimacy between themselves, are at the service of human generation; in their reciprocal love a certain ancestral veneration insinuates itself. The father's love for his son also bears a reflection of filial piety, for the father does not only consider this child as the fruit of his own life, but as the offspring of a whole generation, a new member of the family, and he projects upon him the respect, the love and the devotion which he feels is owing to his ancestry.

We should note that communion of blood is not the whole reason for filial piety, although it is the most obvious. More profound, because spiritual, is that communion of souls of which education is the principle: a human generation finds its specificity and its fulness in that action of the parents' soul upon that of their children. Thus men still speak of filial devotion in the strict sense in the case of adoption, and in a more diminished sense, in the case of the teacher and the student.

Filial piety is an interior sentiment above all else. Nevertheless it has external manifestations of respect and obedience, both being normal expressions of that dependence of the offspring in regard to his origin which the piety acknowledges.

In certain cases, exceptional *per se*, this acknowledgment that is proper to filial piety, will take on the form of a *service* rendered. The respect which, in fact, the son owes to his father makes any disgrace of the father unbearable to the son, and obligates him to bring him help if there is need for it in order that he may continue in the integrity of his being. Thus the son becomes, through a reversal of conditions, the protector of his father, for example in his old age.

Filial piety is not contradicted by Our Savior's saying: "If anyone comes to me and does not hate his father and mother, and wife and children, and brothers and sisters . . . he cannot be my disciple" (Lk. 14:26). Virtues may complement one another; but they are never contradictory. Filial piety cannot be an obstacle to the virtue of religion. However, the requirements of one virtue are capable of modifying the exercise of another virtue. The Church understands it in this way when, in the name of filial piety, she forbids the entry into religious life of a son who must care for his parents. On the other hand, the Religious whose life is definitively engaged by the religious profession in a way which his Rule delimits, will no longer express his filial piety in the same manner as in the days of his freedom, because of his obligations. And furthermore, if he is solemnly professed, his consecration having penetrated to the very root of his faculties, his filial piety does not provide him with any plausible reason for leaving his cloister. Nevertheless, he is obliged, within obedience and the respect for his Rule, to see that those of his own family are not in any need. (Cf. IIa IIae, q. 101, a. 4, ad. 4.)

(b) *Patriotic Piety*

In the Scriptures, God requires of His sons devotion to their country, together with filial devotion. During the whole history of Israel patriotic sentiment appears as a constant factor in the life of the chosen people. The second Book of Machabees is particularly rich in teaching on this subject. The attitude of Jesus toward His country is likewise suggestive, like that delicate feeling of Paul, obliged to appeal to Caesar against the Jews, but with no intention of accusing his own nation (Acts 28:19). Contemporary popes on several occasions have stressed this idea of the fatherland and have emphasized patriotic duty: *Immortale Dei, Summi Pontificatus* give evidence of this.

The word "patria," the Latin term for fatherland, comes from *pater,* "father," and connotes an idea of generation. The fatherland is in fact a moral and civic community formed by men who communicate among themselves in the same heritage of blood, land and spiritual culture. Patriotism is primarily an instinct of becoming rooted in that environment which is a part of ourselves and is our source of life. It is furthermore, on the spiritual level, an attitude of mind and will, an awareness of our involvement in the fruitful unity of the racial community and in its order, with a profound respect for its values of life and the obligations which emanate from them.

Patriotism calls for a *cult* and a *service.* The *cult* is the interior respect, with all its manifestations in regard to the fatherland, and in regard to those who represent it in any respect, whether leaders, compatriots, or the national flag. The *"service"* represents the active share which the citizen must take in the work of conservation, growth, transmittal and defense of the common patrimony. It has various forms. Let us mention those that are principal: *obedience*—community activities can only be fruitful in a well ordered evolution, which implies a "command" and a correlative "obedience": *taxation*—the community of the fatherland is rooted in the earth; it has needs of a temporal kind, and its sons owe it to themselves and to their country to provide for these needs, each according to his status and his condition; *blood*—the service of the fatherland may require the sacrifice of life itself. The fatherland is not merely a community of economic interests; it is before all else a spiritual and cultural community; the defense of the land is thus the defense of a soul. The law of charity, which sometimes prescribes the loving of our neighbor more than our own corporal life, then expresses a kind of justice: there is a *debt of blood.*

Christian patriotism repudiates all *exaggerated nationalism* which tends to make an absolute of the national interest. The pagan theory of the deification of the fatherland or the state was revived in that error which Pius XII denounced in his Encyclical *Summi Pontificatus* (October 20, 1939). Nationalism sins against the citizens, considered merely as "things," and against other human groups who are treated as enemies because they limit the extension of the country. A sound patriotism, fully in the service of the mother country, allies itself on the contrary with the consciousness of the universal solidarity of mankind. This very consciousness is an enrichment of patriotic sentiment, for all fraternal communion is beneficial to the participants. "The nations, in their development and differentiation according to the various conditions of life and culture, are not meant to destroy the unity of mankind, but to enrich it and adorn it by the communication of their particular qualities and the reciprocal exchange of goods, which can only be possible and at the same time efficacious when a mutual love and a charity that is acutely felt unite all the children of the same Father and all the souls redeemed by the same divine blood" (*Summi Pontificatus*). This brotherhood must not be confused with that internationalism which denies all distinction within the human community, and therefore the fatherland. Christian doctrine "teaches that, in the exercise of charity, there exists an order established by God, according to which we must manifest a more intense love and do good to those to whom we are united by special ties" (*ibid*).

The historical evolution of the human community leads us to distinguish two concepts that were primitively identical: the fatherland and the nation. Sometimes they are still identical, as when the native land, juridically organized, has its place as a "nation" among other organized nations. However, these concepts may be so irrelevant to each other that the fatherland has no juridical meaning as a nation, and inversely, the nation in no way represents the fatherland. Such was once the case in Poland, divided into several nations, and such is the case, and even more so, in satellite countries. Similarly, patriotism is distinguished from civic loyalty, the latter being related to legal justice, the virtue by which the member of a collectivity renders to his group his duties of respect and of service without acknowledging in it any origin of being; the former, however, is an acknowledgment of dependence of existences. These two virtues may coincide in their external manifestations, for example, in the payment of taxes, but their interior spirit is different.

An opposition may even arise between the fatherland and the nation. The conflict must then be settled to the advantage of the fatherland. Just as the family, a natural unit of society, takes precedence over the latter, so likewise the fatherland, a quasi-natural group, takes precedence over the nation, a juridical group—to such a degree that the latter has the duty of respecting the life of the former, and in cases of abuse, the devotion of the patriot legitimates his rebellion against the nation. Nevertheless, we must reject that other excess, which endeavors to make a nation out of every fatherland. The common good of the community of men has its exigencies expressed by the historical and psychological laws. The French problem after the treaty of

Brétigny in 1360 was one thing; it was a different problem after the treaty of Ryswick in 1697.

(c) *Deferences*

If every human life has its roots in the family and in the native land, it is developed, however, in a wider temporal and spiritual community in which it is providentially inserted. In regard to this community, by which he lives, man could not deny a certain dependence, which is not without analogy with his first dependence in relation to his family. "Deferences" result from a sentiment of justice which acknowledges this dependence and accepts the duties that proceed from it. They are directed to the community concerned and to those who represent it, the leaders who bear responsibility for it, the citizens of note who, through the excellence of their virtue, their learning, their devotion to public affairs, or their very fortune, forge, so to speak, the soul and body of that community, assure the successful deployment of its activities, and are in some way its *fathers*.

This sentiment which recalls filial and patriotic piety, has normal manifestations, public or private, such as the ceremonial which is customary among all peoples, even the most primitive, according to which they honor their leaders and their great men. The affinities between this ceremonial and the religious liturgy are often impressive; in fact, it is often difficult to discern what pertains to the one and what pertains to the other. In a Christian regime, this virtue has a particular shade of meaning, since as Paul said, the head of the community is the "minister of God."

(d) *Obedience*

Obedience is a particular sign of these marks of respect due to those in authority. But it is placed in the order of action.

The double dependence of men and things in being and action in regard to God, is again found, but at a lower level, in the order of creation, since the Creator, in His liberality, has enabled things not only to exist but also to "cause." A hierarchy of causes corresponds to the hierarchy of beings, and the former, in the human order, appears in the form of leaders and subjects, command and obedience, on both the secular and religious levels.

Obedience consequently appears as subordination of two prudences and two wills. The prudence of the subject borrows from the prudence of his superior all the motives which will enlist his action and sustain it; his personal "order" is wholly informed by the order conceived and willed by his superior. This adoption of the superior order is not made because the subject becomes aware that it is well-founded, which would only result from prudential "counsel," but because this order is "imposed" by the competent authority who has the responsibility for the good to be sought, and the common end to be attained. In itself, obedience makes an abstraction of the liking or the aversion that is felt at the time of the command, as it is compatible with a speculative judgment entirely different from the practical judgment which directs it. The obedience of the judgment, which is sometimes mentioned, only pertains to that full adaptation of the practical judgment to the judgment of the superior, immediately bound up with the action taking place.

Obedience is really a surpassing of self in the sense that it is the linking of an inferior causality to a superior causality, and by the latter to the first cause. It permits passing from a personal level to a broader level, and from an individual good to the common good; it certainly does not equal the theological virtues in dignity, but among the moral virtues it holds a principal rank by this very surpassing which it assures for service in the family of God. On the other hand, we see the evil of disobedience, the ruin of the common order, since there can be no community without order, and consequently, without obedience. Every sin is judged according to its opposition to charity, the virtue of unity; disobedience is therefore judged by the fact that it compromises this unity, and consequently, is opposed to the divine love which embraces the whole family of God constituted upon the earth in many communities: "Therefore he who resists the authority resists the ordinance of God" (Rom. 13:2). However, not every disobedience is equally contrary to the unity of the community; to weigh its gravity we shall consider the superior's intention and the relation of the prescribed means to the common end desired.

Perhaps it would not be useless to emphasize that the virtue of obedience truly involves the citizen on the political level, and consequently, the latter is obliged to obey interiorly the just orders of constituted authority. The Christian is not dispensed from such obedience; his faith does not make him a stranger to the social community or to its order of justice. On the contrary, it provides a new motive for his submission. Nor is this obedience incompatible with the usage of the legitimate freedom of choice and action which every citizen enjoys within the framework of the constitution of his state, nor is it incompatible with resistance to abuses of power.

Obedience to God does not create any difficulties; our faith assures us that God is good, just and wise, and that He is our Father. Obedience to men, however, sometimes creates a problem. The concatenation of secondary causes proceeding from the first cause, is actually susceptible of failures; a superior causality may be an obstacle to the working of a subordinate causality; a causality may tend to exceed its limits. Thus a more important superior may over-rule the decision of one of his subordinate officers; in this case the subject will conform to this superior will, quite like a "motive" which abates under the action of a more powerful "mover."

Besides, every human authority only has a limited jurisdiction, whether these limits originate in nature itself or in a legal constitution. Any exercise of jurisdiction which does not respect its own limits is invalid, and, except in case of scandal, does not engage the obedience of the subjects. No man, for example, has a direct power over the purely interior activities of another man. Every human community is in fact subject to the earthly conditions of time and space, by reason of the structures of our being; its order can only be established, safeguarded and controlled in the measure that it is firmly rooted in the sensible. Therefore it does not involve the interior order of souls except by reaction, when, for instance, the prescribed activity only has meaning by its outlet on the level of virtue, like the requirement of attendance at Mass which necessarily connotes both the intention of uniting oneself with the sacrifice and the attention required for an effective union. On the other hand, within the limits of the constitution proper to the community, all the external acts of the individual are capable of falling under the jurisdiction of the competent authority, except the activities of nature which are at the service of the conservation of the human being and his multiplication: in this respect all men are equals.

However, the defectibility that is proper to all human order, sometimes legitimates a doubt on the subject of the just exercise of authority. When the head of the community has chosen means with a view of the common good, it may be asked, is it applicable? Is it virtuous? Is the superior exceeding his power in the exercise of his office? These are three cases of doubt which may be settled in favor of the authority, but for different reasons.

In the first case, the subject is exceeding his own rights. It only appertains to the person who is responsible for the community, the head himself, to ask the question of the relation of the means to the end, and to decide the matter, since it is his proper duty to preside over all the ordering of the activities of the community, and to decide upon the adaptation of the means to the common end.

The solution of the other two doubts belongs to the subject since it involves the morality of his act. The common good still demands submission.

The second doubt pertains to the morality of the means chosen by the superior. The good intention of the latter is not questioned; one could not deny it except in case of real proof, or at least great probability; the problem is thus reduced to the just valuation of a particular choice. This judgment depends *primarily* upon the one who has the responsibility for the intention of charity in the community. The certain rectitude of his will provides the basic value to the whole moral order which he directs, and prevails over speculative doubt on the subject of the specification of any particular act: respect for this order, commanded by the end, corrects, if necessary, the involuntary error pertaining to the choice of means.

The third doubt whose object is the legitimate exercise of authority is likewise resolved in favor of the superior: such is the excellence of peace among the community values that one can only compromise it in cases of exceptional evidence. But every insubordination is a blow against the order of the community, its unity and its peace.

Nevertheless, the application of these principles does not always bring the desired light; doubts may still hover, and if they are not resolved, there is a risk of jeopardizing the common good. Recourse to higher authority is then required; it is really a question of saving the good of the community through the use of means perfectly adapted to its end, and of strengthening the intention of charity which tolerates no hesitation, and finally of maintaining the real order of the community without which there can be no lasting peace.

The problem of obedience is a problem of order and of the common good. It is in this respect that obedience is related to justice and charity.

5. THE VIRTUES OF CIVILITY

A community lives by the relations established between superiors and subordinates, and quite as fully by those which are forged between its members. After having studied the virtuous order which governs the first of these in the *virtues of veneration*, we must now consider the order which presides over the relations of men, equal to one another: called the *virtues of civility*, which assure its perfection.

(a) *Gratitude*

Can we speak of equality between the members of the same body? Are they not reciprocally dependent? Is not every man the benefactor and the debtor of his brother? The Apostle enjoined the faithful to *edify* one another, and to be "artisans of life" for one another, and consequently to be *subject* one to another in all humility (Eph. 5:21). An elementary justice requires recognition of this dependence in regard to one's brother and the rendering of honor and reverence to him, as to a real principle of good. Such is *gratitude*, which is primarily an attitude of the soul. If however this benevolent brother should some day be in need himself, it could be manifested through "service." We must note, however, that this service only pays the debt of gratitude in part. Gratitude appears as an important factor of the community life of men, and consequently we see how evil is its opposite vice, "ingratitude."

(b) *Vengeance*

The unity of the community of men is achieved by the communion of all of them in the good: it therefore requires that anything which might be susceptible of hindering this should be ruthlessly discarded; resistance to evil, whether personal or social, called "vengeance," is a virtue, the virtue of those in authority, "God's minister, an avenger to execute wrath on him who does evil" (Rom. 13:4), and a virtue of the community's members themselves, who, each according to his position, are likewise obliged to take a stand against evil and to reject it. Vengeance rationalizes and divinizes the instinct of defense which makes every being rise up against evil. Its external expression is called "coercion," which, in the community, has its laws, but which is likewise legitimate, within certain limits, in private cases: as when a father corrects his child, or one neighbor, by some strong gesture, calls an obstinate neighbor to order. Such a virtue is entirely ordered to the common end and has nothing in common with gross *vengeance* which does not strive for the maintenance of order through respect for persons; virtuous vengeance attacks the sin rather than the sinner; its purpose is to restore and not to ruin.

(c) *Truth and Its Opposite Vices: Lying and Indiscretion*

Among the goods which men owe one another reciprocally, *truth* holds the first place. A community life is impossible without this communion of minds and hearts which "veracity" assures. By this virtue each man is frank with his neighbor, opportunely communicating his thought to him through the instrumentality of a word that is always in accord with his thought. In Christianity this virtue possesses a particular savor since the God of Christians is Truth.

Veracity applies its effort in two directions: to tell things as they are, and to tell them opportunely. It therefore moots two problems: that of truth and falsehood, and that of discretion and indiscretion.

We are deficient in the virtue of veracity in speech by lying, and in acts by simulation and hypocrisy. We may also distinguish the simple lie which consists in telling a falsehood, from that lying which is the fruit of vanity, and which exaggerates the case of the party concerned. This is called "boasting," and there is another kind, more subtle, which is used egoistically with the intention of evading one's responsibilities, and consists in underrating oneself; according to St. Thomas, after Aristotle, this kind of lying is given the name of "ironia"—false humility. All these falsehoods in words or in deeds are serious to the degree that they are contrary to the love of God and the love of neighbor. It is an offense against God to falsify the truths of the faith, and a serious detriment to our neighbor; it can likewise be a grave wrong against the latter when simply human truths are distorted. Moreover, to lying properly so called may be added another malicious act from the point of view of the intention: lying in order to hinder the coming of the Kingdom of God, and in order to do evil to other men. Finally, lying may be an evil through the scandal that it causes or because of its disastrous consequences.

However, do not the necessities of daily life compel men to lie? St. Thomas expressed the feeling of everyone by writing: "It is permitted to prudently veil the truth" (IIa IIae, q. 90, a. 3 ad. 4). But can the truth be concealed without lying? What is lying?

In lying, as in every moral act, we shall distinguish its purpose, which is deception, and its object, the declaration of something false. The evil intention may have bearing upon the one or the other. Lying, in its more specific characteristic, does not consist in directly wishing to deceive, but in wanting to say something false. This results in suppressing the normal relationship which exists between the thought and the word which is its sign. To wish to deceive is the cause and consequence of this first bad will. The problem of lying is exactly that of the value of speech considered as a symbol.

Speech is included among the conventional signs used by men and over which they have power. These signs are essentially modifiable, either under the pressure of daily life, or through the connection which is established between various signs and which give different shades of meaning to the symbolism: the gesture or the look either strengthen or diminish an affirmation. With the imbrication of the signs, other conditions are susceptible of modifying their tenor. Speech, however, is a product of the collectivity. After all, not every man is the arbiter of its meaning; as a simple user of this instrument of exchange, the individual is obliged to respect its communal value. He would falsify it by using it apart from the common intention. It follows that no mental reservation may legitimately strain the meaning of a word, or impose a meaning upon it which it does not possess in common speech. On the other hand, like all instruments of exchange, speech is subject to the fluctuations of social conditions; it evolves with the life of the community to the point of enriching itself with new meanings, by the tacit consent of everyone. Thus, when we say "The gentleman is not at home" we commonly mean "The gentleman is not at home to visitors."

At the start of such an evolution, must we necessarily suppose that there is an abusive use of the formula, a real lie? Or is not the situation the same in this instance as in matters of custom, contrary to the law, which acquire the force of law after a certain time? To deny absolutely that there is any sin in the first infractions of this law, like the lie in the first strained use of an expression, would be ingenuous, but it would be rash to affirm that in such cases there is always disobedience and lying.

In regard to *extra-legal equity,* we will note how the common good sometimes requires that we go beyond the letter of the law in order that we may respect its spirit, and how the personal prudence of the citizen is needed to make up deficiencies in the legislator's lack of prudence. Speech is for the enrichment of individuals, as members of the community, in the communion of minds: "Wherefore, put away lying and speak truth each one with his neighbor, because we are members of one another" (Eph. 4:25). Outside of usage, this instrument appears under a rigid form: the strict meaning given in the dictionary. Reimmersed in the activity of the collectivity and of its members, the word loses its absolute sense, and borrows from the contingency of life; this tinges it with relativity: its meaning is relative to the requirements of the totality of the community and the individual conditions which connote the commerce of two men between themselves. The coupling of words varies their respective meaning; the gesture formulates them, and the circumstances of conversation add to these shades of meaning. Such is the case with the handshake, normally a gesture of friendship, which in certain conditions loses its original meaning almost completely and only signifies a vague communion of men among themselves. My partner has taken a position which is not true to him; discretion forbids me to follow him there; my answer, from that moment, will no longer be an answer in the strict sense, but will be a polite attitude. The social conditions of this exchange are such that this formula no longer tends to express my thought on the subject regarding which I am unduly solicited, but expresses that normal interior attitude of one man to another who has the sense of propriety. It is self-evident that such a formula will have to remain within broad generalities; it excludes all fabulations whose character would no longer permit judging it a courteous silence. The person concerned will perhaps not have the intelligence to understand the indiscretion and the reserve which it imposes; my answer will deceive him. This is a case of indirect intention. My intention is not to deceive him, but is the immediate good for which I am responsible, measured within that of the entire community, which authorizes me to tolerate this evil, the error of my partner, quite like the physician who, in order to cure a sick man, administers an effective medicine to him of which one of the secondary effects is however injurious. I have neither deceived in strict meaning of the term, nor lied; I have not spoken contrary to my thought.

We also sin against veracity by not speaking opportunely; there is a time for speaking and a time for silence (Eccl. 3:7). The *fidelity* which men owe one another and which they owe to the community —fidelity without which no social life is possible—imposes discretion, that virtue of the man who knows how to keep a secret. There are secrets whose object is such that to reveal them would be a serious wrong to the integrity of the moral being of the person concerned; his "standing" in the community is compromised and thus the fulfillment of his task as a man. Other secrets are not of such a nature in themselves; however, they have a right to be respected, for they were "confided." The bearer of the secret and his confidant are then involved in a unique movement of willing and living. By the confidence of which he has been the object, the confidant makes all the interests of the other person his very own; he defends them like those that belong to himself. We see how a secret by natural right may also be a "confided" secret, and this is normally the case when a sick person confides his ailment to the physician.

Here again the relations between individuals cannot be judged without reference to the entire community; their good cannot be defined without a comparison with the good of everyone. We understand therefore that *fidelity* to the entire community takes precedence over particular fidelities; no secret can prevail against the common good. Nevertheless, let us immediately note that this same common good requires that private secrets be inviolable, such, for instance, as the sacramental secret in the order of religion, and the professional secret, with various degrees, in the secular order. The common good is composed of the respect for the rights of each person to his fulness of life, within respect for and development of the entire community.

(d) *Courtesy*

If there can be no community life without *veracity,* neither can there be any without pleasure or without joy. Each person *owes it to himself* and *owes* it to his neighbor to put forth his own effort to create and maintain a climate in which it is good to be alive; no one should be unpleasant to his neighbor. *Courtesy* is that disposition of the heart which imposes upon our speech, our actions, and our whole behavior that just measure which results in their being well ordered; it is the virtue of propriety. Aristotle gave this the name of *friendship* by reason of its affinities with the love which closely unites two hearts and imposes upon them an entire order in their external relations.

Contrary to courtesy, in varying degrees, are *flattery* and the *spirit of contradiction; flattery* whose praises do not respect the truth or the occasion, and which deviates from the ultimate measure of all things, the love of God and genuine love for our neighbor; and the *spirit of contradiction* whose intemperances do not originate in antipathy, which would be contrary to charity, but derive from a disordered instinct, always ready to take the opposite stand from the other person without any regard for him.

(e) *Liberality*

The earthly community of men implies continuous exchanges of both their temporal and their spiritual riches. The citizen, and *a fortiori* the Christian, must keep his heart *open* to others; when it is a question of material wealth, we say that he should be *liberal*. Liberality is in fact that virtue which assumes responsibility for the interests of other men to such a degree that it respects not only *their good*—which is pure justice—but it also gives them its *own*, uniquely because it is "proper" to do so; in this respect there is a quasi-debt which is sufficient to legitimate a certain relationship between these two virtues.

The property of the liberal man is to be generous, and yet not thoughtless. He gives according to his means, after having satisfied his personal needs and those of his family, without stinginess. According to Paul's recommendation, he administers his property and acquires more with a view of distributing largess (Eph. 4:28). He gives, certainly; and better still, he *knows how* to give. Liberality is a matter of the soul; it is not measured by the quantity of goods offered but by the dispositions of the man who does the giving; therefore, the propertyless poor man may be more liberal than the rich man; we will recall the liberality of the poor widow in the Temple (Mk. 12:41 and ff.).

The *miser* and the *spendthrift* are the opposite of the liberal man.

The *miser*, so often considered in the holy writings, bears in his heart an immoderate love of possession; for him, riches are not a *useful* good, but an *absolute*. He sins when, to satisfy his passion, he withholds the good of others: this is the common sin of injustice. But his specific sin is in concentrating his entire life upon his belongings, and in loving them, desiring them and taking pleasure in them without moderation.

Experience shows that this sin is more easily a sin of the aged. While their strength is diminishing, they try to make up the deficiency in external goods, and sometimes they go beyond the proper degree. The insistence of the Scriptures in stigmatizing this sin indicates its gravity. In addition to being the principle of many injustices and causing malicious acts, avarice has its own maliciousness in the fact that the love of money is susceptible of making man revolt against God and against his neighbor. Such avarice is a grave sin.

This sin, however, is not equal in gravity to the sins which are directly against God and against men; nevertheless it bears in itself a particular shame since the soul allows itself to be dominated by the lowest kind of goods. And among the sins it also holds a certain sovereignty, which explains its place among the *capital sins,* the kind of sin which gives birth to others. Money exercises an almost infinite attraction upon the heart of man, so greatly does it seem to promise all the goods; to assure himself of money, man lends himself to numerous compromises: betrayals, frauds, lies, perjuries, disturbances, violence and hardness of heart.

While the miser sins against liberality by an inordinate love of money, the spendthrift sins by excessive disinterestedness. The miser was wholly striving for the acquisition and conservation of his good, while the spendthrift is not doing so sufficiently, and wears himself out in wasteful spending. Completely contrary as they may be, these two vices are susceptible of being found in the same heart; a person may be thoughtless in his spending and at the same time avid for gain. We should note that prodigality is not to be judged according to the quantity of goods given up, but according to the excess of this relinquishment. The liberal man may despoil himself more than the prodigal, when necessity requires it; thus the Religious who, in order to follow Christ in poverty, gives away all his goods as alms is not a prodigal, but a liberal heart.

Prodigality is an open road to many kinds of intemperance. This lack of moderation in the use of money is particularly perceptible in the presence of goods which flatter the carnal appetites; as a matter of fact, the person who has no taste for the good of virtue is easily exposed to seeking the pleasures of the flesh.

Of these two sins, avarice and prodigality, the latter is less serious than the former. Prodigality is in one respect less contrary to liberality than avarice, since it resembles it in giving; furthermore the prodigal is useful to others, while the miser is not useful to anyone, not even to himself. Finally, prodigality is more curable than avarice: being less distantly removed from virtue, it can return to it with less difficulty. Age also helps to bring about this return since it is more likely to tend toward avarice; lastly the destitution toward which it points imposes wise solutions; avarice, on the contrary, having its source in the threat of poverty, becomes all the more insistent as the threat increases.

(f) *Extra-legal Equity*

Every community is governed by a law whose purpose is to express the exigencies of the common good and to delimit the duties of the members of the community in the presence of these exigencies. To respect this law is to be *just,* fully in one's place in one's being and in one's action in regard to the whole and to each of its parts.

Nevertheless, can we claim that the law prescribes everything that is just? Does its formula embrace all the rights of the community and of its members to such a point that there can be no perfect justice without blind obedience to that law?

It is the property of a law to be universal, since, by nature, it is addressed to the entire collectivity. It therefore surpasses private cases and only retains their common character. It does not fix itself upon the infinite variations of the contingent. The law is for this very reason condemned as being deficient in matters of justice; its formula is too general to define the rights of each member of the community even unto his ultimate characteristics. Therefore, in certain exceptional cases, to follow the letter of the law is to act badly. It is virtuous to pay one's debts; nevertheless, in the case of a father who is scandalously prodigal to the detriment of his children, justice requires that the reckoning of accounts be deferred to the advantage of the heirs. In such an occurrence, the letter of the law seems too narrow; justice requires that it be surpassed. It appertains to *epikeia* which we call *equity* to bring about this judgment.

This virtue of *equity* which implies a sovereign prudence in its exercise is not in opposition to the law; instead, it is the law's "righting at the point where the law is deficient because of its universality." [3] It certainly does not go contrary to that which is just according to justice itself, but only what may be just according to law. It is not exercised for the benefit of an individual against the good of the whole; it respects the one in order to better assure the other.

Equity will then appear as a species of justice, and as primary. It appertains to justice to render to each man his due, and according as "each man" is, for me, my neighbor; or, for the person in authority who is responsible for the community, one of his subjects, we distinguish *commutative* justice and *distributive* justice. If "each

[3] A. D. Sertillanges, *La philosophie morale de saint Thomas d'Aquin,* Ch. IX. The virtues related to justice, section 9 concerning extra-legal equity.

man" designates for the individual the collectivity of which he is a member, it is a matter of *legal* justice. *Equity* has in common with this *legal* justice the respecting of the common good. It is differentiated from it by the very fact that it goes beyond the letter of the law and intends to safeguard the goods of all men, and of the entire community, and of each of its members. Legal justice thus appears as a participation in *equity,* the latter being the superior rule for human acts.

6. THE GIFT OF PIETY

St. Thomas excels in the analysis of each of the segments which compose the psychology of the Christian. He is no less a master in the reconstruction of this psychology. In this reconstruction he is able to combine all the elements in the unity of charity; and more particularly, all the virtues which resemble one another he knows how to group around each cardinal virtue, as around a distinct organism. In this same effort at synthesis, he studies in regard to one of those mysterious forces which tradition designates by the name of *gifts of the Holy Spirit;* he associates the *gift of piety* with justice.

This is a profound insight of the theologian on the Christian mystery, the mystery of unity through charity which is its center. The treatise on justice is enriched by it with new light.

Certainly, because of its sovereignty, charity communicates a reflection of its own glory to all the virtues; the chastity of the Christian which is governed by his filial love for God, with all its power of spiritualization, is one thing; and that of man left only with the strength of his heart is something else. But justice is still more profoundly transformed.

Justice is in fact the virtue which governs the relations between two human beings, strangers to each other. It makes me respect the good of the *other man.* If this other man is united to me, his good is in some way my own; by respecting *his* good, I respect *my own.* Justice here loses its strict sense as my obligations become heavier, obliged as I am in regard to the *other man* in the same way as in regard to *myself.* Justice is here completely informed by the love which I have for myself to such a degree that it is like one of its elementary signs. This justice governs the relation between husband and wife, between parents and their children, and between friends.

We now see the transfiguration of justice under the influence of charity within the community of the sons of God. In the terms of

Scripture, God is a *father,* a *spouse* and a *friend* for the Christian, and other men, through this union with God, are *brothers.* In all truth *religion* becomes *piety,* and the relations of men between themselves follows from this piety. Every act of justice—whether God or men be the object of it—is, from this point of view, an act of religion, but of that religion which wishes to be the expression of a filial and fraternal sentiment. And just as the Holy Spirit is at the origin of our filial piety in regard to God, according to the Apostle's saying: "You have received a spirit of adoption as sons, by virtue of which we cry, 'Abba! Father!'" (Rom. 8:15), so likewise He inspires all our behavior with fraternal justice in regard to men, our brothers in God. The Christian, in these many acts of justice which form the course of his community life, is under this transforming influence of the gift of piety.

This justice, wholly imbued with charity, experiences tendernesses and makes demands that are unknown to a merely human justice. Under the impulses of the Spirit, the Christian cannot permit the rights of God and those of his brothers to be ignored; he cannot rest until all of them are fully respected; *he hungers and thirsts for justice,* and he is prepared to make any sacrifice in order to give this elementary manifestation of his love to God and to his brothers. At the same time, his justice adopts the measures of love; far from strictly reckoning what he owes to his brother, he gives liberally; he is *merciful,* as he is *gentle,* expelling from his heart all the hard feelings in the presence of unkindness toward himself, the height of justice, under the influx of love, being "to overcome evil with good."

We understand, therefore, that goodness, kindness, and gentleness are characteristics of the Christian soul. They reveal the action of the Spirit within the entire community and in each of its members. They inspire and guide the works of justice which attract, even as they are its fruits, those of the first of the virtues, charity.

REFLECTIONS AND PERSPECTIVES

Everything which pertains to the relationship of one man to another, or of a man to a community, or vice versa, and of one community to another community, is related more or less closely, or more or less distantly, to justice. That is why we place the "social virtues" around the cardinal virtue of justice of which they are realizations or imperfect imitations.

Since it is the function of justice to render *adequately* to others that which is their due, the imperfection, from the point of view of justice, of the virtues which we are studying may derive from the inequality of the contracting parties which prevents the lesser person from *adequately* paying his debt; or from the legal non-determination of the *debt,* which thus becomes a simply moral debt.

Consequently, we may arrange the social virtues, always from the point of view of justice, in the following way:

1. Inequality of the contracting parties:

"Justice" of man towards God: *Religion*
"Justice" of children towards parents:
"Justice" of citizens towards their country: Filial and patriotic *piety.*
"Justice" of subordinates toward superiors: *Deferences* Respect / Obedience

2. Moral debt only.

A. Necessary debt for the maintenance of customs (the existence of good relations between men):

"Debt" of truth in words: *Veracity.* / in deeds: *Justness.*
"Debt" of thankfulness: *Gratitude.*
"Debt" of vengeance for evil inflicted: *Vengeance and Punishment.*

B. Debt that is unnecessary but very useful for the development of of good relations among men:

"Debt" of courtesy: *Civility,* or affability, or courtesy.
"Debt" of not hoarding one's property for oneself, but of being "generous" in its use and distribution: *Liberality.*

To all this we must add "epikeia" or *extra-legal equity,* which is the "sense" of the just deed within and beyond legal formulas.

It is obvious that this classification has a share of relativity; such as it is, however, it sheds a certain light on each of the social virtues. The vices opposed to each virtue may be ordered like this:

Vices opposed to religion Excess in worship resulting from infidelity or falsity: False worship of the true God / Idolatry / Divination / Superstitious observances.
(Superstitions)

Lack of religion ⎰ In regard to God: tempting of God.
or irreligion ⎱ In regard to the divine Name: perjury.
⎰ In regard to sacred things: sacrilege, simony.

Vice opposed to piety: impiety

Vices opposed to deferences ⎰ disrespect
⎱ disobedience

Vices opposed to truth ⎰ in words—lying
⎱ in deeds and attitude—hypocrisy

⎰ One pretends to be more than one is: boasting
⎱ One underrates oneself falsely: false humility

Vice opposed to gratitude: ingratitude

Vices opposed to vengeance ⎰ by excess—cruelty
⎱ by default—softness

Vices opposed to ⎰ by excess—flattery, obsequiousness, adulation
affability ⎱ by default—incivility, boorishness, coarseness,
insolence, effrontery, irreverence

Vices opposed to ⎰ by excess—prodigality
liberality ⎱ by default—avarice

It is interesting to note that the vice *which goes in the direction of virtue,* although it goes beyond moderation, is less serious on account of this fact than the sin which goes in the opposite direction. Thus prodigality, which moves in the direction of the virtue of liberality (which is generosity and sharing), is less serious than avarice. However, this principle must be applied with discretion. What may seem to be the direction of a virtue is not always really so. Determine, for example, the direction of the virtue of vengeance.

The Gospel and humanism. At the beginning of this chapter we mentioned everything that the theology of the social virtues owed to the Gospel, and to the New Testament in general. It would be interesting likewise to show all the borrowings that reason, in search of understanding of the faith and of the believer's behavior, has legitimately made from pagan moralists: Socrates, Plato, Aristotle, Zeno, Marcus Aurelius, Seneca, Macrobus and Andronicus, etc.

The religion and rational equilibrium of the morality which the theologian is thus led to organize is not without its risks. A narrow and closed "evangelism" would lead to a disregard of the splendid virtues which, although they are not literally evangelical, are nevertheless fully imbued with its spirit. An indiscreet rationalism would lead to a disregard for the hierarchy of virtues in relation to charity or to giving more credit than is proper to certain human virtues whose value depends on the charity that inspires them. It is obvious, for example, that "vengeance" does not seem to be an evangelical virtue in itself; however, it may be one if charity inspires and guides it; but the temptation of the "rational" man will always be to make his own *law* triumphant, to the detriment of charity. The Gospel is not the triumph of a law, but of love. From this point of view, evaluate the evangelical quality of every virtue considered. Finally, compare the various exigencies of the Old and New Testaments in relation to these virtues.

Questions that are peculiar to each virtue. Suggestions for study.

Filial Piety

How does it happen that the debt toward our parents cannot be adequately paid? What shall we think about this definition from St. Thomas: "Pater est principium et generationis et educationis et disciplinae et omnium quae ad perfectionem humanae vitae pertinent" (IIa IIae, 1, c): The father is the principle of the generation, the education, the teaching, and of everything that is relative to the perfection of human life. From this point of view, relate the duties of children toward their parents. Can filial devotion disappear if the parents prove to be bad parents? Should parents develop this virtue of filial devotion in their children? "Filial devotion" in the Bible.

Limits of filial devotion (cf. Mt. 10:37). Can a person refuse to enter the Religious life, or delay entrance, through filial devotion? In what circumstances? Can one refuse to be married, or delay marriage, or refuse the person whom one loves, through filial devotion?

The gift of piety. Signification. Theology.

Patriotic Piety

What is the fatherland? History and evolution of this term, and of the sentiments that it evokes. Is the "fatherland" absolutely identical with the "nation" in which one is born and one lives (history of nationalities and nationalism). What does a man receive from his country, and what does he owe to it? Biblical bases of the "theology of patriotism." The limits of patriotic piety. To what point can man abdicate his freedom of choice, of speech, of activity? Is conscientious objection contrary to "patriotic piety"?

Means of formation. Is the State obliged to educate its citizens in patriotic piety? Is it legitimate to arouse greater patriotic ardor? May the State use all the means of propaganda: the Press, Radio, Television, etc.? May the citizens actively defend themselves against excessive stimulation of patriotic worship?

The nations and "catholicity." Fraternity in Christ with all men; does this fraternity give the Christian duties toward other nations and other countries than his own?

Cf. among others, Eric Peterson, *Le problème du nationalisme dans le christianisme des premiers siecles,* and J. Daniélou, *Note conjointe,* in *Dieu vivant,* n. 22 (1952), pp. 87-106.

Deferences and Courtesy

Politeness and the Gospel. Show how the evangelical virtues may be magnificently expressed in certain codes of politeness, and how "worldly vanities" may be contrary to the Gospel. Compare the different social customs of a region, a country, and a people, and appraise them in terms of Christian value.

The "question of rites" in the missionary history of China. What is necessary for religious rites, or merely social rites, if they are to be taken into Christianity? Or if they must be rejected?

The "dowry" in Negro Africa. Is the dowry offered by the fiancé to the parents of the fiancée compatible with "respect" for personality? Should the missionary bless such a custom or try to improve it?

The necessity of honors and social rites to render these honors. Should the honors due to the important people of this world be rendered regardless of their virtue? May they be refused? (The example of King Farouk, who was "dismissed"). In what circumstances? Can there be indignity in rendering excessive honors? (Platitude?)

Honors due to the Saints. Dulia and hyperdulia. Exact theology of "hyperdulia" due to the Blessed Virgin.

Obedience

Principle: The principle source of the theology of obedience is found in Rom. 13:1-7, particularly these lapidary formulas: "there exists no authority except from God, and those who exist have been appointed by God. Therefore he who resists the authority resists the ordinance of God."

In trying to understand this "datum," the theologian discovers an analogy in the government of God between the behavior of "natural" beings and that of spiritual beings. Obedience is the human instance of general submission of a subordinate creature to a superior creature in a divine government which operates hierarchically. Here are some of St. Thomas' formulas:

"Ille qui obedit movetur per imperium ejus cui obedit, sicut res naturales moventur per suos motores" (IIa IIae, 104, 4, c): The person who obeys is moved (set in motion) by the command of the person he is obeying, as natural things are moved by their "movers" (in the philosophical sense that is used here, "mover" is a synonym of "agent," or of "efficient cause"). "Obedientia movetur ad imperium praecipientis quadam necessitate justitiae, sicut res naturalis movetur ex virtute sui motoris necessitate naturae" (IIa IIae, 104, 5, c.): The person who obeys is set in motion, at the command of the person who makes the rule, by a certain necessity of justice, as the natural thing is set in motion, because of its mover, by a necessity of nature. "Sicut actiones rerum naturalium procedunt ex potentiis naturalibus, ita etiam operationes humanae procedunt ex humana voluntate" (IIa IIae, 104, 1, c.): Just as the movements of natural things proceed from natural powers which move them, so likewise human operations proceed from the human will. "Movere per rationem et voluntatem est praecipere" (IIa IIae, 104, 1, c): To set in motion by the reason and the will is to command.

We can sum up this doctrine in the following comparative table; in the top section, that which pertains to the natural order; in the bottom section, that which pertains to the order of human actions:

In Natural Things:	*Excellentia virtutis naturalis:* Excellence or superiority of a natural power	*Movere:* to set in motion.	*Subdi.* subject being (*passive*)	Natural Effect
Corresponding to: (in human affairs)	*Auctoritas:* Authority of the superior.	*Praecipere, id est movere per voluntatem:* To command, i.e., to set in motion by the will.	*Obedire* To obey. (Active Verb)	Human Operation

Example: Just as God, by the heat of the sun (a natural power), assures the growth of the plant and its ripening (a natural effect), so also by the authority of a superior who commands, the particular activity of an obedient subject is assured.

Obedience implies a free dependence; the person who obeys is only reached and set in motion by a word (a precept) which he accepts and makes his own.

Important points: 1. Obedience is a particular virtue and not wholly a virtue. Among the *goods* which are suitable for us, it represents the good of the commanded duty.

2. Obedience represents a portion of the moral life because it is a good. Duty is to be done because it is a good, but not everything which is a good can be defined as a "duty"; not everything which is a good is the object of a determined precept; (on this subject see Fr. Tonneau's introduction at the beginning of Volume III).

3. However, every act of virtue can be the object of a precept. In this case it is related to both the virtue considered and to obedience, but with two distinct motives.

4. Although it is a particular virtue, this does not mean that obedience is not an excellent virtue, on account of its special relationship to charity. (Cf. Jn. 14:15). When friends are equals, they have the same will, and they do not need to obey each other. But when there is a subordinate person and a superior, the identity of wills results in the obedience of the subordinate person and assures the perfection of his love. And when the given command expresses the will of God— and this is the case in every just obedience—the obedience assures the perfection of charity.

Obedience is not a theological virtue (God is not its object, but rather the command), but obedience is that which is the most pervious to love, for the precept expresses the will of God.

Questions Relating to Obedience; Suggestions for Study

It is evident that obedience to God cannot have any limits. Then explain the order given to Abraham (Gen. 22:2), the order given to the Hebrews to carry off the gold and silver of the Egyptians (Ex. 11:2), and the order given to Osee to marry an adulterous woman (Osee 1:2).

The limits of human authority. Are we always obliged to obey established authority? (What is established authority?) Should we refuse obedience in all matters to an established government when it is corrupt? Should obedience consider the virtue of the person who is commanding? Must we obey the State even in questions of taxation, customs-duties and economics? How? Is the Christian obliged to obey more than others? (Cf. Lk. 20:25; I Pet. 2:13; Titus 3:1; Rom. 13: 1-7.) In what circumstances must he refuse to obey? In all these cases show the application of philosophical principles stated above (a comparison of the hierarchy of natural powers with that of spiritual powers).

Is Religious obedience specifically different from ordinary obedience? Show that there is the same virtue, but which is extended to all the activities of life. What are the limits of Religious obedience?

Obedience and education. Show the qualification of a master of the spiritual life with full authority in his domain. Develop this point in particular as it concerns the authority of Religious superiors and that of parents. Can the Religious life be defined as a school of perfection by means of obedience? The theology of education: How far does the authority of parents extend? Should they try to correct all shortcomings, and teach all the virtues? Merits and demerits of tolerant parents? Or intolerant parents?

The "obedience of judgment." What does this mean? Is it a satisfactory formula? Distinguish, in this respect, docility, an act of prudence, and obedience, an act of justice and a social virtue.

Gravity of disobedience. Gravity of servility? If there is no possibility of obeying excessively, show that one can obey someone, or in some matter, that does not call for obedience.

Truth (or Veracity)

Here we mean the "truth," not in the sense of "true" (in this sense it is not the virtue, but the object of the virtue) but in exact sense in which it is the virtue of the truth.

Truth, like justice, is a virtue of the will, since it is an act of the will to manifest the true. The true, in this respect, is considered, like the just deed, the object of justice, under the aspect in which it is a certain good which the will desires.

Words (and even certain gestures, or certain attitudes) are *social signs* of intelligible realities. But they are also rather flexible signs, and according to the way they are used, they may signify different things. There is truth, when there is the will to declare what is true, even with signs that are apparently unadapted, from the moment that no one is deceived by them; there is falsity and lying whenever there is the will to state what is false. Evaluate, according to this principle, the lying in worldly formulas like "Madam is out" to express "Madam is not receiving." What is the purpose of the person who says this?

Truth being a certain "justice," may we consider that there is no longer any truth or lying when the speaker no longer has the "right" to know the truth? (For example: resisting citizens being interrogated by the representatives of an occupying power? Or an enemy being interrogated by an ally? A priest interrogated about the secrets of his ministry?) Is heroic silence on the contrary the only possible escape for someone who is interrogated in these circumstances?

Is truth a sufficient criterion of the morality of the press, of publishing, of the radio and of motion pictures? What kind of performance is objectively true?

What should be thought of "mental reservation"? Or of "playful lying"?

Truth in the Bible. Evaluate the lie of Abraham (Gen. 12:13), and that of Rebecca and Jacob (Gen. 27:6-30). Truth in the New Testament (cf. Mt. 5:37). Particularly the theme of Light and of the "sons of light" in St. John.

Gratitude

Principles: "Gratiae recompensatio attendit magis affectum dantis quam effectum" (IIa IIae, 105, 5, c.): The value of gratitude is estimated more according to the affection of the person who gives than according to what he gives. "Beneficium, secundum quod est laudabile, prout ei gratiae recompensatio debetur, materialiter quidam consistit in effectu, sed formaliter et principaliter in voluntate" (IIa IIae, 105, 5, 1 ad.): The good turn which is praiseworthy and which calls for gratitude consists materially in that which is given but resides formally in the will of the person who gives.

These principles find their greatest application in the religious act of thanksgiving. In this respect, that which is given (or offered) no longer counts except as the expression of the will.

Appraise the different kinds of gratitude and the gravity of ingratitude according to the dignity of the person who gives, or the bond of existing friendship, or the value of the gifts received.

Gratitude (cf. Mt. 18:33; Lk. 7:42) and thanksgiving in the Bible. Comment upon "God loves a cheerful giver" (Prov. 22:8 and II Cor. 9:7).

Vengeance

Principles: "Vindicatio fit per aliquod poenale malum inflictum peccanti (IIa IIae, 108, 1, c.): The role of vengeance is to inflict some punishment upon the sinner. "Vindicatio intantum licita est et virtuosa, inquantum tendit ad cohibitionem malorum" (IIa IIae, 108, 3, c.): Vengeance is licit and virtuous in so far as it seeks to repress evil.

Comment upon Rom. 12:19. May we still speak of Christian vengeance after Paul's precept against seeking to avenge ourselves? In what circumstances?

The qualification for properly punishing, in parents, teachers, and superiors. Must parents punish children for every fault? The instructive role of punishment and of tolerance. How to punish: before the age of reason? after? (It is interesting to note that in ancient times, in this respect, the "age of reason" was synonymous with the "age of puberty." Cf. IIa IIae, 189, 5, c. What should be thought of this estimation?) Is a punishment sinful if it is inflicted because of impatience, or wounded self-love? "Prudence" in punishments. Psychoanalysis of punishment: Formation and evolution of the "super-ego" in the child. Psychoanalysis of unpunished faults, although real, in the child. Theology of corrective punishment. The chastisement of adults. Should the penalty be curative, educational, or simply coercive? Can there be Christian toleration of a prison whose effect would be to corrupt the prisoners? Should every prison be rehabilitative? (On other penalties, particularly the penalty of death, see the treatise on justice.)

Vengeance, as the just exercise of anger. Cf. Jn. 2:15-16. Gentleness and strength of Christ.

Liberality.

Liberality is a virtue which is related simultaneously to justice, fortitude and temperance; to justice because it consists in knowing how to let go of one's possessions when these can be useful to *someone else*, even though nothing is due him in strict justice; it is related to fortitude and to temperance because it also consists fundamentally in putting a generous motive into one's interior *passions*: the fear of risk, the love of gain and of money. Liberality in the *Gospel*. Its end. Comment upon Luke 14:12-14.

Theology of money. Comment upon and explain the parable of

Luke 16:1-14. Cf. Feuillet, *Recherches de science religieuse,* 1947, n. 1. Show the "duty" of rich men.

Poor men and liberality. How can a poor man perform an act of liberality? The spirit of evangelical poverty: is it "liberality"? The poverty of Religious: show that the role of the vow is not to make the Religious "frugal" but "liberal."

Avarice. Its gravity. Why is it a capital sin? Comment upon the saying: "Covetousness is the root of all evils." Avarice and old age: Why is the elderly person more easily avaricious? What reaction is possible?

Epikeia (*or Extra-Legal Equity*)

"Epikeia"—from the Greek word ἐπιείκεια, which means likelihood, expediency, moderation, equity, gentleness, goodness—is not an "imperfect justice." On the contrary, it is the flower of justice.

Equity which re-establishes justice, shows, contrary to the superstition of literalism which is destructive of the common good and prejudicial to everyone, that the law is at the service of man and of the good, and not otherwise.

Cases of equity in the Gospel: concerning the Sabbath and the purifications. Equity and freedom of the Christian.

BIBLIOGRAPHIE

Saint Thomas d'Aquin, *Les vertus sociales,* Trad. de J.-D. Folghera, notes de R. Bernard, Paris, Éd. de la Revue des J., 1932.
Les ouvrages de morale sociale cités au chapitre XII (Justice) seraient également à mentionner ici.

Sur la piété patriotique:

M. Blondel, *Patrie et humanité,* Lyon, Chron. Soc. de France, 1928.
La Patrie, Lyon, Chron. Soc. de France, 1941.
J. Delos, *La communauté nationale dans la communauté humaine,* Lyon, Chron. Soc. de Fr. 1946.
J. Folliet, *Morale internationale,* Paris, Bloud et Gay.
J. Tonneau, *La pape, la guerre et la paix,* Paris, Éd. du Cerf.

Sur l'obéissance:

En dehors des articles de revues (*La Vie spirituelle, Nouvelle Revue théologique,* etc.) et de Dictionnaires, citons seulement:

A. Plé, O. Rousseau, M. Olphe-Gaillard, etc., *L'obéissance et la religieuse d'aujourd'hui,* Paris, Éd. du Cerf, 1951, où l'on trouvera, en références, toute autre bibliographie désirable.

Sur les autres vertus, consulter les ouvrages d'ensemble, les dictionnaires, les revues, et l'intéressant ouvrage de V. Jankélévitch, *Traité des vertus.*

Sur le don de piété:

A. Gardeil, *Le don de piéte et la béatitude de la douceur* in *La Vie Spirituelle,* tome 35, pp. 19-39.

I. Mennessier, *Le don de Piété,* in *La Vie Spir.,* ppl Su., tome 30, pp. 40-42.

BIBLIOGRAPHY

Cranny, Titus, *The Moral Obligation of Voting,* Washington, C. U. Press, 1952.

Cronin, John F., S.S., *Catholic Social Action,* Milwaukee, The Bruce Publishing Company, 1948.

Davis, Henry, S.J., *Moral and Pastoral Theology,* Vol. II, pp. 69-140, 410-426, London, Sheed and Ward, 1941.

Dorszynski, Julius A., *Catholic Teaching about the Morality of Falsehood,* Washington, C. U. Press, 1948.

Farrell, Walter, O.P., *A Companion to the Summa,* Vol. III, pp. 165-246, 303-356, New York, Sheed and Ward, 1940.

Gilson, Etienne, *The Church Speaks to the Modern World: The Social Teachings of Leo XIII,* Garden City, N. Y., Doubleday & Company, Inc. (Image Books), 1954.

Hughes, Philip, *The Popes' New Order,* New York, The Macmillan Company, 1944.

McHugh, John A., O.P., and Callan, Charles J., O.P., *Moral Theology, A Complete Course,* Vol. II, pp. 402-459, New York, Joseph Wagner, Inc., 1930.

McLean, Donald A., *The Morality of the Strike,* New York, P. J. Kenedy & Sons, 1921.

Miller, Raymond J., C.SS.R., *Forty Years After: Pius XI and the Social Order,* St. Paul, Radio Replies Press, 1947.

Moore, Kenneth B., O. Carm., *The Morality of Detraction,* Washington, C. U. Press, 1950.

Regan, Robert E., O.S.A., *Professional Secrecy in the Light of Moral Principles,* Washington, Augustinian Press, 1943.

Sheed, Frank, *Society and Sanity,* New York, Sheed and Ward, 1953.

Sheedy, Charles E., C.S.C., *The Christian Virtues,* pp. 289-316, Notre Dame, Ind., University of Notre Dame Press, 1949.

Sturzo, Luigi, *The International Community and the Right of War* (Trans. Barbara Carter), New York, Richard R. Smith, Inc., 1930.

———— *Nationalism and Internationalism,* New York, Roy Publishers, 1946.

Suhard, Card. Emmanuel, *The Church Today,* Chicago, Fides Publishers Association, 1953.

Williams, Melvin J., *Catholic Social Thought,* New York, The Ronald Press Company, 1950.

Wright, John J., *National Patriotism in Papal Teaching,* Westminster, Md., The Newman Bookshop, 1943.

Fitzpatrick, J. P., S.J., "Encyclicals and the United States," *Catholic Mind,* 53:1-12, Ja '55.

Gill, J. J., S.J., "Apostolate of Patriotism," *Action,* 8:34-39, Ja '55.

Hopkins, V. C., "Nationalism Re-examined," *Thought,* 30:389-401, Autumn, '55.

Murray, J., S.J., "Patriotism and the Next Best Thing," *Studies,* 41:163-174, Je '52.

Newman, J., "Theology of Social Action," *Irish Theological Quarterly,* 22:31-48, Ja '55.

Regan, Robert E., O.S.A., and McCartney, John T., "Professional Secrecy and Privileged Communications," *Catholic Lawyer,* 3-14, Ja '56.

Sheerin, J. B., C.S.P., "The Virtue of Patriotism," *Homiletic and Pastoral Review,* 54:1039-1043, S '54.

Suhard, Card. E., "Blueprint for a Christian Family," *Grail,* 35:38-45, Oct '53.

Thomas, John L., S.J., "The Catholic Family in a Complex Society," *Social Order,* 4:451-457, D '54, 5:69-76, F '55.

Wilms, H., O.P., "St. Thomas' Influence on Piety," *Cross and Crown,* 7:347-357, S '55.

Chapter VIII

FORTITUDE

by A. Gauthier, O.P.

THE THEOLOGICAL PROBLEM OF FORTITUDE

I. THE GREEK CONCEPTIONS OF FORTITUDE
  1. Current ideas
     (a) Courage (ἀνδρεία)
     (b) Austerity (καρτερία)
     (c) Magnanimity (μεγαλοψυχία)
  2. The elaborations of the philosophers
     (a) Man and the world
     (b) The virtues of adversity: courage, austerity,
         magnanimity
     (c) Their classifications
     (d) Their meaning: the exaltation of man

II. BIBLICAL CONCEPTIONS OF FORTITUDE
  1. The power of God given to man
     (a) The vanity of man's strength
     (b) Fortitude, a divine attribute
     (c) The gift to man of God's strength
     (d) The gift received in hope
  2. The deployment of the power of God in man
     (a) Power (δύναμις)
     (b) Assurance (παρρησία)
     (c) Patience (ὑπομονή)
     (d) Longanimity (μακροθυμία)
         Martyrdom, the supreme act of Christian fortitude

487

III. POINT OF CONTACT

Chapter VIII

FORTITUDE

The Theological Problem of Fortitude

There is a theological problem of fortitude, and today it seems to be posed with particular acuteness. Everywhere, in fact, the same accusation arises against Christianity: the accusation that it weakens man and paralyzes his energies. This was Nietzche's accusation—Christianity is the resentment of the weak against the powerful—and it was the accusation of Marx—religion is the opium of the people—and behind these two leaders, in the Germany of yesterday and still in the Russia of today, millions of voices have repeated the accusation which, from those countries, has swept over all the countries of the world. Some have denounced "a debasement of oneself and an attitude without courage" in Christian humility; others seemed to see in Christian hope the principle of resignation which, teaching men "to silently endure an earthly hell in expectation of a so-called heavenly paradise" shatters all willingness to struggle and makes the Christian incapable of any effort.

In the presence of such reproaches, the anxious Christian of today wonders if, in fact, contemporary Christianity has not become insipid. Such insipidity, among too many Christians, is perhaps incontestable. But it does not explain everything. If we go back over the course of history we will see, from century to century, the same accusation repeated over and over. At one point we find it brandished by a Renan and by a Gambetta, who, in 1871, spoke against Christian education which can only form "a softened, weakened kind of humanity, resigned to suffer every misfortune as though they were the decrees of providence"; and again, in the eighteenth century, in the writings of the philosophers, and we find it once more in the closing years of the seventeenth century from the pen of Bayle, and in the sixteenth century in the works of Machiavelli:

Pagan religion only deified men of worldly glory, army generals and leaders of the Republic. Our religion crowns the humble and contemplative virtues rather than the active virtues. Our religion places supreme happiness in humility, abasement and contempt for human things; the other, on the contrary, made the sovereign good consist in greatness of soul, strength of the body, and in all the qualities that make men formidable. If our own requires some strength of soul, it is only to dispose us for suffering rather than for some vigorous action. Therefore it seems to me that these principles, by making men weaker, have disposed them to be more easily the prey of evil-doers. The latter have discovered that they can tyrannize without fear over men who, in order to go to paradise, are more ready to suffer injuries than to avenge them.[1]

But let us go further back and, in the era of the persecutions, we shall find the same accusation again, flung into the face of the Church of the martyrs. There are many evidences which show us the idea that was current in pagan society concerning the first Christians. They were called "exiles from life," "useless persons"[2] recognizable by their "lack of energy"[3] and their "abject inertia."[4] However, these weaklings knew how to die—yes, but as "despairing men" who hurl themselves at death through disgust with life here-below,[5] like "poor fools" who believe that they will find another life after this one,[6] and like "stubborn men,"[7] or as "tragedians,"[8] and not as heroes.

And regarding Christ Himself, the pagan Celsus, about 178, asked how anyone could compare Him with the heroes of paganism, like Anaxarchus for example, or Epictetus. Anaxarchus, ground in a mortar vessel, only felt contempt for this torture and said, "Tan, tan the hide of Anaxarchus, for you will never touch Anaxarchus himself!" This saying was worthy of a truly divine spirit. Epictetus, as his master was twisting his limb, quietly said to him, while smiling, "You are going to break it," and when it was broken, "Did I not tell you that you were going to break it?" But Jesus, in His sufferings was different. What wonderful remark did He make that could sustain comparison with these others? None whatever; He kept silent. Worse than that—He called for help, He complained, He prayed that death, which He feared, might pass Him by: "Father, if it is possible, let this cup

---

[1] Machiavelli, *Discours sur la 1re décade de Tite-Live,* book II, ch. 2; translated by Guiraudet, *Oeuvres de Machiavel,* t. 1, Paris, 1799, p. 323.— See Albert Cherel, *La Pensée de Machiavel en France,* Paris, 1935, in which will be found texts from Bayle, de Raynal, J. J. Rousseau, Quinet, Renan and Gambetta, pp. 175, 237, 238, 272, 298, 300.

[2] Tertullian, *Apol.* 42.

[3] Tacitus, *Histoires,* III, 75.

[4] Suetonius, *Domitian,* 15, 1.

[5] Tertullian, *Apol.* 50, 4; Lactantius, Div. Inst., V, 9; Tertullian, *Ad Scapulam;* Saint Justin, *Apol.,* II, 4, 1.

[6] Lucian, *Peregrinus.*

[7] Epictetus, *Conversations,* IV, 7, 6.

[8] Marcus Aurelius, *Thoughts,* XI, 3.

pass away from me." Truly a pathetic attitude, entirely worthy of a man who was mediocre and weak all during his life.[9] Nor was this the complaint of only one man; his words echoed for a long time, and were repeated, a century later, by Porphyry, the favorite disciple of Plotinus.[10]

Thus, the unbeliever has always reproached Christianity for making men unmanly. And the Church, confronted with these accusations, has always raised her voice to loudly affirm her consciousness of possessing an ideal of fortitude whose value and efficacy have proved to be incomparable. We need only consider the solemn protest made not long ago against the scoffing of the German Nazis by that great pope, Pius XI: "Humility, in the spirit of the Gospel, and prayer to obtain the help of God's grace can be perfectly combined with self-esteem, self-confidence and heroism. The Church of Christ which, through all time and up to the most recent present, counts more confessors and voluntary martyrs than any other moral community, does not need anyone's lessons concerning the heroism of sentiments and deeds." [11]

It is this scandal of a kind of fortitude, proudly claimed by the Church as one of her finest titles to glory, and scoffed at by the wise men of this world as a derisive weakness, which poses the theological problem of fortitude. What then is this Christian fortitude? Does it really deserve the name of fortitude? In other words, what does it have in common with the rational concept of fortitude? Such are the questions which a theology of fortitude must answer before anything else.

To do this, it is necessary first of all to specify the nature of the rational conception of fortitude—we shall turn to the Greeks for this —and in what the Christian conception of fortitude consists—we shall look for this in the Bible; then, we must study their meeting-point, and try from it to extricate laws.

I. The Greek Conceptions of Fortitude

It would doubtless be interesting to examine, even unto their most distant beginnings, the origin of the Greek ideas concerning fortitude and to follow their development in the course of history; but this would lead us too far afield. Let us therefore be satisfied to gather

[9] Cf. Origen, *Contra Celsum*, VII, 53; VI, 15; II, 22.
[10] Fragments, 62 and 63.
[11] *Mit brennender Sorge.*

together the most complete expressions, like those elaborated in the consciousness of the multitudes or by the reflection of philosophers.

1. CURRENT IDEAS

(a) *Courage* (ἀνδρεία)

The word which best expresses the Greek ideal of fortitude is ἀνδρεία. Ἀνδρεία is properly *virility*, that is to say the virtue by which man proves that he is a man, ἀνήρ. If we wish to have an exact description of it, we could not do better than to turn to Aristotle: in this respect, as so often, his *Ethics* only sums up "the tradition of the poets and universal opinion." [12]

Courage, speaking very generally, is a kind of stability which, in the presence of evils which threaten us, will make us remain fearless and steadfast. But there are many counterfeits of true courage, and to distinguish it from these counterfeits, we must specify, in the first place, the *objects* toward which it is exercised, and in the second place, the motives which inspire it.

Not to fear dishonor is one of the first counterfeits of courage, for as a matter of fact there are evils which we must fear, and if we are not afraid of them, it is impudence rather than courage. To be unafraid of poverty or illness is doubtless a praiseworthy attitude, but it still is not courage. What then will be the object that will define courage? Death. But not every death. There are deaths without glory. Not to fear death during a storm or in the course of an illness is not to be courageous. The only thing that can be the worthy object of courage is a death which is *noble*, that is to say a death which is a proof of valor. To act as a man of courage will therefore be to show oneself fearless in the face of a noble death and in all the circumstances in which one almost invariably risks such a death—circumstances which are nowhere more surely found than in war. [13]

To be unafraid of a noble death is therefore the *achievement* of the courageous man. But to be courageous this deed must still be accomplished for a good motive. Aristotle, in this respect, denounces five caricatures of courage: to be unafraid, because one is imbued with the *desire for civic honors*—or to be unafraid, because one has *experienced* danger—or unafraid because one is carried away by *anger*—or without fear because one is sustained by *hope*—and finally to be un-

[12] Festugière, *La Sainteté*, p. 38.
[13] *Eth. Nic.*, 1115, a 10—b 6.

afraid because one is *ignorant* of the peril. In all these cases, as a matter of fact, one accomplishes the external act of courage very well, but it is not accomplished *for its own sake*. The truly courageous man will be one who will accomplish it for its own sake, *because it is noble*. To be unafraid of a noble death, and to remain steadfast in circumstances in which one almost certainly risks death, and without desire, without passion, without hope, and quite lucidly, because it is noble to act in this way and the contrary would be shameful, is real courage.[14]

(b) *Austerity* (καρτερία)

We have now seen the attitude of the hero confronted with death. But he will also know how to face life and his attitude in this respect will be, first of all, a certain *austerity,* an austerity toward himself. In fact, is not life a struggle in which, in order to triumph, one must be austere, and is not this struggle, at the beginning, a struggle against oneself, or more exactly, a struggle against certain parts of oneself in order that one may be truly oneself? Man, as a matter of fact, is reason, the principle of order and the principle of harmony. But, within man, there also exist tendencies and blind, unruly instincts, always ready to pounce upon any pleasure, without discernment, and to flee every hardship, without distinction. If he lets himself go, he is finished as a man: he will no longer be himself; he will be an *indolent* being (μαλακός) to whom everything will happen at random and will leave its mark upon him. If he is to be his true self, and in order that he may leave his own mark upon things, he will have to be austere (καρτερός): it will be necessary for his reason to be mistress within him, and when he instinctively experiences a strong desire for some pleasure which is not in order, his reason must be able to *master* it, which is *continence* (ἐγκράτεια), and if he feels a violent aversion for some hardship which he must endure, he must be able to stand fast against this aversion—and in this instance it is quite definitely *austerity*.[15]

(c) *Magnanimity* (μεγαλοψυχία)

Life however is not merely a struggle for self-possession; it is also, and especially, a struggle for possession of the world. When a man is master of himself, he wants to be master of the world, and it is this

[14] *Ibid.*, 1116, a. 15—1117 a. 26.
[15] *Eth. Nic.*, VII, 8.

aspiration which expresses, in the eyes of the Greeks generally, the term *magnanimity*. Magnanimity is the virtue by which man affirms his greatness. At the basis of this conception of magnanimity there will therefore be a conception of the greatness of man. Man's greatness is manifested in action and in struggle. Magnanimity is therefore primarily the bravery which leads the warrior into the thick of the battle, but it is also the spirit of enterprise, the spirit of conquest, the insatiable desire for vanquishing and dominating, and for making a brilliant display of one's strength and one's superiority. And the reward for greatness thus conquered is honor and glory. Glory is the only dream of the magnanimous man, and dishonor is the only thing that he fears. To acquire glory he spares no trouble; he is prepared to make any sacrifice, even his own life, and to be rid of all dishonor or wipe out the stain of an outrageous insult, he will shrink from nothing. Magnanimity conceived in this way is the virtue of men of action. According to Aristotle's testimony, it is the virtue of Achilles and Ajax, and of Alcibiades also.[16] Philosophers may stigmatize it, but "it is the most noble of folly's names" says the author of the *Second Alcibiades*,—and the multitudes admire it, Isocrates extols it in his portrait of the ideal king (*Evagoras*), and if Demosthenes was indignant on finding it in Philip, a barbarian,[17] it is because he believed that it was the special appanage of the Greeks; he laid claim to it himself.

2. THE ELABORATIONS OF THE PHILOSOPHERS

The conceptions of fortitude which we have just described always remained alive in the Greek soul. But, beginning with Aristotle, and especially with the Stoics, new conceptions were elaborated along with these others, all of which were inspired by an identical preoccupation: to assure man's autonomy in regard to the universe.

(a) *Man and the World*

This preoccupation, moreover, was rooted in the very depths of the Greek soul. There has been a great deal of discussion concerning the serenity and the anguish of the Greeks in regard to life. As a matter of fact, there was such a serenity and anguish among the Greeks, just as there is a serenity and anguish in the Christian. But

[16] *Seconds. Anal.*, II, 13.
[17] *Pour la Couronne*, section 68.

they are quite contrary to each other. The anguish of the Christian is the anguish of sin. The Christian is pessimistic when he questions his own heart, or when he probes his own conscience, or let us say more generally when he sees man trusting to himself alone. For he knows that he is weak, powerless, in himself, to do the good he would like to do, and unable to avoid the evil which he detests. But the Christian is optimistic when he looks outside of man, when he looks toward God and when he considers the world as the creation of God; there is then serenity for the Christian who knows that God makes all things work together for good, for those who love Him. On the other hand, the Greek is an optimist when he considers man; he is then calm and serene, for he has faith in man and in the powers of man's heart to attain to virtue and happiness. His optimism is only hesitant when he looks outside of man and considers the external world; it is then that anxiety arises in his soul. Certainly the Greek loved to contemplate the world's harmonious regularity and the concurrence of all the parts in the unity of the whole which makes of it a κόσμος, that is to say an order, and this order seems beautiful and good to him. But it is a fact that the very law which assures the world its splendid regularity also labors to crush man. The Stoic imagery best expresses the Greek idea. Man is like a turtle which has strayed into the midst of a dancing chorus; the very harmony of the chorus demands that it be destroyed. Thus, the world continually weighs man down with a threat and a yoke. It was in this anxiety about the menace of the world that an immense aspiration was born, which, during the centuries, excited the Greek soul: the aspiration for liberation and deliverance. But while the liberation for which the Christian yearns is a liberation from the yoke of sin, and from one's very self, the Greek is hoping for liberation from the yoke of fate, a liberation from the menace of the world. This liberation could be sought for in two ways: an appeal to the gods, or an appeal to man. It was in this second way that Aristotle engaged Greek ethics: he does not appeal to justice or to the favor of the gods; it is only to the heart of man, and the resources and efforts of man, and of man alone. To man's cry of distress when he is crushed by fate, he does not respond by inviting him to lift up his eyes to a heaven that will finally make justice prevail or which will save him by its grace, but he calls upon him to find within himself the secret of his happiness, and to win his freedom in that way.

(b) *The Virtues of Adversity: Courage, Austerity, Magnanimity*

The philosophical conceptions of fortitude were elaborated in terms of this problem. Aristotle had already improved upon the current concept of magnanimity in this respect. But he had kept, as we have noted, the current and still pre-moral conception of *courage*, the war-like virtue. It was the Stoics who had the merit to raise courage to the rank of a properly moral ideal by their understanding that virile strength is better demonstrated in the struggle of reason against the instincts than in man to man fighting. Far from having death on the battlefield as its only object, courage would hereafter have as its objects, contrary to Aristotle's teaching, all the evils of existence valiantly overcome through fidelity to duty commanded by reason, including those of poverty, those of illness, and those resulting from undeserved disgrace. Likewise, and always because his *Ethics,* far from being a system of pure morality, still made wide provision for extra-moral elements, Aristotle had refused to give *austerity* the rank of a virtue. At the most it was only a half-virtue, he said, for it remains firm against evil instincts, by this very fact it implies their existence; true virtue, in addition to the rectitude of the will, implies that gift of nature which is a balanced temperament, the assurance of a perfect harmony. The Stoics, in this respect also, by their ascent to the level of pure morality, suppressed this requirement of an extra-moral element, and again associated virtue with good will and made a virtue of austerity.

(c) *Their Classifications*

However, when the moralism of the Stoics had in one swoop wiped out the nuances which distinguished courage, austerity and magnanimity, were they not bound to confuse them? Before being willing to accept this conclusion, the Greeks tried to maintain their distinction through subtle classifications.

The first part of these classifications was the work of Chrysippus (third century before Christ). In conformity with a theory that was classical among the Greeks from at least the time of Gorgias, he taught that courage was one of the four *primary* or *principal* virtues —since Saint Ambrose we call them cardinal virtues—and beneath courage Chrysippus placed austerity and magnanimity as *subordinate* virtues, without mentioning still other virtues such as *confidence* (θαρραλεότης). Furthermore, what was the purpose of this classification? It is difficult to state precisely. As early as the first century before Christ, the author of the *De Virtutibus* was bewildered by the divergent interpretations of it, three of which were destined to enjoy a long success: the subordinate virtues are the *species* of a *genus* which is the principal virtue; or else they are the *partial* or *adjuvant* causes of the principal virtue; or they are only *related* to it.

Nevertheless, with Stoicism itself, this classification of Chrysippus was soon questioned again. Toward 140 B.C., the founder of Middle Stoicism, Panetius, raised magnanimity to the rank of a cardinal virtue and assigned courage and austerity to it as parts, and among others, mentioned *security* (εὐθυμία) and *constancy* (εὐτσάθεια) as consequences. In Seneca's time magnanimity could thus claim to be "the most noble of all the virtues," [18] and the "highest virtue." [19]

However, the fondness for these technical classifications was quite rapidly lost. Panetius, becoming free of their yoke, had already preferred combining the three virtues of courage, austerity and magnanimity without any further distinctions in his familiar exhortations, and it was this tendency which, in the new Stoicism, definitely prevailed. According to Epictetus, courage-austerity-magnanimity form an indissoluble triad in which a unique ideal is expressed.

(d) *Their Meaning: the Exaltation of Man*

What was this ideal? It is easy to understand it after what we have said concerning the problem which these virtues were meant to solve. It was their role to assure man's autonomy in regard to the world. To accomplish this, there is only one way: teach man to find within man himself, that is to say in his free will, the whole good of man, that is everything which is not contained within his free will. In other words, find the way to man's exaltation and an affirmation of his freedom in contempt for the world.

Doubtless, there were religious souls among the Stoics—a Cleanthes, a Seneca, and especially an Epictetus—who had the lively sentiment of man's duties toward God, a sentiment that is not found in Aristotle. However, man's great duty, in their eyes, is precisely to justify the providence of God, finding within oneself the secret of one's happiness; for in this way the Wisdom of God and the perfec-

---

[18] *De const. sap.*, II, 2.
[19] Cf. Lactantius, *Div. Inst.*, V, 14.

tion of His work are shown. God does not expect from man any other *testimony* than the evidence of man's autonomy itself.

II. Biblical Conceptions of Fortitude

After our study of the Greek conceptions of fortitude, a surprise will await us if we open the Bible; the very words in which these conceptions are expressed are almost totally absent from the Greek Bible. We would look in vain for words like μεγαλοψυχία or καρτερία, and ἀνδρεία is never found in the New Testament and only appears rarely in the Old Testament. This is only a material statement, but how very significant! By this alone it is sufficient to make us feel that we are entering into a new world. The concept of fortitude is certainly not absent from this world, but it will be expressed in new terms, symbols of conceptions that are likewise new.

1. THE POWER OF GOD GIVEN TO MAN

There are many words which express the idea of fortitude in the Hebrew Bible. They are, for example, *haïl,* which the Septuagint ordinarily translated as δύναμις, a very general term which designates all kinds of *valor,* war-like valor, but also technical and moral valor; or, in a more exact sense, *koah,* usually translated by the Septuagint as ἰσχύς and which properly designates physical strength, corporal vigor, best typified by Samson (Judges 16). Other terms are "ŏ, a poetical term meaning majestic power, for example, the power of a fortified city and of its towers and ramparts, or *gᵉbhurah,* a word in which we might be tempted to see the equivalent of the Greek ἀνδρεία, since it preeminently designates the fortitude of the fighter, and is the quality of a man, of a *gebher,* as ἀνδρεία was that of the ἀνήρ; but the Bible has never given a properly ethical value to this term which the Greeks associated with their ἀνδρεία, and we can only approve the translators of the Septuagint who never render it by ἀνδρεία, but rather like their predecessors by δύναμις or ἰσχύς. Finally, without trying to be exhaustive, let us mention the verbs *hazaq,* which primitively signified *to bind,* and therefore, to make solid, like a bundle well tied together, and the term *ames,* meaning *to be firm,* often combined in the hallowed expression: "be strong and be firm!"

(a) *The Vanity of Man's Strength*

However numerous may be the terms in which the Bible expresses the idea of strength, not one of them has ever acquired the value of a technical term, properly designating a *human virtue.* There is no virtue of fortitude in the Bible.

This is because the Bible does not have great regard for the strength of creatures, and particularly for the strength of man. This is a deceptive strength in which we should not put our trust:

The king is not saved by a great army: nor shall the giant be saved by his own great strength.

Vain is the horse for safety: neither shall he be saved by the abundance of his strength (Ps. 32:16-17).

And yet man is tempted to glorify himself because of this deceptive strength. He is tempted to attribute his successes to himself instead of doing homage to God for them: "By the strength of my own hand I have done it" (Is. 10:13).

The Bible is always warning man against this exulting in his own strength: "Thus saith the Lord: . . . and let not the strong man glory in his strength" (Jer. 9:23; cf. Deut. 8:17).

If this warning is not sufficient, a terrible menace comes upon man: "And I will break the pride of your stubbornness" (Lev. 26:19; cf. Ez. 30:6; 33:28, etc.).

(b) *Fortitude, a Divine Attribute*

The Bible made a *divine attribute* of this fortitude which it refused to call a human virtue. To Yahweh belongs the strength (*koah*) which prepared the mountains (Ps. 64:7) and gathered together the seas (Job 26:12); to Yahweh the majestic power (*oz*), which shines forth in His works (Ps. 65:3) and to Him is offered the homage of all creatures (Ps. 28:1; 95:7; 58:17). To Yahweh belongs the strength (*g^ebhurah*) which makes his enemies tremble (Is. 33:13; Jer. 10:6; 16:21; Ps. 89:11), for He is preeminently the *gibbor,* the strong One, the Hero (Is. 42:13).

(c) *The Gift to Man of God's Strength*

This power which God Himself possesses, as His own, will be readily given to man:

But remember the Lord thy God, that he hath given thee strength (Deut. 8:18).

God who hath girt me with strength . . . with strength unto battle (Ps. 17:33,40).

The God of Israel is he who will give power and strength to his people (Ps. 67:36).

The fortitude which then appears in man is no longer that human strength which Scripture called vanity, but a divine fortitude which does not fail:

Knowest thou not, or hast thou not heard? the Lord is the everlasting God, who hath created the ends of the earth: he shall not faint, nor labour, neither is there any searching out of his wisdom.

It is he that giveth strength to the weary, and increaseth force and might to them that are not.

Youths shall faint, and labour, and young men shall fall by infirmity.

But they that hope in the Lord shall renew their strength, they shall take wings as eagles, they shall run and not be weary, they shall walk and not faint (Is. 40:28-31).

God gives His own strength to man—but this is not saying enough. He makes Himself the strength of man: "My God is made my strength" (Is. 49:5).

(d) *The Gift Received in Hope*

God gives His strength to man, and God becomes the strength of man. But how does man receive this gift? The Bible replies to this question on nearly every page. It is by hope that man received the gift of God's strength.

In this respect also there are many words which express this idea of hope. To hope in God is to *take refuge* in Him, *hasah,* to seek a *refuge* in Him, *mahseh,* like small birds take refuge beneath the wings of their mother when they are frightened—this image is familiar to the sacred writers—or when, in the presence of an enemy, one takes refuge in a tower or a fortified place; this will be *to put one's trust* in Him, *batah:* to place one's *faith* in Him, to find in Him one's *security, betah;* and it will also be to *count upon Him,* and to wait with confidence (*yihel*) or wait with patience (*qawah*) for His help, and make of this help the unique object of one's *confident expectation* (*toheleth*) or one's *patient expectation,* like the taut *cord* to which one clings through every difficulty (*tiq^eah*).

However, whatever may be its shade of meaning, it remains that for man it is hope which is the means of obtaining the strength of God that is offered to him. In the Bible this bond of hope and strength is affirmed very frequently:

The Lord is my helper and my protector: in him hath my heart confided, and I have been helped (Ps. 27:7).

Expect the Lord, do manfully, and let thy heart take courage, and wait thou for the Lord (Ps. 26:14).

Do ye manfully, and let your heart be strengthened, all ye that hope in the Lord (Ps. 30:25).

And suddenly the meaning of the preceding affirmations is apparent, which if they had remained isolated might have led to ambiguity. God gives man *His* strength; God makes *Himself* the strength of man: this does not mean that God gives man a *human* strength, nor does it mean that God makes *man strong*—on the contrary, it is necessary that man be frightened if he is to take refuge in God; a man must be a prey to anguish if he is to put his trust in God: "From the height of the day I shall fear: but I will trust in thee" (Ps. 55:4).

Man must no longer depend upon himself in order that he may depend upon God; in a word, man must renounce his human strength in order that he may receive the gift of God's strength. The entire psalter is full of this contrast; on the one hand, there are cries of fear, cries of anguish, and cries of despair uttered even unto paroxysm, an admission of the nothingness of man's strength, and on the other hand there is the expression of an absolute confidence and unshaken hope, in which the strength which comes from God is affirmed:

Have mercy on me, O Lord, for I am afflicted: my eye is troubled with wrath, my soul, and my belly:

For my life is wasted with grief: and my years in sighs.

My strength is weakened through poverty and my bones are disturbed.

I am become a reproach among all my enemies, and very much to my neighbors; and a fear to my acquaintances.

They that saw me without fled from me. I am forgotten as one dead from the heart.

I am become as a vessel that is destroyed.

For I have heard the blame of many that dwell round about.

While they assembled together against me, they consulted to take away
my life.

But I have put my trust in thee, O Lord. (Ps. 30:10-15).

Frightened, anxious, desperate, and without strength, man is
strong, man is powerful, if, instead of becoming disturbed, as though
he could really accomplish something, and instead of flexing his
muscles and straining his energies, as though he could expect salvation from these, he simply remains quiet and turns confidently toward Yahweh and peacefully waits for His help:

For thus saith the Lord God the Holy One of Israel: If you return and be
quiet, you shall be saved: in silence and in hope shall be your strength
(Is. 30:15).

It is then, indeed, in the place of man, without strength, that God,
the strong One, acts: "Commit thy way to the Lord, and trust in
him, and he will do it" (Ps. 36:5).

God, the Almighty, intervenes. The failures of the expedition of
the king of Assyria, Sennacherib, against Jerusalem in the reign of
Ezechias, offers an excellent example of these divine interventions.

Confronted by an invasion which no human means could stop,
Ezechias took refuge in prayer and put his trust in Yahweh. Yahweh
then intervened miraculously; he roused the king of Ethiopia against
the king of Assyria and sent an epidemic which destroyed the army
which was besieging Jerusalem (IV Kings, 18-19; II Par. 32:1-23;
Is. 36-37). This was a typical intervention of God which the psalmist awaited with confident trust and which he asked for in prayer:

Shew me a token for good: that they who hate me may see, and be confounded, because thou, O Lord, hast helped me and hast comforted me
(Ps. 85:17).

God never refuses these prodigies to anyone who trusts in Him.
And now let the tears be dried and the moanings cease, for God has
comforted (*niham*) the man who, by his tears, was not ashamed to
confess his weakness:

I will give thanks to thee, O Lord, for thou wast angry with me: thy wrath
is turned away, and thou hast comforted me (Is. 12:1).

According to the multitude of my sorrows in my heart, thy comforts have
given joy to my soul (Ps. 93:19).

And then joy bursts forth (*simḥah*):

Thou hast turned for me my mourning into joy: thou hast cut my sackcloth, and hast compassed me with gladness (Ps. 29:12).

A clamorous joy which is manifested in an outcry of jubilation (*rinnah*) and in bounds of merriment (*gil*):

Be glad in the Lord, and rejoice, ye just, and glory, all ye right of heart (Ps. 31:11).

Rejoice to God our helper (Ps. 80:2).

This finally culminates in a song of thankfulness, repeated a thousand times, and in a canticle of thanksgiving:

The Lord is my strength and my praise . . . (Ex. 15:2; Ps. 117:14; Is. 12:2).

Unto thee, O my helper, will I sing, for thou art God my defense (Ps. 58:18).

With expectation I have waited for the Lord, and he was attentive to me. And he heard my prayers, and brought me out of the pit of misery and the mire of dregs.

And he set my feet upon a rock, and directed my steps.
And he put a new canticle into my mouth, a song to our God.
Many shall see, and shall fear: and they shall hope in the Lord.
Blessed is the man whose trust is in the name of the Lord . . . (Ps. 39:1-5).

2. THE DEPLOYMENT OF THE POWER OF GOD IN MAN

The doctrine of fortitude in the Old Testament, as we have just outlined it broadly, is found to be integrally re-stated in the New Testament, except that with God the Father is now associated Jesus in whom God the Son was incarnate, and His Holy Spirit.

The New Testament likewise sees a divine attribute in strength, and this strength of God, which is properly speaking the power by which He created the world and by which He continues to govern it, is tirelessly proclaimed by it (Rom. 1:20).[20] But it shows us this strength specially dwelling in Jesus in its fulness. Isaias had foretold it:

And his name shall be called, Wonderful, Counsellor, God the Mighty, the Father of the world to come, the Prince of Peace . . . (9:6).

And the spirit of the Lord shall rest upon him: the spirit of wisdom, and of understanding, the spirit of counsel, and of fortitude, the spirit of knowledge, and of godliness.

And he shall be filled with the spirit of the fear of the Lord (Is. 11:2-3).

[20] Cf. Mt. 22:29; Mk. 12:24; Mt. 26:64; Mk. 14:62; Lk. 22:69; etc.

St. Peter himself declares that the prophecy was fufilled: God anointed Jesus of Nazareth with the Holy Spirit and with Power . . . (Acts 10:38). Doubtless the power of Jesus will not be manifested in all its glory until His second coming (Mt. 24:30; Mk. 13:26, Lk. 21:27). But even in His earthly life this power was manifested in His miracles; these were incontestably works of power, δυνάμεις— the word is frequently used in this sense. Therefore when the Gospel tells us of the power of Jesus, it ordinarily intends to speak to us about that power of performing miracles which was the most tangible manifestation of the divine power present within Him (Lk. 4:36; 5:17; 6:19; 8:46).

In the New Testament, Jesus gave His disciples this divine power which He possessed in its fulness, just as Yahweh, in the Old Testament, gave it to those who were faithful to Him. The Gospel soon shows Jesus giving His apostles the power to perform miracles during their first mission (Lk. 9:1). This was only the prelude. But before His Ascension, Jesus declared to His disciples that He would send them His Spirit and with His coming they would receive the gift of power in its fulness (Lk. 24:49; Acts 1:8), a power which from that moment would not be *their own* power, but instead, the power of God within them (Acts 3:12; 4:7).

Finally, in the New Testament, as in the Old, it is by confessing his weakness and by trusting to God that man receives the gift of His power. St. Paul said it again in lapidary terms: ". . . the weak things of the world has God chosen to put to shame the strong" (I Cor. 1:27) so that the abundance of power is God's and not ours (II Cor. 4:7) for . . .

". . . strength is made perfect in weakness." Gladly therefore I will glory in my infirmities, that the strength of Christ may dwell in me. Wherefore I am satisfied, for Christ's sake, with infirmities, with insults, with hardships, with persecutions, with distresses. For when I am weak, then I am strong (II Cor. 12:9-10).

However, the New Testament not only re-stated the doctrine of fortitude of the Old Testament; it made definite progress in this doctrine. The Old Testament showed us the strength of God obtained by hope; the New Testament, making this doctrine explicit which was so rich and yet not clear, shows us how the power of God is deployed in man who receives it. By throwing light upon its transcendent object, it sets apart theological hope (ἐλπίς) and brings forth a whole series of attitudes of the soul, also included within it in the Old Testament, which are like its efflorescences on the level of earthly life, and in which it is certainly necessary to recognize what theology calls "infused moral virtues," proceeding from hope and inspired by it. Essentially these will be power or Christian "dynamism" (δύναμις), assurance (παρρησία), patience (ὑπομονή) and longanimity (μακροθυμία).

(a) *Power* (δύναμις)

For the New Testament, and this was a definite progress accomplished in relation to the Old Testament, hope could not have for its object anything human whatever; its unique object is God Himself, possessed in the vision of Heaven. And doubtless it was exactly because hope was raised so high that the moral virtues, destined to assure its radiation on the level of earthly life, began to be distinguished from it in the New Testament.

No doubt we must now distinguish power (δύναμις) from theological hope. Certainly hope is also a kind of power. It is hope which, depending directly upon the power of God (Rom. 1:13), draws its strength from Him, and receives the gift of His power. But hope properly so called is determined by its divine object; it is strength to desire God, and power to attain to God. That is why, in order to encompass all of human life and orient it toward God, it stirs up that radiation of the strength of God which it holds within itself, and which is δύναμις.

What therefore is this power, this δύναμις which gives God to man through hope? Doubtless, in the texts of the New Testament it is primarily the power to perform miracles. This was the power which Jesus gave His apostles, and it was with this power that Stephen was filled (Acts 6:8). It was this power which gave authority to St. Paul's teaching (I Cor. 2:4-5; II Cor. 6:7; 12:12). But this power is not the *whole* of power; it is only the most visible element and, in the last analysis, it is only an accidental element.

If we go to the bottom of the matter, δύναμις consequently is the power of God that is communicated to man to enable him to accomplish a divine deed, to associate him with that great work of God which is the salvation of humanity. This divine power that is present in man doubtless enables him, when necessity requires, to perform miracles. But its field of action is infinitely more vast; it is this power which fortifies us efficaciously for the development of the interior man within us (Eph. 3:16, 20), and qualifies us to be witnesses for

God (Acts 4:35) and to declare that message of the Gospel and that lesson of the Cross which are supremely efficacious because the power of God resides in them also (Rom. 1:16; I Cor. 1:18), and which enables us to suffer for its propagation (Gal. 1:11). St. Paul summed up all of this in a few words: "For God has not given us the spirit of fear, but of power and of love and of prudence. Do not, therefore, be ashamed of testimony for our Lord, nor of me, his prisoner, but enter into my sufferings for the gospel through the power of God" (II Tim. 1:7-8), or even more briefly, "I can do all things in him who strengthens me" (Phil. 4:13).

In conclusion, we may say that the power which God gives to man is essentially a power for action; it is efficiency and efficacy, or as the very word δύναμις says it, it is a *dynamism* which enlists all of human life in order to lead it toward the realization of the work of God.

(b) *Assurance* (παρρησία)

One of the essential tasks which devolves upon the Christian because of the power which he has received, is to bear the message of the Gospel everywhere, and it is primarily in order to accomplish this task that he needs the virtue of assurance (παρρησία). This παρρησία consists in saying everything; it is that freedom of speech, that frankness which says everything that must be said and says it openly in the presence of anyone. But freedom of this kind supposes, in the one who is thus speaking, the boldness that dares, and the assurance which lets no one perplex it, the confidence of a man who is sure of what he is claiming and whom nothing could silence.

Therefore we must not be surprised to find Scripture making it explicitly an effect of hope (Heb. 3:6); it is because he possesses "the hope of producing eternal fruits, in eternal glory" that the minister of the Gospel uses great boldness in his ministry (II Cor. 3:12). Assurance, like the confidence of hope, is rooted in faith (Eph. 3:12) and finding its certain point of support there, it rushes forth toward God. Before being bold toward men, the Christian, however little his heart may reproach him for anything whatever (I Jn. 3:21), is bold toward God first of all; in his relations with Him he puts all the freedom of behavior which marks the relations of a child with his Father. He is not afraid to approach Him boldly (Heb. 10:19), he has full confidence that he will be heard when he prays (I Jn. 5:14). And it was in this confidence in God that the heralds of the Gospel derived their strength, in spite of sufferings and insults, in order that they might speak boldly to men (I Thess. 2:2).

The first Christians implored God to give them this assurance which would enable them to accomplish their mission as messengers of the Gospel, and God, by His Holy Spirit, abundantly filled their hearts with it (Acts 49:29-31). However, the best examples of this were the apostles, Peter and John (Acts 2:29; 4:13), Paul and Barnabas (Acts 13:46; 14:3), and more especially Paul (Acts 9:27-28; 19:8; 26:26; 28:31). As a matter of fact, in the writings of Paul we find a proud claim in this respect: "Having therefore such hope, we show great boldness . . . we renounce those practices which shame conceals, we avoid unscrupulous conduct, we do not corrupt the word of God; but making known the truth, we commend ourselves to every man's conscience in the sight of God (II Cor. 3:12; 4:2).

(c) *Patience* (ὑπομονή)

Nowhere can we see more clearly than in the case of patience the process of dissociation by which this new virtue has emerged from hope. If we turn our attention to the Hebrew Bible, we shall notice that the words which the Septuagint translates by ὑπομένειν, "to have patience," or "to wait patiently" or "endure patiently," are *yihel* or *qawah,* which they most often translate by ἐλπίσειν "to hope," just as the word which they translate by ὑπομονή is *tiq^ewah*, which they generally render as ἐλπίς. In fact, in the Old Testament, patience was still included within hope. In the midst of tribulations, the just man of the Old Testament took refuge in Yahweh, trusted in Him, awaited His help, and at the same time endured and remained steadfast. Hope entailed patience so necessarily and so immediately that they felt no need to distinguish their concepts.

In the New Testament itself, quite often, ὑπομονή, patient expectation, is still confused with ἐλπίς, hope. Examples of this confusion are not lacking in St. Paul: as a matter of fact do we not see ὑπομονή replacing ἐλπίς in his triad of the three Christian virtues? [21] We find this again in St. James when, in the context of an exhortation on the expectation of the Second Coming, he declared that those men are happy who are able to wait, and recalled the patient expectation of Job, an expectation which, by the mercy of the Lord,

[21] Titus 2:2; II Thess. 1:3-4; I Tim. 6:11; II Tim. 3:10.

was not frustrated in the end (Jas. 5:11). Finally, in the Apocalypse of John, which does not use the word ἐλπίς, it certainly seems that the term ὑπομονή is sometimes its equivalent (Apoc. 2:2; 2:19).

But still more often ὑπομονή, although it is closely bound to it, is distinct from ἐλπίς. It will then be that *patient endurance* of trials which is the proper effect of hope—and which in its turn feeds our hope—because we have suffered for Him, we hope to possess God (Rom. 5:3-4; cf. 15:4). We must therefore recognize in ὑπομονή the moral virtue of patience, distinct from the theological virtue of hope.

It is Our Lord Himself who had thus raised patience to the rank of a virtue. On two occasions, consequently, in the Gospel we see Him declaring its necessity. First of all in the conclusion of the Parable of the Sower, a descriptive evocation of the thousand difficulties which the Word of God must overcome in order to bear its fruit: the grain which finally falls upon good ground are they who, with a right and good heart, having heard the word, hold it fast and bear fruit in patience (Lk. 8:15). And it is especially when, in the last days preceding the Passion, Our Lord describes to His apostles the persecutions which they will have to endure: "Then they will deliver you up to tribulation, and will put you to death; and you will be hated by all nations for my name's sake. And then many will fall away, and will betray one another, and will hate one another."[22] Then comes the conclusion, identical in Matthew and Mark: "But whoever perseveres to the end, he shall be saved" (Mt. 24:13, 10:22; Mk. 13:13), and in a slightly different form in Luke: "By your patience you will win your souls" (Lk. 21:19). Patience is obviously in this respect the patient endurance of all those difficulties which overcome those represented by the seed that has fallen upon the road, among the stones or the thorns, or the patient endurance of the persecutions that were foretold, but it is also the patient expectation of the fruit that is long in coming, or the salvation which will be won in the end; in a word, it is the patient endurance of present evils in the patient expectation of future blessings.

And it is this same conception of patience which we find again in the New Testament wherever patience is distinguished from hope. Patience then has for its object the struggle which confronts us here below (ἀγών, Heb. 12:1), and tribulation (θλῖψις, Rom. 5:3; 12:12; Apoc. 1:9), trials (πειραιμος, Jas. 1:2-3), and sufferings

[22] Mt. 24:9-11; 10:17-22; Mk. 13:9-17; Lk. 21:12-18.

(παθήματα, II Cor. 1:6; cf. II Tim. 3:10); Paul made an impressive list of these sufferings: tribulations, hardships, distresses, stripes, imprisonment, tumults, labors, sleepless nights, fastings (II Cor. 6:4-5), but the list is not complete, however, until one has suffered unto blood, after the example of Jesus who, Himself, patiently endured the Cross (Heb. 12:2-7).

All this patience endured, without having deserved it. What glory can there be in patiently enduring punishment if one has acted badly? But if, having acted well, one has suffered and endures it patiently, then there is a basis for grace with God (I Pet. 2:19-20)—patience endures it because it knows that God teaches us through suffering (Heb. 12:7), and also because it knows that suffering is useful and contributes to the salvation of the elect (II Tim. 2:10); it endures it especially because patience is necessary in order to obtain the happiness which has been promised to us by fulfilling the Will of God (Heb. 10:36), and because we must patiently endure tribulation in order to receive the crown of life (Jas. 1:12), and we must be patient with Jesus in order to reign with Him (II Tim. 2:12; cf. Rom. 8:17-18; Apoc. 1:9). In a word, patience endures in the expectation of Jesus Christ (II Thess. 1:3), with eyes fixed upon Him who, after having given us the example of patience, has gone before us into Heaven (Heb. 12:2, 6:20), and in the love of God, for love endures all things patiently (1 Cor. 13:7).

And precisely because it endures through hope and through love, patience also endures with joy. In order to rejoice, the Christian does not need to wait for a new intervention of God, like the just man in the Old Testament. The miracle which saves him, and of which all the miracles of Israel's history were only the figure, was accomplished once and for all upon the Cross when Jesus conquered sin and death. Therefore, the Christian can rejoice at all times (I Thess. 5:16), and he should rejoice more particularly in suffering (Col. 1:24; Phil. 2:17-18). For he is already saved in hope (Rom. 8:24), and God consoles him in the very midst of his sufferings: "Blessed be the God and Father of our Lord Jesus Christ, the Father of mercies and the God of all comfort, who comforts us in all our afflictions, that we also may be able to comfort those who are in any distress by the comfort wherewith we ourselves are comforted by God" (II Cor. 1:3-4). And with comfort (παράκλησις) goes joy, on an equal basis (χάρα), (Philemon 7; II Cor. 13:11; II Cor. 7:4-13; Phil. 2:1-2). Doubtless God can comfort the souls of His faithful people by the agency of external events, the proof of the care which His loving providence takes of them: thus Paul found himself comforted in the midst of the difficulties which assailed him in Macedonia, by the arrival of Titus who brought him good news from Corinth (II Cor. 7:6), just as Titus had found great comfort in the attitude of the Corinthians (*ibid.* 7). Was it not in fact a comfort and a joy for the Apostle to contemplate the good order which reigned among those whom he had evangelized and the steadfastness of their faith (*ibid.;* Col. 2:5; Phil. 1:2)? But the comfort and the joy which God gives to those who love Him are still more a wholly interior comfort and joy. It is a comfort for the soul to think that it is the sufferings of Christ which it must bear, and then, thanks to Christ, comfort is even more abundant (II Cor. 1:5). It is a joy for the soul to hope, and at the very moment when it is patiently enduring tribulation, it rejoices in the expectation of Jesus Christ (Rom. 12:12; 15:13). Then patience becomes easy. It is comfort itself, says St. Paul, which expands and thrives in patience (II Cor. 1:7), in a patience that is entirely spontaneous and wholly joyful.

(d) *Longanimity* (μακροθυμία)

The case of longanimity seems, at first glance, to be entirely different from that of the other virtues which we have just studied. While boldness and patience are only deployments of hope and are not distinguished from it except in the New Testament, longanimity already possesses, in the Hebrew Bible, its own individuality, and the New Testament only needed to borrow the idea from it. Because in the Old Testament, longanimity had no particular relation to fortitude and hope, we did not need to mention it in studying the Old Testament's doctrine of fortitude. The New Testament—and in this respect it is original—expressly brings together longanimity and patience in order to attach them both to fortitude: "May you be completely strengthened through his glorious power unto perfect patience and long-suffering" (Col. 1:11). Let us now look into the past and see in the Hebrew Bible what this longanimity which the New Testament made a sister of patience, and a daughter, with patience, of Christian fortitude.

The word longanimity is merely a copy of the Latin word *longanimitas,* which itself seems to have been contrived by the first translators of the Bible to render the Greek μακροθυμία, and this very word μακροθυμία assuredly used in the common speech of the Hellenistic period, but which was a rare term, only became so frequent in the Bible because it was useful to the Seventy to express a properly biblical concept, that of the *'ôrék 'appaim* (or: *'ôrék rûah*).

The *'ôrék 'appaim,* literally means the *length of the nostrils* (and *'ôrék rûah,* means *length of breath*) which signifies *slowness in becoming angry.* And the angry man, in fact, pants through his nostrils, and consequently, "breath" or "nostrils" are synonyms of "anger."

This slowness in becoming irritated is primarily a *divine attribute.* It is God Himself who, in Exodus, was revealed as the merciful and compassionate God, slow to wrath, abounding in goodness and faithfulness (Ex. 34:6), and the echo of this revelation is prolonged throughout the entire Old Testament and into the New. What then does it mean for God to be long-suffering? It is first of all to tolerate the offenses of man without punishing them *immediately*, and the reason for this toleration is because God is able *to wait.* He has time enough, for a thousand years are to Him as one day. But the menace which, in this respect, subsists in longanimity, can be obliterated. To be long-suffering will then mean that God endures the offenses of man without punishing them at all, and the reason for this endurance will be that God can forgive; for man's offenses, however small or miserable, could never touch His greatness (Ecclus. 18:1-12).

The wise men of Israel made a human virtue of this longanimity, a divine attribute, and the New Testament perpetuated their teaching. Man's longanimity, moreover, is only an imitation of God's. In this respect also, it may happen that the idea of expectation is found on the first level: longanimity will then be slowness in becoming angry, or in becoming impatient or discouraged; it will mean knowing how to wait and how to persevere (Jas. 5:7-8; Heb. 6:12-15). But ordinarily it is the idea of forgiveness which first comes to mind.

This is very plain in the texts in which we see Our Lord teaching longanimity to His disciples:

> Then Peter came up to him and said, "Lord, how often shall my brother sin against me, and I forgive him? Up to seven times?" Jesus said to him, "I do not say to thee seven times, but seventy times seven.

> "This is why the kingdom of heaven is likened to a king who desired to settle accounts with his servants. And when he had begun the settlement, one was brought to him who owed him ten thousand talents. And as he had no means of paying, his master ordered him to be sold, with his wife and children and all that he had, and payment to be made. But the servant fell down and besought him, saying, 'Have patience with me and I will

pay thee all!' And moved with compassion, the master of that servant released him, and forgave him the debt.

"But as that servant went out, he met one of his fellow-servants who
owed him a hundred denarii, and he laid hold of him and throttled him,
saying, 'Pay what thou owest.' His fellow-servant therefore fell down and
began to entreat him, saying, 'Have patience with me and I will pay thee
all.' But he would not; but went away and cast him into prison until he
should pay what was due.

"His fellow-servants therefore, seeing what had happened, were very much
saddened, and they went and informed their master of all that had happened.
Then his master called him, and said to him, 'Wicked servant! I forgave
thee all the debt, because thou didst entreat me. Shouldst thou not also
have had pity on thy fellow-servant, even as I had pity on thee? And his
master, being angry, handed him over to the torturers until he should pay
all that was due to him. So also my heavenly Father will do to you, if you
do not each forgive your brothers from your hearts." (Mt. 18:21-35; cf.
Lk. 17:2-4.)

And, to show the importance which He attached to this lesson, Our
Lord inserted it into the prayer which He taught to His disciples: "In
this manner therefore shall you pray: Our Father who art in heaven
. . . And forgive us our debts, as we also forgive our debtors" (Mt.
6:9-14; Lk. 11:2-4; cf. Mk. 11:25). The longanimity of man is thus
supported by the longanimity of God which it imitates; but while the
longanimity of God, composed of pity for wretchedness which He
dominates, is the generous longanimity of greatness, the longanimity
of man, composed of pity for a wretchedness which he shares, is the
humble longanimity of little man.

It is this teaching of Our Lord which St. Paul repeats when, in
nearly all of his epistles, he recommends longanimity to Christians.
The fruit of the Holy Spirit (Gal. 5:22), the daughter of charity
(I Cor. 13:4), longanimity seems most often to be bound up with
courteous and obliging kindness (χρηστότης),[23] and with humility
and gentleness, mutual assistance and the forgiveness of offenses.[24]
It is a virtue of fraternal love; it is one aspect of the Christian's
charity toward his brethren. Longanimity consists in doing no one
any harm, in not seeking revenge, in not demanding the punishment
of those who have done wrong to us, and in keeping within one's
heart all feelings of anger or irritation—or still better—in not even
having such feelings, keeping calm and unperturbed when someone
offends us, and the reason which St. Paul gives for this is the very

[23] I Cor. 13:14; II Cor. 6:6; Gal. 5:22; Col. 3:12.
[24] Gal. 5:22; Eph. 4:2; Col. 3:12.

one given by Our Lord: we must forgive one another even as the Lord has forgiven us (Col. 3:12-13).

We readily understand why μαϰροθυμία, defined in this way, is the equal of ὑπομονή (Col. 1:11) according to St. Paul. The two concepts, as a matter of fact, are similar. Μαϰροθυμία and ὑπομνή are both a kind of patience. But μαϰροθυμία is one type of patience and ὑπομονή is another. Ὑπομονή, as we have said, is the patient enduring of present evils, in the patient expectation of future blessings; in the midst of sufferings it is the expectation and hope of the realization of divine promises, and it is this hope which is the raison d'être of endurance. Μαϰροθυμία is very different, both in its attitude and in its motives. Ὑπομονή is the patience that endures suffering without flagging because it hopes; μαϰροθυμία is the kind of patience which endures injury without rendering it, because it is aware that it also has much to be forgiven.

Martyrdom, the Supreme Act of Christian Fortitude

Martyrs have always been, and are still today, the living incarnation of the biblical doctrine of fortitude, such as we have just presented it.

The word μάρτυς, in the common Greek tongue, meant a *witness*, in the legal sense of the term; μαρτύριον or μαρτύρια was the testimony, and μαρτυρεῖν was *to witness*. And it is still almost exclusively this idea of witnessing which these words evoke in the language of the New Testament. The apostles are the most outstanding witnesses; they were chosen precisely in order that they might observe everything that was done by Our Lord, and especially to verify His resurrection, and thus be in a position to give their testimony officially.[25] However, in some texts there already appears in combination with the idea of witnessing the further idea of suffering and death which this very witnessing may entail for the witnesses. Our Lord predicts these things to His official *witnesses:* "They will arrest you and persecute you, delivering you up to the synagogues and prisons, dragging you before kings and governors for my name's sake. It shall lead to your bearing witness" (Lk. 21:12; cf. Mk. 12:9). St. Paul, in a sermon reported in Acts, and St. John, in his Apocalypse, show us other *witnesses:* Stephen, Antipas, who sealed their testimony with their

[25] Lk. 24:48; Acts 1:8; 1:22; 2:32; 3:15; 5:32; 10:39, 41; 26:16; I Cor. 15:14-15.

blood (Acts 22:20; Apoc. 2:13; cf. 11:3,7; 17:6). It is this new idea which, very soon, was destined to pass into the foreground of Christian speech: the martyr will no longer be a witness, or even a witness who is ready to bear witness, if necessary, even unto death, but he will be *someone who dies* in order to bear witness, a person whose death itself is a testimony. The new meaning of the word, which appears as early as the first century in the letter of Clement of Rome to the Corinthians (5:4-7), seems established by the middle of the second century, and as early as the end of the same century it becomes so exclusive that we find a new word, that of confessor (ὁμολογητής) making its appearance to designate those who had confessed their faith before the judges, under torture, but without having death seal their testimony.

Martyrdom is therefore death undergone in order to bear witness to the truth of the Christian faith; and this is preeminently the act of Christian fortitude. Very precisely, it is the act of ὑπομονή, Christian patience: the very first text in which we find the term martyrdom in its technical sense is in the Letter of St. Clement of Rome which explicitly affirms it two times: it is an illustrious model of patience which the apostle St. Paul has left us by his martyrdom. *The Letter of the Churches of Lyons and Vienne,* which reports the death of the martyrs of 177, is no less explicit: it is everywhere ὑπομονή, the patience of the blessed, which is celebrated, without ever mentioning, in their regard, the Greek virtues, ἀνδρεία, καρτερία or μεγαλοψυχία.[26]

Nothing is more enlightening than this association of martyrdom with the biblical virtue of ὑπομονή, and nothing could more surely enable us to understand the contempt of all those who thought they could confuse the ancient or modern martyrs with the ancient or modern pagan heroes. When the pagan dies heroically, it is a display of his ἀνδρεία, καρτερία or μεγαλοψυχία—courage, austerity or magnanimity—and it is the sentiment of his virility, his strength or his greatness, in a word the sentiment of his manly dignity which sustains him. If the pagan's death can be a testimony, it can only be a testimony rendered to *men.* When the Christian dies as a martyr, it is his hope for a better life that sustains him: "I love life," said the martyr Appollonius to his judge, "nothing is more precious than life, but I mean eternal life." It is his trust in the help of Christ who suffers within him, and it is especially his love for

[26] Eusebius, *Hist. Eccles.,* V. 1, 4, 6, 7, 16, 20, 27, 39, 45, 51.

Christ whom he is imitating and whom he is going to meet, and his love for God into whose company he will soon be admitted. Consequently in the martyr there is that mingling of trembling sensibility and overflowing joy, so different from the impassibility of the pagan hero, but which is the mark of ὑπομονή, Christian patience. And that is why the martyr is a witness *of God,* a witness of the truth of the Christian faith.

And that is also why, from the very beginning, the Church has recognized in martyrdom one of the highest points of Christian perfection. It certainly was not manly strength which the Church admired in the martyr, but rather, through his patience which was its fruit and visible sign, she admired his faith, his hope, and above all his charity. "Greater love than this no one has, that one lay down his life for his friend" said Jesus (Jn. 15:13) and He gave an example of this greater love. In the martyrs the Church recognized imitations and very similar likenesses of that true love,[27] and that is why she venerated them, as disciples and imitators of the Lord.[28]

III. The Point of Contact

1. OPPOSITION OF THE GREEK IDEAL AND THE CHRISTIAN IDEAL

At first glance one can only be struck by the antithesis which seems to contrast the Greek and Biblical conceptions of fortitude in an irreducible contradiction. On the one hand, there is an affirmation of the strength and the greatness of man; on the other hand, there is an admission of his weakness and his smallness, with praise only for the power and greatness of God. On the one hand, a hopeless impassibility whereby man's own dignity is safeguarded; and on the other hand, an endurance full of hope whereby one bears witness to one's faith in God and one's love for Him. On the one hand, a contempt for the world which is an exaltation of self; on the other hand, a contempt for the world which is also a contempt for self and an exaltation of God alone. On the one hand, a haughty boast of man's autonomy; on the other hand, a humble prayer to God from whom one waits for everything. Celsus, certainly had seen clearly: there is a big difference between the Stoic hero parading his sufferings and Christ who

[27] *Saint Polycarp,* Ad. Phil., I, 1.
[28] *Mart. Polycarpi,* 17, 3.

weeps and prays, and the martyr who calls for help: "Christ, help me, Christ, have pity, I beseech thee, Christ, give me strength. . . ."

(a) *Their Apparent Confusion in the Fathers*

How surprised we shall be to find that, very early, the Greek ideal and the Christian ideal were apparently confused: The *Book of Wisdom* had already appropriated the Stoic list of the four principal virtues, and so we find the Greek ἀνδρεία introduced into the Bible (Wis. 8:7). With the Fathers, the confusion seems to triumph. As early as the dawn of the third century, Clement of Alexandria does not hesitate to identify purely and simply the Stoic conceptions of fortitude with the biblical conceptions, and he can only explain this apparent coincidence by the theory of Greek plagiarism of the Bible. The Greek Fathers followed his lead. The ὑπομονή of the Bible will be assimilated to the καρτερία of the Stoics, the μακροθυμία with the μεγαλοψυχία. More flagrant still will be the confusion found in the Latin Fathers. Even before St. Ambrose, in his *De Officiis,* made a theory of it, they were expressing it by a confusion of vocabulary. Whereas in Greek it was easy to distinguish the group of Greek virtues—ἀνδρεία, καρτερία, μεγαλοψυχία—from the group of biblical virtues— δύναμις, ὑπομονή, and μακροθυμία, in Latin everything was confused. *Fortitudo* is variously the Greek ἀνδρεία or the biblical ὑπομονή; *patientia* is indifferently the Greek καρτερία or the biblical ὑπομονή; and it is also these two same virtues which form *perseverentia.* The Greek μεγαλοψυχία and the biblical μακροθυμία are also absorbed, in one respect, into *patientia;* however, the Latin language possessed two neologisms to translate them, which were contrived one by Cicero and the other by Christian translators: *magnanimitas,* and *longanimitas.* But these technical terms themselves were confused: the most ancient Christian translators, such as the first translators of the Bible, in translating μακροθυμία used the word *magnanimitas* instead of the proper term, *longanimitas.* In a word, there was an indescribable confusion in which there was a disappearance of both the delicate nuances and the blunt contrasts which were so well emphasized in Greek vocabulary. This confusion passed from the Latin language into our own.

(b) *Elimination of the Greek Ideal*

We must not, however, allow ourselves to be deceived. Under the appearances of this confusion are hidden the triumph of one ideal and the exclusion of the other. And we must emphasize this because people are often mistaken about it. It is the Christian ideal which has triumphed, and the Greek ideal which has been excluded. Doubtless the words, the formulas, the external attitudes, may sometimes be illusory. But we must look to the bottom of things—to the depths of the heart—and there the illusion is dissipated.

According to St. Clement of Alexandria, the perfect Christian is *impassible*, and in this respect the Stoic conceptions of fortitude are evoked. But of what is this impassibility composed? Of contempt for created things and the hope of living some day with Christ. Or better still, it is made of love, of that love which has only the purpose of pleasing God. And then, it is a gift of the grace of God. . . . Now, the further we advance in history, the more is this exclusive triumph of Christian conceptions confirmed. It reached its culminating point in the Middle Ages. Patience, fortitude, constancy, magnanimity, longanimity, all these virtues, according to David of Augsburg, only differ between themselves by imperceptible nuances, and finally they are identified with humility, the great Christian virtue. As a matter of fact, what does it mean to be strong? It is to have contempt for the world. And what does it mean to be humble? It is to feel contempt for oneself. But these two contempts are only one contempt, the contempt of the creature and of his nothingness (*nihileitas*) in the presence of his Creator. . . . So speaks St. Bonaventure.

The Christian, we may also say, is a conqueror; he also dreams of accomplishing great things. A whole conception of fortitude was elaborated in the twelfth century on this theme, from Abelard to Chancellor Phillip and including the *Moralium Dogma:* And here there was an evocation of the magnanimity of the Greek conquerors. . . . But the conquest of which the Christian dreams is the conquest of the Kingdom of Heaven, and the great things which he undertakes is the practice of the evangelical counsels, and he does not count upon his own strength to do this; on the contrary, the less self-confidence possessed by the believer, even in little things, the more he hopes from the power of God, even in greater matters. "I can do all things in him who strengthens me" is the motto of the magnanimous Christian. Thus speaks St. Bernard, and here again, and in conformity with biblical inspiration, there is an affirmation of the power of God alone which is manifested in the weakness of man: this time "magnanimity" is identified with the theological virtue of hope.

(c) *Integration of the Greek Ideal in Christian Thought*

It was therefore the proper task of St. Thomas and his new approach to integrate the principal affirmations of Greek reason into Christian thought. St. Thomas was first in offering us a theology of fortitude which united the lesson of the Greeks to the lesson of the Bible, and combined the exaltation of man.

2. A THEOLOGY OF DYNAMISM

Doubtless if we wish to have an understanding of this theology that is profound to any degree, we must not be too concerned about the frameworks within which it is enclosed. These are the old frameworks of which Chryssipus once posed the principle, and of which scholastic arguments, prolonged during the whole of the twelfth and thirteenth centuries, failed to establish the interpretation. Around the cardinal virtue of courage were ranged the related virtues, magnanimity with confidence and security, magnificence, patience with longanimity, perseverence with constancy; but are these virtues elements of fortitude, "degrees in which this virtue ascends and benefits," or are they distinct virtues although related to courage? Men argued this point in the first century before Christ, and were still arguing about it in the thirteenth century. St. Albert, against Chancellor Phillip, had vigorously defended the second point of view. St. Thomas did not dare to choose. But it does not matter. We are not interested in this. Nor are we interested in the idea of St. Thomas concerning each of these virtues; it is a strange amalgam of anomalous elements, combined or dissociated at random in Latin translations, as we have already noted regarding the vocabulary of the Latin Fathers. But under this finery of the past is hidden a profound thought, a doctrine by which our time also may live, for its import is eternal.

(a) *The Exaltation of Man*

Human Hope

This doctrine will be inserted into the very depths of human psychology. There is in man a natural love of himself. This natural self-love normally develops into a natural love of his own greatness. Man does not only desire, with natural desire, his good, but also desires to find his own perfection in this good. However, the idea of perfection immediately summons forth the related ideas of excellence and greatness. Excellence is a perfection which confers upon us a superiority, a primacy. Greatness is elevation itself, the height and eminence of perfection. We may therefore say that a natural desire for perfection proceeds from self-love, as also a desire for excellence and greatness. A love, a desire . . . but this is not saying enough. We must say even more, and say it better: a *hope*. For the love and the desire do not move if they are not completed in hope.

What then is hope? Primarily it is an *intense* desire, whetted and fortified by the greatness of its object, and brought to its point of maximum tension: consequently one only hopes for great things. Next, it is an *efficacious* desire. One only hopes for what is possible, that is to say one hopes for *what can be accomplished by oneself*. And precisely because one has measured one's strength before hoping, and this strength has been found sufficient, can the hope, and only hope, command the action. It is preeminently the motivating passion. An intense desire, an efficacious desire, and a mover—hope is all these —and it is still more. For by its very greatness, the good which one hopes for is difficult to attain; it is very high, separated from us by its very height, and also by a thousand obstacles which we must conquer before we can reach it. And that is why hope is not only desire, but also struggle and conquest. It is the rush of generous blood, the leap of a soul which becomes alert in the presence of difficulty; the impetus and the impulse of the appetite which expands in order to grasp its object, the effort and elevation of the soul which aspires to the greatness of the good. Hope is full of joy, not yet the joy of possession, but a taste for the effort in which the faculty is fully exercised, and the thrill of the search which is certain of success, and the intoxication of discovery and conquest. And all this—the impetus which carries us through the difficulties, the impulse which lifts us above ourselves, the expansion of the soul, this utter joy—all this makes of hope a passion that is captivating and exciting. Perhaps the word hope no longer evokes for us all this wealth of feeling, but we must learn to find it again and to see in hope the enthusiasm which makes for great hearts.

Magnanimity, the Virtue of Human Hope

This rush of hope, natural to the heart of man, needs to be governed. Hope is an impetus; hope is an enthusiasm. But a blind impetus and enthusiasm. It can go astray or become falsely excited— in this way are born the vices of vanity and presumption—or it can weaken and fail—thus is born the vice of pusillanimity. To govern it, a virtue is necessary: magnanimity. Vanity leads to error; it allows itself to be seduced by false magnitude which, in reality, will ordinarily be only meanness. Presumption, however, really seeks true greatness, but it becomes mistakenly excited: it goes beyond its own powers. Pusillanimity, on the contrary, does not make use of all its powers. Magnanimity is able to discern true greatness and knows how to seek it according to its strength.

The real greatness of man is primarily greatness in virtue. For virtue is not a discipline which limits our field of action. It is an enrichment, an abundance of energy which enables our faculties to operate fully and to give their full measure. Virtue is the expansion of human power. The greatness of man is therefore first of all to perform the most perfect virtuous actions. But the greatness of man is also the greatness of knowledge, and it is the greatness of the gifts which make the leader and the man of action. It is likewise the strength of the body, health and power, sources of self-confidence and means of action. The greatness of man is completed by external goods, honors, wealth, power. . . . In a word, the greatness of man is the complete expansion of the human person, the will and the intelligence, body and soul, and it is its radiation in the world.

It is this true greatness which magnamity is seeking. To do this, it must first of all become aware of its own powers. Consciousness of his own value is an essential element of man's perfection. From this self-awareness proceeds self-confidence: when we are sure of our means of action, we are also sure of attaining to the goal and this firm conviction gives our hope that strength, that new energy, which is confidence. Aware of its own power and trusting in it, magnanimity does not fear the obstacles that may rise up on the way. It is sure of conquering them, and for its hope this is still additional strength; it is alert and without anxiety. Finally, magnanimity watches jealously over this hope thus magnified. It combats everything that might dry up the sources, whether impurity, laziness, depressing sadness—for great souls are only fashioned in purity, in work and in joy—it strengthens the soul in order that it may always be inaccessible to despair even in the most difficult circumstances.

The role of magnanimity, as we were saying, is to regulate hope. But we see that to govern hope is not to lessen it but to magnify it. It is to exalt it by enlightening it. Magnanimity sees true greatness and knows that it can attain to it. By adding the light of reason to its impetus of enthusiasm, magnanimity lifts human hope to its summit.

Magnanimity, a Way of Life

The greatness of man is the end pursued by magnanimity. Now the greatness of man contributes to all the human goods and in every human good man may seek his own greatness, and seek this naturally. Magnanimity may therefore order to its own end the greatness of man and all human activity. In the first place, magnanimity may "command," that is to say foster for its own end all the virtues. It inspires all of them with a new impetus, and breathes into them a new order; it leads them all into its aspiration to greatness and compels them to surpass themselves. But let us clearly understand that the magnanimous man is seeking, and is considering in all the virtues, not their own nature, but whatever is great within them, the perfection which they bring him, and the expansion of his personality which they achieve. Likewise, in vice the magnanimous man is fleeing from pettiness, diminution, and the disgrace which this entails.

And it is this which assures a preferred place for the virtue of magnanimity in the moral life. Doubtless it is not a cardinal virtue. But the primacy of the cardinal virtues is of a purely *conceptual* order; courage is a cardinal virtue because, even better than magnanimity itself, it realizes the *concept* of strength of soul, realizing it in the very presence of death. But if we place ourselves on the level of life instead of the level of logic, it is to magnanimity that the primacy belongs, because it is a *general* virtue, that is to say a virtue which is capable of orienting an entire life and leaving its mark upon it. Magnanimity defines *a way of life*, a personalist way of life, wholly placed beneath the sign of the expansion of human personality.

Let us note, however, that from this very point of view, it cannot be isolated and there is room at its side for other general virtues which also will leave their mark upon the whole life of man. The highest ends which man's heart can solicit are three in number: man's greatness, the welfare of the community, and the honor of God. There will therefore be three great general virtues, three lines of strength in the moral life: magnanimity, social justice and religion. Thus magnanimity embraces all human activity to order it to the greatness of man; social justice embraces all human activity to order it to the welfare of the community, and religion, for the third time, embraces all human activity to order it to the honor of God. Between all these aspirations there is no conflict, but harmony, for the human person only finds his greatness in the service of the community and in the worship of God. Magnanimity cannot disregard these imposing perspectives. Man wants to be great for the good of the community and for the honor of God.

Magnanimity, an Aristocratic Virtue

Magnanimity is primarily defined by its object: greatness. Now, if the quest for greatness is to be reasonable and virtuous, there must be some proportion between itself and the person who aspires to it. That is why no one can be magnanimous unless he has received exceptional gifts. It is the privilege of an elite not to surpass one's own powers in seeking greatness. Magnanimity is the virtue of the strong. Modesty is more fitting for others. If it be true that the Thomist conception of magnanimity defines a humanism, this humanism is an aristocratic humanism.

(b) *The Exaltation of God*

It is the greatness of man for which magnanimity strives, and the powers on which it depends to attain to it are the powers of man. It is therefore most certainly the Greek ideal in its deepest meaning, that of a salvation of man by man, which is here integrated within Thomist morality. How then can we overcome the contradiction between the Greek conception of fortitude and the Christian conception, a contradiction which we denounced? This remains to be seen.

Magnanimity and Humility

First of all reason itself is sufficient to teach man that he is a creature and that his greatness as a man and his manly powers have all been received from God, his Creator, and from this new consideration the virtue of humility will be born. The domain of the virtue of humility is exactly the same as that of the virtue of magnanimity. Humility, like magnanimity, has the rule of governing human hope. And yet, far from hindering each other in any way, the two virtues reinforce each other reciprocally by combining. This is because if both govern human hope, they do not do so from the same point of view: magnanimity governs hope *in terms of man*; while humility governs it *in terms of God*.

Human hope must consequently be governed from a double point of view. First, in consideration of the real capacities of the subject.

And in this respect humility can accomplish nothing. It is not its role to say whether or not a particular individual, considering what he is in himself, has the right to aspire to greatness; it is not its role to direct him in the conquest of this greatness if he is capable of it himself. In this respect, he must be magnanimous in order to see clearly and behave properly, and it is only when he is magnanimous, first of all (or modest, if such is the case) that he will also be able to be humble, for humility *supposes* this first regulation of hope, and it *adds* a second to it which does not destroy the first, but perfects it: it notices that the very powers thanks to which the subject strives for greatness are a gift of God, and consequently, he only moves toward it by a gift of God and could not so move without God. Therefore, it only hopes to arrive at greatness by a gift of God and it does homage to God for this greatness which it owes to Him. Let us therefore conceive of one and the same man who is both humble and magnanimous; in so far as he is magnanimous, he will measure his powers, and having found them adequate, he will judge himself worthy of greatness and confidently undertake to reach it; in so far as he is humble, he will judge himself unworthy of any greatness without the help of God, but this reflection will in no way result in shattering his enthusiasm since he knows that God really exists and has granted him great gifts. It will not diminish the fervor of his hope in any way, but will imbue it with gratitude toward God who allowed it. The act of humility by which man recognizes the blessing of God in his own greatness and strength, is not the denial of that greatness or that strength. It is the oblation of it, and consequently it is the sanctification of it.

Infused Magnanimity

This first corrective applied to the Greek theory might have been perceived by the Greeks themselves—in fact, among the last of them, an Epictetus, a Marcus-Aurelius, obscurely foresaw it. But we must go further—where only faith can advance. Because, as faith alone reveals it to us, the nature of man is wounded. It follows that man's task itself cannot be fully undertaken by man in his own strength alone. He must first be healed of those wounds which sin inflicted upon his very nature, and this can only be done by the grace of God. This brings us to the level, still human but already theological, of infused magnanimity, which is properly Christian magnanimity.

What then is infused magnanimity? It is magnanimity which God "infuses," pours into, the soul on the day of our baptism and at the same time as He diffuses grace in it, and this magnanimity, to regulate our hope, does not seek support in the light of naked reason, but in the light of reason enlightened by faith. And everything is transformed. Reason dreams of a harmonious development, of an expansion that is wholly in line with our faculties. Reason enlightened by faith knows that this is only a dream, that our faculties, injured, wayward, and inclined to evil must be righted and healed before being developed. Reason dreams of leading man to greatness by his manly powers alone. But reason enlightened by faith knows that this again is only a dream, and that these very powers, weakened by sin, must be restored by grace. Infused magnanimity therefore still aims at the greatness of man, but a greatness which is more of a restoration than a development; it still depends upon the powers *of man*, but powers that are healed by grace. And then it enters into a new order. Natural magnanimity puts the greatness of man in the service of the community and makes an offering of it to God. Infused magnanimity, itself, is in the service of charity. It is through love for God that it pursues within itself the restoration of the work of God.

The Gift of Fortitude

Infused virtues respect the mode of human action and yield to its conditions. Therefore magnanimity, even infused, remains an aristocratic virtue. Doubtless every Christian receives it in baptism. But only a select few can exercise it. In other men it remains inactive. This aristocratism, however, could not be the last word in a Christian theology. The doctrine of the gift of fortitude will enable Thomist theology to avoid it even on the human level. By the gift of fortitude man measures his activity no longer by his own powers, even when restored by God, but by the very power of God placed at his disposal. It is upon this power that he depends for undertaking the greatest and most difficult actions, even when they are not in proportion to his strength. Consequently, even if a saint is *humanly* the most mediocre of men, nothing prevents him from undertaking and successfully completing many enterprises which, *even humanly*, are included among the greatest successes in human history.

Theological Hope

Magnanimity, even infused, remains a confidence in self—in oneself as created by God, in the self healed by God—but finally in oneself. The greatness to whose conquest it aspires is still the greatness of man. The gift of fortitude itself can be exercised on the human level, putting the power of God to the service of man. This is still not true Christian fortitude, the fortitude of dynamism that is wholly supernatural, which St. Paul preached about. However, this dynamism is not absent from the theology of St. Thomas. But it is called hope, and it is a theological virtue. To complete the theology of fortitude we must then turn to the theology of the theological virtue of hope. This time it is no longer the greatness of man which is the goal one sets out to reach, but it is the greatness of God Himself, of God attained and possessed in common, in a loving contemplation, by the whole family of men. And for this conquest, most certainly, the powers of man, even the greatest of men, are absolutely of no importance, but the power of God alone, His wholly gratuitous grace, is important. Pure trust in God, with no mixture of confidence in self, will therefore constitute the divine hope. But it will still be a principle of action, a supernatural dynamism, which will lead the Christian to the winning of God, which, consequently, will make him work enthusiastically for the coming of His reign upon the earth. For only those will enter Heaven who will have worked to make the earth more noble and more worthy of God.

Theological hope therefore appears to us as a supernatural magnanimity which is given to crown human magnanimity. But this is not saying enough. In reality, it is the very *condition* of the complete development of human magnanimity. Does not magnanimity require in man the full equilibrium of his faculties and their greatest efficacy? Now, as we know, without grace this cannot be, and the finest human qualities are always lacking in some respect. But there is only one grace, the one which lifts man higher is also the one which heals him; the one which causes divine hope to be born in man's heart is also the one which causes infused magnanimity, the expansion of human hope, to be born in human hearts. The conclusion is inevitable: the man who, to obtain the greatness of God depends upon God alone, is also the only one who is justified in depending upon himself to reach greatness as a man, in dependence upon God. The man who looks to God for his salvation—the only real salvation, which is above man and is divine—is the only one who has the right to depend upon his own powers, redeemed and sustained by God, in order to save the human in man. Now, the divine hope is offered to everyone. And consequently, as by the gift of fortitude, the aristocratism of natural magnanimity is found to be shattered, so the only mass humanism which is not utopian, and which in fact is no longer humanism but rather "divinism," can then be established.

CONCLUSION

What solution, finally, does theology teach us to bring to the problem of fortitude, such as it was presented to us? A double solution.

First of all, there are typically Christian conceptions of fortitude. And, on this level, no theology will ever suppress the scandal of Christian fortitude. On the contrary, the role of theology will be to throw full light upon this scandal. Reason, consequently, could not recognize in these Christian conceptions the ideal of fortitude such as it would itself conceive, for these conceptions must be situated at the start on a level to which mere reason has no access, a supernatural level. For anyone who does not have the faith, this will always be foolishness. But that which is a scandal and foolishness for reason without faith, is an adorable and admirable mystery for reason enlightened by faith. And this is the first response of theology—of all theology—to reason: there is something in this which is beyond you; bow down and believe. . . .

However, while the Fathers and the Augustinian theologians remain there, St. Thomas wished to accomplish more and bring a second response to reason, and this is the originality of his theology of fortitude: Christian conceptions *do not exclude* the human conceptions of fortitude; their apparent opposition only arises because they are not found on the same level, the first pertaining to the realization of a work that is properly religious and supernatural, while the others are useful for the realization of secular and natural tasks. Furthermore, they are in perfect *harmony*, and it was a stroke of genius for St. Thomas to have introduced self-confidence and confidence in God into a common psychology, that of hope.

At the same time, St. Thomas brought to the theological problem of fortitude the solution which our time demands. For if the first response, that of Augustinian theology, was sufficient for an era when, as during the Middle Ages, the sacred having absorbed the secular, all human activities were transposed to the supernatural level, it could not be adequate for an era which, like our own, has granted autonomy to secular activities. If it was sufficient for the formation of clerics whose activity is deployed on the supernatural level, it is not adequate for the formation of laymen, devoted to temporal tasks. It was precisely the major error of the seventeenth century to return by an unpardonable anachronism to the Augustinian morality of the Middle Ages, thereafter out of date, and it was this error which formed a type of Christian man in modern society who was not the kind it needed and who was bound to seem ineffectual. The Thomist theology of fortitude, by teaching Christians and particularly Christian laymen engaged in temporal tasks, that they *may* legitimately and that they *should* bring to these tasks that self-esteem and self-confidence, proposed to them by Pius XI, which are the conditions of a genuine efficacy, is the only theology in a position to fashion the kind of Christian man which modern society needs.

REFLECTIONS AND PERSPECTIVES

Modern Conceptions of Fortitude

The preceding account was limited to the examination of the Greek conceptions of fortitude, a typical example of human conceptions of this virtue. We should also examine the modern conceptions of fortitude, that of Nietzsche, and that of certain surrealists which Michel Carrouges reveals in *La Mystique du surhomme* (Paris, N.R.F., 1948), or that of the sociologists whom J. Folliet denounces in *L'avènement de Prométhée* (Chron. soc. de France). It would then be necessary to begin with what they contain in the way of human truth or deviations, and to show how their content of human truth may agree with the Christian conceptions of fortitude.

The question is asked: "Has Christianity deprived man of his virility?" Could it not also be asked, in an era which is already called the "era of the organizers" or that of technicians: "Has Christianity deprived humanity of the qualities of woman?": those qualities of a complementary kind of which woman has a certain prerogative, if not the monopoly—kindness, tenderness, gentleness, life and an exuberance of life (are our churches exuberant with life?), and joy (are our Christians more joyful than others? Do they seem to be "more saved"?), natural beauty and grace (does the simple beauty of nature have anything in common with certain church interiors which resemble a pawn-shop with their accumulation of gadgets and artificial things?), maternal care for our neighbor considered as an individual (do our modern apostles, engaged in works that are increasingly collective, sometimes forget the individual and personal "case" of each Christian?), etc.

The true Christian possesses the opposite virtues of firmness and gentleness, of pride and humility, of trust and fear of God, of magnificence and spiritual poverty.

Fortitude and Martyrdom

The preceding account has indicated how martyrdom is related to Christian "Upomone" and how we may find in this the principle of solution for most of the very complex questions which the theology of martyrdom poses.

The canonical conditions of martyrdom, that is to say the external conditions which canon law requires for a martyr to be canonized as a martyr. It is obvious that, even in the absence of these conditions, there may be authentic martyrdom in the eyes of God who sees the hearts; but we will readily understand that the Church must surround the official recognition of martyrdom with precautions, since it is not the external, visible act which constitutes martyrdom, but the invisible motives which clearly distinguish Christian "Upomone" from pagan fortitude. Cf. on this subject the article *Martyre,* in *Dict. de théologie catholique,* volume 10, col. 223-233.

Apologetical value of martyrdom. This question is very delicate for the same reasons. Cf. E. A. de Poulpiquet, *L'objet intégral de l'apologétique,* Paris, 1912, pp. 148-187.

Martyrdom and the baptism of blood. We have just laid stress upon the invisible motives and the interior intention, which distinguish Christian fortitude from pagan fortitude. Men were less aware of this interior aspect during the first Christian centuries. Or, at least, they were more aware of the fact that in determined conditions the external aspect of martyrdom (the shedding of blood) was the sign, sometimes even the sacrament, of its interior aspect (the grace of God, who gives the martyr His charity and patience). The Holy Innocents were recognized as blessed not because they had the actual intention of giving their life and offering themselves to God, but because "massacred in hatred of the Lord" they had truly received the sacrament of His Passion, they had been sacramentally configured in Christ who shed His blood for us. The catechumen's shedding of blood before the oppressive public authorities is like immersion in the baptismal font, an imitation of the death of Christ, and for this reason a baptism of regeneration. This does not mean that the "intention" of the martyr is of no further importance, but it must be sought in the same way as that required of the catechumen who presents himself at the baptismal font. On this subject, cf. Ch. V. Heris, *"Le salut des enfants morts sans baptême"* in *La Maison-Dieu,* n. 10, pp. 90-105.

Martyrdom and confirmation. Much has been written on the grace of the sacrament of confirmation which is said to be a sacramental grace of fortitude that is capable of sustaining the candidate in every profession of public faith. Is this exact? The thesis at least deserves to be varied slightly. On this subject, see *Force chrétienne,* opus cit. and also the articles of Fr. L. Bouyer in *Paroisse et liturgie* (1952, n. 1, and n. 2), "Que signifie la confirmation?"

Christian martyrdom and pagan martyrdom. What should be thought of the specious objection of certain communists: "Our martyrs are greater than yours, because they are disinterested. We do not believe in immortality." What is the meaning of interest and disinterest, in faith, in hope and in love? (See the chapter on Hope.)

Fortitude and the Struggle of the Christian

It would be useful to develop the Pauline and monastic theme of Christian life as a duel. This was a Gospel theme, moreover, before being Pauline (cf. L. Bouyer, *Theology Library*, volume II).

On this theme, concerning the Christian's battle against Satan and the powers of evil, refer to the writings of St. Paul, cf. Eph. 6:10-16; Rom. 13:12; II Cor. 6:7; I Thess. 5:8; etc. The military virtues, the athletic virtues, the "virtues of the stadium," are particularly liked by St. Paul.

On the monastic theme of combat against Satan, see the *Rule of Saint Benedict,* especially the Prologue, chaps. 1, 2, 58, 61. The monk is a "Domino Christo vero regi militaturus," a man who must fight for Christ the King. The monastery is a school of combat where one is trained "thanks to the support of many brethren to fight against the devil. And when one is well trained, he goes out from this fraternal militia to solitary combat in the desert."

But it is especially in the closing hours of life that the Christian's struggle is increased in intensity. It is then, truly, an "agon" (an agony, from a word of Greek origin meaning combat) in which the part of the Evil One and the whole of the Christian is played out to a finish.

Concerning the monastic theme of the martyr-monk, and more generally, on the theme of Christ, the martyr of truth, read the very fine book of Dom A. Stolz, *L'ascèse chrétienne,* Chevetogne, 1948, particularly chapters 3 to 5. Numerous sermons of the Fathers could also be mentioned.

Christian Pride

On this theme we can only cite the sermon of St. Leo which the Latin Church reads every year at the Matins of Christmas: "Recognize, O Christian man, thy dignity, and having shared in the divine nature, keep thyself from returning to the evil ways of the old man through unworthy conduct. Remember of what Head and of what Body thou art a member. Remember that rescued from the powers of darkness, thou hast been transported into the light and the kingdom of God."

If there be a Christian honor, it is the honor of God. The greatest magnificence is that of working for the honor and glory of God. This belongs to the Christian.

Fortitude and the Passions

The Thomist theology of fortitude is governed by a certain psychology of the passions, particularly the passions of the irascible which, as we remember, St. Thomas classifies in the following way:

Confronted by an arduous and difficult good:

> Man tends toward this because he sees the good: the passion of *hope;*
> Man avoids this because he judges it difficult: the passion of *despair.*

Confronted by an evil which overwhelms him:

> Man avoids it, in so far as it is evil: the passion of *fear;*
> Man experiences it and rebels against it: the passion of *anger.*

Thomist psychology, to the degree that it rests upon the elementary and solid apperceptions of common sense, will keep its value. However, it can only gain by being thought out again in terms of the discoveries of modern psychology. The theology of fortitude has everything to gain in this respect.

A scientific analysis of the passions which fortitude must discipline, and of character which it must form, will also help the theologian to specify useful pedagogical methods for acquiring the human virtue of fortitude and preparing for the Christian virtues, which grace infuses, a basis on which they may be deployed without being constantly contradicted by the revolts of temperament.

The Elements of Fortitude and the Associated Virtues

This is how St. Thomas classifies the latter. It is clear enough not to require commentaries.

St. Thomas distinguishes two acts of fortitude: *aggredi* (to attack), and *sustinere* (to sustain, or to be steadfast against adversity) which is the most characteristic of the virtue of fortitude.

(The opposite vices are indicated between brackets.)

Aggredi

Integral parts (or elements of the virtue):
- for the preparation of the soul: confidence (timidity)
- for the execution of the work: magnificence (pettiness)

Potential parts (imperfect realizations of the virtue of fortitude):
- Fortitude of someone who incurs great expenses: magnificence (meanness)
- Fortitude of someone who is obliged by honors: magnanimity, greatness of soul, assurance.

> Vices
> - by excess: presumption, ambition, vainglory, arrogance;
> - by default: pusillanimity, timidity.

Sustinere
- Against imminent difficulties: patience (impatience);
- Against the long duration of hardship: perseverance, longanimity, constancy, and final perseverance.

> Vices
> - by default: Instability, inconstancy;
> - by excess: Vicious pertinacity, stubbornness.

The gift of fortitude

Theological bases and study. The gift of fortitude in the saints.

BIBLIOGRAPHIE

Le chapitre qui précède n'est, pour une large part, qu'un résumé de: R.-A. Gauthier, *Magnanimité, L'idéal de la grandeur dans la philosophie païenne et la théologie chrétienne*, Paris, Vrin, 1950, dans lequel on trouvera la justification et le développement de la plupart des points de vue brièvement indiqués ici.

532   THE VIRTUES AND STATES OF LIFE

Sur la position du problème de la force, voir: *Le christianisme a-t-il dévirilisé l'homme?* Enquête de *Jeunesse de l'Église,* n° 2, pp. 65-103; n° 3, pp. 35-58; n° 4, pp. 9-42.

Sur les conceptions grecques de la force: A.-J. Festuguière, Ὑπομονή *dans la tradition grecque,* dans *Recherches de Science Religieuse,* XXI (1931), pp. 477-486, et, du même auteur, *La Sainteté,* Paris, 1942, ch. 2, "Le héros grec."

Sur la conception biblique de l'ὑπομνή: C. Spicq, Ὑπομονή, *Patientia,* dans la *Revue des Sciences Philosophiques et Théologiques,* XIX (1930), pp. 95-106.

Sur le martyre: Hippolyte Delehaye, *Sanctus, Essai sur le culte des saints dans l'antiquité,* Bruxelles, 1927, ch. II, "Martyr et confesseur," pp. 74-121; M. Viller, "Martyre et perfection," in "Revue d'Ascétique et de Mystique," VI (1925), pp. 3-25 et "Le martyre et l'ascèse," *ibid.,* pp. 105-142, articles repris, sous une forme simplifiée, dans: Marcel Viller, *La spiritualité des premiers siècles chrétiens,* ch. II, "Le martyre," Bibliothèque catholique des sciences religieuses, Paris, 1930.

Signalons enfin, parmi les ouvrages plus directement pratiques:

L.-M. Dewailly, G. Gourbillon, etc., *Force chrétienne,* Coll. *Cahiers de la Vie spirituelle,* Paris, Éd. du Cerf, 1943.

BIBLIOGRAPHY

Davis, Henry, S.J., *Moral and Pastoral Theology,* Vol. I, pp. 264-267, London, Sheed and Ward, 1941.

Farrell, Walter, O.P., *A Companion to the Summa,* Vol. III, pp. 357-402, New York, Sheed and Ward, 1940.

McHugh, John A., O.P., and Callan, Charles J., O.P., *Moral Theology, A Complete Course,* Vol. II, pp. 465-483, New York, Joseph Wagner, Inc., 1930.

Pieper, Josef, *Fortitude and Temperance* (Trans. Daniel F. Coogan), New York, Pantheon Books, Inc., 1954.

Sheedy, Charles E., C.S.C., *The Christian Virtues,* pp. 317-326, Notre Dame, Ind., University of Notre Dame Press, 1949.

Tanquerey, Adolphe, S.S., *The Spiritual Life,* pp. 505-517, Westminster, Md., The Newman Bookshop, 1948.

Chapter IX

TEMPERANCE

by P. Laféteur, O.P.

I. A VIRTUE MODERATING CARNAL DESIRES

1. Signification of carnal desires
   - (a) The likenesses of God in creation
     - Resemblance to Him Who is
     - Resemblance to Him Who creates
     - Resemblance to Him Who endures
   - (b) The instincts of the creature
     - Natural gravitations
     - Hierarchy of the gravitations
   - (c) Carnal desires are fundamental desires
     - To maintain and to grow
     - To maintain the species

2. Signification of temperance
   - (a) The rational direction of sensible life
   - (b) Definition of temperance
     - A virtue which moderates
     - *A* virtue, not *the* virtue
     - A cardinal virtue
   - (c) "Libido" and the noble virtue
     - The lower inclinations
     - Possible defeat of reason
     - Reason in the service of the flesh and of sin
     - Carnal disorder and original sin
     - The shameful vice
     - The "noble virtue"
     - Temperance among the other virtues

3. The measures of temperance
   - (a) Objective measures
     - Principles of judgment
     - Avoiding subjective attitudes and judgments

Chapter IX

TEMPERANCE

I. A Virtue Moderating Carnal Desires

Because there is no virtue without all the virtues—and especially because there are no independent virtues but only virtuous men—we must begin by reviewing a few general points: to define a virtue is also to situate it. Even if we seem to do this rather deviously, it will not be merely a repetition of what has already been said.

1. SIGNIFICATION OF CARNAL DESIRES

"And God created man to his own image" (Gen. 1:27) and this was the crowning of creation. But every creation is already a reflection of God.

(a) *The Likenesses of God in Creation*

Resemblance to Him Who Is:

The creature is a reflection of God primarily because *it exists:* this is the basis of everything and that is why we call a creature a "being." This is the first resemblance to "Him Who Is," *Yahweh.* But there are no two beings who resemble Him equally or in the same way. Very roughly, we are accustomed to distinguish those which exist only materially, in a word, the mineral world; and those which, furthermore, (it is important to remember in a practical way that it is *furthermore*) are alive: vegetation; and those which, moreover, know and feel: the animals; and finally man, at the summit, who thinks and wills.

Resemblance to Him Who Creates:

God is not only He Who Is; he is also the One Who acts, and, going straight to our present object, God is *He Who creates,* the One Who projects His being outside of Himself (we must make use of inadequate expressions in speaking of God) and allows His being to overflow upon others who are born of this radiation. Every being, in a certain way, acts, moves others, calls them forth into existence;

the universe is not merely an immense museum but instead a field of actions and reactions, in which beings are constantly giving of themselves to one another and receiving from one another. In the measure that each one gives, he is the image of the God Who projects Himself, of the God Who creates, and of the God Who begets. At the top of the hierarchy, the living creature is never more fully the image of God the Creator than when he *begets:* he is then the source of being for another living creature who is equal to him. What greater thing could he do? When he has attained to his greatest dimension, when he is an adult, he reflects the being of God to the greatest possible degree within himself, according to the richness and modalities proper to his species: he can only do more by "procreating," that is to say by allowing his own richness to overflow upon others to the point of giving them the impetus that is necessary in order that some day they may equal him as images of God.

Resemblance to Him Who "Endures":

By this action the living creature attains to another resemblance to God. He Who *Is* and Who is infinitely, He who is *action* and infinite action, is also the *Eternal One:* He Who had no beginning and will not cease to be—or better still, He Who is above time. By generation, the living creature obtains the means of *enduring.* Although the law of his material being is to be born, to grow, and then to decline and finally to die, generation will prolong him. And while any particular being or individual must disappear, at least the species does not disappear and consequently it continues to be the image of immutable being of God in order that it may continue to show forth in its own way the richness and beauty of its creator. This is the superiority of the species which endures over the individual who passes away.

(b) *The "Instincts" of the Creature*

Natural Gravitations:

A being could not be the image of the God Who is free, the God Who is infinitely *spontaneous* in His creative activity, if the activity of that being were artificial, so to speak, or if it were in God's hands only a kind of inert puppet that had to be moved from outside itself. Every creature *bears within itself the "law"* according to which it acts; every species plays its role under the impulse of an internal impetus of which we would have to analyze the modalities in their diversity and in their hierarchy, but which may roughly be reduced to a few types: the gravitations or affinities of material beings; kinds of vital impetus which make them develop "according to their species," if they are vegetables; and for beasts, there are instincts (using the word in a very broad sense) which are impulses toward action which finally become sensible and conscious in the form of "appetites," cravings, and desires for a foreseen enjoyment which will accompany the action; and finally, for man, there is freedom. It must be understood, and it is essential for our purposes, that these are things which are additional, and which envelop one another, and do not replace one another, and therefore man continues to be "material, vegetative and instinctive" while also being intelligent and free.

Hierarchy of the Gravitations:

In a well constructed universe we conjecture that these impulses, these "gravitations," and these desires for enjoyment, will be *all the stronger because they correspond to the more essential functions,* and to the more radical needs of the being that possesses them: the very force of these attractions and the dimension of the promised enjoyments more irresistibly ensure the most necessary actions.

Such are the landmarks which we had to find again in order to situate the virtue of temperance and to indicate its conditions. And now we need only to gather and classify.

(c) *Carnal Desires Are Fundamental Desires*

To Maintain and to Grow:

The first condition for any creature is to exist. Before being this or that (it is obviously not a question of a "before" in time) it is necessary *to be.* The most radical need of a creature, the image of Him Who is, is to maintain itself, and to develop itself if possible.

To maintain itself primarily against every enemy: this is the universal law of self-defense. In the living creature it will be called cicatrization, coagulation, the secretion of anti-toxins or phagocytosis, etc.; in the sensible animal it will be accompanied by the pain or the well-being which the individual bears, by simple desire for relief or a sensible satisfaction in seeking conditions that are more favorable to his conservation. But merely to stay alive is not sufficient; there must be *growth,* by means of an effortful search and quest if necessary and if the being is capable of it: we need only think of the plant which extends its leaves and its roots. *Hunger and thirst* are one aspect of this instinctive need which the animal has in order to endure and to grow in his individual being. We might almost call them "pains," the pains which put the animal on guard against the danger of his destruction, if the word pain did not connote something more passive than hunger and thirst. The "pain" only calls for relief; hunger and thirst only disappear by taking in something. The scholastics say "appetites," and we still use the word, but contemporary speech has greatly reduced its meaning. "Desire" does not express the force of these interior movements sufficiently. "Covetousness" is the word which we conserve by preference, while removing the slightly pejorative nuance of envy which seems to have tainted it. The most radical need of the individual, the necessity of maintaining himself and growing is therefore expressed by a supremely demanding desire, and its satisfaction brings an enjoyment of which the most superficial observation immediately recognizes the universality.

To Maintain the Species:

However, as we have already stated, the species is in some sense superior to the individual: by its perennity, first of all, and also by the stability of its perfection, since in the species, at all times, we find all the richness in act which is proper to it and which, in a certain measure, must be shared by the individual being, no one having all the "talents" of the species, nor even possessing fully during a whole lifetime those with which it is endowed. It will not surprise us, therefore, to find impulses toward the reproductive function more profoundly inscribed in the living creature than in all others; we shall see it guaranteed by unimaginable deployments of adaptations and precautions of nature (we need only think of the number of germinal seeds, and all the devices which assure their conservation or their development in fruit and grain—or in a mother) and finally, in the animal, by a desire and an enjoyment of exceptional force.

We said, the *superiority of the species over the individual:* it matters little, therefore, if the individual perishes, provided that the species endures, since another individual takes his place. The more so as the *reproductive instinct* is expressed by powerful desires of

such violence as hunger and thirst rarely experience, and its satisfaction is accompanied by a shock which often deprives the animal
of his self-control. It happens sometimes that the instinct of individual conservation is prevented from functioning; in certain species
it happens that the male dies after the reproductive act, and it is not
unknown (even among men) that males kill one another for the
possession of a female. These almost irresistible impulses are the
psychological aspect of the magnificence surrounding an action
which is, in the animal, as the summit of his power of being and
acting, the summit of his likeness to God, Who is, Who endures,
and Who creates.

This is not the place to describe the fulfillment of all this in human love and the sacrament of marriage. This is done elsewhere.
Our purpose is more humble, but it would be regrettable for the
reader to forget these fulfillments, for it would perhaps falsify his
judgment concerning the values in question.

2. SIGNIFICATION OF TEMPERANCE

These considerations concerning living beings are useful to man
as a corrective, or as an addition, both considerable and essential,
which we have provisionally left in the background.

(a) *The Rational Direction of Sensible Life*

Man is not merely "material, vegetative and instinctive." Above
all this and enveloping it, he is intelligent and free, a small "providence," it has been said. If the stone is moved according to its internal law which is its weight, and the chemical product according
to its affinities, the plant according to its vital forces and the animal
according to its ultimately sensible instincts, man alone, while also
having weight, vegetative forces and instincts, *"moves himself,"* in
the full sense, by considering his destiny, by determining the means
for realizing it, and by freely choosing the acts to be done. He must
govern himself reasonably, and this is the very definition of his virtue. He cannot allow his life to be spent at the mercy of his instincts;
he cannot let it become oriented, without control, toward blind
enjoyments.

He must prevent this especially because he must not only govern
his animal nature in a reasonable way, but his spiritual nature (that
nature which is *also* and supremely spiritual, but not *only* spiritual)
gives him objectives and issues which *surpass the carnal condition,*

in the full measure in which the spirit properly so called, intelligence and free will, dominate and surpass matter, even animate matter, the vegetative life and sensibility.

It follows, be it noted, that the human person who, being intelligent and loving, treats directly with God, has a proper value which contradicts the "superiority of the species over the individual." But we need not touch upon all this here. It must be remembered, however: it is the mystery of man (and perhaps his drama) to be, in his very nature, both carnal and spiritual, and furthermore, both social and personal. The whole theology of marriage and its practical spirituality, and more generally the whole behavior of man, are marked by it. We shall find several applications of it. The mystery of the Mystical Body, that tremendous solidarity of all men in the unique person of Christ, which leaves each man his whole personality, and more importantly which is the condition of each man's ultimate fulfillment, is the supernatural mystery that is the culmination of the aspect which we have in mind concerning the mystery of man. It is difficult to define it theologically and to live it practically in its double aspect: communal and personal, the stumbling-block being to choose one of the two aspects at the expense of the other.

(b) *Definition of Temperance*

Temperance is the virtue of that government which man must exercise over himself.

A Virtue Which Moderates:

The word *tempero* often connotes the idea of a mixture, of a compensating alloy, and consequently of a mitigation. We think primarily of a moderation, a reserve, and a discretion, and this is not false. However, only one step is needed to call temperance a weakness or a "mediocrity," just as men refer to humility, clemency or chastity in such terms, but this is a caricature.

Unless we only think of temperance in the vulgar sense as a moderate use of strong drinks—and that would not be false either. But it would then be taking a part, and a small part, for the whole.

With moral tradition we are now speaking of a virtue, and it is a cardinal virtue. It is therefore a matter of strength and not weakness; we are concerned about an "axis" of the moral life and not about some detail.

For *tempero* also means to govern, and even to reign. The relation to mixing, compensating and moderating is visible; the one who governs, in so far as he commands and fosters the activity of his subjects, must balance their respective forces and their mutual relations in order to enlist all the forces of his state in a full and calm mastery; *he must keep everything perfectly in hand.* He must compensate some particular richness by another that is complementary; he must prevent some particular subject from extending his overly independent activity alone at the risk of introducing disorder and perhaps resulting in catastrophes that are all the more serious because it is a question of a subject who is less commonplace and more enterprising. All of this is "to order," which means first of all to establish an "order," *ordo,* and then to carry it out (we may think of prudence which sees, deliberates and chooses before giving commands). To govern is to foresee, to organize and *foster,* whereby the leader is the image of Providence, which foresees and, by seeing, creates. But these things cannot be done if the authority is too soft and if it occasionally hesitates *to repress.*

The analogy, which is clear, now definitely lets us see what the virtue of temperance must be. Call it moderation if you will; or equilibrium and the golden mean, certainly. But these constitute mastery for the sake of perfect efficiency.

"The virtue which moderates carnal covetousness." In this way it has often been defined in its narrowest sense. This is quite correct if we do not limit the meaning of "moderation." Perhaps it would be better to say that this virtue governs, since it is a question of a virtue which enables reason, grappling with passionate instincts, to retain control over life. It will often be necessary to restrain the anarchical instinct; it must always be guided and maintained in the right direction, and sometimes it must be aroused (we say sometimes, not because it is less moral, but because man is so made that, in matters we are now considering, a voluntary inducement is rarely necessary). If moderation or control mean all this, our definition states what is necessary very well; the following will throw light upon it.

Several remarks are necessary now.

A Virtue, Not *the* Virtue

First of all let us remember that temperance is *a* virtue and not *the* virtue. It is not a question of placing the whole moral life under the sign of temperance. It would not even be a virtue if it were not allied in man with all the others which are, in regard to moderation, organizing, fostering and "encouraging" virtues, and which, furthermore, would not be virtues without it. This modest remark is not new to the reader; but it is not useless if we judge it by what the term virtue means for most people. Many lives, more or less consciously and completely, have been built, and many educational systems established, upon this error which consists in seeing only temperance as virtue or in placing too much emphasis upon it, or else in giving all the other virtues the form of restraint that is proper to temperance alone. This is regrettable.

A Cardinal Virtue:

It must not surprise us that we entrust this "moderating" mission to a virtue which moral tradition emphasizes as a *cardinal* virtue. For reasons already mentioned, carnal desires are the strongest that an animal nature experiences—and man is an animal: the functions which they control are in fact *the most fundamental,* for lack of which the creature denies itself by self-annihilation. We should therefore expect that their control by reason will be a laborious matter in which we must enlist the activity of a virtue of a more prominent kind which, by this very fact, will be able to serve as a type for others. This is exactly what is meant by a "cardinal virtue." It is a common experience that these desires practically hold an incontestable place in man's moral (or immoral!) life, and that the disorders to which their force inclines men heavily impose themselves upon the moralist's attention and upon the efforts of the man who desires to keep his life under control.

(c) *"Libido" and the Noble Virtue*

The Lower Inclinations:

When we speak of "passionate desires" and even of disorders, it is not meant that the strong and demanding inclinations are evil in themselves. All of our preceding remarks say the opposite and it is important to emphasize this at the very beginning of this paragraph rather than elsewhere, against a prejudice which we must not too readily suppose to be dead. Furthermore, even if they were evil in themselves, it would not be a question of moderating, restraining or controlling them, and even less of arousing them from time to time, but quite definitely of destroying them. We must not therefore let current speech delude us when it qualifies these desires as "low," or when it calls them "the lowest." Certainly that is what they are. If the purely vegetative movements and material gravitations are still humbler and lower, they do not come within the sphere of virtue because they are wholly unconscious or at least automatic and un-controllable. This is below the moral sphere into which they enter in a roundabout way at the very most. They are tendencies to which man may freely yield or not, and which he may watch over, curb, or permit intense development, or against whose unguarded awaken-ing he may possibly defend himself. These are therefore most cer-tainly "the lowest." But we must not overestimate the pejorative character of this attribute: even if the basement is the lowest floor in the home, it does not mean that it is necessarily a shameful place.

Possible Defeat of Reason

It follows that if man completely yields to these desires, and if he does not control them, but only submits to them, he is denying that which defines him among other carnal creatures: his power and duty of governing himself—in the fullest sense of this word, accord-ing to reason, and according to the nature of things. Furthermore, experience proves that such a fault contains within itself its pro-portioned punishment; one is engulfed by it. In the most realistic way, man is incapable of keeping himself at the level of the beast: if he does not keep himself above it, which is according to his na-ture, he falls below it. It is a matter of experience, in fact, that if man acquires the habit of *yielding* to carnal desires instead of con-trolling them, which is the capitulation of freedom to instinct, he is not far from *seeking* their satisfaction and of thus spontaneously putting his free will at the service of that which is lowest in him: reason at the service of the flesh, the "angel" at the service of the "beast."

Reason in the Service of the Flesh and of Sin

In these matters, merely bestial remissness may lead and often does lead straight to pleasure-seeking and to repugnant perversion which is unknown to the beast, and is finally able to make man fall into that most extreme degree of disorder: applying his intelligence to overthrow the world's order by seeking carnal enjoyments that are not only *outside* of their ultimate purpose, but even *against* their ultimate purpose, artificially avoiding the effects of an act in order

to retain only the enjoyment which was meant to ensure performance. This is the disorder, for instance, in every form of onanism,
whose abasing aspect, especially in solitary vices, is known to everyone; the more "systematic" disorder of contraceptional practices,
which implies more deliberate pleasure-seeking whereas the other
was only weakness; the supreme disorder of abortive practices in
which the intemperance, in this latter case, is doubled by a real
murder, often coldly consented to, in an action which was meant to
procure life. The moralist, in such matters, is constrained by the
facts to a great and terrible realism which he cannot consider fleeing,
whether because of a false modesty or the legitimate desire to have
no part in certain awkward kinds of preaching; morality is a *science
of life*. His theology only results in making him acquire a more realistic and more serious sense of disorders into which the sinner puts
his "providential" power (his reason, his freedom, and occasionally
his knowledge) to destroy the natural order of things which requires
that inclinations and the enjoyments connected with their satisfaction should lead to the necessary and fruitful actions as a means
intended to procure the desired end. The first perversity is to seek
the enjoyment for itself, with no concern for the end and *without
measuring* everything in relation to this end. The supreme perversion
is *to prevent* the effects *artificially* in order that these, with their
various demands and their consequences, should not lessen by encumbering it, the pure enjoyment desired for its own sake.

Carnal Disorder and Original Sin

We wanted to tell of the greatness and the excellence of the instincts which temperance is required to "moderate," and we wanted
to remove any pejorative sense from the word *low* which qualifies
them, and yet we have not been able to avoid mentioning serious
and debasing disorders at the very start. It must not surprise us that
the popular sense often confuses original sin with these sensual inclinations, especially with the reproductive instinct, and "sin" itself
with the "sin of the flesh." There is a reason for all this: because
these inclinations are carnal, the enjoyment which they entail is immediately sensible, and because they are fundamental, the enjoyment is considerable. Now, original sin, or to speak more precisely,
its "wound," consists of an interior anarchy which deprives reason
of the facility and the suavity of its control over the "passions"; at
the point where the mind ought to govern and impose its law, it is

matter which tends to impose its own in a thousand ways, which, moreover, we need not analyze now and of which certain ones go beyond the object of morality. Such a reversal of values can only be more sensible (it does not follow that it is always more serious) precisely in those slightly sinful acts in which man is grappling with the deepest and strongest tendencies of his carnal nature. We are at the junction point of human nature, precisely where the linking up ought to be foolproof.

And yet these tendencies are not evil in their nature; they are not original sin, to such a degree that we should not imagine that they were absent from the state of innocence, or suppose that their satisfaction, which is proper in marriage, would be an obstacle to sanctity. However, if original sin is not in these tendencies, at least it is most brutally shown forth in them and men meet with original sin most frequently because of them. That is why it is necessary, while also correcting it, to side with this common judgment in so far as it is well-founded and accept the *practical* importance of temperance.

The Shameful Vice

The virtue which gives man the necessary mastery to control this passionate and restive nature is consequently found to be twice reasonable. On the one hand, it makes us exercise reasonable control over the desires that proceed from hunger, thirst or from the sexual appetite, which are its proper object, but on the other hand the passions which it moderates are of such strength and are so easily unruly that remissness in such passions becomes a kind of tyranny and establishes a chaos in man which, in his own person or around himself, overthrows everything: intelligence, prudence, justice, fortitude. These disorders, from drunkenness to depraved love affairs, introduce all the forms of "degradation" into man, from the fury of the beast to its feebleness; everything has resulted from these: war, assassination, lying, slavery, theft. That is why temperance, which is reasonable in itself like any virtue, is likewise found to be the indirect establishment of the reasonable security of the other virtues in their own domains; it is by the lack of temperance, on the contrary, that man loses his human countenance most crudely. The unscrupulous fellow who pushes himself into the first places, ready to trample upon rights of others and to violate justice, remains less vile than the debaucher because he is more reasonable, both in his organizing prudence, and the strength that he deploys and in the works he undertakes, which may be opportune and fruitful. He does not degrade himself like the person who stoops down to the level of the beasts, or below it. The popular sense is still not completely mistaken when it gives its admiration, almost in spite of itself, to the ambitious person who is intelligent and efficient, regardless of his injustices and his pride, while it scorns, even good-naturedly, the drunkard lying in the gutter who has never violated the rights of others: the unscrupulous fellow himself corresponds to this popular judgment by not having any feeling of shame for his sin which the drunkard feels for his.

In regard to "fashionable vice" we shall have to make analogous appraisals later on, but with attention to the different variations and degrees, and concerning shame, we must state our reservations upon the nature of popular judgment in these matters.

The "Noble Virtue"

Bearing in mind the reservations that are necessary, it is the degrading and shameful conditions of intemperance which have contributed to the usage of designating the opposite virtue, especially in its aspect of chastity, as the "noble virtue." In some circles this is a usage from which no one would dare to deviate as if the very name of temperance and especially of chastity had already been stained by the impurity from which that virtue protects us! Even though it is frequently used in a tone of voice which quickly reveals certain errors concerning the nature or the proportions of things, this epithet "noble" attributed to the virtue can however no more be rejected in the sense given, than the reality which it expresses. If beauty is a matter of proportions, harmony, and rhythms, temperance is certainly a—and even *the*—noble virtue; and more especially if we understand it in its full meaning which we shall develop later; for assuring man the hierarchies of interior values, temperance establishes the "unity of order" in a well-made organism.

Temperance Among the Other Virtues

Let us however be on guard against the temptation of giving this virtue precedence over all the others at the risk of neglecting them. Moderating carnal appetites in man, it remains humble, considered in itself, compared with fortitude, which is dynamic, conquering, and so fruitful in behalf of the common good, or compared with justice which makes us live with consideration for others, or with prudence in which the image of divine Providence is fully confirmed in man, and much more so, obviously, when compared with the theological virtues.

I should say, quite willingly, in summing up these remarks in a rather schematic way, and which must consist entirely in various shades of meaning, and are not out of place in a domain in which "sentiment" and prejudices tend to reign: man cannot be man if he consents to being bestial, wayward, or dissolute, and this is the importance of temperance. But *not to be bestial* is finally nothing unless he intends *to be a man* (and a Christian)—and this is the greatness of the other virtues which are based upon temperance. Furthermore, to intend positively to be a man is doubtless the best means of giving oneself a loathing for bestiality, and striving to be a man in a constructive manner is the best means of ridding oneself of many enemies of temperance. The virtues are related and arranged into a hierarchy.

3. THE MEASURES OF TEMPERANCE

A virtue which puts order and discipline within *myself,* and whose proper role is to give *my will* mastery over *my* passions could hardly be more subjective at first glance. Will everything be reduced to this introspection, and be based upon it and be completed in such a construction of my "self" that whatever happens within me will be the measure of everything? Will such a virtue become a vicious circle? Nothing could be more false, and, like every virtue, it is upon objective values, but which are objective in their own way, that the temperate man will measure his moral attitudes.

(a) *Objective Measures*

Principles of Judgment

Since carnal desires, that is to say the attraction of the enjoyments connected with the functions of the conservation of the individual and the race have as the reason for their existence the accomplishment of these necessary functions, then to follow these attractions, and to desire and accept these enjoyments will be reasonably good in the exact measure in which they will lead to the natural accomplishment of these acts or will be their natural accompaniment. We do not repress merely for the sake of repressing, nor do we moderate merely for the sake of moderation: this would be "meaningless"—

understood in the most formal manner: it would take us no where, and lead to nothing, and therefore, it is outside morality. Pleasures and attractions are meant to assure functions: they are therefore good in the measure in which they assure them; we are not then to deprive ourselves of them or be ashamed of them; it may even be appropriate to arouse or develop these attractions in order to better assure the corresponding function.

The person who simply takes the pleasure attached to an act which he had to perform objectively is not therefore sinning—nor is the person who desires this pleasure; he is doing what is good. It is not sinful for a person to make his food "appetizing," or to do the same for his relations and friends, nor is there sin when a man, in the married state or with marriage in view, makes himself desirable to his spouse or to the person who may become his spouse: that is the nature of things. It is good. But the person who seeks pleasure for its own sake in such conditions that the end is thwarted, is sinning obviously, as already stated, and as a general rule the sin is serious, for he is going against the stream; as an example we may mention the person who voluntarily becomes intoxicated and clouds his reason which makes him a man although food and drink are meant to maintain him in his being as a man, or the person who seeks the pleasures of the generative act in conditions which thwart it either in its direct nature (we gave examples of this above) or in its essential conditions (for example outside of marriage).[1] The person who, without thwarting the purpose of his act, indiscreetly increases the pleasure derived for its own sake with no relation to the perfection of the act is generally sinning venially, for he is not going against the nature of things but is letting himself be more or less swept along—for example the man who is immoderately concerned about the pleasure of the table or excessively fussy about them.

Avoiding Subjective Attitudes and Judgments

These remarks are simple; it is to be hoped that they appear obvious. However, they are not useless, for it is not uncommon to

[1] It is obvious that such matters are complex and that their "casuistry" is difficult and even confusing. We can only give a general outline, and it seems that it is the soul of things which ought to be presented in an introductory study rather than a material résumé which would be an unintelligible catalogue of particular cases and concrete determinations.

find men judging more or less confusedly and more or less generally concerning the goodness of acts by the lack of pleasure contained in them, a kind of morality of pleasure in reverse. However, at the present time there exists in certain Christian circles, and they are not always the least sympathetic, an inverse tendency which sometimes would go so far as to take the opposite position from traditional morality in its fundamental orientations, but which finds itself hindered in fact by an unreasonable attachment to accepted positions: for it is most difficult to hold fast to the crest line of the "golden mean" of a *reasonable* morality, and not allow oneself to be led either to the right or the left. It is good to notice that, if it seems less fortunate in its consequences (it is far from being always so), the first error is an error nonetheless, and at bottom the same: an act is not more moral because it is pleasing, and therefore it could not be moral because it is painful. An act is to be considered good when it is in accord with the *nature* of things and the objective necessities. It would be fortunate if it were automatically pleasing— and the development of virtue within us definitely makes moral acts more and more easy and delightful (even if it be only a matter of spiritual delight at the beginning).

It is not necessary for us to repudiate a self-styled morality of "sacrifice" (i.e. a self-styled sacrifice) which, measuring every action by the "renunciation" which it demands instead of measuring it by its usefulness, by its efficacy, and by what it will accomplish for others (even if it be the glory of God) finally becomes strangely egocentric. This morality, moreover, contains an error concerning the meaning of sacrifice of which it mutilates the essential value.

(b) *"Human" Measures*

An important explanation is necessary now because it touches upon a very practical point.

The Secondary Purposes

Pleasure is legitimate and desirable, as we believe, if it procures and normally accompanies an act that is normally necessary, an act which we ought to perform. We must still recognize that there are different kinds of necessity, or, if we prefer, different kinds of purpose. Let us state the matter concretely; it will be more obvious.

For example, there is an instinct which has always induced men to make eating not only a nutritional function, but in regard to meals in common, an act of fraternal cordiality. To take our food from the same dish surely signifies our common nature and the human solidarity which binds us to one another. The Latin terms *"convivium"* (designating our common meal) and *"convivere"* (meaning to live together, and to share a common life) are very rich expressions. "We are one body," said St. Paul commenting upon the teachings of Christ—and this is already true, in large measure, according to nature itself and not only according to grace. Did not a contemporary French artist one day have the inspiration to recognize a "sacrament of humanity" in the act of Parisian workers who were "having a drink" together? In this very human spectacle he saw, as though in dual perspective, Christ celebrating the Last Supper with His disciples and he felt himself compelled to make of this banquet the next of his works of art. He saw truly, and this fraternal act of the common meal was consequently in readiness to be raised by Christ to the high level of communion, the authentic and very real "sacrament of humanity," the symbol and means of the unity of all men in the mystical body of Christ. It is therefore perfectly natural that, without having the primary intention of feeding them, we love to invite our friends to this fraternal sharing and that we make these "love-feasts" somewhat extravagant, and this may seem rather needless at first glance, but it is the symbol of our cordiality and the sign of the politeness with which we desire to establish our fraternal or family relations. Men do not go to a family dinner merely in order "to eat together at the same time," and it would be offensive and wrong not to use a "liturgical" manner, so to speak, in presenting oneself; the forms will vary according to the circumstances, the environment and the occasions. Sometimes one will attend little formal meals, almost without any nutritional value, which will only have the signification of an act of courtesy, for example, an afternoon tea. It would be quite unrealistic to call this intemperance under the pretext that it does not nourish and because in all likelihood such studied elegance does not increase the chances for good digestion! We now leave the proper and strict purpose of a meal—nutrition— and we pursue *another value naturally inscribed* and instinctively discovered in the common meal: brotherhood. In these matters an inhuman rigidity in the determination of what is "necessary" would be unrealistic and a lack of understanding, and could not pertain to true morality.

The reader himself will realize the application that can be made of such principles to other matters which also pertain more or less directly to temperance, like the care of our personal appearance or a certain luxury in the furnishing of our home.

However, we must not forget that we are referring to "moderation" and that everything must remain moderation. It is not a question of justifying extravagances that are offensive to the poverty of others (and they are more easily offensive than is commonly thought), nor are we trying to justify absurd wastes of time; nor are we canonizing the rather spectacular competence of the guest who knows and uses, to the admiration of the company, all the means of not losing a single crumb of delicate pleasure (?), and who slowly caresses his glass of liqueur in the correct way to show appreciation for its fragrance and never runs out of details in discussing the quality of the food. Our preceding remarks place us in another world: the spiritual world. Gilded gluttony ought to be called gluttony as fashionable sensuality should be called sensuality.

Temperance: a Way of Life

As an illustration of what has just been said, I could readily see a perfect example of the virtue of temperance in that elderly priest who, so very simply, sat down at the family dinner table of his parishioners. In his plain and simple way he accepted the things they offered him affectionately, as though consuming them and yet not touching them, and rather more slowly than the others (so that no one ever insisted when, with a smile or a barely visible gesture, he refused to let anyone serve him a second time), knowing how to show his appreciation for what had been done for him by a kind and rather discreet word, and indicating that the effort of the cook had not escaped his notice, yet all the while his detachment was clearly apparent and quite naturally, therefore, and without any embarrassment, the conversation could at the same time turn to God and the things of God, including the poor of the village, and no one would ever have thought for a moment that he had merely been satisfied "to eat a good dinner." In a word, his mere presence filled the whole house with such an atmosphere of ease, simplicity and reserve that it was a spiritual event for the family gathered around the table, and imposed its own formality upon everyone. He was so simply dressed, even so poorly, and yet with such natural distinction, that he did not mar the beauty of the chatelaine's salon in which he was so perfectly at ease that, without thinking about it, or the others either, it was he who set the tone, but he could then, without any change in himself, go to the poorest of his parishioners where he was quite as gracious if they asked him to accept a glass of milk or wine (unless he said: "No, thank you, not today" and no one insisted further); and there, as everywhere, his visit was a spiritual occasion. Nobody received or treated his fellow-men with greater kindness, and the most unfortunate person could arrive unexpectedly: he only needed to sit down in order to be perfectly at home for he was obviously in the home of another poor man.

To put a portrait in the place of a dissertation is perhaps to abandon the expected procedure in an "introduction to theology." But we will make no excuses for this: in matters in which everything must be *human* (wouldn't this ultimately be the profoundest definition of temperance in its broadest meaning?), a portrait is of greater worth than scholastic categories in characterizing virtue. Nor need we excuse ourselves for having abandoned "carnal desires" in doing this, in order to describe a way of life: it is the force of things which thus makes us aware, concerning some particular case, of the unity of the virtues which gravitate around a cardinal virtue as well as the informing of all the virtues by charity; we have opened the perspective which the second part of our study on temperance will enlarge.

The Joys of Sexual Love

Analogous developments could be made regarding conjugal love. It would be a crude and absurd simplification to reduce conjugal love to the attraction of the generative act; as the rather coarse but very expressive formula puts it, marriage does not consist in a "process of mating," but in *living* a fruitful human love. The mutual attraction of husband and wife, when it deserves the name of love, is a subtle and complex thing, although one, as the complex nature of man is one. Sensible and even carnal elements are involved in it, which, in the thinking of the husband and wife are not always subordinate to the generative act. Generation is the "end" of marriage in the sense that it is the fruit, without which the marriage would have no metaphysical purpose. We may say the marriage is not a generative act that is abstracted from its context and from its psychological sublimation; it is rather a question of a total atmosphere of life. The overflow of mutual love-making, a certain richness—delicate—of sensible relations, and the pursuit of whatever maintains desire, all this is for the best, even if the generative act did not need to be perfected by it. To renounce this, and especially to impose such renunciation upon the other person, would not be perfection but generally an error. A would-be virtue which denied these values or feared them, and which repudiated them as unfounded or unfortunate, and took refuge in the abstract and cold insensibility of a so-called spiritual love (which, being disincarnate, and therefore negative, would not necessarily be spiritual, which is positive) and of generative acts which would become sporadic and take on the aspect of cysts, would no longer be human love but rather—and may I be excused for saying this—a paradoxical mixture of angelism and breeding. Neither the one nor the other is *human*, and a St. Thomas does not hesitate to brand as sinful the kind of insensibility which is the systematic rejection of desires, passions and consequently of pleasures, because it is contrary to the nature of man.

A Human Virtue Is Not a Mediocre Virtue

Since it is quite naturally appropriate at this point, we should note that this term "human," which sounds badly in certain ears as if it necessarily implied a remissness or an accommodation which one must regretfully accept through condescension, certainly does not in itself have this pejorative sense, and definitely will not have this sense in what I write here. It does not qualify a *wretchedness* but a *greatness:* the greatness which consists in not forgetting half the problems and in not reducing life to the proportions of a skeleton. A more "human" morality has a more flexible aspect, and is less "categorical" (this is the right word): a living person is more flexible than a corpse. This is a general statement which, like the preceding one, is worth more than ever when we speak of temperance and which we should certainly keep in mind at the moment when we broaden the idea of this cardinal virtue.

(c) *Reasonable Restrictions*

Must we for this reason condemn partial or total abstinence from "moderate" carnal pleasures?

Anti-human Renunciations

In the measure in which these pleasures correspond to a *necessity* of nature, we must vigorously reply: this abstinence is never licit. A person who lets himself die of hunger under the pretext of totally depriving himself of the pleasures of eating, could not claim to be performing a virtuous act—no more than a person who refused to help his neighbor under the pretext of . . . renouncing the joy which he finds in it! The same must be said in regard to a total and universal abstinence from generation, which would compromise the very existence of the human race. The very effort of reserve, and of the interior denial of pleasure, as a kind of vigorous and systematic renunciation by the will of a pleasure which, naturally, is attached to a necessary and proper function, would be an abnormal attitude and contrary to nature. It is an attitude which as a general rule, we would have to declare foreign to virtue. Furthermore, is it even possible? Does the counsel pertaining to such abstinence, which is sometimes given in cases which we cannot now examine, have any practical significance for the ordinary man?

Human Renunciations

But we must be greatly on guard against any schematism which would quickly become false.

If mankind, in its totality, cannot do without generation and therefore cannot purely and simply renounce the pleasures of sexual love and of the procreative act, the race is not compromised in its existence by the abstinence of this person or that. Nor is the life of some particular man compromised by a certain abstention, even "excessive," in matters of eating, or by an exceptional rigor in depriving himself of everything which might be a pleasure that is not absolutely necessary—doubtless nobody being able to renounce the pleasure of eating when very hungry, even if the things are not very appetizing.

These procedures must not however be in any way an ascetical or penitential "game," a renunciation for the sake of renunciation: anything which "has no sense," we repeat, can have no moral value, and may be immoral if it is contrary to nature. Therefore, in the cases which we have just mentioned, it could only be a question of renunciation with a higher end in view.

Penance, which moreover only takes on the fulness of its meaning in a supernatural atmosphere, normally leads the sinner to privations that compensate for illicit pleasures, formerly accepted and sought. Even if there is no longer any *sin* to expiate, a restrictive asceticism is also legitimate and necessary, as an exercise, to correct excessive or wayward *tendencies:* anyone who wants to straighten out a twisted bar of iron must forge it in the opposite way; what we have said about original sin is sufficient to show that an asceticism of this kind is appropriate for everyone. But a more radical asceticism, and which has, so to speak, a uniquely positive scope, may legitimately incline us toward a higher good: everyone is familiar with the example, mentioned by St. Paul, of the man who practices such asceticism with a view of winning the prize in the stadium. Father Sertillanges says, somewhere, that the intellectual cannot "spend his life in one long series of fasting," and he commends a great richness of temperance of all kinds to the apprentice thinker. A quite rigid asceticism for the purpose of conquering oneself and with a view of higher human fruit-fulness, should not be condemned. With these renunciations, we are within the reasonable best, and therefore within authentic morality.

Super-human Renunciations

The analogy of the athlete leads us farther. This is the place to remind ourselves of a preceding remark: namely, that properly "spiritual" ends are proposed to man, which, in all their dimensions, surpass the body. It is thus that the consecration of virginity, which, be it noted, "sacrifices" not only the carnal but the whole of conjugal love, will become legitimate if it has the religious sense of an exclusive dedication to God and represents an engagement in a life of more total and more perfect contemplation. It is not therefore directly a matter of a renunciation but rather of the pursuit, which this renunciation facilitates, of an end which is higher than that to which the rejected pleasure was ordered. It is finally a displacement of human riches to a higher level, and not a mutilation; it is the putting of all man's power of self-giving and loving at the disposal of supernatural life. A simple natural contemplation, supposing that it was actually possible, would already doubtless justify such renunciations and such a consecration, and more especially a Christian contemplation, the fullest possible development of the theological life. However, in this respect, we must not fail to mention that it could only be a question of exceptional ways; furthermore, the dangers are not lacking and we are aware of the most immediate, and perhaps the most serious: that these renunciations will only result in dryness (the causes matter little here) and will only be a mutilation. The mutilation is this: the man or the woman whose celibacy has been consecrated to God, turning into the hardening of the "bachelor" or the "old maid," if I may be allowed these expressions.

We must say the same thing, proportionately, in regard to the renunciation of the pleasures of taste. Certain "excesses" in these renunciations may be legitimate; certain uncommon procedures may be appropriate. For example, those who are called to the contemplative life must specially avoid everything which might be vain attachment or carnal preoccupations—or even simply material encumbrance. A systematic and constant severity at table, which would be incongruous in a family, could not be reproached in monks who have established themselves in society precisely with the intention of cultivating penance and the contemplative life exclusively.

The renunciation of pleasures, licit in themselves, may finally be a pursuit of "the cross." The superficial observer might perhaps see in this a renunciation desired "for its own sake," but nothing could be more false, for it is a matter of a special assimilation to the mystery of the Passion, with a loving and redeeming purpose. It is not foolishness, it is not immorality, nor is it egoism; it is instead an excelling. The life of the saints is the magnificent proof that, however disconcerting such a spiritual way may seem to the worldly person, it has nothing to do with a morbid taste for death or the systematic extinction of everything that vibrates in man. These processes are, to some degree, a part of ordinary Christianity, and the Christian cannot completely disregard them. Even in their rigorous and exceptional forms, these attitudes of renunciation do not contradict the rule which we have set forth and which is the basis of all morality in these matters: they have an *objective* measure, and are proportioned to an end which is supremely worth attaining, and which they actually procure in the measure and according to the manner in which it may be said that human means procure such an end. Whatever may be abnormal in them only emphasizes the complexity of the human vocation. This vocation, already complex according to nature is all the more so when super-nature opens up its infinite perspectives. Furthermore, the person who practices these exceptional processes is in fact only applying, in another direction, the same principle which would allow us to justify those refinements that are supposed to be useless, which we mentioned before. He is not retired into a subjectivism which would make him center everything upon the concern of pursuing his passions; he is a being exceptionally inclined toward God in a total religious purpose. We must still admit that we are here in the domain of an infused temperance, in the full life of grace. We are also in a domain in which an easy casuistry would not only be entirely vain, but in which the actions are beyond common measures, and in which inspiration prevails. Finally, we are in a domain in which reason, without which there is not any virtue, even infused, may cease to be "reasonable" and in which, to the astonishment of the worldly person, we can no longer make any reply other than the famous reply of St. Augustine: "Give me someone who *loves* and that person will *understand*."

4. THE BROADENING OF THE IDEA OF TEMPERANCE

The domain of the influence of the virtues is not something whose limits are sharply marked. Nor their concept either.

(a) *Ramifications of Covetous Desire*

We have situated the virtue of temperance by defining its most marked point of application: "carnal desires." Many things remain to be said, of which the first is that this virtue is not exercised only in regard to covetous desires properly so called. Let us consider a few specifications.

The Passions of Sympathy

If some good appears before me, a "*love*" springs up within me. My "appetite," that is to say my power of loving this or that (using "to love" in the widest sense, from "loving wine" to "loving" in the sense of conjugal human love), the possibility which I possess of being inclined toward this or that is found to be determined. A habit is formed, a resonance established: I am in "sympathy" with this object of my love. It is this object and not something else which now captivates me, more or less completely, and impels me. If this good is in any way distant from me, I have the desire for it, I covet it as the thing which will fill an emptiness within me. When at last I have been able to get hold of it, I rejoice: the term is attained, love rests in a satisfied complaisance, in the joy of possession.

We see how these things hold together: if a resonance had not begun within me, I would not have desired this thing or this person that now marks my life with its impress.

There is, furthermore, in this respect, only one moral and psychological path: the same virtue of temperance will therefore enable me to govern my life reasonably when I am grappling with all these emotions. It is evident that, of these elements, it is desire, covetousness, which is the most delicate or the most difficult to manage; it is an impetus whose power threatens to lead me into blind excesses, and the evil will then be done. In any case, we have made it the *principal* object of temperance. But the rest also falls under its moderating control. If I do not let an injudicious love become crystallized within me, if I turn away in time from this penetration of an object whose impress will later release troublesome passions, I am temperate, apprehending the evil at its source: the control of temperance over the initial emotion of love. Let us note, furthermore, that I am likewise temperate if I let an excellent love impress itself within me and if I do everything to make its imprint indelible: control is not only repression.[1]

If, letting myself go in the opposite direction, through consent or by surprise, in loving and desiring an object which was unworthy, and then getting possession of it (even if it be a purely imaginary possession)—and this is also entering into a reality that is too well known—and if there results within myself a joy and a satisfaction which are of an evil kind, I must now try to escape from this very satisfaction. I must try to cut short its invasion. In any case, I will have to take hold of myself, and find the light of my judgment again, and going against the stream, I will have to strike hard against the root of the evil by striving to stifle this malevolent love, or forget it. Even in a legitimate joy, moreover, the excessive lack of restraint may be harmful, clouding up my reason and leading me to foolish deeds.

The same virtue which made me resist devious commitments, and dominate and control seductive desires, enables me to remain in possession of myself—or to take possession of myself again—in the midst of seductive satisfactions. All of this is the object of temperance.

The Passions of Antipathy

But this is not all. These emotional mechanisms may function, inversely, in regard to "antipathetic" objects which appear to me as a source of suffering. It is not longer good for me, but bad; it is an evil. My "appetite" does not remain indifferent to it; it is marked by it also, but not with "love"—but by "hatred" instead. There follows an attitude of rejection, a propensity to be rid of this or to avoid it, an *aversion* which risks, nearly in the same way as desire, making me do foolish things or polarizing everything towards itself by depriving me of judicious control of my actions. The simple effort of virtuous ac-

---

[1] We should note that this is valid for every aspect of permissible loves, for example, for the aspect of conjugal love. We have already met with this and will meet with it again: it is a duty to maintain whatever is good, to cultivate an insufficient desire. It may be necessary to think seriously about this duty if a person, who is married, is temperamentally "cold" (physically or psychologically), and if he is thus in danger of failing in justice or charity toward his or her spouse.

tion, with what is always painful in it, easily becomes at times the object of such an aversion. For lack of temperate control, this hatred, this aversion, will defeat the resolutions that were prudently made and will obstruct the timely accomplishments. More violent reactions may even follow these antipathies in certain cases and lead to irreparable catastrophes. What finally shall we say about *sadness*, about suffering, those depressing passions, which are at least quite as overwhelming as joy? They are the term of a hatred and an aversion to the object we have not been able to elude and whose object, whether a person or an event, has finally imposed itself upon us in a presence which hurts us and grieves us.

A Unique Virtue Moderating Several Passions

We see how the same control remains necessary in our lives, either because these passions have conquered us or because we wish to avoid their development, whether it is a question of the passions or sympathy or antipathy. It is quite as difficult, and it demands the same force and the same adroitness, to control a mob drunk with power which runs to pillage, as a mob which believes itself attacked and is seized with sudden fright, and the same excesses are to be feared. Finally, we are quite as poorly guarded by an army broken by its defeat than by victorious troops intoxicated with their success, and the same control is required of the commanders who must avoid both stumbling-blocks or extricate themselves from either extreme. Without describing anything, let us say that we must always resist seductions and those movements of sensibility which risk sweeping us into their excesses by hurling us into regrettable ways, as do unwholesome desires or those that are simply irregular, or by making us give way to destructive discouragements. There is always and everywhere a need for control, for "moderation," and for government, in movements which pertain to emotivity that is under the influence of the passions: this is the more widely measured object of temperance.

Once more, let us note that the temperate man is not always a destroyer of emotions: if he must overcome a destructive sadness, it will be done by having in view an object of joy and desire and by arousing this desire. Let us only point out, for example, that *to resist* sadness is almost exclusively the work of temperance, whereas to throw oneself into stimulating tasks rather depends upon the courageous virtues: in this latter case, temperance therefore must specially step aside, which is not a minor role.

Let us finish this paragraph quite simply with a few words of Paul Claudel which describe the virtuous man in his self-control, which is at once prudence, fortitude and temperance, but especially, in this case, temperance.

"The man who derives his understanding and this thought from temporal things little by little

—Renews the unity of his powers and puts himself in the presence of God,

—Is like the commander of a warship who has taken his stand in the conning-tower,

—And he listens, and all his means, under him, are around him awaiting himself who is both energy and cause."[1]

(b) *The Fringes of the "Carnal"*

It is from another point of view that we must now distinguish the objects of temperance and extend our concept of it. No longer by distinguishing the *levels of the emotional act* which the virtue moderates nor the positive or negative attitude of our reaction before the object which is presented to us (this is what we have just done), but by considering the *peripheral zones of this object*. Later we shall have to study temperances in a very broad sense; it will not be a question then of a carnal domain and we shall give these virtues other names. But for the moment it is still a question of "carnal" desires, but in a somewhat enlarged sense; and next it will be a question of desires (with love and joy naturally) which are still corporal but with no direct relation to nourishment or generation.

The Pseudo-gluttonies

In beginning, let us briefly consider matters which border upon the "carnal" by resemblance, envisaged thus far, and whose place is difficult to specify: namely, the pseudo-gluttonies like the use of tobacco. When it becomes a passion, an encumbering or injurious habit, we cannot tolerate it any more than alcoholism—in regard to its gravity. As a moderate excitant to work or effort, or even as a relaxation in a moment of fatigue, or as a ready sign of social cordiality, we could not condemn it any more than a cup of tea or a glass of liqueur. There is no need to insist upon this. In our study there are more serious subjects although the latter, or others that are similar, should not be

[1] *La Messe là-bas, Credo,* Gallimard, 1936, p. 39.

kept outside morality on the pretext that the great moralists of the Scholastic period do not mention them—and for good reason. We could also consider the difficult problem of narcotics, but we cannot touch upon everything.

The Scope of the Sin of the Flesh

Carnal desires and their satisfaction comprise a strong, essential and basic emotion, and, by way of retinue, surrounding it and leading toward it, there is a whole array of secondary emotions. We have briefly touched upon this in regard to the glutton who relishes his wine as a connoisseur. It is easy to see what extravagant pleasure may be, and often not without elegance, surrounding sexual concupiscences (we have in mind especially those that are disorderly): studied affectation in clothing, perfumes, poses, balls, "worldly" parties, subtle pastimes that trouble the spirit which introduce us into a particularly difficult domain in which classification, once again, is absolutely impossible and judgments of value are often difficult. There is a great difference between a slight flirtation, an impure kind of fun and therefore intemperance—but a superficial intemperance through lack of a perverse involvement of the will or because the impure acts are only begun—and the clever and refined provocations which are the sign of a fixed will which seeks, suggests and develops the temptation, increases it, and refining it, sets traps for others by this very refinement, which are all the more certain because they are more concealed beneath their external tenderness. There are moreover no barriers in between; the paths are not rectilinear, but thickly intermingled, and consequently they are impossible to mark out. These appraisals are especially difficult for the moralist because nothing would be more erroneous than to draw conclusions, as the ordinary person does too readily, from external attitudes that are materially similar to identical intentions, and it is in this direction that codifications are inclined. The uncertainty of these paths and the complexity of this world of intentions that are often poorly recognized by the subject himself, in which the latter's honesty is most of the time too uncertain to allow for recognition and to call things by their proper names, and in which the allurements and associations of ideas and emotions are variable —all this and many other things obviously justify the radical and decisive strictness of most spiritual guides in regard to these alarming considerations, a strictness which is generally the result of the best empiricism. But the moralist cannot be satisfied with this, whose clientele does not only include those who are definitely determined to journey to the summits, and he must, supposedly, consider everything and judge it. When the physician has inveighed against some particular excess, he must still attend to those who have allowed themselves to be seized by it, and first of all he must diagnose their illness. Now then, it may happen that the moralist will here use common sense in order to pass a refined judgment upon things which accompany these desires or acts whether they are licit or not in their fundamental value. This may happen, moreover, starting from other premises than those of "common sense" and in any case without making so many unwise concessions.

Spiritual Values Preserved in the Midst of Carnal Sin

Elegant sensual vice, for example, is less repugnant than coarse bestiality, and the gourmet's affectation is less than the degradation of the drunkard who "drinks for the sake of drinking." It is notorious that indulgence is more quickly obtained where the sin is attractively arrayed in lace. This judgment does not seem to be a complete rejection, for the lace may be beautiful even when the sin is not. Apart from the case to which we alluded before, a case in which the elegance was only an ignoble trap, authentic spiritual values are often involved in the same paths as carnal sin; furthermore, even if it goes astray, the spiritual in its very nature remains obviously more human than the bestial and therefore, everything else being equal, less immoral. It may even keep a wholly positive value—art which is born of an impure love, for instance, and which perhaps has sustained it, continues to be art which is a human value. It is not even necessarily suggestive and is not always lacking in paradoxical purity, or one might almost say candor. As a comparative description, if the cruelty of the cat is cruelty, although ever so elegant, and we must judge it as cruelty, its elegance continues to be elegance even in the cruelty and it must be evaluated as beauty. Applying all this in a practical way, we may think of a floor-show that is very daring, with an ingenious staging, a clever use of lines, a choreography which wonderfully interprets the music in spatial expressions, and music which is quite as full of authentic harmony as the whole production is replete with human values (however perverse), but all of this, which pertains to art, does not always justify its exhibition and, in fact, it may be necessary to forbid it; but the direct or indirect immorality of the spectacle cannot mean that it is not true art.

One trembles in having to suggest these reflections briefly. They only emphasize the urgency of a true *virtue* of temperance that is objective, reasonable, sound and sanctifying, and of the quasi-instinct which it gives us, like every virtue, and which alone can finally assure the correctness of our appraisals and our behavior in such complex matters. Everyone knows that artistic performances, notably choreography in all its forms, but even others that are much less "carnal" in the literal sense of the term, pose moral problems which vary enormously, according to the subjective dispositions of each person.

The modern world, to an extreme degree, shows forth the scope of this morality, but the principles can only continue to be those of the traditional authors who were very much aware of these variations and emphasized this complexity. In this respect, everything is casuistry, if we understand it in the proper sense of the term: a matter of individual cases; but not at all in the banal and deformed sense of a congealed codification, indefinitely extended. No domain will be more fully that of *virtue* or less properly that of ready-made *legalism,* for in taking objective measures as we said above, temperance remains, in its very concept, a virtue of *the interior order of the subject.*

(c) *Morality in Sports*

Let us further extend the domain of this virtue.

Corporal Well-being

There are desires of the body which have no direct relation to hunger or the sexual appetite. There are other kinds of bodily well-being than those which man finds in nourishment or reproduction—in the highest degree, although very difficult to define in abstract terms, that of an organism in healthy equilibrium. It seems quite natural and its legitimacy as such should not be questioned, even by someone who admits that this matter eventually leads to exercises of an asceticism of redress or to the "foolishness" of the cross. The cult of the body has been fairly stigmatized, along with all semi-nudism of which the athletic fields and the beaches are the privileged place, and which are far from being irrelevant to the well-being we are considering. These matters have not been overlooked in moral studies. What then is the joyful well-being of a human being who turns his body toward the sun and breathes deeply of the fresh air, a well-being which sometimes becomes a kind of exaltation? "Nearer to Thee, my God": in a pagan magazine which however did not seem to be pornographic, this inscription accompanied the picture of two feminine bodies reaching toward the sky in an exultant gesture. We could find abstract metaphysicians who would approve of this pursuit without further question: everything that is expansive and joyful makes for the happiness of the creature and therefore the glory of God; certain moralists would condemn it with the same measure of certainty and absoluteness. But if we wish to be realistic, we will be more reserved, and, if we are obliged to pose the problem, we are less inclined to offer a solution.

Indications of a Solution

As far as the body is concerned, it must remain the servant: if a primary value were made of its cult, or only an encumbering one, there would be a displacement of values and disorder. This is obvious, and it is the first indication which marks a proportion in things in the ensemble of life and intentions.

If it were a matter of deviated exaltation which issued in sensuality (one should perhaps not be upset about a casual, unwholesome emotion, if one is not yet accustomed to the customs and dress of the athletic field or the beach—and likewise, it is not unheard of that the beginning physician must also quite simply rise above certain disturbances which will later pass away: we are considering things that are desired and accepted), *a fortiori* if this sexual emotion was deliberately sought and one came there, not for the sport but for this other purpose, it would also be obvious. A second indication.

Apart from this, here again, with an example: consider an athletic event, or more exactly a gymnastic event, in which some two hundred young men simply wearing short athletic trunks took part in group demonstrations or in individual exercises, magnificently coordinated and with great esthetic significance, accompanied by commentaries and timed to musical executions of a rare quality: and I do not mean bands or buffoons who habitually haunt athletic events! It would be difficult to imagine a more artistic spectacle, or more inspiring, healthier and at the same time more captivating, one might even say, disregarding the apparent paradox, more spiritual and spiritualizing. In the opinion of those who usually understand spiritual matters, we would carry away an impression of human strength, and moral "health." It would only be slightly spoiled by the proximity of a lawn on which spectators (only men) much more fully clothed, certainly, than the athletes, but dressed carelessly, would be sprawled all over the ground:

their partial nudity, quite discreet materially speaking, would give us a painful impression of very unwholesome sensuality.

This easily imagined contrast now enables us to know unequivocally which well-being we are discussing here. There are dilating athletic sensations as there are (analogically) dilating intellectual emotions and dilating pleasures of love. Allowance being made, a satisfied body should be happy as a satisfied soul; there is nothing intrinsically abnormal in this. In addition to a total intention that is obviously fundamental (one can make a magnificent machine with the purpose of killing one's neighbor) the moral quality of these things, as of all things, is measured by their adaptation to the human end which is proper to them. It is here a question of control of the body, of the excellence of bodily powers finding expression in bodily joy. "Making handsome beasts," it is said, but sometimes not without an intention of disparagement. Be it so: handsome beasts; the normal man ought to be one unless there is providential indication to the contrary, and the formula ought to be kept in mind *if it is not restrictive of something else* which is dominant in man. A strong virility, in control of itself, ordered, disciplined, is that which gives positive moral qualification directly to the development of the body, and consequently to its natural exigencies and its dilating emotions. The athletic field experienced in this way is moral and even moralizing; the body is there reduced to servitude: that of a tall, handsome, efficient and enthusiastic servant. Indirectly, this authentic corporal well-being is moreover, by its very nature, the best preventive (or remedy) against the morbid desires and unwholesome impressions which only too often accompany poor health. (With regard to the still more indirect moral value of the athletic field: mastery of the will, team spirit, etc., this is not the place to dwell upon it but we mention it in passing.) One would have to be abnormal, keeping in mind the customs of the times or the sense of well-being found in these places, for the clothing conditions reasonably required on the athletic field or in the swimming pool to become disturbing, provided that people are indulging in real sport. But we may also say that it is sufficient to be normal, on the contrary, for such disturbing thoughts to result from lazy loitering, indolent languidness, lack of energy and equivocal liberties. A great cleanliness of soul is necessary, and it must be served by a virtue of *mastery*.

These reflections may help us see what ought to be the "morality of the beaches" or the approaches to the beaches which are sometimes the entire town. It is the disturbing atmosphere of night clubs which defiles the beach and not the contrary; it is not because people wear swimming suits which debase it, but rather because they revel in such attire.

Social Pressure and Prejudices in Judgment

May I be permitted to close with a remark which seems to require once again the realism to which we have tried to adhere? It will simply recall the basis of the strictness or the falsity of certain judgment which are too material in these matters. The Freudian psychologists would have a field day here. Let us simply mention one example: imagine a person for a long time inveighing against the idolatrous cult of the body and the indecency of the apparel that was worn for tennis; this continues until the day when a happy evolution in local customs and the disappearance of this same person's timidity which was only a cultural prejudice would now allow him to play tennis like everyone else, and wear the same "indecent" costume. It would not result in lewdness and the satisfaction of this very legitimate desire would be sufficient to put an end to his undefined uneasiness and wipe out every problem as if by magic. It is not rare to find more disturbing repressions intervene than the one which was mentioned in this case, and we could find old maids (and bachelors?) who would say that the most authentic forms or manifestations of love are immoral. However, keeping to our subject, let us say that those whom conventions or legitimate and timely obligations, or sometimes prejudice, will deprive of certain things, must be mindful of this psychological phenomenon in their judgments. They would avoid shocking and sometimes upsetting others in this respect, and also avoid being judged (to be called stupid would be nothing: the judgment which they draw down upon themselves is more humiliating). They would possibly avoid the blunders which compromise the authentic moral message which they may want to deliver.

(d) *The Morality of Sensations of Touch*

With our last remarks we enter into the domain of temperance in the strictest sense: the moderation of the sexual appetites. But this is only by way of reminder. The whole of the section keeps us on the contrary within the scope of a temperance in the extended sense, that is to say a virtue of broader animal well-being, a real temperance however since it is still moderating appetites and pleasures which, to

avoid ambiguity, we have no longer called carnal, but corporal—
"secondary objects" of a true temperance, to use the traditional language of moral theology.

In a study of these "corporal" pleasures, we would have to introduce other analogous questions, although still more subtle and moreover in general less embarrassing morally, like that of the liking for
fragrances, or sensations of touch. We know that St. Therese of Lisieux was very sensitive to the odor of a flower or to the touch of
velvety fruit and that her attitude evolved in this matter from the
severity of abstention to full acceptance. Once more, we cannot say
all that needs to be said: an introductory study is not a catalogue but
a beginning. The reader may furthermore judge these matters himself
by way of analogy; he must not neglect to allow everyone the lati-
tude which his "individual differences" require.

(e) *Beyond the Carnal*

Our subject matter flows through our sections and our categories,
like the life that men wish to enclose within a cage. We have already
had a glimpse of these "sensible" pleasures toward which those which
we have just mentioned are leading us, but which we can in no sense
call "carnal" nor even "corporal" without abusing current speech:
these include every esthetic emotion, the joy of music or the beauty
of lines and colors. They are already the sources of the joys of the
intelligence. The latter no longer pertain to temperance in the first
sense, while the former still pertain to it as though to its farthest limit.
But here also "gluttonies" are possible (don't men speak—and they
do exist—of gluttonies in the life of prayer and in the properly religious emotion, or even the mystical emotion?) and here again however, nothing is evil in itself. It is conceivable that some men may
renounce these pleasures, through the "foolishness of the cross," or
simply through absoluteness of the faith which brings God to us, that
is to say everything, and that some will enclose themselves for life
within the silence of an oratory or a cell with bare walls. It is also
conceivable that other men will accept them and that they will lead
them to God. Their possible disadvantages are less burdensome than
those of the pleasures previously studied, for they are more spiritual;
however, to deny their disadvantages would be a lack of realism. Their
quasi-spiritual value will enable us to apply to them what we shall
later consider in regard to curiosity.

What law shall we follow? None at all. Unless it be a moral sense and a Christian sense. The safest thing we can say is doubtless that each man has his own vocation and that the supreme rule is to seek God and His Kingdom during his entire lifetime. An honest man, even if he is only groping his way and sometimes stumbles, will always finally find his way, and from God will come, at the proper time, the necessary purifications (God is most often "Providence" in His most ordinary emotions). A great honesty of soul, a determined zeal in the service of God and neighbor, an exact faithfulness in everything which obviously pertains to the divine will, without the obstructions of any subjectivism or any wilful self-seeking, a profound and sincere desire, often brought before God in prayer, for anything which will purify our life of irregular attachments and "sensualities," and also the willingness to seek counsel: this is doubtless the real solution of a problem which cannot be logically or abstractly clarified. Once again we must say that there can be no moral life without virtue, nor any virtue without all the virtues; only a *virtuous life* can solve what theoretical morality is unable to solve *practically*. Observations of this kind are always necessary, and they alone place the question on its true ground. This point, at least, had to be made.

5. CONCLUSION

We can state our idea of temperance precisely if we briefly review the ground covered thus far.

We said that it is a virtue that moderates carnal desires. We should prefer to say that it is a virtue of "control" of carnal desires, for the word "moderation" in our language implies the idea of repression too exclusively. Certainly, in fact, its role will often be to curb desires which would be unrestrained without it.

We shall never fail to repeat that in the face of sins of sensuality there is a place for sins of insensibility, as we have said before. However, to return to an example already used, if it is a mistake for the head of a community to allow overly enterprising subjects to conduct their business wrongly and irregularly, at the expense of the common good and the peace, it would also be a mistake, and quite as serious, for him to bully worthy subjects and to destroy their creative enthusiasm.

1. First observation: it is primarily upon *covetousness* that the action of temperance must be brought to bear, and not upon the sensation connected with a particular act. A voluptuous sensation is a psychological fact, not a moral case. That which comes under the

scope of morality, and in this case, specifically the virtue of temperance, is first of all the desire for the sensual sensation that is still absent, in circumstances where it is not normal for the latter to occur and when attachment to this sensation has become present, the pursuit of sensual pleasure for the sake of sensual pleasure. This is of practical importance. There are voluptuous sensations attached to good acts, the generative act, for example, or eating; it is not a question of repressing them by a virtue. There are voluptuous sensations (real or imaginary) which are necessary for us: it is our emotion in their presence or the possibility of our experiencing them which must be watched. But this very emotion, whether it be a desire or an interior disturbance, can not always be repressed; it is then in the refusal of the acts to which it solicits us and in the attitude which we shall assume in order to escape them if possible, that our virtuous action will be situated. It is not unprecedented that we may have to receive voluptuous impressions that are due entirely to a physical condition, or to seasonal or atmospheric conditions, or to fortuitous encounters with disturbing objects: our virtuous rectitude will often consist not in "driving them away," but in bearing them patiently by trying not to pay attention to them or develop them.

2. Second observation: It is primarily in the presence of desires relative to eating or to generation that temperance has something to say. The old moralists, for example St. Thomas, referred to the *sensations of touch*. The sensations of generation and those of taste are certainly, in fact, the most "epidermal," if I may use this term with the shade of meaning that it commonly acquires in familiar speech. These are the deepest and strongest movements which the most forcefully give this cardinal virtue its proper aspect. But they are also the movements which give the most immediate satisfaction, the most surface impression and at the same time are the least refined and the least proximate to intelligence.

With regard to the objects of the other senses, it is possible that the delights or desires which they enable us to experience fall under this ascendancy of temperance properly so called, in the measure in which they produce "carnal" sensations; for example, a particular look because it arouses a sexual passion, or a particular fragrance because it causes a favorable disturbance of the libidinous emotions (we know how greatly this is exploited), or some melody or musical rhythm.

It is only within the scope of a broader "temperance" that other objects may be included, still "carnal," but of a more subtle nature; by way of example, in an order of increasing spiritualization: the corporal euphories of "kinesthesis," the gratifications of the sense of smell, those of hearing (music), and those of sight (the play of lines and color, etc. . . .).

Such is the study which we have outlined up to this point.

In a still broader sense we may speak of temperance again in regard to every passionate desire, even spiritual, for example the love of glory or of knowledge. But this will be considered later in our study.

3. We should notice that if it is a question of "temperance" in the broad sense, it does not necessarily mean that it is a matter of secondary things in the moral life. Although they are less common and less "epidermal" moral problems, they are still very important moral problems. It is sufficient to think of the importance which spiritual tradition attributes to self-love and to curiosity, and to the necessary purification in these domains, if we wish to attain to a profound and positive spiritual life.

Finally there is much that could be said to "decant" visual or auditory pleasures and distinguish within them what is truly more spiritual or on the contrary more carnal (I mean "tactile") as for example the craze for movies and the hubbub of the radio. There are here moral domains that have been little explored.

II. The Parts of Temperance

In a few lines let us recall what are the integral parts, subjective and potential, of a virtue. These are practical and traditional categories.

The *integral parts* are the necessary conditions of a virtue, the spiritual attitudes which are necessarily part of the countenance of the man who is animated by the virtue in question. For example, modesty will be an integral part of temperance: every temperate man is modest, but this is only an integral part, for modesty is not sufficient to be the whole of temperance. To describe the integral parts of temperance is to obtain the portrait of the temperate man.

The *subjective parts* are the different species of one and the same virtue; they are differentiated according to the objects, like sobriety which is temperance in regard to drinking, and chastity, in regard to generation.

The *potential parts* are related virtues which merely have the manner of the principal virtue but which retain only a part of its difficulties, because of the fact that their object is secondary. The potential parts of temperance are temperances in the broad sense: virtues which mark the life of a man with a form of moderation, but without having as their object the desires of the "sense of touch" which are the proper object of this cardinal virtue. Among them, the virtue of temperance properly so called is like an elder sister, or like the perfect type which is directed toward the most serious and most characteristic object, and of which the related virtues take up the idea in their own way, but less strongly marked. The illustration which we gave above in sketching the portrait of the temperate man led us to put a total way of life in the wake of this virtue: this was probably the best way to make known the "potential parts."

1. THE INTEGRAL PARTS

Many things that could have been said here were said in the first part in order to "situate" the virtue of temperance. We shall only present here a few complements concerning the virtue of chastity.

(a) *The Fear of Shame*

It is very difficult to translate the word "verecundia," of which the French form is "vergogne," and the English form, now rarely used, is "verecundity," which do not express the idea strongly enough. "To act without verecundity" is a negative formula meaning "to feel no shame." Commonly, shame is the feeling which makes us blush because of some disgrace, and whose sin is hidden. There are people who do not experience this feeling; there are others in whom it is impure in the sense that they would willingly commit sin if it could be kept safely secret; and there are still others in whom it borders on the virtue because it is reasonable, measured, and is therefore an authentic help to the still imperfect virtue. The fear of shame which we are now considering should make us think not so much of the feeling experienced *after* the disgrace, but rather of the kind of emotional shock which may *repress* the sin beforehand because of the thought of the disgrace which would result if the sin were known, and this is even more properly a way of *considering* what is "shameful" in the sin than a matter of saving one's reputation. This feeling obviously should accompany every virtue, but more especially temperance and chastity: the term "shameful sin" is sanctioned through usage in this matter. There is something instinctive about shame which seems to be sufficiently explained by the degrading character of the sin and especially the sin that is contrary to chastity. It often happens that the mere thought, "If someone knew!" has held back certain wavering virtues from secret sins, even in cases in which it was unlikely that anyone could ever learn of them.

The counterpart of this just "shame" is a psychological reality that is quite commonplace: the difficulties experienced by many people in confessing these faults. Such a feeling of shame is so profound that even in men who have fallen very low it still subsists; for example, in the form of painful astonishment in the presence of the revelation of a wretchedness similar to their own in someone whom they respected.

We must admit that the perversion of certain milieux has checkmated this quasi-instinctive character of "shame"; it sometimes happens that men glorify sensual vice. Are "virtuous" people responsible for this because of the rather cowardly aspect which they sometimes have given to this virtue which is not a fear—no virtue is a fear—but is properly self-control? Even if the shame of these miseries has been lost, this does not diminish their debasing character: a "reasonable" reaction is often necessary and it must be aroused, for very weak consciences are easily corrupted by these indulgent attitudes. More seriously still, it is impossible not to be alarmed by the facility with which men excuse the most serious perversions, like abortion, because they have an outward appearance that is less repugnant than vulgar debauchery; but this does not excuse it, in spite of our previous observations, for we can hardly see what human value has been preserved by this less heavy grossness. It is not rare that the shame disappears entirely and that a murder is covered up which would be deservedly stigmatized if it happened to a young child who was born normally. The Christian cannot forget the seriousness of a murder, within a mother's womb, of a human being who has not been able to receive baptism and of whom the least that can be said is that a disturbing mystery hovers over its eternal destiny.

The attenuation of the shame, in the measure in which the subject is responsible for it by the systematical perversion of his conscience, or even the simple repetition of the sin to which he becomes habituated with no effort of conversion, only *aggravates* the fault by leaving the will more and more abandoned to the evil. It is a sign of perversion and this is the condition of those who, in the sense commonly used in morality, are called "habituals." In this domain, a great share must be attributed to collective responsibility for which everyone ought to feel concern. Inversely, moreover, this lax common conscience often partly excuses *thoughtless* sinners who have but little personal moral reaction. It is so true and we must say it again, that practical morality is complex and that judgments *pertaining to persons* must be infinitely varied: however, be that as it may, it in no way changes the proper and objective gravity of the act committed and as far as the moralist is concerned, it only makes for an additional duty of presenting an objective teaching, a teaching of values.

(b) *Modesty*

We have not said everything about *"verecundia"* in speaking of the fear of shame. The latter is connected with a deeper feeling which is, so to speak, foreign to the sin itself: modesty.

Certainly there are kinds of modesty that are false and frightened, and grave errors of judgment have deformed certain consciences or profoundly perplexed others. Modesty is however an authentic and instinctive feeling which is a kind of shock not only in the presence of anything sinful but in the face of anything which is simply an indiscreet allusion to the things of the flesh, even if they are simply natural and in good taste. One does not have to be prudish to experience an instinctive uneasiness, emphasized by a well known physiological reaction (blushing, for instance), which accompanies remarks that are too bold, or attitudes that can only be condemned for their indiscretion. In this respect it is difficult to distinguish between the conventional and the natural, the false and the true, the theoretical and that which a practical prudence suggests or requires; there seems to be no end to the discussion concerning what should or should not be said about this matter in the education of children. In any case, it seems that we must associate this feeling not only with the sense of weakness inscribed in man's flesh and which demands a great reserve in anyone who does not want to compromise his virtue, but much more profoundly, with the mysterious character of sex. The very persons who are the least inclined to yield to false and morbid prejudices relatively to the nature of marriage and who, most readily, extol not only the natural values but also the sacred values among all its aspects, including generation, for the very reason of their esteem for this mystery "which is great" (Eph. 5:32), are also frequently most inclined to make every attitude a closed secret and avoid any remark which would be an illusion to sex and more generally to sensual love itself.

This is not all. The idea of Christian modesty would be incomplete and variations in its practice would be lacking if we forgot the consecration, not only of the soul, but of the body by baptism, and its value as the temple of the Holy Spirit (I Cor. 6:15) and its call to the glorious resurrection; or if we also forget the quasi-sacred character of Christian virginity, even when it is not officially consecrated or is not destined to be immolated in marriage. A certain unconstrained and brazen eagerness to exhibit one's body (this does not, on the other hand, contradict what we have said about a healthy and frank liberty in attitudes that are justified and timely), a certain levity in manners or remarks quickly betray the absence of this *Christian* modesty even where nothing could be materially classified in a reprehensible category.

Instinctive modesty in all cases brings to the establishment of the virtue of temperance an assistance through the aversion or at least through the uneasiness which it arouses in the presence of impure desire or when confronting imprudence in matters of chastity. *Controlled and confirmed,* it is a part of the countenance of the temperate man.

(c) *Integrity*

This is the literal translation of a common term which has not passed into English in this exact sense, except in the negative form: men commonly speak of "dishonest" things, attitudes or customs. An excellent definition was borrowed by St. Thomas from Isidore of Seville: "Honestus dicitur qui nihil habet turpitudinis": "A man in whom there is no aspect of turpitude." This latter term, in its Latin meaning, expresses both that which is ugly or deformed and that which is depraved and shameful. Temperance, as we said, is the "beautiful virtue."

Let us briefly think of the clear, straight look of the chaste young man—when I say chaste I am unable not to think of virile also— so different from the disturbing, stealthy look of the person whom the shameful vice is devouring, or the falsely affectionate look that is so quickly embarrassing to the person whose sensibility is not in order in regard to others, as also the insolent and "shameless" look of the "daughters of Sion" who, we are told, "are haughty, and have walked with stretched out necks, and wanton glances of their eyes, and made a noise as they walked with their feet" (Is. 3:16). In the presence of this "upright" look we are as far from the insolence of the libertine as from the false and conventional prudishness which insists that purity must be expressed by lowered eyelids and downward glances. It is not in our time that the rapprochement of purity and frankness has been most apparent. Without contempt for the fear of shame, or beyond this, for modesty, we are aware that we are now in the regions of a virtue that is well-established and sure of itself. Frankness and openness are words which also perhaps express our meaning, and which are unknown to the man who is not temperate. This is purity in the largest sense of the term.

We see immediately that this would quickly lead us, like everything which we have said about temperance, into an atmosphere of life surpassing the object of chastity. We have been able to define all sanctity by purity, the transparency of the soul before God.

Fear of shame, modesty, and integrity are truly "integral" parts. Without them we should not have completed the portrait of the temperate man, but instead we might have deformed it.

2. THE SUBJECTIVE PARTS

Two parts: temperance applied to drinking and eating; temperance applied to matters of generation. The usual vocabulary of books of morality use the term abstinence in referring to temperance applied to eating, and speak of sobriety in reference to the temperance whose object is drinking; chastity is the virtue of sexual desires.

(a) *Abstinence and Sobriety*

We must not confuse the meaning which we are now giving to the word "abstinence" with the much narrower term used in canonical language: abstension from meat on certain days.

The Virtuous Attitude

A saying of St. Paul, in a context that is really a little more particular, perfectly situates the problem: "Commend us to God. For neither shall we suffer any loss if we do not eat, nor if we do eat shall we have any advantage" (I Cor. 8:8). To eat food or abstain from it has no value in itself, materially. These acts acquire moral value according as they conform to reason enlightened by faith.

We have related the essential thing above: in speaking of human and superhuman measures of temperance, we defined its meaning. What is reasonably necessary is to give the body what it needs, like providing fuel for a machine in order that it may function, without clinging to the restriction as to a superstition or to a sport in which one is proud of excelling, and especially without considering it as the whole of virtue. We remember the prophet's saying:

Behold in the day of your fast . . . you exact of all your debtors.
Behold you fast for debates and strife, and strike with the first wickedly. Is this such a fast as I have chosen:

Is not this rather the fast that I have chosen? loose the bands of wickedness, undo the bundles that oppress, let them that are broken go free, and break asunder every burden.

Deal thy bread to the hungry, and bring the needy and the harbourless into thy house: when thou shalt see one naked, cover him, and despise not thy own flesh (Is. 58:3-7).

The counterpart that is needed is not to seek pleasure for its own sake or cling to it gluttonously, and the best measure of our virtue in this respect is doubtless "the evenness of soul with which we accept the disadvantages or privations that are unforeseen or imposed by circumstances or duty" (St. Augustine). What is necessary is not to encumber with gastronomic preoccupations a lifetime which has better objects on which to spend itself; it is also to correct within ourselves what ought to be corrected. Super-human measures may require more, but this must never be at the expense of that which is necessary in order to accomplish our duty suitably—or simply in order to preserve the good humor which fraternal charity demands.

The Positive Law

In these matters it is important to have an exact conscience. We must distinguish: 1) on the one hand the natural law, permanent and valid for all men: we are obliged to practice the virtue of abstinence of which we have just indicated the aspects; 2) on the other hand, the positive law, obligations gravely imposed by the Church, a law which, in the matters now under consideration, is hardly more than the memory, quasi-liturgical, of ancient rules that were otherwise severe. These obligations comprise abstinence in the *strict sense,* which is abstension from meat, and the fast which consists in only one full meal each day with the possibility of "collations" in the morning and evening. Authority alone is competent to fix or specify these rules. The dissertations or foolish formalities in these matters that we find in certain manuals can only be particulars that are often very unreal, and never obligations. Furthermore, these laws allow for many dispensations. Today they are such that in matters pertaining to fasting, they are so liberal that they hardly require anything which is beyond the simplicity habitually practiced each day by persons in modest circumstances. Christians whose table is easily filled with more than is necessary would do well to take care and not be so quick to consider themselves dispensed from laws which require nothing heroic from them, and still less nothing imprudent!

Everybody knows, without doubt, that persons who are tired or burdened with excessively hard tasks are ipso facto dispensed from the law of fast. Persons more than sixty and less than twenty-one years are expressly dispensed by the law, but no one is dispensed from acquiring the virtue of abstinence in the sense defined in the preceding paragraph.

Drunkenness

Let us set up a few landmarks that will enable us to judge the gravity of faults in a matter in which they are perhaps more currently serious than is the fault of gluttony.

The clouding of reason by intoxication is obviously a serious evil since it deprives man of that which makes him a man and an image of God and sometimes leads him to tragic excesses. Such a sin is mortal by its nature. We say *by its nature*. We could not therefore say that involuntary intoxication, happening unexpectedly, is sinful. But if the possibility of intoxication has been completely and coldly accepted by someone who knew that it would occur and who conducted himself accordingly, he would not, in principle, escape the seriousness of mortal sin; and more especially if the intoxication is systematically sought. Everything intermediate belongs to venial sin according to the gravity of the imprudence and the extent of consent.

A more delicate case to judge is that of the drunkard overpowered by his vice. On the one hand, it must be said that the total disappearance of temperance by accumulation of consents opposed to this virtue, expressed by the disappearance of healthy reactions of conscience and of all effort, aggravates the fault since it indicates a more and more total involvement in the vice. But on the other hand, we must agree that neurosis, which is nearly always the basis of these conditions of disgrace, should incline us to considerable mercy in our judgment: from the moment that the subject is sincerely repentant (the shame of his condition is already a repentance) and if he is constantly falling, but is sincerely sorry, this neurosis is an excuse since it constitutes an obstacle opposed to a will that has become upright again. Merely to have gotten near these people who, in a tragic way, struggle (like exhausted men will struggle), and accuse themselves and fall again and again, is enough to see to what extent we must be careful in our judgments, assuming that it is necessary to judge at all.

The judgment to be made concerning the gravity of sins committed while intoxicated requires the same carefulness. Theoretically, intoxication excuses sins which it causes in the measure in which it is total, since these sins were committed without the intervention of reason. But there can be indirect responsibility precisely to the degree in which the subject is responsible for the intoxication himself. This responsibility is transposed to the sins that are committed under the influence of intoxication. It is an aggravating circumstance for a person who may have foreseen as possible or probable the abuses which result from intoxication to take no notice of them. It is a matter of maximum gravity for a person to become totally or partially intoxicated (i.e., to give themselves "nerve") in order to commit excesses which, when they are sober, their consciences would venture to forbid. This is a typical case of "indirect willingness." And these are principles which must be applied in each particular case.

(b) *Chastity*

This is the virtue which governs the desires and pleasures connected with the generative act. We must not be mistaken about its scope. A common expression, "the vow of chastity," can deceive us: the vow is a consecration of virginity or at least the consecration of a total abstension from the things of marriage; it is therefore one of the possible forms of chastity, but not the whole of chastity. Since the main lines have been indicated above, let us take up a few particular points.

1. Virginity

Material and Spiritual Virginity

Materially a virgin is someone "whose flesh is untainted"; this reality is quite concretely material in the woman. More generally, the man like the woman, is a virgin if the generative act has never been performed,—*a fortiori* a person who has never committed an abnormal act voluntarily or an immoral act of such nature as to arouse carnal sensations and physiological movements similar to those which are produced in the consummation of the generative act. *Virginity of soul* is the state of the person who moreover has never sought or accepted the "sensual" pleasures of the flesh, whether on the occasion of pure imagination or of actions.

It is obvious that nobody can prevent normal physiological phenomena which entail no less normally the sensible emotions that are analogous to those of the generative act, emotions which cannot be prevented and which should neither grieve nor disturb us. We must accept these things as simple facts without moral value. Neither can we escape, at certain times, under physiological influences or because of external circumstances, from certain sensual impressions which may be very piercing and acquire the weight of solicitations or temptations. None of this touches the virginity of the body, and certainly not that of the soul, since whenever it is a question of virtue, it is a matter of *will* (the will which arouses or the will which delights in accepting), and the virginity of the soul is the absence of *seeking* and of *unwholesome acceptance* of sensual sensations. Practically, we must never forget that the simple acceptance, *de facto,* of the sensual impression, in so far as it is a psycho-physiological reality of nature—this remark could be readily translated: "That's the way it is, and I can't do anything about it"—could not constitute the moral consent which destroys the virginity of the soul; but that other acceptance which delights in finding in such sensations, originally involuntary, a kind of substitute for impossible carnal acts, would certainly destroy it. There is therefore no need to exhaust ourselves in vain and absurd struggles against a part of ourselves which acts and reacts outside the influence of the will. The pretense to "drive away" these natural impressions which our organism imposes upon us, and the efforts in which it exerts itself, are doubtless the surest way to becoming entangled in irremediable difficulties.

There may be a virginity of the body, factually real but only material whereas the virginity of the soul is already destroyed. Inversely, the virginity of the soul may be preserved even when that of the body has been lost, as the result of violence. We will recall the proud reply of Lucia, the virgin of Syracuse, addressing her judge, in a dialogue which the acts of the martyrs have preserved for us:

Paschasus asked her, "Is the Holy Spirit within you?" (She had just invoked His help), and she replied, "Those who live in chastity are the temple of the Holy Spirit." And the judge said, "I am going to issue orders that you be brought to the house of prostitution; your Holy Spirit will leave you then." But the virgin told him, "If it be against my will that you have me violated, my chastity will be accounted double in heaven." (Breviary, December 13).

Corporal chastity is nothing, morally, if it is only material, and the same may be said of its loss. United to virginity of soul, which alone has positive importance, it keeps however a symbolic value which is maintained by a holy tradition that tells us that the Virgin Mary gave birth miraculously in such conditions that her carnal integrity did not suffer from it.

Outline of the Mystical Meaning of Virginity

Let us refer to the first part: "the super-human measures of temperance": consecrated virginity is not a mutilation, but a surpassing. This renunciation of human love—and not merely the carnal pleasures of love—does not signify a kind of moral game desired for its own sake, an equilibrium of chastity, as someone has humorously said, but primarily a liberation which permits the soul to apply itself directly and uniquely to divine contemplation. "And the unmarried woman, and the virgin, thinks about the things of the Lord, that she may be holy and in spirit. Whereas she who is married thinks about the things of the world, how she may please her husband" (I Cor. 7:34). For the priest, celibacy is a liberation which enables him to be "all things to all men" by renouncing all conjugal and family affection; but this is the second aspect of the same commandment.

More profoundly, however, the consecration of virginity has the value of oblation, offering, holocaust: the "spouses of the Lamb" to whom their entire life is directly surrendered, are the firstfruits of the Church being offered to God. Speaking pictorially, they are, within the mystical body of Christ which is the Church, the offering which is burned upon the altar symbolically represented by our holy candles which burn before God and for God alone; other Christians, who attend to matters of the world for the love of God are like those other offerings which, given to God, will however actually serve to alleviate the miseries of the world: the symbolical value of the first offerings is obvious—but they must not for this reason eclipse the others which keep their own value. From this point of view, consecrated virginity has always been considered in the Church as a vocation of choice. St. Jerome attributes the hundredfold to virginity, in relation to widowhood and marriage, to which he allows sixty and thirty for one—a vocation which he compares to martyrdom, to which, however, St. Augustine attributes the first place with a hundred for one as against sixty to virginity and thirty for one in the case of husband and wife.

Consecrated widowhood and consecrated celibacy whose purity may have been recovered after sin, have the same import. But with a slight distinction, or even a difference which St. Jerome strongly indicated and which preserve all the value of the Christian tradition of virginity. But some explanation is necessary in regard to this, and it is difficult to give, moreover, for these are matters which "the heart knows better than reason."

It is not a question here of despising marriage. The latter is not only a sanctifying state, but it is holy. Marriage also is a consecration, like every form of Christian life and especially as the sacraments are. The best way to define its sacramental value would perhaps be to say that each of the spouses symbolically represents God in receiving the other as an offering. Like the priest who absolves, while remaining a man with the fulness of this personality, represents the merciful Christ to the penitent to such an extent that in confessing his sins, it is to God that the penitent confesses them and when the priest says, "I absolve thee," it is God who absolves—and thus, analogically, the husband is for the wife a presence of this God who has a right to the homage and the service of our entire selves; by giving herself to her husband, it is to Christ that she devotes herself. We cannot exalt these mystical values of the sacrament of marriage too highly.

It is no less true that the husband and wife will live these spiritual realities by humanly showing their mutual love, and they will give themselves to God in and through their marriage by giving themselves, body and soul, to each other in a way which, alas, may finally to some degree diminish their gift to God. This is what St. Paul had in mind when he spoke of "division." Even in Christian marriage, the "fine point" of the spiritual life surpasses the scope of the mutual gift and remains a mystery between each person and God which the other spouse can at best surmise, but which is beyond understanding. If the wife has given herself to God by giving herself to her husband, and if she consummates this gift to God by living this gift to her husband every day, it does not hinder her husband from being quite really a man and it is therefore to this man that she has given the intimacy of her body and her heart, and very humanly, although once again as a sign of the gift of herself to God. This "ambassador" of God has remained himself while being an ambassador, and the mystery of this virgin has been offered to *someone* who was not God alone in His invisible divinity. The holocaust of virginity signifies that everything has been reserved exclusively for God, and burns only for Him and has never been offered for any use, even sacred, which was not strictly that of rising toward God as "a sacrifice of acceptable fragrance." The biblical expressions, "A sealed fountain" and "An enclosed garden" will perhaps enable us to understand the mystery of virginity better than any other impossible expressions.

If consecrated widowhood must itself feel the effects of this loss of virginity which marriage entailed and assume a particular nuance, how much more will this loss of virginity make the consecration to God which follows it something different from that of virginity. This is so true that a special congregation was to receive into the contemplative life those persons whom the sin (not only against the sixth commandment, but especially that sin) had touched. And it has been correctly observed that even those persons whose disgrace had remained completely secret felt more at ease in communities of this kind than in monasteries established principally for virgins. Certainly the mystery of God accomplishes many things, as His goodness does also, and it was a Mary Magdalene, a sinful woman, whom Jesus lifted to her feet to designate her as a model of love. It is true, however, that the chef-d'oeuvre is not the Magdalene but the Virgin Mary. But the case of the Magdalene remains simply a chastizing lesson for those men and women who take advantage of their virginity in order to glorify themselves or to dispense themselves from the other duties of holiness. This pharisaical virginity was stigmatized by St. Gregory in a famous homily. No one is holy because of virginity. However, all things being equal, virginity gives to the halo of sanctity a special radiance, particularly expressive of the holocaust and the exclusiveness of God's rights over man; it was this which led the Church to give virgins a special place among the saints in her Office.

A final observation: virginity does not hold the same place in masculine sanctity as in feminine sanctity. Just as the sin of the flesh is spontaneously held to be not less sinful but of less consequence in man than in woman—and this difference in evaluation is not merely the result of simple prejudice—so likewise virginity holds a different place in the sanctity of just men than that which it occupies in the sanctity of the "spouses of the Lamb." This natural difference is due to the varying mentalities and roles which both sexes possess within the Body of Christ.

2. Sins Against Chastity

The Matter of the Sin

We shall now present a few principles of solution. In the domain of acts, there is serious sin, theoretically, when serious carnal emotions, accompanied by characteristic physiological movements, *a fortiori* "consummated" actions, have been systematically aroused and pursued, outside of marriage, with the intention of experiencing its pleasures. There is likewise serious sin whenever a person has deliberately consented to remain in situations which were bound to make him fear these emotions as very probable, without having sufficient external reasons for the acceptance of these situations and, all in all, it is the prospect of sexual sensation which accounted for his remaining in them.

Imaginary sensations obviously can only be serious sins to the extent that they constitute, by their nature and their gravity, a kind of "substitute" for acts which are committed and which are systematically sought or deliberately accepted along with the unwholesome sensation which they entail. The typical case would be that of a person who was held back from committing these impure acts by a cause independent of his own will and who, furthermore, delights and wallows in their desire or their memory (cf. Mt. 5:28). We are now in a domain in which perplexities of conscience and scruples possess excessive freedom and in which we must refer everything to the conscience of the individual if there is too much freedom, and provide liberating appeasements to persons whose conscience is timorous or falsified. In any case, it is unlikely that there could be serious sin by imagination when a struggle, a kind of interior dissension, persists with the disturbing imaginations, and this is a sign that the will is not completely involved. The calm consideration without immoral desire, the cold and rather "theoretical" representation of a natural or slightly sinful reality, like the simple view of the human body by a "nature lover" could not be a sin if it does not entail either immoral will nor the grave danger of impure pleasures, whether recognized or accepted.

In the domain of physiological movements that are unsought and are not directly aroused as in that of imaginations, venial sins may be caused either by whatever is artificial in the impure sensation, or because gravely impure sensations when one could not reasonably foresee that they would have such a consequence are produced as the result of disturbing attitudes voluntarily assumed. There would therefore have been partial surprise, because an incomplete consent was accorded to the sensual emotions which both occur and recur in the presence of movements and impressions which are thus half accepted and half sustained.

It is apparent that there is no sin whenever strong sensual emotions, or even "consummated" phenomena, are the result of involuntary or necessary circumstances and in which the will has not directly or formally seized upon these emotions as though they were a kind of windfall, so to speak. A typical case: the impression which accompanies nocturnal physiological phenomena wholly involuntary and in no way incited either during sleep or in the moment of waking which they cause. The carefulness of the moralist is not without an authentic virility of judgment.

The Hierarchy of Values

(a) *The gravity of the sin* is all the greater according as the action committed is, all things being equal, more *contrary to the nature of things*. Within a same domain, the sin is less serious if it is a matter, not of an action, but of a simple desire or imagination. From the point of view of the nature of the actions, we must classify these sins in an increasing order of gravity:

Fornication, the relationship between two unmarried persons.

Onanism, either individual or between two persons of different sex, whether married or not (a "fraudulent" conjugal act; on the sin of Onan, see Gen. 38:8).

Sodomy, a parody of the conjugal act between two persons of the same sex, or between two persons of different sex but in postures gravely contrary to the nature of the human conjugal act (cf. Gen. 19:5).

Bestiality, the parody of the conjugal act committed upon an animal.

Among these wretched practices solitary onanism, especially in the case of young boys, sometimes assumes disastrous proportions, and it must be admitted that it is an evil that is much more common than certain parents suppose. With regard to sodomite tendencies, we must say that carnal attraction between persons of the same sex is also an evil that is less rare than people will admit. It may only be the carnal and delayed projection of a very extensive psychological reality on which psychoanalysts insist under the name of homosexuality. If it is a disposition that is obviously pathological (but not very rare) in collectivities that are too "confined" it often assumes an abnormal frequency which, without leading to repugnant actions, nevertheless entails much psychological and moral weakness. Educators must be informed about it, be watchful for it, and especially avoid believing that it is in narrow methods of education and surveillance that the remedy lies. It is by "airing out" that "secret and hidden" illnesses are best treated, for they would not often originate in broad daylight.

(b) *Aggravating circumstances* of fornication, all things being equal:

The fact that at least one of the sinners is married, the sin against chastity becoming at the same time a sin against justice toward the spouse, and a sin against the sacramental sanctity of marriage.

The fact that at least one is consecrated by the vow of chastity: this also makes it a sacrilege.

The fact of consanguinity between the sinners: incest.

The fact of unwillingness on the part of the person whom the sinner compels to submit to his outrages: rape.

(c) The aspects against nature of the sin (first paragraph) and the aggravating circumstances (second paragraph) being realities of different natures, we could not classify all these sins in one line of increasing gravity, even by taking them according to their abstract and theoretical import: differences of nature are not resolved in more or less.

(d) In a study like this one, we are unable to dwell upon adequate analyses and therefore we do not know where to classify facts of extraordinary appearance: matters usually placed in the category of masochism (the pursuit of suffering that is self-imposed or which the person will have imposed upon himself by others)—and sadism (a liking for cruelty inflicted upon others)—all of this being connected with desires that are sexual and often perverse and against nature. Monstrous cases are too well known, especially in regard to sadism. Concerning these matters the psychoanalysts have not yet said their last word. It is obvious that it is often a question of unhealthy tendencies, but there seems to be an attraction for many people, and there may be useful and sometimes serious indications to be kept in mind about this, either in the education of children or in the direction of souls. It seems that the taste of daily newspaper readers or movie-goers for stories of crimes and, correlatively, the tendency of journal-ists or script writers (even certain highly esteemed novelists) to dwell on them at great length, or else the love which certain children have for making animals suffer may in some cases pertain to the sixth com-mandment. Obviously proportions must be kept and there should not be excessive generalization. Nor can we overlook the taste of certain persons whose practice of spiritual life is expressed in carnal mortifica-tions or spiritualities of suffering which contain a measure of unfortu-nate sublimations, or else are a sign, of these disturbing tendencies. Being vigilant is not being a pessimist nor having morbid tendencies.

Abstract Theory and Living Practice

These "increasing gravities" or these aggravating circumstances are *theoretically* understood in the sense of *abstractly* considered sins. But there are no abstract sins in life.

Theoretically, the solitary sin, for instance, is more serious than simple fornication. But in "reality" it often happens that fornication is doubled by a scandal (a sin against charity which consists in being a tempter of the other person or at least an occasion of sin); it sup-poses a more deliberate purpose by all the conditions which its doing requires; and finally, the solitary sin is frequently exculpated from a part of its gravity by the circumstances in which this vice has taken hold in someone's life, as well as by the kind of neurosis which it frequently involves; the latter, when the will is corrected, intervenes as an "antecedent passion" which more or less excuses and to the ex-tent that the person whom this weakness overpowers always carries the temptation with him. And who can tell the part of congenital tendencies of simple temperament, often quite semi-pathological, in these moral difficulties?

There should also be many variations in judgments bearing upon solitary onanistic acts of children who do not clearly discern their seriousness. Sometimes there is a case of "invincible ignorance." The same may be said about so-called "sacrileges" committed by children who conceal this sin in confession.

Conjugal onanism, which is a serious sin *by its nature* (cf. Encycli-cal, *Casti Connubii*), is however difficult to qualify exactly in *fact*. It is often impossible to really compare the disorder which it represents

in the entirety of a Christian life with that which some other sin in-
jects into it. After all, who could exactly qualify, in a concrete case,
the gravity of the sin committed by one of the spouses when, the other
having made himself or herself directly the tempter of the other, there
is finally consent (and not only "materially")?

Many things could be said of common-law marriages of which the
theoretical situation, in regard to chastity in the most literal sense, is
obviously that of "public sinners," and in which, however, it happens
that so many human values are respected. Does not the mere fact of
refusing promiscuous union and desiring civil marriage often indicate
a mistaken kind of conscience and the existence of a half-faith which
can only perplex anyone who might wish to make a judgment no longer
concerning the *material* facts, but regarding the *persons* themselves.

All this shows us that we must distinguish three kinds of judgments:
the judgment of the moralist who considers the nature of the act taken
in itself and apart from the circumstances which may excuse or ag-
gravate it; the practical judgment of the psychologist (or the priest), a
complex judgment which can only pertain to what is *seen* and in which
the subject himself is very often a poor judge; finally the judgment
of God which we do not know and which alone takes exact account of
the conscience of the subject who is the principal in the matter (even
a mistaken conscience obliges): one must take a stand which these
three judgments often do not cover. This observation, of course, does
not justify any erring conscience which would prefer to be erroneous
or remain so, or which might bear some responsibility for error in an
indirect way.

3. Chastity of Marriage

What we have just said brings us back, in concluding, to the chastity of marriage. The current use of the term "vow of chastity," or
even "state of chastity" lends itself to error; there is a chastity not
only of celibacy but also of marriage.

In this respect, a fear of carnal pleasures would be false or pathological. It would also be a rejection of all sensibility. There is a nature
of things to be respected. There are also "degradations" and shocks
to be avoided, because they lower marriage to the level of a bestial
and wholly carnal life. Doubtless it is sufficient to remember that marriage in all its acts, even the most carnal, is a sacred reality, a sacrament, a memorial of the espousals of Christ and His Church, if finally

we understand that there is a difficult harmony in the practice of marriage and that this harmony is the highest form of chastity in this state.

4. Sex Education

The very difficult and often painful problem that is commonly called "sex education," which is too narrow a term, and which is also too narrow to be classified in a chapter on chastity, is complex and thorny. We present it here *as an open question*, without claiming to do more than suggest themes for reflection and pose a few indications of certainty in the midst of a teeming swarm of prejudices and errors.

Responsibilities

(a) It is criminal to solve this problem by flight or nothingness. In every way it poses itself as a problem and the capitulations of educators (parents and teachers) lead to the worst psychological and moral catastrophes.

(b) It is capitulation for parents to leave the problem to those who can only solve it in part; properly, parents cannot leave this charge entirely with teachers or confessors. The teachers can often only act "in general" when, more than in other matters, there is need for a vigilance that is proper to each case; with regard to confessors, their role is not and should not be a role of universal informers, and can anyone seriously claim that they should assume such a responsibility in regard to young girls? All these roles are complementary, and the parents must agree that their role is, by right, the principal one.

(c) We must, however, be realistic. After having exhorted the parents to do their duty, and after having assisted them in this respect by counselling them, if possible, it must be admitted that *many fail to do their duty* and will continue to neglect it through inability, timidity or negligence, and sometimes unworthiness; they therefore need substitutes. Realism thus seems to make it necessary, in fact, to seek other solutions, which however, must be provisionally qualified. Nothing will have been solved by being modestly indignant against the search for these solutions or by declaring that it is absurd or perverse to have this education given by the teacher when the latter possesses the full confidence of the child. Experience seems to condemn the point of view of those who prefer nothingness to such teaching and justice requires that no one should suspect, *a priori*, the educators for fulfilling this troublesome duty. It remains true, however, that parents who are conscious of their duty and able to accomplish it (in fact the minority) must do it.

Matter

With regard to the matter itself, it seems that we must distinguish what may be called "the natural history of generation" and the subjective aspects of the problem. In reality sexual education is only one aspect of the education of love and of all the powers of love. The educator must see to the sound growth of a love which, at first terribly and tyranically egocentric in the small child, must some day become a capacity for self-effacement and for giving oneself generously to a person of the other sex in "oblative love." The successive impregnation of this growth of love in the sensibility of the adolescent, his sensuality, his emotional make-up, and especially his intelligence and his "spirit," must be taken into consideration, it would show great contempt for "man" to consider only the development of the sexual organs or forms of the body.

Two points must therefore be kept in mind:

Sex education, while including a measure of objective information, must be an education in interior growth. It should tend to favor rather than "forbid" the growth of a positive reality, rich in many virtualities. Sex education is inseparable from education as such. It is one aspect of the education of love.

Methods

Here again are a few indications:

(a) This education, like all education, must be progressive. This is obvious in regard to the subjective part which it includes and which we have just mentioned. But it is also true concerning the information which must be imparted at various stages, according to the child's capacity and long before certain obsessions of certain serious problems of sexuality have arisen. The prejudice according to which it is then a matter of things which children do not need to know, and that it is best for them not to know such things as long as possible, in their innocence, is false. It is difficult to see how innocence enters into a matter which, by its very nature, is good. Above all else, this objective information must not be imparted on the occasion of perverse solicitations at an age when sexual and sentimental problems already arise; this would be stirring up trouble in muddy waters. There are souls which have never recovered from this.

(b) The delicate turning-point to be used for imparting information is the appearance of physiological phenomena which can no longer fail to pose the problem in all its acuteness. The moment has then come to complete the information and to speak frankly and confidently to the young "man" or the young girl.

(c) It is not wrong to have the required objective information given at least in part by the teacher; we have already said this. But the instructor's teaching must then be completed by a discussion at home where, in an atmosphere of frank intimacy, the child will feel personally understood, helped, loved, and we must add, listened to. He must be able to ask questions freely. This is of the highest importance in this turning-point in his life.

(d) This frankness in discussion requires that there should be no theatrics, nor any air of mystery which results in raising untimely questions in the adolescent's mind. "Magic" must be banished from these explanations, and one must not create the impression that this domain is taboo and cannot therefore be approached except by means of certain rites. . . . Questions must be answered, not by silence nor by evasive explanations, and certainly not by lying (for lying has never been an educational means)—but very firmly, with great sensitivity for the soul and the heart of the child, in regard to everything which he asks and according to his capacity and his way of understanding. It should be remembered that the child sometimes possesses other sources of information which are clandestine and ordinarily not very moral. It may happen that his curiosity will be aroused by the answers which he receives, in the family setting, and that he will seek this information himself, in places where this information is not provided by his teachers and when no effective education has been given him in the family home.

To sum it up, education that is called "sexual" requires the collaboration of the teacher who instructs and informs (this may naturally be the father or the mother) at each age level according to the child's capacity for reception, and the parents who continue to watch over his affective education—an education which, although it includes sentimental and sexual components, is not less an education of the heart, primarily, and finally collaboration with the priest whose proper role is spiritual and moral and consists in supporting with his counsels the personal apprenticeship in virtue.

3. VIRTUES RELATED TO TEMPERANCE (POTENTIAL PARTS)

There is a wide measure of relativity, or even purely academic concern, in the classifications of the moralists. We are not trying to defend them now. We are merely using their arrangements in order to set forth the virtues which we must still present for consideration.

(a) *The Virtues Which Moderate Anger*

1. Gentleness (*Mansuetudo*)

The *mansuetudo* which we translate as gentleness, for lack of a better word, is a virtue which moderates and controls anger within us. Everyone is familiar with the nervous uproar which accompanies this passion and the clouding of our reason which ensues: "the blood rushes to our head." Therefore it deserves to be placed parallel to carnal passion; the least heedful person would know that we can no more play with this passion with impunity than with the latter and that it can lead to the worst excesses of bestiality, brutality, and injustice, and at the same time to weakness in judgment and decision.

The virtue of "gentleness"—would we not rather call it serenity today? It is regrettable that we have lost the sense of such an evangelical word (cf. Mt. 5:3). It puts us on guard against angry behavior and against all carnal emotion. It is a mastery of ourselves, a being on guard which cannot only dominate, but put an end to those sudden changes of disposition. It is a kind of foresight which can even be expressed by bodily attitudes of stability and calm confrontation, and this strongly emphasizes the overlapping of the moral and the physical. When this disposition becomes habitual, and this being on guard becomes almost instinctive, and our vigilant foresight keeps us calmly prepared for every encounter with injury or contradiction, then it is the virtue of gentleness which is operative in us.

2. Clemency

If gentleness is prolonged in an affectionate and charitable comprehension of the contradictor which not only prevents us from treating him too harshly under the effect of the emotional impact, but on the contrary makes us soften our reply or diminish the chastisement he deserves, we are then showing clemency. Gentleness and clemency are excellent examples of virtues related to temperance, and of mastery and moderation, which makes us manly and noble, and show forth our interior movements. Brutal severity, even if it is perfectly in conformity with the texts of the law, is never human; the key to human relations is that reciprocal understanding which love gives. The movement of justice which inclines us to punish misdeeds must be compensated by a movement of clemency toward the malefactor, and clemency implies that we know how to dominate the psycho-physiological movement of anger.

3. The Caricatures of Gentleness and the Holy Angers

We are especially considering virtues, therefore, tendencies of the soul that are voluntarily controlled or established within ourselves and likely to make us act reasonably. There are people in whom gentleness is natural (so much the better), and others in whom it is acquired. But there are also some people in whom it becomes a lack of energy, apathy, and eventually weakness in moments of necessary confrontation or repression; at this point it is no longer a virtue but a fault. It has even been proposed as a chef-d'oeuvre of self-control that men should attain to a universal indifference which leaves man's disposition changeless in the presence of anything whatever and forbids him any external attitude of visible disapproval, irritation or anger. But nothing could be more false, nor, consequently, more unfortunate. In this respect we must now repeat what was said regarding the control of the carnal passions and insensibility: moderation and mastery are not destruction but *utilization*. The problem is not to allow oneself to go to excess or to be carried away by the passions, and not therefore to suppress them. If anyone needs to be convinced of this he need only refer to the example of Jesus driving the money-changers from the Temple with blows of the whip, or flaring up against the Pharisees. Certain kinds of behavior cannot fail to arouse this interior agitation in the virtuous man whose very violence is the sign of his attachment to the true and the good. Certain reprimands by being expressed in a peaceful manner would only indicate moral laxity or a natural apathy. Better still: certain clashes and certain disapprovals require this upset of the human emotions in order to acquire their necessary, reasonable, proportionate and therefore moral vigor. Even if it then gives vent to itself to the point of provisional clouding of self-control, such anger is and continues to be moral: it is the visible, and so to speak the carnal aspect of an attitude of strength which calls upon the physical for assistance. If everything has remained moderate and controlled from the start, and if the self-mastery which the virtue of temperance (gentleness and clemency) assures also guarantees that there will be nothing immoderate or excessive, it matters little that a provisional and rational eclipse of control may ensue; it is not necessary for emotion to be repressed. It is often when he is "beside himself" and when his emotion finds full expression that the artist or the orator is admirable; the strong man, the leader, and the "avenger" may be admirable in their anger and eminently moral. Perhaps there are weak persons who ought to cultivate their aptitude for anger in order to call it to their rescue when they feel that an attitude of vigor is required and that they will be unble to maintain it coldly.

On the sides of every virtue there are two opposite faults which must be feared; in this case the expression of an anger which may govern without control, and apathy. It pertains to the virtue, in this matter, to keep to the "center" (the crest-line between two precipices) and to avoid these two faults. It would be a serious mistake to think that it should only keep us from the first, and that it can be accommodated to the second. Its role, as a virtue, is precisely to keep us from outbursts of such a kind that we no longer risk falling into inertia (or taking refuge in it).

(b) *Humility*

We are getting further away from the passions which have a certain reverberation in our flesh. Anger is still a physical passion, carnal in large part. The desire for greatness is much less so, and in any case, less directly so. There is however an unwise desire of elevating oneself which a virtue ought to moderate. It is a question of an attitude of soul, a judgment brought to bear upon ourselves, and not merely of external acts or attitudes which would always make us seek lesser roles. It is also a matter of gratitude, both simple and objective, for the gifts which God has given us, both natural and supernatural, and which must not be disregarded either theoretically by questioning their existence or practically by refusing to put them to work. In such matters, a welcome acceptance of the judgment of others concerning ourselves may be a great help and the sign of an authentic humility. Finally, it is a matter of virtue which, quite simply, makes us accept the places and roles which Providence has reserved for us, even if they may eventually be the first in rank. It is definitely not humility to put oneself stubbornly in the rear ranks when it is perhaps ourselves whom others are expecting to lead the column and when it is at the front that men are killed. The virtue of humility, because it is a virtue, could not be destructive; it cannot be separated from magnanimity which directs us toward great works to the extent that they are intended for us. There are false humilities which are only weakness and pusillanimity, and others which are only pride and vanity. In effacement they only find a refuge from difficulties and humiliations which the action may strew along our path.

It is finally toward a total disinterest in our own person, and in our rank or the esteem received from others, that humility will lead us, and consequently to a complete freedom of soul which enables us to act with a perfect objectivity and lift ourselves just as high as our calling requires in order that we may likewise descend just as low as others will place us, thus accomplishing everything that God expects of us. Humility is the virtue of the soul which constantly lowers our natural pride in order to put us in our rightful place *before God*. The consideration of the infinite greatness of God is never absent from the person who is humble. It is essential to him.

Pride

Pride is the opposite of humility. It is not merely a vain complaisance in our talents and a rather silly joy in seeing them recognized by others. This may only be vanity which means "empty" and is merely childishness. It is no more real pride than excessive abasement is humility. The basis of humility is that knowledge that we are nothing before God, and that we are nothing by ourselves, but that all that we are is God's doing, and nothing can be terminated in ourselves but everything must end in God. Consequently, pride is a love of our own excellence which makes us wish for impossible greatness or undertake possible deeds with the intention, in both cases, that our own person may gain esteem, as if everything should finally lead to ourselves and everything were made for us alone. It is therefore an opposition of man to God, an elevation of ourselves against God whose excellence, as omnipotence and last end, diminishes our own. It practically becomes a negation of our situation as a creature.

The First Sin

We now understand that the sin of the first man was a sin of pride, man exalting himself in his own excellence, and finally desiring to be the equal to God whose infinite excellence overshadowed man's. In the same instant man denied his dependent status in relation to the

Creator which alone constitutes his greatness—like a mirror that desired to turn away from the sun in order to be a source of light by itself. Pride, inclining man to be delighted with himself, and to consider himself as an end, cuts him off from the source and reduces him to his proper measure which is nothingness, if we may so speak.

It is interesting to note that the first sin was a sin of pride and not a sin of sensuality, as is sometimes stupidly supposed. It would be truer to say that it was a disobedience, but this itself is really only a second aspect of Adam's sin. Pride is at the root of every sin in each of us as well as in all humanity taken as a whole. Man could not sin by gluttony or by intemperance, by injustice or disobedience, as long as sensibility, sensuality and all the physical powers were harmoniously submitted to reason. There had to be a first disorder introduced into a beautifully structural and ordered nature which God had created. This first disorder was the pride with which man wished to exalt his freedom by freely denouncing the bond of dependence which attached him to God. The spirit of man no longer being submitted to God, the flesh itself was in some way emancipated, and no longer had any natural master, nor any curb, and began to "militate against the spirit" which it considered as an intruder. The gate was open to all the disorders and all the sins.

(c) *Studiousness* (*studiosity*)

A traditional distinction, derived from St. John, recognizes three parts in concupiscence in the pejorative and somewhat sinful sense of the term: the concupiscence of the flesh, the concupiscence of the eyes, and pride of life. Temperance properly so called restrains the first, and humility curbs the third; there remains the concupiscence of the eyes.

The moralist considers concupiscence of the eyes as "an immoderate desire for information and knowledge." Some virtue is necessary to moderate this desire and this is studiousness.

It is significant that the very name of this virtue makes us think less of a repression, in the way of the virtues which gravitate around temperance, than of an impulse, in the manner of the potential parts of the virtue of fortitude. This indicates once again that a virtue is an exact center between two excesses and that studiousness which moderates the appetite for knowing is not meant to lead to inaction or inertia. If it checks a concupiscence of the eyes of the body which do not need to see everything or look at everything, and a concupiscence of the eyes of the mind which do not need to know everything, it is likewise capable of imposing upon the mind the necessary effort of attention for considering and learning what is really good to know. Consequently it is familiar with two stumbling-blocks: laziness and curiosity.

Laziness

As the living image of God, and not merely a dead or passive image, man cannot reject effort. No more than the sun can refuse to give heat, according to its nature, or the plant refuse to grow according to its own, man cannot refuse to know, think or act: for lack of these the world would not be what it ought to be. God will not do the work which the world refuses, for it is not in the manner of God to over-rule the secondary causes which He has made: He does not destroy what He has created (cf. Wis. 11), and it would practically be a de-struction of man if he were dispensed from being a little providence in the world; and it is self-destruction for man to renounce this and reduce himself to vegetating (half-bestial, half vegetal). His work does not therefore conflict with God's, nor does it compete with it or harm it, but he is the instrument of God's work and renders glory to his creator. We are never so completely in His hands than when we act the most completely as men: intelligently and freely.

Psychologically, it is good to observe that there are two kinds of laziness opposite in manner. The "virtue of work" is the virtue which permits the patient, continuous and efficient efforts which prevent both inaction and superficial trifling.

The Vice of Curiosity

There is a good and legitimate curiosity, therefore desirable, the kind which an educator seeks to waken in his students: an interest, an attention to the things of the world and attention to God, a desire to penetrate their mystery. But even in current speech "curiosity" connotes the idea of a defect, an indiscretion. In this respect, what is the source of the disorder of the sin?

The knowledge of truth is good in itself: the intelligence in its own domain, and the senses in their domain, are made for it. It cannot occur without a legitimate joy, the kind that the satisfaction of every appetite gives us. But the desire to know may be vitiated and vicious, that is to say degraded. It is so, for example, if this concern for know-ing is in reality a desire to surpass others and to glorify oneself. It is then arrogant. It may even in certain cases become blasphemous. It happens that some men apply themselves to the knowledge of God, not in the attitude of infinite respect and religious considerateness which such an object requires, but rather from the position of looking downward, so to speak, as if it were a question of just any object of analysis submitted to man.

Solicitude for knowledge may also be vicious through a disorder in the choice of our objects. A few examples: a person who gives up a difficult and timely study in order to turn to less useful matters, but of more pleasant access; or someone who applies himself to studies above his reach with the possibility of delusion, or understanding wrongly, for lack of patience and refusal to recognize at least the provisional limitations of his means, and finally the person who is unable to restrain himself from turning toward every passing object haphazardly, and always drops whatever he has once begun. What acquisition could be expected from this? There is the example of the student who by not making a judicious choice of teachers hazards his intellectual formation. All this, and other things too, require control. A necessary discipline of life, which is related to a temperance, is always to the advantage of a certain enrichment and efficiency.

(d) *Modesty*

Under this term, understood in a broad sense, we shall place several virtues of refinement that are admittedly of social import. They are still temperances because they are moderations and discretions.

1. Good Manners

It is a virtue to maintain, in one's attitude, a "moderation" which both expresses what we are, and what others mean to us and to our mutual relations. It must be admitted that certain generations have been too steeped in formalisms and that there are people who seem too constantly arrayed in frock-coats. This is an error; either because these attitudes becomes hypocritical, or because they are content to be empty and vain. But it is also an error not to keep the minimum of "conformity" which constitutes a kind of language of politeness and which we could call a liturgy of social life, when it possesses its proper measure. With regard to practical determinations, they may include a share of conventions (why do civilians greet one another by lifting their hats while between soldiers only the hand is lifted?) and especially a great deal of relativity; they vary according to the places and the persons. Good manners makes us observe the moderation which the elite of our society has established, and it prevents us from acting like a boor or from being cumbrous by excesses of gesticulations and prattling. Courtesy is a word full of meaning.

2. Propriety of Clothing

We must now give the word to St. Francis de Sales:

Propriety of clothes and other ornaments depends upon the matter, the form and the cleanliness. With regard to cleanliness, it must always be the same in our clothing on which, as far as possible, we must not leave any kind of stain or dirt. External cleanliness represents, in some way, interior integrity. God Himself requires corporal integrity of those who approach His altars and who are principally responsible for worship.

With regard to the matter and the form of our clothing, propriety should be considered in relation to various circumstances of time, age, qualities, company, and occasions. One ordinarily dresses better on holidays, according to the greatness of the day which is celebrated; in times of penance, as during Lent, one makes drastic changes in dress; for weddings, one wears marriage garments, and at funerals mourning clothes; in the presence of princes one enhances one's appearance and diminishes this among domestics (i.e., the persons of our household and not the servants). The married woman may and should array herself attractively for her husband, whenever he desires it. . . . We allow more fineries to young girls because they may lawfully desire to be pleasing to a number of persons, although it is only in order to win one of them by a holy marriage. . . . People always mock elderly folk when they try to prettify themselves: this is an extravagance which is only tolerable in young people.

Be proper, Philothea, let there be nothing upon you which drags or which is poorly arranged. It is contempt for those with whom we are conversing to go among them in unpleasant dress; but keep yourself carefully from affectations, vanities, curiosities and wanton attire. So far as possible keep yourself on the side of simplicity and modesty which is doubtless the greatest ornament of beauty and the best excuse for ugliness. St. Peter warns young women primarily not to wear their hair excessively frizzled, curled, ringed or wound. Men who are so weak as to amuse themselves with this foppish behavior, are everywhere decried as hermaphrodites, and vain women are considered to be imbeciles (without strength) in regard to chastity; at least, if they possess chastity, it is not visible among so much rubbish and so many baubles. It is said that nobody thinks ill of it, but I reply, as I have done elsewhere, that the devil always thinks about it. For myself, I should like my devout man or devout woman to be always the best dressed of the flock but the least pompous and least affected, and, as the Proverb says, that they might be arrayed with grace, propriety and dignity . . . St. Louis says in a word that one should dress according to one's state of life, so that the wise and the good may not say: "You go too far," nor young folk say, "You are not doing enough." But in case the young folk are not willing to be satisfied with propriety, one must insist upon the counsel of wise men.[1]

[1] *Introduction to a Devout Life,* part III, chap. XXV.

Can we do better than to listen to the remarks of this man of the world who was at once a humanist, a great bishop and a saint, keeping in mind the three centuries which separate us from him? He agrees with Father Lacordaire in saying that order and cleanliness are quasi-virtues. And we are far from the time, thank God, when, apparently, care of the body was held, in certain houses of education, to be sensuality and an irregular interest directed toward the flesh! If clothing must be clean, *a fortiori*, the body which wears it . . .

May we draw out of these reflections a morality of elegance, fashion and usages? Here at least are a few suggestions:

Fine clothing, and a beautiful dress chosen with taste and which is becoming to the woman who wears it, puts into human society that variety, that beauty, and sometimes that splendor which the Creator has put everywhere in the world. A reasonable elegance is restful to the eyes, and is the youth and health of society. It is a virtue in the same way that it preserves moderation. It is not harmful to society; on the contrary, and even among people at work it does no harm to see beautiful clothing; but the attractive and simple clothing for work will be one thing, and holiday clothing will be something else.

The temptation of the woman, however, and it is for her that the virtue of elegance will be the most useful, consists in wishing to be too noticeable. The excess which is most to be feared is not that she will seek to make herself unattractive, but rather adorn herself immoderately. The virtue of elegance consists in keeping, with the best taste of which one is personally capable, the moderation which is suitable in the society in which one works, one plays or one lives. While the contrary vice, which is foolish and sometimes sensual flirtation, no longer considers the best that is within herself and which it is a matter of expressing simply, nor even the good or the approbation of society, but seeks above all else to make herself seen, and to attract glances to herself and arouse the desires of the senses. If elegance is capable of expressing what is best in society, a certain bold ostentation is capable of showing what is most vile in the human being.

The distinction between elegance and flirtation is however less simple than it appears in theory. And this proves to us, once again, that the moderation of the virtue is not a static datum established once and for all, but that it is in some way created by the intelligence in terms of all kinds of external, social, and personal data. The elegance of Sundays will be different from that of work-days; that of the city from that of the country; that of the fiancee with her young man from that of a woman who has renounced marriage for the Lord. In this respect, a stupid conformity in regard to a tyrannical fashion may be quite as immoderate and therefore vicious as a provocative originality. And, inversely, a simple and flexible submission to the best taste of a period, and therefore to a standard of fashion considered as a kind of liturgy, may be quite as virtuous as a measure of liberty taken in regard to this fashion. The moderate usage of make-up may be approved in such circumstances for some particular person; while other make-up will be disapproved, if only because of the time and resources that are lost because of it. And clothing which is suitable for the beach is obviously not proper for going to church.

To suggest things by way of illustration, it is not to be doubted that today mothers of families who are most Christian appear in public in clothing whose degree of exposure would not have been tolerated fifty years ago. It seems, in fact, that it is by the clothing's unusual and astonishing aspect in a certain context, and consequently in its "shocking" appearance, in the etymological sense, and finally in its arousing character, that it is the most objectionable rather than by its form, its length—or its absence—according as these are accepted or legitimately required. This is a delicate matter. Once more the need for a reason to give to virtue its right balance.

3. Good Disposition

In the conferences of the Fathers we read that the apostle St. John, when certain persons were scandalized to find him playing with his disciples, asked one of those who was carrying a bow to shoot an arrow. After he had shot several, St. John asked if he could continue doing it indefinitely. The man replied that if he continued the bow would break. And St. John drew this lesson from it: "Thus it is with man's soul which would break if it were never relieved from its tension. Aristotle says the same thing: In this life we must give ourselves some rest in play" (IIa IIae, q. 168, a. 2).

Temperance is control for the sake of better efficiency. Work no longer "yields" if man always wants to keep himself under strain. Relaxation is necessary and current speech excellently calls it "recreation": we are "re-created." The proverb tells us, "The man who desires to travel far will spare his mount." It pertains to the virtue of relaxation, related to temperance, to give us these necessary respites with the moderation that is fitting in order that the recreation may be neither laziness nor superficiality.

All forms of labor have need of "rest periods." This is obvious in regard to the activities of the mind. Over-work is an error or a sin; it hinders better performance. This is still truer of manual labors which not only fatigue the muscles, but run the risk of stupefying the mind: consequently there is need for rest which enables men to renew their awareness of spiritual values. This is the positive meaning of the precept which forbids servile work on Sunday.

By way of suggestion a word will enable us to outline the morality of "leisure": recreation is to re-create us, not to wear us out. Anything that would be stupefying, degrading, or exhausting, and anything which, far from giving us rest and putting us "in good form" (physically, intellectually or spiritually) would make necessary the recovery of oneself, before we could take up again fruitful works, would be a poor kind of "recreation." The free relaxation of leisure time or the gratuitous gift of self which is made in games or sport does not mean that one is forsaking his intelligence, but that he is applying it to things that are calming, pleasant or restful to reason. If a game has not purpose in itself, the pleasure that results from it does have one, and this is rest and recreation for the soul. The word "eutrapelia" could very well be translated as the virtue of good humor. It is at once amiability, sociability, light-heartedness, joviality, and still more radically, the virtue of good fellowship. It makes us avoid attitudes which are unnatural, strained, artificially austere and a certain heaviness which is so depressing in society. In spite of prejudice, thank the suffering God, sanctity is neither stiffness nor a composed face, nor being a wet-blanket; it is even the very contrary since it is "grace" (the term gracious comes from this), and it is in the naturalness and the elegance of the good deed that the fulfillment of the virtue is found. "A saint who is sad is a sad saint."

Eutrapelia makes us moderate in pleasantry and smiling, and in relaxation; it makes us spontaneously find the attitudes that are most suitable according to the occasions and the persons. Stiff seriousness, grumbling, the mania for seeing and stressing the dark side of everything, are in this case sins of default. The heavy joking of the "traveling salesman" or the wisecracks in army barracks are sins by excess.

Thus it is an eminent virtue to maintain in oneself and in others both good humor and relaxation, for its puts facility and efficiency not only into everyone's life but into social life also. Many dissensions are resolved, and many difficulties overcome, because of a good word spoken opportunely, because of a sally or teasing remark, or because of the cordial atmosphere of a laborious discussion. Eutrapelia, the virtue of leisure time, games, and the temperance of diversion, and of sane pleasures, is often a marvelous expression of charity. We cannot end this section more suitably.

III. The Gift of Fear and Temperance

The gift of fear is quite close to the virtue of hope and is its support. This is not therefore the place to study it. But a venerable tradition, of which a St. Thomas and his commentators have made themselves the witnesses, insists upon the closeness of the spirit of fear and of temperance. There is a lesson in this which must not be rejected.

1. FEAR AND TEMPERANCE PROPERLY SO CALLED

Fear may, in fact, be a very useful help to our weakness in time of temptation. Let us not scorn it. The man upon whom the humiliating attraction of improper pleasures weighs heavily would be quite out of place to reject as unworthy of himself a thought of the suffering which carnal vices will bring upon him whether in this world or in eternity. An authentic form of this fear may even be quite simply the thought of the disgrace (degradation or illness) which debauchery may entail, for there may finally be in this very fear, a respect for the order of things as God has willed them to be, and for the greatness which He desired for man—and this is a good sign, even if it be imperfect. From this point, nothing will prevent a man from rising to a more filial and more loving attitude toward his Creator (cf. Ecclus. 1 and 2).

2. FEAR AND HUMILITY

But we must go further. The spirit of fear is fundamentally the sense of the infinite greatness of God, of His transcendence, of His omnipotence, and of His absolute rights over the creatures. Humility and fear are bound up together. Man being nothing and having no strength by himself, can only build upon God; and he must build upon God as greatly as his love for God will prompt him, that is to say without limit, and this is the virtue of hope whose "moderation," as in every theological virtue, is "not to have any moderation" since it is dependent upon the love and the infinite mercy of God. "Abyssus abyssum invocat" (Ps. 41:8): Deep calleth on deep. Wherever humility gives us the sense of the nothingness of the creature, digging within us an abyss of nothingness under the inspiration of "fear," the abyss of the divine mercy gives us the excitement which is called hope. Those who feel their own nothingness, either directly by the sense of the greatness of God or more humbly by that of their own wretchedness—the weight of the flesh is definitely meant to give the sense of this wretchedness—are very near throwing themselves "desperately" into God's arms: the Kingdom is open to them (cf. Mt. 5:3).

REFLECTIONS AND PERSPECTIVES

The question of temperance is one of the points by which the "healthiness" of a theology is recognized. Man is not, in fact, only spiritual or only carnal, but he is spirit and flesh. A "discarnate" theology which might wish to ignore the body or "sex" would be a false theology. A theology of dualistic and Manichaean tendency which would be inclined to attribute all evil to the body and to sexual matters—like that of certain Cappadocians for whom the division of the sexes was the fruit of original sin and would not have existed in a condition of original justice—would be very dangerous and certainly false in part. A theology which would not have place for the normal development of sex and of good sensuality in the adolescent and then in the adult would be in error. On the other hand, a theology which would materially establish the measure of chastity in certain external behavior and apart from all reference to the spirit, would likewise be false. Or else a theology which would too strongly emphasize the health of the body, the glorification of the cosmos, to the detriment of the spirit and of living union with God, would be dangerous. A sound theology makes room for all the requirements of the spirit and all the natural exigencies of the flesh which God also created.

However, man has sinned and always carries within him the wounds of this sin. "The flesh warreth against the spirit." For his salvation, which is the salvation of both the spirit and the body, man is called upon to "crucify his flesh with its evil desires." The theologian must therefore maintain on the one hand the goodness of everything which God has created, including sensuality and the natural desires of one sex in regard to the other (it matters little that we cannot "picture" to ourselves psychologically what these desires might have been in a condition in which the flesh would have been dependent upon the spirit, harmoniously and spontaneously), and on the other hand, the high legitimacy of asceticism, and the contempt of the body, and of attitudes which, externally, may resemble the behavior of dualist thinkers, but to which the Spirit gives a very different signification.

Temperance, a cardinal virtue. It is the function of temperance to "temper," that is to say to moderate, to impose a measure. But this function is that of every virtue; temperance would be only an aspect of every virtue—the aspect which consists in putting the measure of reason into every action—if it were not otherwise defined. Temperance is a special virtue, distinct from the others, and as such a cardinal virtue, the axis of numerous virtues, only when the "putting measure" (in the sense of moderating and tempering) is of the greatest difficulty. Everybody can hammer a nail; but not everybody is for that reason a carpenter: a trade, a technique, a profession are necessary for this. Likewise, every man of ordinary virtue is capable of moderating his liberality, for example (in the sense in which the latter is a passion): nature itself helps him in this; but this does not mean that he is quite as capable of moderating certain desires: he requires a very special mastery in order to "put a measure" into these passions whose tendency is to always lead him beyond every measure. The cardinal virtue of temperance has precisely for its object the control of the appetite in relation to that which leads him thus and which the ancients called the "delectationes tactus," the pleasures of *touch*.

A whole philosophy of the "sensation of touch" would have to be undertaken and presented here. It is obvious that the touch in question is not simply the fifth of the external senses; it is a very general sense which is also found in sight and in the other senses. Just as the first of the senses, sight, is inversely found in all the others also. When a blind man touches an object and discovers its identity little by little, he says, "I see what it is." When a sailor perceives from afar an unusual object which he is still unable to identify, he simply says, "I have contacted something." Sight is the most synthetic sense, the most immaterial, and also the most abstract. It represents whatever knowledge there may be in every other sense. But touch is the most concrete sense, the most affective, the sense of experience; it represents in every other sense a kind of impregnation of the sensibility of the body by the object that is sensed: it is the least differentiated sense and is spread over the whole surface of the body (the qualities recognized by the sense of touch are variously the hard, the soft, cold, hot, the rough, the smooth, etc.).

The touching which brings pleasure—and arouses desires—of the strongest kind is that of carnal contact which the procreative act requires. To a lesser degree there is next the touch of "taste" which communicates to the palate all the pleasures of drinking and eating. The first is necessary for the life of the species, the second for the life of the individual. All desirable kinds of touch—whether of sensuality or the sensibility of the palate—pertain to these two fundamental types of touching; it is to the degree in which they are so related that temperance has the function of moderating their attraction. Attractions of smell (perfumes); attractions of sight (including picture-magazines, billboards, films); attractions of hearing (music that is called "sensual"), etc. The role of the Christian and of the educator—and of the theologian—is to be able to unravel these subtle relations in the sensations which are presented to him and to denounce the "motives," whether hidden or not, of these sensations. Morality of films, of pictures, of fashions, of perfumes, etc. Consider well that nudity is not always that which is exciting for the senses; certain apparel, certain perfumes, certain behavior, definitely "studied," are often more so.

Temperance puts man in a position to govern the usage of these various kinds of touch (or to abstain from them if their usage is contrary to his state in life) and to discard all the false imitations and counterfeits. It likewise moderates the attraction of the pleasures which accompany these kinds of touch.

The Beautiful Act

Honestas, according to the ancients, is one of the important elements, and even the most important, of the virtue of temperance. But we must not translate *honestas* by honesty; the vernacular derivative of our time is an illegitimate child of a virtue which is otherwise great and human. *Honestum* is "quod nihil habet turpitudinis," that which is composed of nothing shameful, or better stated, that which is beautiful. The intemperate act is the shameful and ugly act, ignominious, which merits disgrace and makes men blush, the infantile act (which St. Thomas calls "puerile"): because the flesh has overpowered the spirit, man then becomes in some way carnal even in his soul. The temperate act is the beautiful act, clear, clean, doing honor to man; spirit then triumphs over the flesh without destroying it, but simply by keeping its mastery, and man becomes in some sense spiritual even in his flesh; he is then luminous. While the intemperate man becomes ill (cf. I Cor. 11:30), the temperate man is more fully man.

Theology of education in these matters begins with the value of "beauty." Learn to do what is beautiful (the beautiful gesture, the fine act, the beautiful thought, the beautiful sentiment) and to detest what is ugly. Develop the sentiment of shame: the fear of anything that is ugly and shameful.

Intemperance and confession. The sacramental economy of penitence requires that man make reparation for his sins by confession. The sanctifying shame of confession will therefore correspond to the humiliating shame of the intemperate act. St. Augustine thought that shame constitutes the greatest part of penitence; and St. Bernard said, "the discovery of a precious jewel does not cause man as much joy as the blush on the face of the repentant sinner procures for God." With respect to the sinner, therefore, regret for his sin normally prevents him from repulsing the shame of this humble confession, simple and chaste, by which the grace of chastity is restored to him. But the attitude of the priest must be one of mercy and discretion, following the example of Our Lord in the presence of the adulterous woman. If it be necessary to interrogate, let it be by necessity and with discretion, for the good of the guilty person and without curiosity.

Feminine fashions: Sensual appetite inclines man to be particularly attentive to the body of woman, and inclines the woman to be particularly attentive to making herself noticed, to be pleasing or even desirable. Therefore, feminine apparel is of primary importance in every society.

This principle is just. It would however be false to conclude by reducing the moral problem to a question of the length of dresses or sleeves. Virtues are not material reckoners and there is no worse education than that which is satisfied to impose rules for external attire, without considering the changes in times and places. The virtue of chastity is, like every virtue, a quality of the spirit; it is communicated or at least is taught by the spirit. It is only acquired by means of sustained effort of the spirit laboring for harmonious mastery over the flesh; this is also to say that it usually experiences many successive approximations and tentative procedures, and that certain regretted failures may be of more benefit to it than an attitude that is perpetually conformist in which the spirit has no part.

Nevertheless, this does not mean that mastery of the spirit over the flesh (that is to say chastity) can be indifferent to all external behavior. However reduced it may be, a certain correspondence remains between outward appearance (clothing, bodily posture, etc.) and interior feeling. The outward appearance expresses the sentiment and often creates a certain climate for it. And this "correspondence" is particularly true in young people; this explains the role of the uniform in education.

Christian moderation in fashions and apparel will therefore be inspired primarily by the concern to express a certain mastery of the spirit (chastity), and next and secondly, in regard to external appearance—it might even be in order to inspire them better—will manifest the intention of following the customary and sound norms of the society in which one lives. The make-up which is considered "bad taste" in certain country areas may be "question of attire" in certain urban centers.

Christian asceticism. The different "procedures" to acquire the chaste mastery of the spirit over the flesh have varied in the course of time, and also according to countries, climates, and environments (monastic and lay). A geography of these ascetical means might be undertaken, along with their history. On this subject, see *L'ascèse chrétienne et l'homme contemporain.* Collection entitled *Cahiers de la Vie Spirituelle,* Paris, Éditions du Cerf, 1951.

It seems that for several years, and partly under the influence of Saint Therese of the Child of Jesus, a renewal of these procedures is under way. It would however be harmful if a too sudden reaction, although justified (if we take into account the changes in the organism, the temperament, and the nervous wear and tear of modern man) against traditional methods of mortification were to make Christians of today forget the imperishable principle of mortification itself. The liking for hygiene, in particular, is good; a certain obsession for hygiene, common today, often indicates a lack of moderation in the appreciation of that which ought to be sought for.

The principle of asceticism, in every state, is that it is not so much the body which must be mortified as the spirit which is expressed in certain corporal postures, as in certain acts or desires. The degree of mortification is to be found by each person separately, but no one can avoid it, not even the sick person—even if it be only by the constraint of his illness, and this is ordinarily sufficient. On the subject of the ascetical "principle" among monks, one should read the fine book of Dom A. Stolz, *L'ascèse chrétienne,* Chevetogne, 1948.

Chastity and one's state of life. Without going all the way to the hazardous determinations of certain systems of casuistry, a theology which desires to be practical must prolong the declared principles unto the most concrete, possible application to different states of life. Work projects: chastity of the priest; chastity of Religious; chastity in the apostolate; in the priest's relations with women (how reconcile the exigencies of the love of charity and of the mercy which the priest owes to all the lambs of Christ, particularly sinners, with the requirements of chastity?). Chastity of Nuns; advantages of the cloister and its risks in relation to psychism; "possessive" love, psychology, effects. (On this subject read *Chastity,* Newman Press, 1955. Education in chastity for adolescent boys and girls, young men and young ladies, male and female educators. Education in the home, in the school. Chastity in marriage, the chastity of engaged couples (cf. Marriage, volume VI). The chastity of maternity. The chastity of celibates. Education in chastity among non-Christian peoples (viz. the African missions): what practices and what customs can be tolerated or not tolerated in matters of chastity?

Education in chastity is particularly difficult in regard to young girls, because of the fact that their sensuality is very diffuse, unconscious, and often undistinguishable from sensibility properly so called and from affectivity. Feminine sensuality is furthermore still poorly defined both medically and psychologically. The education of sensuality (and of sensibility) will therefore consist not in stopping all the effective or sentimental impulses but first of all in opening the mind in order to learn how to discern the play of intentions and drives behind desires, inquiries, imagination and dreams, attitudes and friendships; and then in helping the subject to acquire the control of all interior powers not by seeking to break them or by placing oneself in some way against the stream, but rather by placing oneself at the head of the stream in order to integrate them generously within a voluntary love, and therefore primarily spiritual, including everything which is worthy of being humanly loved.

Modesty and humility. These two virtues, which are really only two aspects of the same virtue, are characteristic of Christianity, and the very basis of our spiritual life. Show the basis in Scripture, and especially in the Gospel. Humility according to the Gospel. Humility in tradition. The "degrees of humility" and the apprenticeship of humility in St. Benedict's Rule, in St. Bernard, and St. Ignatius Loyola. The motive of humility and its cause. Education and practice of humility. Relations of humility to chastity, of pride to intemperance ("pride of the flesh"), and of pride to cruelty.

The evangelical virtue of modesty. Christian modesty according to St. Francis de Sales (read this completely). Theological judgments concerning certain "styles" that are apparently not "modest." Baroque style (cf. on the subject, P. Roques and P. R. Regamey, *La signification du baroque,* in *La Maison-Dieu,* n. 26), the style of certain giant monuments, and of certain images. Compare primitive Romanesque art, Gothic art, Baroque and Rococo arts.

Christian joy. Temperance, a virtue moderating human sadness. Chastity and joy. Intemperance and the sin of sadness. Qualities of Christian joy. Laughter and joy. Sensual laughter and Christian joy. Philosophy and theology of laughter. Joy in the Gospel.

The sin of Adam and Eve. It is not true that the first sin was a sin of intemperance, as is sometimes said. Or at least, if there was gluttony in the first sin, this was only a secondary aspect of an act which was primarily a sin of pride. "For pride is the beginning of all sin" (Ecclus. 10:15). The temptation offered to Adam and Eve was furthermore: "You shall be as Gods" (Gen. 3:5). The psychology of this sin. The state of original justice, and the state of sin.

Theology of the punishments of sin: Expulsion from paradise (meaning, content of the punishment); loss of the privileges of original justice; punishments inflicted upon women: sufferings of childbearing, the pain of child-birth (Gen. 3:16); enslavement to her husband (explain: "thou shalt be under thy husband's power, and he shall have dominion over thee" (Gen. 3:16); the punishment inflicted upon man: the cursing of the earth, work in the sweat of his brow, thorns and thistles. Punishment inflicted upon the soul: the emancipation of the flesh which is no longer under the domination of the spirit, and the shame of nudity (Gen. 3:7); the separation of the soul from the body by death. Concerning Gen. 3, cf. the explanations of R. de Vaux in *La Genèse,* Collection *La Bible de Jérusalem,* Paris, Éditions du Cerf, 1951. Concerning the hostility between the serpent and womankind, cf. in particular F. M. Braun in *La Mère de Jésus dans l'Oeuvre de Saint Jean,* Revue Thomiste, 1950, III, especially pages 467-479 and 1951, I, pages 5 ff. Can we

compare the sin of Adam and the sin of Eve, the punishment of the one with that of the other?
Theology of temptation beginning with Gen. 3:1-6. Psychology of temptation. How can temptation be avoided?

BIBLIOGRAPHIE

Saint Thomas d'Aquin, *La tempérance,* trad. et notes de J.-D. Folghera, Paris, Éd. de la Revue des J., 1928 (La question 154, *De partibus luxuriæ,* a été curieusement laissée en latin sans être traduite).
Le livre du P. Sertillanges, *La vie intellectuelle,* Paris, Éd. de la Revue des J., intéresse le problème de la studiosité mais aussi tout le problème de la tempérance auquel il élargit le débat.

Citons enfin: Saint François de sales, *Introduction à la vie dévote,* livre classique qui est en même temps un véritable bréviaire de la discrétion.

Sur la chasteté, on lira d'abord des ouvrages positifs de documentation tels que:

J. Carnot, *Au service de l'amour,* Paris, Éd. Beaulieu.
Ch. Combaluzier, *Science biologique et morale sexuelle,* Paris, Spes.
Docteur Biot, *Éducation de l'amour,* Paris, Plon, 1946.

Il ne manque pas d'études et d'articles sur l'éducation de la pureté ni sur celle, plus fondamentale, de l'amour:

M. Nédoncelle, *Vers une métaphysique de l'amour,* Paris, Aubier, 1946.
J. Lacroix, *Personne et amour,* Lyon, Éd. du livre français, 1941.
G. Madinier, *Conscience et amour,* Paris, Alcan, 1938.
S. Kierkegaard, *Vie et règne de l'amour,* Paris, Aubier, 1946.
A.-D. Sertillanges, *L'amour chrétien,* Paris, Lecoffre, 1924.
R. P. Bessières, *L'amour et ses contrefaçons,* Paris, Spes, 1920.
R. P. Bessières, *Les lois éternelles de l'amour,* Paris, Spes, 1944.
Ch. Viollet, *Relations entre jeunes gens et jeunes filles,* Paris, Assoc. du mar. chrét.
Fr. Charmot, *L'amour humain de l'enfance au mariage,* Paris, Spes, 1936.
E. Rolland, *Sexe et psychologie,* Paris, Éd. Fam. de Fr., 1947.
Ch. Viollet, *L'éducation de la pureté et de l'amour,* Paris, Éd. Mar. et Fam.
M. Oraison, *Vie chrétienne et morale sexuelle,* Paris, Lethielleux, 1952.
A. Arthus, H. Bissonnier, etc., *L'éducation sexuelle,* Paris, 31, rue de Fleurus.
Jacquemet, *L'éducation de la pureté,* Paris, Bloud et Gay.
Docteur Abrand, *Éducation de la pureté et préparation au mariage,* Paris, Ass. du mar. chrét.
W. Foerster, *Morale sexuelle et pédagogie sexuelle,* Paris, Bloud et Gay, 1920.
M.-S. Gillet, *Innocence et ignorance, Éducation de la pureté,* Paris, Lethielleux.

Certains ouvrages de morale traitent de la pureté et de l'éducation de l'amour sous le titre général *De sexto* (ce qui signifie: Sur les actes que prohibe *le sixième* commandement). Cette manière d'envisager la chasteté est malheureuse. Être chaste ne consiste pas essentiellement à éviter certains péchés, mais à posséder, dans la force de l'Esprit, la tranquille maîtrise de ses passions. Faire l'éducation de la pureté selon ces principes légalistes est ordinairement désastreux et relève d'une morale de la Loi plus que d'une morale de la grâce. On se méfiera de ces ouvrages qui, au surplus, réduisent la morale à n'être qu'une casuistique.

Sur la chasteté conjugale (chasteté des époux), on lira:

Claude Serviès, *La chair et la grâce,* Paris, Spes.
H. Rambaud, *La voie sacrée,* Lyon, Lardanchet, 1946.
G. Thibon, *Ce que Dieu a uni,* Lyon, Lardanchet, 1947.
Docteur Jouvenroux, *Témoignage sur l'amour humain,* Paris, Éd. Le liseron, 1948.
P. Chanson, *L'Œuvre de chair,* Paris, Éd. fam. de Fr., 1948.

Sur la virginité, la chasteté et la vocation virginales:

Th. Camelot, *Virgines Christi,* Paris, Éd. du Cerf.
P. Chanson, *La vocation virginale,* Paris, Éd. du Cerf.
La chasteté, à paraître aux Éd. du Cerf, 1953.
J. Perrin, *La virginité,* Coll. *Cahiers de la vie spirituelle,* Paris, Éd. du Cerf, 1952.

Enfin, sur les vertus "modératrices," annexes à la tempérance, nous ne signalerons parmi les ouvrages modernes que:

Dom Bélorgey, *L'humilité bénédictine,* Paris, Éd. du Cerf.

BIBLIOGRAPHY

Buckley, Joseph, *Christian Design for Sex.* Chicago, Fides Publishers Association, 1952.
DeSales, St. Francis, *Introduction to the Devout Life* (trans. John K. Ryan). Garden City, N. Y.; Doubleday & Company, Inc. (Image Books), 1950.
Doe, John, *Sobriety and Beyond.* Indianapolis, SMT Publishing Co., Inc., 1955.
Dohen, Dorothy, *Vocation to Love.* New York, Sheed and Ward, 1950.
Doyle, Charles H., *Cana Is Forever.* Tarrytown, N. Y., Nugent Press, 1949.
Fitzsimons, John, *Woman Today.* New York, Sheed and Ward, 1952.
Ford, John C., S.J., *Man Takes a Drink.* New York, P. J. Kenedy & Sons, 1955.
Haley, Joseph E., C.S.C., *Accent on Purity.* Chicago, Fides Publishers Association, 1948.
Hull, Ernest R., *The Formation of Character.* St. Louis, B. Herder Book Co., 1949.
Joyce, G. H., *Christian Marriage.* New York, Sheed and Ward, 1953.
King, J. Leycester, S.J., *Sex Enlightenment and the Catholic.* London, Burns Oates & Washbourne, Ltd., 1947.
Kirsch, Felix, O.F.M., Cap., *Sex Education and Training in Chastity.* New York, Benziger Brothers, 1930.

Kothen, Robert, *Marriage the Great Mystery*. Westminster, Md., The Newman Bookshop, 1947.

LeClercq, Jacques, *Marriage and the Family*. New York, F. Pustet & Co., 1947.

Lindworsky, Johann, *The Training of the Will* (trans. A. Steiner and E. A. Fitzpatrick). Milwaukee, The Bruce Publishing Company, 1929.

McCarthy, R. C., *Training the Adolescent*. Milwaukee, The Bruce Publishing Company, 1949.

McHugh, John A., O.P., and Callan, Charles J., O.P., *Moral Theology, A Complete Course*. New York, Joseph Wagner, Inc., 1929.

Magner, James A., *The Art of Happy Marriage*. Milwaukee, The Bruce Publishing Company, 1949.

Meersch, E., S.J., *Love, Marriage, and Chastity*. London, Sheed and Ward, 1939.

O'Brien, John A., *Sex-Character Education*. New York, The Macmillan Company, 1952.

Sertillanges, Antonin D., O.P., *The Intellectual Life*. Westminster, Md., The Newman Bookshop, 1948.

Sheedy, Charles E., C.S.C., *The Christian Virtues,* pp. 327-354. Notre Dame, Ind., University of Notre Dame Press, 1949.

Sheen, Fulton J., *Three to Get Married*. New York, Appleton-Century-Crofts, 1951.

Sheppard, Lancelot C. (Tr.), *Chastity*. Westminster, Md., Newman Press, 1955.

Valentine, Ferdinand, *For Better, For Worse*. Oxford, Blackfriars, 1948.

Von Hildebrand, Dietrich, *Marriage*. New York, Longmans, Green & Co, 1942.

————, *In Defence of Purity*. New York, Sheed and Ward, 1935.

Wayne, T. G., *Morals and Marriage*. New York, Longmans, Green, & Co., 1936.

Welton, Thurston S., *The Modern Method of Birth Control*. New York, Grosset & Dunlap, 1943.

White, Lynn, *Educating Our Daughters*. New York, Harper & Bros., 1953.

Canavan, F. P., S.J., "Finality of Sex," *Catholic World,* Ja '54.

Ford, J. C., S.J., "Temperance and Purity: Liquor Problem," *Messenger of the Sacred Heart,* F '56.

Peters, G. E., "Virginity and Marriage," *Worship,* Aug '53.

Ryan, M. P., "Sex Education," *Worship,* S '53.

After having considered the division of all the virtues, theological as well as merely moral, the theologian must turn to the particular situations in which people find themselves animated by these virtues. St. Paul tells us, as a matter of fact (I Cor. 12:4-6), that there are varieties of gifts, varieties of workings, and varieties of ministries. The theologian takes note of these and then goes from them to those varied and particular conditions in which the Christian finds himself placed by the will of God in order to attain his salvation. For it is necessary that each one be informed of what is asked of him, not only in a general way, but in that which concerns him personally.

We shall not consider these "particular situations" within the framework of a community or society. We might indeed consider the particular situation of professions: of leaders in industry, in medicine, in law; of age: the young man, the young girl, the adult, but this would not, properly speaking, constitute a new chapter in our theology. The appropriate virtues of the man in such and such a profession are only the virtues already considered. So all that remains is to make a concrete application of them. The appropriate virtues of the head of a company, of the governor of a state, are those of justice and prudence (we are speaking, of course, of the prudence which is a virtue and which we have already defined as a "virtue of enterprise and of responsibilities"); the virtue befitting the doctor is also that of a very special prudence in the practice of his skill. The "answer" to all these "situations" would be to elaborate, with regard to them, the chapters of the virtues already analyzed. These elaborations, we might add, are far from being superfluous, and it is well for each one to apply them to the responsibilities which concern him.

We shall consider the particular situations which are inscribed in the structure of that society which is the Church. The Church is at once a society and a living organism, and even more precisely a society and the Mystical Body of Christ. Considered as a society, it possesses, like any society, a juridical order. Considered as the Mystical Body of Christ, it has the unity of a living organism with a head, a body, and members who are not interchangeable. Each Christian in the ecclesiastical society receives a hierarchical situation, but he also receives, insofar as he is a member of Christ, a life, an inspiration, particular gifts, a vocation, even perhaps, a special task in the Mystical Body of Christ. These are the situations which we are considering in this last section of moral theology.

We shall study first of all the differences of grace in the Mystical Body, and in order not to confuse them with the personal graces which each one receives for his own salvation, we shall call them, according to the custom established elsewhere, the *charismata*. These are the graces given to men not so much in view of their own sanctification—although that is not excluded—but in the service of the Christian community in which they live.

We shall then study the different types of *life* which a Christian can lead in the Mystical Body of Christ: a contemplative life, of a more intellectual kind, and an active life, of a more social kind. These ways of life, like the vocations which correspond to them, are not mutually exclusive and can be realized everywhere—within the present boundaries of the religious state or outside of any institution.

Lastly, we shall consider the offices, duties and states in the Mystical Body of Christ. Attaching ourselves above all to "the state of perfection," we shall try to understand what that means theologically and how the *pastoral state* and the *religious state* fulfill its requirements.

Chapter X

THE CHARISMATA

by J. V. M. Pollet, O.P.

Chapter X

THE CHARISMATA

By charismata we ordinarily understand certain particular graces granted by the Holy Spirit to chosen individuals in view of the over-all good of the Church. This simple definition shows us that here we leave the realm of general morality, which concerns the general effects of grace for the sanctification of mankind in general and each of its members, and enter the field of particular morality, i.e. that part of morality which is preoccupied with concrete, individual action—showing its vitality and its finality (tract on charismata), relating it to this or that kind of life or activity (tract on functions, offices and states).

Within this framework St. Thomas assigned a place of distinction to the charismata. It is regrettable that he has had so few imitators among theologians, and that his text itself has inspired so few commentaries. Let us briefly point out the origin of the question and what theological tradition more clearly teaches us on the subject of the charismata. We will then show what charismata are in themselves, then what the different levels are in which they are found, or the order of activity to which they belong. Finally, we will conclude with a few remarks concerning their moral value.

I. Origin and Development of the Doctrine

1. The first epistle of St. Paul to the Corinthians contains a whole passage devoted to "spiritual gifts" or charismata (12-14), which, if we join to it parallel passages,[1] is the "theological locus" of the question. Not that the charismatic phenomenon had special significance for the Pauline Churches founded in the midst of the Gentiles; the Gospels [2] and the Acts of the Apostles [3] attest to the action of the Spirit which is properly charismatic. But at Corinth more than anywhere else, the development taken by manifestations of this kind was such that they threatened the order and the discipline of the

[1] Rom. 12:3-8; Eph. 4:7-16; cf. I Pet. 4:10-11.
[2] Mk. 16:17-18; Lk. 21:15; Mt. 17:19, etc.
[3] Acts 2:1-13; 5:12; 6:10; 9:31, etc.

Church; it also affected certain aspects of Christian morality and even of dogma—notably that expression of the collective life of the Church in Christ which has received the name of the Mystical Body.

2. Was a phenomenon which seems so essential to the life and to the constitution of the Church doomed to disappear with the mystical enthusiasm characteristic of Christian origins? The Fathers of the Church were able only to establish the transiency of the charismata, at least in the collective form which they appear to have assumed in the Pauline communities. On the other hand, they delighted in attesting the permanence of the action of the Spirit in the Church, being manifested notably by wondrous deeds, whose apologetic value was indisputable. To the faithful who were endowed with these signal graces (prophecy, revelations, visions, working of miracles, etc.), they did not fail to recall with St. Paul their true end: common interest (I Cor. 12:7), moderation in keeping with their custom (Rom. 12:3), primacy of charity and of sanctifying grace (I Cor. 12:29).

From the testimony of the Fathers, it also follows that the efflorescence, even the manner of distribution and the exercise of the charismata, are not unrelated to the level of the Church's prevailing fervor in a given period. It is an exact indication and one which shows that the charismata, as they are seen in St. Paul, are not to be taken as absolute—let us go so far as to say invariable—notes of a scale which either would be repeated indefinitely according to the same tonalities or would cease altogether. These are rather manifestations of the Spirit, of a special order which it will be fitting to determine, whose rhythm and modalities are adapted to the necessities of the life of the Church.

3. In the Middle Ages the glossarists and commentators of St. Paul themselves give witness, indirectly at least, to this truth. Interpreting the text of St. Paul in relation to the state or decree of the Church which was under their very eyes, they assimilate one part of the charismata to ecclesiastical offices or functions. Again, they emphasize the exceptional character of the charismata which, like the gift of miracles and the gift of prophecy, fit in the category of the miraculous.

Theologians of the 12th and 13th centuries were first interested in the mystical aspect of the charismata. They wondered whether or not each of them constituted a gift of the Spirit, in the active sense of the word; that is, a grace by which the Spirit gives Himself to the subject as it happens with sanctifying grace and with the aforesaid gifts of the Holy Spirit. Considering the lack of inner consistency of the charismata and their essential relationship to the Christian collectivity, for whose service they are granted, the answer can only be negative. At the same time, the charismata belong to sanctifying grace and are on a lower plane than the latter. This is also the position which they occupy in the *Summa Theologiae* (Ia IIae, q. 111, a. 1) and which they seem to have kept ever since. When, farther on (IIa IIae, q. 171 to 178), St. Thomas broaches the subject of the charismata specifically and for their own sake, he is trying to work out a synthesis—he relates them all or almost all to the gift of prophecy—rather than an analysis according to their own nature which would disengage the elements which enter into their structure. This second aspect of the theological task is no less important than the first. Until the present it does not seem to have caught the attention of the theologian.

4. In modern times, the charismata are enjoying a return to favor in the camp of the apologists and mystics. For the former, because of the preternatural character in which they mostly appear, they furnish weapons for the fight against rationalism. Considered from this angle, miracles, prophecies and other charismatic phenomena which accompany Revelation take on the value of *signs* of God's intervention which clearly manifests itself in them. That is to say, attention is here turned less toward the charismata themselves than toward Revelation, for which they are witnesses. Speaking analogically, it is the same when the charismata come under the rule of mystical theology. Here, the charismata are valued for their indication of sanctity; they appear as "the concomitant sign of election to plenary grace" (M. Lot-Borodine) without their demonstrative value being always and strictly absolute.

For its part, moral theology scarcely treats of the charismata except in an appendix to sanctifying grace and in order to underline their inferiority in relation to the latter. Keeping in mind common usefulness rather than the good of the subject, the charismata do not directly affect the sanctification and the spiritual progress of the individual exercising them. Consequently, the idea that is formed of one's salvation and roads leading to it is limited and strictly individualistic and therefore it is not difficult to neglect the charismata as being an accessory part of the theological system. It has happened in the course of these last decades that the charismata have had to fight, if not for their existence—they have not ceased to exist in the living consciousness maintained by the Church and animated by the Holy Spirit—at least for recognition on the part of theologians. Father Prat doubtless was only expressing the tacit "consensus" of the writers of his generation, when he wrote: "Granted by reason of the common good rather than on behalf of individuals, the charismata could one day disappear without depriving the Church of any indispensable organ." [4]

5. Does not part of the embarrassment experienced today by the theologian who treats of the charismata come from the fact that he is obliged to prove the existence of his object in the measure in which he attempts to explain it and to discover the secret resources of it? More often therefore he resigns himself to speak of the charismata in the past, lest he incur the reproach of archaism—in a word, to leave the matter to biblical or positive theology. Contemporary opinion seems, however, more and more disposed not only to recognize in speculative theology a rightful place for the charismata, but to make a rather large place for it.

Is it necessary to speak of a return to the viewpoint of St. Thomas, which puts the charismata in the very heart of his moral synthesis whose mystical aspect they reveal? Absolutely not. Rather, we are sensitive to the vital, organic aspects of the charismata which, you will have noticed, are constantly associated by St. Paul with the idea of the "Mystical Body." The charismata play an essential role in the internal development and external expansion of the Church considered as Mystical Body.

The recent Encyclical "Mystici Corporis Christi" confirms this belief. It is not content, in fact, to praise the "charismatics, those men with the marvelous gifts, whose presence will never be lacking in the church." [5] It links the charismata to the immanent and revivifying action of the Holy Spirit, the soul of the Church. "It is the Spirit of our Redeemer, who, as a source of graces, gifts and all the charismata, refills the Church for ever and internally, and acts upon her." [6] We shall be all the more curious to investigate this idea of charism of which, in retrospect, we have already given several outlines. In order to do this more earnestly, we shall first distinguish

[4] P. Prat, La Theologie de saint Paul, 1920, vol. I, p. 521.
[5] P. 11, French edition.
[6] P. 34.

the different orders of the charismata, and try later to unite them under a common denominator.

II. Various Kinds of Charismata: Nature of the Charismata

A. Analytical Aspect of the Doctrine

As they are shown to us in St. Paul and theological tradition, the charismata are distributed among the various orders or collective levels of existence and of activity in the Church.

1. IN THE ORDER OF WORSHIP

(a) According to their first and original expression, the charismata are related to the development of "worship in spirit and in truth," as it took concrete form in the Church or, rather, in the Christian congregation. In that spirit we must read chapters twelve to fourteen of the First Epistle to the Corinthians.

The charismatic function which goes by the name of "speaking in tongues" and which has something of almost mystical virtuosity about it, belongs to the part of the service called "assemblies of words," a prelude to the eucharistic worship. Already the gift of tongues granted to the Apostles on the day of Pentecost had for its end to glorify God and to extol His benefits for the various classes of listeners (Acts 2:11). The "speaking in tongues" or "glosses" (idomatic expressions, at times scarcely articulated sounds), wrongly confused with the miracle of Pentecost, of which it was only a rather pale substitute, had also a very marked ecstatic character. It was directed toward the praise of the greatness of God, too exclusively so to the liking of St. Paul, who complains about the lack of communication established between his subject and the audience, and of the lack of spiritual edification which resulted from it. Sensational as this gift was in certain aspects, so highly prized by the Corinthians, it was nonetheless judged on the common level of its general usefulness, therefore indicative of a certain real poverty. And St. Paul, for tactical reasons, was inclined to depreciate it still more.

(b) In our thinking here is revealed an essential aspect of the charismata which has been too neglected ever since. The charismata are an ornament of the Church, the temple of the Holy Ghost, the Spouse of Christ, the assembly of the faithful gathered together for the glory of the Father. Without our having already penetrated "beyond the veil," the charismata allow us to discern, beneath the shadows which surround them, the true reality of the Church. In her, the fullness of grace which is in Christ is poured out and "is manifested," "expressed," in the exact sense of the word which exceeds the simple meaning. The charismata tend precisely to act out this expression, revealing certain potentialities of the grace which, without them, would remain veiled in mystery. Imperfect though it may appear, compared to the brilliant light of the beyond, this Revelation, nevertheless, makes us sense the glorious state for which the Church is promised and to which she reaches out unceasingly as toward the term of that spiritual stature of which the charismata themselves are one of the most efficacious signs (Eph. 4:12-16). With these various titles, the charismata have more than a mystical flavor: they surround the Church with an eschatological halo.

More immediately, however, the effusion of the Holy Spirit on the early Church, distinguished by the gift of tongues, marked the beginning of the messianic era, which, as we know, contains in it a promise of eternity.

(c) The early Church, which was content to appear as the organ for the praise of God on earth in the hands of the Spirit, received in abundance the gifts of speech, in the category of "glossolalia," or speaking in various tongues, thanks to which she translated her inner religious emotions into inspired language. In proportion as the worshipping congregations became more numerous and worship was disciplined, or if we may express it thus, rationalized (Rom. 12:1; I Pet. 2:2), the words of mystical praise and of mutual edification, which were described in the First Epistle to the Corinthians, had to give way to more sober, hieratic forms of worship. The most notable of these have been preserved in the liturgy.

St. John Chrysostom notes this transition in a passage stamped however, with a certain bitterness. St. Paul had said: "Such are my instructions for all the Churches of the saints." About this the former writes: "Can one conceive anything more horrifying than these words? Yes, the Church was then a heaven; the Spirit ruled her as master, He directed and inspired each one of her dignitaries. Today there remain for us only the symbols and remains of these gifts. In fact, in our days also, we speak each one in turn, two or three, and when one is silent the other begins (cf. Cor. 14:27). But these are only signs and a commemoration of what was happening then. Therefore when we pronounce the prayers the people respond: with thy Spirit (Spiritu tuo), as if to signify that formerly they spoke thus, moved not by their own wisdom, but rather by the Spirit, which has ceased to exist, at least as far as I am concerned." [7]

(d) But if the Christian congregations have lost much of this "pneumatic" character which they had originally—there remains, nevertheless, a part of inspiration in the texts of Holy Scripture and liturgical works themselves—the charismata have not ceased to be what they were then. The most exalted spiritual gifts which are the allotment of mystical souls (spiritual prayer, discourse on wisdom and science, etc.) perpetuate this note of esctatic praise, these souls who personify the Church on earth by what comes closest to the celestial Church, who are wholly concerned with the praise of God. In their turn, the gift of miracles, the gift of prophecy and other marvelous gifts which set in action the omnipotence, the knowledge and the infinite sanctity of God, are made up of these attributes like partial revelations (as much as possible in the scale of created being) which have no other end than to allow creatures to glorify God in His works.

2. IN THE ORDER OF DOCTRINE

(a) The intellectualism of St. Thomas and his school has thrown a bright light on the doctrinal character of the charismata. "The charismata," states the former, "are a function of faith and of the spiritual doctrine which they aspire to manifest" (IIIa, q. 7, a. 7). Suarez sees them "as accidents or instruments of faith." It is this aspect which tempts us to group them around prophetic illumination, of which they are as so many emanations, faith having no other effect than to engender in us a certitude equivalent to that which springs up spontaneously in the consciousness of the prophet.

We can push the analysis further and try to underline the role which devolves upon each charism in that work of divine pedagogy, which, in the wake of Revelation itself, constitutes Christian catechism. On the doctor of the Church the Holy Ghost bestows, with full knowledge of the things of faith, the means of informing others about them (gifts of elocution); then He makes up for the lack of evidence and rational proofs with signs (gifts of miracles); finally, He suppresses accidental obstacles raised by the disparity of language between the preacher and his audience. On the whole, we see

[7] *Hom.*, XXXVI, n. 4, *P.G.*, vol. 61, col. 312.

a classification of the charismata according to the manner and categories of teaching, which would almost be the following one.[8]

(b) Division of the charismata according to their object, defined as the instruction of one's neighbor in matters of faith:

I. They give the power of stating divine things.
- *faith* or special certitude about fundamentals made communicative.
- *word of wisdom:* shows the principal conclusions known by the First Cause.
- *word of knowledge:* illustrates divine realities with the aid of examples and effects taken from secondary causes.

II. They confirm Divine Revelation
- by works
  - gift of *healing*
  - gift of *miracles.*
- by knowledge
  - *prophecy*
  - *discerning of spirits.*

III. They assist in preaching the Word of God
- *gift of tongues*
- *interpretation*

(c) If such is the case, we are not far from the thought of St. Paul in affirming that in the Church the charismata are linked to magisterial teaching, whose efficacy and infallible rectitude they assure. The "charism of infallibility" transmitted to the ecclesiastical Magisterium in the exercise of its high office [9] lies in this context. In any case, it is in facilitating and in supporting the proposition of revealed truth that the charismata achieve their end, i.e. inner growth of the Mystical Body and its outward extension. And because there is no Christian, especially in modern times, who is not called to do some work (whether as a catechist and teacher in regard to Christians insufficiently instructed, or as witness to the Christian truth, announcer and propa-

[8] Cf. Sum. Theol., Ia IIae, q. III, a. 4. Beginnings and conclusions are taken from the analogy of the sciences; here they directly designate articles of faith and subsidiary truths.

[9] *Conc. Vatic.,* sess. IV, chap. 4, Denz.-Bannw. 1837.

gandist of the Gospels with respect to unbelievers), neither is there anyone, not even a layman, who may not some day lay claim to the charismatic assistance of the Spirit. Doubtless this assistance is graduated and specified according to the personality of the subject, the form and necessities of the teaching of faith, and it remains, in any case, unforeseen and mysterious (Jn. 3:8). This much is certain: to it must be attributed first of all, the inner assurance and fullness of conviction, then the clearness and efficacy of the testimony of the confirmed Christian.

(d) But the activity of the charismata goes beyond the realm of everyday faith. They are also, we have said, at the service of "spiritual doctrine." By this we must understand the spiritual paths which, blazed by the saints, attract souls enamored of perfection. While enhancing the virtue of the saints, the charismata, or particular graces of a mystical order, consecrate it in our eyes; at the same time, they sanction the value pattern of example which sanctity possesses and the value of doctrine included, or annexed to it, as is the case with the masters of spiritual doctrine.

3. IN THE ORDER OF CORPORATE LIFE

Or the order of the organic functions and collective tasks and services of the Church.

(a) Finally, the charismata are affected by an entire order of duties, functions, services, whose end is to procure the spiritual (even the material, but in conjunction with the spiritual) welfare of the faithful. St. Paul brings it to mind by a word when he inserts "services of help, power of administration" in his catalogue of the charismata (I Cor. 12:28). In a Church in reduced circumstances, the common good scarcely presented any complications, and in the meantime, the Apostle is not afraid of attributing the benefit of a charism to first one and then another who dedicate themselves to it. How many more must there be like this in an age where the Church has become coextensive with the Universe, and where the good of the whole can be procured only by a multitude of functions and services ordered among themselves and graded.

The sacred functions are assuredly the most typical, and there is no reason to refuse their bearers not only the privilege of a sacramental grace or of a grace according to their state in life, but, in the strict sense, the privilege of a charism. Except for these functions, how many are there who, having been immediately aroused by the Holy

Spirit and corresponding to the needs of the Church at certain time, should also be able to claim for themselves a charism? At times even these attempts (which are only too soon declared to be happy and truthful) are normalized, socialized, and regulated, just as charitable works and associations are. Others live rather in the state of movements or of currents (apostolic movements, spiritual, liturgical, biblical currents, etc.). There is, without a doubt, in these various forms of the ecclesiastical activity in which the laity participate, a charismatic manifestation of the Spirit. Can we define it and within what limits must we circumscribe the operations of the charismata?

(b) The charism has for effect:

i. to arouse the vocation to such a permanent state or form of life as to have canonical status in the Church (priestly state, religious state) or to an expectation of such status in the case of categories of works or of activities to which we may dedicate ourselves in a transitory way;

ii. once the call is received, to *orient* the activity of the subject toward such a privileged aspect of the real common good of the Church, to be sought for individually or in conjunction with others of the faithful who have heard the same "vocational" call.

iii. to assign to this activity its *norm* and its *rhythm* by a secret instinct, the Holy Spirit remaining master of the activity of the Mystical Body and of each one of its members, whatever may be the domain over which it is exerted: thought or action, worship or apostolate.

iv. to impregnate the efforts displayed by those who throw themselves into a task; e.g. of edification and spiritual renovation, of missionary propaganda, or again of charitable assistance, whose amplitude and difficulty certainly go beyond the means which they arrange. Let us note that what *efficacy* is in the category of speech, *fecundity* is in that of action. These, then, are the two most striking aspects of the work of the charismata.

Such are the different levels in the life of the Church on which the charismata are found. We may state, at the close of this rapid examination, that if the present day Church yields to the early Church with regard to the charismata of the first order, she triumphs over her regarding the charismata of the third order, while the charismata of the second order (prophecies, miracles) represent rather the constancy of the charismatic phenomenon. By this title the foundation of Christian Apologetics is laid.

There is, moreover, in the sum total of the manifestations in the life of the Church, a charismatic aspect which, with the Vatican Council, permits the Church herself to be considered "as a great and perpetual motive for credibility—in the admirable method of its propagation, its outstanding sanctity and its inexhaustive fecundity in every species of goods, its unity joined to its catholicity, its invincible stability."[10]

The charismata are, as a matter of fact, both ornaments which cause the sanctity of the Church to shine and forces which assure her stability; actually many rather than one in their source, they are factors both of unity and of catholicity. Finally, they coincide directly with the propagation of the Gospels and with the extension of the Mystical Body.

B. Synthetic Aspect of the Doctrine

1. INSTRUMENTAL FUNCTION OF THE CHARISMATA

(a) Can we proceed and gather under a common denominator the spiritual phenomena which have just been briefly mentioned? Here theology, it seems to me, hesitates and starts to stammer. It has no specific name at all for designating the charismata. So, it stops at the generic term grace, which it multiplies as it were by itself: grace freely given (gratia gratis data). Such is the classic name of the charismata according to the terminology honored by the Scholastics. This name means less by what it affirms, namely the gratuity of the supernatural dispensations, than by what it denies, namely that between sanctifying grace, common to all regenerated souls, and grace "freely given," there is no ambiguity, but rather there exists a certain affinity, a community of nature which permits them to be classed within the same category. They are both equally an effect of divine favor; at one time it overtakes human nature, raises it up and transforms it from within (sanctifying grace); then again it speaks rather to the personality and, without substantially modifying it, takes hold of it for a moment and turns its activity toward an immediate spiritual good to be procured for the benefit of the Mystical Body.

(b) This means that charism does not designate a stable disposition conferred on a subject with a view to elevating it in the scale of being and activity (habitus), but, rather, a fleeting, transitory movement, which, passing through its words or its gestures, causes them instrumentally to produce an effect which surpasses their natural vir-

[10] *Conc. Vatic.,* sess. III, chap. 3; Denz-Bannw. 1794.

tue. This effect is first of all of a physical order, hence the miracle; but it can also be of a moral nature (for the charismatic scope extends that far) namely, the soul's conversion. But it would be well to distinguish here that which depends on the immediate action of the Holy Spirit and that which represents the original contribution of the human agent, i.e. preacher or apostle.

The latter, working on minds and hearts through persuasion, expands beyond his catechesis; that is, seeks to impress them favorably and to incline them to the faith, but he cannot move them completely. The Spirit who seconds his efforts—using this display of truth in order to work in the innermost part of the soul and to make understood the "consolation" or inner word—is the real mover of conversion. The charismata are not instrumentally, then, causes of faith, for the same reason that we say of the sacraments that they cause grace instrumentally. They have no less a real virtue, of an intentional kind, and being inserted into the process which leads to conversion, they influence the latter, at least by virtue of a disposing cause.

Thus they are indeed "manifestations of the Spirit in view of the common good" (I Cor. 12:7), at least in that sense in which they give to the Divine Spirit the opportunity to be manifest and to act sovereignly. At times we shall attribute to them the total outcome; i.e. the edification of the Church in faith and charity (Eph. 4:13-15); but at times we shall also try not to consider the series of secondary causes and of the created intermediate ones which the Spirit uses in order to better attain His ends, and we shall attribute the merit of the result obtained directly to the interior action of the latter; cf. Acts 9:31: "The Church was in peace and was being built up, walking in fear of the Lord, and it was filled with the consolation of the Holy Spirit."

2. CHARISMATA, GIFTS OF THE HOLY GHOST, AND GRACE OF STATE

(a) The sublimity of the work accomplished contrasts undoubtedly with the scarcity of the charismata. Is it not because the charismata have a "wilful" being, fleeting, transient, that we have so much trouble in defining their nature? In order to define them, it is necessary to be able to determine them, but to determine them would be to take away from them their quality of instrumental movements whose entire value of being goes back to the sources from which they are drawn, that is, the sovereign virtue of the Holy Spirit (I. Cor. 12:4). Even now we are already closing the gap which separates the charismata from the gifts of the Holy Ghost, as also from those graces which take on a special aspect and with which we have at times, and often wrongly, confused them, namely, the graces of one's state of life.

(b) Gifts are "habitus" or permanent supernatural dispositions, deep-rooted in us, which make us ready to receive the movements of the Holy Ghost and to let ourselves be carried by them. When these movements are felt, our faculties, thus sublimated, adopt them and conform to their modalities or to their rhythm. The result is an effect which correctly belongs in the order of personal sanctification. With the charismata the result is quite different. Here the touch of the Holy Spirit catches us unawares; it touches us lightly, and passes through us rather than affecting us. Beyond our own person it sights an effect whose amplitude greatly surpasses our comprehension, namely, the collective sanctification of the Church. Nevertheless, because this is the same Spirit who works through gifts and through charismata, and because He takes into consideration, in the progress of His action, the law of human psychology, we shall see that the charism will have for its object to communicate to others what the soul has acquired under the influence of the gift—from the words of wisdom and of knowledge and of the discerning of spirits, correlative to the gifts of the same species (wisdom, knowledge, counsel).

(c) In their turn, the graces of one's state of life (vocational graces) furnish a new division. Their name suggests that the organism of virtue is modeled, in its concrete determinations, on the state or condition of the person; upon the latter are grafted accidental aids or actual graces which allow the subject to meet virtuously the circumstances in which he is placed according to the whims of fate. In all this it is only a question of individual behavior. It is otherwise with the charismata belonging to society—which have in view certain effects concerning the spiritual common good of believers and which affect individuals as well as members of the Church. For the same reason, we shall distinguish in charism the disposition imprinted by the sacraments of confirmation and of Holy Orders, although here again these realities often overlap, and although there may be reason to see in every priest or confirmed layman faithful to his vocation, a "pneumatic" (spiritual) being. The disposition is concerned with the liturgical validity of the actions which it lays down and which result in Christian worship. On the other hand, charism properly concerns the efficacy of Christian testimony.

(d) Finally, it appears that the charismatic phenomenon, thus defined with respect to the instrumental motion of the Holy Spirit, is two-fold: subjectively, it is translated in the mind of the one who is the beneficiary by a special kind of assurance (of which we find many traces in the Acts of the Apostles and the Epistles of St. Paul) which may be illustrated in numerous ways (charismatic certitude of faith; knowledge of revelation in the prophet; assurance in the preacher; confirmation in grace in the mystic). Objectively, it is manifest by the quality, also special, of the result obtained: miracle (physical order); efficacy of testimony or of preaching, and success of work (moral order).

3. TRUE EVALUATION OF THE CHARISMATIC PHENOMENON

(a) From the preceding considerations it is apparent that the charismata are inseparable from the action of the Holy Ghost who illumines, impregnates and animates the Church, builds it from within and urges it to greater expansion without. The charismata are like the points of greatest intensity of an action diffused throughout the entire body of the Church and which, in order to attain more surely its ends, is distributed among its various members and chooses certain ones of them in preference to others so as to make them the instrument of a more efficacious action. That is to say, if the perpetual presence of the Holy Spirit in the bosom of the Church is undeniable—denying it would be to go back to questioning the spiritual nature of the Church —it is subject to certain vicissitudes, to changes of administration and changes of method which coincide with the different moods which are made responsive by the constant assistance of the Holy Spirit.

(b) An invariable law, however, presides over the distribution of the charismatic forces within the Mystical Body of the Church, that is, the law of the communication of truth which normally is established among the various members of the Mystical Body, and which aims beyond the Church at the world—more generally, the law of collaboration and of mutual aid in view of salvation. The charismata have no other end, in fact, but to contribute to the collective return of redeemed mankind toward the Triune God, seconding the attempts which set in motion or accelerate this process and supplying what is lacking in our natural possibilities, even though enriched by grace. As this return is not accomplished by chance and without order, the beings closest to God, by grace or by office, will take the greatest part in it. In the Church, the hierarchy, who are the best instructed Christians, having come of age in the faith (maiores), will also be those who will be most endowed with the charismata. St. Paul had called for moderation; St. Thomas preaches order. "All which proceeds from God, is accomplished with order" (Ia IIae, q. 111, a. 1; cf. Rom. 13:1). Order governs the very principle of distribution of the charismata, and measures it by the rule of usage. Finally, the cooperation of man with man in the work of salvation rests on the collaboration of God with man in view of a particular saving effect to be obtained.

Far from being an obstacle, we see how much the graces "gratis datae" contribute to increase in each member of the Mystical Body the radiance of his charity and of his personal grace. The charity of one member includes virtually all the others, and, thanks to it, a communication of spiritual goods (prayers, merits, satisfactions) is established among all those who are united by the same supernatural bonds. The wholly gratuitous graces concern rather a basic exchange—communication in faith and revealed truth, which is the origin of the other. That is why they contribute not only to the edification of the Mystical Body, but to its external growth by the addition of new members. Nevertheless, the fact remains that it is indeed through the charismata, and not immediately through charity, that St. Paul proposed and developed the analogy of the Mystical Body (loc. cit.).

(c) Again going beyond this framework, we are allowed, following St. Thomas (*C. Gentiles*, bk. III, ch. CLIV), to contemplate the charismatic phenomenon as a moment in a more general phenomenon which envelops the entire universe, angelic creatures not at all excepted. The believer is not an isolated being; he is a part of an organized universe; he is hemmed in on all sides by forces which have the same origin and same end as he; he also has to defend himself against influences which tend to draw him aside from the straight path of spiritual progress. These interactions take different names according to the level of being on which one is placed: in the case of the angels, they bear the name of illumination; in the case of men, charismatic action. In proportion to the interference of the bad angels, one part of this last group will be turned aside so as to produce a virtue of discernment (gift of discerning of spirits), while the good angels will act upon the elite of the charismatics by way of prophetic illumination (IIa IIae, q. 172, a. 2). On the same level with the human race, the charismata will facilitate communication, not only of man to man, but of one generation to another. With Holy Scripture and Tradition serving as a link between believing generations, the charism of *inter-*

pretation, correlative of initial *inspiration,* will maintain or will restore understanding of them.

Briefly, in this field of conjecture extended to the dimensions of the universe, the charismata acquire a cosmic significance. Now, in this universe Christ occupies the summit: the fullness of the charismata also falls to Him as "to the first Doctor and Principle of faith" (IIIa, q. 7, a. 7). "Of this fullness we have all received, grace for grace," and charism for charism (cf. Eph. 4:16; St. Thomas *loc. cit.*). It behooves us to lend ourselves to this influx and to the charismatic action itself. Because they provide us with the means of collaborating efficaciously in the collective good of redeemed humanity, the charismata postulate for us not only the rectitude of the will, but a certain promise of ourselves in the service of the common good which meets the spontaneous tendency of grace and charity ("gratia tendens in alios" said St. Thomas). Herein lies their moral value.

III. Moral Value of the Charismata

A. Criteria of the Moral Value of the Charismata

1. It is not in vain that we have classified the charismata within the framework of moral theology. St. Paul himself, when he touches on the subject, does so as a man preoccupied above all with safeguarding authentic moral values. "Now concerning spiritual gifts, brethren," he writes, "I would not have you ignorant. You know that when you were Gentiles, you went to dumb idols according as you were led. Wherefore I give you to understand that no one speaking in the Spirit of God says 'Anathema' to Jesus. And no one can say 'Jesus is Lord,' except in the Holy Spirit" (I Cor. 12:1-4). This is to put the faithful on guard against any counterfeiting of these gifts, as sometimes happens not only with the pagans but in the case of the mystics. The test of the authenticity of the charismata shall be the true faith as the Church preserves the depository of it (Cf. Rom. 12:3). Hence, no one can invoke some "pneumatic" impulse or mystical communication and go against this norm which regulates the function of each charism.

2. That is not all. The charismata, ordered at the same time for the edification and for the good of the whole Church, are unable to oppose one another. Common finality, in dictating to each its needs, assigns at the same time the law of its behavior. And since the attainment of such a lofty end is not in the power of one alone, but rather

of all working together, and each in his place, under the motion of the Holy Ghost, we expect each charismatic to be faithful to his particular vocation and to live strictly along the line which is indicated by the Holy Spirit. This will be the means of administering to all the gift which has been received, according to the instructions of St. Peter: "According to the gift that each has received, administer it to one another as good stewards of that manifold grace of God" (I Pet. 4:10; cf. Rom. 12:6).

From this viewpoint again, the charism falls under a rule which, in assigning to it the sphere of activity beyond which it cannot spread, helps to sanction its moral value. It is for having transgressed this rule and for having forgotten that they were only individuals in the services of the Christian group, although magnificently gifted, that the glossologists of Corinth saw themselves called to order by St. Paul. The danger of mystical individualism has not disappeared since that time. Originally, the sects which gravitated toward the Catholic Church may have possessed an authentic charism which the beneficiary then abused by setting up, for instance, as a general and always valid maxim, that which could and should only be the spiritual experience of a subject placed in those given conditions and in a given environment.

3. That is why, among all the charismata, there is one which is recommended to us as having a higher moral value, and this is the gift of discerning of spirits. In the charismatic organism it holds an analogous place to that which goes back to prudence and to the gift of counsel in the order of virtues. That is, it belongs to it not only in distinguishing true inspirations of the Holy Spirit from false ones (attributable to the spirit of lying), but again in discriminating between what is suggested by the Spirit of God everywhere and always infallibly, and that which proceeds from the very sense which is subject to error. (So it is with the prophet.) Also useful to whoever receives a call from the Holy Spirit for determining a true "vocation," it permits him to determine in advance the proper course of his action among the multiple activities of the Mystical Body and put his entire life under the control and rule of the Holy Spirit. Finally, invaluable for a simple believer, this gift is most earnestly required by the hierarchy, to whom it comes as a last resort for judging the authenticity of the charismata and for orientating them, each one in its class and according to its own measure, toward the common end, i.e. the spiritual good of the Church.

4. Lastly, what permits us to state that the charismata have a deeply moral value, if not the fact that their dynamism, powerful and original though it is, does not suppress the exercise of human freedom. St. Paul affirmed this about the charism in which divine inspiration was the most apparent—the grace of prophecy: "The spirits of the prophets are subject to the prophets" (I Cor. 14:32). We shall recognize then, the authentic charismatic Christian by these signs: docility to the Holy Spirit, respect for the norm, and lively feeling for the exigencies of the common good, to which the exercise of the charismata is subordinated.

B. Charismata and Hierarchy

1. It is in this spirit that we must tackle the question of the relationship of the charismata with the hierarchy. A celebrated question which is asked especially apropos Christian antiquity, but which, in truth, belongs to all ages.

We might have asked whether the charismatics of whom St. Paul speaks, and especially the triad of the teaching Church (Apostles, prophets, and doctors), took the place of a hierarchy at a time when the Holy Spirit ruled as master in the Church and when the distinction between authority and charism was still not very pronounced. Within the limits of this article it is not possible to throw light on a difficulty which is due more to the absence of texts for the period of the early days of the Church than to the very nature of things. Let it suffice for us to remark that above the little world of the charismatics of Corinth towers the immense height of the Apostle who united in his person both grace and authority, the latter received by a direct mandate from Christ. Do we not hold here the key to the solution: the development of the hierarchy within the Church, from the early apostolic group?

2. But the question of the relationship of the charismata with the hierarchy has more than a historic interest. It brings face to face two principles which belong equally to the essence of the Church and which compose her very complex structure: the *personal* principle and the *institutional* principle. We have said that in opposition to sanctifying grace (which qualifies nature in us), the charism is attached to the person of the Christian. In other words, the charism, while sublimating original aptitudes, depends on them and on what concerns the very personality of the subject that which makes it individual and irreducible to any other than itself. We can affirm it, moreover, without deny-

ing the gratuity and transcendence of the charismata, for at the origin
of these dispositions peculiar to each one we must place God's ordination. According to the remark of Cajetan: "God did not choose
Moses, David, Isaiah, Jeremiah in order to make prophets of them,
because He found a suitable disposition in them." But rather: "According His gifts to each one subject to His good pleasure, and especially to the prophets, who are the object of a more attentive selection,
God has turned them toward this gift conferring on them the fitting
disposition." (Comm. on IIa IIae, q. 172, a. 3, no. II.)

This truth finds quite a wide field of application in the charismata
of the last order which enables certain offices or functions indispensable to community life to be filled within the Church. If it is true that
the charismata are governed in their exercise by the law of this whole,
the fact remains that they constitute for each subject a particular vocation, which corresponds to his inner aspirations and to the reactions
of his soul to the presence of God, who speaks to him. "Wherever
this contact with the Lord with the individual is established, as we
think is normal, so that a call results from it, we are dealing with a
beginning of an authentic charism, discreet, silent and rudimentary
though it may seem" (H. Rahner).

3. Does not the exercise of a charism risk encountering an order
constituted outside of itself whose guardian is the hierarchy? And,
consequently, will not the individual be urged to choose between his
loyalty to the Holy Spirit and the duty of obedience to the hierarchy?
It is an especially painful choice, which we would like to think is
chimeric, if history itself did not show us its lessons here on earth.
Let us think of the example of a Joan of Arc and a Margaret Mary.
But the fact that momentary conflicts can arise between charismatics
and representatives of the hierarchy does not weaken the law in any
way.

The later authorizes us to assert that charism and hierarchy, far
from being diametrically opposed to each other, complement and depend on one another, like two indispensable principles in the life of
the Church, one of which gives the stimulus, the other the direction.
Without the charismata, the Church would soon be no more than a
spiritual administration, always performing the same actions, and applying the same prescriptions, regardless of the actual exigencies of
the environment in which it is called to live and grow. On the other
hand, without the hierarchy, the charismata would produce strong

trends first in one direction, then another, held in place only by the inherent law of their progress, from which the individual may always escape, without any exterior link between them. It is true, then, that "the charismatic factor is incorporated into the very substance of the Church like an element of dynamic discontent, if not of revolutionary upheaval" (K. Rahner), yet it is a fact that it needs to be tempered by the hierarchical factor which balances it.

4. How is this harmony, this synthesis of two principles realized concretely? There is reason to think that if the Holy Spirit, being master of His gifts, dispenses them to whom He wishes, priests or laymen, He will take into consideration the general interests of the Church in giving them preferably to those who are entrusted with greater responsibilities. Thus it is that the teachings of the Church are endowed with the privilege of infallibility. The assistance of the Holy Spirit in the field of administration is shown also by inspirations or by illuminations which prepare for major decisions. From top to bottom in the hierarchy, the dignitaries who, urged on by the Holy Spirit, have entered upon an ecclesiastical career, know that for as long a time as they shall be faithful to the original call or "vocation," they will benefit from an assistance of the Holy Spirit which will double the efficacy of their word, will add to the inspiring strength of their example, will increase the productivity of their works, and, finally, will make them spiritual men. Laymen who in their turn, moved by the Holy Spirit, throw themselves into the conquest of the modern world with a view toward leading it back to Christ and the Church, need never fear to dovetail their efforts with those of the hierarchy. If, however, there are disagreements or differences of opinion, it is necessary to maintain that, according to the precedent created by St. Paul at Corinth, Authority does prevail.

It remains, then, for those who believe themselves entrusted with a mission or called to spread a new spirit to yield and to reconcile their action with the norm of the whole—as determined at each turning-point of history by the hierarchy. They can rely on the Holy Spirit to guarantee that the decisions of the hierarchy will do justice to their legitimate claims. Finally, the orderly growth of the Mystical Body and its unceasing expansion in the world, which include both stability and progress, depend strictly on the assistance which the two principles embodied by the charismata and the hierarchy give, and on the harmonious development which the two principles build up.

C. Charismata and Sanctity

1. If submission of the charismata to the law laid down by the hierarchy is not foreign to its moral value, that moral value will be perfectly established only when we have established the intimate relationship which exists between grace, "gratis data," and sanctifying grace, which is to say between the charismata and sanctity.

Here we must put an end to a misunderstanding. This concerns the Holy Spirit who shows His sovereign mastery and the gratuitousness of His gifts by using as instruments sinners as well as the just and who distributes His charismata as it pleases Him—to sinners as well as to saints. Since sanctifying grace is reserved for the just this misconception concludes that the charismata do not depend at all on grace, either in their distribution or in their modalities and their administration. This conclusion is unwarranted. Sinners, in fact, benefit from the charismata only by virtue of being members of the Church and by virtue of Christian truth held by the Church, to which they give witness, if not by their actions, at least, occasionally in their speech. The charismata are, then, the normal accompaniment of the total grace invested in the Church. So they manifested themselves at the first moment of her existence on the day of Pentecost and throughout the apostolic period, which, for the subsequent life of the Church, has normative value, i.e. the abundance of the charismata, which could be verified at that time, was like the magnificent fruit of collective fervor.

The case of the just who are endowed with the charismata furnishes the counterpart of this truth. With regard to sanctity, the charismata play only a subsidiary role, the proof being that in the beatification process, miracles and other spiritual or marvelous phenomena serve only as additional proof, sanctity being attested to by the heroic quality of virtues. What does this mean, if not that even in the saints the charismata show off the collective sanctity of the Church, whose distinguished members they are, rather than the personal sanctity of their owners? The Encyclical "Mystici Corporis Christi" expressly teaches this: "Certainly our pious Mother shines with a faultless light . . . in the heavenly graces and supernatural charismata by which she engenders with untiring fecundity innumerable troups of martyrs, confessors and virgins" (p. 36).

2. This is only natural. The charismata are properly divine effects which are impressed on certain privileged members of the Mystical

Body by the Holy Spirit, the soul of this Body. On the other hand, we may not forget that the presence of the Holy Ghost in the body of the Church is realized through sanctifying grace. His immanent motion being like a continuation of His presence, it is normal for the charismatic action to issue from the fullness of sanctifying grace and for it to be subject to the same variations as the former. To periods of fervor in the Church will correspond, then, moments of charismatic brilliance.

What is true concerning the Catholic Church as a whole, can be stated with as many reasons for each one of its parts or cells (the parish), or for the movements and currents which are born and develop in her bosom; their apostolic efficacy will ordinarily be a function of the fervor of their members. Finally, even in individuals this statement can be verified. The Holy Spirit is pleased to visit and to fill with His charismata those souls most united to God by charity. Thanks to them, the potentialities contained in charity are given free play and are indicated by results on the order of those which we have described. St. Thomas hints at it: "When in effect the virtue of charity is intensified, then by the same reason of charity, the subject obtains the collation of a new effect of grace (usus gratiae), such as the gift of miracles or that of conquering all temptations without difficulty, or any other spiritual gift of this kind" (in *Sent.*, D. XX, q. 5, a. 1, sol. 2).

It is no less true that by virtue of the law of association of Christians in the Mystical Body, the charismata do not necessarily ask for any charity in their immediate subject, and, in any case, the moral value of the charismata "which disappear" is subordinated to that of the charity "which remains" (I Cor. 13:8).

REFLECTIONS AND PERSPECTIVES

"Charism," in the meaning in which it is theologically understood, is by definition a favor freely given to a soul, not in view of its sanctification, but for the good of the universal Christian community. There is danger, nevertheless, under a pretext of obtaining clear and distinct ideas, of separating these two finalities too much. It is "normal" for the charism which is destined to sanctify a great number of souls to begin by sanctifying the one who is its subject. The preacher is the first beneficiary of his own preaching. It happens that the Church discerns false charismatic favors while affirming the malice of the subject apparently laden down with favors. If, therefore, theology explains the charismatic phenomenon by the "good of the community," that does not mean that the good of the favored soul may be excluded from it.

It is, moreover, a general law in ecclesiology that one must distinguish but never separate the hierarchical principle of administration and the principle of spiritual assistance, or "pneumatic" principle. There is no opposition between the gifts of the Holy Spirit and the government of souls. Authority is itself a charism and "pneumatic (spiritual) enthusiasm," if it truly comes from the Holy Spirit, will always be preserved from insubordinate illuminism. One and the same Spirit inspires Christians and their leaders, awakens spontaneities and controls their harmony. (Cf. L. M. Dewailly, *L'Esprit et les chrétiens dans l'Église du Christ*, in *Le Saint-Esprit, auteur de la vie spirituelle*, Paris, edition Cerf, 1944, p. 70. The entire article has been cited elsewhere.) On the activity of the social (and of the hierarchical) and of the spiritual elements in the Church, compare the studies of Y. Congar (a restatement of the problem which is out-of-date but easy to read, in *La Vie intellectuelle*, Nov. 1947, pp. 6-40), and *Notre communion fraternel*, in *La communion des saints*, 2nd part, Paris, edition Cerf, 1945.

Charismata in particular. Explain literally and theologically I Cor. 12:28-30; Eph. 4:11-16. Are the lists complete? Charismata in the early Church.

The charism of *apostolate* (cf. I Cor. 12:28). Meaning, theology. Who receives this grace? What does it entail? Definition of "apostolate."

The charism of *prophecy* (I Cor. 12:28). Meaning and theology. Prophecy may be, in the words of St. Paul (I Cor. 11:5) a grace given to women; cite examples in the Old and New Testaments. What is a prophet? What is prophecy? Is the prophet aware of all the truths that he teaches and of all the implications of what he says? Dispositions to be a prophet? A whole "treatise on prophecy," starting with the Scripture, should take place here.

Inspiration: How to recognize the books which are inspired and those which are not? History of the canon on the sacred books; definition of the scriptural canon; history of the determination of "inspired" books. What is inspiration? How does sacred inspiration differ from the natural assistance of God with the intellect in its action? Who should be called the author of a sacred book? Is there a prophetic inspiration different from scriptural inspiration? Definition of "sacred writer." To which faculties (intellect, will, executive power, etc.) does inspiration extend? Does inspiration extend to the compilator of the books which are inserted in this way in the Bible? Does inspiration affect the author who is simply quoted by the sacred writer? The author whom he mainly summarizes or whom he copies? Does inspiration extend to non-religious truths uttered by the sacred writer? Can we establish degrees in inspiration? or in prophecy? or in *revelation?*

Infallibility: To what does it extend? Definition. Who is the subject of it? *Meaning of the Scriptures:* literal meaning (definition), spiritual meaning (are they determined by the author? name, value, and use of these meanings), secondary, consequent, adaptable meanings (interest and value?) Ecclesiastical directives. Textual, historical *critiques.* Rules of exegesis. *Reading of the Bible.* Must one be inspired in order to read the Bible? Can everyone read the Bible and understand it? Reading of the Bible in the Church: rites, place and time of Bible reading. *Literary genres.* Should we distinguish literary genres in the reading of the Bible? How? Which ones? On all these questions, see especially St. Thomas, *La Prophétie,* French translation by P. Synare and P. Benoit, Paris, Ed. de la Rev. des J., 1947, in particular the second appendix of P. Benoit, pp. 269-376. The theology of the Word of God has just been revived in an excellent issue of *Lumière et vie* (no. 6): *L'Église et la Bible.* Read in particular M. E. Boismard, *La Bible, Parole de Dieu et Révélation.* On prophecy in the Old Testament, see the classical Biblical introductions: Vigouroux, Bacuez, Brassac, *Manuel biblique,* A. T. Paris, 14th edition, 1917–1920; L. Dennefeld, *Introduction à l'ancien Testament,* Paris, Bloud et Gay, 1934; A. Robert and A. Tricot, *Initiation biblique,* Paris, Desclée, 1939; J. Chaine, *Introduction à la lecture des prophètes.* For the New Testament, read L. M. Dewailly, *Jésus-Christ, Parole de Dieu,* Paris, edition Cerf, 1945. On Bible reading one should read especially C. Charlier, *La lecture chrétienne de la Bible,* Maredsous, 1950, and Th. G. Chifflot, *Que pouvons-nous trouver dans la Bible?* in *La Vie Spirituelle,* Oct. 1949, pp. 232-261. Nothing has been said yet on the regulation of biblical "reading" *in the Church*; a theology of this regulation could be made; one of the bases for it would be Lk. 4:17-21.

Private revelations. Nature, discernment. Does the Church canonize certain private revelations? Value of these revelations. Value of the revelations "of the Blessed Virgin" at Lourdes, La Salette, Fatima, etc. Read on this subject K. Rahner, *Notations théologiques sur les révélations privées,* in *Revue d'ascétique et de mystique,* no. 98-100,

Av. Déc. 1949; *Mélanges Marcel Viller,* pp. 506-514, and V. Bassett, J. Boutonier, *Faut-il croire aux révélations privées?* in *Suppl. de la Vie Spir.,* August, 1947, pp. 181-193.

On dreams and the premonitory value of dreams, consult D. J. Lhermitte, *Le sommeil,* Paris, A. Colin, 1931, and Dr. Osty, *La connaissance supra-normale,* Paris, Alcan, 1923. Theologically, it would be well to read especially the notes of I. Mennessier (especially pp. 402-404) in St. Thomas Aquinas, *Le Religion,* vol. II, Éd. de la Rev. des J., 1934, and Synave-Benoit, op. cit. Likewise on the prophecy of pagans and, in particular, the sybelline prophecies.

The charism of the *doctor of the faith* (I Cor. 12:28). Exegesis of the term doctor in St. Paul. Respective roles (throughout history and in theology) of priests and laymen in the teaching of the faith. (On this subject cf. Mandonnet-Vicaire, *Saint-Dominique,* Paris, Desclée de B. 1937, vol. II, p. 13-48.) How does this teaching constitute a charism? Is it necessary to have a vocation for it? Is a vocation sufficient to be able to teach? Vocation and hierarchical power. Role of women in the teaching of the faith? Teaching of faith and liturgy (on this subject, read A. G. Martimort, *Catéchèse et catéchisme,* in *La Maison-Dieu,* no. 6, pp. 37-48, J. LeClerq, *Le Sermon, acte liturgique,* in *La Maison-Dieu,* no. 8, pp. 27-46 and C. Rauch, *Qu'est-ce qu'une homélie,* in *La Maison-Dieu,* no. 16, pp. 34-42).

The gift of *miracle-working* (I Cor. 12:28). What is a miracle? Miracles of the Old Testament and of the Gospels. The working of miracles as a "sign"; the working of miracles as "proof." Working of miracles and apologetics. Cf. in particular, apropos the Resurrection and the miracles of Jesus: C. Lavergne, *Les miracles de Jésus,* in *Apologétique,* Bloud et Gay, 1948, pp. 410-424.

The gifts of *healing,* of *charitable help* (I Cor. 12:28). Of what do they consist? Should works of mercy in the Church depend on a particular gift?

The gift of the *power of administration* (I Cor. 17:28). Should the hierarchical power depend on a charism? Does the Church give the episcopacy to those who have the charism, or does the Holy Spirit communicate the charism to those whom the Church delegates to hierarchical duties? Make in this connection, and in a completely general way, a "theology of the *graces of one's state in life.*" The *magisterium* and charism. The charism of *infallibility* in the

Church, in the Councils, in the pope. Object and limits of infalli-bility. Scriptural foundations and history of the dogma.

The gift of *tongues* (I Cor. 12:28-30) and the gift of *interpreta-tion* (I Cor. 12:30). Of what do they consist? Usefulness. On the gift of interpretation and translation, cf. J. Travers, in *La Maison-Dieu,* no. 11, pp. 32-33 and the authors already cited. The entire article of J. Travers, *Le mystère des langues dans l'Église,* is cited elsewhere.

On the religious life, understood as a gift, or as a "pneumatic order," cf. J. LeClerq, *Points de vue sur l'histoire de l'état religieux,* in *La Vie spirituelle,* June 1946, pp. 816-833.

On *ecstasy* and the charismatic phenomena of the "mystical" union, read at least St. Teresa of Avila, Autobiography, edition de la vie spirituelle, Paris, and from the viewpoint of theological anal-ysis, A. Poulain, *Des grâces d'oraison, Traité de théologie mystique,* 11th ed., 1931 (certain vocabulary in this book is already partly outdated).

On the charismatic power given to certain souls against devils (the Curé of Ars, Marie Thérèse Noblet, in modern times), cf. *Satan* in *Études carmélitaines,* Paris, Desclée, 1948. On the charismatic phe-nomena of conversation with the angels (e.g. St. Françoise Ro-maine), read J. Daniélou, *Les Anges,* Chevotogne, 1951; the studies of Benoist d'Azy on the angels (especially in *Bull. de la litt. ecclés.,* Toulouse, 1943) and the unpublished theology of Ch. V. Heris, *Les Anges* (treatise of St. Thomas Aquinas translated and anno-tated, published by the Éd. de la R. des J.).

Gifts and hierarchy. To whom does the judgment belong: can the "prophet" in the Church "judge" certain acts of the hierarchy? Should and can the hierarchy judge all the words of the "prophets," of "private revelations"? In a more general fashion, can the "spir-itual" in the Church judge the "hierarchical"? According to what cri-teria should the "hierarchical" judge the "spiritual," or the "mysti-cal"?

BIBLIOGRAPHIE

Pour plus de détails, nous renvoyons à l'ouvrage: *Charismes et Corps mystique* (de J. V.-M. Pollet), à paraître aux Éd. du Cerf, dans la collection *Unam Sanctam.*

En attendant la parution de cet ouvrage, il n'existe rien de plus complet que saint Thomas d'Aquin, *La prophétie,* trad. de P. Synave, notes de P. Synave et de P. Benoît, Paris, Éd. de la Revue des J., 1947, 400 pp. Ce petit volume d'apparence modeste contient près de 280 pages de notes explicatives et de renseignements techniques qui sont un véritable traité.

Consulter aussi:

A. Lemonnyer, article *Charismes,* dans le *Supplément Dict. Bible,* Paris, Pirot, 1928 (point de vue exégétique).

R. Garrigou-Lagrange, *Les trois âges de la vie intérieure,* Paris, Éd. du Cerf, 1938.

X. Ducros, art. *Charismes* dans le *Dict. de spiritualité,* Viller, 1940.

Dom B. Maréchaux, *Les charismes du Saint-Esprit,* Paris, 1921. C'est un recueil littéraire des textes des premiers siècles.

Ces trois derniers livres intéressent le point de vue "mystique." Voir enfin, au point de vue historique, les "histoires de l'Église" un peu détaillées (par ex. Fliche et Martin, chez Bloud et Gay) et G. Bardy, *La théologie de l'Église de saint Clément de Rome à saint Irénée,* Paris, Éd. du Cerf, 1945 (en particulier l'introduction et le chapitre III).

L. Cerfaux, *L'Église des Corinthiens,* Coll. Témoins de Dieu, Paris, Éd. du Cerf, 1946.

L. Cerfaux, *La théologie de l'Église suivant saint Paul,* Coll. *Unam sanctam,* Paris, Éd. du Cerf, 1942.

BIBLIOGRAPHY

Amabel du Coeur de Jesus, Mother, *To Love and to Suffer.* Westminster, Md., The Newman Bookshop, 1953.

Carroll, James F., *God the Holy Ghost.* New York, P. J. Kenedy & Sons, 1940.

Gardeil, Ambrose, O.P., *The Holy Spirit in Christian Life.* London, Blackfriars Publications, 1953.

Garrigou-Lagrange, Reginald, O.P., *The Three Ages of the Spiritual Life.* St. Louis, B. Herder Book Co., 1948.

Grandmaison, Leonce de, *We and The Holy Spirit,* Chicago, Fides, 1953.
———, *Come Holy Spirit,* Chicago, Fides, 1956.

John of St. Thomas, *The Gifts of the Holy Ghost.* New York, Sheed and Ward, 1951.

Kelly, Bernard J., *The Seven Gifts.* New York, Sheed and Ward, 1952.

Vann, Gerald, O.P., *The Divine Pity.* New York, Sheed and Ward, 1946.

Wollen, C. J., *The Twelve Fruits.* New York, Joseph Wagner, Inc., 1950.

Chapter XI

THE ACTIVE LIFE AND THE CONTEMPLATIVE LIFE

by Th. Camelot, O.P. and I. Mennessier, O.P.

I. ACTION AND CONTEMPLATION IN CHRISTIAN TRADITION
by Th. Camelot, O.P.

II. SPECIFIC ASPECTS OF CHRISTIAN LIFE: Active and Contemplative Life
by I. Mennessier, O.P.

A. Fundamentals Orientations
B. Dominant Occupations: contemplative, active and mixed works
C. Action, Contemplation and Personal Equilibrium in Life
D. Contemplation
   1. An activity of possession
   2. The role of love
   3. Affected knowledge and gifts of the Holy Spirit
   4. Mystical experience and theology
   5. Acquired contemplation

REFLECTIONS AND PERSPECTIVES

BIBLIOGRAPHY

Chapter XI

THE ACTIVE LIFE AND THE CONTEMPLATIVE LIFE

I. Action and Contemplation in Christian Tradition

The Treatise on "active life" and "contemplative life" is put—by St. Thomas, whom we are following here—at the end of moral theology, the science of human behavior. After having studied the virtures common to all human conditions and their opposite vices, he comes to what belongs to individuals in particular: "charismata" or gratuitous gifts given for the benefit of the Church; "ways of life" which are men's principal occupation and their every concern: exterior activity, or contemplation of truth; "functions" and "states" whose diversity show the beauty of the Church, and especially, the "state of perfection." The treatise on the charismata and the one on functions and states of life is referred to expressly by St. Paul; [1] that on ways of life is referred to in the gospel episode of Martha and Mary; [2] Martha is concerned with the cares of serving, Mary is seated at the foot of Our Lord, listening to His words. [3] What is the value of this reference, and what, in Christian tradition, is the value of this distinction between "active life" and "contemplative life"? It is worth the trouble to examine this problem before setting forth the teachings of theology on this point.

For the problem does exist, and more acutely than St. Thomas' very tranquil account would make one suspect. We will speak at length on *contemplation,* and the *contemplative life.* These words have acquired status in Christian Society, but the Gospels do not use them. The word *contemplation* (*theôria*) is found only once in the entire New Testament (Lk. 13:48), and it has the every-day meaning of a *spectacle* which one looks at: it treats of the crowd which has gathered to look at Jesus' torment—*ad spectaculum istud,* according to the Vulgate. The verb *to contemplate* (*theôrein*) is found

[1] I Cor. 12:4-11, 28-30; Eph. 4:11.
[2] Lk. 10:38-42.
[3] IIa IIae, q. 171, prol., and cf. q. 182, 1.

some fifty times in the New Testament, but it also has the current meaning of *to behold, to see*—the Vulgate translates it most often by *videre*. Foreign to the vocabulary of St. Paul, the verb is particularly frequent in St. John (twenty examples) where it is colored at times with a religious shade of meaning; i.e. it treats of a spiritual knowledge of Christ, the Messenger of God, a knowledge which is possible only in the eyes of faith, as, for example, John 6:40: "Whoever *beholds* the Son and *believes* in Him" (cf. again 14:17, 19; 17:24). But this shade of meaning depends on the context and on the object of this vision more than on the word *theorein* itself, which designates neither a special manner of knowledge nor a fixed state of life.

We shall speak again of the peace and tranquillity of contemplative life, which removes all earthly cares in order to be satisfied with a very simple look at the contemplation of divine truth (for example, q. 180, 1, 2 ad., etc.) But nowhere in the Gospels do we see that it is necessary to be isolated and separated from the world to give oneself up to contemplation. On the contrary, the whole ideal of the Gospels, and of St. Paul, is an ideal of *charity, agape,* which is first of all love of neighbor, a working and merciful charity dedicated to the active and eager service of one's brothers. Higher than the knowledge of all the mysteries and higher than all gnosis, is charity: gnosis will one day be reduced to nothing, charity alone remains (I Cor. 13:1-13).

But if the Gospels do not speak of contemplation and contemplative life, this distinction and this very decided opposition between ways of life, "active" and "contemplative," was familiar to the Greeks. Next to the *active* (or *practical, bios practicos*) life—a life of moral action, a life of the man who mingles with the things of this world, with the bustle and confusion of the family, with the securing of a livelihood as a worker or with city affairs—they offer the ideal of the wise man, the *contemplative* (or *theoretical,* speculative, *bios theoreticos*) life: freed from all material cares, from all worldly activity, the philosopher is able, with a peaceful and unified gaze, to contemplate Ideas, the Beautiful, the Good, and thus to rise to the contemplation of the one who is beyond all idea and all essence, the One, God. It is easy to show the grandeur and the nobleness of such an ideal; it is also easy to oppose strongly this ideal, very intellectual and also very aristocratic, even, indeed, quite egoistical or proud, with the Gospel of sweetness and of humility, which testifies to a very sharp distrust in regard to all "gnosis," to all superior knowledge reserved for an elite of scholars and wise men, or the initiated: it is to all the little ones that the secrets of the kingdom of God have been revealed (cf. Matt. 11:25).

To the living, God is invisible, and all of Holy Scripture affirms that man is unable "to see God." [4] The claim of being raised to the "contemplation" of God is foreign to the Judaic-Christian tradition.

Nevertheless, there is in the Fathers of the Church—we could almost say in the majority of them—a broad, deep stream, whose source is visibly Hellenic, in which we find again this ideal of contemplation and contemplative life. It starts with Alexandria, that center of Platonic culture and religiosity, where Philo the Jew had already strongly hellenized Jewish tradition, and where Clement, confronted with gnostic errors, tries to construct an orthodox gnosis, a superior knowledge that will be a contemplation, an immediate recognition of God contemplated face to face, an "unveiled contemplation, recognition and comprehension of the Divine essence, a gnosis of the Divine essence . . . eternal and immutable state of contemplation." [5] It is Clement again who expresses in this way his ideal of contemplative life: "In the contemplative life *one is occupied with oneself,* with giving worship to God, and, by a sincere purification, one contemplates piously the Holy God. The temperance which looks at itself and observes itself, contemplates itself unceasingly, renders itself as much like God as possible." [6]

Origen, who must not be thought of purely and simply as a disciple of Clement, expresses an analogous ideal. More systematically than Clement had done, he transposes the degrees which Greek philosophy, Stoic as well as Platonic, placed in the progress of knowledge in order to apply them to the stages of spiritual ascent: he claims to recognize them in the three sapiential books of the Hebrew Bible; e.g. Proverbs teaches moral doctrine, Ecclesiastes knowledge of nature, and finally, the Canticle of Canticles leads to mysticism, to the *contemplation* of God (Commentary on the Cant. of Cant., prol.). Underneath this rather artificial biblical veneer is the traditional distinction between ethical, physical, and theoretical, which is thus applied to the realities of Christian living. Origen is the first to interpret the Biblical episode of Mary and Martha according to hellenic

[4] Gen. 33:20; Judges 6:22; 13:22; Is. 6:6; Jn. 1:18; I Tim. 6:16.
[5] Stromate, V, 10, 66; VI, 7, 61.
[6] Stromate, IV, 23, 152; cf. Plato, *Theetete,* 176 b.

formulae so as to recognize in it the distinction between active *life* and contemplative *life:* "Mary is the symbol of the contemplative life and Martha that of the active life" (*In Joann.,* fragm. 80). It is again Origen who applies to individual mystical experience and to the efforts of the soul to embrace God the conjugal images of the Canticle of Canticles, which St. Hippolytus before him understood as the union of Christ and the Church. We cannot exaggerate the influence of Origen in the development of the contemplative life and Christian mysticism, even in that of the monastic life; but we can not forget, either, that it all is strongly tinged with hellenism.

After Origen we can follow that platonic (or if one prefers, neo-platonic) vein throughout the entire history of ancient spirituality. We can do little more here than list a few names: In the East, Gregory of Nyssa, and after him, the author of the writings attributed to Dionysius the Areopagite and his commentator, St. Maximus the Confessor; the Origenistic Evagrius who gives to the rather meager experience of the monks of Scete its intellectual structure; linking the East and the West is Cassian, the disciple of Evagrius, whose influence on all medieval monastic spirituality is known. In the West St. Augustine, who was able to know Origen through St. Ambrose and through the translations of Rufinus, and who had read the books of the "Platonists" (Plotinus); St. Gregory the Great who brings St. Augustine into common use of all medieval Latin countries. St. Augustine and St. Gregory are the ones who are the most frequently quoted by St. Thomas in the treatise on ways of life.

After this it is easy to place primitive Christian spirituality against that of the Gospels and of St. Paul, of St. Ignatius and St. Irenaeus, wholly centered on Christ and the union of Christ with the Church —a scholarly and intellectualist spirituality, founded on a platonistic psychology and anthropology; the soul aspires to flight from the world and the evasion of the sensible in order to be absorbed in the contemplation of the Intelligible, and to contemplate in its proper essence the Divine Light. Again, it is easy to show that when we speak of contemplation and the contemplative life we are, unknown to ourselves, victims of a tradition more Greek than Christian, and that we must return to the Gospels and St. Paul, to the Christian ideal of *agape,* and away from the platonic *eros,* the selfish aspiration of the soul which is seeking to grasp and contemplate God in order to find in Him its proper beatitude (see for example, the articles of Fathers Hausherr and Festugiere, cited in the bibliography).

We have concealed nothing of the problem presented by the *sources* of the classic treatises on the active and contemplative life, and even more basic, the very existence in Christianity of the forms of life thus characterized. To attempt to answer these problems will be to help make the consequent doctrine better understood.

We shall readily agree that this doctrine is expressed in terms borrowed from Greek philosophy, and that the Christian ideal of contemplation and contemplative life was first developed and formulated in hellenic surroundings. This is a historic factual situation, no question about it, and one which enters into the providential economy of salvation its human historic conditions. We could say *a priori* that if God desired those fixed historic conditions, they have not been able to determine the development of Christian thought and life to the point of modifying and radically disfiguring the evangelic message. But we must look closer.

If it is Greek philosophy which has given Christian contemplation its framework and its formulae, if not indeed, its primary inspiration, we could not deny that it is a profoundly *religious* philosophy. Such is, as a matter of fact, the dominant character of the philosophy, at once stoic and platonic, which is current in the Second and Third centuries. In the words of St. Justin, the desire to see God is the goal of the philosophy of Plato.[7] But is not this desire natural to the human spirit, which seeks spontaneously to know God, and asks of philosophy—or of myths and mysteries—the secret of this knowledge "which leads to God and unites us to Him"?[8] The knowledge to which the Greek thus aspires is not pure speculation, it is a profound union and a vital communion.

It is an authentically *religious* aspiration, which encounters a profoundly *biblical* and *Christian* aspiration. Religion is not simply worship nor solely request and supplication, nor even, it must also be said, solely the department of widows and orphans (cf. Jas. 1:27); it is a deep-seated movement of love of God, which is translated into an ardent desire to see God (Ex. 33:3). But if man cannot see God, God makes His goodness known to man; in Christ He shows Himself still more than on the rock of Horeb, and the

[7] Dialogue I, 3; II, 6.
[8] Ibid., II, 1.

faith of the Christian can contemplate the glory of God upon the face of Christ.[9]

If the Gospel is the message of salvation and of redemption, as well as a revelation of the mystery of love which is in God, this implies a knowledge; i.e. knowledge of faith, founded on a gratuitous revelation, and not the expression of an attempt at an intellectual ecstasy (Matt. 11:25); a still partial and obscure knowledge, which is not yet the face to face vision (I Cor. 13:12; I Jn. 3:2); a knowledge wholly impregnated with love, that which makes of it a vital and enjoyable experience, but a knowledge, assuredly, which of itself tends to be developed into a clasp and an embrace of its object, and to that intimate union in the vision which shall be eternal life (Jn. 17:3). To lead all Christianity back to the one brotherly *agape,* and to exclude from it every intellectual element, every desire for knowledge and "contemplation," would be to impoverish it singularly, and to deprive it in particular of the whole contribution of the writings of St. John. The love of God for man stirs up and creates in the latter a love of God which by its own movement ends in the desire to know God more intimately, to be united to Him by the most intimate union, and to "dwell in Him." A Christianity which would not comply with that deep-seated need of the soul would be neither a human religion nor a divine religion.

Thus, neither the similarity of vocabulary nor the analogies of structure between philosophic contemplation and Christian contemplation should cause us to mistake that which is deeply original and authentically founded in revelation.

A detailed comparison between these two forms of contemplation would end in analogous conclusions. We shall be content here to underline three points.

1. The object of Christian contemplation is not "the God of philosophers and scholars," the One, the superessential Monad, but the "God of Jesus Christ." It is the Triune God, revealed by Jesus Christ. We could quote Origen here as well as Evagrius or Cassian: "Is it another perfection of science—of *gnosis*—, that of knowing the Father, the Son and the Holy Spirit"? [10] "Perfection of the spirit is spiritual knowledge, as the Fathers say, and its consummation is

---

[9] Cf. II Cor. 4:6; and St. Irenaeus: "What is invisible in the Son, is the Father; what is visible in the Father, is the Son" (*Adv. Haer.,* IV, 6, 6); there is knowledge and contemplation of God only in Christ.

[10] Origen, *Hom. sur les Nombres,* X, 3.

the knowledge of the Holy Trinity." [11] And this assures us that this contemplation is quite another matter than platonic ascension through degrees of being to Being. It is, *in faith,* an enjoyable and very simple knowledge of the Triune God which has been revealed in Jesus Christ. Christian contemplation is both Christological and Trinitarian, if we may use these words, and that is what assures it of its specific originality.

2. In this contemplation (in this contemplative life), *charity* plays a conspicuous and outstanding role. We have already pointed out that love is the starting-point of this desire of knowing. It is because "his love of Jesus cannot be content with an ordinary and irrational knowledge" that Ambrose, the friend of Origen, let himself be led astray toward the speculations of the false gnosis. Origen still held that "spiritual charity prefers nothing to the knowledge of God." [12] The purifications of asceticism, with which (we shall repeat) the "active life" tends to be identified, have for their end to prepare the soul in the realm of charity while correcting morals and calming passions. *Apathy,* whatever may be the disagreeable echoes contained in this word—the apathy of the Christian is not quite the same thing as the apathy of the Stoic; it is, says Evagrius, "the calm of a rational soul, made of humility and of chastity." [13] We could translate this, as we did recently, "interior freedom." By this lone example we see to what point Christian thought makes free use of the concepts and formulae borrowed from philosophy.

Charity, which is the starting-point of the struggle toward contemplation, and which sustains the labors of the ascetic, is also the end and the consummation. We might have hesitated at the exact thought of Clement of Alexandria on this point, although he has precise passages: "Gnosis, ending in charity, reunites here below, as friend to friend, the one who knows with the one who is known." [14] But Origen, in a previously cited passage, tells us that "mysticism rises to the contemplation of God by a sincere and spiritual love," and, furthermore, that gnosticism "is a spiritual love." [15] Evagrius maintains the same thing, and St. Gregory, in whom all Western tradition is summed up, says that the grandeur of contemplation can be

[11] Evagre, *Centurie* III, 15.
[12] *Sel. in Ps.,* 119, 9. This text is perhaps to be credited to Evagre.
[13] *Centurie* VII, 3.
[14] *Stromate* VII, 10, 57.
[15] *Comm. sur les Prov.* VII, 3.

granted only to those who love,[16] and that love itself is a knowledge.[17] Here we find all the elements of a theology of "mystical" and affective knowledge by connaturality.

Coming after St. Gregory, and very intimately inspired by him, St. Thomas sees love as the beginning and end of contemplation: as the beginning, because love desires a more and more intimate knowledge of the beauty of its object; as the end, because from contemplation bursts forth the joy which makes love itself more intense. Christian tradition has integrated contemplation into charity which is primary.

Let us add that it is also a question of brotherly love. It would be easy to cite exquisite accounts of the most remarkable charity with which the *Lives of the Fathers* of the desert and the *Apophtegmes* are filled. It would also be necessary to recall how many monks became bishops and to show that the monastic and contemplative life has been for the Church the center of the most ardent charity. It is especially necessary to quote St. Augustine and St. Gregory, who have here again furnished St. Thomas with some of the most important elements for his treatises. "If love of truth seeks holy *leisure,* the requirements of charity know how to burden themselves with a fitting occupation. . . . If this burden is imposed on us, we must accept it for the requirements of charity." [18] "It is necessary to know that if a good program of life suggests that we pass from the active life to the contemplative life, it is nevertheless often useful for the soul to return from contemplative life to active life *so that the flame which has been lit in the heart of contemplation shall give all its perfection to action.* Thus the active life leads us to contemplation, and, also, the contemplative life, from what we have considered silently, will recall us to action." [19] To go back to an image familiar to the Fathers, the apostle passing from the embraces of Rachel to those of Lia will join the fecundity of action to the chaste solitude of contemplation. *Contemplata aliis tradere.* But charity comes first.

3. Finally, for that very reason, the relationships between active life and contemplative life are profoundly modified. The active life is no longer merely the *bios practicos* or *politicos,* dedicated to

[16] In *Ezech.* II, 5, 7.
[17] *In Evang. Hom.* III, 37, 4.
[18] *City of God* XIX, 19.
[19] *Hom. sur Ezechiel* II, 2.

works and trades and occupations of the city; it is, as the Greeks had already pointed out, the *moral* life; it is the struggle between vices and the acquisition of virtues, all "the loving labor of the ascetic," the purification of the sensible passions, an indispensable preparation for contemplation, a life which we could not view with scorn. It is no longer a question of opposing two irreducible ways of life to each other, one inferior, the other more perfect, but to distinguish in the spiritual progress two stages, successive no doubt, but in continuity with each other, and both equally necessary. Origen, Evagrius, and Cassian after him, are the sources here of a unanimous tradition.

But the active life is also an exercise of *charity*. The great bishops of the 4th and 5th centuries, many of whom, not to say almost all, had begun by being monks, fashion the type of an *episcopal* sanctity which shall later be called *apostolic*. The latter prevails over the purely contemplative life, because, *by love for God,* and without ceasing to be nourished by the loving and delightful contemplation of the word of God, it adds to love for God the overflowing fulness of an active love for one's neighbor. Active life and contemplative life, again, are no longer opposed like two types of life absolutely foreign and irreducible, one given to the service of one's neighbor, the other turned selfishly on itself in the contemplation of ideas. They are both two forms of the same life of charity; the distinction between the two ways of life is made now in the interior of the one charity.[20]

Finally, it is necessary to add that in the viewpoint of St. Augustine, who is here still the great master, the active life and the contemplative life are opposed to each other as a life of work and a life of repose, a life of suffering and a life of happiness, a present life and a future life, a temporal life and an eternal life. It is only in the other life where there will be no more hungry to be fed, sick to be visited, quarrels to be appeased, ignorant to be taught, after we have given ourselves to works of action that we shall be able to enjoy the reward of contemplation. The meaning of *time* and of history which Christianity introduced in human thought, and eschatological perspectives, have here also radically replaced the axis of Greek thought. But we must not forget to say that if the contemplative life will be perfectly realized only in Heaven, it is from this earth, it is for those who are called to it and have, like Mary, received the better part,

[20] Cf. St. Thomas, IIa IIae, 182, 2.

like an anticipation and a first prophetic realization of the life of the blessed. In virtue of this it has an irreplaceable role in the Church.

These reflections would be worth developing. We should above all support them with references to texts. Several of them are found in the studies indicated in the *Bibliography*. We should like to sum them up here by saying simply that the doctrine of the two "ways of life," classic since the 3rd century in Christian tradition, may well indeed depend in its vocabulary and in its very structure on Greek thought, but that, for that very reason, it finds a profoundly human and religious reality, and that, after all, it has inflicted profound modifications on that Greek doctrine, by which is affirmed its deep-seated originality and its authentically Christian character.

II. Specific Aspects of Christian Life

ACTIVE AND CONTEMPLATIVE LIFE

Leaving to the historian the care of discovering the various meanings which the terms "active life" and "contemplative life" have had in the past, we would like here simply to situate these ideas, and the realities which they represent within the general lines of our theological synthesis.

The problems which the relation of action and contemplation, and sometimes their difficult balance, can pose to Christian experience, are clarified, we believe, if we take the trouble to distinguish the different planes on which they may be considered. One fundamental idea is set off by the systematization which finds not only its framework, but its principles, in the second part of the *Summa Theologiae* of St. Thomas. It is the idea of *life*. We shall easily see the importance of this viewpoint. By it we are placed from the first on the plane of *interiority*. We are not content to look at the exterior. Life bursts forth from within. It is the fundamental inclination in which the nature of a being is primarily revealed and which prompts it toward all operations by which it attains its end. Nothing is more profound, nothing is more organic. Life supposes a unity of organized activities. There is in it a necessity for unification, for synthesis. When we distinguish action and contemplation as two aspects characteristic of human life, we must, at the same time, see in which sense life will be unified. This is why we can, it seems, imagine the relation of action and contemplation on three planes:

(a) These actions themselves; how to reconcile these very diverse activities, which are the act of contemplating, with the occupations of a practical order; i.e. in terms of personal equilibrium;

(b) A certain general organization of life, according to the predominance given to this or that order of occupations;

(c) The fundamental structure of Christian life.

Let us begin with this last point.

A. *Fundamental Orientations*

We are on the plane of life. Our theology, in gathering here the ideas of active life and of contemplative life, provides an inherited distinction of Greek thought, as well as of Christian tradition. The movement of life expresses, by its very orientation, what is most specific and most intimately personal in life. Each one's life is depicted, according to Aristotle, by the quality of its dominant pleasures; it is characterized by that which makes up, above all, the object of its cares, by that very thing which by preference it intends to share in living together with its friends.[21]

By virtue of this, we perceive very quickly that, discarding the "voluptuous life" as infra-human, the great tendencies of men carry them toward disinterested liking for truth or toward activities of a practical order. Human nature seems, moreover, so radically made that the human spirit can be at one and the same time incited by the attraction of pure knowledge or by the application of knowledge to action. Speculative activities of the spirit, organizing activities, even fabricating activities are apparently the great components of a strictly human life. If we state, then, the pure and simple primacy of the "contemplative life," the reason is that life being defined by the most characteristic activity of a human being, the one in which he is ultimately consummated, the contemplation of truth appears as the supreme operation of the highest powers of man. To Aristotle it seems necessary to order all social life so as to assist the leisure of those few rare privileged individuals who are the success of the species, the wise men.

But, if the essential structures of human nature do not change under the rule of grace, it is quite necessary, no doubt, to expect that such ideas will undergo several transpositions. For the essence

[21] "Vita uniuscujusque hominis videtur esse id in quo maxime delectatur, et cui maxime intendit, et in hoc praecipus vult quilibet convivere amico," St. Thomas, IIa IIae, 179, 1.

of Christian life is to love. Its innermost movement is that of the "pondus amoris" which places the object of supernatural charity in us.

Certainly, all life is an inclination, *appetitus,* and that, of course, is not sufficient to characterize it. We must see exactly to what this movement inclines, and, if it is a question of happiness in the life of a conscious being, in what kind of happiness it is achieved: *id in quo maxime delectatur, et cui maxime intendit.* What then is the supreme act in which our love stops growing and comes to rest? Obviously, for the Christian it is the vision of God. The Christian life—and our moral theology begins by making us sure of it—is wholly an aspiration toward the *blessed life,* which we know consists in the vision of God. Let us say, then, that it is love which inclines to an eternal vision in which it will find its accomplishment and its definitive state.

This single statement is important, for when we affirm again the pure and simple primacy of the contemplative life, we mean by that: that all Christian life is fundamentally contemplative in the sense that it inclines to the vision of God. Such is the *intendere* which characterizes it. We do not forget, however, that we do not see God here on earth and that characterized by the light given it Christian life is essentially a love en route. The few glimpses received here below are given only in order to enlighten it in its search and to lead it on still further, not in order that it may rest here permanently.

Now, this love en route, if it requires above all by the very reason of its end a sense of God and an intimacy with Him, in which this life of togetherness required by Divine friendship begins, it also meets on its way a whole series of requirements which will, no less, characterize its activities. In any case, this supernatural charity, inner principle of Christian life, introduces us into Divine friendship only while assimilating us to Christ, Who with it communicates to us the very movement of His own love. And Christ came to save the world. Is not Divine love itself, when it inclines toward us, this merciful descent: "God has so loved the world that He has given His only Son . . ."?

The movement of Christian life is also characterized by that proximate, immediate object: the human miseries of all kinds which for love of the world it is necessary for us to succor. The terms *vita activa* will embrace all this order of charitable activities. In its fullest meaning this will be apostolic fervor, the zeal for the salvation of souls which must animate all Christian life. But all kindnesses are also found therein. In any case, under whatever form it may be, from the humblest almsgiving to the most characterized apostolic activities, it is really always a question of "active life," including the inevitable care of organizing, providing for and facing the multiple needs of the world—a quite different attitude from the "return to the one" in which the movement of contemplative living takes pleasure.

We see that on this plane, if we say that Christian life is both active and contemplative, it is for other reasons than merely those taken from Aristotle. It is more than the structure of the human spirit which is suited to that two-fold yearning for pure speculation and for organizing activities, with personal inclinations more or less marked in one sense or another. It is the very object of love that desires it thus—its two-fold object, God and neighbor; its two-fold movement, intimacy and service. And, of course, we see beyond theoretical discussions on the pre-eminence of one or the other term, action-contemplation, that species of inner anguish which the charitable soul experiences and which is truly resolved only in the very elevation of its love. St. Paul expresses it: "all my desire is to cast off the moorings and be with Christ," and elsewhere, "I wish to be anathema far from Christ, separated from Him for my brothers . . ."

Theoretically, to be sure, the *vita contemplativa* triumphs over the *activa vita;* that is to say that for love God is the first object—and, we repeat, the most fundamental movement of supernatural life is the longing for the blessed vision of God. But in the order of priorities this love en route which is our condition, contemplative activities and the leisure which conditions them must often yield to that greater urgency of need which solicits us. It is on this plane of activities that contemplative leisure and charitable service share the heart of the Christian.

There will always be the problem of unifying one's life in love. But to understand that there is no other primacy except that of love, is precisely to find the principle of that inner unity. Is St. Paul, who wished himself "far from Christ" in order to belong to his brothers, ever closer to Him than when he dedicates himself to their service? But is it not true that the inner debate which he expresses parallels not so much beneficent activities and contemplative leisures which share our earthly life, but even more radically the eternal possession of God and the present moment? It is because the present moment is at all time the moment of service. In his longing for blessed deliverance, Paul points out the way of genuine love which consents to the labors of life here on earth.

B. *Dominant Occupations: Contemplative, Active and Mixed Works*

Here is a new point of view. It is no longer a question now of visualizing Christian life in its essential components—that two-fold movement which in the unity of the life of charity implies the apparent dilemma which Father de Guibert once translated in these words: "To Enjoy God—To Serve God"—but to see it differently arranged, in this person or that one, according to a given preeminence in a particular order of activity.

We shall speak then of contemplative life, of active life, or again, of "mixed" life, in order to designate a certain way of living, a certain spiritual course resulting from the more or less marked specialization for activities or for works which we shall qualify according to these same categories: active, contemplative, mixed.

The predominance of studious activities, of the exercise of mental and vocal prayer, the application to multiple works, themselves different from charitable benevolence, the whole gift of self to apostolic demands (whose very means can be extremely varied), will suppose various organizations in life which are *typical* of their state in the different forms of the religious state. The latter will be studied by itself in the chapter devoted to "states of perfection." But we can henceforth see in the diversity of religious orders the most characteristic circumstance of this organization of life in terms of this or that dominant concern for contemplation or for action. Rather than of contemplative, active or mixed life, we shall speak next of contemplative, active or mixed religious Orders.

Here let us note simply that, beneath this diversity of proximate goals, which in diversifying religious institutions, gives to each one its particular features in the very arrangement of traditional means which make up the economy of the religious state, lies this essential finality: the inclination to the perfection of charity.

It follows that the great essential laws of the life of charity are these afore-mentioned ones. Whatever may be the particularized form according to which regular life is organized, the great aspects characteristic of Christian life must find in it their full place. That is why, even in the most "active" orders, a minimum of spiritual exercises destined to safeguard intimacy with God and to maintain the fundamental "contemplative" basis of supernatural life are provided. But contrariwise, because always it is a question of promoting the life of charity such as it is "in via," apostolic concern cannot be absent even from the most contemplative forms of religious order. If he is not concerned about his brothers, would the most contemplative of hermits still be a Christian?

In this last point of view, these are the *means,* in which are reflected the distinction of the ways of active, contemplative or mixed life, which love chooses in order to exercise the fulness of its radiance here on earth. For if "contemplatives" are not less concerned than others for the salvation of the world, their means of providing for it is, above all, that of prayer and of the offering of their life of sacrifice. A powerful means, which makes of the "contemplative life" of the cloisters an efficacious agent of apostolic action. There one deals directly with God, so to speak: "He who prays for another, does not act by addressing himself to the interested person but by turning to God directly." [22]

As for the *vita mixta,* it is characterized not by a scholarly mixture of contemplative activities and of mixed activities, but by its ordination to mixed works; that is to say, in that class of activity in which contemplation and practical application are found intimately mingled *ex objecto.* Such are the properly apostolic activities in which the work of research and of communication of Divine Truth has no meaning unless dominated by the contemplation of the latter. The unity of contemplative life and of apostolic action is then maintained by the very character of the latter; to communicate divine truth is, in one sense, never to leave it and to remain lovingly attached to that intimately assimilated and possessed truth. The image of Jacob's ladder which the angels ascended and descended translates this ideal. It is also expressed in the famous formulae: *contemplare et contemplata aliis tradere.*

This profound unity of contemplation and of action in the exercise of the apostolic life supposes an orientation of contemplation rather different, of course, from what it would be for the true contemplative. At the heart of Christian contemplation there is the love not of pure ideas, but of God and of our brothers. The apostolic vocation is born directly of a charity which human misery sets in motion. Also, the ideal of the *vita mixta* is not that of the chaste philosopher who leaves his speculative leisure to offer his contem-

[22] St. Thomas, IIa IIae, q. 181, a. 3 ad. 3.

poraries his new theory, nor of the poet who sings his sublime intuition: let him who will, hear, let him who is able, understand.
This would really be to misunderstand the *contemplata aliis tradere*.
The contemplation of the apostle, which is born of a love that is
willing to help, is oriented by reason of the spiritual misery which
calls for help. The apostle must go deeply into the knowledge of
God. But it is in unceasingly ascending and descending Jacob's ladder, and in order to communicate it usefully by means of a whole
human work of adaptation, which makes St. Thomas say: *Docere
est opus activae vitae*. Quite symptomatic is the anguish which seizes
St. Thomas himself on the eve of assuming his duties as a teacher.
William of Tocco has left us the theme of his prayer on that night
in which this born contemplative, preparing his first teaching assign-
ment, proved what a wrench from the serene contemplation of the
One the work to which he had dedicated his life brought with it:
*Salve me Domine quoniam diminutae sunt veritates inter filios homi-
num!* (Save me, O Lord, for I must descend among the sons of men
where truth is to be found only in small bits.)

C. *Action, Contemplation, Personal Equilibrium in Life*

The preceding reflections concerned the ideas of active and contemplative life in relation to the general organization of a life, dedicated to the characteristic occupations of one or other of these
aspects. If the religious state, in the diversity of its institutional
forms, has furnished us the type of these different ways of life, it
goes without saying that, analogically, individuals not engaged in
the religious state will be able to organize their life in terms of those
same dominant concerns. But the fact remains that, whether within
the limits of a religious rule or outside of it, the problem "action-
contemplation" is still a problem of personal equilibrium to be
sought between the two-fold entreaty of contemplative peace and
quiet in divine intimacy and active service of one's neighbor. Quite
a few psychological conflicts may at times present themselves which
are not, alas, only those born of the attractions of grace among
present labors, but also those of the individual temperament, even
of the temptations of the age.

How many contemplatives, or even contemplatives by "state,"
dream in their cloisters of an exterior activity in which they could
spend themselves. But the reverse is likewise true. And, once again,
the attractions of grace are sometimes difficult to distinguish from

those of nature! Of course, it is necessary above all to counsel each one to do well what he has chosen to do, or better still, what God has chosen for him.

In any case, one of the elementary problems of spiritual life is that of being united to God among the more or less absorbing occupations of temporal life. Let us consider here just this obvious law, that, on the plane of activities themselves, we cannot do two things well at the same time. The application of the spirit to some organizing activities (I do not say only the time spent in occupations of material order, for the latter can at times allow freedom of spirit) is naturally incompatible with the actual thought of God. The solution is not in the multiplication of acts of actual attention to God, in interrupting application to exterior tasks which have been undertaken, but in deep inner orientation, which though only "virtual," will be actualized at the opportune time. Inner unity is on the plane of profound *life* and not simply in combinations of schedules. For the rest, and St. Augustine called attention to it very well, we must not let the attachment to divine intimacy be destroyed by an excessive activism:

> The love of truth aspires to holy leisure; the demands of charity charge us with necessary works. But if this burden is not imposed on us, we must use our freedom of spirit to search for and to contemplate truth. If it is imposed on us, we must welcome and bear it: charity demands it. But under this weight let us not forget entirely the joys of truth: deprived of that sweetness we would be crushed.[23]

With respect to the display of temperaments more or less disposed to contemplation or to action, a delightful passage of St. Thomas commenting on St. Gregory lead us to this pleasing advice:

> Passionate people by need of activity have a spirit easily in movement and have more aptitude for an active life than for contemplation. Certain individuals, says St. Gregory, have a spirit so restless that, far from comforting them, the absence of occupations overwhelms them. Their hearts suffer a tumult all the more painful because they have, in addition, the leisure to think. . . . But, elsewhere, you will find a clearness of soul, a tranquility, which denotes a natural aptitude for contemplation. Put those people entirely into action, they will suffer grave injury as a result of it. Certain ones, St. Gregory says again, have so inactive a spirit that, thrown into exterior occupations they are quickly submerged. But, he continues, one often sees slothful spirits take heart in work, through love, and fear to maintain in contemplation the impetuosity of others. The temperaments most suited

[23] St. Augustine, City of God, c. 19. Cf. St. Thomas, *Summa theol.,* IIa IIae, q. 182, a. 1.

for active life can, then, by their very activity and the moral effort which it requires, prepare their souls for contemplation; and the naturally contemplative temperaments, far from suffering injury in being trained for the active life, will leave this trial more suited to contemplation.[24]

Finally, let us note that we are also speaking of "contemplative life" in order to designate more particularly, in terms of a certain concept of "infused" contemplation, the turning-point which spiritual life takes when, by an action of divine grace to which corresponds a growing inner docility, the acts of this so-called "infused" contemplation are multiplied. About these souls we shall say that they have "entered into contemplative life," whether or not they are in other respects dedicated to active works, or whether they lead the ordinary Christian life among secular occupations in the life of the world. This leads us to study briefly contemplation in itself.

D. *Contemplation*

1. An Activity of Possession

Essentially an intellectual act, contemplation is not pure repose (the latter is its condition, if we understand it as the leisure which allows us to contemplate; or its completion, if we understand it as the love which reposes in the possession of God), but an activity of spirit characterized by these words: *motus qui est actus perfecti*. That is, not a movement of search, of acquisition, but an activity of possession in which we simply enjoy that which we possess in exercising that possession which, in the order of truth, is the act of knowledge. Thus it is a simple glance at the end of an entire activity of search and investigation (motus imperfecti) that, gathering together all the wealth of thoughts by which we have access to contemplated reality, takes possession of the latter.

Intuitus simplex veritatis: better yet, let us say, *contuitus.* In its simplicity, this glance, rich in all the abundance which it seizes upon, gathers together multiple aspects of knowledge which it restores to that synthetic unity in which intelligence is perfected.

An entire intellectual preparation is thus normally presupposed for any kind of contemplation. This is consistent with the structure of human intelligence. Christian contemplative life, in that which is most authentic about it, is far from neglecting this preparation of the spirit in its step toward the delightful and disinterested possession

[24] *Summa Theol.,* IIa IIae, q. 182, 4, 3 ad.

of divine truth. The Middle Ages made a place among the spiritual exercises for these "degrees" which, for example, Guigius the Carthusian expresses in this way: "reading, meditation, prayer, contemplation." Richard of St. Victor for his part defined these stages: "Contemplation is the clear and free dwelling of the soul upon the object of its gaze. Meditation is the survey of the mind occupied in the search for truth. 'Cogitation' is the mind still in process of search." Thus contemplative life is pictured in its various stages by a sculptor of the 13th century on the north portal of Chartres: recollection, reading, prayer, and finally, union with God. Again contemplation is free, simple and penetrating gaze, only because it supposes possessed truth. Its activity is indeed *actus perfecti;* that kind of "movement" in which the human being does not gain, but manifests in its action the perfection which is thenceforth its own. This activity also enjoys a magnificent, sovereign freedom, as well as simplicity. The more perfect spiritual activity, the more it ascends to simplicity, for the privilege of the spirit is that of unifying and synthesizing what is of itself multiple and diverse. It is the preparatory activity which is complex. Possessed, penetrated by itself, truth lets itself be savored in this simple and free gaze or *intuitus*.

2. The Role of Love

But, above all, spiritual men and theologians proclaim the role of love in Christian contemplation. Having defined the contemplative act as the exercise of a possession can, no doubt, make us understand that that very thing which is the object of possession interests us only insofar as our heart is fond of it. What I possess is my good: it is by virtue of this that I am pleased with it. But still it is necessary in Christian contemplation to see what one is fond of, of what our heart is really enamored.

It is necessary to discern what is the profound attraction of the contemplative. We may take pleasure in looking at something with the eyes of the body or of the spirit for two reasons: through love of the reality which attracts our gaze (there where thy treasure is, there thy heart is . . .), but also through a liking for the spiritual satisfaction which is found in the end of its search. One then understands why St. Gregory made contemplative life to consist in the love of God Himself: it is by loving God that we are aflame to gaze on His beauty. As delight is born of the possession of that which is loved, contemplative life grows in joy and thus finds its end in the activity of love—which is, moreover, only a start for a new and more ardent thrust of love.[25]

[25] St. Thomas, *Summa Theol.,* IIa IIae, q. 180, a. 1.

This is a good description of that tension between the natural attachment to pleasure we find in exercising that "perfect operation" in which the life of the intellect is completed, and the taste of God loved for Himself. Spiritual Christians are very attentive to that purity of the contemplative gaze, which is not only a stripping away of vulgar images in order to reach highly spiritual truths, but a detachment from the satisfactions which bring sublime knowledge to the spirit in a sublimation of self where God is loved more than anything. The teaching of a St. John of the Cross finds in this many of its essential principles. Let us add that we do not see God here on earth, and that we must accept the fact. Contemplative Christian life is basically an untiring search for God, in which repose in His presence is never, as we have said, merely a stopping-place along the way.

3. Affective Knowledge and Gifts of the Holy Spirit

But spiritual theology is not content thus to situate the contemplative act within the movement of love. It is not enough to say that the latter, eager for possession, moves us to contemplate and to seek, for that reason, every trace of God Who is loved. Nor is it enough that contemplation, drawing to a close in a movement of the heart which clings to the Sovereign Good, is accompanied by joy, an act of love resting in its object.

Taking as a fact the spiritual experience of Christian contemplatives and mystics, theology endeavors to explain the psychological idea of contemplation by showing what love brings to knowledge. On the other hand—and that is one of the beautiful aspects of the classical treatise of John of St. Thomas on the gifts of the Holy Spirit—this psychology is linked to the theology of virtues and gifts, and we see in the exercise of the intellectual gifts of the Holy Spirit the immediate principle of "infused" contemplation.

Psychologically, this is the theme of affective knowledge. Love not only moves us to know, but enriches knowledge itself by a singular penetration, by an intimate and wholly personal sense of the reality of the object loved. *Amor transit in conditionem objecti,* says John of St. Thomas. That is, the object of knowledge carries as it were the enjoyable reflection of this love which makes us recognize in it the same one which moves our heart. A subjective element— what theologians still call *connaturality* here—, which clings to this sympathy, this affective union which love effects with its object, comes into play here. And so, drawing from the subjectivity of the lover this character of intimacy, of personal experience that is peculiar to him, affective knowledge lays claim at the same time to a greater objectivity, at least to more profound realism. For he who loves truly goes out of himself, submits with a more complete receptivity and thenceforth judges others for themselves and not for himself.

Such is the role applied to the knowledge of God which charity plays in that exercise of living faith that is Christian contemplation. Faith assures us of the reality of its object with a wholly divine certitude. It is thus the principle of all supernatural knowledge which we have of God and which we can maintain only because of his revelation. Nothing, moreover, will add to its certitude founded on the very word of God. But this knowledge, whose principle is faith, is itself to be irradiated under the influence of that love of charity which, in uniting us to God, establishes that connaturality we have spoken of.

Theologians believe, therefore, that this is the role of the gifts of the Holy Spirit, that they are, as it were, the organ of this irradiation of love in the life of faith. It is under this aspect that John of St. Thomas conceives the psychology of the gifts of understanding, knowledge and wisdom. Considering in these gifts the aspect by which we are rendered docile to these "operating graces," by which the "instincts" of the Holy Spirit are understood, theologians see a justification of the idea of "infused" contemplation. The latter appears to them, consequently, not as an extraordinary gift, but within the *normal* line of development of a spiritual life in which the entire organism is active—virtues and gifts born of grace. But it is no less important, we believe, to see clearly that the "movement" of the Holy Spirit is exercised in consideration of charity, and that it is indeed by way of love that there comes into the soul this understanding, or better, this delightful, although generally obscure sense of the reality of God of which spiritual men are said to have experience.

The gifts proceed, believes John of St. Thomas, "in genere mystico et affectivo." Hence the character at once intimate and secret of this "inspiration." The intimate movement of charity unites us to that wisdom which is hidden in God Himself and which is communicated in that delightful experience wherein God proves Himself the real object of our love. The exercise of the gifts of understanding, knowledge and wisdom, in view to the realities which faith makes us recognize, seems, then, a kind of appreciation—beginning with this movement of the heart—of the reality, the agreement, the transcendant fulness of God.

"Understanding" corresponds, therefore, to that sense of reality with which every love provides its object. Whatever may be the etymology given to *intellegere: intus legere,* to read into—or more exactly, *inter legere,* to choose among—, it is still the same idea of penetration, at the same time as a placing in relief, among all other beings, of the one to whom our heart has been given. Supernatural understanding, the sense of the reality of divine things, no longer allows us to be satisfied with any created thing. To the gift of knowledge may be ascribed, according to our theologians, that appreciation of things created in relation to God and always beginning with the love which we have for Him; likewise, through knowledge we obtain appreciation of the value of faith, in spite of its inability to move us to embrace God.

The gift of understanding causes us to say: "How real it is!" The gift of knowledge causes us to declare: "How true it is!" But wisdom would be expressed in these phrases, for example: how truly God explains everything, how God suffices for me: God is my all! The affective union with God Himself—summit of the knowledge of love, supernatural wisdom, gift of the Holy Ghost in whom all others originate and end—is the source of that delectable appreciation of divine fulness in which the mind and heart now find an appeasement. It is the announcer of eternal joys. The gift of wisdom is therefore, according to our theologians, the formal principle of Christian contemplation in its most prominent acts.

4. Mystical Experience and Theology

This theological effort, we see, endeavors to reconcile an experimental fact, as it is translated in the confidences of the mystics, with a certain conception of the spiritual organism of the soul in a state of grace. We must not forget, however, that the language of the mystics proceeds from a dictionary—that of experience, and of an experience which they themselves call ineffable—other than the traditional theological language. We shall watch out then for too easy agreements between a John of the Cross, for example, and a Thomas Aquinas. Each one must be appreciated on his own level. Jacques Maritain, in *The Degrees of Knowledge,* has tried to give the principles of that proper discernment which permits us to "distinguish in order to unite."

For the fact remains that if a John of the Cross goes beyond simple experience in order to make a certain systematization of it, he does so while remaining on the level of the "expert in contemplation." And we understand very well that this level itself is subordinated to the judgment of theological "knowledge" striving for an explanation, whose principles are taken *ex propriis rerum,* that is, in the event of the very reality of the state of grace.

It is along this line that a theologian like Father Gardeil has tried to "explain" mystical experience (while assuming it to be that very thing which is most characteristic of it in the descriptions of spiritual persons, who describe it as a kind of contact with God during the night) not only by beginning with the gift of wisdom, but, seeking the final reasons, by making it the very *structure* of the soul in a state of grace.

Without being able here to set forth all the aspects of this profound doctrine, let us say simply that the experience in question seems to belong to the tension between charity's longing to see God, in that immediacy of the blessed vision which determines charity's every movement, and the condition of faith whose law is to conceal from us again the God whom it reveals to us and whom we attain only through its images, *per speculum, in aenigmate.* "Where then hast thou hidden thyself, beloved who hast left me to weep," sings John of the Cross. "I have gone to thee crying and thou wert gone . . ." God, he comments, is hidden in Himself. Such, it seems, is the reason for that negative and at times painfully purifying aspect which the movement of contemplative life takes.

The theologian endeavoring to judge it on his own level (not on the level of behavior of a soul but on that of explaining a structure *in genere*), will be particularly concerned, then, to state precisely within what conditions the relation to God (object of immediate knowledge and of full fruition which *defines* supernatural life) is combined with the "intentional" phase of faith. We are made for the vision of God. Charity is in us that love whose entire nature has to blossom out in the vision of God. This divine junction cannot be realized here on earth. But what we are living is a supernatural life which stretches out to it, and would we not be capable of experiencing that in a certain way? If, then, there is introduced in the very heart of our most sublime knowledge of God a "that's not it, that's

not He!," isn't that as it were the return shock of a positive inclination toward the divine Object as He is in Himself? Let us note well
that this "negation" which comes in the case of the mystic to extin-
guish, so to speak, his most beautiful thoughts about God, is not a
work of intellectual reflection, like the *via negationis* of the analog-
ical method: it is a kind of instinctive reaction, a translation of a
singular experience which would be the very same thing in our life
of grace.

Would mystical experience otherwise always be only that anxious
quest for God, that "negative knowledge" in which the soul would
find appeasement only in the humble acceptance of the present condition, in the accepted renunciation of seeing God? There is more,
it seems, and it is there that we shall find again the gift of wisdom.
For in the heart of this negation which is the supreme intellectual
step in mystical wisdom, love already is enjoying God. Obscurely,
certainly, but the spiritual person feels in this going beyond all limits, the transcendence of that Good whom he recognizes as his own
in the movement carrying him toward Him.

More simply, let us say that at the time the feeling seizes him
nothing of what he knows about God is himself; he knows himself
loved by that Infinite One whom he is powerless to grasp. Then for
an instant this anguish of search for God is calmed and the soul
lets itself simply be carried by that love which surrounds it, understanding that God wished nothing else of His creature but that it let
itself be loved by Him and be opened to that fulness. "Receive my
love with love," says God to Catherine of Siena. God is love. Does
the Christian contemplative try anything else?

5. Acquired Contemplation

In thus connecting mystical experience and supernatural contemplation to the structure of the soul in a state of grace (Gardeil),
and more directly to the exercise of the gifts of the Holy Ghost
(Garrigou-Lagrange), our theologians have meant to state that from
the most humble experiences of spiritual life to the peaks of contemplation, there is continuity.

That is to say, what appears to us with a particular intensity in
the mystics is not of a different species than what normal development in the life of grace implies. Hence it is in order to avoid the
misunderstanding which assumes the existence of two spiritual ways
—the one ordinary, whose peak would be a so-called *acquired* con-

templation, the fruition and the end of a methodical meditation principally connected with a virtuous asceticism; the other exceptional and pre-supposing special graces—that theologians like Garrigou-Lagrange reject the term acquired contemplation. There is no true Christian contemplation unless infused, in the sense that proceeding from gifts of the Holy Spirit it supposes that amenability, that passivity in regard to divine action, in which the life of grace finds its full meaning.

But we can admit, without risk of falling into denounced error, the rather relative character of the distinction of the acquired and the infused. Let us not see in it, however, the distinction of something more or less essentially supernatural. The act of living faith, even if the gifts of the Holy Spirit animate it only in a very latent way, is no less essentially supernatural; and the gifts are not substantially superior to the theological virtues: they are in their service.

Now, the exercise of the most essentially supernatural virtues supposes, in the development of the habitus, an acquired knowledge which allows us to speak very justifiably of an acquired contemplation, fruit of the habit which we assume in practising our faith. But we will normally see in this "acquired contemplation," fruit of the patient and even methodical exercise of theological prayer, a *disposition* to some of the graces of contemplation which normally prepare for that contemplation which is called infused *in order to designate a form of prayer in which predominate the exercise of the gifts of understanding and wisdom*. It is in this sense that certain Carmelite authors of the 17th century made this idea of acquired contemplation coincide with the active prayer of recollection described by St. Teresa. Father Huguenay, in certain articles of *La Vie Spirituelle* (November, 1933), characterized acquired supernatural contemplation by the more or less frequent repetition of the "*contuitus*" of living faith, fruit of analytical meditation, of reading and of prayer. The gifts of the Holy Spirit already enjoy it, in a more or less secret way, but the greatest part, in this opulent gaze of all meditated thoughts, still clings to the attempt which we have made and which, beyond our prayer, the action of the Holy Spirit consummates.

We return, therefore, to all that has been said about the intellectual preparation of the contemplative act. But if we do not forget that Christian contemplation is the fruit of living faith, we attach a still greater price to the purification within us of charity in order to dispose ourselves to a truly contemplative life. The practice of prayer is certainly indicated by all spiritual persons as the preparatory step toward that interior recollection of the soul in which is enjoyed the delicacy of the love of God. But spiritual theology insists quite as much on the required moral preparations. The *vita activa*, understood in the sense that we today call asceticism, is required as the stable foundation of the spiritual dwelling: "the moral virtues enter into the movement of contemplative life by reason of aptitudes to that final act. It is hindered, as a matter of fact, by the violence of the passions, which, diverting the soul from its spiritual diligence, recall it to the sensible, and by agitations from without. . . ."[26]

But above all, it is the purification of the heart, the true unselfishness that is the immediate condition of that experience of love which is the very basis of life with God. From that viewpoint the *vita activa*, understood this time by loving devotion to one's neighbor, and, notably, by the apostolic life, may, by the detachment of self which it implies, favor, if not a contemplation of speculative form, at least an experience of intimacy with God not always known in the same degree by souls who, under pretext of contemplative life, seek their own peace of mind. Certainly exterior activity can include some encumbrance of the spirit. But is not the laying bare of the heart the essential thing?

There are three degrees in charity: God must be loved above all for Himself. There are people who willingly, and without it bothering them very much, let go of divine contemplative leisure in order to take part in the affairs of the world. They do not display a great love, perhaps not even for anyone. But there are those who enjoy this divine leisure to such a point that they do not wish to give it up in any way, even in order to dedicate themselves to the service of God by serving their neighbor. Others, however, ascend to such a summit of love that even the divine contemplation which they enjoy so much is put aside to serve God by working for the salvation of their brothers. . . . They also are symbolized by the angels, ascending the ladder of Jacob in contemplation and descending in the concern which prompts them to save their neighbor.[27]

REFLECTIONS AND PERSPECTIVES

Temptations of the theologian. The treatise on contemplative life ordinarily offers the theologian a twofold temptation. On the one hand is the "Greek" temptation: too concerned about being faithful to the Greek tradition which they have borrowed and not worrying enough

---

[26] St. Thomas, IIa IIae, q. 180, a. 2.
[27] St. Thomas, *De caritate*, XI, 6.

about other traditions with their categories of "active life" and "contemplative life," certain theologians succeed in making Christian contemplative life an "intellectual" life, even a philosophic life, in which love no longer holds the place of honor which it must have in Christianity. On the other hand, there is the "mystical" temptation: certain theologians, doubtless making reference more to particular centers of contemplative life and especially to feminine communities whose theological and even intellectual culture is often mediocre, have a tendency to make Christian contemplative life an amorous one and, as it were, one without definite subject matter, a life whose fervor is applied to putting into action all the forms of sensible affectivity and of emotivity, rather than to giving life to the intellect while laboring to "know" its good. The first group forgets that it is the appetite of faith and the love of God which, in Christian contemplative life, move the understanding and lead it to the search for truth; the second group forgets that all contemplative life is essentially of the intellectual order, although its principle (that is, its motif in the etymological meaning of the word) and its end (the joy which accompanies the possession of the true—or the possession of God) belong to the movement of the will (and of charity).

But the latter and not the former are right: the quality of knowledge and the interior penetration that we can have of our Object in the exercise of faith which is ours here on earth are in proportion to the love of charity which makes us apply the understanding in the search for God. In heaven, on the contrary, when we shall see God as He is, our joy in possessing Him will be in exact proportion to what we shall possess, by a gratuitous gift of God, in understanding. A sound theology must maintain simultaneously the rights of the intellect and the demands of love in the bosom of Christian contemplative life.

Perhaps those theologians with the mystical bent have been too much influenced by the names given to religious communities. Nowadays we are accustomed to call contemplatives those cloistered communities who have no other work. But the life of a community is not defined by the exterior and juridical conditions of that community. In the current fashion we also define "monastic life" as "contemplative life." That is certainly not untrue; but it is good to note the relative character of this identification. St. Benedict, patriarch of Western monks, never speaks of "contemplative life" in his Rule. And in the 12th and 13th centuries still, even if no one denied that monks could also be contemplatives, it is necessary to point out that they were far from being accorded the privilege.

Theoreticians of the canonical life (Canons Regular) for example, define monastic life as ascetical life, that is, in the terminology of St. Thomas Aquinas, active life (one trained in the acquisition of virtues) as opposed to canonical (i.e. Dominican) life which, they say, answers more exactly to the definition of contemplative life. St. Thomas [28] declares that the ceelbration of the divine mysteries, to which the canonical order is "directly ordained," being the principal work of contemplative life, it is the order of Canons which realize contemplative life better than orders of monks.[29]

Thus there is always a need to be wary of hasty designations and to be careful in all that the latter signify. The criterion of contemplative life lies in this definition which St. Thomas gives of the "life" of each man: *Id in quo maxime delectatur, et cui maxime intendit, et in quo praecipue vult quilibet convivere amico.*[30] In this way only the *community* whose intention and principal occupation refer to the works of contemplative life really has the right to be contemplative. In other words, the celebration of the divine mysteries—the reading, study, research, as it were, of truth which provide the "opus Dei," the work of God—may be considered less an exterior handling of objects of worship than a body of signs constituted by these things whose contemplation turns the attention of the spirit unceasingly to what they signify.

It is necessary, finally, to point out another temptation of the theologian—that which consists in comparing a "treatise on the contemplative life" and a "treatise on perfection." We must say again here that the essence of perfection lies not in contemplation but in the charity which is exercised in the active life and in the contemplative life. If the contemplative life, of its nature, is superior to the active life (St. Thomas gives eight reasons which he borrows from Aristotle but all of which he links very judiciously to patristic and biblical tradition), it does not follow that such an active life cannot be more charitable, and thus more perfect, than such a contemplative life; nor that

---

[28] IIa IIae, q. 189, a. 8 and ad. 2.

[29] Cf. on this subject A. M. Henry, *Moines et chanoines,* in *La Vie Spirituelle,* Jan. 1949, pp. 60 ff. The issue is dedicated to *Reguliers et seculiers.*

[30] IIa IIae, q. 179, a. 1. (The life of such a *man* will be) that in which he finds his greatest joys, that to which he most applies himself, that which he most loves to communicate to his friends and to share with them.

in every contemplative life, charity must, from time to time, take leave of contemplation for the good of one's neighbor.

In the same way again, it is a temptation and an excess to attribute the contemplative life all the silent acts of the spirit. Examination of conscience, precautionary investigation, meditation terminating in "practical resolution" and decision, belong, by virtue of the very word which determines them, to the active life. It is otherwise in the case of theological prayer or the meditation which is used to understand the Word of God and to go to the Divine embrace: these on the contrary, are acts of contemplative life.

In short, we can consider on the one hand, as depending on the same order, the expressions of active life, virtuous life, ascetical life, human life (man's life as a whole), social life, political life (man's life considered as a member of a city or of a country), militant life (the Christian's life on earth), life which provides for the necessities of one's present existence, life of service, life of prudence. On the other hand, we can consider the expressions of contemplative life, studious life (studies leading to contemplation), heavenly life, divine life (this is in fact God's own life and that of the blessed), life of friendship and intimacy, a wholly free life. The contemplative life here on earth is always imperfect and mingled with the active life; the acts which belong here on earth to the active life (such as mercy and justice) arise in our Heavenly home from the unique contemplative life (called the beatific vision). As for the "mixed life," it is not just any mixture of active and contemplative life, but an overflowing of contemplative life which is communicated to one's neighbor through a teaching action.

Schools of Contemplative Life

The idea of life is an idea of interiority; it appeals to what is most personal and most profound in each man; i.e. his fundamental task, his vocation, his destiny, his innermost "nature." It is also easily applied to persons and with more difficulty to institutions which are defined above all by the exterior laws and the constitutions governing them. The idea of *state* which will be defined in the following chapter is quite the contrary. It is principally an idea of exteriority; it is also applied first to institutional and next, by reference to these institutions, to persons for example, a religious is in a state of perfection not because he is in himself perfect, but because he has officially joined an exterior state or an institution of perfection. We shall also speak more correctly of Orders, congregations, societies, companies, institutions, communities in reference to *states* rather than *ways of life*. Whatsoever may be the intentions of the legislator, it happens that the so-called contemplative communities are not composed only of contemplatives, and it is rare that there are not some true contemplatives in active communities. In order to recall, on the contrary, the ordinary characteristics of certain "currents" or of certain "movements" in contemplative life, we shall speak more definitely about *schools* than about Orders or congregations.

A "school" is the expression of a common spirit, and at the same time the guide of this spirit. It is the same expression which is used, for example, in painting when one speaks of the Flemish school or of the Italian school of the Renaissance. Contemplative life also includes certain "schools." Most of them bear the name of the great religious Orders, but they are not completely coextensive with these Orders, and, like the spirit whose expression they are, their influence overflows the banks of these Orders and may cover several of them; or, on the other hand, one and the same Order may introduce several "schools."

The distinction according to "schools" in the heart of contemplative life has become classic since the 16th and 17th centuries; there is a certain anachronism in "applying" it to the Middle Ages. Not without reason does the historian distinguish between the 12th and the 15th centuries; for example, the Benedictine school (Masters: Peter the Venerable, Rupert of Deut, St. Hildegard); the Cistercian school (Masters: St. Bernard, William of St. Thierry, Joachim de Flora, St. Gertrude, St. Brigit); the School of St. Victor (Masters: Hugh and Richard); the Franciscan school (Masters: St. Francis of Assisi, St. Bonaventure, Blessed Angela of Foligno, Raymond Lulle); the Dominican school (Masters: St. Dominic, St. Thomas Aquinas, St. Albert the Great, St. Catherine of Siena, St. Vincent Ferrer); the Rhineland school, likewise Dominican (Masters: Eckhart, Tauler, Henry Suso, and, because of his spiritual kinship, we must add John Ruysbroeck, who was neither Dominican nor Rhenish); the school of Windisheim (Gerard Groot, Thomas a Kempis); the Carthusian school (Masters: Ludolph of Saxony, Denis the Carthusian).

At the end of the 16th century, we shall distinguish over and above these old schools for example, the Ignatian school, characterized by the *exercises* of St. Ignatius; the Carmelite school (Masters: St. Teresa of Jesus and St. John of the Cross); the Berullian school (Masters: Cardinal de Berulle, Father de Coudren, Father Bourgoing, M. Olier and the founders of St. Sulpice) from which also rises in France a part of Carmel; the Salesian school (Masters: St. Francis de Sales and St. Jeanne de Chantal) the School of Charity (St. Vincent de Paul, St. John Eudes, St. Margaret Mary). These schools are the principal ones; we could name others, and in particular, develop the list of their "masters" from the beginning up to the present. It belongs to theology to study the characteristics and special marks of these schools.

Areas of work. Can we say that the "priestly life" is a contemplative life? Or an active life? What should the priest be? And the bishop? Can the contemplative life be led in the world? Under what conditions? Can a married woman be a contemplative (in the technical sense in which we have defined it, where contemplation represents not only principal intention and deep liking for, but also the principal occupation)? Isn't a holy active life rather the normal fruit of matrimonial grace? Try to define the essential virtues of the spouses and sketch the general outlines of their "spirituality." Life of teachers: is it a contemplative life or an active life?

Value of the different works of contemplative life: Celebration of the Divine Office, listening to the Word of God, mental prayer, reading, study, meditation; can we compare these different activities with each other? Which is the better? Can a contemplative life dispense with any of them? Which activities are the most useful at the beginning of each contemplative life? Do asceticism and the correction of faults which are ordered for the stripping of self and for a greater love of Divine truth (which the contemplative seeks) arise from the active life, or from the contemplative life? Value of the different works of active life: obedience, asceticism, mortification, brotherly correction, etc. Can we establish a hierarchy among active congregations from works like teaching poor and abandoned children, teaching of the wealthy, care of the sick or the infirm, cathechizing, visiting the poor, visiting prisoners, welcoming guests, assisting the parochial clergy, social assistance, etc.? What is the principal of the value judgment? Comment on the words of St. Augustine: "He loves you less, Lord, who, at the same time as you, loves something else which he loves not for you."

Biblical "types" of active and contemplative life: Rachel and Lia, Martha and Mary. Explanation and value of these symbols. Doctrine of the sapiential books on the "contemplative" life. Evangelic doctrine: show, especially from I Cor. 1:18, the role of Christ crucified in the progress of the contemplative in the knowledge of the Truth.

The fruits of contemplative life, its distinguishing marks: peace, joy, beauty of soul; the beatitudes which accompany it. Renunciations and "crosses" which it normally knows—for instance, the doctrine of the "nights" of St. John of the Cross. Does the active life also normally know certain "nights"?

Contemplative life outside the Church. Since there can be no contemplative life without grace (and without charity), can there be a contemplative life outside the Church? Explain certain facts (cf. L. Massignon, *La passion d'Al Hallaj, martyr mystique de l'Islam,* Paris, Geuthner, 1922; and L. Gardet, *La connaissance et l'amour de Dieu selon quelques textes sûfis des premiers siècles de l'hégire,* in *Revue thomiste,* Jan.-March, 1946, pp. 120-151).

Principles and Definitions. To conclude these reflections and meditations, we present here a general view of principles and of definitions which refer to the theological ideas of human life, active or contemplative life. The Latin being more concise, we shall quote them first in Latin:

Unumquodque vivens ostenditur vivere ex operatione sibi maxime propria ad quam maxime inclinatur: the life of a living being is revealed in the operation which, more than any other, is his alone and toward which his principal inclination carries him.

Vita humana attenditur secundum intellectum. Intellectus autem dividitur per activum et contemplativum: quia finis intellectivae cognitionis, vel est ipsa cognitio veritatis quod pertinet ad intellectum contemplativum; vel est aliqua exterior actio, quod pertinet ad intellectum practicum sive activum: Human life is defined as a function of the intellect. And the intellect is divided into active intellect and contemplative intellect; intellectual activity has for its end, as a matter of fact, either to know the truth (which is the concern of the contemplative intellect), or to act exteriorly (which is the concern of the active or practical intellect.)

Ex hoc ipso quod veritas est finis contemplationis, habet rationem boni appetibilis et amabilis et delectantis. Et secundum hoc pertinet ad vim appetitivam: From the fact that the end of contemplation is truth, the latter takes on value as being quite able to set in motion the voluntary appetite, able to be loved and to give pleasure. And it is in this way that truth interests the voluntary appetite.

Vita contemplativa unam quidem actum habet in quo finaliter perficitur, scilicet contemplationen veritatis, a quo habet unitatem: habet autem multos actus quibus pervenit ad hunc actum finalem:

Contemplative life consists of that unique act in which it is finally made perfect and which is the contemplation of truth; i.e. it is from that final act that it receives its unity, but it includes many other acts by which it journeys to that supreme one.

Contemplatio pertinet ad ipsum simplicem intuitum veritatis: Contemplation pertains to the simple intuition of truth.

Ultimo perfectio humani intellectus est veritas divina: The ultimate perfection of the human intellect is divine truth.

Vita contemplativa dicitur manere ratione charitatis in qua habet et principium et finem: (In spite of the interruption here on earth of the acts of contemplation) we say that the contemplative life dwells in a soul because of the love in which that life finds its beginning and its end.

BIBLIOGRAPHIE

Les pages du P. Camelot en tête de ce chapitre reprennent l'essentiel d'un article déjà publié par lui: *Action et contemplation dans la tradition chrétienne,* in *La Vie Spirituelle,* tome 78 (1948), pp. 272-301.

Sur ce même problème on lira les remarques pénétrantes de A.-J. Festugière, *L'enfant d'Agrigente,* 2ᵉ éd., Paris, Plon, 1950, et dans un genre un peu différent: P.-I. Hausherr, *Les grands courants de la spiritualité orientale,* in *Orientalia Christiana Periodica,* I (1935), pp. 114-138.

Sur le caractère eschatologique de la distinction entre les deux vies, voir l'excellent article de Mlle A.-M. La Bonnardière, *Marthe et Marie, figures de l'Église d'après saint Augustin,* in *La Vie Spirituelle,* tome 86 (1952), pp. 404-427.

Théologie des "vies":

Saint Thomas d'Aquin, *La vie humaine, ses formes, ses états,* trad. et notes de A. Lemonnyer, Paris, Éd. de la Revue des J., 1926. On remarquera que le P. Lemonnyer a mis sous un même titre deux traités fort différents: celui des *Vies* et celui des *états,* Cette réunion des deux traités en un même volume, et sous un même titre, prête à une confusion fâcheuse dont la tentation est déjà forte en beaucoup d'esprits. Rappelons donc ici une fois encore que le traité des vies n'est pas un traité de l'état de perfection. La seule considération du plan de la somme théologique (voir tome 1, p. 388) montre bien d'ailleurs que saint Thomas envisage les "vies" et les "états" comme deux conditions aussi opposées les unes aux autres que les "charismes" et les "vies."

Sur la vie contemplative: il est difficile de distinguer les ouvrages sur la vie contemplative proprement dite, de ceux sur la vie d'oraison, la vie mystique, la "spiritualité," la "théologie spirituelle" (selon une terminologie moderne), voire même la vie monastique ou "vie parfaite." Voici quelques livres sur ces problèmes:

THE ACTIVE LIFE AND THE CONTEMPLATIVE LIFE   679

D. Joret, *La contemplation mystique d'après saint Thomas d'Aquin,* Paris, Desclée de Br., 1923.
J. de Guibert, *Lecons de théologie spirituelle,* Toulouse, 1946.
É. Gilson, *Théologie et histoire de la spiritualité,* Paris, Vrin, 1943.
Y. de Montcheuil, *Problèmes de vie spirituelle,* Paris, Éd. de l'Épi, 1950.
A. Poulain, *Des grâces d'oraison, traité de théologie mystique,* Paris 1931.
A. Gardeil. *La structure de la connaissance mystique.* (Revue thomiste, 1924-25).
R. Garrigou-Lagrange, *Perfection chrétienne et contemplation,* 2 vol., Saint-Maximin, Éd. de la vie spirituelle, 1923.
R. Garrigou-Lagrange, *Les trois âges de la vie intérieure,* Paris, Éd. du Cerf.
J. de Jaegher, *Anthologie mystique,* Paris, Desclée de Br.

Il est souvent remarquable que les ouvrages sur la vie contemplative fassent peu mention de la lecture et surtout de l'étude qui sont normalement, pour saint Thomas, des moyens essentiels d'accès à la vie contemplative. Tenir compte, le cas échéant, de cette différence.

Les écoles de vie contemplative (et de vie spirituelle):

Nous avons déjà dit qu'il était difficile de distinguer des Écoles proprement dites de spiritualité avant les xive-xve siècles. Bien que les dénominations d' "École d'Alexandrie" et d' "École d'Antioche" soient courantes en histoire de la théologie, ces Écoles caractérisent surtout les tendances théologiques et exégétiques des Pères grecs des iiie-ve siècles. Elles sont moins des Écoles de spiritualité au sens moderne du mot. Aussi rangerons-nous sous le même titre, "la spiritualité des premiers siècles," tout ce qui concerne la vie spirituelle tant du clergé que des moines ou des fidèles, de l'Orient ou de l'Occident, des 10 premiers siècles.

1. La spiritualité des premiers siècles:

M. Villier, *Spiritualité des premiers siècles chrétiens,* Paris, 1930.
Dom Germain Morin, *L'idéal monastique et la vie chrétienne des premiers jours, Maredsous,* 6e édition, 1944. Cet ouvrage, qui rassemble simplement les instructions d'une retraite, est un très beau livre de spiritualité.
G. Bardy, *La vie spirituelle d'après les Pères des trois premiers siècles,* Paris, Éd. Bloud et Gay.
Dom Anselme Stolz, *Théologie de la mystique,* Chevetogne, 1947.
Dom Anselme Stolz, *L'ascèse chrétienne,* Chevetogne, 1948.
L. Bouyer, *La vie de saint Antoine,* Saint-Wandrille, Éd. de Fontenelle, 1950.
Très beau livre, et qui présente admirablement la spiritualité du 3e siècle.

2. La spiritualité des xiie-xiiie siècles. Cette spiritualité est à peu près la même dans tous les milieux. On note cependant une tendance d'opposition entre l'ordre monastique et l'ordre clérical ou "canonial" qui semble à cette époque prendre conscience de son ensemble (ou de son "Ordre"). On note aussi une opposition naissante entre la spiritualité des cisterciens (principalement de saint Bernard dont la tendance "mystique" fera école) et celle des Clunisiens, ou des autres bénédictins (tel Suger à l'abbaye de Saint-Denis). Enfin au xiiie siècle apparaissent les Ordres mendiants que le genre de vie tout nouveau va opposer, parfois vigoureusement, aux moines, ou au clergé, séculier ou régulier, des églises particulières.

a. École clunisienne et bénédictine.

Dom J. Leclercq, *La spiritualité de Pierre de Celle,* Paris, Vrin, 1946.

Dom J. Leclercq et J.-P. Bonnes, *Un maître de vie spirituelle, Jean de Fécamp,* Paris, Vrin, 1946.

Dom J. Leclercq, *Pierre le Vénérable,* Saint-Wandrille, Éd. de Fontenelle.

Marcel Aubert, *Suger,* Saint-Wandrille, Éd. de Fontenelle, 1950. D'un point de vue plus particulier, lire *L'amour du cœur de Jésus contemplé avec les saints et les mystiques de l'Ordre de S. Benoît,* Coll. Pax, Desclée De Br.

b. École cistercienne.

Les textes de saint Bernard peuvent être lus soit dans la patrologie de Migne, soit en traduction, dans les ouvrages de morceaux choisis tels que ceux de E. Vacandard (*Vie de saint Bernard, abbé de Clairvaux,* Paris, 1895); de Dom Alexis Presse, 1947; de M.-M. Davy, Paris, 1945; de E. Gilson, Paris, 1949. Nous citerons en particulier Pierre Daloz dans sa traduction de *La considération* (Grenoble, 1945) et le *Traité de l'amour de Dieu,* Coll. Pax, Desclée De Br., Sur saint Bernard, lire:

E. Gilson, *La théologie mystique de saint Bernard,* Paris, 1934.

Dom J. Leclercq, *Saint Bernard mystique,* Paris, 1948 (Dom. J. Leclercq prépare une édition critique des œuvres de saint Bernard).

J.-Ch. Didier, *La dévotion à l'humanité du Christ dans la spiritualité de saint Bernard,* Paris, 1929.

P. Aubron, *L'œuvre mariale de saint Bernard,* Paris, 1929.

Dom A. Presse, *La réforme de Cîteaux,* Paris, 1932.

J. Berthold Mann, *L'ordre cistercien et son gouvernement des origines au milieu du XIIIe siècle* (1098-1265), Paris, Éd. de Boccard, 1945. Livre particulièrement remarquable qui éclaire d'un jour nouveau les origines de Citeaux.

D.-J. Othon, *Les origines cisterciennes,* Ligugé, 1933.

c. Écoles prémontrée et dominicaine.

Nous rangeons sous un même titre les "spiritualités" prémontrée et dominicaine; les deux ordres sont issus pratiquement des mêmes mouvements: canonial et "apostolique," et ont au XIIIe siècle la même spiritualité. Cependant le caractère monarchique de l'institution prémontrée, la condition mendiante et itinérante des frères prêcheurs, créeront peu à peu une distinction.

F. Petit, *La spiritualité des Prémontrés aux XIIe et XIIIe siècles,* Paris, Vrin, 1947.

P. Mandonnet, M.-H. Vicaire, *Saint Dominique, L'idée, l'homme et l'œuvre,* Paris, Desclée De Br. (1938).

On trouvera dans ces ouvrages la bibliographie désirable.

Bien que sainte Catherine de Sienne soit seulement du XIVe siècle, nous citerons ici aussi comme exemple de spiritualité dominicaine, son *dialogue,* trad. Hurtaud, 2 vol., Paris, Lethielleux, 1913.

d. École franciscaine.

Les "vies" de saint François sont innombrables. Citons simplement:

Saint Bonaventure, *Vie de saint François d'Assise,* 1951.

O. Englebert, *Vie de saint François d'Assise,* Paris, 1947.

R. Guardini, *Der heilige Franziskus.*
J.-R. Moormann, *Saint Francis of Assisi.*
Jean Vignaud, *Saint François,* Paris, 1950.

Les écrits de saint François peuvent être lus dans les *Opuscula* dont une édition critique a été publiée à Quaracchi, 1904 - et dans les *Opuscules,* Paris, Libr. Saint-François.

Les *œuvres spirituelles de saint Bonaventure* ont été publiées en français (6 vol.) à Paris, 1854-1855.

Les œuvres de Raymond Lulle: *Opera omnia* à Mayence, 1721-1740, 10 vol.

Lire aussi:

A. Gemelli, *Le message de saint François au monde moderne,* traduit par P. Mazoyer, Paris, Lethielleux, 1948.

Vitus a Bussum, *De spiritualitate franciscana; aliqua capita fundamentalia,* Rome, 1949.

e. Les ermites:

Guigues le Chartreux, *L'échelle du paradis,* Paris, Éd. du Cerf.
Jean-Berthold Mahn, *L'ordre cistercien et son gouvernement,* op. cit.
A. Giabbani, *L'eremo, Vita et spiritualita eremetica nel nonachismo Camaldolese primitivo,* Camaldoli, 1945.
Catechismo camaldolese, Camaldoli, 1951.
Dom Jean Leclercq, *Un humaniste ermite, le bienheureux Père Giustiniani,* Camaldoli, 1951.

3. L'école rhénane et l'Imitation de Jésus-Christ.

Bienh. Henri Susso, *L'Œuvre mystique,* trad. Lavaud.
J. Denifle, *La vie spirituelle d'après les mystiques allemands du XIVe siècle,* Paris, Lethielleux.
L'Imitation de Jésus-Christ, texte latin, trad. française de Lamennais, Intr. Chenu, Paris, Plon, 1942.

4. L'école ignatienne.

Saint Ignace de Loyola, *Exercices spirituels,* Paris, de Gigord.
Hugo Rahner, *Saint Ignace de Loyola et la genèse des exercices,* Toulouse, Apostolat de la prière, 1948.
J.-P. de Caussade, *L'abandon à la Providence divine,* Paris, Gabalda.
L. de Grandmaison, *Écrits spirituels,* Paris, Beauchesne.
P. de Jaegher, *La vie d'identification au Christ-Jésus,* Paris, Éd. du Cerf.

5. L'école carmélitaine.

Sainte Thérèse de Jésus, *Vie par elle-même,* Paris, Éd. du Cerf.
Sainte Thérèse d'Avila, *Œuvres complètes,* par le R. P. Grégoire de Saint-Joseph, Paris, Éd. du Seuil.
Saint Jean de la Croix, *Œuvres complètes,* par le R. P. Grégoire de Saint-Joseph, Paris, Éd. du Seuil.
Saint Jean de la Croix, *Avis et maximes,* Carmel de Monte-Carlo.
Laurent de la Résurrection, *La pratique de la présence de Dieu,* Paris, Desclée De Br.
S. Thérèse de l'Enfant Jésus, *Histoire d'une âme,* Carmel de Lisieux.

A. Combes, *Introduction à la spiritualité de sainte Thérèse de l'Enfant Jésus,* Paris, Vrin.

Soeur Élisabeth de la Trinité, *Réflexions et pensées,* Fribourg, Impr. Saint-Paul.

A quoi nous ajouterons toute la collection *La vigne du carmel* que publient les Éditions du Seuil.

6. École française, École de "la charité," École salésienne.

Card. de Bérulle, *Opuscules de piété,* Paris, Aubier.

Card. de Bérulle, *Vie de Jésus,* Paris, Éd. du Cerf.

Saint François de Sales, *Traité de l'amour de Dieu,* Paris, Lethielleux.

Introduction à la vie dévote, éditée par A. Fleury, s. j., Tours, Mame.

L. Cognet, *Les origines de la spiritualité française au XVII⁰ siècle.*

Enfin sur le P. de Foucauld, on lira particulièrement:

Ch. de Foucauld, *Écrits spirituels,* Paris, de Gigord.

M.-M. Vaussard, *Le Père de Foucauld, maître de vie intérieure,* Paris, Éd. du Cerf.

R. Voillaume, *Les fraternités du P. de Foucauld,* Paris, Éd. du Cerf. Sur la spiritualité des petits frères, lire R. Voillaume, *Au coeur des masses,* Paris, Éd. du Cerf.

BIBLIOGRAPHY

Caussade, J. P., *Abandonment to Divine Providence,* St. Louis, Herder, 1921.

Chesterton, G. K., *St. Francis of Assisi,* New York, Sheed and Ward, 1930.

Eugene of the Child of Jesus, O.C.D., *I Want to See God,* Chicago, Fides, 1953.

———, *I Am a Daughter of the Church,* Chicago, Fides, 1955.

Faber, Frederick, *All for Jesus,* Baltimore, Murphy and Co., 1954.

DeSales, St. Francis, *Introduction to the Devout Life* (tr. John K. Ryan), Garden City, New York, Doubleday and Company, Inc. (Image Books), 1950.

———, *The Love of God,* London, Sands and Co., 1931.

Gabriel of St. Mary Magdalen, O.C.D., *St. John of the Cross,* Westminster, Md., Newman Press, 1946.

Garrigou-Lagrange, *The Three Ages of the Interior Life,* St. Louis, Herder, 1948.

———, *Christian Perfection and Contemplation,* St. Louis, Herder, 1942.

Gilson, Etienne, *The Mystical Theology of St. Bernard,* New York, Sheed and Ward, 1940.

Grandmaison, Leonce de, *We and the Holy Spirit,* Chicago, Fides, 1953.

———, *Come Holy Spirit,* Chicago, Fides, 1956.

Guibert, Joseph de, S.J., *The Theology of the Spiritual Life,* New York, Sheed and Ward, 1953.

St. Ignatius Loyola, *The Spiritual Exercises,* New York, Benziger Brothers.

St. John of the Cross, *Complete Works* (tr. E. Allison Peers), Westminster, Md., Newman Press, 1945.

Maritain, Jacques, *The Degrees of Knowledge,* New York, Scribners, 1938.

Marmion, Columba, O.S.B., *Christ the Ideal of the Monk,* St. Louis, Herder, 1934.

————, *Christ the Life of the Soul,* St. Louis, Herder, 1922.

Montcheuil, Ives de, *For Men of Action,* Chicago, Fides, 1952.

Tanquerey, Adolphe, S.S., *The Spiritual Life,* Westminster, Md., Newman Press, 1948.

St. Teresa of Avila, *Complete Works* (tr. E. Allison Peers), New York, Sheed and Ward, 1946.

St. Therese of the Child Jesus, *The Story of a Soul,* New York, P. J. Kenedy and Sons, 1926.

Thomas a Kempis, *The Imitation of Christ,* Garden City, N. Y., Hanover House, 1955.

Tissot, J., *The Interior Life,* New York, Benziger Bros., 1913.

Voillaume, R., *Seeds of the Desert,* Chicago, Fides, 1955.

Chapter XII

FUNCTIONS, STATES AND ORDERS IN THE CHURCH

by A. M. Henry, O.P.

Chapter XII

FUNCTIONS, STATES AND ORDERS IN THE CHURCH

The actual position of the Christian in the Mystical Body of Christ may be determined in several ways. We have studied the *charismata*, which are the special graces bestowed upon a particular individual in view of the common good; next, the contemplative, active and mixed *ways of life*, by which the destiny of each baptized person is developed here on earth. But that is not enough. Setting aside virtues and grace (the study of which is common to all Christians), there is still in the Church of God a diversity of *functions* or offices, a diversity of *order* or dignity, a diversity of *state* or condition. One priest has care of souls which another does not have; one believer is a layman, another is a tonsured cleric, still another is higher up in "orders"; finally, this baptized person finds himself called by Our Lord to follow Him in the *state* of continence or virginity, while that one must serve Christ within the bonds of marriage.

The role of theology in relation to these situations—functions, states, orders or degrees—is to define them, to find their raison d'être, their usefulness or their necessity, to offer a guide for those who find themselves in these situations and, as far as possible, to pass judgment on their comparative value.

I. Functions, States and Orders Considered in General

A. DEFINITIONS

Function, state, order are terms which can be applied to every human situation but when they are attributed to certain specifically and uniquely Christian situations, a special theological meaning must be defined.

According to St. Isidore, the word "office" is derived from efficiency; the *e* was easily changed to *o* for the sake of euphony. This is a simple way of suggesting that office belongs to action. Offices are diversified by the acts which characterize them: the office of the judge, the teacher, or that of the doctor. On the whole the word is quite close to "function." In the Church we come upon the offices of *parish priest* (one who has care of souls), *preacher*, etc. Let us note immediately that the acts of which we are speaking here—acts which separate the different functions—are not, like those which separate *lives* into active or contemplative life, acts considered absolutely without reference to anything but the active subject. The word function is a relative term and the acts which separate functions are acts relating to others.

Order, or degree, brings to the interior of the same office, or the same state, a difference in eminence, in mastery or in dignity. Almost every profession includes different degrees which one reaches by merit or by seniority. The Church, which is a hierarchical body, also possesses different orders, from those of catechumens and baptized persons among the laity, and those of porter and lector on up to those of priest and bishop among the clergy.

State is a more difficult idea to define. State—in Latin "status"—is that permanent position of a thing which most deeply corresponds to its nature. The state of a man, considered as a living animal, is to be upright; that is in conformity with his nature; the state of a corpse is to be supine. In order that a business may be stabilized, it is necessary for it to find its balance in regard to raw materials, sales, clientele, etc. The state, healthy or unhealthy, of a business is a question of balance. How, then, are we going to define the state of man considered not only as animal but as a person, that is to say, as a being endowed with autonomy? Between total dependency in being and in acting there is a balance to be found and that balance establishes man in his condition or his state.

Let us note well that this is not a question of a temporary balance but of permanent balance. The fact of serving does not make one dependent and does not constitute a state. But the fact of being a slave, throughout life until death, truly constitutes a state.

The fact of being rich or poor does not constitute a state, for nothing changes like wealth or poverty, and these can affect very diverse conditions. There are poor middle-class persons, and there are rich wage earners who live in the same manner as other working men; what a middle-class person most fears is not so much poverty as coming down in the world. The struggle of the classes appears as a struggle for independence and autonomy. But while it is true that only servitude or independence fix man in a permanent condition, it remains difficult to better his condition without wealth.

Likewise, a raise in rank can better the condition but does not formally constitute a state. One can lose his rank and keep his social position, or at least his autonomy.

Finally, although there may be so-called "liberal" professions, neither is this the function which determines one in a state. The stockholder who renounces his profession does not lose his position in the world. A professional group is composed ordinarily of all social classes, that is, of all positions. And the work of those who direct is often more obligating than that of others. What the free man dreads above all is not so much work as servile work.

Thus, everything is reduced in brief to the two-fold idea of freedom (or independence) and of servitude. Whereas *function* is defined with respect to acts, or to the collective service that is undertaken, and *order* refers to excellence or to dignity, the *state* of man is determined by his degree of freedom or of servitude. Among Christians one speaks of a *state of grace* that is the state of those who have the freedom of the children of God, or of a *state of sin* that is the state of those who are under the yoke of sin, or slaves of sin. One likewise speaks of the *religious state*, that is, the state of those who have established their life in such a way that they may be, in the words of the Apostle, "free from cares" (I Cor. 7:32) in the midst of the world.

If these three notions are different, nothing prevents an individual from being able to make as it were a triple hit in relation to them. Thus, the priest promoted to the episcopacy enters in a new function (a new *office*), attains a new *state* of freedom and is established in a new *order* or a new dignity.

B. DEGREES WITHIN THE STATE OF FREEDOM

State, therefore, deals with freedom or servitude. We may then consider in spiritual life a double kind of freedom and a double kind of servitude, namely: a servitude of sin and a freedom in relation to "justice," that is, to spiritual rectitude; a servitude of justice and a freedom in relation to sin. We are slaves of sin when we are dominated by evil inclinations; we are slaves of justice when we are dominated by a virtuous love. The just man is restrained, or restrains himself, when he accidentally sins; the sinner is free in his habitual sin.

Let us consider, furthermore, that there is freedom and freedom. In contemplating our nature, vice is an added individual characteris-

The Church, being at the same time of the world and out of the world, expresses in her action the two-fold movement corresponding to her state. On the one hand, she goes toward the world through her preachers, her missionaries, her Christian families, bearing the Word of God and taking on the elements of the world—water, bread, wine, oil, consent, vow—in order to constitute her sacraments. On the other hand, she retires from the world, in the desert or the retreat, as is still testified by the Egyptian monastery of Dair al-Sourian, where she had taken up residence with the hermits at the beginning of the 3rd century.

If her radiating action toward the world is true, if her harvest outside the world is also true, the Church is not less fascinating, we would say captivating, for souls in the second movement than in the first. It suffices for us to remember those monastic colonies which from the 5th to the 10th centuries converted Europe not by sending out missionaries from each colony, but, on the contrary, by "intussusceptio," attracting by their silence, their recollection, their evangelic simplicity, those new lambs of Christ and then receiving them into their retreat. The Church is at once missionary and pastoral.

The Church carries the Word of God, but, the Word having been proclaimed, she must still help and protect the silence of the soul. Where would conversions be if the Word were not proclaimed everywhere? Where would the converts be if there were no living communities, true Thebaids of the faithful, in which believers can express their own faith and their thanksgiving—their Eucharist—to the living God who has called them?

Monastery of the Mother of God, *Walidat Ilah,* now called the monastery of the Syrians, *Dair al-Sourian,* in the desert of Scete-Nitrie (6th century). On this monastery, read L. Gardet, *Un monastere copte,* in *Suppl. de la Vie Sp.,* Nov. 1951.

tic—exterior and accidental as it were. Since the virtuous act is defined as an act according to reason, the virtuous inclination is more in conformity with our pure spontaneity, that is to say, with our freedom. The freedom which lets this second nature that is a vice appear is a shallow freedom, an exterior freedom which disguises and snuffs out true freedom. Grace, on the other hand, lights up all our primary spontaneity which is the love of good and which blends with our most fundamental and most authentic will to live. Thus real freedom is that of the just and real slavery, that of sinners. "Now the Lord is the spirit; and where the spirit of the Lord is, there is freedom (II Cor. 3:17). Our Lord Himself says: "If you abide in my word . . . you shall know the truth and the truth shall make you free" (Jn. 8:31-32). To be a slave of the truth, the light and the will of God is to find at last one's true self, and it is to be united to that source where being, drawing on its native freedom as a creature, is free from all possible restraint.

But that "slavery of justice," and that freedom which results from it, is in a way a frontier state. The Christian arrives there only after much zeal and many efforts. Likewise, we distinguish several stages or several degrees within the state of fredom, namely: the degree of *beginners,* those who have made up their minds to serve truth, to shape their life henceforth to that which is right and good; the degree of the *advanced*, those who are fixed in virtue and progressively acquire a greater freedom; finally, the degree of the *perfect.*

Two remarks—these three stages overlap those of charity; this is normal since charity is that by which we shall free ourselves from sin. These three stages are also called degrees which means that a change of state corresponds here to an ascent, to a new dignity.

C. REASON FOR THE EXISTENCE OF THIS DIVERSITY

This diversity of functions or of ministries, orders and states is not without reason. It contributes to the perfection of the Church. A true poet has only one thing to say but he is always prolific. With greater reason the divine artist, in order to imitate his own plenitude, must multiply his creatures in every way. "And he himself gave some men as apostles, and some as prophets, others again as evangelists, and others as pastors and teachers . . " (Eph. 4:11). This distributes the work and allows a happy accomplishment of it.

Finally, this diversity contributes to the beauty of the Church whose variegated dress shines at the same time with the doctrine of the

Apostles, with the testimony of martyrs, with the purity of virgins, and the tears of penitents.

But, you will say, is not this diversity an obstacle to the unity of the Church in which all members are equal? Why do women not attain the pastoral ministry? Why are certain services appropriated by certain offices? The unity of the Church is the unity of faith, of charity in the Holy Spirit, and this charity is expressed in the diversity of the services which the members render among themselves. The inequality of functions takes away nothing from the quality of the persons and contributes to form the unity of love. We must not attribute to the diversity of cares but to the lack of charity and to the lack of a "catholic" spirit, the fact that a pastor, jealous of his own administration or of his ministry, is reduced to acts which destroy the unity of the Church.

The fact remains that if charity is the bond of diversity, it may also come to suppress certain diversities where these no longer arise from the motives we have spoken of. Charity will thus be able to "reunite" certain religious congregations whose ends, means, habits, sentiments overlap. It will also be able to diminish the number of honorary titles of prelates or canons when they would flatter the vanity of the subject more than they would serve the "beauty of the Church." But in this field nothing must be exaggerated. Diversity, even if its origin is doubtful, gives the members the opportunity to prove that their unity is beyond these differences, i.e., within the Holy Spirit who animates the Church.

D. THE STATE OF PERFECTION [1]

The special study of the different *ministries, states* and *orders* within the Church is not to be undertaken here *in toto*. The consideration of *orders*, major and minor, calls attention to the theology of the sacrament of Holy Orders which is presented in Volume VI of *Theology Library*. The ministries are studied partly in connection with *Holy Orders*, and partly in connection with the *state* which those who exercise this or that ministry are in. There remains, therefore, the study of states. And since every movement is determined by its term, we give the principles of what is to be said regarding beginners and "advanced" while studying only the *state of the perfect*.

[1] What we are saying briefly here, under a form which suits the purpose of this chapter, will be taken up again in another way in the concluding chapter of this volume which will include many useful details.

This study can be divided into two parts: perfection and the state of perfection.

1. *Perfection*

Beginning and end coincide, i.e., it is in going back to the beginning that a being finds its end and its perfection. Man, created by God, finds his ultimate perfection in God. Charity establishes us in God who is Himself Love: "... he who abides in love abides in God, and God in him" (I Jn. 4:16). Charity is "the bond of perfection" (Col. 3:14). On the plane of grace, as on the natural plane, the law of progress like the law of perfection, is the very law of love.

Let us immediately point out that this perfection of love also leads to perfection of judgment. In order "to live in perfect harmony," St. Paul urges us "to be united in one mind and in one judgment" (I Cor. 1:10), to be "in mind mature" (I Cor. 14:20). But the perfection of judgments which refers to the truths of faith has its root in charity. The more we are united to God, the more we acquire the spiritual meaning of what is true.

It also involves, at least in the beginning, perfection of all the virtues. We may, in fact, speak of perfection in two ways: a being is perfect, absolutely speaking, when nothing is lacking to his nature, like an animal who has all its members and organs in good condition. But, relatively speaking, perfection can be understood from what is added outwardly; thus the whiteness or the quality of a tint can bring a "certain" perfection. The Christian is perfect, absolutely speaking, when he is in charity, since charity lets him abide in God and assures him of the life of the soul. The virtue which is added to charity brings only a relative perfection since, without charity, it is incapable of leading the soul to its end. But inversely, the charity which assures absolute perfection gives value and life to the virtues founded on it. Just so a body in good health gives color to the complexion, causes the voice to be firmer and assures a sweet breath. Charity is mother and "form" of all the virtues.

Let us go a step further in the consideration of perfection and ask ourselves if it is possible in this life, and in what way.

Since perfection consists in charity, we can distinguish several kinds of perfection according to the limits which charity is capable of attaining.

First: charity is complete not only with respect to the one who loves but also with respect to the one who is loved. God is loved as much as He is lovable. This perfection is possible only in God.

Second: charity exhausts the capacity for love of the created being. He is borne toward God without halt and with all his power. Such is the perfection of the elect in Heaven.

Third: charity excludes all that which is repugnant here on earth in the movement of divine love. And that itself can be understood in two ways: either that charity rejects all that which is opposed to divine love, such as mortal sin—the result is a perfection necessary to salvation; or that charity rejects also that which prevents it from being carried toward God with all its momentum; this is not the perfection of beginners or even of the advanced but of the "perfect" who put all their resources into increasing their fervor of love. This two-fold type of perfection is found also in the love of neighbor: the perfection which is necessarily that of salvation consists in having nothing in one's heart that may be contrary to the love of neighbor. The perfection of the "perfect" is realized in three ways: 1) by way of extension, it consists in loving not only one's friends but even strangers and enemies (cf. Mt. 5:46); 2) by way of intensity, it consists in giving not only of one's goods but of one's self, even to the point of paying for one's love with one's life (cf. Jn. 15:13); 3) by way of efficacy, it consists in giving not only temporal goods but especially spiritual goods and in sparing oneself no trouble in gaining souls for Christ (cf. II Cor. 12:15).

Finally, one last question: is perfection a matter of precept or of counsel only?

We have said that perfection consists in charity. Now, charity, which is to say the love of God and of neighbor, is the very object of the first two precepts. Perfection, therefore, is a matter of precept. It is even important to note that love does not fall under the precept according to a certain measure only, the surplus being as it were of counsel. We are commanded to love God without measure. If we love only up to a certain point, we do not love and we are not saved. From the moment love is seen in terms of end, there is no longer a problem of measure: the doctor must be prudent in his remedies, but he can not desire the health of his patient too greatly.

Counsels are useful, not necessary. Just as the commandments, other than the first two, are destined to make us reject all that is opposed to the very movement of charity, counsels offer us means destined to facilitate the movement of charity as well as to assure it a more certain success. All do not understand these counsels, but only those whom the Lord calls: "Let him accept it who can (Mt. 19:12). Counsels remain counsels, and are not the only way. But whichever may be the paths that are followed, all must be united in the end which is charity.

2. *The State of Perfection*

On the one hand we have tried to define "state" (a permanent condition of freedom or of servitude); on the other, in what perfection consists (in charity). But we must make the link between these two notions in order to determine who is in the state of perfection.

Immediately, two kinds of states of perfection must be considered: an interior state which, in the eyes of God, is the state of those who are spiritually free—who have rejected the chains of self love, egoism and sin, and have become voluntarily the slaves of Jesus Christ living in His Spirit. This state, being by definition spiritual and invisible, does not create noticeable differences among men—the habitual state of grace, or the state of sin, may pass unnoticed. This state is also considered in that part of our theology where we discuss the particular situations of men in the ecclesiastical society.

The second kind of state of perfection—the only one we shall dwell on—is an exterior, social, ecclesiastical state of perfection. It is no longer the inner disposition that is considered, but the exterior acts by which men contract a certain apparent servitude in order to acquire the perfect inner freedom of the sons of God. This contract necessarily includes two elements: first, *perpetual* obligation to the state of perfection (a temporary service does not make a slave). Secondly, an *exterior*, public, even solemn obligation. The perpetual obligation of which we are speaking cannot be merely a private, personal and inner matter, or it would revert to the creation of an inner state which is not our concern here. It is necessary then that the contract be perpetually and publicly made.

Thus understood, we easily perceive that the state of perfection does not always coincide with perfection. The state of perfection is an exterior thing, a profession, in the sense in which we speak of a profession of faith, whereas perfection is essentially an interior thing. Nothing, then, prevents certain ones from being perfect who are not in the state of perfection, and others from being in the state of perfection who are still far from being perfect.

Since the state of perfection is defined by the *perpetuity* and the *public* character of the contract, we find it verified in two ways: either in the episcopal state, or in the religious state.

On the day of his consecration the bishop solemnly gives himself to his flock. He becomes as the husband of his diocese, which is the reason for wearing a ring. He takes the responsibility of the salvation of all and promises, according to the text of the *Pontifical*, to lay down his life, if necessary, for his sheep. He thus makes a profession of the greatest love (for there is no greater love than to lay down one's life for one's brothers) and is established in a *state of perfection*.

On the day of his profession, the religious renounces, through love of God, all that which may legitimately belong to him: worldly goods, the human possessions of marriage and a family, the free disposition of his activity. All that, offered to God through love, represents an exterior profession of perfect charity. The religious is thus placed in a state of perfection.

The episcopal consecration like the religious profession is an exterior state, a social state within the Church, and not an interior state. The religious commits himself by vow, publicly and perpetually, to certain concrete conditions of poverty, variable from one order to another but in which there is always that common bond between those who possess nothing in their own right. The religious likewise promises to remain celibate for the Lord; he binds himself to a specific rule, or to a specific institution, with specific superiors. But he does not take a vow of poverty in spirit only, nor does he vow with respect to the virtues of chastity and obedience. Still less does he take a vow of charity, or of humility, or of patience. Charity, like the other virtues, is the end of the vows, it is not the substance of them. Just as we have said elsewhere, the perfection of charity is obligatory for every Christian, and not only for the religious. There are not two gospels. What is interior—the spirit of poverty, chastity, the spirit of devotion to God—is asked of all because that directly concerns perfection. What is exterior is the means and can only be counsel. To enter the Kingdom of God, everyone is not obliged to put himself into a like exterior situation, although it may be a privileged means —or even, for certain ones, the only means. But there is no inner perfection that does not carry with it possession of all the virtues, even evangelic poverty. We shall come back to this in respect to vows, but it is not out of place to mention it here in order to give an exact idea of the state of perfection of which we are speaking.

E. COMPARATIVE SITUATIONS OF PARISH PRIESTS AND RELIGIOUS

At the end of this analysis we would like to compare, from the viewpoint of perfection, certain functions or ministries, certain orders and certain states. This comparison will have, furthermore, the advantage of giving more precise information on these subjects.

Let us compare, then, the situation of a parish priest with that of a religious.

The parish priest is called a "secular" (which is his *state*); he is obviously a *priest* (which is his order); and he has *care of souls* (which is his *office* or function). We shall compare him successively with an order priest who does not have care of souls, and with a religious not a priest (lay brother, coadjutor brother, etc.).

1. Parish priest and order priest having care of souls (religious abbot, superior of a "mission," etc.). The only difference between them is a difference in states: one is secular, the other regular. It is obvious that, in considering things by their nominal definitions, the condition of the order priest triumphs over that of the parish priest. The order priest is consecrated to God; there is in him a state of absolute consecration, and that state prevails over all others.

Is it not true, however—if we do not consider the words, secular and regular, but the states in their concrete reality—that the parish priest is in a state of consecration and total servitude in relation to God? The term "secular" which we are using in regard to him is not quite exact except for designating Eastern rite priests who are married and of whom no renunciation is asked. Our Latin rite priests, who vow celibacy for the Lord, pass for monks in the eyes of the Eastern rite Catholics. As a matter of fact, they are from this point of view. And they are still more, in contrast to the Eastern priests; for the latter have not given obedience the pre-eminence among the virtues of a monk, as Benedictine tradition has done in the West.

The fact remains that the religious has the benefit of his profession. If the priest achieves an exterior state of "quasi total" obedience, it is not up to this point that he has dedicated himself, at least explicitly. Whereas the religious has dedicated himself totally; he has completely renounced all personal property and all personal behavior in his activities. From this point of view, his profession (his state) is better than that of the secular priest and remains so.

2. Parish priest and order priest without care of souls. Here, two

differences: of state and of function. The condition of the religious is better than that of the parish priest from the viewpoint of state, inferior from the viewpoint of function, and equal from the viewpoint of order.

Can we go still further and ask ourselves which of these two predominates—that of state or that of function? We can, in fact, compare both on two points:

From the viewpoint of jurisdiction. In this respect the religious state, at least of those who are not bishops, must be put above the care of souls. The parish priest actually is not bound to his parish for life; above all, the care of souls which is entrusted to him does not relieve him in the last resort from his responsibility. The parish priest, although he may have ordinary power over his parish, is a subordinate official in regard to the bishop. His responsibility is limited to private acts. Whereas the religious, by his profession, must be a priest to all. He is completely dedicated to the service of God within the order he has entered. Religious state and parochial office are, in their relationship, like universal and particular. Note, however, that this comparison only takes into account two ways of life considered in themselves. That does not prevent, obviously, a certain parish priest from being holier than a certain Benedictine. A work less valuable than another in itself can become more meritorious because of the greater charity which it inspires.

From the viewpoint of difficulty. In this respect the pastoral responsibility offers more difficulties than the religious life. The pastor must instruct, preach, catechize, be perpetually concerned about the salvation of his own people and this not only by praying but by evangelizing. Living in the world, he is more acquainted with exterior temptations. He runs more risks when he has erred, for example, because he is responsible for many. On the other hand, he is not bound by the strictness of religious observances like the order priest. Religious life is more austere and more secure, pastoral responsibility more difficult and more vulnerable. In addition, none can take the office on his own—he must be assigned to it and receive it from whoever, within the Church, has full responsibility. What counts, in brief, is conformity to the will of God.

3. Parish priest and lay-religious. It is evident that the dignity of the priest prevails over that of the layman. On the other hand, the priest, by the very fact that he celebrates the Sacrament of the Altar, is bound to a higher interior sanctity than that of any other person

It is necessary for reality to go with the symbol, for the life of the priest to correspond to that which he expresses sacramentally.

But the superiority of dignity is not the final criterion of value. The priest is a priest not for himself but, first of all, for others. The priesthood is a service; whereas the monastic life is useful first of all for the monk. If we compare on the one hand the spiritual support and help which the exercises of his order brings to the priest, and on the other the support which his rule and its regular observances bring to the religious, we ascertain that the priesthood brings to the priest more demands but that it does not give him the support possessed by the religious of community and observances.

II. Pastoral Responsibility

The pastoral function can be considered from several points of view in theology. We can look upon it, first of all, as one of the ministries of the Church as a whole—from the viewpoint of ecclesiology; we can see with what sacrament it is connected and how it proceeds from it—then it can be viewed in terms of the study of the sacrament of Holy Orders; we can, finally, consider the personal state of the one who has charge of it (here we are placing ourselves in the point of view of the moralist).

A. WHAT IS A PASTOR?

The pastor is, in the Church, the one who possesses the *cura animarum,* that is, the one who has care of souls and who assumes the responsibility for their spiritual conduct.

Such was the care of the Apostles who were chosen by the Master and sent out by Him to announce to the whole world the Gospel of salvation and to bring the message of truth. The Apostles appointed their successors; these were the bishops—the true and unique pastors of the Church. The bishops, however, were surrounded from the beginning with co-workers and servants. The co-workers were the priests; the servants were the deacons. In early liturgical ceremonies, while the deacons always stood ready to receive the orders of the bishop, the priests who surrounded him were, like him, seated. They were the council and senate of the bishop as well as his co-workers. They prayed with him, facing the altar and facing the people; where there was only one Mass they celebrated with him; where the bishop could not go, he delegated a priest who celebrated in his name. The priest actually had the same power of order as the bishop; he offered the same sacrifice to the Father, that of Christ in the name and in the place of Christ. But he did not have care of souls directly. Only the bishop had that responsibility and the corresponding jurisdiction.

In the first centuries of the Church the bishop did not have such a ministry that it was necessary for him to shift a great deal of the responsibility onto his priests. The bishop personally baptized, reserved for himself the right to preach, to instruct the faithful, to expel penitent sinners solemnly from the church at the beginning of Lent and to reconcile them on Holy Thursday, to confirm and to ordain. The duty of the priest, in the episcopal church to which he was attached, consisted principally in standing near the bishop in all liturgical functions and in celebrating collectively each day the divine office of that church.

From age to age pastoral functions have been extended and multiplied; the bishop, therefore, has shifted responsibility little by little to his co-workers who have become more closely associated with his responsibilities, more and more actively pastors. Baptism is rarely administered today by the bishop, but almost always by the priests of the "parish"; Sunday Mass at the cathedral is more and more rarely celebrated by the bishop, and the priests have inherited in the liturgy of the solemn High Mass rites formerly reserved for the bishop.[2] Since the Irish monks in the 7th century spread auricular confession, the administration of the sacrament of penance has become an ordinary duty of the priest, and it is even quite a heavy one today in certain parishes. The responsibility of priests concerning marriage has become important since the Council of Trent obliges the spouses to present themselves to the parish priest or his delegate for the validity of their sacrament; it has become still more important since a preliminary instruction is obligatory. Furthermore, in the complex situation of modern Christendom, parish life is filled with all kinds of preaching,[3] organizations, "movements" and meetings. Finally, history and recent decisions concerning confirmation administered by parish priests or assistants, show that the sacra-

---

[2] Cf. Jungmann, *Missarum Solemnia,* Vol. I, p. 249, Ed. Aubier.

[3] Preaching was reserved for the bishops in the early days of the Church. Although in Gaul, this privilege was granted to priests and sanctioned by a Council (Vaison, 529), it was not, from the 6th to 13th centuries, extended elsewhere.

ments whose administration is reserved for the bishop are so only by virtue of a reservation in fact and not in law.

Before the evidence of these facts it would be lacking in realism not to recognize today the pastoral power and duties of certain priests. Although dependent on that of the bishop, their responsibility is more and more increased. Numerous African bishops in the 2nd, 3rd, and 4th centuries had a less far-reaching influence and less weighty cares than many of the parish priests of today. We must even go further and recognize that, paralleling the increased responsibility given to priests, we have been watching for several centuries a decrease in the responsibility granted to bishops. If a few priests today wanted to gather around the bishop, vow obedience to him and lead a regular life under his crozier as did the clerics of St. Augustine, or the canons of Arles or Chartres, they could no longer do so; the initiatives of the bishop in matters of religious are more and more reduced. Likewise the bishop is no longer sole master of the diocesan clergy, of its canonical regulations; he can no longer on his authority—like St. Martin for example—go off to pagan lands to convert the heathens: this is no longer within the jurisdiction of bishops attached to the Holy See. Finally, the bishop, at least in the Latin-rite West, monopolized by administrative cares, is further and further removed from souls. Although he alone wears the ring of the Spouse married to his Church, he is usually more easily moved from one diocese to another than certain parish priests upon whom canon law confers irremovability.

The "pastor" whom we are considering here is not, therefore, only the bishop, but any priest—diocesan priest, exempt * priest or "apostolic" missionary—any priest in charge of a territory or chaplain in charge of a specific category of faithful, etc., *according to his participation* in the apostolic ministry. Only the titular and resident bishop, or the pope over mission territories has still the full responsibility of pastoral office.

B. DEDICATION AND PERFECTION

We have already shown that the bishop is in a state of perfection by the fact of his episcopal consecration which dedicates him *solemnly* and *forever* to feed his flock. Just as the religious is the slave of God, the bishop is the slave of his Church. For her he is held to

---

* *Exempt* from the jurisdiction of the ordinary of the diocese, as, the Dominicans, etc. (Translator's note).

an unlimited charity: 1) extensively, by which he is held to the love of even his enemies as were the Apostles whom the Lord sent as sheep in the midst of wolves (Mt. 10:16); or 2) intensively, by which the bishop is ready like the good shepherd to lay down even his life for his flock, or 3) efficaciously, by which the largess of the bishop includes not only temporal goods for the poor and infirm but, above all, spiritual goods, namely, his teaching, his example, his prayers. The bishop is so possessed by his task that he is completely dispossessed of himself from the time that he assumes it; that is what his state of perfection implies.

It goes without saying that this state is fully verified in the resident bishop, head of a diocese. It is verified especially in the pope, who assumes all responsibility, and who does not even have the possibility of being moved to another diocese. It is less true in the so-called bishop "in partibus," whose diocese is fictitious and whose title is at times honorary. It is verified, proportionately speaking, in all those who collaborate in the task of the bishop and have received a part of his responsibilities: the parish-priest at the time of his "installation," the director of Catholic Action at the time of his nomination; it is also verified in the abbot within his monastery, etc. The state of perfection (it is always a question of the exterior state of perfection which is promised inwardly by the one who enters into it but which does not automatically make him perfect) of each one is proportionate to the importance of his individual cares and responsibilities. In broad outline we may show these functions in this way:

The pastor is like Christ, and in His footsteps, priest, king, prophet. As a priest, he offers Christ's sacrifice to the Father in the name of his Church and of his flock, and he administers the sacraments of salvation. As a king, he exercises a "royalty of sweetness." He knows each one of his flock by name, directs them and gathers them into the unity of faith and charity: he defends the freedom of his Church against public authorities and can be led to fill in the insufficiency or deficiency of governments to exercise "stop-gap measures" such as teaching, care of the sick, education of the retarded or crippled children, etc.; lastly, he always takes care of the poor. As a prophet, he unceasingly, on every occasion, to those in his Church as well as to those outside it, speaks the Word of God.

The characteristic virtues of the pastor are those of solicitude and fidelity.

One remark in closing: Let us be wary of confusing priesthood and pastorate. The priesthood gives the power to offer the eucharistic sacrifice and to administer the sacraments; it does not constitute a state of perfection (if a sacrament of perfection exists, it is baptism which must be considered as such and not Holy Orders. We shall take this up further on). The pastorate gives responsibilities and cares over the Mystical Body; it constitutes one in a state of perfection in the measure in which the pastor's responsibilities *bind* him to his Church.

C. THE VOCATION OF PASTOR

St. Paul declares that it is good to desire the office of bishop (I Tim. 3:1). Does that mean that the pastoral responsibility depends on the liking and desire of each one? The answer to this question carries with it all kinds of fine points.

The pastoral function usually comprises several things: the pastoral ministry properly speaking, the rank or grade with which those who have pastoral responsibility are invested, and the honors resulting from it. It is obvious that neither honors nor rank (honorary canon, prelate, vicar general, etc.) but only the apostolic work should be desired for itself.

On the other hand, the care of souls depends in the first place not on any one individual, but on Christ and on His Church. The Holy Spirit can indeed urge some candidate to wish to be pastor but that is not enough for him to become one in actuality; it is still necessary for him to be invested by the hierarchy. And, inversely, those whom the hierarchy wishes to invest may be urged by the Holy Spirit into other paths; thus it is that certain ones take a vow of not accepting the office of bishop, or that others, following the example of Moses (Ex. 4:10), submit to their superiors the obstacles or difficulties which they see in undertaking pastoral responsibilities. The pastorate is not an individual necessity for salvation. We have even seen a Pope (Celestine V) tender his resignation in order to find monastic solitude again, and holy bishops beg to be dismissed from their cares so as to enter religious life. The fact remains, however, that it is easier for the hierarchy to bestow the office of bishop upon a monk than the monastic life upon a bishop, since the common good, if the Holy Spirit does not appear to contradict it, has to come before the particular good.

Two viewpoints are to be considered, then, in what can be called the pastoral vocation, namely: the viewpoint of the hierarchy who invest, and the viewpoint of the candidate who is interiorly called.

History teaches us that the hierarchy did not always wait for the candidate to present himself or to feel himself called. The Church of Milan took Ambrose in spite of himself and he became its bishop. Many are the analogous examples in antiquity. Where there is no absolute obstacle, the Holy Spirit can very well begin to speak through the voice of the institutional Church.

But, on the other hand, history shows us that the hierarchical institution is more and more respectful of each person's vocation. And that, contrariwise, it cannot force a situation which rises from an unforeseen and inalienable movement of the Spirit in the soul of the individual: his will to remain celibate for the Lord or to follow some evangelic "counsel." Let him who can understand, but only the Holy Spirit can make such a call "understood." Also, insofar as the pastoral office requires celibacy, must the Church wait for the candidate to appear with a prior "vocation." Having tested the spirit which urges the subject to work in the Lord's vineyards, the Church hires him for the harvest according to his abilities.

D. PASTORAL POVERTY AND GENEROSITY

Up to what point is the state of perfection obligatory for the bishop, and, *mutatis mutandi,* for each pastor or apostle?

Our Lord said to His Apostles: "Do not keep gold, or silver, or money in your girdles, no wallet for your journey, nor two tunics, nor sandals, nor staff; for the laborer deserves his living" (Mt. 10:9-10). Is this advice suitable for every apostolic worker? It must be noted that St. Paul himself received a subsidy from other churches so that he could preach the Gospel to the Corinthians (cf. II Cor. 12:8). Our Lord's order is aimed directly at the Twelve Apostles for their special mission among the Jews in the Land of Israel. His instructions are not to be taken to the letter but in the spirit. The bishop, whose charity obliges him to set an example and who must provide for the livelihood of his priests, for their perfection, for the responsibilities of his churches and for the care of the poor, cannot, without scandal, lead a mode of life that may be offensive to the extreme poverty of certain priests or the distress of certain poor people. But the responsibilities which he assumes also require that he be free from material tasks. Poverty of the bishop is a matter of the spirit, not of external rule.

The bishop must give his life for his flock; does that mean that he must never abandon it, for example, in case of persecution? There again it may be that the departure of a bishop and his replacement by another may be the means of avoiding a general persecution or of assuring a better shepherding of the flock. It is the salvation of the flock, the pastoral responsibility, that must be considered above all and which must indicate to the pastor his line of conduct.

E. PASTORAL OFFICE AND LAITY

Must the pastor be necessarily ordained? Yes, since certain sacraments are necessary to salvation, and since all are useful. No one can give salvation if he is not capable of administering the sacraments.

However, the layman can participate in the pastoral care as far as he is inclined, according to the spirit which invites him to do so and the mandate which he receives. A laborer can "win over" his pagan comrades by his prayers, his example, his zeal in presenting the Gospel to them and, little by little, lead them to the Church. He then well deserves to be called apostle or pastor, by participation. The extent of his powers is determined by the Holy Spirit and by what he can give to others before, or after, reception of the sacraments although he cannot confer the sacraments.

Among the institutions for laymen, marriage is especially consecrated by the Church for a certain pastoral task. The spouses are solemnly committed, without any time limit, to the instruction and spiritual education of their children. They are to carry the word of God to anyone, even baptized, who would remain in ignorance except for the priest. The priest can do little effectively without them.

F. PASTORAL INSIGNIA

The bishop is defined by the apostolic powers which have been transmitted to him by those possessing them officially and by the Church whose care is entrusted to him. The public character of his consecration, which puts him in a sacred state, is designated by certain rites and insignia which vary according to the liturgies. The essential ritual is always the laying on of hands (cf. I Tim. 4:12; II Tim. 1:6). Two bishop co-consecrators are necessary; they represent the apostolic succession.

The other rites in the Latin Church are: 1) the imposition of the Book of the Gospels: this rite, which comes from the Greek liturgy, is still found on page 380 in the book of apostolic constitutions; 2) the anointing of the head: a rite of the Carolingian liturgy which resembles the royal anointing; 3) the tradition of the ring and the crozier; 4) the tradition of "goods," in the form of landed property, a symbol of the episcopal patrimony; 5) the tradition of the Book of the Gospels; 6) the tradition of the mitre (11th century) and of the gloves (10th century).

III. The Religious State

The bishop is bound to the flock whose pastoral responsibility he has undertaken. The religious, in order to become wholly the slave of God, is bound to an exterior state which cuts him off from everything that can alienate him from the love of God. The religious, as the word indicates, is in such a state that he is totally bound to God and to His service. Each Christian is religious from the sole fact that he worships God, but the religious in the highest sense of the word is the one for whom the name is reserved absolutely. Likewise, the word "devout," which today is applied indifferently to all sorts of pious persons, was formerly reserved for the dedicated kind of life; what the liturgy still calls *devotus femineus sexus* signifies *the nuns*.

But whatever may be the words used to designate this way of life (ascetic life, monastic life, apostolic life, etc.), the one whom we now call "religious" is the one who, in order to be united *entirely* to God, offers *everything* without keeping anything for himself. By his sacrifice, his offering, his vows, the *entire* life is henceforth placed under the seal of the virtue of religion; nothing escapes the service or the worship of God. No doubt it is through love that he thus becomes a servant of God, but his love is such that he wants to be obliged in justice (for the virtue of religion is a certain justice as are the acts of religion which are oblation, worship, the vow) never to leave him. By means of a promise, his entire life is offered lovingly to God, and, having made the promise, he *must* fulfill it in the same love.

It goes without saying, once again, that the religious is not made perfect by the simple promise. He may be in the state of perfection only a beginner or someone more advanced. But his exterior state testifies that he inclines toward perfection and has undertaken all the means of attaining it.

A. RELIGIOUS STATE AND BAPTISM

The profession of the religious offers many analogies with baptism.

Baptism is a renunciation of Satan, of his worldly attractions, of his works; it attaches us to Jesus Christ forever. It is in its way a servitude, the first liberating servitude of the Christian. But the baptized person lives in the midst of the world; he is attracted by all kinds of "good things" which, without ceasing to be good things, can awaken his unholy desires and tempt him to no longer follow Christ. The religious is a baptized person who takes his baptism seriously and radically suppresses all that which, though good, can compromise the fruits of it. Religious profession is a second baptism, a "repeat" of baptism. The monk is essentially a *conversus,* a convert, like the baptized person.

This doctrine that religious profession is a "second baptism" has been traditional since the 4th century.

It is expressed in the rites of profession which are patterned on those of baptism; the theme of death for the old man and of the birth of a new man plays a leading role in it. Even today, we can recognize several baptismal themes in the ceremony of consecration of virgins which the *Pontifical* still retains. Finally, the ceremonies of profession (or investiture) and of consecration of virgins have been considered for a long time—since the 12th century—as sacraments, in the manner of baptism or martyrdom, and produce the same effects.

Actually, for the early Christians the "perfect" man was the martyr. The martyr was also proclaimed blessed, without any further ceremony, and no one else except he was considered to enjoy eternal bliss. Even after Constantine, that is, after the persecutions, martyrdom remained the measure of perfect piety; it had a profound effect on the conception of monastic life which was developed by St. Athanasius (cf. *The Life of St. Anthony),* St. Basil, St. Jerome, Cassian. After the peace of Constantine, the monk who offered his entire life to Christ appeared as the ever necessary *witness,* the martyr of the new times. Theologians of the 12th and 13th centuries remained faithful to that tradition in attributing to the solemn profession of the religious effects that were analogous with those of baptism; for example, religious profession takes away sins like baptism. It consecrates and patterns the religious to Christ in His state as servant of God and in His condition as victim and holocaust. It designates him for the worship of God and obliges him not only to assist at Mass and to participate in certain celebrations, but to make his entire life a worship of God.

B. HISTORIC MODES OF THE RELIGIOUS LIFE AND OF ITS INSTITUTIONS

Before touching on the theology of the religious life, it is necessary now to take a look at history and to learn from it how this "baptismal totalitarianism" attributed to religious life has appeared throughout the centuries.

We can distinguish six stages:

1. The Preaching of Jesus Christ

Our Lord offers one and the same ideal of perfection to everyone. There is not one gospel for some and another for others; the same gospel is offered to all. The writers of the Gospels frequently observe that Christ "calls the crowd together" (Mt. 8:34), that He "said to all" (Lk. 9:23), or to "great crowds" (Lk. 14:25). It was for all His disciples that Jesus prayed to the Father and asked that they all might be one (Jn. 17:21). It is to everyone that He says: "You therefore are to be perfect, even as your heavenly Father is perfect" (Mt. 5:48); "If anyone wishes to come after me, let him deny himself, and take up his cross daily, and follow me" (Lk. 9:23); "If anyone comes to me and does not hate his father and mother and wife and children, and brothers and sisters, yes, and even his own life, he cannot be my disciple" (Lk. 14:26); "Whoever tries to save his life will lose it; and whoever loses it will preserve it" (Lk. 17:33). Although at times Jesus Himself sets the example of retiring to the desert or upon a mountain, whether to pray or to speak to His disciples (Mt. 5:1), He does not instruct anyone to leave the world, but only to keep himself from evil (Jn. 17:15).

Moreover, certain particular vocations must be noted in the Gospels, e.g. that of the rich young man: ". . . go, sell what thou hast . . . and come, follow me" (Mt. 19:21); that of certain disciples: "Follow me . . ." (Mt. 8:22; 9:9, etc.); that of the man from whom the devils had gone out who wished to be Christ's follower but whom Jesus instructed to return to his own people (Lk. 8:39); that of those "to whom it has been given" to hear and to understand a certain word, for all do not understand it (Mt. 19:11).

In brief, it follows from the Gospels: 1) that the Christian is one who is called, summoned (Christ does not cease to call, to summon those to whom He wishes to speak); he is an elect, or, according to the word which St. Paul is so fond of, a saint (through the initial efforts of God and baptism); 2) that salvation is for everyone salvation by the cross; i.e. it is false to think that some are to be saved by sacrifice and renunciation while others will be saved by the life of the world as the world leads it; 3) that variations in the kinds of vocations do not affect the end but the means; i.e. to each one the Spirit of God Who is the Spirit of Christ imposes a personal way of following and of imitating his Savior.

2. The Apostolic Time

Immediately after Pentecost we see in Jerusalem a group of Christians selling their possessions, sharing the receipts and adopting an integral communal life (Acts 2:44-47). ". . . Not one of them said that anything he possessed was his own, but they had all things in common" (Acts 4:32). In the abundance of the gifts of the Spirit bestowed upon the young Church, we see certain Christians spontaneously giving this testimony of poverty and of brotherly communal life. The Lord had not laid down anything that clear-cut, but the spirit of the Lord was in them and imperiously suggested that they "follow" the Lord in this way.

For centuries the Church of Jerusalem is the type and model of communities and of religious Orders. Up to the 15th century and even later, we can say that the desire of almost every founder (Augustine of Hippo, Benedict of Nursia, Robert of Molesmes, and Stephen Harding, Norbert of Xanthus, Francis of Assisi, Dominic of Osma, etc.) was to establish an institution in which the first community of Jerusalem would somehow live again in the very terms in which it is presented to us in the Acts of the Apostles (chaps. 2 to 5). Hence it happens that, until the 13th century, the phrase *apostolic life* is synonymous with *regular communal life,* or *monastic life* in the case of cenobites. St. Thomas does not hesitate to write that "every form of religious life took its beginning from the disciples after the resurrection (*Summa Theol.,* IIa IIae, q. 188, a. 7).

All, however, do not know that call of the Spirit to put everything in common in one perfect charity. If Ananias and Sapphira were punished to death (Acts 5:1-11), it is not because they were blamed for keeping something back, but because they lied. A distinction is thus made between the "charismatics" of this generation (cf. I Cor.

13:28-31). But it is the same Spirit who gives to each one his gifts and inspirations. And it is the same gospel that everyone wants to hear and to follow.

3. From the 1st to the 6th Century

The distinction of "gifts," on the one hand, the increase of hierarchical offices on the other, and lastly, the great number of those who have not received any special vocation and do not have any function in the Church, rapidly created a three-fold category of the faithful. This triple division is suggested in the Acts, and very plainly in the Apostolic Writings. Tradition has recorded it in the liturgy; for example, in the mass of Good Friday the celebrant prays for all the needs of the Church according to the following formula: "Let us pray for all bishops, priests, deacons, sub-deacons, acolytes, exorcists, lectors, porters, confessors, virgins and widows, and for all the people of God." The three Orders of the Church are these: 1) the clerical Order (here very well developed, but whose origin goes back to the Apostles); 2) the ascetical or mystical, or charismatic, or "pneumatic" Order (from the Greek, *Pneuma,* Spirit, and *pneumatikos,* animated or invigorated by the Spirit); this is the order of all those who have received a private call from the Spirit prescribing for them a greater renunciation; lastly, 3) the lay Order (from the Greek *Laos,* the holy people).

From the 1st century, even before a hierarchy was formed at the side of the twelve apostles who were legally and actually the heads of the Churches, we see these first "charismatics" appear. They were called *ascetics* or *confessors;* virgins or widows. They lived in the world, separated from each other, without any bond between them and without any institution. As soon as they were resolved to adopt this way of life, they simply stated it to the Church who consecrated their decision in a ceremony. They prayed and devoted themselves to works of mercy. The Church considered herself so honored by them that she gave them a special place in the nave; hence it happens that all the sermons of Ambrose, of Augustine, of Gregory on virginity, treat also of humility.

In the 3rd century we have St. Anthony, the father of all "monasticism." Anthony was born around 250 A.D. in Egypt. At the age of twenty, upon entering a church, he heard the word: "Go, sell what thou hast, and come, follow me." Anthony followed the Gospel to the letter, and disappeared into the desert like Christ after His Baptism. This was the "conversion" of St. Anthony. He lived on herbs and vegetables from a little garden around his hermitage. Soon disciples came to see him, to ask his advice and to establish themselves around him. He died in the year 356 A.D.

With Anthony begins that form of asceticism which we call anchorite. Until this time ascetics lived in the world with other Christians. Anthony fled the world. Why? Because the Spirit moved him to do this. The rule of effective secession from the world is not written in the Gospels; but the rule of Christians is not a formula that can be written on tablets, it is written on our fleshly hearts (II Cor. 3:3): It is the Holy Spirit Who has been given to us, as He is given to the whole Church. Without Him, no one can say: Jesus is Lord (I Cor. 22:3). With Him alone, we can read and understand the Gospels.

The desert was soon to be as populous as the valley of the Nile. The "spiritual" men were to become counselors, fathers, abbots (from the Hebrew, Abbas, which means Father) of a large number of disciples eager to listen to counsel. Soon abbots and disciples formed groups which would become veritable colonies of hermits.

Hermits, however, were not all prudent or wise. The desire for a vigorous asceticism, the ambition to suffer everything for Christ, drove them to every extravagance; for example, the extravagances of the acoemetae who deprived themselves of sleep, of the stationaries who did not move, of the siderophores who wore fetters or chains, of the stylites who lived on top of a pillar. Although there may be some saints among them (e.g. St. Simon Stylites), there were also all kinds of eccentrics.

St. Pachomius (292–346 A.D.) was the first legislator of monasticism and the founder of cenobitism (from the Greek *koinos bios,* communal life). He withdrew around 320 A.D. to an island of the Nile and organized a monastery to which he gave his rule (the Coptic Rule of St. Pachomius has been translated by St. Jerome). The Pachomians were obliged to prayer, fasting, manual labor, and the reading of holy books. Large monasteries, both for men and for women, were organized.

St. Basil, who was born in Cappadocia around 330 A.D., took up Pachomius' idea again and organized monasteries in his country. Or at least he organized houses of communal life, called *cenobia.* He wanted so much to react against the dangers of the anchorites that he refused his institution the very name of monastery (from the

Greek *monos,* alone). Originally the monastery was a gathering of solitaries in huts.

Then, in 480 A.D. in Nursia, near Rome, St. Benedict was born. A fervent disciple of Basil, Benedict organized cenobitic life at Subiaco, then at Monte Cassino where he settled around 525 A.D.; it was there that he wrote his Rule. He died in 547. St. Benedict denounced the illusions of eccentrics and tramp monks. He emphasized obedience and made it the principal instrument of perfection.

The West still knew many other abbots and other Rules (St. Aurelian's, St. Colomban's, St. Augustine's and St. Cesarius' of Arles for women). Only that of St. Benedict survived for monks, Charlemagne having imposed it upon all the monks of his empire.

4. From the 6th to 12th Century

From the 6th to the 12th century, the East and West knew only one form of religious life, which was the monastic life. Even at the end of the 12th century the West did not "practically" know any except the Benedictine life.

These were the monks who, often without premeditation, went to convert the towns and countries of Northern Europe. Let us mention St. Martin, St. Boniface, St. Anscarius, St. Eric, etc. The monks swarmed in, founded a little colony which cut down trees, cleared the land, tilled the soil, and received peasant families seeking food and work; soon the colony of settlers would turn into a little Christian community whose master was the lord-abbot.

In the 12th century asceticism, which had entered the solitude of the desert with Anthony and the cloisters with Benedict, was to leave its enclosures and return to the world, as in apostolic times, but this time along organized lines. The occasion for their return was the crusade. The crusade created *military orders, orders hospitallers* (for the poor and sick of the Holy Land), and orders intended for the *ransoming of prisoners.* But the crusades were not the only ones concerned. In the 12th century we witness the birth of a whole world which, little by little, freed itself from signorial tutelage. This is the world of merchants or middle-class persons, certain of whom, especially in Italy, were to amass colossal fortunes. As a reaction against the intoxication of riches the *friars minor* came into being. And in order to guide this world religiously and intelligently in social revolution the *preachers* were formed (12th century). We see fervent Christian life organizing outside the cloisters and creating all kinds of new forms in secular life, i.e. Third Orders, brothers of the common life, convents of Beguine nuns, etc.

A more important point also has to be noted. We said that antiquity had recognized three "orders" of faithful: the clerical or hierarchical order, the ascetical, spiritual order, and the secular order. This convenient division corresponds but very imperfectly to reality. At the end of the 8th century, and especially under the influence of St. Benedict Anianus, a great number of Western monks received holy orders, while at almost the same moment, and especially in the 11th century, many chapters of "canons" (clerics enrolled in the canon of a particular church) undertook to reform by adopting monastic garb and observances. The monastic influence was so great that the office of the churches was transformed by it; e.g. in place of the ancient cursus of two hours a day, matins, lauds, and prime, all the canons adopted the monastic cursus of seven hours daily.[4]

In the 11th and 12th centuries, it was often extremely difficult to distinguish a community of clerics, or of canons, from a community of monks. They were recognized especially by the color of their habit (white for clerics, black for monks, at least until the birth of Citeaux), by their liturgy, by their rules. The priests, as a matter of fact, whatever the place where they were established, did not have all the ministry that they have today; that is, their main function was to celebrate the Divine Office according to the title by which they were attached. The two orders, clerical and ascetical, whose characteristics seemed so distinct and so clear during the first six centuries, were thus little by little becoming fused. There were, however, from the 4th century fruitful exceptions that must be noted; e.g. St. Augustine of Hippo, as well as St. Eusebius of Verceil, St. Martin of Tours, St. Victricius of Rouen, and others lived "monastically" with the clerics of their churches.

The Augustinian order of priest-monks (or of cleric-monks) was prolific. The "regular" canons of the 11-12th centuries, united in congregations like those of St. Rufus or of Prémontré, or members of an autonomous community, could rightly claim kinship with it. The cloisters which we see still situated beside certain cathedrals (for example, Notre-Dame du Puy or St. Trophimus d'Arles), bear witness to this glorious part of canonry. From this clerical tradition spring religious families such as, in the 13th century, that of the

---

[4] Cf. Martimort, *Les Offices du dimanche soir;* in *Le Jour du Seigneur,* Paris, Laffont, 1948, pp. 246-249.

preaching friars (Dominic was a reformed canon of Osma) and in the 16th all those of the *clerics regular* (Theatines, Jesuits, etc.).

But if the priest-monks did not seem very different, at least in certain eras, from the monk-priests, their origins, their traditions and their vocations remained different. Should a crisis occur, a reform become necessary, or should the Church have need of new apostolic workers, both will react differently. "In the history of monastic families, says Dom Doyere, most of the movements of reform are placed under the sign of a return to the eremitical life and to solitude." The clerical families, on the contrary, developed their pastoral responsibilities within the lines of their tradition, in conformity with the requests and needs of the whole Church. At a time when the priests had scarcely any other duties than that of celebrating the liturgy, the regular canons had no more, either; but today there is no priestly function within the immense gamut of ministries which may not also be assumed by "regulars." There is, therefore, reason always to distinguish among the existing Orders, the Orders of priests who have taken monastic observances in order to become better priests, and the establishments of monks to whom the priesthood had been given (the custom becomes more and more wide-spread) without their having ceased to be monks and without their ever becoming pastors or apostles by appointment.

Above all specialization, however, is the supreme rule of the Gospels. The words of Stephen of Muret (1046–1124) to his religious are significant in this regard: "If you are asked what Order you belong to, tell that person of the Gospel which is the basis of all rules. Let this be your answer to all those who inquire thereupon. As for me, I will not suffer to be called either monk, canon, or hermit. These titles are so lofty and so holy, and imply such a measure of perfection that I would not presume to apply them to myself." [5]

5. From the 12th to the 20th Century

The 12th century saw the birth of two great Orders; one of monks —the Cistercians—which appeared as a reform of the monastic Order, and one of canons—the Premonstratensians—which was a reform of the canonical Order and which in numerous points (solitude, labor, contemplative life) differs little from the Order of Cistercians.

[5] *Sermo de unitate diversarum regularum,* in Martène, *De ant. Eccl. rit.,* Venice, 1783, vol. IV, p. 308, chap. 2.

The new Orders of the 13th century were different. They no longer exiled themselves far away from the world; on the contrary, they were in close contact with the people and in communication with them. Originally, a number of the Friars Minor were artisans and so earned their living in small market towns. The Preachers taught everywhere—in the pulpits of the churches, in the newly-formed "universities" or in their own schools. Both were now exempt from episcopal jurisdiction and were soon to form the shock troops of the Apostolic See in all the "missions of the world." Their very flexible administration no longer included abbots (elected for life, a sort of feudal lord in spiritual and temporal things concerning their abbey), but simply priors, first among equals, continuously reelected and controlled by "chapters." The creation of Preachers was one of the first steps in this Roman centralization attempted by the monastic Order of Cluny, and which ended in the 16th century in the *Society of Jesus* and, in modern times, in all those religious associations joined together under the Roman congregation of religious.

The evolution of the religious life of the women in this period calls for a remark. We have already said that there had taken place among the men a kind of fusion between "the hierarchical order" and "the ascetical order." There was nothing similar for the women. Until the 18th century the type of regular life for women, whatever their Order, was monastic. Since Boniface VIII, the rules of enclosure have become even more strict for all the monasteries. These rules, however, have not hindered monasteries of cloistered nuns from existing or from becoming hotels, and later schools. But if, toward the 16th century, many young ladies were instructed in the cloisters, it was because the cloistered nuns received them within the convent, and did not go out. We find nothing more similar to the institution of deaconesses or to that of widows in apostolic times.

In the 16th century a few congregations were formed with exterior action as their end. But wishing to be nuns also, they were restrained by the rules in use and quickly ended up being no more than contemplatives. Such is the history of the Visitation nuns of St. Francis de Sales who were originally destined for the "visitation" of the sick. In the following century St. Vincent de Paul was to evade the difficulty by grouping his daughters outside of any order and any religious rule.

Times have changed. Today, among congregations of women, we

must distinguish, even where there are fewer outer dissimilarities, the establishments which are monastic by origin and by tradition (that is, where the nuns have no other end than to attain perfection in their baptismal life), and establishments dedicated to particular works of mercy whose Sisters have adopted monastic garb and observances, and who are the organized heirs of the deaconesses and widows of apostolic times.

The particular works being indefinite in number, and, likewise, the extent of application of these works (children, young men, young women; Christian land, mission land, this diocese or that one, etc.) and the choice of the means and instruments of perfection, the congregations are able to change ad infinitum. In the 19th century the proliferation of diocesan congregations and, to a lesser degree, of missionary congregations, resulted in an enormous increase in religious establishments.

6. From Lay Brothers to Secular Institutes

We have seen a fusion take place, little by little, aided by both the monastic influence and the custom of more liberal administration of holy orders in the monasteries, between the "clerical order" and "the ascetic or monastic order." We now have to consider another kind of fusion—between "the ascetic order" and "the secular order" of the faithful. This kind of fusion was inevitable from the moment that the monks, who originally were never priests, ceased to inhabit the desert in order to live in the midst of already populated countries. But here again it is not always easy to discern the limits of "the monastic order."

Historians assign the birth of the "lay brothers" to the abbey of Hirschau in Germany, around the 10th-11th century. From the beginning of the barbaric invasions, a number of individuals and families, homeless, without work, without food, were happy to find their refuge and livelihood close to a monastery. Little by little the big abbeys were surrounded by a huge populace. There were families, but there were also unmarried men and young people. Certain ones, attracted by the monastic life, were not content to give their labor to the monastery, and offered all their possessions; others went still further and asked to offer themselves wholly, to the end of their days, in the service of the abbey: these were the oblates (the name formerly reserved for children offered to the abbey), wards or domestics, confreres, regulars, etc. In time certain ones were given, by the monks, the name of *conversi*, lay brothers, which had formerly been reserved for monks. These "lay brothers" differed from the monks in that they lived outside the enclosure, "in the world"; they could be employed in the cultivation of the distant lands owned by the monastery, or in the exchanges of correspondence and of commerce with another abbey or with lay people. These were the religious "ex-claustro."

The 12th century, especially with Citeaux and Premontre, is the great century of the lay brothers. They worked alone in the distant "granges" owned by the abbeys and in many of the workshops adjoining them. But their institution had changed. Their religious life ceased in part to be centered around that of the abbey; they formed as it were a monastery within a monastery with their particular superior, chapter, habit, and above all, their divine office. In the 13th century, the Order of Preachers also received into it "lay brothers," but these were simply religious laymen (non-clerics) dedicated to all the material tasks of the convents. These tasks, it must be added, were extremely numerous and varied because of the fact that convents were still maintained in relative self-sufficiency.

Truly, the institution of lay brothers, oblates, semi-oblates, and "wards" was the perfect answer to the yearning of the peasants of the 7th to 11th centuries whom the invasions had driven everywhere and robbed, and who found refuge and work only around monastic centers. These rough men, pagans or demi-pagans, fascinated by the monastic life, gave themselves to God by offering themselves, according to the extent of their generosity and their abilities, in the service of the abbey.

In the 13th and 14th centuries, when the lay brothers had practically ceased to live in the world, lay Christians found other ways of giving themselves to God in new forms better adapted to the times, i.e. Third Orders, confraternities of laymen, later the convents of Beguine nuns, brothers of the common life, etc.

It is interesting to note that all these institutions leaned on religious Orders or imitated them. It is to the credit of St. Francis de Sales in the 16th century that he showed the possibility for the devout life to be practised in the world. "Those who have treated of the devout life," he wrote in the preface of his *Introduction*, "have almost always considered the teaching of persons altogether retired from the world, or at least have taught a kind of devotion which leads to that retreat. . . . It is heresy to wish to exclude the devout life from the company of soldiers, from the shops of artisans, from the court of princes, from the household of married people."

The logic of this teaching, which unites over the centuries that of the Apostles, led to the formation in modern times of "pious societies" and of "secular institutes," while at the same time it assured a productive development of the doctrine and grace of Christian marriage.

The members of secular institutes lead the common life or live separately; they earn their living or live at home; they live "in the world and with the means of the world" having offered their lives to God and vowed "perfect chastity." Certain ones still depend on religious orders which give them the benefit of a greater spiritual support, but they run the risk of compromising their secular character; others are completely autonomous, though under the control of the hierarchy.

C. THE RELIGIOUS COMMITMENT

Although the commitment to perfect chastity had been from the beginning the characteristic of the "ascetics," we do not find, at least in the West, before the time of St. Benedict an oral and written promise intended to be officially preserved.

The Rule of St. Benedict brought forward the famous triad: *Conversio morum, stabilitas, obedientia:* conversion, stability, obedience. The act by which one pledges oneself to this is called *propositum* or *votum,* or "monastic profession" (or holy or religious profession) which duplicates as it were the "Christian or baptismal profession." The ceremony was patterned after that of baptism: renunciation of Satan, profession, prostration in imitation of the death of Christ and of the immersion of the catechumens, and reception of the new habit.

The canons were to adopt an almost analogous formula. Here is the formula of canonical profession classic at the end of the 10th century: Ego frater N. offerens trado meipsum Ecclesiae S.N. et promitto conversionem morum et stabilitatem meam in loco . . . Promitto etiam obedientiam usque ad mortem.

It is interesting to observe in the 12th century the original formula of Premonstratensians who promised to live "according to the Gospel of Christ, the apostolic institution and the rule of blessed Augustine." Let us make no mistake, these words do not mean what we would attribute to them today. "To live according to the Gospel of Christ" means to live according to the gospel of St. Mark, chapter ten; especially according to the rule of St. Matthew, 10:9-10, that is, to make a profession of poverty in preaching; "to live according to the apostolic institution," is to live in conformity with the *Acts of the Apostles* 4:32-35, that is, to make a profession of communal life.[6]

The growth of theological reflection on religious life led, by the end of the 13th century, to replacing the Benedictine triad by the triad of poverty, chastity and obedience which is almost universal today with the Western cenobites.

D. ESSENTIAL ELEMENTS OF THE RELIGIOUS STATE

The history of religious life is revealing. The religious is a man who has heard a call, a "vocation," and he is the witness of that indefinable call. The clerical Order includes *functions* in the Church; the ascetical Order represents an aggregate of various *vocations,* fruits of the sole grace of the Spirit which the hierarchy can only approve and control, or whose non-evangelic forms it can reject. The variety of forms of religious life, of ascetic means, bear witness to the manner of this freedom of the Spirit which makes each one understand and asks of him what He wishes in order to make him attain personally the perfect stature of Christ.

Theology invites us to pick out of this history several enduring elements. The religious hears the gospel of Christ and wants to follow the Master everywhere He goes. If he is not detached but enters a religious "institution," what are the fundamental elements which constitute the latter?

It is certain that the religious will follow the precepts, especially the precept of charity. Every religious institution proposes as its end to shape its members in the perfection of charity.

As for counsels, we must distinguish two kinds: first, those which arise as a consequence of perfect charity, as, for example, *blessing one's enemies* (Lk. 6:28). The religious institution cannot pretend to impose such actions on every one and at all times. The religious, as a matter of fact, is not a perfect Christian but a Christian who desires as much as he possibly can to become perfect; he must, therefore, be disposed to perform such works if the occasion arises, but he is not obliged to anticipate these occasions, unless by a spe-

[6] Cf. Petit, *La spiritualité des Prémontrés aux XII⁰ et XIII⁰ s.,* Paris, Vrin, 1947, pp. 200 ff.

cial call from the Holy Spirit. He is obliged, however, not to scorn better works than those which he does, which would be to resist spiritual progress. The other kind of counsels comprise those which are the means and dispositions for the perfect fulfillment of charity, such as abstinence, continence, voluntary poverty, etc. The religious is not obliged to undertake them all, but only those of the rule he has adopted. Three among these, however, have been gradually imposed by spiritual masters, and by all religious institutions; they are poverty, perpetual continence, and obedience.

Poverty, because Our Lord said: "If you wish to be perfect, go, sell what thou hast . . ." (Mt. 19:21, 23; 13:22). Indeed, cupidity is opposed to charity; in order to free the will completely from the love of earthly goods, it is necessary to take away the free disposition of them.

Let us not object that the poor man is at times more covetous than others; the poor religious is not a poor man in spite of himself, but is a *voluntary* poor man. Let us no longer say that the religious is deprived of giving the alms required by the Lord which is so good for the one who gives it; the religious, in giving everything, gives a universal alm, better than all private ones.

Continence, as the Lord gave His disciples to understand it (Mt. 19:12), and as the Apostle Paul formally counseled it (I Cor. 7, and particularly 7:32). The violence of pleasures and of temptations of the flesh indeed pre-occupy the spirit and easily prevent it from belonging entirely to God. Married people can embrace a certain state of poverty, even adopt certain religious observances, as we can see in the "family groups" ("groupes de foyers"), but they are not religious properly speaking. However, Our Lord, in calling Peter, who was married, to the apostolate, shows that it was a counsel only, and that the Spirit of Christ does not impose it on anyone.

Obedience, because Our Lord in order to make reparation for the disobedience of Adam wanted to become uniquely obedient and "obedient to death, even to the death of a cross" (Phil. 2:8). Man is a social being and, whatever he may make of his life, he must always obey. God leads us hierarchically. It is one thing to obey in certain spheres of one's professional, religious, civic, or family activity and another thing to submit all one's activities and one's whole life to another person—to obey in every sphere, such is religious obedience. It makes the religious in a way a slave, and constrains him in justice to do what is asked of him (obedience is a certain justice); but this constraint does not lessen the merit, on the contrary it increases it, since the religious freely willed it and can always freely will it.

Hermits who live alone do not have the merit of obedience, although, nevertheless, they are subject to the Sovereign Pontiff and to ecclesiastical controls. Their state is more like that of an already acquired perfection than that of a disciple of perfection. That is why they are not ranked among religious properly so-called (canon 487). But the Holy Spirit who calls both knows what is suitable for each one and how to instruct inwardly and without an intermediary those whom He truly leads to solitude.

It is not enough, however, to adopt these counsels and to follow them for a moment. In order to become perfect, one must follow them always: "No one, having put his hand to the plow and looking back, is fit for the Kingdom of God" (Lk. 9:62); a person must commit himself whether it be by vow, by oath or any other form of promise: life is successive as a matter of fact, and the only way of offering it entirely is to enter into a contract covering all consecutive days. The day to day offerings which the Christian can renew do not add up to the sacrifice, made once and for all, of one's whole self and the definitive (and free) renunciation of that freedom to dispose of oneself anew.

These three vows form, then, the essential part of the religious state. Let us consider the latter as an exercise tending to free one from all the obstacles which are opposed to the perfection of love, for the vows deliver one from attachment to exterior things, from concupiscence of carnal pleasures, from instability of the will. Let us consider the religious state as a freedom from exterior cares (I Cor. 7:32), for vows free one from the administration of goods, from the management of a home or of one's own life; let us consider it, finally, as a holocaust, for vows offer to God all that a man can give: the use of his goods, the enjoyments of the flesh, the free disposition of his activities. They form a perfect trilogy to which, it seems, nothing can be added.

It is understood, of course, that if the interior acts (of charity, humility, patience) in which perfection consists are not mentioned among the vows, it is because they are the end of them. The religious is attached by vow in order to become perfect in charity, patience, and humility, in that state of poverty, in continence and to a particular superior under a particular rule. This three-fold state constitutes the subject matter of the vows, not the end which remains the end of every Christian.

Among these vows, that of obedience is the most perfect, on the one hand because of what it gives—free disposition of activities; it is the most precious good that man can offer; and, on the other, because it contains in a certain sense the other two; and finally, because obedience, by the acts which it requires, has a closer affinity to charity, which is the end of the vows.

E. THE SINS OF THE RELIGIOUS AND THE SINS OF THE LAYMAN

Before comparing the sins of the religious and those of the layman, let us try to evaluate the gravity of the sin "against the Rule."

One remark is called for: everything does not have the same value in the Rule. The Rule indicates the *end* of religious life; it legislates on the *observances* and the means. To sin against the end of the vows, which is charity, is of itself a serious sin (a mortal sin if the matter of charity and the subject are gravely involved); to sin against observances likewise constitutes a serious sin if these observances are the subject of the vows of chastity, poverty and obedience. In the case of other observances, the seriousness of the sin would come only from the precise scorn which the religious might have toward them, or from a disobedience to a formal precept that the superior makes in certain cases. It is evident, in this respect, that life "according to the rule" must be understood more or less rigorously according to what the rule itself states. Certain rules are understood as strict models to which one must pay as much attention as possible in every detail; others distinguish a few precepts which alone seriously oblige. Still others, finally, like those of the Preachers, do not oblige in such a way that those under them sin if they deviate from them, but in such a way that they must undergo a punishment; these are purely penal rules.

Can we say, then, that the sin of the religious is more serious than that of one who is not a religious? It is evident that the religious sins more gravely if he sins directly against his vows (theft, fornication, etc.), if he sins through scorn of spiritual progress because he is ungrateful toward the benefits of God, and finally, because many watch how he lives and have a high esteem for his state, if his sin can cause scandal.

Nevertheless, in view of the fact that everyone sins and that the religious is not exempt, the sin of the religious is, in general, less serious than that of the non-religious. The venial sin of the religious is quickly effaced, caught up in the momentum of charity of his life. Even mortal sin is less serious for him, because it goes against his habitual intention and because the religious, to overcome it, always has the help of his brothers.

It really is necessary to say, however, that if sins of weakness scarcely affect the soul of the religious, scorn soon makes him worse than others: "Since I have begun to serve God," says St. Augustine, "I have experienced that, if it is difficult to find holier people than those who have profited in monasteries, it is also difficult to find worse ones than those who have fallen in monasteries" (Sermon 78).

F. THE LIFE OF RELIGIOUS

The activities and the conditions of religious are varied. We see some preaching, others keeping perpetual silence; some lead an apparently easy mode of life, others wear miserable habits; some earn their bread largely by dint of hard work, others beg, etc. What are we to think of this diversity?

1. *Preaching.* The religious state is not opposed as such to spiritual functions. But a layman is not permitted to preach, which is rightly the office of the priest. It is not insofar as they are monks that certain religious preach or teach theology, but insofar as they are at the same time priests and that their Order was intended for this function.

2. *Mode of Life.* The management of riches easily produces greed; that is why it is forbidden for religious to own individually; it is dangerous for communities to have great wealth. But the charity which religious owe to every man can lead certain ones to go into the palaces of kings, the houses of powerful men of this world, and to lead an easier life than other religious. They should nevertheless keep all the necessary discernment and discretion.

3. *Manual Labor.* Manual labor has many advantages in religious life: it assures a livelihood, it does away with idleness, mortifies the body, and allows alms-giving. We must remark, however, that a livelihood can be assured in another way, that there are other means of struggling against idleness and of mortifying oneself, and that alms-giving is not so recommended except where it is possible. Manual labor is not obligatory everywhere. The precept given by St. Paul (I Thess. 4:11) is directed at men in general and not each one in particular.

The case of preachers deserves, as a matter of fact, a special mention. It is normal for those who work hard for the spiritual good of all to be dispensed from also working with their hands, so that their preaching does not have to suffer any detriment. It is true that Paul himself did manual labor; but this was so that false apostles might not imitate him by not working, and also so that he might not be a burden and set the example. These reasons and others can still, at certain times, lead a few preachers into doing manual labor. As for those who are contemplatives without being preachers, there would be no reason for dispensing them from working with their hands.

4. *Gifts and Honorariums.* Religious can receive gifts if necessity obliges them to; for example, if the infirmity or incapacity of many make work non-remunerative, or if the services rendered make them worthy of it; preaching and the ministry of the altar of order priests can justify these gifts on condition that they remain gifts and are not exacted, which would be simony. Order priests, more than any other priests, must be less demanding in this respect.

Communities must beware, however, of growing rich in receiving gifts or considerable legacies. It is more suitable to their state for them to receive small gifts than big ones. If the custom of the religious dowry has spread to the point of becoming canonical, communities of women should not forget the original reason for it and should remember that there was a time when parents who gave something to the monastery in order to have their daughter enter it were considered by some as simonists.[7]

5. *Mendicancy.* Begging in itself is not to be condemned. If the goal intended is commendable, begging is likewise commendable, on condition of its being made with direction and without a spirit of greed. The shame often attached to the one who begs can then promote a healthy humility.

6. *Habit, Lodging, Bed, Board.* All these exterior things are usually codified by the Rule. Still it is necessary to know the spirit of them, for it happens that the Rule, for example, prescribes a particular modest material for a habit, at a given period. But this material, becoming rare in another era, or being better tailored, may end by making the same habit luxurious.

Religious must also be unpretentious, scorn honors, and behave as men who have renounced the world. The originality which consists in "disfiguring their faces" (Mt. 6:16) or in wearing vile garments in order to be seen, is as contemptible as vain affectation in dress, food,

---

[7] Cf. A. Duval, in *La pauvreté,* Paris, Ed. du Cerf, 1952, p. 117.

or manner of wearing the habit. Avarice and negligence are likewise to be condemned.

In general, religious wear a habit that is the sign of their profession. But the latter can very well be represented only by a badge or some other distinguishing mark. In this case, it is fitting for religious to have simple habits, which correspond to their work: as laborers, for example, or of peasants in the manner of the first disciples of St. Benedict, or of other occupations.

G. DIVERSITY OF RELIGIOUS INSTITUTIONS

We understand here by religious institutions, an Order, an autonomous monastery, a congregation, a company, a society, etc.

It is normal that there be many religious institutions. They are distinguished, in fact, not by the total gift which religious make to God, but by the services (or the worship) that they wish to render, either to God or to neighbor, and by the way in which they prepare for it. But there would be confusion if several religious institutions pursued the same end, gave the same services (e.g. training and education of youth), by the same means (schools). The interest of the Church, and the charity synonymous with it, invites them, therefore, to join forces.

Religious institutions intended for works of mercy (Jas. 1:27) must not be afraid to re-enter the world, not in spirit but in body—"using the world as though not using it" (I Cor. 7:31). A religious institution to serve the crusade would scarcely be understood today. But there have also existed religious institutions of bridge-builders (pontiff friars). A Franciscan, Father Kolbe, set up a printing-press and printing establishment with workers entirely given to God who did not want any salary. Religious institutions can also be different because there are different and legitimate ways of serving one's neighbor.

The diversity of purely contemplative religious institutions is justified by the difference of worship and of the means used: liturgies, study, manual labor, means of mortification, ascetic exercises, etc.

The hierarchy of religious institutions is established in the following way: in first place are the preachers of the faith who are priests as well as religious, then the contemplatives, and lastly, the active orders. This hierarchy is sufficiently justified by the superiority, which has already been established, of the contemplative life over the active life. Equal in rank, a contemplative religious institution will, for example, prevail over another if it indulges in better works: prayer, for example, is better than simple reading, divine office is more precious than corporal asceticism. It can be better than another, also, if its means are better, that is, better adapted to its end. A good knife, indeed, is not the one which is made of gold, but the one which cuts. Likewise, one asceticism is not better than another from the sole fact that it is more rigorous, if it interferes with attainment of the end instead of facilitating it.

This last remark should put one on guard against too hasty judgments. In order not to take only the example of poverty, it stands to reason that a purely contemplative monastery, a house of preachers, and a congregation of male nurses have very different needs. It is as important for contemplatives to be strictly poor, as it is useful for preachers to have books and the necessary working tools, and as it is necessary for nurses to have the implements and medicines of their profession. Every judgment on the collective poverty of an institution must be referred to the end of that institution.

H. ENTRANCE INTO RELIGION

The theology of what we call "vocation" must first of all consider two things: on the one hand, the vocation properly so-called which is the inner call of the Holy Spirit, and on the other, the fact that this or that religious institution allows the candidate to enter its doors and receives him. In other words, the candidate and the religious institution which he is entering.

The call of the Holy Spirit can be expressed in this way: the person called is a man who is seeking God and desires to give himself wholly to Him. St. Benedict in his rule asks those who supervise vocations to ascertain merely whether the candidate "truly seeks God." But it may be that the call is increased two-fold by another call or at least is expressed in a very concrete form: seek God in a *particular* monastery; give oneself to God in becoming an apostle of God, for God; give oneself to God in a particular service of one's neighbor.

The role of the priest, or of the master of novices, is thus two-fold. He must first see *if the candidate is seeking God*. It matters little whether he is barely a beginner in virtue, or one who is advanced. Neither is it necessary for the subject to have decorously observed all the precepts before wanting to embrace also the way of the counsels; no more than it is necessary to have been married to keep virginity appropriately. Only the call of the Spirit Who urges the candidate to seek God with all his being matters (Ecclus. 8:8; I Thess. 5:19; Acts 7:51). On the other hand, the candidate may be mistaken in his own attitudes in keeping celibacy, for example. Even St. Paul, who eulogized virginity to the Corinthians, writes to Timothy: "But refuse younger widows. . . . I desire therefore that the younger widows marry, bear children, rule their households . . ." (I Tim. 5:11, 14). Medical, hereditary and psychological indications may intervene here. It may still be that the candidate is held back by certain obligations: that of helping his parents who could not without him supply their needs, that of his ministry if the candidate is already a priest and has not received a dispensation from his Ordinary (Canon 542, 1st and 2nd; 981, 1st). However, it would be scorning Providence to close the door on a priest under pretext that the service of souls must be assured above all. The same would be true of the fear that entrance into religion and refusal to marry will bring about depopulation. It is up to God to preserve the human race and to see that His Church is not bereft of pastors. Let each one act as the Spirit moves him. The Director who, with the Holy Spirit, desires the best government of the Church, must simply ask himself what the Spirit also requires of a candidate.

The role of the spiritual director is easier if it is a question of seeing not whether the candidate "truly seeks God" but *if he is suited to the functions* or to the ministry of the congregation. The candidate may sincerely desire such a congregation, but does he have the aptitude for it? It is immediately necessary to distinguish among institutions the monastic ones which have no ministry. Here requirements for admission should be less "difficult"; the aptitudes required, when it is recognized that the candidate truly is seeking God, need be only those of health and the ability of the subject to keep the rule. If the subject is incapable of preaching and unteachable because, for example, he is mute, he will not be accepted in an Order of Preachers. If he lacks judgment and psychology, he may not become a priest. Discernment here refers especially to human data, and it is not so necessary to "test the Spirit."

When the candidate has made his profession, it may happen that he wishes to change religious institution. This is in principle not completely recommendable nor praise-worthy; thus many religious institutions refuse a candidate who has already been professed elsewhere. The Holy Spirit, however may demand it, and those responsible must also "test the Spirit." Vows, in fact, are never expressed idly: they attach the religious to his congregation; it is a serious thing to break them while asking for dispensation from them. On the other hand, one usually benefits more in the religious institution in which one has been accustomed to live, and there may be cause for scandal for those left behind. However, there are good reasons, as, for example, illness, or a desire for a more perfect life, or the need for a more austere order (the excellence of a religious institution being valuated, as we have said, according to its end or its works).

Canvassing for vocations. We have said that entrance into religion comprises two aspects: the vocation proper which is the inner desire (desire of the will) of the subject and the acceptance by the anticipated religious institution. The desire of the subject is ordinarily first. But the Holy Spirit Who makes everything coincide with His ends can cause this desire to be born in a thousand ways, among which we can count education, upbringing, the environment in which one lives, the presence of priests and spiritual masters. Instead of being merely passive and receiving the request of the candidate, religious institutions can also discreetly solicit it and cause it to be born.

Formerly these kinds of "solicitations" were carried on less delicately than today. In the time of St. Benedict it was acceptable for parents to "offer" their children to the monastery, much as one bequeaths a legacy to the Church. From the time of St. Paul (I Cor. 7:37) and through the centuries parents have decided on the "vocation" for their daughter. Even in the 17th century, Angelique Arnauld wept copious tears in her convent before she became converted to her "vocation" as a cloistered nun. There exist today centers for the promotion of vocations: these are the minor seminaries,[8] apostolic colleges, certain junioriates. And a good many priests, monks or nuns, consciously or unconsciously, cultivate this form of the apostolate.

The tree is judged by its fruits. If the vocation is genuine, because it is good, one can do no better work than to induce someone to embrace so excellent a state. But it must be remembered that in reality we "induce" nobody, that God alone is master of hearts; we are, we can be, but an instrument. We can only dispose and encourage vocations. The duty of priests and of superiors is to test all the more rigorously those vocations which they have solicited. What St. Benedict says—"not to receive readily those who enter religion and to be assured that it is the spirit of God which urges them into it" (Rule, chap. 58)—holds true *a fortiori* for these kinds of vocations.

The canvassing for vocations is, therefore, good in itself, but it is

[8] In all these questions, we compare fully the so-called "secular" (diocesan) clergy with an Order or a congregation. Cf. *supra.*

extremely dangerous and many dubious motives can be mixed with it: for example, the possessive instinct of clerical or religious institutions and their excessive desire to increase. This can be a grave fault if, for example, a candidate is deterred from entering an order elsewhere where he may have better opportunities or better instruments of perfection. It is a fault equally grave if the society which has taken so much trouble to "recruit" subsequently offers the candidate only a mediocre instruction and education, whether religious or clerical. Such situations would then deserve, proportionately speaking, Our Lord's reproach to the Pharisees (Mt. 23:15).

Priests, religious, or nuns "charged with vocations" must be disinterested. Christ alone, by His Holy Spirit, is master of vocations. He alone determines the number of clerics, or of religious, that is right for each society. The choice is His. To Him belong the hearts of those who have been called.

REFLECTIONS AND PERSPECTIVES

The abundant material of the treatise on *states*, which the theology of St. Thomas Aquinas brings together here seems, in a more recent perspective, to need a different ordering. On the one hand, what concerns the functions, hierarchical degrees and states (officia, gradus, status) assumes its true proportions in the light of a theology of the Church (see Vol. V). It is a question there of the Christian social order, of the role and rank of the episcopacy, of the determination of various ministries, of the place of institutes of perfection, and of the place made in the Church for the laity. Remaining here on the plane of moral theology, we have not considered in the course of this chapter the structures and institutions of the Christian social order in themselves, but more precisely that which in them concerns the personal and moral problems of those gathered together by this social order. An exception must be made, however, for the religious state which is defined by the institution in which the religious has dedicated himself, and whose theology goes beyond the limits of an ecclesiology.

Before beginning our reflections on the pastoral office and the religious state, we can ask ourselves if there would not be room to consider a "special morality" according to the situations which contemporary ideas of environment, mode of life and profession define quite well. The greater awareness by Christians today about the demands of a Christianity which should animate all aspects of human life causes this kind of problem to crop up. Should there not be, for example, a formulation of a Christian deontology of different professions? We can refer here only to various publications in which this research has been attempted: *Cahiers Laënnec* for doctors; *Cahiers chrétiens de la Fonction Publique* for everything concerning public service within State administrations; *Cahiers universitaires catholiques, Équipes enseignantes*, for professors and teachers; *Recherches et débats*, for intellectuals; the excellent review *Promesses*, for high-school students; and even *Cahiers du clergé rural* for apostles in a rural environment and, in a more general way, for this entire group; *Cahiers de l'aumônerie militaire*, for the Army; *Masses ouvrières* for the workers, etc. Let us add, however, that at this stage of moral consideration we are more on the plane of the concrete practice of Christian prudence than of the theological preparation of even a "specialized" morality. Jacques Maritain, in order to situate this kind of consideration, once spoke of the "practically practical" stage of moral science, distinguishing it from a "speculatively practical" stage in which moral knowledge would be organized and formulated after the experience itself. But doubtless there must always be mistrust in such cases of a casuistry conceived according to too rigid forms. It is advisable to remind Christians that, whatever may be their particular commitment, a Christian conscience draws all its lucidity and its strength from its affection for final ends and the exercise of all the virtues. The most concrete determinations, particularly those of moral requirements of professional competence, are, if not secondary, at least second in regard to these fundamental principles.

The Pastoral State

Theology includes under the one name, "state of perfection," the pastoral state—first and foremost, the episcopal state which in each individual Church is the sovereign pastor to whom everyone is responsible—and the religious state. It is important not to let oneself be deceived by this kind of "identification" and to compare, for example, from the viewpoint of perfection, a diocesan priest who might have pastoral cares and responsibilities with a religious. It is from a wholly different, even opposite, point of view, that the pastor and the religious are in the state of perfection. We could compare both of them, on the one hand, to parents who have the care and responsibility of educating their children, and on the other, to the children who hold in a family the position of the ones who are going to be educated and instructed. With this difference, however: that parents are not the ones ultimately responsible in the Church for the salvation of their children (they need those who administer the sacraments and they are subject to the hierarchy) and that children have neither chosen their way nor are, properly speaking, in a school of perfection (the family institution has for its end simply to direct in a suitable way the growth of children). Neither is truly in a "state of perfection," but they are a reflection of a representative relationship: on the one hand the bishops in relation to their flock, and, on the other, religious in relation to the institution which they enter. This viewpoint is important for the "preferential orientations" which should be given to certain "undetermined" vocations. One does not name just anyone to the office of professor or teacher: there must be natural ability and preparation; it is equally good for spouses to be prepared for their paternal and maternal responsibilities and to be instructed about them. Likewise, we should not direct to the "pastoral" clergy, holy though this state may be and even if the subject is virtuous and desirous of becoming holy, anyone who would not have natural talent for the pastorate (for scriptural and theological studies, for preaching, etc.). Whereas those who, without any other special talent, "truly seek God" always have a place in the religious state; they may even have a place in the clerical state of monastic institutions where the priest-monk has no ministry.

Priesthood and pastorate: hierarchical value of the *priestly and episcopal* duties. Is not the pastoral office the most important one of the priest? Origins of the different pastoral responsibilities entrusted to "lower echelon" priests (so-called sometimes in contrast to the bishops). What are the duties which the bishops have little by little unloaded onto their assistants? What are the most important duties of the bishops? Those which they must retain at any price? To what degree could the bishop get rid of his administrative duties?

Episcopal recruitment. Episcopal appointments among members of the "secular" clergy and among members of the regular clergy in the course of history. Reasons for favor given to one or the other clergy in the course of history. Origins of the preference given to the secular clergy in modern times and in the Latin Church. Merits and demerits of the Eastern practice by which bishops are usually chosen from monastic circles.

Bishops and temporal power. Should bishops speak out and protest against temporal powers each time the rights of the people are assailed? Each time there is an unjust deportation or maltreatment? To what extent? Should the bishop take sides against the wealthy in

order to maintain the rights of the poor if that is the only way of up-holding those rights? Against the poor in order to uphold the "rights" of the wealthy?
Mode of life of bishops. Origins and history of their titles, preroga-tives, insignia, privileges, honors, robes, heraldry, etc. Present ad-visability of these privileges.
Pastors and *priests*. History of community life of the clergy: the presbyterium in the first six centuries; country churches entrusted to archpriests and their clergy; chapters of canons at the end of the 9th century; canons regular and secular at the end of the 11th century. Reform movements of the secular clergy at the end of the 16th cen-tury. Present community movement. The non-resident pastor. Origins of this state. Opposition of the councils, against the lords and against their chaplains, at the beginning of this practice. Possibilities of the "missionary deanery." Present possibilities of "canons regular." On this subject read the decrees of the Council of Trent about the re-establishment of the hierarchy (major and minor orders) in cathedrals, collegiate and parish churches, about the possibility of replacing cler-ics of minor orders with married persons. ("Quod si ministeriis quatuor minorum Ordinum exercendis clerici coelibes proesto non erunt, suffici possint etiam conjugati, vitae probatae, dummodo non bigami, ad ea munia obeunda idonei, et qui tonsuram et habitum clericalem in Ecclesia gestent" (Sess. XXIII, *De Reform, Can. XVII*). On com-munity life in the clergy, read especially Dom P. Benoit, *La vie des clercs dans les siècles passés*; Paris, Bonne Presse, 1914. On canons regular today, read Y. Bossière, *Symptômes de renaissance canoniale*, in *Suppl. de la Vie Spirituelle*, Nov. 1947, pp. 259-268. On pastoral formation and priest community, read A. Duval, A. M. Henry and Th. Suavet, *Sacerdoce et pastorat*, in *Suppl. de la V. Sp.*, August 1948, pp. 121-222; and, A. M. Henry, *Charité et communauté*, and J. de Feligonde, *Notes practiques sur les comportements religieux du clergé paroissial*, in *Suppl. de la V. Sp.*, Feb. 1949, pp. 363-417. Means of sanctification of the clergy outside community life: celibacy; origins and history of ecclesiastical celibacy; its reasons for existence from the viewpoint of the priest's personal sanctification and from the viewpoint of the pastoral life. The breviary; origins, history, nature of the obligation (cf. A. G. Martimort, *L'obligation de l'office* in *La Maison-Dieu*, no. 21, pp. 129-153); is it necessary to adapt the rhythm of canonical hours to the present rhythm of pastoral life, or the rhythm of pastoral life to the rhythm of the hours of the brevi-

ary? (Cf. in particular the investigation of *La Vie Spirituelle,* Jan. 1947, and, more recently, *La Maison-Dieu,* no. 21: *Le trésor de l'office divin: vers une réforme du bréviaire?*). The breviary in the life of the priest; administration of the sacraments, means of sanctification for the priest (Cf. M. Glanndour, *Le ministère du baptême,* and J. Bonduelle, *Porteurs d'esprit,* in *La Vie Sp.,* July, 1952, pp. 8-36; this installment contains also on p. 37 a bibliography on the ministry, source of sanctification); prayer in the life of the priests: necessity, time, methods; reading and study: usefulness of courses for young priests; reasons for existence and possible adaptations, as a function of the needs of pastoral life, of "examinations of young priests"; study and "reading" of holy books in the life of the priest. Comparative values of these means of sanctification.

Deacons and *deaconesses,* in the beginning of the Church, exact role in pastoral life. Survivals and present roles.

Laymen and pastoral life. Do laymen have the right to preach, to perform a pastoral action? (See the chapter on Charismata.) Do laymen have the right to go from door to door in the manner of certain sects (Baptists, Jehovah's Witnesses, etc.) to promote the Word of God? "Pastoral" role of fathers and mothers of families toward their children, instruction they must give them. Apostolic and "missionary" role of laymen in Catholic Action. Does one have the right, when in danger of death, of confession to a layman? Value (non-sacramental) of this confession (cf. on this subject the very interesting book of P. Teetaert, *La Confession aux laïcs dans l'Église latine depuis le VIIIe jusqu'au XIVe siècles,* Louvain, 1926). Direction of conscience exercised by laymen: spiritual direction exercised by superiors on their religious, history and present legislation; counsels collected from "men of God" and "spiritual persons": tradition of this practice in the Church; role of "starets" in the Eastern Church.

Biblical foundations of a pastoral "spirituality." Cf. C. Spicq *Mystery of Goodliness,* Chicago, Fides Publishers, 1954 (Priestly Spirituality according to St. Paul).

The Religious State

The state of perfection of which we are speaking here is not the state of masters in perfection, but the state of those who are starting out in the school of perfection in order to attain it themselves. It is not futile to go back to this in order to clear up a still current confusion: we cannot compare, from the viewpoint of the state of perfection, what is called at times "the sacerdotal state" and the religious state. The sacerdotal state itself does not give the means of acquiring perfection but of communicating it to others—except in the sense that you learn or acquire well only by communicating it to others. But that is an incorrect way of speaking: What is true specifically of persons is not necessarily true of states; if it is true, for example, that the teacher learns a great deal, in fact, from teaching, we cannot define "the state" of the teacher as a state of apprenticeship. It is also certain that the sacerdotal state of priests in the Latin Church includes numerous means of personal sanctification (celibacy, discipline, breviary, etc.), but this results from these priests having retained for themselves some rudiments of religious life, as, for example, celibacy. It is notable, too, that the breviary is in the Church more of a personal obligation of those who have dedicated their celibacy to the Lord (in the consecration of virgins, the bishop gives a breviary to the cloistered nuns in order to signify for them the function to which their new state ordains them) rather than of pastors as such (married priests of the Eastern church are not obliged in the same way). In short, if there is a "sacrament" of perfection to be acquired, that is, of conversion, it is traditionally baptism and not the priesthood. But nothing prevents priests, whether they are parish priests or have an extra-parochial ministry, from being also in the state of perfection (let us say, rather, to avoid ambiguity, the state of conversion) while committing themselves to the communal life in the sharing of goods. (On the history of religious institutions read the article which we have mentioned so frequently: J. LeClerq, *Points de vue sur l'histoire de l'état religieux*, in *La Vie Spirituelle*, June, 1946, pp. 816-833, and July 1946, pp. 127-137.)

Having distinguished priesthood and religious state, it is still necessary to distinguish *way of life* and *state*. Let us state definitely here (cf. chapter *Ways of Life*) that state is a matter of dedication to the purity of celibacy, the community of goods, and obedience within a specific institution, and that, in itself, it does not prejudge the life that is led in this state. Way of life is a matter of intellect which is sometimes active, sometimes contemplative. Certain states, however, oblige subjects to a more active life; others to a life necessarily more contemplative. The commitment in such states must then take into account the dispositions of intellects (we shall refrain from overestimating the role of "the intellect" among candidates in certain monasteries of contemplatives; we have already spoken, in the chapter on *Ways of Life,* of the part of the will in Christian contemplative life).

A study of the word *religious.* At what period was the word applied indiscriminately to monks and priests (linked by the vows)? In the 12th century, when people argued about the relative superiority of monks over canons or of canons over monks, they did not seem yet to see that the two states considered were "religious." Rupert of Deutz, arguing for the superiority of monks, never seems to have recourse to the word *religious.* Origin and history of this word. Analogous studies of the words monk, lay brother, oblate, devout person.

A study of the terms by which these religious themselves are qualified: Order, congregation, company, society, union, solitude, etc. Origins, history, difference of these words, not from a judicial point of view, but from the point of view of the origins and the internal structure of the different institutions. Analogous study of the words: abbey, monastery, priory, collegia, chapter, convent, residence, etc.; abbot, provost, guardian, superior, "Father" or "Mother," etc.

Entrance into religion. 1. Vocation. Theology of the vocation. (Cf. *Le discernment des vocation,* Paris, Éd. du Cerf, 1950, especially the chapters by A. Motte, *L'obligation de suivre sa vocation,* and by A. Bonduelle, *La vocation religieuse, ses éléments de discernment.* And, in a more general way, Y. Congar, *Au monde et pas du monde,* p. 16, in *Suppl. de la Vie Spir.,* Feb. 1952). It is advisable to distinguish throughout between "vocations," and "conditions for admission" in a particular religious institution; the position of the subject, and the position of the religious superiors of the institution which he enters: both are necessary for "entrance into religion," but a theology of "vocation" is needed to distinguish them. Christian vocation (study the numerous passages in the New Testament where there is a question of vocation of divine choice, of election; among others: Mt. 20:16; 24:22, 31; Mk. 13:20, 22, 27; Lk. 6:13; 18:7; Jn. 6:71; 13:18; 15:16, 19; Acts 1:2, 24; 13:17; 15:7, 40; Rom. 8:33; 16:13; I Cor. 1:27, 28; Eph. 1:4; Col. 3:12; II Thess. 2:12; II Tim. 2:10; Titus 1:1; Jas. 2:5; I Pet. 1:1; 2:4, 6, 9; Apoc. 17:14); vocation and predestination, vocation and divine government; Christian vocation and baptism (why is it necessary to refuse the alternative: Is it baptism which gives the Christian vocation or is it the Christian vocation which leads to baptism?); baptismal vocation and the vocation to perfection (signs, criteria of discernment); "contemplative vocation," "active vocation"; vocation to celibacy, "vocation" to marriage (can we speak of a vocation to an involuntary celibacy?). Can a person refuse to "follow his vocation" (in the double sense of the word: to be able to, to have permission to, *can, may*)?

2. Extrinsic motivations of entrance into religion: fear of marriage, Oedipus complex, disillusioned human love, attachment to mother, desire for intellectual life, for "missionary" life, etc. Are these motivations always counter-indications to entrance into religion? Counter-indications resulting from character or from temperament: instinct of domination, jealousy, absence of docility, spirit of contradiction, etc. (To what extent in accounting for or not accounting for it?); too violent appetite of the flesh (how do you interpret the words of St. Paul: "But if they do not have self-control, let them marry, for it is better to marry than to burn"? I Cor. 7:9). Can the absence of dowry constitute a sufficient obstacle to being a "choir religious" in a monastery or convent?

3. Cultivation of vocations. Problems of minor seminaries, juniorates, apostolic schools. At what age can we legitimately recognize the "vocation" of a child? What do you think of parents who, in order to respect the "vocation" of their children, never speak to them of the religious life, all the while instructing them, as they should, in the things of marriage? What do you think of parents who, through devotion or generosity, send their child at a very early age to the minor seminary, without any sign shown by the child "that he may have a vocation"? What should be the attitude of parents toward the future of their children? Is there only one attitude possible? Vocations to monastic life, to clerical, apostolic, missionary life? Formation in an enclosure when it is a question of future apostles—is this recommendable on all points? Recruiting of vocations and propaganda: dividing line. Distinguish in this field between monastic and missionary congregations. Can an institute issue a call for "vocations" by poster, movies, advertising, notices, etc.? Preaching for vocations. Should the religious life and virginity be preached to the "detriment" of matrimony? How to preach to the faithful so that Christian spouses may be more imbued with the beauty and grandeur of their "vocations"—and so that "the rich

young man," or any other, may at the same time understand the Master's call to a more perfect renunciation?

Religious life in the biblical and patristic tradition. Study traditional biblical "types" in monastic life: the prophets, John the Baptist, the Apostles (cf. on this subject the fine work of J. LeClerq, *La Vie parfaite,* Turnhout, Éd. Brepols, 1948). Study traditional themes of monastic life understood as *Return to Paradise,* as *School of Christ, School for the service of the Lord* (Rule of St. Benedict); "Carta Caritatis" (the Chapter of charity of the Cistercians); *School of perfection* (St. Thomas Aquinas); as *angelic life* (cf. Agnès Lamy, *Bios angelicos,* in *Dieu vivant,* no. 7, pp. 59-77); or *seraphic life* (the Franciscan theme of the seraphic life), *apostolic life,* etc. The theme of retreat and the theme of *desert* in religious life (cf. Jules Monchanin, *La spiritualité du désert,* in *Dieu vivant,* no. 1, pp. 47-52). Eastern monasticism: Biblical traditions in Eastern monasticism; characteristics.

Virginity. The mystery of Christian virginity. Virginity of the Church, virginity of Mary, virginity of the soul, consecrated virginity. Theology of virginity. Cf. on this subject Th. Camelot, *Virgines Christi,* Paris, Éd. du Cerf, 1944; A. M. Henry, *Ève, l'Église et Marie,* in *La Sainte Vierge, Figure de l'Église,* Parıs, Éd. du Cerf, 1946, pp. 96-136; and Raymond D'Izarny, *La virginité selon saint Ambroise* (mimeographed thesis, at Saint-Sulpice Seminary in Lyons). Consecration of virgins; history and explanation of the rite; sacramental value; why is the bishop reserved for this consecration? The office of virgins in the Church. Virgins and public prayer (Breviary); virgins and prayer; virgins and good works. The habit of virgins. Origin of the veil; significance. The "crown" of virgins (cf. R. D'Izarny, *op. cit.*). Wedding ring of virgins.

Monasticism. The "monachatus" formerly considered in the manner of a sacrament: study of the ceremony; significance of the rites. Meaning of the "profession." Priesthood of monks: origins, particular end; Mass of the monks (in what sense could it be said that the individual Masses of all the monks of a community are worth "more" than the conventual Mass?); monastic office (exact place of the *divine office* in the monastic institution; is it truthful to say that the monk is made for the office?); evolution of the monastic office in the time of St. Benedict of Anianius; influence of the monastic office on the office of clerics; work of monks (origin; evolution. Cf. on this subject A. M. Henry, *Moines-ouvriers,* in *Rythmes du monde,* 1950, no. 2, pp. 32-43), the monastic habit (origins; adaptations; customs; symbolisms of the colors black and white in monastic tradition). We shall not fail to study also, in order to compare with it a clearer and purer conception of Christian monasticism, the non-Christian monasticisms. Cf. the Hindu Ashrams, the monasteries of lamas in Tibet, the centers of Zen buddhism in Japan, etc. (Cf. *Rythmes du monde,* 1950, no. 2, *op. cit.*)

Canonical life. Origins of the regular life of the clerics. Evolution. History of reformed chapters at the end of the 8th century; institutions of canons regular at the end of the 11th century. History of the canonical office. Priesthood and canonical life: evolution of the ministry of canons. Role of canons in preaching, ministry, mission, in the Latin Church in the 12th and 13th centuries. Canonical spirituality and monastic spirituality (show similarities and contrasts). Read on this subject the fine work of F. Petit, *La spiritualité des Prémontrés au XIIe et XIIIe siècles,* Paris, Vrin, 1947.

The Hermit. Can hermits be considered religious? Canonically? Theologically? Perfection and imperfection of this state from the viewpoint of "the religious state" considered as a dedication in a specific institution. On hermit life read *Bienheureuse solitude,* in *La Vie spirituelle,* Oct. 1952.

Secular institutes. Theology of the secular institute from the viewpoint of the state of perfection. How to understand the practice of the vow of poverty and the vow of obedience in isolated laymen engaged in temporal affairs?

Vows of religion. 1. Vow of chastity. Education in chastity of young religious and nuns; inherent difficulties in the present-day world (cf. on this subject *La chasteté,* in the series *La religieuse d'aujourd'hui,* Éd. du Cerf, 1953). Practice of chastity, means of mortification. 2. Vow of poverty. Religious poverty: monastic poverty, poverty of preachers. Religious poverty compared to the poverty of poor people in the world. Cf. on this subject: P. R. Regamey, *La pauvreté religieuse,* in *Suppl. de la Vie Spir.,* Feb. 1948, pp. 371-389 and Nov. 1948, pp. 243-269. (In a more general way, it will be worthwhile to read the fine work by the same author: *La pauvreté,* Paris, Éd. Aubier, 1941); and *La pauvreté,* series *La religieuse d'aujourd'hui,* Paris, Éd. du Cerf, 1952. It will be asked in particular if the actual forms of poverty of certain congregations correspond to the founding spirit of poverty. 3. Vow of obedience. In what does religious obedience differ from the obedience of a sub-

ject in any kind of society? Theology of religious obedience; show
superior quality of the vow of obedience over other vows. 4. Dispensation from vows: origins of this practice, history. How to give vows
their absolute gravity despite this possibility of dispensation. Temporary vows; can institutes with temporary vows only found a
"state" of perfection?

Observances. Origins, history, detail of the observances. Monastic
observances, canonical observances, observances of the regular
clergy. Theological judgment from the viewpoint of the end of institutions. Theology of silence.

Monastic premises: cloister, chapter: origins, usefulness, significance. Places of silence and especially sacred places (outside of the
church) of the monastery: traditional symbols in the refectory; rites
and prayers of the refectory; are poverty, and sacred character of
a place terms which exclude one another? Architecture of monasteries; theological considerations on the evolution of this architecture (the early dormitorium which was later divided into "cells";
altars of the church which were increased; the abbot's apartment
detached from the rest of the monastery, etc.).

Categories of religious. Origins and history of the different categories: monks and lay brothers; oblates, domestics, etc.; choir nuns,
lay sisters, portresses, etc. Original reasons for the existence of these
different categories. Present justification. (On the origins of lay religious, cf. J. Bonduelle, the article *Convers,* in the *Dict. de droit
canonique.* On the problem of lay religious today, read *Religieux
laïcs,* in *Suppl. de La Vie Spir.,* Nov. 1949; J. Bonduelle, *Dialogue
sur les frères convers,* in *Suppl. de La Vie Spir.,* Feb. 1950, p. 519;
and J. Bonduelle and A. Motte, *Les soeurs converses,* in *Suppl. de
La Vie Spir.,* May, 1952, pp. 168-191.)

BIBLIOGRAPHIE

Saint Thomas d'Aquin, *La vie, ses formes, ses états,* op. cit. (Voir chapitre
XI).
   Sur la notion d'*état,* on lira l'excellente note de J.-A. Robilliard, *Sur la notion
de condition (status) en saint Thomas,* in *Revue des sc. phil. et théol.,* 25ᵉ année
(1936) n. 1, p. 104-107.

   Sur la perfection:

R. Garrigou-Lagrange, *Perfection chrétienne et contemplation,* 2 vol., Saint-
Maximin, Éd. de la vie spir., 1923.

A. Janvier, *La perfection dans la vie chrétienne*, 2 vol., Paris, Lethielleux, 1924–25.

B. Lavaud, *Amour et perfection chrétienne selon saint Thomas d'Aquin et saint François de Sales*, Lyon, Éd. de l'Abeille, 1942.

Vytantas Balciunas, *La vocation universelle à la perfection chrétienne selon saint François de Sales*, Annecy, 1952.

Sur l'état pastoral:

On lira d'abord la belle *Règle pastorale* de saint Grégoire qui fut pour les pasteurs pendant tout le moyen-âge un peu ce que fut la Règle de saint Benoît pour les moines. Une traduction en existe dans la collection *Pax*:

Saint Grégoire le Grand, *Le Pastoral*, Maredsous, 1928.

Voir aussi:

Mgr Hedley, *Lex levitarum, la formation sacerdotale d'après saint Grégoire le Grand*, Trad. Labbé, Maredsous; et l'*Enchiridion clericorum*, Herder (Vatican), 1938.

Sur l'évêque lire:

J. Colson, *L'évêque dans les communautés primitives*, Paris, Éd. du Cerf, 1951.

A.-G. Martimort, *De l'évêque*, Coll. La Clarté-Dieu, Paris, Éd. du Cerf, 1946.

G. Bardy, *La théologie de l'Église de saint Clément de Rome à saint Irénée*, Paris, Éd. du Cerf, 1945—et *La théologie de l'Église de saint Irénée au concile de Nicée*, Paris, 1947.

M. Kuppens, *Notes dogmatiques sur l'épiscopat*, in Revue eccl. de Liège, 1949, pp. 355-367 et 1950, pp. 9-26, 80-93.

Sur l'office et la sainteté pastorale des "prêtres de second rang", Dom Columba Marmion, *Le Christ idéal du prêtre*, Maredsous, 1951.

G. Thils, *Nature et spiritualité du clergé diocésain*, Paris, Desclée de Br., 1946.

J. Le Presbytre, *A la croisée des chemins: vie laïque, vie sacerdotale, vie religieuse*, Tounai, Casterman, 1949.

R. Fuglister, *Die Pastoraltheologie als Universitatsdisciplin, Eine historisch-theologische Studie*, Bâle, Gasser, 1951.

E. Masure, *Prêtres diocésains*, Lille, Éd. soc. du Nord, 1947.

On lira utilement aussi, surtout à propos de ce dernier livre: *Sacerdoce et pastorat*, numéro spécial du *Supplément de la vie spirituelle*, Août 1948, avec des articles A. Duval, A.-M. Henry et Th. Suavet (celui-ci à propos des stages ouvriers de séminaristes).

F. Mourey, *Réflexions et suggestions:* Tome 1, *La préparation au sacerdoce;* T. 2, *Sacerdoce et apostolat;* T. 3, *Les qualités du pasteur d'âmes*, Paris, Spes.

G. Thils, *Mission du clergé*, Paris, Desclée De Br.

Le problème pastoral ne peut être évoqué sans renvoyer également aux études du P. Congar. On lira l'article très suggestif *Faits, problèmes et réflexions à propos du pouvoir d'ordre et des rapports entre le presbytérat et l'éspiscopat*, in *La Maison-Dieu*, n. 14, pp. 107-128. Pour les autres études de Y. Congar, nous renvoyons aux revues *La Maison-Dieu, Le Suppl. de la vie spir., Irénikon*, et la *Revue des sciences religieuses*, 1951, n° 2 (Avril) et 3 (Juillet) où le P. Congar publie et commente la thèse de l'abbé Long-Hasselmans sur le sacerdoce.

Sur l'état religieux et les vœux:

R. Lavaud, *L'idée de la vie religieuse; l'état religieux dans la vie chrétienne et dans l'Église,* Paris, Desclée De Br., 1939.

A. Vandenbunder, *De statu perfectionis religiosorum,* Collect. Brug. t. 48, 1952.

J. Leclercq, *La vocation religeuse,* Tournai, Casterman, 1951.

Sur la vie monastique, les ouvrages sont innombrables. Nous citerons simplement du point de vue qui nous intéresse en théologie:

Saint Benoit, *La Règle des moines,* trad., introd. et notes de Dom Phil. Schmitz, Maredsous, 1945.

Saint Grégoire le Grand, *La vie du bienheureux Père saint Benoît,* trad. par les bénédictins de Paris, Beauchesne, 1922.

Fr. Vandenbroucke, *Le moine dans l'Église du Christ, essai théologique,* Louvain, Mont-César, 1947.

Dom J. Leclercq, *La vie parfaite,* Turnhout, Brepols, 1948.

L. Bouyer, *Le sens de la vie monastique,* Turnhout, Brepols, 1950.

Dom Stolz, *L'ascèse chrétienne,* Chevetogne, 1948.

H. Mogenet, *La vocation religieuse dans l'Église,* Paris, Téqui, 1952.

C. Butler, *Benedictine Monachism,* Londres, 1919 (Le monachisme bénédictin, trad. par C. Grolleau, Paris, 1925).

M. Hergott, *Vetus disciplina monastica,* Paris, 1726.

D. Martène, *De antiquis monachorum ritibus,* Maredsous, 1922.

D. U. Berlière, *L'ascèse bénédictine des origines à la fin du XII*^e *siècle,* Maredsous, 1927.

D. U. Berliàre, *L'ordre monastique des origines au XII*^e *siècle,* Maredsous, 1921.

D. Phil. Schmitz, *L'Ordre de saint Benoît,* 6 vol., Maredsous, 1942–1948.

H. Marc-Bonnet, *Histoire des ordres religieux,* Paris, P. U. F., 1949.

Dom Knowles, *The Monastic Order in England,* Cambridge Un. Press, 1940.

A. Mayer, J. Quasten, etc. *Vom Christlichen Mysterium,* Gesammelte Arbeiten zum Gedächtnis von Odo Casel, Dusseldorf, Patmos, 1951; lire surtout les pages de Dekkers, *les anciens moines cultivaient-ils la liturgie?*

Dom Marmion, *Le Christ, idéal du moine,* Maredsous, 1922. (Voir aussi les ouvrages mentionnés, chap. XI).

Une bibliographie abondante pourra être constituée en suivant les revues: *Revue bénédictine* (Maredsous), *Revue Mabillon* (Ligugé), *Irénikon* (Chevetogne).

Les Règles des grands Ordres religieux ont été publiées en allemand par Hans Urs von Balthasar, *Die grossen Ordensregeln,* Einsiedeln, Benziger, 1948 (Règles des saints Basile, Augustin, Benoît, François, Ignace).

Sur l'ordre canonial, on lira d'abord l'article *Chanoines* de Ch. Dereine dans le *Dict. de droit canon,* et les nombreuses études de cet auteur, en particulier, *Saint Ruf et ses coutumes aux XI*^e *et XII*^e *siècles,* in *Revue bénédictine,* n°s 1-4, 1949, pp. 161-182.

Lire aussi J.-C. Dickinson, *The Origins of the Austin Canons and their Introduction into England,* London, S. P. C. K. House, 1950, et F. Petit, *L'ordre de Prémontré,* Paris, Letouzey, 2e éd., 1927.

Sur l'Ordre prêcheur, lire M.-A. Ricaud, *Frère prêcheur,* Préf. de E. Gilson, Toulouse, 1950.

Pour une vue d'ensemble de tous les Ordres, nous renvoyons au livre simple et pratique de H. Marc-Bonnet (voir plus haut).
Sur les Congrégations missionnaires du XIXe siècle, lire surtout B. de Vaulx, *Histoire des missions catholiques françaises,* Paris, A. Fayard, 1951.
Sur les moniales enfin, on lira d'abord les documents pontificaux récents: Pie XII, *Constitution apostolique* Sponsa Christi, trad. dans la *Nouv. Revue théol.* t. 73, 1951. Et les commentaires des différentes revues (Revue des communautés religieuses, 1951, pp. 73-88; La Vie spir., etc.)

Sur les instituts séculiers:

R. Petit, *L'Église et les instituts séculiers,* Paris, Bonne Presse, Enfin, les *Atti e documenti del primo convegno internazionale delle religiose educatrici,* en cours de publication aux Éd. Paoline, à Rome, sont une véritable somme à l'usage des religieuses.

BIBLIOGRAPHY

Butler, Cuthbert, O.S.B., *Benedictine Monachism.* London, 1919.
Carr, Aidan, *Vocation to the Priesthood.* Washington, C.U. Press, 1950.
Colin, Louis, C.SS.R., *Practice of the Vows.* Chicago, H. Regnery Co., 1955.
Dickinson, J. C., *The Origins of the Austin Canons and their Introduction into England.* London, S. P. C. K. House, 1950.
Duffey, Felix, D., C.S.C., *Testing the Spirit.* St. Louis, B. Herder Book Co., 1948.
Dukehart, Claude H., *State of Perfection and the Secular Priest.* Washington, C.U. Press, 1950.
Farrell, Edward, O.P., *Theology of Religious Vocation.* St. Louis, B. Herder Book Co., 1951.
Garrigou-Lagrange, Reginald, O.P., *Christian Perfection and Contemplation.* St. Louis, B. Herder Book Co., 1947.
Hedley, Bishop John C., *Lex Levitarum.* New York, Benziger Brothers, 1905.
Kelly, Bernard J., C.S.Sp., *Progress in the Religious Life.* Westminster, Md., The Newman Bookshop, 1953.
Knowles, Dom, O.S.B., *The Monastic Order in England.* Cambridge, Cambridge University Press, 1940.
Marmion, Columba, O.S.B., *Christ the Ideal of the Monk.* St. Louis, B. Herder Book Co., 1934.
————, *Christ the Ideal of the Priest.* St. Louis, B. Herder Book Co., 1953.
Masure, Eugene, *Parish Priest,* Chicago, Fides, 1955.
Merton, Thomas, *The Waters of Siloe.* New York, Harcourt, Brace and Company, 1949.
Meyer, Wendelin, O.F.M., *Pastoral Care of Souls.* St. Louis, B. Herder Book Co., 1944.
Spicq, Ceslaus, O.P., *The Mystery of Godliness,* Chicago, Fides, 1954.
Stockums, Wilhelm, *Vocation to the Priesthood.* St. Louis, B. Herder Book Co., 1937.
Vocational Institutes. Notre Dame, Ind., University of Notre Dame Press, 1948, 1949, 1954.

The preceding expositions of volumes *III* and *IV* have followed in their general outline the plan of St. Thomas Aquinas in the second part of the *Summa Theologiae*. Its diagram is clear. The ultimate finality implied in every action and the conditions in which human action is directed to its beatitude lay the foundations of our ethics: an ethics of good and of integrity and not an ethics of obligation, as Father Tonneau pointed out so firmly at the beginning of volume III. The study of human behavior is pursued profoundly. The voluntary aspect of the human act and its rational integrity are assured by the spiritual organism of the virtues and gifts in which sanctifying grace blossoms.

When the last end has been recognized, human behavior analyzed, and the virtuous organism described, it is fitting to re-compose all this in the light of the movement of life. This is the richest aspect of those classical treatises on *charismata, ways of life,* and *states.* In it we perceive man, destined for eternal life, endowed with virtues and gifts, in the very movement of his actual life, in his ascent to the perfection of charity as he may pursue it here on earth. We discern the noble means he may take and the social limits within which he may settle in order to sustain his attempts at interior emancipation.

Under the heading "Christian Perfection," Father Mennessier now endeavors to gather into a brief synthesis the major elements of moral doctrine developed in these volumes. A few theologians may be tempted to see in it an outline of "spiritual theology." So we must again explain our position with respect to this expression.

When Father de Guibert [1] tries to give to this part of theology its place, he claims for it a strict unity—excluding the distinction into two disciplines of "ascetical" and "mystical." Then he distinguishes it from "moral theology," whose sufficient object would be merely the good deed, while "spiritual theology" would envisage Christian perfection and the means of realizing it. It is plain, however, that in St. Thomas' view on theology (which is ours), all the problems posed by spiritual life and its evolution enter again into that *consideratio moralis* which has but one object: man on the way

[1] Refer to *The Theology of the Spiritual Life,* already cited in connection with Chapter XI.

to his blessed destiny. And we know quite well now that this way is not imposed on man from without—after he has been instituted in his nature. No. "God did not create a heavy body in order to notify it afterwards of the law of gravity, nor man to notify him afterwards of the precept of behaving as a man." Ethics is radically inscribed in the very nature which God has made. And it is one.

In meeting again in this concluding chapter the initial considerations of Father Chenu and Father Tonneau, and in pointing out how the two ideas of "precept" and "counsel" are concretely presented in relation to the Gospels, a synthesis is arrived at which takes the form of a conclusion of all ethics.

Chapter XIII

CHRISTIAN PERFECTION

by A. I. Mennessier, O.P.

I. WHAT IS THE PERFECTION OF CHRISTIAN LIFE?
  A. In what sense do we speak of perfection?
  B. Constitutive element of Christian perfection: charity
  C. Conditions of perfect charity
  D. Beginners, advanced and the perfect

II. PERFECTION IS IMPOSED ON ALL: PRECEPTS AND COUNSELS
  A. The Gospel and Christian experience
  B. Theology of the counsels
    1. Their nature
    2. Their meaning

III. CHRISTIAN SANCTITY
  A. Steadfastness in the union with God
  B. An undivided heart

Chapter XIII

CHRISTIAN PERFECTION

All Christian perfection consists in the perfection of charity. What that implies—what never-ending tension here on earth, what ways and aids are prescribed for it—is what we want to point out briefly.

I. What Is the Perfection of Christian Life?

A. IN WHAT SENSE DO WE SPEAK OF PERFECTION?

This term, perfection, is used in the Gospels; we know the phrase of Mt. 5:48: "Be perfect as your heavenly Father is perfect." "If you wish to be perfect . . ." our Lord says again to the rich young man in Mt. 19:21. Actually, the whole morality of the Gospels appears to us as an appeal to a constant transcendence of self, an ideal of perfection. St. Paul also uses the words τέλειος, τελειότης to designate the fullness of Christian life with respect to its beginnings; so a state of infancy leads to maturity. But how define more precisely this perfection? A being may be called perfect when it possesses all the constitutive elements of its own nature—initial, constitutive perfection. Rightly, the state of grace appears on the supernatural plane as a fundamental perfection. But the idea of perfection is not conceived solely from the point of view of being established in being. It signifies also the state of being "which is such that one could not perceive any progress in the order considered" (Lalande). This is the ultimate flowering of the living being. We already know that supernatural life finds its completion in eternal bliss. We cannot, therefore, speak of perfection of Christian life here on earth except in a sense which always remains relative to this final and transcendent flowering. We are on the way, *en route.* But it is the very movement of this *route,* in its tension and its unceasing transcendence, which is indicated here.

We speak, then, of a state of perfection on this interior plane of life, not to designate a terminus but a certain condition of permanence that guarantees progress. We speak of it as already having a certain fullness, a certain indication of the blessed life in the practice of the great meritorious acts which end in it. Thus the evangelical beatitudes stand for certain mountain tops in Christian life, and express, at the very door step of the Gospels, that call to a spiritual elevation which is its entire law. But the latter is summed up above all in the commandment of charity. Thou shalt love the Lord thy God with thy whole soul, and thy whole mind, and thy whole heart. This totality required of love, as well as the transcendence of its object, which is God Himself, do they not imply that call to a perfection whose principle is charity itself? When the new precept is joined to it, in which Christ commands us to love our neighbor not only as ourselves, but as He Himself has loved us, we are given a model, an ideal of exemplary perfection. Theologians are concerned primarily with defining how perfection of Christian life consists in charity and what aspects it may include here on earth.

B. CONSTITUTIVE ELEMENT OF CHRISTIAN PERFECTION: CHARITY

In assuring us first of all that perfection of Christian life consists essentially in charity, theologians intend simply to eliminate, in the concept of the order of Christian values, what would be only a partial view or false perspective in which the means would be taken for the end. The intellectual superiority of Gnosticism under all its forms; the taste for the extraordinary; the confusion between perfection and feats of mortification, even the practice of absolute poverty; the identification, especially in the various forms of quietism, of perfection with passivity or the gifts of contemplation: all these are so many errors which make the essence of Christian perfection consist in what is only an accidental aspect, condition or effect.

It is, finally, always this place made for charity, says Father de Guibert, which puts an abyss between Christian spirituality and spiritualities derived from various idealistic, positivist, pantheistic philosophical systems which are based on a moral autonomism, an absorption of the human personality in a more or less conscious absolute, a vague altruism sacrificing individual perfection to an indefinite progress of human collectivity. Opposite these ideals Christian dogma clearly marks the limit of man's inner ascents in the fullness of God's love, a limit never attained here below, but whose unending pursuit during the time of trial conditions the degrees of the satisfying possession of God in terms of eternal life.[2]

This doctrine theology obtains from the Scriptures themselves. St. Paul untiringly affirms this primacy of charity, "bond of the perfection" of love, "fullness of the law." The great text of the Epistle to the Corinthians sets forth the supreme value of charity in relation

[2] Leçons de théol. spir., p. 139.

to all the gifts and charismata, "major autem caritas." And one has only to re-read the first chapter of St. John to be convinced of the essential place of charity in Christian life: "Who abides in love, abides in God and God in him" (I Jn. 4:16). St. Thomas Aquinas forcibly gives the theological formula which is that of all Christian tradition, in these words:

> The pure and simple perfection of spiritual life is that of charity. One may speak of perfection in two meanings: the being whose essential properties have reached their conclusion is perfect, purely and simply. The one in whom an accidental property has alone attained that final blooming is perfect in one point only. . . . If it is then a question only of attached qualities, their perfection, real though it may be, is not perfection. On the plane of spiritual life, perfection in the absolute sense of the word will cling to that which forms the essence of this life. . . . Now spiritual life consists essentially in loving. Without charity one is nothing spiritually.[3]

Perfection of other virtues is only a relative perfection. As a matter of fact, charity alone (this is the argument of the *Summa Theologiae*) unites us to God, our last End, and there is no perfection for a being except when he attains his proper end.

C. CONDITIONS OF "PERFECT" CHARITY

But in what does this perfection of charity itself consist? This is what St. Thomas again sets forth vividly in his treatise on the *Perfection of the Spiritual Life.* God can only receive from Himself the measure of love which He deserves, and, finding in Himself a love equal to His goodness, He shows us the ideal of all perfection.

The only perfection that is possible for us is that which, expressing the capacities of the subject, causes us to give our entire measure of love in a total sincerity. This is the meaning of the great commandment as it is formulated in Deut. 6:5. Thou shalt love the Lord thy God with thy whole heart, with thy whole soul and with thy whole strength. St. Luke adds (10:27) and with thy whole mind, thus completing the picture of all that is necessary to surrender to love: the heart, which is to say the deepest orientation of our inclinations; the mind, with all its understandings; the soul, with all its sentiments; strength, with all its realizations.

Let us note, however, that there are two ways of fulfilling this ideal.

One is total, complete, without the least defect. To put all one's

[3] St. Thomas, on the Perfection of the Spiritual Life, Chap. 1 (English Tr.: *The Religious State, the Episcopate and the Priestly Office*, Newman Press).

heart, all one's soul, all one's strength and mind into loving God, supposes that there is no longer a deterrent to that ardor which carries one toward God in an actuality of love which thoroughly possesses. This kind of perfection cannot be obtained by people enroute as we are here on earth: it is the perfection of the Blessed who see God. "No," says St. Paul (Phil. 3:12), "not that I have already obtained the prize, or already have been made perfect, but I press on towards the goal. . . ." He will be perfect only when he shall embrace God at the hour of receiving the crown of the Blessed. This embrace [étreint] is not that embrace [embrassement] which would enclose its object, restrain it completely. In the latter meaning God is outside the grasp all creatures and thoroughly "incomprehensible." St. Paul simply points out that the end of the pursuit, the goal is attained and possessed. This is the beatitude of heaven, where in an endless act of understanding and love the soul throws itself on God and enjoys Him: this is not a simple disposition to act, but, in its very perfection, an activity. The soul has found its last end, God, the supreme Truth. Behold it united to the One who must direct all our desires, and towards whom all our activities are ordered. We may then speak of loving God with all our heart: this is the blessed perfection in which the soul, thoroughly possessed, gathers all its thoughts, all its loves, all its works into the single ardor which carries it towards God. With all one's mind: for God offers Himself to the intellect in a vision without end; it is in Him that the intellect knows all things, in the light of divine Truth that it judges all truth. With all one's soul, in an unceasing ardor of love in which affectivity is wholly aroused and in which nothing is loved except for God. With all one's strength, or with all one's might, acting only for a unique motive, the tender and divine love [dilection].

Such is the measure of love proper to the Blessed: this is the second degree of perfection.

Behold now another way of understanding this totality which must be put into the love of God. When our love is flawless we love Him again with all our heart, with all our mind, with all our soul and with all our strength: there is nothing in our actions or our dispositions that does not attract us to God. This is the perfection implied by the precept of charity. What does it demand of us? First, that God become effectively the goal of all our actions. "Whether you eat or drink," says St. Paul, "or do anything else, do all for the glory of God" (I Cor. 10:31). We fulfill this condition when we put our life in the service of God. Through this fundamental orientation, all the acts which spring from the will are virtually directed to God—unless, naturally, their object is repugnant, as is the case of the sin that turns us away from God. In this way do we love God with our whole heart.

It is necessary next to submit our mind to God, clinging by faith to what He reveals to us. St. Paul speaks in this sense of the mind brought into captivity and wholly obedient to Christ (II Cor. 10:5). This is to love God with our whole mind.

Thirdly, it is necessary to love in God all that is loved, and to center in Him all our affective life while unifying it in divine love. St. Paul again writes: "For if we were out of our mind, it was for God; if we are sane, it is for you. For the love of Christ impels us" (II Cor. 5:12-14). It is with all our soul, then, that we love God.

Finally, all our exterior acts, our words, and our works must draw their strength from this source of divine love. Let all your works be done in charity (I Cor. 15:14 [sic]). Thus we put all our strength into loving God.

Such is the third degree of perfect love. It is imposed on all, being made obligatory by the precept itself. The preceding degree is not accessible to anyone here on earth, unless he shares in this earthly life the state of heaven, as did our Lord Jesus Christ.

Let us recall now the words of St. Paul: "Not that I have already obtained the prize, or already have been made perfect, but I press on hoping that I may lay hold of it. Let us then, as many as are perfect, be of this mind" (Phil. 3:12-15). These words give proof to the evidence that if the perfection of the elect is not possible for us here on earth, it remains the ideal for which we must strive and for which we must have the desire to conform inasmuch as our state allows.

D. BEGINNERS, ADVANCED, AND THE PERFECT

Having considered the objective ideal of perfection, there is another order of considerations: we are looking now at the human being himself in the development of his spiritual life: This is a matter of discerning the general laws of his development. Certainly, these conditions are varied according to individuals. With the help of spiritual direction each one may be enabled to discern the ways of his own progress and to act as a person. But theology strives to recognize, as we have just said, the common conditions of every spiritual ascent.

One essential principle appears from the beginning: spiritual life follows the rhythm of all life. Its development comes about by successive degrees. There are "ages" of spiritual life which comprise the concerns proper to each one and the activities consistent with the actual state of growth. Molinos' proposition denying this gradation in spiritual development has been condemned (cf. Denz. 1246). Does not St. Paul himself speak (I Cor. 3:1-3) of the different food which he must give to "spiritual men" and to those who are still only "little ones in Christ"?

Christian tradition, from the teachings of the Fathers, has reduced to three "degrees" these great stages of spiritual life: beginning, progress, and perfection. Later came the distinction of the three ways, called purgative, illuminative, unitive. The very vocabulary here is originally that of the pagans and it is only in the 13th century that agreement in the gradation of beginners, the advanced, and the perfect begins to be established. St. Thomas Aquinas takes care to link this progression to that of charity, whose various degrees will be distinguished later by the successive preoccupations inspired by this progress in love. The concern of the beginner is above all to withdraw from sin and to resist the covetous desires which would turn him away from God. By analogy with the first age, it is a question primarily of "feeding" and of protecting—*fovere* (translated: incubate, hatch)—that charity which has all the frailty of infancy. Progress is affirmed in the advanced by intense application to everything which may develop the strength of their love. The perfect, delivered from all these immediate cares, have only one concern: to dwell united to God in a more and more ardent yearning toward the divine and eternal enjoyment of the God whom they love.[4]

Spiritual ascent, then, appears as the inner enjoyment of a soul more and more fixed in its orientation toward God. Extracting part of St. Paul's text (Rom. 6:20-22), "For when you were the slaves of sin, you were free as regards justice. . . . But now set free from sin you have become slaves to God," St. Thomas Aquinas was to see in the stages of this liberating submission many *states* of spiritual life. We shall speak, then, not only of degrees, but of the *state* of be-

---

[4] St. Thomas, IIa IIae, q. 24, a. 9.

ginners, the advanced and the perfect, indicating by this that the essential thing is inner liberation whose principle is charity.[5]

The notion of state implies, as a matter of fact, the idea of a permanency which is defined relative to freedom or to servitude. We find it again in its most appropriate meaning—when defining the exterior states of perfection. But on the plane of interior life, the use of this word puts the accent on that growing liberation which can clearly be best defined with respect to the great spiritual means of perfection. Thus Christian asceticism is, above all, a liberating effort. The evangelic counsels have no other meaning.

It is a question, writes St. Thomas, and this is an obvious psychological law, of unifying one's heart in order to intensify its ardor. We should be all the more wholly given up to the love of God as we disengage ourselves from earthly attractions. The poison of charity, says St. Augustine, is the ambition of acquiring or of keeping worldly goods. But we see charity grow in proportion as we desire less. It attains perfection when desire dies. Such is the meaning of the counsels that we are invited to follow in order to attain perfection: it is a liberation of the soul which, in tearing itself away from perishable temptations, has but one goal—God, contemplated, loved, served, in all His desires.[6]

II. Perfection Is Imposed on All: Precepts and Counsels

Here is a classic theme of spiritual theology: does perfection consist in the fulfilment of precepts, or does it require the practice of what are called the evangelic counsels? A rather simple problem, really, if we do not yield to a wholly legalistic concept of ethics, which, conceiving everything in terms of obligation, sees in the fulfilment of the counsels only an optional ideal. This ideal is seen as relative to a minimum perfection, a perfection at reduced rates, strictly obligatory and limited to the observance of the commandments. Our theological view must then reassert this distinction between counsel and precept in the context of a moral science in which the necessity for each one to reach to his own good forges a line of conduct whose integrity is finally assured by virtuous prudence. Precept obliges. Counsel is an invitation which leaves us the choice of following it or not. It is proposed, not imposed. But obligation of precept and invitation of counsel have their meaning only relative to that prudent conduct in which the interior call of good is first, and in which everything on the supernatural plane must be measured by the same requirement of charity in a desire for the supreme good.

[5] *Ibid.*, q. 183, a. 4.
[6] St. Thomas, on the *Perfection of the Spiritual Life,* chap. 6.

A. THE GOSPEL AND CHRISTIAN EXPERIENCE

The Gospel places us immediately into such perspectives. In truth, the distinctions of obligatory legal regulations for everyone and simple counsels does not seem at first glance conspicuous. This discernment is that of Christian tradition and theology. However, these distinctions join together the Gospel dicta in a useful way if we keep them exactly within the proper horizons, which are those of the common call to a perfection which each one pursues in proportion to his generosity. Rather than strict regulations, an ideal is offered. This seems indeed to be the meaning of the sermon on the Mount. Morality of "the soul which is open" wrote Bergson. When we try to interpret the Gospel texts as categories of precepts and counsels, we discover in reality a universal call to perfection which imposes, along with renunciation, the service of Christ with an undivided heart, the service to one's neighbor in the likeness of Jesus. Such is the law of the kingdom. But the demands of interiority and of spiritual elevation which the charity of the sons of God requires leaves in the detachment, in the very ways of service, a free initiative which expresses the movement of the heart in answer to the call of the master.

The gift of the heart to God—such is the essential answer of those who hear the tidings of the Kingdom of Christ. The remainder is on the plane of abilities; but Christ's invitation to leave everything in order to follow Him shows that there is no limit to the generosity of the disciple. Christ's answer to the young man who, according to Matt. 19:16, asks what he must do to possess eternal life, having observed all the commandments—"If thou wilt be perfect, go, sell what thou hast, and give to the poor . . . and come, follow me"— indicates, it seems, at one and the same time a summons to a perfection which is optional for no one, and the individual character of a choice which corresponds to the personal vocation of each one.

The words of the Lord concerning total renunciation of riches and those where He invites whoever can understand to renounce marriage (Matt. 19:10-11) have greatly influenced the form of life of ascetics and virgins, as well as the origins of monastic life. Thus it is that Anthony retires into the desert after having heard the gospel of the rich young man. But even those who so intensely live the ideal of Christian perfection care very little about distinguishing precepts and counsels! The imitation of Christ, that of the Apostles, the magnanimous example of the martyrs—this is what arouses the ardor of those who can understand. Primitive monastic life does not bother, moreover, about the distinction of evangelic counsels, in which medieval theological systemization sees one of the characteristics of the religious state. The most ancient rules concerned simply with setting forth the conditions of a Christian life led according to evangelic laws.

One cannot fail to observe, writes Dom J. LeClerq, that St. Benedict, quoting the entire Bible and the Gospels, never takes into account the texts which are said to be the foundations of what are called evangelic counsels. . . . This is because St. Benedict, in continuity with ancient monasticism, does not clearly distinguish the requirements of salvation and those of perfection.[7]

The theoretic distinction of precepts and counsels arose out of the need, felt by doctors of the Church, of determining the exact balance of Christian conduct as a counter to the over-simplifications of heretics who saw in celibacy or absolute deprivation a universal requirement for salvation, or of detractors of evangelic poverty and Christian virginity. It was a question of showing that if there is no universal requirement, these ways of life facilitate Christian perfection in a way not to be overlooked. Augustine, Irenaeus, Jerome and Ambrose furnish later theologians with texts. They distinguish that which is imposed on all, that which the precept intimates, from that which, without being the requirement of all, facilitates the approach to perfection to which all must tend. By this distinction they mean indeed to note that the law of grace, while inviting to the heroism of love, requires from each one a conduct proportioned to his strength. An admirable passage of St. Ambrose in his treatise *de Viduis* (11-12, *P.L.*, 16, 255-257) contains all the essential things that can be said on this subject.

B. THEOLOGY OF THE COUNSELS

1. Their Nature

Before even pointing out their role in the pursuit of perfection, it is the place of counsels among the divine aids (His law and His grace) that our theology has to define. Precepts and counsels make up, each in its own way, a part of these divine aids which come to the help of our conduct in conforming to the demands of the moral good.

[7] *Points de vue sur l'histoire de l'état religieux,* in *La Vie Spirituelle,* vol. 74, June 1945, p. 825.

Precept does this by imposing on us an obligation. Let us note furthermore, that if precepts can require anything, it is not simply in virtue of the voluntary authority which imposes them, but, first of all, by expressing the necessary bond of our actions with the ends which we must pursue. The moral requirement is first and foremost inscribed in the nature of things. The usefulness of the precept is to make this good explicitly known to us, and, in compelling us to act, to sustain with all the force of divine authority our sometimes failing will.

Counsel itself imposes nothing formally, precisely because no necessary bond exists between what it proposes and the end to be obtained. It does not point out a specific good to be realized here and now: this determination belongs to us. What it proposes is a possibility. Also, counsel cannot oblige us to do what it invites us to do. But our choice is moral, when maturely weighed, and corresponds to what our prudence shows us as befitting the attainment of the end to which we are striving. The act of commanding and the act of counseling are thus formally different. One requires our obedience; our prudence has only to surrender itself to it while seeing therein the immediate rule of its determinations. The other requires our attention and the personal exercise of prudence, whose choice is here determined by our own inner needs.

Consequently, it seems altogether fitting that the system of relations with God established by the "Law of grace" should include this manner of divine intervention which we call counsel. What is it in fact but the law of grace, *lex gratiae?* There would be a great subject for mediation in what St. Thomas tells us about this law which moral theologies use perhaps too little. The Law of grace does not mean that grace accompanies the Law like an inner help joined to the exterior statement of the precepts. It is within the supernaturalized heart itself, as an intimate requirement, before being expressed in formulae, that the new law, *lex indita cordibus,* is written. And, truly, it is living charity that must speak in us. The law of grace is the law of love. That is likewise the reason why it is a requirement of perfection as well as a law of freedom: it does not command so much from without, with all that array of punishment and temporal promises which characterized the old law, as it works from within. More exacting in its interiority than the old law with its numerous precepts, it also leaves more to the action of personal prudence: consequently, counsels are perfectly appropriate there. Counseling is the act of friendship. The free sons of God (which we are) find in Christ's friendship, along with His example, the counsel which will help them in the pursuit of perfection.

2. Meaning of Counsels

The law of grace, law of love, is a law of inner freedom. It is in virtue of this that there are counsels. But they themselves lay down for us the ways of that growing liberation which is one of the aspects of the ascent toward perfection. As a matter of fact, theology has especially applied itself to these counsels of poverty, chastity and obedience which make up the matter of the three traditional vows of religion. We have already spoken of the tardiness of this systemization. Let us note in this regard that it is quite different to find in the Gospel a set rule of counsels of obedience as they are practiced in religious life. It is only by reflection that we have been led to distinguish this obedience from that common to all Christians, as a special manner of submitting one's life to another, in relation to "counsels" of perfection. Whatever it may be, the interpretation, for example, which St. Thomas gives of the suitability of these three counsels in a state of life where one is dedicated to striving toward the perfection of charity, illuminates clearly this liberating aspect on which we insist: religious celibacy is considered, on this plane, as a freedom from the domestic difficulties of married life, as well as from the sentimental complications in which the will is dispersed; poverty, as a deliverance from the numerous worries of business. And in obedience we see a remarkable simplification of life, by the elimination of so many petty, personal decisions in which fancy finds its place and in which we linger uselessly.

All that we have said about the nature and role of counsels should keep us from yielding to the somewhat oversimplified view: precept is that to which one is obliged; counsel, that to which one is not obliged, that which is "supererogatory." Let us understand well, then, that counsels do not merely set forth an optional surplus of perfection which is recommended with respect to an obligatory minimum as minimum. It is the order necessary to the last end that requires the fulfilment of what the precept imposes on us in the form of obligation. This is all that remains *undetermined,* and thus deferred to our prudential determination, in the order of the means of attaining the supreme end. This supreme end becomes the object of the counsels according to which we guide ourselves effectively. Perfection is not rendered optional because the means of choice which we have of attaining it are proposed to us under this form of counsel. Very much to the contrary, it only makes manifest the inner requirement of a grace which, while deferring to our personal generosity the choice that is expedient for us, shows by the very perspectives of detachment and heroism which these "counsels" express, the loftiness of the end that we are destined to achieve.

Moreover, theology in reflecting again on the relationships between the counsels and the precepts notes well that, on the whole, it is the precept of charity itself that forms the obligation of perfection, if not the means of pursuing it. The classic doctrine is thus summed up quite well in these few propositions:

Christian perfection consists essentially in charity and is included as an end in the precept which is given to us of loving God and our neighbor: to strive toward perfection is the very law of love that is commanded us.

Perfection of charity, implying a spiritual liberation through a more complete service of God, is the counsel which is proposed to us as the most suitable means of securing this inner freedom in the service of perfect charity.

Precepts, other than that of charity, are themselves ordered to the latter as a condition sine qua non of the perfection toward which charity strives. The counsels are subordinated to the precepts as a way of their perfect fulfilment required by charity itself.

In short, there is not a twofold ideal of Christian life: one ordinary and imposed by the precepts, the other additional—to which we would be invited by the counsels. There is only one goal, life eternal; only one longing, charity; only one law of the supernatural being: to be perfect in the image of the Heavenly Father. The gospel is itself that call to the free generosity of a soul which, if it loves, always wants to do more. And everything is brought around, finally, as the first Christian generations had so well understood, to the imitation of the Savior. His law, like His teaching, is first and foremost His very person. The friendly counsel which we receive from Him only puts into relief the personal aspect of a moral science and a spirituality in which He is everything: he who wishes to be my disciple, let him leave everything—let him renounce *self* and follow *me*.

III. Christian Sanctity

The perfection of Christian life goes by the name of sanctity. If we distinguish it by this word, it is because it is marked by certain characteristic features which the word expresses. Thus it is these features that must be clarified first. We may depart from the definition given, for example, by St. Thomas, when he wonders [8] if the words *religion* and *sanctity* are equivalent. In one sense yes, he says, for sanctity shows that which is in relation to God—that which implies purity and steadfastness: Steadfastness in adherence to the immutable; purity—the liberation from everything that through earthly complexity is incompatible with the simplicity of God. As a token of this, holy things and consecrated persons are separated from the profane in worship, in order to be definitely reserved for divine uses alone. But the word sanctity, still more than the idea of religious worship, includes spiritual values. One can perform an act of religion without putting any sanctity into it. The latter is the spiritual part of religion, that of the soul.

In his book, *La Sainteté,* Father Festugière is careful to note that the Greek idea of sanctity considers primarily the object of veneration which provokes the mysterious feeling that is the meaning of the sacred thing; sanctity may be applied to places and objects of worship, but it is not attributed to persons. The ideal of personal perfection is that of the hero and of the wise man, of the courageous man whose fate can even be, like that of Hercules, to brave the jealousy of the gods. Making sanctity the essential attribute of God, attributing it likewise to men who have dealings with Him and who participate in the sanctity which He communicates to them, is a characteristic of Judeo-Christian semantics. Finally, it is through Christ that this sanctity which He possesses is communicated, not by mere participation but by being. Christian life, a life of so-called sanctifying grace, solicits sanctity because it is the new life which, tearing us away from sin, makes us participants of the divine life in Christ.

Our proposal is to show, in the various aspects that the lives of the saints may take, the permanent features that make their heroism sanctity. The two features of steadfastness and purity in the union with God outline the plan of these reflections.

[8] IIa IIae, q. 81, a. 8.

A. STEADFASTNESS IN THE UNION WITH GOD

Steadfastness of soul seems to express itself in the aspect of *heroism* which Christian perfection must have in order to be declared *sanctity*. It is required for the canonization of a saint that he have manifested in his life heroism of *all* the virtues. From the brilliancy communicated to them by those virtues whose own object is to face the greatest difficulties, even the greatest dangers the saints must radiate courageous magnanimity, fortitude that recoils before nothing. The courage of the saints is one of the first features we can recognize in them. But still it is necessary to see how their heroism is distinguished from that which Greek antiquity gave as an ideal to the man worthy of this name.

Virtue of fortitude: "I am certain, said St. Paul, that neither death, nor life . . . will be able to separate us from the love of Christ" (Rom. 8:39). And we know also that at the beginning of the cult of saints there was the martyr: it is in his indefectible fidelity that Christian heroism takes cognizance of itself. Later, when the era of persecutions had ended, it became the custom to measure perfection in terms of martyrdom.

But the exterior aspect of the deed that plays so important a part in legends of the saints is not what should restrain us. Christian courage is the sign of sanctity, not of a merely human heroism. The martyr is a victor, but his victory seems at first like a victory of God. And no doubt the meaning of so many marvelous tales is that of stating almost symbolically, by the accumulation of extraordinary proofs, that such a resistance witnesess an intervention from God Himself. Still more, there is soon seen in the martyr's victory the victory of the Cross. This heroism of the martyr appears then before all as the sign of a total fidelity to Christ, expressive of a charity without measure.

Christian sanctity, heroism of all the virtues, originally signified by martyrdom, appears thus clearly above all as the manifestation of love: perfection of Christian life is always that of charity. It follows that if in the ordinary man and in the saint the virtue of fortitude can produce the same obvious acts, both the motivation for them and interior attitude toward them are quite different. Humility is first and foremost. The saint can be asked to face great battles. He will do it counting less on himself than on the grace that sustains and animates him. "The Lord has said: My grace is sufficient for thee . . ." (II Cor. 12:10; cf. 1:8-9).

But, above all, the steadfastness of the saint appears as the fidelity of a love in which the *interior* virtues take first place over exterior and spectacular manifestations. The patience of the saints is often hidden from the glances of men—at times, under the exterior appearances of what we could take to be despondency. No inhuman stoicism—apparent weaknesses, but no turning back; contradictions, the triumph of mediocrity—there is scarcely any saint who has not had to be proved by adversity before casting off self in order to be fixed in God alone.

Finally, this inner courage of love is often revealed in the continuity of an obscure and completely unobtrusive life. Sanctity is thus composed of small daily fidelities, each one of which may seem mediocre in itself, but which are the substance of the highest virtues. One thinks of a Thérèse of Lisieux whose most heroic courage is made up of that self-effacement before God in the continuity of a life without brilliance, with none of the possibilities of realizing any of the great adventures with which her childish dreams adorned the image she was forming of sanctity. To be a warrior, missionary, martyr—she had wanted all that, but the only thing left for her was to sweep the cloisters and strew rose petals on a crucifix. But one day she understood that the sole value was that of love. And it was then that her concept of sanctity underwent a transfiguration: it was no longer incompatible with the experience that she felt daily of her littleness, of her very imperfection. M. Van der Meersch has, in his biography of the saint, left this essential meaning of love somewhat obscure. But in other respects he has vigorously thrown into relief what is heroically courageous in consenting to accept herself and her nothingness before God, rather than to strive towards a spectacular and often artificial ideal of sanctity.

In a different connection Van der Meersch has raised another problem: If the essential thing is fidelity to God even in the endurance of one's own afflictions, would sanctity be compatible with certain afflictions of a moral nature? Is sanctity compatible with the afflictions which the Christian endures in a continued effort to begin anew—a fidelity which is no less heroic for being only an ever-repeated appeal to divine mercy? On this point let us go back to the dictionary article on spirituality: *Sanctification of the abnormal,* and let us say simply that Christian sanctity is not, first of all, the victory of a moralism but rather of an indefectible love.

B. AN UNDIVIDED HEART

It is in this manner that the aspect of "purity" which comprises Christian sanctity must be understood. The heart that loves God must be undivided. But what does this mean? Here we must take care not to confuse with our concept of spiritual sanctity the ideas which would refer rather to the order of what should more correctly be called sacred. In this last case sanctity is actually defined by distinguishing it from the profane: things and individuals dedicated to worship are intentionally set aside, reserved for divine service. The ambiguity comes from what the two aspects of sanctity can join together in one and the same being. But the ideas are not necessarily co-extensive. On of the plane of personal sanctity, the principle of interior renunciation, of uprooting self is still perfection of charity. *Abnegation* appears, then, as the other side of that preference which the saint gives to God. And it is essentially that *abnegatio sui,* that purification of the love of self which spiritual men pursue, in all its deviations, to the innermost recesses of the soul.

That in order to attain this it is necessary to undergo many exterior detachments, is a law which the lives of the saints show us—even with all the diversity of temperament, circumstances of environment and of time that they represent. Everyone must know, sooner or later and more or less brutally, this reversal of created values which is the law of the beatitudes. John of the Cross and Teresa of Avila vigorously express the principle that two opposites cannot coexist in one and the same subject: one must choose God or oneself.

This purification is that of love: the more it is free of all alloy the more the charity of the saints responds to the very ideal of love, for its ardor then carries it toward all that retains the image of God. It is not at all a separation from, but an openness to all. No one is more in love with the reality of the world than the saint: he has ceased to become a screen between the creature and God. Moreover, his sanctity is that which Christ imparts to him. In him man and God are reunited, and it is the whole of creation that he assumes in order to gather it together in Him. In one sense nothing is any longer profane, or more exactly, everything must return to Christ and be sanctified by the charity of the saints.

Several problems remain: we have scarcely spoken of a "new type" of sanctity, sanctity turned toward the "sanctification of the profane," in opposition to that deemed medieval, a sanctity of the cloisters dominated by separation from the world.

That in the course of time there may be diverse conceptions of the ways offered to Christian perfection is undeniable. But still it is necessary to establish that divine grace mocks our classifications and that the latter retain a great relativity. If we are less tempted in our times to make sanctity and separation from the world equivalent, it is again necessary that this happen above all in terms of knowing how to distinguish what is essential from what is only accidental. That done, many problems still present themselves: for example, that of "separation"—which really implies the state of the person consecrated to God. What activities are possible to those whom religious life has radically separated from the world? We know the debates which in the 13th century the activity of new orders dedicated to the apostolic life stimulated. The solution given at that time by St. Thomas Aquinas is not to be neglected. Recalling that the religious state exists only for the perfection of charity, he concludes that all the works of perfect charity are within reach of those who are consecrated to them. Not less real is the problem of the kind of separation which the consecration to the priesthood and the specialization of its duties imply.

Returning to our proper object, which is the detachment which interior sanctity implies, we can ascertain by the example of the lives of the saints that their spiritual ascent, even among the most extremely active ones, often includes phases of exterior detachment and of retreat from the world. But no doubt we can also establish that it is when they have found God—after whatever necessary detachments and sacrifices—that they finally possess that supreme independence, that security which allows them to return unharmed to the world they are to save. A Teresa of Avila, who stumped up and down Spain founding monasteries is an example. But still more striking perhaps is a Catherine of Siena, who, intent at first on a zealous search for divine intimacy, takes to the road relying only on keeping that intimacy in the "interior cell." The saint is a soul liberated by the fervor and plenitude of its love.

BIBLIOGRAPHY

Adam, Karl, *Christ Our Brother* (trans. Dom Justin McCann, O.S.B.), New York, The Macmillan Company, 1939.

Aquinas, St. Thomas, *The Religious State, the Episcopate and the Priestly Office* (On the Perfection of the Spiritual Life). Westminster, Md., Newman Press, 1950.

Caussade, J. P., *Abandonment to Divine Providence,* St. Louis, B. Herder Book Co., 1921.

Chautard, J. B., O.C.S.O., *The Soul of the Apostolate,* Gethsamani, Kentucky, 1946.

DeGuibert, Joseph, S.J., *The Theology of the Spiritual Life* (trans. Paul Barrett, O.F.M. Cap.), New York, Sheed and Ward, 1953.

DeJaegher, Paul, *One With Jesus* (trans. Louis J. Puhl, S.J.), Westminster, Md., The Newman Bookshop, 1951.

DeSales, St. Francis, *Introduction to the Devout Life* (trans. John K. Ryan), Garden City, N. Y., Doubleday & Company, Inc. (Image Books), 1950.

Garrigou-Lagrange, Reginald, O.P., *Christian Perfection and Contemplation* (trans. Sister M. Timothea Doyle, O.P.), St. Louis, B. Herder Book Co., 1942.

Marmion, Columba, O.S.B., *Christ the Life of the Soul,* St. Louis, B. Herder Book Co., 1922.

Rodriguez, St. Alphonsus, S.J., *The Practice of Christian Perfection* (trans. J. Rickaby, S.J.), Chicago, Loyola University Press, 1929.

Tanquerey, Adolphe, S.S., *The Spiritual Life.* Westminster, Md. The Newman Bookshop, 1948.

Carney, E. J., "Priesthood and Sanctity," *American Ecclesiastical Review,* 120: 469-474, Je '47.

Cartmell, J., "Nature of Sanctity," *Life of the Spirit,* 8: 87-96, Aug-S '53.

Condit, A., "Increase of Charity," *Thomist,* 17: 367-386, Jl '54.

D'Amato, A., O.P., "One Commandment," *Cross and Crown,* 4: 405-420, D '52.

Farrell, A., O.P., "Perfection and Imperfection," *Life of the Spirit,* 9: 63-67, Aug '54.

Farrell, W., O.P., "Destiny's Master," *Cross and Crown,* 6: 16-26, Mar '54.

Gleason, R. W., "Layman's Obligation to Perfection," *American Ecclesiastical Review,* 125: 284-292, Oct '51.

Greenstock, D. L., "St. Thomas and Christian Perfection," *Thomist,* 13: 1-15, Ja '50.

Hughes, D., "Dynamics of Christian Perfection," *Thomist,* 15: 247-288, Apr '52.

Matthijs, M., O.P., "Christian Holiness," *Cross and Crown,* 4: 209-221, Je '52.

Sturzo, Luigi, "Spiritual Life of the Average Man," *Spiritual Life,* 1: 201-209, D '55.

GENERAL BIBLIOGRAPHY

Aquinas, St. Thomas, *Summa Theologica* (3 Vols.), New York, Benziger, 1947.
Connell, Francis J., C.SS.R., *Outlines of Moral Theology.* Milwaukee, The Bruce Publishing Company, 1953.
Cronin, John F., S.S., *Catholic Social Principles.* Milwaukee, The Bruce Publishing Company, 1950.
Davis, Henry, S.J., *Moral and Pastoral Theology* (4 vols.), London, Sheed and Ward, 1941.
DeGuibert, Joseph, S.J., *The Theology of the Spiritual Life.* New York, Sheed and Ward, 1953.
DeSales, St. Francis, *Introduction to a Devout Life* (tr. John K. Ryan), Garden City, N. Y., Doubleday & Company (Image Books), 1950.
Farrell, Walter, O.P., *A Companion to the Summa* (4 vols.). New York, Sheed and Ward, 1940.
Carrigou-Lagrange, Reginald, O.P., *Christian Perfection and Contemplation.* St. Louis, B. Herder Book Co., 1942.
————, *The Three Ages of the Spiritual Life.* St. Louis, B. Herder Book Co., 1948.
Howell, Clifford, S.J., *Of Sacraments and Sacrifice.* Collegeville, Minn., The Liturgical Press, 1952.
Marmion, Columba, O.S.B., *Christ the Ideal of the Monk.* St. Louis, B. Herder Book Co., 1934.
————, *Christ the Ideal of the Priest.* St. Louis, B. Herder Book Co., 1953.
————, *Christ the Life of the Soul.* St. Louis, B. Herder Book Co., 1922.
McHugh, John A., O.P., and Callan, Charles J., O.P. (translators), *Catechism of the Council of Trent.* New York, Joseph Wagner, Inc., 1954.
————, *Moral Theology, A Complete Course.* New York, Joseph Wagner, Inc., 1929.
Prat, Ferdinand, *Theology of St. Paul* (2 vols.), New York, Benziger, 1947.
Scheeben, Matthias J., *The Glories of Divine Grace.* Cincinnati, Benziger Bros., 1886.
Sheedy, Charles E., C.S.C., *The Christian Virtues.* Notre Dame, Ind., University of Notre Dame Press, 1949.
Smith, George (editor), *The Teaching of the Catholic Church* (2 vols.), New York, The Macmillan Company, 1954.
Suhard, Card. Emmanuel, *The Church Today.* Chicago, Fides Publishers Association, 1953.
Tanquerey, Adolphe, S.S., *The Spiritual Life.* Westminster, Md., The Newman Bookshop, 1948.
Thomas a Kempis, *The Imitation of Christ.* Garden City, N. Y., Hanover House, 1955.
Vann, Gerald, O.P., *The Divine Pity.* New York, Sheed and Ward, 1946.
Von Hildebrand, Dietrich, *Fundamental Moral Attitudes.* New York, Longmans, Green & Co., 1950.
Vonier, Anscar, *The Collected Works of Abbot Vonier* (3 vols.), Westminster, Md., Newman, 1951–1954.

INDEX OF PROPER NAMES

ANALYTICAL INDEX

Abnegation, 763
Abortion, 545
Abstinence, 554, 555, 576-7
Accident, 273n
Action, apostolic, 657-8
Acts, human, 42-3, 44, 46-7, 221, 222-3, 231, 253, 259, 269, 520
Virtuous, 520
Adjuration, 417-8
Adoration, 406
Adversity, virtues of, 496
Agape, 135, 145, 146, 151, 167-70, 647, 649, 651
Divine, 138, 139-40, 140, 143, 147-50, 150-1, 153
St. John, 146-54
Agnosticism, 37
Alms-giving, 189-90
Alterity, 273-5, 293-4
Angelism, 554
Anger(s), 213, 511
Holy, 593-4
Antipathy, passions of, 559-60
Apathy, 652
Apocalypse, The, 26, 88-9
Apocatastasis, 94
Apologetics', 627
Apostles' Creed, 27-8
Apostasy, 43-4
Appetite(s), 163, 164, 224, 539
Irascible, 119
Sexual, 567
Appetitive faculties, 221, 225
Aptitude, 212
Art, 225-6, 267
Artistic process, 267
Asceticism, 184, 555-6, 711, 712, 713, 754
Assurance, 505, 506-7
Augustinians, 713
Austerity, 493, 496, 497, 514

Authority, 34, 236, 237, 348, 349, 351-2, 368, 462-3, 542
Duties of, 350-1
Avarice, 238, 469-70
Aversion, 559-60

Baptism, 7, 8, 255, 708-9
Beatific Vision, 95
Beatitude, 94-5, 99, 101
and Hope, 102
Beatitudes, The, 36, 76-7, 748-9, 763
Belief, 4, 13, 17, 31
Meaning of
Benedictines, 713
Beneficence, 189
Bishopric, The, 700-3
Duties of
Virtues of
Blasphemy, 38
Against Holy Spirit
Body, The
Cult of, 564-5, 567
Mastery of, 565-7
Brétigny, Treaty of, 459-60
Brotherhood, 551

Charismata, 632-3, 646
Defined, 618
and Doctrine, 624-6
and Freedom, 635
and Hierarchy, 635-8
and Life of Church, 622-3, 626-8
and Sanctity, 638-9
in Worship, 622-4
Charismatics, 710, 711
Charity, 22, 25, 145-6, 154-62, 178-81, 181-4, 184-6, 187, 255, 303, 315, 396, 404, 447, 448, 452-3, 463, 472-3, 515, 553, 559n, 632, 633, 639, 647, 652, 653, 654,